White

Collar

Fictions

White Collar Fictions

Class and Social Representation in American Literature, 1885–1925

Christopher P. Wilson

The University of Georgia Press
Athens & London

Athens, Georgia 30602

Designed by Richard Hendel
Set in Berkeley
by Tseng Information Systems
Printed and bound by Thomson-Shore
The paper in this book meets the guidelines for permanence and durability of the Committee on Production Guidelines for Book Longevity of the Council on Library Resources.

Printed in the United States of America
96 95 94 93 92 C 5 4 3 2 1

Library of Congress Cataloging in Publication Data
Wilson, Christopher P. (Christopher Pierce), 1952–
White collar fictions : class and social representation in American literature, 1885–1925 / Christopher P. Wilson.
p. cm.
Includes bibliographical references and index.
ISBN 0-8203-1367-X (alk. paper)
1. American literature—20th century—History and criticism. 2. American literature—19th century—History and criticism. 3. White collar workers in literature. 4. Social problems in literature. 5. Social classes in literature. I. Title.
PS173.W45W55 1992
813'.409355—dc20 91-19791
CIP

British Library Cataloging in Publication Data available

Photo: O. Henry Memorial, Greensboro, North Carolina

for my mother and father

Contents

Acknowledgments

The idea for this book originated in the classroom, during a one-semester course I had titled—a bit too generically—"The American Business Novel." At the time we were just wrapping up Theodore Dreiser's *The Financier* (1912) and moving on to Sinclair Lewis's *Babbitt* (1922). At this juncture, I asked my students to draft an additional scene for Lewis's novel—a scene that Lewis might well have written himself. Much to my delight, one student chose to recast an actual episode from *The Financier,* in which the young Frank Cowperwood, coming of age in antebellum Philadelphia, learns about the survival of the fittest by watching the lobster tank at his local fish market. Day after day, he witnesses a copperish-green lobster terrorize, encircle, and ultimately devour a squid; the latter is described as "pale and waxy in texture, looking very much like pork fat or jade," its only defense a cloud of ink. Dreiser remarks that the example stayed with the boy all his life "and cleared things up considerably intellectually. . . . 'That's the way it has to be, I guess,' [the boy] commented to himself. 'The squid wasn't quick enough.'" The addition that my own student made was that alongside the young Frank Cowperwood was a smallish, pink, bespectacled boy who all the while was sympathizing with the squid. His name was George F. Babbitt.

Thus began my own study of the Americans who, observers often say, are the elusive, protean people who generate "ink" in our society, and—depending on whom you ask—either cloud the social tank or clear it up. Since that time, a good deal more ink has been spilled. I am grateful to those friends and colleagues who have provided insight and support along the way. During the summer of 1985, I participated in a National Endowment for the Humanities Summer Institute at the University of California at Berkeley, taught under the inspiring example of Michael Fried and Walter Benn Michaels. It was here, surrounded by an unusually supportive group of friends and critics, that I first tried out my ideas and found so many of them drafty. Later, John Crowley shared his enormous knowledge of American literature in commenting on Chapters 3 and 5 particularly; Eugene Leach read my material on Robert Grant in its early phases; Richard Ohmann and Christine Bold provided similarly thoughtful reactions to Chapter 1. In 1989–90 I was fortunate enough to join a small reading group: here I would like to thank Teresa Murphy, Louis Masur, David Jaffee—and especially Cynthia Taft, who went to the extraordinary length of actually reading a few Edna Ferber novels. Richard Fox, as always, provided editorial assistance and comradeship throughout. In addition, a number of my colleagues in English and American Studies at Boston College have provided comments, sanity, or just plain solace in regard to particular chapters. I would especially like to thank Rosemarie Bodenheimer, Nancy Boisvert (who made me rethink the ending of "The Trimmed Lamp"), Paul Doherty, Carol Hurd Green (who first pointed me to Edna Ferber), Dayton Haskin, Paul Lewis, Nancy Palmer, Richard Schrader, Judith Smith, and Judith Wilt. A Boston College Faculty Fellowship in the spring of 1990 allowed me to complete the manuscript. For professional and personal debts somewhat less tangible but no less meaningful, I would also like to thank Michael Anesko, Martha Banta, Lois Brown, Robert Chibka, Greg Conti, Marjorie DeVault, Albert Duhamel, Emory Elliott, Amy Kaplan, Gary Kulik, Jackson Lears, Ethan Lewis, Robin Lydenberg, John Mahoney, Roberta Pressman, Joan Shelley Rubin, Mark Seltzer, Michael Smith, Dennis Taylor, Andrew Von Hendy, and James Wallace. The staff of the University of Georgia Press, particularly Matt Brook and Malcolm Call, have been generous with their support and patience; Gwen Duffy was a constructive and sympathetic copyeditor.

A number of libraries and historical societies have provided expert assistance and permission to cite from their collections: The Greensboro Historical Museum, especially J. Stephen Catlett; The Harry Ransom Humanities Research Center, University of Texas at Austin (and Mr. Norman Zelenko, executor of the Elmer Rice papers); The Collection of American Literature, Beinecke Rare Book and Manuscript Library, Yale University; The Lilly Library at Indiana University; The State Historical Society of Wisconsin; The Thomas P. O'Neill Library at Boston College; The Houghton Library at Harvard University; The Princeton University Library; the Libraries of the University of Massachusetts, Amherst; The Boston Athanaeum; The Minnesota Historical Society, especially Harold L. Miller; The Boston Public Library, including The Rare Book and Manuscript Division; and The Industrial Relations Collection, Littauer Library, Harvard University. Substantially revised portions of chapter 3 were previously published as "*Unleavened Bread*: The Representation of Robert Grant," vol. 22, no. 3, *American Literary Realism 1870–1910,* © McFarland & Company, Inc.; substantially revised portions of chapter 4 first appeared as "Sinclair Lewis and the Passing of Capitalism," *American Studies,* 24 (Fall 1983): 95–108.

Finally, I would like to thank Greer Hardwicke, who lent her spirit and support to the level of every day's most quiet need. For this, for Jesse, and much else besides.

White Collar Fictions

Introduction

Representing Main Street

What must be grasped is the picture of society as a great salesroom, an enormous file, an incorporated brain, a new universe of management and manipulation. By understanding these diverse white-collar worlds, one can also understand better the shape and meaning of modern society as a whole, as well as the simple hopes and complex anxieties that grip all the people who are sweating it out in the middle of the twentieth century.

—*C. Wright Mills,* White Collar

This is a study of turn-of-the-century representations of class, "mass," and commonality—specifically, literary treatments of and by the "new middle classes." Of course, it can no longer be said, as C. Wright Mills once did, that these were the Americans who "slipped quietly" into modern history.[1] In the four decades since Mills's classic study, these Americans have made their presence felt in an enormous (and enormously contentious) sociological literature and in a growing number of studies in the new social history. To date, however, their new prominence within American literature after 1900—despite their creators' often-unrivalled contemporary popularity—has received little attention. As if following the fate of white collar workers themselves, writers like O. Henry, Edna Ferber, Robert Grant, Elmer Rice, and even Sherwood Anderson and Sinclair Lewis have been splintered away from each other, assigned to the various lesser-known offices of the critical enterprise: studies of American humor, of the grotesque, of satire, or regional local-color writing. In part, this reflects the fact that, in contrast to the upsurge of current interest in gender, ethnicity, and race, studies of *class* in American literature have remained relatively undeveloped.

Of course "class," it has often been observed, has rarely slipped easily off the American tongue—and "middle class" all *too* easily.[2] In its own day, the literature discussed in this book often went out under a variety of critical labels: as the literature of "typical" Americans, as "clean fiction," *Saturday Evening Post* stories, literary "Main Streeting." Moreover, this diverse body of literature itself frequently denies the pertinence of class to the Americans it describes. Within individual texts, authors rarely begin with the exclusive intention of class portraiture. Even Sinclair Lewis's *Babbitt* (1922), for example, often seems more intent on constructing its protagonist out of mass-cultural fantasies, suburban routines, local headlines; as Vernon Parrington and Alfred Kazin observed, Lewis somehow wants us to see his hero as "*genus Americanus,*" a "kind of monstrous incarnate average" of American life as a whole.[3] It is not merely, then, that Babbitt is new "middle" *class;* rather he is cast as "middle" in the sense of an arithmetic mean of culture, a norm embodied, literally personified. Lewis's cultural "averaging" is only one of several turn-of-the-century literary strategies, in fact, which enfolded white collar representations within cultural rhetorics of commonality, "human nature," or middle Americanness. If these disparate rhetorical strategies became pivotal to the development of American languages of class, then an inescapable part of their contribution was often a heartfelt "denial of the existence or reality of classes" altogether. It is on this pervasive yet elusive paradox of what Anthony Giddens has called "class awareness" that this study centers.[4]

Much has already been written about American writers' responses to the social dislocations of the turn-of-the-century years. Recently a number of important new studies have revitalized critical interest in late-Victorian and Progressive-era literature by redescribing American writers' engagement with the social, technological, and cultural disruptions of late-industrial society: the extension of market values, the cultural fascination with the industrial dynamo, or the emerging spectacles of modern mass culture. Yet the representation of white collar strata per se has rarely been in the foreground of these studies. In part, this reflects a continuing focus on realism and naturalism to the partial exclusion of other styles; these two prominent genres, even now, are the ones to which late-industrial capitalism has been genetically linked. However, from another perspective, realism and naturalism can seem equally evocative of what Raymond Williams has called "residual," nineteenth-century cultural motifs: in their habitual descriptions of the class structure in polarized "halves"; in their sometimes overbearing Victorian moralism, masculinity, and hierarchical social values; in their succumbing to melodrama and sensationalism; in their often-celebratory embrace of imperialist adventurism. By contrast, I mean to address, within varieties of what I have called literary and cultural "averaging," a series of newly emergent twentieth-century situations: the expansion of the middle ranges of the social register; the diverse occupations (bank teller, saleswoman, lawyer, publicity writer, advertiser) that characterized these white collar ranks; the tensions between dependence, professionalism, and social reform within such classes-in-formation; the refashioning of modern liberalism to account for such citizens, often cast in normative, mass, and middle-class terms.[5]

To begin with, therefore, I am interested in how various languages of class, "mass culture," and normality informed the literary practice and cultural allegiance of American writers who engaged in white collar portraiture. How did such writers define "average" Americans, and why did white collar workers (by no means the social or even arithmetic mean in these years) so often fit the bill? Why did white collar classes so often double as representations of the "typical" mass citizen? How do we account for such prosaic titles as *The Job* (1917) or *The Girls* (1921), or (conversely) for such white collar antiheroes as Selma White, Mr. Zero, or George F. Babbitt? How is it that conservatives and liberals were often engaged in this portraiture? How did various writers modify literary forms—political fable, novel of manners, expressionist drama or satire—in order to *engage* their audiences in this representational project? What was the relationship of such projects to the white collar lives—particularly the work experiences—these authors portrayed (and often lived)?

No such accounting can ever be comprehensive. Ideally, of course, as Stephen Greenblatt has suggested in a quite different context, one would hope to assemble various white collar literary fictions along a spectrum or hierarchy of genres (which Greenblatt has called "the aesthetically codified stock of social knowledge"). Yet this study attempts nothing so ambitious. The more literary history I write, the more it seems, as James Clifford has observed about ethnographic truths generally, histories are "inherently partial—[partial in the sense of both] committed and incomplete." I have not meant to posit a single, encompassing idiom, or a unitary tradition, or a unified class culture among the different writers discussed herein. This was hardly a seamless cultural project—but rather, a variety of literary manifestations of what Harry Braverman has called the "short-term relative expression" across white collar class awareness and experience, little more.[6] I have not broached, for example, questions of taste or canonicity, and I have spared the reader the by-now-customary programmatic conclusion, proclaiming where contemporary criticism "must" head given my findings.

Meanwhile, since I have been partly bound to what white collar literature will admit to—that is, in a literal sense, allow *into* its vision—naturally my study has blind spots and omissions: technical and managerial employees; government employees; secretaries; those aspects of class generated beyond the work experience on which my own analysis centers. Similarly, although this study covers some writers widely read in their own time, it says nothing about *really* popular novelists such as Harold Bell Wright or Zane Gray; nothing about mass literary forms like detective fiction or romance, where class is also represented; nothing about the intersection of "white" collar vocabularies with the invidious languages of racism and ethnic exclusion. We must also remember that the intraclass depictions examined here were hardly uncontested by other social groups; one historian has reminded us, for instance, of unionized Boston clerical workers protesting that "We're no Kitty Foyles."[7] These writers are so involved with lateral or intraoffice horizons that they often neglect or obscure interclass tensions—and, as some would no doubt suggest, this is perhaps the biggest fiction of all. But even these absences provide some clues about how and why certain writers were "admitted to" (in the sense of gaining access to) a larger field of discussion about class. In the following chapters I mean to trace the negotiation between literary forms, implied audience engagement, and the class portraiture writers attempted—how the "idioms" that writers fashioned served to negotiate the quite material class experiences they had often shared with their audiences.[8] In more technical terms, my goal is to investigate the interaction between what Jonathan Culler has called "cultural *vraisemblance*"—verisimilitude that occurs when writers apply a shared knowledge of popular-cultural typification—and the often divided social life they propose to describe.[9]

| | |

To even begin to discuss such "middle" American groups or "classes," of course, is to enter into what one critic of the field rightly calls an "unstable," "disconcertingly heterogeneous" grouping with a "polymorphous" and tangled character—and set of interpretations.[10] Not that it is difficult to enumerate changing occupational categories in this period. American historians and sociologists have long recognized that the half century or so after the Civil War witnessed a major alteration in the national social structure. As if confounding predictions (republican and Marxian) about postbellum social polarization, after 1870 the middle strata between capital and labor expanded rather than contracted. As the percentage of Americans employed in manufacturing continued to grow gradually, this era also saw a drastic reduction in agricultural labor and a rapid expansion in clerical, professional, and sales work. For instance, agricultural laborers constituted roughly 53 percent of the gainfully employed in 1870; by 1900 this had dropped to 35 percent; by 1930, to 21 percent. In the same span, clerical occupations rose from less than 1 percent to over 8 percent; those in the professions nearly tripled in number; the number of salesmen in stores expanded over six times. In the years when the total U.S. population tripled, and the workforce expanded between three and four times, the number of clerical workers alone expanded nearly fifty times. Similarly, revisionist historians have pointed to the strategic cultural role played by the expansion of new middle-class professions in this period—growth generated largely by modern universities and professional schools. In real numbers, for instance, the number of American lawyers grew by nearly 20 percent in the two decades after 1900.[11]

The challenge comes, however, in translating these sheer body counts into meaningful configurations of class structure, culture, consciousness, or awareness. Fortunately, American historians have begun to move beyond the days when, as several commentators have observed, the term "middle class" was tossed about "with gay abandon"—or perhaps worse yet, simply assumed.[12] Lately, historians such as Mary Ryan, Stuart Blumin, and others have begun to describe the emergence of a middle stratum more concretely, as part and parcel of the broad revolution in class relations originating within the industrial economy in the late-Jacksonian era. This earlier, formative period brought several important social changes: the disintegration of the patriarchal, corporate family that had once been the center of household production; the displacement of such production by commercial agriculture, the cash economy, and the factory system; the growing transparency of middle-class differences with journeyman artisans and laborers in work relations, neighborhood organization, and public entertainment. With these changes came the slow emergence of white collar employees—salaried managers, professionals, retail clerks, and office workers—to staff ever-bigger industrial and commercial operations. To date, Blumin has made the boldest set of claims regarding the developing split between the broader horizontal social relations of manual and nonmanual workers in the nineteenth century. He has documented the increasing alignment of nonmanual work with entrepreneurship and salaried (as opposed to wage-earning) employment, the increasing specialization of firms in the nonmanual sector, and the growing physical separation of manual from nonmanual work. Manual and nonmanual work environments were increasingly distinguished from each other by means of architecture, interior design, and the location of firms within urban space. Following this trail into the postbellum years, Blumin also finds a hardening of blue and white collar lines around patterns of consumption, voluntary association, domesticity, and other spheres of life.

Meanwhile, social and cultural historians have also delineated the social values gradually contributing to the hardening of class lines. To historians like Paul E. Johnson, David Montgomery, or Sean Wilentz, more centrally concerned with changes in work relations per se (and vertical class exploitation), the significant middle-class divide derived from *within* the political culture of antebellum republicanism, and was manifested in the rising tensions within a producer's ethos—its conflicting egalitarian, mutualist, and individualist strains among journeymen—and the growing centrality of "free labor" preferred by masters and entrepreneurs. All the while, the upper middle strata were molded by successive waves of evangelization and reform, which helped concatenate a broad ideology of free will, deferral of gratification, and female domestic nurturance—ideals that served as forms of social restraint and self-control.[13] Thus the genteel performance of the Victorian parlor was set against the pragmatic street knowledge of working women; the male bourgeois ideal of Christian character, a man who (in the words of Charles Rosenberg) "tested his manhood in the fires of self-denial," against the "Bowery B'hoy" and his veneration of rough amusement and honor; the family reading provided by *Harper's* or *The Century,* against the thrilling story papers and dime novels read by young artisans. Likewise, scholars such as Alan Trachtenberg, Amy Kaplan, and Elsa Nettles have demonstrated how even Howellsian realism of the commonplace was set off against the "below the line" underworld of the cities.[14]

Even accounting for differences of chronology, region, or city size, I can hardly hope to arbitrate the various interpretations above—which perforce I have summarized much too briskly. Nearly all of these interpretations acknowledge the distension, fragmentation, and new formations taken on by "middle classes" in the later period covered by this study (1885–1925). Nor can any single sociological label adequately encompass all of these new middle sectors. The often-simplistic equation of occupational categories with the concept of class is itself part of the problem; rather, in the turbulent late-capitalist system in which nonmanual work came to occupy a variety of positions, it was the contesting of the meaning of turn-of-the-century "middle-classness" which single occupations—and the resulting literary fictions—often vivify.[15] For the purposes of this study, C. Wright Mills's usages—"white collar" and "new" middle classes—will be retained, if initially as heuristic terms. I employ these particular labels for three reasons: "white collar" to designate those nonmanual workers who existed principally as employees—not owner, master, or employer—or as office and sales workers; "new" middle class to differentiate these workers from the classical risk-taking entrepreneur or *petit bourgeois;* and finally, both terms, to retain Mills's sense of the contradictions (even the social oxymoron) built into "White Collar." Even four decades after the fact, Mills's terms, however fatalistic or ironic, still seem preferable to those more orthodox or more fashionable labels that have periodically arisen to challenge them. Moreover, "white collar" retains what other more neutral or traditional labels lose: Mills's recognition of the continuing existence of exploitation—exploitation that the modern white collar employee, paradoxically, both experiences and creates. Mills's investigation, as subsequent chapters will try to show, was beset by male-centeredness, hyperbole, republican nostalgia. In all its expressionist vigor, *White Collar* is perhaps closer to Elmer Rice than Balzac.[16] But even given its deficiencies, Mills's hard-edged attention to work relations, in particular, is still preferable to those more recent accounts that discount (or deconstruct) the republican telos altogether. Perhaps most important for this study, Mills's book remains a devastating counterpoint to the popular American mythology of the "Little Man"—the figure he called the "senator's fetish of the American entrepreneur" (35)—one of the social vocabularies I reexamine.

I also mean to employ Mills's "white collar" (coming into usage in this period) and "new middle class" heuristically in order to better understand the dynamic process of cultural and literary representation.[17] If one begins cultural analysis by imputing a fixed historical backdrop—rigid occupational categories, a unified class culture, or a given class consciousness—often the best one can do is argue how literary forms respond passively, either as reflections or mystifications of social processes (either filter-down or bubble-up reactions).[18] On the first score one risks, as Cathy Davidson has observed, tautological reiteration of given cultural-historical paradigms and documents (collapsing literature into history); on the second, one often neglects literature's positive cultural work, its meaning-making activity in trying to refashion readers' horizons. Today, even our best critical studies too often portray History (usually capitalized) as a static backdrop, with literary forms (or an imputed political unconscious) standing only in a reactive relation to social change. Yet as Michael Denning has argued, we need to ask not merely what can be learned about the situating of narratives in a class context, but what can be learned *from* them about contemporaneous class formations and ideology. One does not have to be an apostle of the hermeneutic circle to recognize that, in order to open up this imaginative terrain *as* history, it is necessary to shuttle back and forth between cultural forms and their social situating. Literary forms often pose a cultural horizon or set of historical givens to be interrogated, brought into conflict with each other, dramatized in dreamlike explorations; through these imaginary transformations, sense and nonsense are made of new social determinants and their possibilities.[19]

The word "fictions" in my title, consequently, refers not merely to a plurality of narrative forms (including drama), but to the linguistic and material conditions that served to "make up"—both mystify and constitute—white collar life itself. In each individual study, I hope to draw together job experience and vocational strategies with the narrative conventions and social vocabularies that served to negotiate tasks and problems faced by individual white collar Americans. Each Part takes up a "determining" social condition bearing upon white collar life. Part I considers the matter of dependence or service—in its simplest sense subordination to others in the workplace—as it was represented by two popular writers, O. Henry and Edna Ferber. Perhaps the most commonly observed condition, dependence has been ascribed to white collar workers by analysts of virtually all political persuasions.[20] Part II considers the role of professionalization in the liberal refashioning of political theory and authority in this era; here I ask how two writers, Robert Grant and Elmer Rice, crafted new literary forms to negotiate a growing conviction at the heart of liberal thought: the hypothesizing of new "middle" Americans swayed more by fantasy and symbol-making than appeals to their rational self-interest. Unlike the deliberative citizen of the republican tradition, this new "average person" is akin to a reader on the run, motivated not by reason but by habits and attitudes.[21] Part III discusses two better-known writers, Sherwood Anderson and Sinclair Lewis, who created perhaps the most enduring representations of "Main Street" culture—and who were also engaged in what have been called the "culturalist" dimensions of new middle-class work: advertising, public relations, even book production and publicity itself.[22]

Though these chapters are thus cross-referenced around white collar issues, I have tried to make each reasonably self-sufficient, recognizing that many readers may wish only to consult my discussions of individual authors. I also address particular subtopics that may be of more specialized concern: O. Henry and human-interest journalism; Ferber and the modernization of women's sentimental fiction; Robert Grant and our current understanding of realism and liberalism; the problem of narrative voice in *Winesburg, Ohio* (1919). My larger hope would be, in the plan of the book as a whole, to bring together methods in social history and literary theory which recently have shown signs of going separate ways. In recent years, despite the explosion of research in local history, gender and class studies, and labor history, literary critics have become—under a range of provocative new interpretive techniques fostered by the climate of postmodernism—much more interested in textual and ideological decoding, often to the exclusion of this new research. In some quarters, even under the banner of the new historicism, the New Critical distrust of biography and intention escalated into the "death of the author," as criticism gravitated instead to mapping out cognitive fields of ideology, discourse, systems of representation and belief. If one critic calls for examining a "micro-foundation" of social conditions influencing literary practice, many others favor the "speculative" and "relational" interests that once marked classic American criticism, transcending the local and the merely visible.[23]

There have been enormous gains on both sides, and certainly the field of historical criticism is large enough to contain a variety of approaches. Yet my own view is that there have also been costs incurred by a too-exclusive emphasis on what E. P. Thompson has identified as the seductive "idealism" of discourse analysis (or rigid ideological decoding). Cultural vocabularies are commonly cut loose from their class moorings and accents; literary critics betray little interest in the material dimensions of history; cultural holism returns, often surreptitiously, in the guise of totalizing theory; criticism returns to brittle reassertions of a given writer's "subversiveness" or "complicity" (usually based solely on rhetorical grounds).[24] Wherever possible, as Clifford Geertz writes, I have tried to keep "the analysis of symbolic forms" as close as possible "to concrete social events and occasions, the public world of common life"—if only to see *which* social vocabularies and literary forms acquired conventionality, dominance, or resistance in and around local contexts. Such local occasions, at the very least, provide a needed corrective against taking gestures of commonality, writerly patronage, and particularly discursive power at face value—even, alas, our own.[25]

| | |

As I have said, these white collar literary fictions have not figured very prominently in recent scholarship; of the writers considered herein, only Sherwood Anderson has had a full-length scholarly biography since the early 1970s. Elsewhere, with a few worthy exceptions, critical interest (in O. Henry, Ferber, or Grant, for example) is practically moribund. In part, this reflects the fact that some of these writers were once canonized by a series of loosely connected narratives in Progressive literary history, only to be subsequently attacked in New Critical, counter-Progressive criticism. Several of these writers remain, of course, as pantheon figures in literary history's "Innocent Rebellion" against Victorianism; as rebels in the "revolt from the village"; as "smart set" debunkers of bourgeois culture inspired by H. L. Mencken.[26] At this late date, however, it is of little use to rehearse in detail my reservations about these histories—for instance, the common tendency to portray Lewis as representative of a generalized intellectual rebellion. Suffice it to say that this earlier scholarship organized cultural history into a dialogue or competition between competing metaphorical paradigms, an approach with thoroughly discussed strengths and limitations; these histories usually positioned writers as dissenting from mainstream/Main Street assumptions, or (worse yet) in a space somehow outside culture—a claim I reexamine in my later chapters particularly. These older histories also tended to view writers as passive recorders of cultural life, discounting their social and vocational framework by characterizing them as cosmopolitan wits (or, conversely, intuitive writers)—and overlooking what Hans Robert Jauss has called the "horizon of expectations" set by private and public institutions of cultural reception and audience.[27] Even a brief reimmersion in the literary history of this period raises other problems: that, contrary to the notion that these idioms were by-products of the disillusionment following World War I, experimentation in white collar portraiture predated 1900; that, contrary to the more recent idea that these writers were "closet" conservatives, many (Lewis, Anderson, Ferber, Grant, Rice) thought of themselves as progressive liberals; that these decades (even the 1920s) were full of affirmative, and highly popular, portraits of middle-class Americans.

To a degree, the persisting narratives of intellectual rebellion—including histories of naturalism and muckraking—have disguised the rather consistent popularity of "middling" social representation in this era. Many contemporaries acknowledged the recurrent demand for what was variously called "Main Street in Fiction," "clean fiction," *Saturday Evening Post* stories, or fiction of "typical" Americans.[28] One thinks, for example, of Chicago humorist George Ade's newspaper sketches of the unpretentious, informal urbanite who was putatively freer than either of his proletarian and plutocratic counterparts—portraits that, as Burton Bledstein observes, typified a nascent American interest in middle-class behavior and mores.[29] Likewise there is O. Henry (William Sydney Porter), the so-called "caliph of New York," who habitually denigrated class labels in his stories, specializing instead in human interest, small-scale portraits of clerks, stenographers, shopgirls, and other employees. Before his death, O. Henry had sold nearly five million bound volumes of his stories (most of them previously published by Joseph Pulitzer's *New York World*); as late as 1922, even Fred Lewis Pattee, although upset by O. Henry's journalistic flavor, had to admit he still dominated the age's tastes in short fiction.

O. Henry, of course, would have a series of self-conscious protégés like Edna Ferber, William Saroyan, Christopher Morley (*Human Being* [1932] and *Kitty Foyle* [1939]), and even (briefly) Elmer Rice and H. L. Mencken. Meanwhile, the success of O. Henry and Ade provided a set of expectations that would affect other writers, such as Ring Lardner, Sherwood Anderson, James Thurber (first in his Mr. Munroe tales), and Sinclair Lewis (notably in the Lancelot Todd advertising tales of the teens). Portraits of the American "national character" in these years—in which everyone from E. A. Ross to Robert Grant or Nicholas Murray Butler participated—often explicitly linked their normative portraiture to the world of business, to a singular "middle" American type who was a prisoner of cultural convention and taboo. Mencken's infamous *boobus Americanus,* a figure so axiomatic to cultural descriptions of the American businessman in these years, actually took shape in a series on "The American" (1913–14), which contributed to this national character debate.[30] In literary representations, one thinks as well of such resolute portraits of American middleness as Mr. Zero of Rice's *The Adding Machine* (1923); the citizens of Anderson's *Windy McPherson's Son* (1916) and *Winesburg, Ohio* (1919), each of which had its own Main Street; the stenographers and secretaries of Dorothy Parker. Such portraits of "average" white collar Americans made their way into popular media as well: contemporary films with titles like *The Clerk* (1914), *Making a Living*

(1914), and *The Eternal Grind* (1911) centered on commonplace, commuting, office-bound Americans such as the horned-rimmed hero of Harold Lloyd's *Safety Last* (1923). Lloyd and Hal Roach explicitly aimed to create a "regular fellow" distinguishable from the Chaplinesque tramp, that icon of social polarization with his gentlemanly charm and yet ragged appearance, so they adorned Lloyd with oversized, horned-rimmed glasses. "I would be an average recognizable American youth," Lloyd remembered, "and let the situations take care of the comedy." Similarly, newspaper readers were treated to cartoons like "Blondie" (begun in 1930), or those by "the American Hogarth," Gluyas Williams, presenting the suburban small-fry.[31] This set of expectations even had a role to play in the standards set down by metropolitan arbiters like *The Smart Set* and *The New Yorker*. The normative middle-class existence, sometimes equated with everything "primitive" in our national culture, not surprisingly became a foil for intellectual rebellion in these years. Mencken's *Smart Set,* in fact, defined itself as "for minds that are not primitive," just as *The New Yorker* said it was "not for the lady from Dubuque." As one commentator on modern intellectual magazines remarked in 1923, "the *intelligentsia* are perpetually lamenting that shift in emphasis, in the modern dispensation, which has made the average man not only the center of the political system, but the arbiter, to a very considerable extent, of literary and artistic destinies as well."[32]

Such complaints, meanwhile, were borne out by best-seller statistics. As *Publisher's Weekly* surveyor Irving Harlow Hart observed at the time, popular literary tastes in hardcover fiction had been markedly Americanized since the 1890s. Reversing the rule of the nineteenth century, of the hundred best-selling authors from 1900 to 1925, sixty-nine had been of American birth. Hart also went out of his way to observe that novels "distinctively American in setting" had been among the most consistent best-sellers in the first quarter-century. Grant's *Unleavened Bread,* which satirized a "middle" parvenu named Selma White, was a national best-seller in 1900. Ferber had established her celebrity with her *American Magazine* serial about businesswoman Emma McChesney in the teens. Booth Tarkington, by Hart's estimate, had been the fiction leader since 1910 and by 1920 was already third in total sales since 1900. In the quarter-century marked by the Progressive reform movement, the Russian revolution, and World War I, the longest running best-seller in America was Eleanor Hodgman Porter's *Pollyanna* (1913).[33] After the war, this pattern continued. Spending some sixteen weeks on best-seller lists, Lewis's *Main Street* was not only the #1 hardcover fiction best-seller for the postwar era, but for the entire period from 1900 to 1925 (and *Babbitt* would eventually outdistance its sales). Lewis himself was the #3 overall sales leader from 1919 to 1926, going on to have five national best-sellers in a single decade, refuse the Pulitzer (and later serve on its jury), and become the first American writer to win the Nobel Prize. Ferber had, by 1926, become the most popular female fiction writer in America, winning her own Pulitzer for *So Big* (1924) and breaking into the best-seller list three times in the twenties. (In hardcover best-selling, Ferber was the tenth most popular writer in America between 1919 and 1926; by comparison Edith Wharton was fourteenth; Scott Fitzgerald, fifty-fourth). Tarkington made the best-seller lists six times by 1928, and was crowned twice with the Pulitzer Prize—in 1922 for *Alice Adams*, the story of a midwestern middle-class socialite turned office worker, often considered a response to *Main Street* itself.

It must be remembered, of course, that even these seemingly pure manifestations of popular American taste were partly molded by literary institutions. For instance, the Americanization of best-seller lists, Irving Hart observed, was no accident; rather it was a direct consequence (and intention) of the protectionist provisions of the International Copyright Law of 1891.[34] Similarly, Ferber, Mencken, and Christopher Morley turned to O. Henry as a model partly because he was perhaps the first American writer to have received such an *institutional* memorializing upon his death in 1910. As I will discuss in Chapter 1, O. Henry's own white collar life was sanitized in several testimonial volumes, biographies, and memoirs, by the founding of the O. Henry Hotel in his home state, by the posthumous O. Henry short-story prize.[35] Likewise, the fact that writers such as Tarkington, Ferber, or Lewis dominated the Pulitzer Prize lists was, as a few contemporaries recognized, partly a reflection of the specific intent of the prize itself. Extrapolating from Joseph Pulitzer's original deed of gift, prize boards were directed to select a novel reflecting the "whole," or alternately the "wholesome," atmosphere of American life, as well as "the highest standard of American manners and manhood." In its first decade and a half after its inception in 1917, the prize was dominated by Columbia University's Nicholas Murray Butler, whose pronouncements on "national character" in texts like *The American as He Is* (1908) were echoed in Pulitzer selections. In this collection of speeches given at the University of Copenhagen, Butler claimed that the "ninety millions of American people are at bottom a single and recognizable type"—essentially a "good citizen," conservative, loyal to native institutions—and easily "seen at its purest and best in any one of the hundred or more small cities and towns in the Middle West." In addition, Butler chose critics and authors for Advisory Board members—William Allen White, William Lyon Phelps, Richard Burton, Bliss Perry, Hamlin Garland, Stuart Sherman, to name just a few—usually well disposed towards novels broad in scope and particularized in manners, depicting virtuous money-making by modern yet simple folk of pioneering stock. Robert Grant himself had joined the Pulitzer board as juror, where he backed books in the *Main Street* vein.[36]

Finally, there were the changes in literary taste, production, and distribution inaugurated by the new breed of editor and publisher—Joseph Pulitzer himself, George Horace Lorimer, Edward Bok—who had brought "Main Street" commercial values to mass-market publishing. Several of these entrepreneurs initially became sponsors of reform writing, popular naturalism, and muckraking, and to this their initial fame as promoters of Jack London, Upton Sinclair, and other writers is often tied.[37] But within a decade after popular naturalism's heyday—indeed, as muckraking was simultaneously subsumed under a broader turn to topical magazine content—contentious rabble-rousing, heightened passions, irresponsible raking of the "muck" was soon contrasted to a supposedly saner path. It was not unusual when Charles Dwyer, editor of *The Delineator,* announced as early as 1904 that "[w]hatever the function of magazines may be, the function of this magazine is not to exploit so-called 'problems.' We stand for the home . . . though it may be necessary at times to strike the minor chord, it is the alert, helpful note that travels farthest and does the most good in the world." In a short time, the high circulations of magazines with names like *McCall's, Everybody's, The Saturday Evening Post,* and *The Ladies' Home Journal* reflected the reinvigorated cultural centrality of family life, safe breadwinning, and middle-of-the-road normality. Even reforming was tied to efficient management of consumption, curtailing patent medicine ads, offering designs for middle-class homes. Edward Bok of the *Journal* repeatedly pleaded with readers to recognize "the element of romance in our everyday life," spoke out against the "willful and reckless criticism of other people's doings and motives," and argued that reform legislation meant little without individual reform on one's own doorstep. As if mining Main Street logic himself, Bok (like Butler) declared that the real American life existed outside the urban centers, in small cities like Albany, Troy, Syracuse, New Haven, or Hartford. Here—ostensibly—home life and domesticity were preserved, religious faith was stronger, and common sense prevailed.[38] Indeed, as the somewhat fragmentary market research materials available from these years indicate, such magazines self-consciously cultivated an audience in the new cities of the Midwest, often aiming (as *McCall's* editor Burton Rascoe recalled) explicitly at salaried white collar workers and their wives. When Robert and Helen Lynd surveyed their own Middletown (Muncie, Indiana) in 1924, aggregate circulation for the *Post* and *Journal* was roughly sixty times that of older magazines like *Harper's* or *The Century*.[39] (These were the new magazines and audiences that could inflame Robert Grant's ire in creating Selma White; inspire Ferber to try her hand at shopgirl stories; make Sinclair Lewis, writing about office employees, into what Lorimer would call a "household word.")

Not only was business fiction actively sought by editors like Lorimer at the *Post*,[40] but business and professional leaders were increasingly solicited for magazine articles or interviews in magazines with workaday titles like *The World's Work*, or *The American* (satirized in *Babbitt*), or *Everybody's* (the first patron of Ferber). Editors were in fact typically awed by business achievement; in 1926 Lorimer would declare that there was "no finer product of modern civilization than the modern businessman"—by which he usually meant a more generalized white collar citizen. Lorimer defined his average "American" as a middle-aged man who "has gained a fair degree of material success," yet not one given over to "bookishness and ripe culture."[41] "The stuff of literature," Lorimer declared, "is human character, and the stuff of gossip is human character—or the lack of it. What people are, what they have done, what they are doing or going to do—that is the prime interest of every normal being."[42] Editorially, the *Post* was dedicated to what it called "The Plain American," caught between capital and labor (though clearly more loyal to the former). Resurrecting an aphoristic, Franklinesque style, Lorimer (son of Baptist evangelical George Claude Lorimer) preached for "law enforcement, for cleaner living, and sounder thinking"; allowed no liquor, cigarette, real estate, or financial ads; ran his longest series on "Your Savings"; and handed out advice to the young man who was a private, lieutenant, or aspiring captain of industry. Always astride the top of circulation lists for Lorimer's thirty-eight year tenure, the *Post* declared that "successful money-getting calls for soberness of living and evenness of mentality." (I discuss this platform further in Chapter 1.) "Given moderate ability and fair health—the endowment of the average man—and any youth with good staying power may still work through to the fore." "Nothing succeeds like common sense," Lorimer advised, "and common sense is an expression of sound morals." Again, a key component here was that social contentiousness was discounted, "hyphenated" Americanism belittled, meddling reform seen as bolshevistic. Lorimer proclaimed the end to rough and tumble business ethics, identified the distribution of wealth as the main achievement of the American system, and called for human cooperation in the spirit of "good gossip" and "professional Pollyanna"-hood. (Bok, similarly, compared his stories to "mental sunshine.") In its capsule biographies of the successful businessman, the *Post*'s publicity proclaimed, such a figure was shown to be "a human being, made of the same sort of dust as the doctor or village blacksmith."[43] This style of commonality, in fact, was what Edith Wharton ridiculed as the "just folks" reflex exhibited by the proliferating Main Street novels in the twenties—in which, Wharton complained, Howells's famous defense of "the whole of human nature" had degenerated into a relentless literary homage to "that hollow unreality, 'Man.'"[44]

These lists can only begin to suggest the range of cultural representations surrounding the new "common mean" of American life in its new habitats. If, as Stuart Blumin has suggested, late-nineteenth-century social languages were increasingly marked by polarized, two-class descriptions of American social structure—and at best an "unsaid" center—these newer cultural fictions point explicitly to an expanding middle register, indeed propose (in some cases) a society virtually without traditional class distinctions.[45] But my point is not that "common people" or white collar figures numerically outnumbered other characters in this era's "imagination," nor that they personified a turn-of-the-century Zeitgeist. Nor do they provide a ready list of character traits that supposedly reflect the norms of an ostensibly symmetrical (much less classless) "American" culture. (To follow any of these lines, in fact, would be simply to replicate some of the normative rhetorics that still inhibit the writing of cultural history itself.) For one thing, cataloging the sheer volume of cultural images tells us little about the common idiomatic forms such representations of white collar Americans often took. Such portraits were often marked, for instance, by various strategies of cultural *vraisemblance:* by an emphasis on normative, "synoptic," or "paradigmatic" cultural delineation (simply put, a single character who putatively embodied a social average); by insistence on the ordinariness of such characters, whether to their credit or detriment, and on their subjection to habit and routine; by a dependence of such characterization on what Mencken dubbed "common American"—that is, mass vernacular idioms or testaments that blended malaprop, slang, first-person monologue—and occasionally self-indicting confession.[46] These portraits were often strikingly cultural rather than historical or biological; they were portraits in the now, describing the normative behavior of an ostensibly average citizen with narrow horizons and limited options, a "regular fellow" (or woman) governed by habit, taboo, cultural fantasy, and nationalist cliché. In sentimental forms or in the most extreme caricatures, these citizens were often daydreamers, closet romantics in a struggle with their routinized existences. In this way, members of a white collar class were made to embody "mass" social life at large. At the heart of Main Street's literary popularity, as Wharton partly discerned, was an act of nationalist cultural and class synopsis. As what she called "middling clay" became the soil of literary representation, to be "American," "just folks," middle-class, or "mass" were simultaneously seen as one and the same thing.

| | |

In singling out a cause for the "just folks" reflex disseminated by popular imitators of Sinclair Lewis, Wharton pointed to the rapid standardization of American social life. Complaining that writers only focused on the "common mean" (649) of experience, Wharton blamed a social system in which "degrees of culture and conduct" had simply been "Taylorized" (650) out of existence. But the social vocabularies underwriting the cultural synopsis she described—particularly the linking of white collar to a cultural "mean"—were by no means an inevitable by-product of any broad-scale social homogenization. Even by using the broadest definition of white collar classes—in terms of income, percentage of population, and so on—one does not arrive at anything like an arithmetic average of society as a whole even by 1920. Not until the late 1950s would the number of nonmanual workers in America exceed that of manual employees.[47] Nonetheless, from the very start, contemporary critics subsumed the writers who worked literary Main Street under a naive, unitary, mimetic claim: that their writing mirrored its times. Quite commonly, for example, Lewis was positioned by critics as a native realist who wrote "great novels" made up of "great masses of the veritable stuff of existence" (Carl Van Doren), a "documentarian" writer (Mencken's description). Even notorious opponents of naturalism like Stuart Sherman acclaimed Lewis as "a leader in the famous revolt of the Younger Generation" who employed "objective narration" to fashion "representative" Americans in the first truly "national" narrative style. In 1940, Alfred Kazin described Lewis as having "led so mimetic an existence that his works have even come to seem an uncanny reproduction of surface reality. Not so much revelations of life as brilliant equivalents of it." "Mirror," "photography," "mime" were common generic descriptions; structural lapses were deemed the cost of embodying actual life. In subsequent years, persisting current labels like "debunker" only extended this claim. As Theodor Adorno has suggested, the dissenting "debunker" label and the naive mimetic claim actually coexist quite peacefully. The debunker often describes himself as a "seer" who is not "taken in" by the illusions of the "Mr. Knownothing" he ridicules; his vision is consequently described as a realistic one, the penetrating eye of the satirist who sees behind events, dethroning bunk.[48] Questions of the contingencies and revisions of style and genre are thus omitted altogether, and we are presented with transcriptions of, or "equivalents" to, white collar life which are somehow also not of it.

In this study I hope to follow a different approach to writers, texts, and cultural representation. Works such as Grant's *Unleavened Bread* (1900), Ferber's "Sisters Under Their Skin" (1915), or Lewis's *Babbitt* are hardly spontaneous or autonomous responses to externalized cultural values or myths; rather they are created within a network of highly charged and often competing social, political, and aesthetic demands on representation. Consequently, we need to recapture these writers' intellectual vocabularies, the genres they identified as their models, the social issues they deemed most pressing, and how they engaged their audiences in those issues. We need to look at the cultural institutions in which writers were produced (and reproduced themselves): Sunday newspapers, law schools, advertising firms, the agencies of literary publicity, memorialization, and even decanonization itself.[49] As Greenblatt has suggested, writers' intentions, genre choices, and historical situations interpenetrate one another; these forces enter into alliance, struggle fiercely with one another, reform each other within the text and without—but not arbitrarily. Literary texts offer an imaginative arena in which prevailing social vocabularies, personal fantasy and anxiety, political intentions, and social repercussions are tested out, brought into contest. (In fact, if white collar fictions have a signature, it is the daydream—examples of which I will explore.) Because the text's cultural and "dream" work is often a locus of this conflict, it is often read by audiences in radically different ways.

This last point is an important one. Perhaps my most difficult challenge is to explore how such a conflict, even in aesthetic terms, was contiguous with the struggle of turn-of-the-century new middle classes to define themselves.

I have therefore consciously chosen six writers who—despite the relative silence of literary history on the matter—all had significant engagement (indeed, in some cases ongoing engagement) with the modern determinants of white collar life. Of course, this was not representative of all writers working literary Main Street—a phenomenon of taste, to be sure, with any number of causes. But this engagement does point to an important confluence taking place at some of its strategic points of production—in effect, an inside story that may explain how new social vocabularies negotiated a changing social life, naturalized its contradictions, indeed became a cultural "Main Street" to begin with. For it is not only that the turn-of-century years witnessed a widespread commerce, overlapping—or if you will, "imbrication"—between art and business due to changes in literary markets, but rather that many of the skills we commonly associate with imaginative literature—drafting effective prose, anticipating an audience, creating a credible, authoritative, or personable voice—had already been incorporated into the Main Street practices of modern capitalism.[50] In this sense, literary Main Street did not merely reflect changing patterns of taste, or regional pride, or intellectual nostalgia for a disappearing way of life, but a rewriting of class languages and norms of social representation within the everyday practices of white collar life itself—within what E. P. Thompson has called the "raw material of experience" and consciousness that derive from common experiences as a class.[51]

My use of "fictions" is thus, again, meant to suggest the open borders between narrative, ideology, languages of class, and white collar experience, as is my resorting to the currently derogated field of biography. In this period, in fact, writers readily acknowledged the open borders they hoped to create between life and art, seeing their literary work as social "potions," intraclass allegories, patronage of social classes, and scripts for living. Consequently, to understand these open borders, this study examines American writing beyond that commonly deemed "literary"—for instance, Grant's juvenile novels or legal writing, Lewis's publicity writing, Anderson's advice to agricultural advertisers—but not simply to flout any currently prevailing canon. Rather, my idea here is to move into white collar worlds and out again, to cross the boundaries critics have usually assumed existed between these writers and routine existence. The current challenge of literary history, rather than to continue hypothesizing about the constitutive role of texts in history, is to throw such idioms in social relief within (not just against) historical process. What I want to explore here is the striking contiguity or "imbrication" of literary and white collar practice in this period—several developments, literary and nonliterary, that collaborated in vitiating the ostensibly separate space of literary culture and made this body of American literature constitutional in the reformation of class description itself.

Naturally, then, I have tried to pay attention to how writers were read, promoted, and critically received in their own day. Throughout I want to relate my findings to the recent theoretical speculation about the "cultural work" popular texts may do. In part this term has been coined to describe the way in which popular or critically prominent authors, in their own day, articulate and propose solutions for the problems shaping their historical moment, thus providing their readers a way of ordering the world and attributing meaning to it. The term has been applied especially to currently marginalized authors—nineteenth-century sentimental novelists, James Fenimore Cooper—who, like so many of the writers in this study, were deemed "tedious and safe" by succeeding generations of critics. Philip Fisher, for example, has speculated that the most potentially "radical" works are those that do the mundane cultural work of reforming ways of seeing, and fashioning consensus, in their own day. Similarly, in an invaluable discussion of Antonio Gramsci's notion of hegemony, T. J. Jackson Lears has argued that we must examine how certain ideological "codes" "establish the plausibility of their discourse," in "cementing a given group's social prestige" and purveying notions of "common sense."[52] In the chapters that follow, I want to rephrase this critical interest in cultural work—which is almost always a matter of informed guesswork—to what I will call the "cultural solubility" of writing. I am interested in how authors and texts fashion commonsensicality and marshall typification, gather authority and engage their readers, make the "literary" look like a livable fiction. The memorial to O. Henry in Greensboro, North Carolina (see photograph, page *i*) perfectly suggests this relationship: in the "pages" of a bronze statue representing an O. Henry volume, a reader (or character?) peers across a permeable text boundary. Rather than seeing these writers' literary gestures towards fashioning "common sense" and "human nature" as merely false consciousness or sentimentality, I want to take their construction seriously. As a literary historian, naturally, I am primarily interested in how social life was represented in literary subject matter. Yet beyond this, I am also interested in tracing the how of discursive power as much as the what, in visualizing the different strategies of power inhering in white collar literary fictions themselves: in the modeling of a "commonsensical" social vocabulary; in the control of psychological space and, therefore, social perspective; in the "scripting" (projecting a social pattern) of a developed or "capable" white collar life. By so doing, we may begin to understand how these literary representations may have themselves entered into and become part of what one historian has called the "thick ideational cement" of middle-class awareness itself.[53]

Rather than hold their popularity against many of these writers—as final critical proof of their supposedly minor status—I want to explore the social designs and potential power inherent in the simple fact of their solubility. Today, when such figures of putative national "averageness"—Babbittry, the "little man," Walter Mitty, even the "Middle American"—remain so much a part of national folk wisdom, we have neglected their prehistory as cultural constructions. In one sense, much like the Americans Mills described, these mythologies and social vocabularies—as I will discuss in closing—did enter quietly, as if in the back entrances of cultural reasoning, in the manner Robert Lynd (quoting historian Carl Becker) once hypothesized. In time, Lynd predicted, such "assumptions" come to be "regarded as so much 'of course' as hardly to require proof; they are passed readily from hand to hand like smooth-worn coins."[54] These writers aimed for a kind of power we all too often overlook: the power of becoming axiomatic.

Part I Family Trials

One **Over the Counter** O. Henry and the Loyal Employee

Not very long ago some one invented the assertion that there were only "Four Hundred" people in New York City who were really worth noticing. But a wiser man has arisen—the census taker—and his larger estimate of human interest has been preferred in marking out the field of these little stories of the "Four Million."

—O. Henry, The Four Million

The epigraph above is from O. Henry's first volume of New York City tales, *The Four Million,* published by McClure in 1906; most of the stories had appeared previously in Joseph Pulitzer's Sunday *New York World* magazine section. In posthumous Authorized Editions, this epigraph would be preceded only by the title page and a photograph of a street scene: a crowd shot from several stories up so that everyone is scaled down, faceless—shielded by straw boaters, the hat typically worn by male office workers—flanked by the commuter's trolley and a stone-faced office building.[1] In many respects both the photo and the epigraph served as O. Henry's career prolegomenon. In an oracular pronouncement, he appoints himself recorder, and moreover patron, of the mass: he is for them even before he begins, a loyal representer. He identifies himself with the census taker (itself a white collar job), a recorder of a plurality of occupations—and with his door-to-door, mathematical matter-of-factuality. O. Henry's portraits are "estimates," not "inventions" of mere assertability; his "little stories" are most meaningful when taken in the mass. They work, in the lexicon of Pulitzer's journalism, to estimate "human interest," and less obviously, perhaps, to take notice of readers themselves. In a very real sense, O. Henry is indeed "marking out a field" for himself before he begins; in return, his little stories of little people often made readers feel proprietary. "Having O. Henry's writing there at all," William Saroyan later wrote, "was like having a living thing that was one's own. He was a nobody, but he was a nobody who was also a somebody, everybody's somebody."[2]

At first, the elusive significance of O. Henry (the pen name of William Sydney Porter) seems to reside in this seemingly paradoxical gesture: that, somehow, he made his mass patronage into a specialized trademark. What distinguished O. Henry, his contemporary supporters said repeatedly, was that he was for everybody.[3] Such a conclusion might easily await anyone tracing through successive generations of his memorialization. To his colleagues in publishing and journalism—the pallbearers at his funeral were a virtual *Who's Who* of mass-market publishing—O. Henry was the "Caliph" of "Bagdad-on-the-Subway," a man who had arrived an unknown in New York and yet mastered its mysteries. That Alphonso Smith's biography (1916) followed the format more typical of the nineteenth century—mixing life and letters with scrupulously sanitized testimonials—only exemplified this carefully managed adulation. His stories were reissued in exotically bound "Bagdad" editions, in special memorial volumes, in pamphlets from Doubleday which indexed his tales and critical reviews. A hotel was founded in O. Henry's name; a campaign began to build a statue in Columbus Circle in New York; another memorial was erected in Raleigh, North Carolina, in 1914; finally, the O. Henry Prize was established in 1918. For the next seven decades, despite O. Henry's belittling in the academy by New Critics and literary historians alike, the public enshrining of his skills in "human interest" continued.

It was supposedly a mass idiom without modern origins—so contemporaries claimed. Typically, such admirers enfolded O. Henry's origins instead within the nostalgic cracker-barrel mythology of Poor Richard. O. Henry's memorializers often recounted how the young Will Porter, having worked as a clerk in his uncle's pharmacy, had assimilated the wide array of "human nature" that passed through the store seeking relief from the pain of life. Porter did in fact draw sketches of his townspeople at the time, often composing limericks about customers on the back of pencil drawings.[4] This legend inspired such testimonials as Christopher Morley's poem, "O. Henry

—Apothecary," which called Porter the "master pharmacist of joy and pain," a writer shrewd about human foibles yet sympathetic to private injury. Porter was even said to have found his pen name "O. Henry" from the *United States Dispensary,* having copied the name of a noted French druggist. In these ways, O. Henry's humanizing of "average" New Yorkers—in a manner akin to what Edith Wharton would later call the "just folks" idiom of the twenties—was linked to shrines of preindustrial, precorporate, familial capitalism: the pharmacy, the country store counter, the realms of store-bought wisdom and gossip. Laissez-faire trade became the crucible of his craft; little wonder that he was revered by George Horace Lorimer.[5] That O. Henry had in fact never been the mythical apothecary; that pharmacies had been only one of his clerical jobs; that in his fiction the over-the-counter potions often backfired or did not work—all this was overlooked. Instead, contemporaries said O. Henry's census-taking balanced "human nature" and the imprint of urban life. O. Henry's is a prosaic, episodic, consensual realism of human equivalence with and among "ordinary" citizens—a style later imitated by writers like Edna Ferber, William Saroyan, Robert Benchley, James Thurber, and Morley himself.[6]

This was only part of the story, however; in his own time, O. Henry's "human interest" was achieved originally through his representation of class. O. Henry's enterprise begins from the bottom border of the middle class, from the world of clerks, salesgirls, cabdrivers, stenographers; his photo frontispiece confines itself to the downtown and does not extend to the outskirts or factory workers. He was commonly dubbed the "little shop-girl's knight." At least one shrewd contemporary reviewer, Chicago critic Frances Hackett, credited O. Henry with conveying "a humorous yet profound understanding of a phase that has not yet been treated before in American art. . . . O. Henry accepts, with a mixture of irony, wit, and sympathy, the distressing fact that a human being can be a clerk, the remarkable fact that a clerk can be a human being." In fact the writer himself had reportedly remarked, upon visiting a gathering of department-store workers, that "if Henry James had gone to work in one of those places, he would have turned out the great American novel."[7] That is, much of O. Henry's power resided in his humanizing of current social differences, his covert revisions of class description itself. In contrast to so many nineteenth-century writers, he offered to make the "mass" safe, to give it a human face. Francis Hackett thought O. Henry was not "patronizing"; to reread this unintentional pun, one might say O. Henry worked along the border of sales and employee relations, toying with the tensions about dependence, "loyalty," and identity that are created within the store or office or across the counter—to use his word, within their "curriculum."

| | |

Perhaps the most frequently discussed social determinant of white collar work is American workers' putatively new dependence—in its fundamental sense, subordination to others. In the implication of the word "employee," this condition is often thought of as a loss of earlier freedom or autonomy. For years, historians and sociologists have emphasized how the prudential ethos of "middling" Americans—which had enjoined the value of free labor, craftsmanship, manual work, and property holding—eroded in the Gilded Age and after. In a republican jeremiad extending from Thorstein Veblen to C. Wright Mills and beyond, analysts viewed white collar workers as having "fallen," as it were, into salaried employment, paperwork, and consumer borrowing. Certainly the recurrent metaphor of "wage slavery," an idea as close to the heart of Abraham Lincoln as to Karl Marx, may well have reflected how turn-of-the-century white collar workers experienced what Cindy Sondik Aron sees as a "defensive" posture, a feeling of "psychological sacrifice" on the job.[8] Corporate employment, many historians reasoned, was bound to have deleterious effects on the traditional character traits—thrift, sobriety, self-control, future-mindedness, and perseverance—undergirding the middling classes in the past. Indeed, there did seem to be signs of change in material conditions and popular ideologies. Like factory workers, clerks encountered the rationalization and scientific management of their work; modest property holding was, even among the salaried clerical workers of the federal government, rare enough indeed (Aron, 22–25). Taken as a whole, clerks now seemed to settle into a permanent white collar workforce with limited chances to rise. In such a climate, Horatio Alger's familiar justification for his hero's pluck and perseverance—rising upward—seemed to become an anachronism.

This is not an unfamiliar story. On the other hand, the traditional way in which "dependence" has been seen—as a decline from middle-class "independence"—may be a little schematic and misleading. If clerical workers did come from failed businesses and faltering families, then the old middle-class world hardly looks so stable itself. If white collar employees shuffled from job to job, as many did, then working for others was hardly a new experience. Moreover, there were several status advantages commonly accorded white over blue collar work. For instance, working conditions in offices or stores tended to be cleaner than those in factories; sales jobs provided proximity to the glamorous world of goods and often an affluent clientele; from a nativist standpoint, clerical employees mixed less frequently with the newer (Southern European) immigrants, since clerks (partly because of the language needs of their work and prejudices of their clientele) were usually native born. Historians sometimes also cite the status of being identified with a prestigious store or corporation. Clerical pay in 1900 was also roughly double that of transportation and production workers.[9] Meanwhile, many historians of turn-of-the-century success literature have reminded us how durable the older ideologies of thrift, sobriety, self-control, future-mindedness, and perseverance actually were well into the twentieth century. Newer emphases on "personal magnetism" or professional competence did not take hold automatically. Although commercial academies (such as Elmer Rice and Sherwood Anderson would attend) had begun to train tens of thousands of students by the 1890s, specialized education of this kind still failed, in the judgement of Donald Meyer, to stimulate the public imagination. When New York editor and lecturer Albert Shaw, in *The Outlook for the Average Man* (1907), urged his readers to acquire the "science, invention, skill, special training" of the professions and technical vocations, the book apparently fell on deaf ears.[10]

What all of this suggests is that the problem of white collar dependence was more subtle, and the alterations in middle-class ideologies less cataclysmic than may be supposed. For "dependence" could mean not simply a loss of entrepreneurial energy or a putative freedom to act, but something that went to the core of cultural justifications for character, loyalty, even selfhood itself. It could mean disappearing into a corporation's identity at the expense of one's own; it could mean a threat to the borders between what was legitimately inside work and outside of it; it could signify identification with the corporation, loyalty to the commodity, at the expense of other loyalties to family or community. The turn-of-the-century usage of "wage slavery" elicited associations not just with ill-treatment or confinement, but with a loss of agency, with the displacement of familial loyalties, with loss of an imprint on one's world.[11] Clerical dependence interacted with concerns that were just as properly, indeed originally, issues of personal and familial socialization: matters of personal loyalty, of trust in others, being able (in the older entrepreneurial or artisanal traditions) to put one's name on one's work. In a period in which many family businesses increasingly gave way to larger corporate entities, dependence in clerical occupations quite literally spoke to problems of identity. It is this dimension that may well be at the core of anxiety over dependence expressed not only by popular success manuals but by clerical unions and corporations themselves.

More recent historical descriptions of turn-of-the-century clerical life emphasize a fluid and unstable climate that exacerbated these problems of social self-denomination. As Aron has argued, white collar employees emerged adjacent to an old middle class "that, before it was barely formed, was already being transformed" (17). Many things contributed to the dislocations and blurred "collar line." Some workers migrated from rural villages or small towns; others came from within the local urban workforce (DeVault, 174). Many came from faltering middle-class families (as did O. Henry, Edna Ferber, Elmer Rice, and Sherwood Anderson); many from families of manual workers. Taken as a whole, the clerical workforce was also made up of sons and daughters from many levels of American society. This variegated backdrop may well explain why clerical workers seemed especially both "individualized" and yet "mass." As Robert Wiebe writes, "the growing number of clerks and salesmen and secretaries" shared little more "than a common sense of drift as they fell into jobs that attached them to nothing in particular beyond a salary, a set of clean clothes, and hope that somehow they would rise in the world." Perhaps most of all, clerical workers often encountered a lack of social definition about the character and class level of their labor. To many eyes, the clerk was not exactly a wage earner but a salaried employee, not a member of management but not exactly labor either, more "independent" financially yet with little or no autonomy or republican "freedom to act." Even unions seemed to throw up their hands. "For many a long day," a leading clerical union journal complained after the turn of the century, "the poor clerk has been told again and again that he is a nobody. He has no trade, he has no skill, and, the greatest lack of all, he has no tools."[12]

This apparent lack of social definition carried over into what E. P. Thompson has called the "raw" material of day-to-day class experience. Jürgen Kocka reports that many clerical workers lived in boardinghouses or with families in rented rooms. They were usually paid bimonthly or weekly and thus could be easily fired or laid off. During the era when this workforce was increasingly feminized, clerical work was regarded by many women (and employers) not as a career but as a temporary way station (often to marriage)—a view that may have extended to some male clerks as well.

Although the fact that women in offices worked in close proximity to men was exploited for its romantic possibilities by popular writers like O. Henry and Ferber, "new womanhood" could create new frictions and job instability as well.[13] Given the insecurities of living independently—or, on the other hand, trying to juggle a dazzling night life and the tedium of routinized work—this could indeed seem a fluctuating and uncertain world.

Not surprisingly, then, historians have generally found little evidence of anything approaching clerical "class consciousness" in this era.[14] American clerical unions stressed professional ideologies as much as labor-conscious platforms; what clerical unionizing existed tended to be the occupationally based (hence fragmented), bread-and-butter unionism of the American Federation of Labor, which stressed upward mobility over class solidarity. Even this modest degree of organization seems not to have been particularly characteristic of American white collar workers as a whole. The Retail Clerks' International Protective Association, the first American salesclerk trade union (founded in 1890), never organized more than about 5 or 10 percent of its potential membership; by 1919 it had garnered only about 2 percent. Meanwhile, though there is some disagreement over whether the economic disparities between white and blue collar workers in this era were enlarging or dwindling,[15] Kocka and DeVault argue persuasively that the American working classes, themselves quite heterogeneous, provided much less of a negative reference group than in comparable European contexts. Within turn-of-the-century corporations, for instance, although there were some differentiations in cafeteria plans or vacations, or within employer welfare and personnel policies, on the job distinctions between blue and white collar employees, Kocka reports, were not at all as commonplace as one might think. In fact the very word "employee," still appearing during this era in its French root *employé* (meant originally as an adjective to be applied only to men), was itself used as a term for lumping manual and service workers together.[16]

Americans would use a variety of new social languages—for example, "Positive Thinking," or the popular writing of Elbert Hubbard—to label this new white collar world. Yet it is important to realize that the more traditional success vocabularies did not disappear. Rather, a subtle alteration occurred, most notably within corporate texts, as the secular ethos of thrift and sobriety was reemployed, or rather literally "incorporated," into a new framework. Particularly within the industries that experienced an explosion of clerical work, the trait Donald Meyer says counted "above all others"—

the quality of perseverance—was refitted to describe the productive and reliable employee. Republican virtues once resonant of individualism and free-thinking were now enshrined under the rubric of loyalty and accountability. As the advertising firm N. W. Ayer put it in 1896: "The way to handle our business is to cultivate responsibility and accountability in individuals. . . . The great essential is that each [employee] should be faithful, dependable, and capable."[17]

This renewed emphasis on perseverance was reflected in contemporary advice manuals like Edward Bok's *Successward: A Young Man's Book for Young Men* (1895). Published under the aegis of New York Plymouth Church, where Bok had served as Henry Ward Beecher's protégé, this book counseled that ambition was a "capital servant [now close to a pun], but . . . a poor master." Instead, Bok said success was available at every social level, as long as one set goals and stuck to a slow, steady rise in business. As if refashioning Beecher's own Protestant veneration of self-sacrifice, Bok said the young man must seek not self-reliance but a "forgetfulness of self" in work. He must avoid needless social interaction (especially the discussion of religion and politics), become married, stay steady—virtues enshrined in the author's own autobiography, *The Americanization of Edward Bok*. Ask yourself, Bok advised, how you can deserve a higher salary.[18] Concurrently, as noted earlier, George Horace Lorimer redesigned the *Saturday Evening Post* to promulgate precisely this new prudential complex, emphasizing "soberness of living and evenness of mentality." As with Bok, traditional providential justifications were secularized once again, as good works now meant corporate membership—if not advancement, then security, modest material reward, and belonging.

This readaptation of providential perseverance bears directly on the matter of dependence, because "loyalty," a term more conventionally associated with personal, family, and community relations, was now appropriated to suit corporate designs. Within popular advice manuals, domestic analogies were easily transposed with business responsibility while, in turn, business advice was often cloaked in paternal garb. In one of the era's biggest best-sellers, Lorimer's *Letters from a Self-Made Merchant to His Son* (1902), advice to employees was couched in the form of personal letters from an old self-made bourgeois to his employee son. (Lorimer in fact had modeled his book's narrator on his own corporate mentor, P. D. Armour, rather than on his father.) Lorimer's advice covered how to manage conversation with co-workers, how to maintain agreeability, how to acquire and disseminate information in the modern office. Bread-and-butter unions hardly provided a different set of expectations or advice. Kocka has surveyed the advice literature from this period which was aimed specifically at white collar workers, including that offered by union journals like the R.C.I.P.A. *Advocate,* and arrived at a profile entirely compatible with Bok's and Lorimer's. In this literature, the ideal clerk was one who accepted competition as part of his or her job; who exhibited steady effort, firm purpose, and self-control; and who demonstrated "[c]omplete identification with his firm, enthusiasm, self-confidence, [and] optimism."[19]

A number of contexts reinforced this reformulation of producer perseverance into employee loyalty. In the heyday of pooling, industrial trusts, and what Alfred D. Chandler has dubbed the "visible hand," corporations normally emphasized long-term growth instead of short-term profit-taking. Developing service industries also, by their nature, emphasized continuity of personnel. (N. W. Ayer, quoted earlier, was addressing the problem of employee turnover.) The rationalization of office routines also buttressed sober traits and hence more easily replaceable ones. Loyalty was obviously also designed as an effective counter to more aggressive labor organization itself; this design was entirely reflective of the new corporate paternalism that stressed an employee's belonging, security, and morale.[20] Above all, the new emphasis on employee responsibility reflected the idea that clerical employments—sales, bookkeeping, accounts, writing letters to clients—necessarily involved a particularly close identification between the corporate entity and the employee, between job and person. In this new "family," the persons in sales, those who kept accounts, those who generated ink, became the public face of the corporation, not just its personnel but its personae. Loyalty was, in other words, the rhetoric by which the generalized term "employee" became a badge of distinction, membership—a value unto itself. When General Electric founded its own in-house white collar periodical, David Nye reports, it was simply called *The Monogram.*[21]

"Loyalty," however, was not as innocuous as corporate enthusiasts suggested. One must remember, as Nye writes, that such paternalistic benevolence—even the virtual tribalism of a G.E.—only mystified competitive and even cutthroat management practices. Nor did expanding consumer horizons outside the workplace necessarily support refashioned prudential values, though historians are constantly recording how safe and sane even the most exotic of new consumer habitats could be.[22] Even more to the point, one is struck, as Harry Braverman has observed, by how responsibility and "loyalty" often slid over into "accountability" (the term, again, Ayer uses). Analyzing the stream of paper characteristic of monopoly capital, Braverman shows how an increasing portion of labor in this period was devoted to the accounting of value—a practice that is the specialization of banks in particular. Indeed, Braverman shows how, as the number of intermediaries between production and consumption increased, and elaborate record keeping and double bookkeeping were instituted, accountability in fact now defined both intercorporate and inner (employee) relations. He notes with considerable irony:

> The normal presumption in intercorporate dealings is not one of honesty, but of dishonesty, unverified records are not considered adequate or trustworthy for any purposes but those of the institution which keeps them. . . . That which appears on the books of one [corporation] as a credit shows in the books of the other as a debit. Since, when disputes arise, the burden of proof is shuttled back and forth between the parties in accordance with the available documentation, each set of records is as a rule a private affair to be used not for helpful coordination but as a weapon.
>
> The internal recordkeeping [double bookkeeping] of each corporate institution is, moreover, constructed in a way which assumes the possible dishonesty, disloyalty, or laxity of every human agency it employs; this, in fact, is the first principle of modern accounting. [303]

Accountability, in other words, stood for a new mode of internal supervision, an enforcement of person as job; it implied anything but familial trust. Adrian Forty, for example, notes how Victorian rolltop desks, with cubbyholes that constituted both privacy and responsibility for the nineteenth-century clerk, were replaced by efficient tables with shallow drawers so as not to impede the flow of paperwork. For secretaries, "tub" desks were designed which could be viewed by an elevated supervisor. Conversation, likewise, was dismissed as gossip distracting to work. In such settings, Braverman notes again ironically, professional accountants—those who "make a profession of honesty"—were also employed to check up on employees, again reflecting the rather negative corporate presumptions about its own clerical workers.[23]

Will Porter was never employed in a large corporation, nor was his experience in any way typical of clerical workers as a whole. But he had been a clerk who moved from his own family's business, left home and the identity it had given him, only to be found accountable in committing a clerical crime (one discovered, in fact, by a professional bank examiner).[24] As is well known, on 10 February 1896, Porter was indicted for embezzlement while working as a teller for the First National Bank of Austin, Texas. He fled Austin, lived underground in Houston and New Orleans, and then exiled himself to Honduras before returning in January, 1897, to face trial. During the preparations for the trial his wife had died, despondent over her public shaming; Porter was subsequently found guilty, sentenced to five years (then the lightest sentence under the law), and spent roughly three in the Ohio State Penitentiary. It was in prison that he adopted the pen name "O. Henry" professionally; from there, he went to New York. When he confided in others about his background at all, he always maintained his innocence. In New York, the episode was safely guarded from the public, which gobbled up the legend that O. Henry had previously been a wanderer, a vagabond, a rootless rolling stone.[25] He conducted only one interview in his lifetime (and lied there); he avoided being photographed; he preferred cash to checks from his editors. Even when taken to the hospital on the night he died, Porter concealed his actual name—now a "somebody" who preferred to stay a nobody.

He knew how fragile his job identity could be. While evading his trial in Houston, he wrote these stanzas for a poem called "Fly Time":

> Only a little fly;
> But it stopped the fielder's pay,
> For he muffed the ball,
> And he let it fall,
> And he was released next day.
>
> Only a little fly,
> But the plate of soup was spoiled,
> And the cook got fired. . . .[26]

At the time, of course, he was "on the fly" himself.

| | |

Critics have quite naturally focused on O. Henry's criminal experience as a rupture that marked his temperament permanently. By and large, they have emphasized the guilt and secretiveness that resulted in Porter's personality and the role secrets, vindication, and imposture consequently play in his writing. Naturally, much curiosity has been focused on his guilt or innocence. But here I would like to shift the prevailing focus to the content of what Porter was charged with, thereby to frame his trial in terms of his class training and outlook. There is a direct emotional conduit between white collar accountability and O. Henry's literary idiom. He detached himself from his past initially to erase the accounting capital itself had done.

The bare facts of Will Porter's background are reasonably well known.[27] Born during the 1860s, he had expended much of his boyhood energy coping with the declined status of his father. A. S. Porter had once been a well-to-do physician-turned-druggist who had married the granddaughter of a Connecticut clock company representative and set up a practice in Greensboro, North Carolina. But he had declined, in the years of Will's youth, into a tippling dreamer who slept half the day away. Instead of attending to his patients and practice, Dr. Porter had instead wiled away the hours on far-fetched inventions—for instance, on what others remembered as a perpetual motion machine. Will apparently felt shame at his father's irresponsibility; the son grew into a sickly, awkward, diffident, and remote boy (like a "monkey with a toothache," he later said) prone to cartoon drawing and pranks—pranks that included, apparently, sneaking into his father's room and trashing those inventions.[28] Because of his father's indisposition, and his mother's early death (when the boy was only three), Porter was raised by his grandmother and aunt and forced to leave school at fifteen. At that time, he became a prescription clerk in his uncle's drugstore (in reality a general store) and worked long hours there until he was nineteen.

There is considerable evidence to suggest that Will Porter felt restricted as an employee; as an older man he remembered clerking as "agony" and confinement. In contrast to the easygoing, cracker-barrel image of the drugstore promoted by his memorializers, druggists of this era (not to mention drug clerks) actually occupied an ambiguous middle ground between professional medicine and commercial potion peddling—a problem one of Will's limericks, cited earlier, explicitly mocks. Only in 1881 did North Carolina begin to require pharmacists to register with the state, the same year Will and his uncle signed up. A. S. Porter's descent into dreamy quackery may have provided a living parody of his own son's employment in potion selling. Though Will apparently built up enough social capital to earn recommendations for reliability, after four years behind the counter he chose instead to travel west with a doctor friend and try something else. (In fact, this began a persistent pattern in Porter's life: while on the fly, Will was recurrently aided by older doctors who picked him up and helped him on his way.) His letters home from Texas speak of not "crawling" back to North Carolina until he had at least the air of success.[29]

From the accounts of those who knew him in Texas, it seems that Porter tried resolutely to find that air. Outwardly he adopted many of the sanctioned attributes of the modern white collar employee. Quick with words and numbers, an expert draftsman able to write with an exquisite hand, Porter's copying skills themselves signified the applicability of literariness to the new clerical occupations. By all accounts he was a serious, steady worker who, again, fit the male profile of his day: a young married head of household, with little property of his own, hoping to rise. One friend later remarked that Porter's demeanor was "steady, even calculated" in its appeal to a "high class" of employer. At first he did not drink, sang in the local barbershop quartet, and kept his politics resolutely Independent (and anti-Socialist and anti-Populist), even earning a local political appointment.[30] Yet, there was also some unevenness here—not the least of which was Porter's apparent indecision about whether to continue in his father's and uncle's profession. He kept up his pharmaceutical registration in North Carolina, then let it lapse. Porter then went through the drift that marked the experience of so many white collar apprentices.[31] He moved from job to job with only meager change in status, from headwork to handwork and back again. In rural Texas, he was a part-time cook, mail gatherer, peripheral ranch hand; in 1884, he moved to Austin, took a job as a drug clerk, then as a bookkeeper in real estate, then as a draftsman in a land office, a cigar-store bookkeeper, a drug clerk again—all before landing his fateful job as a teller. After a while trouble set in: Porter's marriage began to go badly; he began to drink and carouse; he bought into a journal once titled *The Iconoclast,* which subsequently siphoned off his cash. According to his most reliable biographer (Gerald Langford), Porter's life prior to the trial had reached an impasse—indeed, he was suddenly threatened by the possibility of recapitulating his own father's downturn.

Porter's legal trial was not, then, altogether the rupture his memorializers would insist. Despite its seemingly comic banality, the trial only brought home Porter's persistent dilemma of occupation. Charged with diverting bank funds for private use, early on he had doubted whether the jury could demonstrate "understanding enough of the technical matters presented to be fair"; his only error, he said from prison, had been that he had kept a "position that I could not successfully fill." In other words, Porter maintained that he might be accused of negligence—lapsed accountability—but not criminality. It is rather remarkable, however, that Porter instructed his family and friends to stay away from the courtroom and that he did not speak in his own defense.[32]

The tendency to belittle the actual crime—perhaps a white collar bias—needs, nevertheless, to be adjusted for hindsight. In the late nineteenth century, the grounds for proving culpability were commonly more stringent, but punishment was often more severe than today; decades prior to the probation system, criminal law did not distinguish between white and blue collar crime as it does now. To the Austin judge, the moral error surrounding Porter's crime was a matter of great community concern. As the judge said in his directions to the jury: "The crime of embezzlement is a species of larceny. . . . It involves . . . first, a breach of trust or duty in respect of the moneys . . . and secondly, the wrongful appropriation thereof to his own use. In other words, there must be an actual and lawful possession or custody of the property of another, by virtue of some trust, duty, agency, or employment, committed to the party charged." The judge added: "Evidence has been introduced touching the general reputation of the defendant for honesty, uprightness and integrity prior to the commission [of the crime charged]. . . . Upon this point, you are instructed that good reputation and good character are generally facts proper. . . . If, however, the guilt of the accused is plainly proved to the satisfaction of the jury, notwithstanding his good character has been given its weight by them, it would be their duty to convict him, irrespective of such proof of character" (Langford, 118–19).

Sorting out Porter's guilt or innocence, already clouded by years of mythmaking concerning Porter's protection of another individual, and the informality of the bank's methods, has obscured this basic point. What the judge's directions elucidated, and Porter's own comments reaffirmed, was that the overriding issue was Porter's accountability as an employee. Moreover, these instructions suggested that Porter had not only failed to be loyal in discharging his assigned duties, but that he had essentially bankrupted his entire social capital.[33] He had, the judge said, a certain reserve of character on account; yet now it was simply marked off the community's books. The crime, in other words, only recapitulated Porter's long-standing vocational dilemma. The trial only exposed his utter dependence upon the personhood of employment, his dependence on its definition of his character.

That this was the significance of the trial is brought home by Porter's behavior in prison. Naturally, he was severely humiliated to be thrust among men who were treated like animals; he wrote of being surrounded by death, suicides, the beating and hosing down of prisoners who refused to work. His imprisonment would definitely have registered a decline in status, since inmates in the Ohio Penitentiary tended to be laborers and semiskilled workers. (Hard labor, as well, was still the primary means of enforcing discipline, although the fact that, by the 1890s, it had been stripped of its antebellum rehabilitative faith is certainly relevant.) That he was forever marked by the prison years seems indisputable; one physician in the "O.P." who had encountered tens of thousands of prisoners said Porter was the most humiliated he had ever seen. While in prison, Porter kept his whereabouts a secret from his eight-year-old daughter, concocting elaborate ruses to convince her that he was out on the road, working as a salesman. His main defensive strategy was to become entirely unobtrusive: "[h]e strove to have his personality appear as a negative, neutral one," one observer remembered, "which would merge, indistinguishable, with all the others." He was not, in fact, assigned the normal routine of prisoner life; rather, once his pharmaceutical background was discovered, he was put to work in the medical dispensary and then in the steward's office, keeping books. In other words, in prison O. Henry became a clerical employee again, and by all accounts, he became a unreservedly loyal one. Once again, he was befriended by a local doctor who took Porter on his rounds. In one memorable episode, Porter exhibited fierce loyalty by leaping over a counter and punching a convict in the doctor's defense. Eventually, Will was moved to a separate building and allowed to roam; his sentence was eventually shortened for good behavior. One letter speaks of being much "more independent than an employe would be."[34]

On the contrary, O. Henry's prison term was penance of a particularly appropriate kind. Here, in what is commonly known as a "total institution," Porter very nearly mimics the modern Millsian employee, staying out of sight, revering loyalty to his job, achieving a small degree of in-house freedom. His fiction, which explores employment as an account of the self, continued to wrestle with the justice such a life held out for clerks and other lower middle-class nobodies. The facelessness of O. Henry's urban "four million," or indeed of his own narrative persona, is thus not a reflection (as is so often argued) of urban anonymity, but an exercise in imaginatively negotiating and subverting the labels imposed upon an unstable social status.[35] To modify Francis Hackett's terms, O. Henry is both member and patron of his nobodies: reverberating with their doubts that the self one acquires over the counter is real, offering to save them from the imprint of job accountability by reemploying himself as their representative. In his fiction, as well, there is a profound ideological solvent working not only upon the polarized, nineteenth-century languages of class but upon the persona who gives voice to those languages.

| | |

It is not insignificant that, while fleeing his pending indictment in Houston, Will Porter disappeared into what Denning has termed the "unauthored prose" (24) of mass-market journalism—the medium that displaced the dime novels of the Gilded Age (and perhaps their "mechanic accents."). At a time when the by-line was uncommon for all but the established journalist, O. Henry found refuge in anonymous columns of witticism—"Tales of the Town," "Postscripts and Pencillings," "Some Postscripts"—urban sketchery, afterthoughts supposedly authored by events themselves. For good or ill, O. Henry's craft has always been linked to the modern newspaper. His humanizing power, as enthusiasts described it, epitomized journalistic "human interest"; his journalist friends faithfully remembered his skills at Bohemian vagabonding and mimicry of his urban informants. On the other hand, critics like Fred Lewis Pattee found his journalization breezy and shallow, designed for readers rendered jaded and blasé by the *World*'s sensationalism. Ironically, both of these critical approaches have directed attention to the ground of realism against which O. Henry's art—sentimental, lacking in interiority, contrived in its snapper endings—is often found wanting.[36] These notoriously nebulous critical standards, however—realism, sensationalism, human interest—can seriously misconstrue O. Henry's journalistic style.

Why O. Henry was sought out by the *World* in 1903 is still largely a matter for speculation. Initially, editor F. L. H. Noble solicited him to write brief introductions to Sunday *World* specials, "whatever sort of preface, whimsical, philosophical, or serious" as the writer "deemed proper"; he was given news or story copy first and encouraged to extemporize. On the second go-around, editor Nelson Hersh sought such "bully yarns" as O. Henry's magazine productions and specifically ordered up New York tales. One of Pulitzer's rare comments on his fictional fare suggests a guiding rationale; ridiculing other papers' efforts to include "serious literature," Pulitzer instead said his papers offered "bright, sparkling, varied, amusing, and attractive" material.[37] When the *World* paid tribute to O. Henry upon his death, it singled him out as a writer who did not write about "problems" (a codeword for muckraking), but who wrote actual "lives," "cameos" of his Four Million, combining "truth, simplicity, directness and humor." Praising O. Henry's disdain for the "high-class" magazines and his preference for "popular mediums" that went "directly to the millions for whom and of whom he wrote," the *World* dubbed O. Henry the unrivaled "interpreter" of "the *moods and motives* of the American masses." None of this indicates O. Henry was sought for his realism or his shopgirl knight-errantry (or on ideological grounds), since these kinds of tales had yet to appear; rather, his editors sought a folksy commentator, in the tradition of the cracker-barrel humorists whom they had been publishing for years. Hence another connotation of O. Henry's apothecary image; as medical historian J. Worth Estes has recently shown, patent medicines were accepted by contemporaries as generalized palliatives, mixtures of bitterness and sugary sweets, part modern cure-alls and part backwoods quackery that relied much on the will of the patient.[38]

As many critics have recognized, O. Henry adapted many strategies from vernacular humor. In many of his journalistic ploys, O. Henry skillfully evokes what Clifford Geertz has called the "tonal shadings" of "commonsensicality."[39] For example, O. Henry tends to overplay literariness in language by troweling on figures of speech, alliteration, or allusion, often to court distrust of a given character's hubris. Of a lawyer he writes: "Surely it might be permitted Lawyer Gooch to mitigate the bore of brief, the tedium of torts and the prosiness of processes with even so light a levy upon the good property of humor" (1112).[40] Here O. Henry recoups a sly (tax) metaphor after discounting others (prosy processes); his voice acquires a practical, commonsensical edge that usurps the lawyer's own expertise. Similarly, like earlier dime novelists, O. Henry will often explicitly enjoin the reader into the process of literary production—talking outright about editors, their tastes, how to contrive a plot, even typesetting—as for instance: "A favorite dodge to get your story read by the public is to assert that it is true, and then add that Truth is stranger than fiction" (1094). Again, this device seems to provide inside dope and ridicule of formulae. O. Henry will also often downplay his own tales' melodrama, undoing their tension by euphemism and self-ridicule, as in this description of climactic violence: "He quickly bestowed upon Freshmayer a colorado-maduro eye in the return for the ardent kick that he received from the dealer in goods for cash only." His plots are often pointedly flattened out in this way, downshifted from epic to a quotidian gear. O. Henry's frequent use of the second person similarly performs a colloquial and identifying function: "you" are placed in the protagonist's (usually worn) shoes and spirit.

All of these maneuvers contribute to the way O. Henry courts what Geertz terms "immethodicality." In ways that look forward to Sherwood Anderson, O. Henry's tales often begin by stating a proposition, or endowing (in fablelike way) a character with a philosophical and psychological "conceit." Such a hypothesis is often capitalized as a Truism, which is subsequently punctured in the course of the plot—much like O. Henry's own metaphorical "conceits," which often collapse (intentionally) of their own attenuation. Some of this immethodicality comes through invocations of randomness or mere contrariness, seizing upon "condensed philosophy" (1257) and dismantling it. A story may open with: "Likely as not the world is flat" (1138), or "Cupid shoots blindfolded" (1152). (In fact this is a main consequence of O. Henry's frequent resorting to love as his subject matter, because love more than anything ostensibly defies hypothesizing.) Occasionally, as well, immethodicality is played off conventional sociopolitical faiths, like moral uplift or the power of the press.

In sum, O. Henry appropriated a cracker-barrel, "common sense" style of humor to address the problems of his urban protagonists and audience. In part, he was channeling a quarrel with modern social accountability into a voice that was not so much affecting rural byways as it was mocking the pretensions of urban expertise: commercial, professional, even literary. Even at the level of his own voice—as it were, in the texts' preliminary gestures—O. Henry's own self and literary job are distanced from one another; he proposes to show lives, not "art." Given this, it perhaps should not come as a surprise that, when it came to his literary ideology, O. Henry resisted any analogizing of authorship to a specific trade, yet covertly embraced a salesclerk's idiom.[41] At first it can seem as if he gave his literary vocation no figuration at all. He ridiculed intensive background research, once comparing it to a man who tries to win the long jump by taking a three mile start. In another moment of pique, he said his "recipe" for a successful story involved, primarily, mixing a strong drink. In his tales he belittled the contemporary designations (e.g. "local colorist") that sprung up around him (and still do). Yet he also called his craft simply his "bread and butter stunt"; in the lexicon of trade, he called his stories "samples" and "the goods."[42] Again, this vocational self-description may have allowed O. Henry to act as if he were devoid of a platform or program yet sustain a man-in-the-street presentation by invoking the mundane demands of the job. This double gesture may have been the reason that his contemporaries did not find O. Henry "patronizing"; implicitly, he fashions an equivalence with his subjects and readers by seeming to de-skill and "humanize" his own craft and voice. He is disfigured and refigured—as Saroyan suggests, a self-made nobody.

Important as these genre precedents like cracker-barrel humor are, they can obscure the modifications O. Henry made within the *World*'s own style. The Sunday paper, created in its modern form by Pulitzer in the 1880s, partly to respond to the growing demand for department-store advertising, was a pastiche of crime and scandal, political and financial news, comics, write-in contests, puzzles, theatrical gossip, dress patterns, self-help, personality profiles, and much more. The *World*'s Sunday edition regularly outsold its dailies; want ads called for single young men and women; the *World* ran features on famous immigrants; papal authorities merited cover stories. In part, as Robert Park once surmised, Sunday papers succeeded by appealing to those for whom the only reading matter had been the family story paper or the cheap novel, which had often couched working-class ideologies. In this broader view, the Sunday newspaper's function was thus not only to supplant these fading cultural forms but to draw upon the readerly expectations associated with them. Moreover, the *World* extended a century-long displacement within the languages of class by both newspapers and story papers. As Dan Schiller has written, penny presses in the antebellum era succeeded in part by appropriating the language of artisanal republicanism and transposing it to the language of the public sphere. In the 1830s, James Gordon Bennett had pitched his penny paper not to classes but to "the great masses of the community," trumpeting that his only guide would be "common sense," not ideology or partisanship but that which was "plain," obvious, and purportedly accessible to the common man. (Bennett's claim to "truth" and "independence" likewise appropriated, for different ends, values within artisanal culture.) Pulitzer, similarly, told his writers to write in "plain" language for the man on the streetcar; he pitched his paper to the "masses" rather the "classes," not just to elites or laborers, but to a "public." Even as it turned to lighter fare, the *World*'s cultural and political aims shaped O. Henry's "common sense" about class relations.[43]

Gilded Age conservatives' reaction of horror to the Sunday papers' presumed invasion of the Sabbath can easily conceal the fact that the edition articulated rather safe and sane activity for that day. Diversified family fare, puzzles and contests, serialized dreams of adventure and celebrity all implied regular family gatherings around leisure activity, activity pointedly devoted to both evaluating and fantasizing about the romance of social status (want ads and prize contests, as it were, engaging the same desire). The Sunday newspaper reinforced ideological procedures very much akin to personal or familial accounting, "taking stock," if in a dreamlike way, of chances missed and taken. In fact, this in itself is highly characteristic of O. Henry's characters; their social status is revealed only by adding up the external parameters of their lives—the fact that they are rural emigrants, that they get paid by the week (and are behind in paying their bills), that they frequently move from tenement house to furnished room. They are rarely if ever seen at work—hence their apparent mass denomination—as if they are the Sunday sum of their exterior accomplishments and possessions. Several tales—such as his well-known "The Furnished Room"—play off the "X marks the spot" murder stories of the *World,* reconstructing identity by evidence in exterior items, often in tragic ways. (Similarly, O. Henry himself explained why he wrote about the salesgirl after hours; "[y]ou can't get romance over a counter," he said.)[44] In other words, O. Henry's apparent disinterest in interiority is a reflection of how much he is concerned with exteriority—as his Sunday audience was liable to be, with the tangible fruits of labor—a kind of shallow horizon, a questioning of what one has at the end of the day, week, or year. Alternatively, these tales consider what one might have had given another twist of fate. For instance, the famous tale "A Gift of the Magi" is partly a meditation on something resembling familial double-bookkeeping, where prudential icons (a watch, a comb) are so treacherously close to back-breaking assets and debits for an urban dweller with limited means.

In certain respects, the Sunday *World*'s sensationalism has obscured this more mundane function of dreamlike accounting. Of course, sensationalism was not simply a figment of conservatives' paranoia; in one edition in which an O. Henry tale appears, eight of the nine front-page headlines detail fraud, violent street crime, or murder.[45] Yet even these items represent the melodramatizing of personal catastrophe or turnabout, a bringing down of the famous, an intrusion of chance into a commoner's life. The Sunday *World Magazine* section, in which O. Henry appeared, focused on such moments, albeit in a much lighter, gaudier, indeed Ripley's-Believe-It-or-Not vein.[46] Here is a slightly annotated list of contents (excepting ads) from the issue in which O. Henry's "Madison Square Arabian Night" appeared in 1904:

A survey of the success rate of 21 young men who came to New York
"Romance of a Green Housemaid Who Won a Millionaire's Heart and a Fortune"
A story concerning the heroism of a blind judge
A story of a man who sued the Pennsylvania Railroad for 2 cents
An entire page on the importance of walking for fitness (including an essay by New York Mayor McLellan)
An essay by a confessed gambler
"How to be Happy in a New York Flat" (adjacent to the O. Henry story)
A full-page story on the curiosity of mid-winter sea-bathing
The story of a boy who made it rich and "The Power of Money to Buy Romance in Real Life"
A women's page devoted to dress patterns
The cover story, on the Pope's right-hand man
An essay on home economics in the public schools
An essay on trade schools
A portrait gallery of current theater favorites (framed portraits which could be cut out of the paper)

It is not easy to generalize from such a list. Yet it is apparent that one thing that provoked "human interest" in *World* terms was a steady fare of middle-class self-help seasoned with romance—with oddity, paradox, the elements of chance that put a different spin on the everyday, especially upon divisions of wealth and social status.

This interest in the mundane and the uncanny sheds light on why O. Henry called his fiction—his stories, in fact, were a *rarity* amid all this Ripleyesque fare—"semifiction." Like their *World* context, these stories inhabited a boundary between journalistic fact and the uncanny—and thus should not be measured in realistic terms. In regard to his contrived plots and snapper resolutions, one might take the lead from historian Neil Harris's argument that P. T. Barnum's audiences were fascinated with the showman's "operational aesthetic," knowing they were to be hoodwinked but fascinated by how it was to be done. Even now, when one reads O. Henry's tales successively, the snapper becomes part of the expectation. This is of no small importance: the reader has in some sense complied in the resolution's occurrence; chance, for a *World* reader, becomes part of what is expected. Often this providential reversal, or the intrusion of chance, functions to inaugurate dream-work or to return life to an even keel. In the *World* as a whole, "human interest" often involved pulling a rabbit of prosaic humanity out of the hat of celebrity or infamy, or the reverse: stories ran about "Men of Millions Who Are Soldiers," "Society Women Who Drive Their Own Cars," a "Murderer Who Went Home for Christmas Dinner," a "Young Multi-Millionaire Who Clerks in a Ticket Office By His Own Choice." Such stories habitually created paradox by infatuating the reader with social masks of celebrity and then juxtaposing mundane domesticity or scandal.[47] O. Henry's tales often turn on the same kind of juxtaposition, for comic or tragic ends alike. In "From the Cabby's Seat," for instance, a hack driver sees his customers as little more than "goods in transit," as "Fares" (68), until his bride takes him all over town. In "The Romance of a Busy Broker," a boss is so unravelled by his day that he forgets he has married his stenographer the night before. (Thankfully, the tale relates, remembering prevents him from having to fire her.) In both of these tales, romance redeems the indifference and angularity of trade and office relations by an intrusion of "human interest," chance, and circular irony. "Circles," of course, are O. Henry's trademark geometric shape.[48]

By the same token, much of the *World*'s naturalization devolved upon crucial moments in class mobility, as O. Henry's own fiction often did. The Sunday *World* paid considerable attention to turns in the life cycle, to the fragility of celebrity, and to safer strategies for getting ahead and staying there. Fate and self-help thus worked hand in hand. Such semifiction played up the element of luck as much as "pluck" in social success stories. It emphasized the element of chance that lent both romance and danger to aspirations for rising. By counterpointing John D. Rockefeller with a news deliverer who grew up in the same neighborhood, by writing about a millionaire brought to humility and scandal by his own millions, these tales highlighted the chance moments in the everyday that made or broke someone. In many ways, the *World* toyed with the romance of accountability, exploring moments of release into a different fate, gestures of reassurance of commonality for those bypassed by that chance. O. Henry's tales often pivot on a condensed life juncture hidden in a commonplace urban episode, a chance missed or misunderstood, a department-store girl who misses her millionaire or the reverse. Given his own background, O. Henry can easily be understood as someone fascinated by this problematic: by the paper-thin quality of the boundary between success and scandal; by the vulnerability of having left family and those loyalties behind; by the way the theatrical workings of chance rendered life like a series of cameo encounters, chances to get the "goods"—achieve "class"—or be recorded as one of the Four Million.

| | |

There are six O. Henry tales that are commonly singled out by his memorializers as representative of his shopgirl knight-errantry, four of which appeared in *The World*—stories that Theodore Roosevelt said "started [him] on [his] campaign for office girls."[49] The question of O. Henry's politics—praised by Soviet formalists, yet discounted as timid or contradictory by liberal historians and critics—has often confounded his readers. While sentimentally rendering the pathetic plight of the "working girl" (notably highlighting the "Satan" [1441] lurking for girls if they "fell") and revering the mass or "proletariat" that a famous tribute identifies not as a "rabble" but "brothers seeking the ideal," O. Henry seems just as frequently dismissive, even denunciatory, about social reform efforts aimed at improving his "brothers'" lot.[50] In "Elsie in New York," for example, the daughter of a "faithful old employee" for a cloak and fur company, seeking work after her father's death, wanders from job opportunity to job opportunity, only to be put off at each turn by reformers: a "burly cop" who mistakes her conversation with a marriage-conscious westerner for a prostitute's pitch; a "Miss Ticklebaum" who dissuades her from using an employment agency; a "black and steel lady" who prevents her from being a cashier at a candy shop, because it sells brandied sweets; a solemn man, dressed in black, who turns her away from the "regalia of Satan" in the theater; and—finally—a union organizer who prevents her, by threat of force, from being a scab. Ultimately, she ends up at her father's own employer, who lines Elsie up as his new mistress. "Lost," O. Henry cries. "Lost, Reformers and Lawmakers, born with heavenly compassion in your hearts, but with reverence of money in your souls. And thus lost around us every day" (1483).

This generalizing moral, following upon such a Bunyanesque plot, captures the way O. Henry frames his semifiction in part as fables of class. If, as Denning hypothesizes (72), working- or lower-class audiences were liable to read in an allegorical fashion, so much the better. O. Henry's tales—which often have only one or two characters—invite an allegorical reading, not just by individuating representatives of class polarities (employer/employee, landlord/tenant), but by creating a narrative containment that renders coincidence always apt; the girl a character meets on the ferry is the girl who lives in one of the tenements he owns. Similarly, many of O. Henry's tales are very much in the vein of pleas, if not ministerial, then chivalric or protective appeals. He writes on behalf of his shopgirls, but not *to* them. He asks for his reader's forgiveness, for the reader to see these women, and their crimes or "lost" state in a more forgiving light. Coincidence is, in fact, what conveys forgiveness; through circular workings of providence, O. Henry reconstructs both "individuals" and a social process that delivers "samples" (shopgirls), individuals representing more generalized social states.

His shopgirls are "products" (samples, goods) in a number of senses, as derogatory as this may seem at first. To be sure, these women are presented in quite sentimental terms. They are usually pastless people (when one does see their parents, they are often negligent or lost themselves); his girls are often young adults who work along, as Elsie does, on the border of blue and white collar work, varying from small entrepreneurial enterprises to work in "The Biggest Store" with 1,999 other salesgirls (1262). Quite commonly O. Henry gives his shopgirls only a rural first name (Elsie, Dulcie, Maisie), while employers have Dickensian last names: Blinkers, Piggie, the firm of Otter and Fox, Posey and Trimmer. His shopgirls often fix up their boardinghouse walls with newspaper photograph galleries such as the *World* itself provided in its pages; they are nobodies who want to be somebody. These women dream of the romance of far-off lands and famous people. The diminutive "girls" implictly evoked the aura of paternalism which the author wants to turn to his advantage by provoking guilt. The shopgirl is presented, as historians have been quick to note, as a victim.[51]

On the other hand, at other moments, these shopgirls are very much cameos, thin and undernourished, yet also self-reliant and sharp-edged. At first glance, O. Henry may seem completely uninterested in these women's work per se. The label "shopgirl" itself suggested both employment in small-scale work environments or sales jobs, but for O. Henry, the term "shopgirl" is also very nearly oxymoronic. First of all, he seems to mean a "girl" both stranded between the longing to shop, to have and to own, and the experience of being on the other side of the counter, selling to other shoppers. Each shopgirl brings to the tale (already produced in her) the ambivalence of knowing the falsity or artificiality of over-the-counter sales, yet she is fully acquainted with the longing that goods hope to address.[52]

When seen in this light, it becomes evident why O. Henry sees these shopgirls as "clear-eyed." Though longing themselves, they also see through things, both through products (e.g., the baubles offered by suitors) or the pitches in the theater of social life. Their first reflex is often "don't buy the line," particularly with potential suitors who (in a gallantry that is O. Henry's own dark antithesis) propose to "take them away from all this."[53] In "Brickdust Row," for example, a hat trimmer named Florence initially wards off the approach of a man named Blinker (the antithesis of clear sight), who, the story reveals, is actually the landlord of her slum tenement. She is so lacking in private space in her "home" that she has been forced out on the streets to begin with. (Naturally, this fact undercuts Blinker's gentlemanly and hypocritical disapproval of her street assignations.) Yet she plays off Blinker, in O. Henry's retelling of their dialogue, with a clear eye and knowing wit. Florence even doubts the authenticity of Blinker's name, playing off his implied accusation by calling him "Smith," and even turning up the heat when she senses he is backing away from intimacy. Moreover, O. Henry drapes her defensive wit in figures of job employment and reductions in social status:

> "Are you going to Coney Island?" asked Blinker. [They are *on* the ferry.]
>
> "Me?" She turned upon him wide-open eyes full of bantering surprise. "Why, what a question! Can't you see that I'm riding a bicycle in the park?" Her impertinence took the form of drollery.
>
> "And I'm laying bricks on a tall factory chimney," said Blinker. "Mayn't we see Coney together? I'm all alone and I've never been there before."
>
> "It depends," said the girl, "on how nicely you behave. I'll consider your application until we get there."
>
> Blinker took pains to provide against the rejection of his application. He strove to please. To adopt the metaphor . . . he laid brick upon brick . . . until, at length, the structure was stable and complete. The manners of the best society come around finally to simplicity; and as the girl's way was that naturally, they were on a mutual plane of communication from the beginning. (1406–1407)

This byplay is of a piece with Florence's unsentimental eye in recognizing that, for example, a lifeboat life preserver is poorly manufactured and useless—an emblem that mocks Blinker's hope to "save" her.

By the same token, this suspicion of "goods" developed over the counter cuts in another direction when, on one of those life-cycle pivots that fascinated *World* writers, such skepticism causes the shopgirl to miss an actual prince—as in "The Lickpenny Lover," or in "The Ferry of Unfulfillment," which is almost a mirror reversal of "Brickdust Row." In "Ferry," when a rancher asks a shopgirl what she values in life, she inadvertently blurts out "cash" (1474), having already dropped off to sleep—and dreaming, no doubt, about a customer who had asked for credit back at the store. (Conversely, in "Springtime a la Carte," a typist literally orders up her lost lover by unconsciously printing his name on the menus she types.) It is important to see that such skepticism does not, to O. Henry, represent poor judgment on the shopgirl's part, or low horizons, or Coney-jaded dreams; rather, it represents the penetration of the job into the self, the shop into the girl. Even O. Henry's representation of the shopgirl's fall into prostitution, as sentimental as it may seem, is instead a sign of this complete surrender to cash requirements.

That O. Henry places these women on the borders of criminality and scandal, on the one hand, and romance on the other, testifies to the importance of the *World*'s audience horizon and the author's own personal investment.[54] Yet O. Henry's rewriting of criminality, his attempt to reproduce a common social product, is done largely in terms of accountability. In the first place, one cannot say enough about how O. Henry's own preliminary accounting procedures in his tales, in a rudimentary arithmetic sense, establish a commonsensical familiarity with his subjects, an identification with their putative clear-sightedness. O. Henry repeatedly denigrates any attempts at "moral" reform and prefers instead simply to list the essential, arithmetic requirements of life: shopgirls cannot live on eight dollars a week; landlords should not charge what they do; people need a place to work, young women a place in which to meet young men. What is a sin, "An Unfinished Story" explains, is the six-dollar wage and the life it brings (76). In this light, O. Henry implies, moral reform is itself destructive when it impedes these basic, immediate, arithmetic rights.

Likewise, the outcomes of his tales often feel like marks in ledgers that he and his readers will keep in private, and his snapper endings function as a kind of providential bookkeeping (that looks forward to the more radical speculation in Elmer Rice's *The Adding Machine*). One of O. Henry's best-known passages is the final "celestial Court-Room" scene in "The Guilty Party," in which a shopgirl murderess is pronounced "Discharged" (1446) because she had originally been sent to the streets by an uncaring father who was tired at the end of his day. O. Henry plays off the ultimate accounting, and also the doubtful fantasy, of being able to sort out the original crime: the father who did not love you, the landlord who denied you space and set you out on the street. Not infrequently, those who propose to "save" are found to have committed the original crime.

This fantasy of reversing accounts, I think, went even deeper: that is, into the mechanics of character itself. In a tale like "The Trimmed Lamp," it is as if O. Henry delineates the Protestant ethos with eraser as much as pencil. The tale examines the love lives of two working girls who are friends. It begins this way: "Of course there are two sides to the question. Let us look at the other. We often hear 'shop-girls' spoken of. No such persons exist. There are girls who work in shops. They make their living that way. But why turn their occupation into an adjective? Let us be fair. We do not refer to the girls who live on Fifth Avenue as 'marriage-girls' " (1365).

This is very much in the spirit of O. Henry's naturalizing, "human interest" motive. The tale turns upon the very problem of social designation (in a sense, *employé* as an adjective) and its relation to the character of the employee. The "question" to which O. Henry may refer is the debate, within popular ideologies, over the relationship between a given temperament and styles of employment. O. Henry elaborates at length in this vein:

> Lou is a piece-work ironer in a hand laundry. She is clothed in a badly fitting purple dress, and her hat plume is four inches too long. . . . Contentment radiates from her. Nancy you would call a shop-girl—because you have the habit. There is no type; but a perverse generation is always seeking a type; so this is what the type would be. She has the high-ratted pompadour and the exaggerated straight-front. Her skirt is shoddy, but has the correct flare. . . . On her face and in her eyes, remorseless type-seeker, is the typical shop-girl expression. It is a look of silent but contemptuous revolt against cheated womanhood; of sad prophecy of vengeance to come. (1366)

Even within single sentences here, O. Henry disclaims types and defies the reader's fondness for them; he takes them away, then returns them with a precise familiarity that he claims is "owned" by the reader. Interiority, similarly, is withheld for a purpose; like so many of O. Henry's tales, this one invites the reader to fill in the personality traits commonly associated with a given occupation. O. Henry entitles his readers by assuming *their* "inside dope," and importantly, his comparison divides right along the social border area—blue and white collar work—that his "Elsie's" and readers traversed.

The subtext of the associations in this tale are expectations about handwork and headwork generated by prudential values. The story evolves into a debate about the two girls and the relative merits of their work. Lou is innocently thumping away in the noisy laundry, tied to the routine of her iron; she earns a good wage and has a thirty-dollar-a-week electrician as a boyfriend. Nancy, educated by the "curriculum" (1369) of the department store, is surrounded by silks and jewels and laces, is proud and fastidious, and a dreamer who hopes a millionaire will cross her path. O. Henry neatly eases his way into popular expectations about the relative merits of manual labor and sales work and their effect on America's republican heritage. As if replaying the judge in his own trial, O. Henry places each character's employment against broader questions of what kind of social character they have on account.

As it turns out, however, the story is built around one of O. Henry's trademark double-reversals. Lou and Nancy effectively swap temperaments and futures, as the contented Lou (the iron worker) is enticed into the charms of a millionaire (only perhaps marrying him), and Nancy (the shopgirl) falls in with the electrician. O. Henry is explicit, in closing, that "something better than prosperity" has descended upon Nancy; she had already discovered that millionaires are often liars, and it is Lou who sobs "turbulently" as the tale ends. At first glance, as is so often the case with O. Henry's stories, this would seem a neatly packaged instance of Protestant moralism—the poor are truly happy, and providence has certainly worked in mysterious ways—but notice, not for the plucky, industrious, "independent" (in spirit) hand laborer Lou.

In particular, it is the "curriculum" of the department store that has worked in mysterious, yet class-marked ways. For Nancy, in a fashion Thorstein Veblen would have recognized, the store teaches a "copying" of upper-class manners and dress—a scrupulous "aping" of style and a management of taste that is itself compared to writing, to Stevenson's playing the "sedulous ape" (1369)—and the mastery of that formula to the extent that it seems "personal." Moreover, this skill is mobilized in a "campaign" of hunting (1369) and sizing up the person, whether it be customer or courtier—and one cannot tell the difference—across the counter. But in its core curriculum, the store has taught a more central lesson. Reversing contemporary expectations about the virtues resulting from blue or white collar labor, O. Henry demonstrates the lesson:

> In the steaming laundry there was nothing but work, work, and [Lou's] thoughts of the evening pleasures to come. Many costly and show fabrics

> passed under her iron; and it may be that her growing fondness for dress was thus transmitted to her through the conducting metal. (1370–71)

> But another lesson [Nancy] learned, perhaps unconsciously. Her standard of values began to shift and change. Sometimes the dollar-mark grew blurred in her mind's eye, and shaped itself into letters that spelled such words as "truth" and "honor". . . .
>
> So, Nancy wondered sometimes if Persian lamb was always quoted at its market value by the hearts that it covered. (1372)

This comic providence, in short, denies the terms of accountability that popular ideologies were liable to stress. Instead, O. Henry implies that hand work can be the devil's workshop, and that, as a salesclerk, one might actually recoil from the insubstantiality and truthlessness at the core of sales and commerce. Like the *World* fare that bracketed it, O. Henry's tale is both "pedagogic" and uncanny; even as he offers an instinctual rejection of the magic system of servicing commodities, O. Henry implicitly endorses a disciplined scrutiny of "style" that the store inculcates.[55] For all its duplicity and disciplines, the "counter" does indeed produce, to O. Henry, a better, more human, clearer-eyed character. At the end of the story, a "new order" (1374) is introduced; even as she introjects "fashion" sense, Nancy rises above "hand" work and dismisses millionaires. She is "clear-eyed" and, importantly, "middle" class.

To some of his readers, O. Henry may well have offered pharmaceutical consolation in this more specific form of narrative "entitlement." To be sure, as the residual chivalric label of "knight" may suggest, O. Henry crafted "protective" appeals for his shopworkers; the R.C.I.P.A. *Advocate* reprinted one of his stories in 1910, calling it "a bit of real life," seeing it as an implied appeal to action. The assertion of what a reader like Hackett saw as the "human being" status of the clerk had a place not just in nostalgia but in the labor politics of his time. As labor surveys repeatedly showed, as many as 70 percent of department-store women earned less than eight dollars a week and had little or nothing left over for leisure.[56] At the very least, this kind of power certainly belies O. Henry's current reputation in the academy as a mere humorist or "local color" writer.

On the other hand, O. Henry contributed to new languages of commonality and universality that might well escalate his style into an even broader distaste for reform. There can be little doubting which side of O. Henry his twentieth-century memorializers preferred to remember. Insurance companies in Porter's hometown lobbied to have his conviction set aside; local historical groups reconstructed his uncle's drugstore (which actually had been bought out by the founder of Richardson-Vicks, another local son). In 1963, O. Henry's legacy became an issue in the Cold War, as supporters petitioned both Dwight Eisenhower (an apt choice) and the 88th Congress to issue a commemorative stamp, having been already beaten out by the Soviet Union a year earlier. The most evocative memorial, as mentioned earlier, is the sculptural group now standing in a Greensboro corporate plaza: the solitary figure of the author, dressed in a middle-class suit with sketch pad in hand, stands adjacent to a bronzed, person-sized open book, in and out of which peer readers or characters alike (one cannot tell the difference, and that is the point). The O. Henry celebration in 1985 received the following appreciatory telegram: "His message is irresistible and even instructive: that interesting things are happening all around us, and that every one of our neighbors is someone special. Anybody is a candidate to be an O. Henry hero or an O. Henry heroine." The note was from Ronald Reagan.[57]

One could certainly make too much of this collective act of historical amnesia, or even of O. Henry knighted by an anecdotal, amnesiac president (and white collar dissembler), affirming "anyone" can be a "candidate" in modern America. Over time, O. Henry's tutelage could lead in several directions, as this final testament suggests. (One thinks, for instance, of the former president's desire for a "color-blind" America.) In a number of ways, O. Henry's craft *was* too easily reducible to census-taking, to focusing on the mathematical, even demographic rudiments of existence—implying universal terms of equality amid all the plurality of vocations, yet all the while resolving employees and employers into a singular mass profile. This is a writer so interested in unsettling accounts that he often confines the lineaments of dignity to "average" mathematical needs, or he elevates those needs to romantic longings that are inaccessible to all but the politics of symbol. Reagan's testimonial registers the modern standards of political representation that, as Sheldon Wolin suggests, have changed the "conception of the citizen as a bearer of rights, who in principle could exercise his capacities to speak, petition, write, and associate . . . to a conception of a wholly new kind of being whose existence consisted of indices which told him what his condition was objectively: an index for prices, another for wages, inflation, unemployment, consumer spending, and, most grandly, 'a misery index.'"[58] The potential limits of O. Henry's representation are perhaps even more obvious when one reflects on the constitution of his shopgirls. At one level, his shopgirls suggest an American citizenry that later expressionistic portraits (like those of Grant, Rice, even Lewis) only made more explicit: a citizenry in some sense made out of the Sunday newspaper's discourse of semifiction—very much, as the *World*'s obituary put it, a populace of "moods and motives." These are shopgirls conceived as readers: when clear-eyed, of want ads; when not, of *World* romances.

In part, however, these political extensions of O. Henry's social portraiture may conflate, as Howard Horwitz has written in another context, a social "commitment" and a "future application."[59] Will Porter is not responsible for how his work was employed by posterity—although, in a limited way, such use indicates how potent his revision of languages of class could be. And becoming a writer hardly exempted O. Henry himself from what has been described here as white collar disfiguration. The *World* was only the world. Though widely successful, O. Henry was constantly short of cash, fretted over the tedium of his work, and became increasingly unsure of his abilities at the end of his life.[60] "I'm a failure," he now began to say. "I always have the feeling that I want to get back somewhere, but I don't know just where it is. My stories? No, they don't satisfy me . . . [the label 'celebrity'] seems like such a big label for such picayune goods. Sometimes I feel that I'd like to get into some business; perhaps some clerkship; some place where I could see that I was doing something tangible, something worth while."[61] This desire for a more tangible form of goods, the longing to return to clerk status, is intriguing, for in so many respects, O. Henry as a writer—in his sending out of samples, his preference for cash payment, his rushing to meet contracts set by others—remained the quintessential employee. In the end, he could not be loyal even to his own potions.

Two

The Submerged Server

Edna Ferber

"And so," *the story writers used to say,* " they lived happily ever after."

Um-m-m—maybe. After the glamour had worn off, and the glass slippers were worn out, did the Prince never find Cinderella's manner redolent of the kitchen hearth; and was it never necessary that he remind her to be more careful of her finger-nails and grammar? . . .

It is a great risk to take with one's book-children. These stories make no such promises. They stop just short of the phrase of the old story writers, and end truthfully, thus:

And so they lived.

—*Edna Ferber, Foreword to* Buttered Side Down

Although O. Henry was often dubbed the "shopgirl's knight," his chivalric male voice rarely addressed her. Rather, in a Dickensian manner (his "Lost, Reformers and Lawmakers" a direct echo of *Bleak House*), he enlisted the sympathy of a more secure reader—literally a reader, one presumably saturated with sentimental stories. He addressed the urban passerby, the acquaintance, the onlooker; unfortunately, little is known of actual shopgirls' reactions to his pleas. But it is common knowledge that he inspired the young Edna Ferber, who had clerked in her parents' dry-goods stores on the Main Streets in Midwestern towns, family establishments run by her dynamic mother Julia. Edna had been an omnivorous reader of stories and had sent her first fable, a story about a salesgirl called "The Homely Heroine," to the first magazine (*Everybody's*) she had found on her mother's living-room table; from that day on, the shopgirl had claimed O. Henry as her mentor. The sometime salesgirl, full-time middle-class daughter seemed to project herself easily into O. Henry's cracker-barrel class mythology: even her book titles, like *Buttered Side Down* or *Roast Beef, Medium* (1913) blended the homely and the domestic with the snappy wit of urban, commercial byways. To Ferber, as to O. Henry, such writing brought enormous popularity, even the mantle of protector of the American commonality. From having begun, in her mother's parlor, to write "hard, tough" stories about the "Little People . . . those who got the tough end of life," Ferber rose spectacularly, becoming in all likelihood the most popular female writer in America for the next two decades.[1]

Ferber is all but forgotten by the academy today—much less recognized as a successor to O. Henry.[2] When she is remembered at all, it is as the creator of "Emma McChesney," the woman who succeeded in the world of sales, or as the author of larger-than-life, intergenerational, middlebrow novels—and film extravaganzas—such as her Pulitzer-Prize winning *So Big* (1924), *Showboat* (1926), or *Giant* (1952). From the 1920s to World War II, she would become one of Doubleday's highest-paid authors; be privately invited to sit on the Pulitzer board; break onto best-seller lists several times; earn an honorary degree from Columbia; eventually have thirteen movies based on her novels, seven on her short stories, five on her plays. Across this expansive career, most of all, she would become fully identified with the Main Street literary phenomenon of the twenties. Ferber's literary trademark became heroic sagas, usually of women battling the odds in a man's world—a triumph her own career seemed to signify. She was a celebrity who seemed, to her supporters, never to have lost the common touch. In the twenties, Ferber was praised both as an archangel of "mother love" and "success," an upbeat, loving portraitist "unafraid to reveal her love" for "common folk." Ferber was a devotee, in Louis Bromfield's eyes, of those "solid, sometimes humble people who are the very essence of American life." "And heaven knows," close friend William Allen White wrote for *The World's Work,* "Edna Ferber has never had a grouch on life. She has never gazed steadily and moodily into life, to learn it well that she might scorn it more deeply."[3] Looking back nostalgically from the politicized 1930s, she said she came from a time when "people were 'folks,' not The People" (12). Indeed, Ferber liked to say her favorite fantasy was to be seated in an "invisible arm chair" on "any Main Street in America."[4] Yet as the O. Henry tutelage suggests, Ferber's mature idiom did not derive from the rough soil of national commonality, but from an early career that struggled over the meaning and place of "little people" in the modern American class system. Literary Main Streeting emerged only at the end of Ferber's youthful negotiation of her own cultural identity and that of other "submerged servers"—including her own mother.

To Ferber's important if difficult imbrication with actual white collar poetics, the matter of gender must be added. Ferber's literary work broaches a wide range of issues about familial and sororal duties for female salesworkers, about their fears of becoming "mannish" in male-dominated occupations, and, particularly, about the gendered meanings of service. Early on, her representation of clerical experience—depictions of saleswomen, stenographers, department-store workers, and others—was cast within familial and female tropes: Cinderella stories, fables of sisterhood, fairy-tale ruminations on "the girls" of successive generations. Her own experience, meanwhile—itself another, different kind of Cinderella story—allowed her to project herself into the drama of white collar women working outside the home. In this respect, if O. Henry was Ferber's literary father, her literary mothers would seem to be those authors in the American sentimental tradition: writers like Fanny Forrester or Louisa May Alcott—the latter to whom Ferber explicitly alluded.[5] Her own tortured vocational struggles recalled those of these predecessors: curtailed intellectual opportunities as she grew up; severe ambivalence about her mother's sacrifices; subjection to that sacrifice herself. Over time, Ferber stitched together her short-story fables into a modern patchwork novel, trying to represent the range of options—and obstacles—for working women beyond the home.[6]

This was not, however, a seamless ideological recrafting of the sentimental tradition. In part because of her gender and class, Ferber found herself bound *to* and separated *from* women's clerical work in often contradictory ways: cast back upon it as a family dependent when she did not survive alone in the city; rising out of that status by managing her career as the literary patron of "Little People"; ingesting some of the dominant idioms of her class, and then claiming to have transcended them. Even after she had arrived, Ferber would be a volatile mixture of self-made hubris and persistent, private self-denigration. In fact Ferber's revised "Cinderella" stories might well be read *against* those of her predecessors—particularly someone like Laura Jean Libbey, the author of sentimental dime-novel "thrillers," with their portraits of forlorn yet beautiful working girls and their vocabulary of sin, sacrifice, and redemption.[7] Ferber would succeed not by disseminating self-sacrifice or passive Victorian influence but, rather, by aggressively domesticating the public world. As such, her modernization of sentimental domesticity was part of a much broader project. Working out from

O. Henry's base, she attempted a broad revision of her readers' languages of class—originally, by envisioning a matriarchal family as the model of modern class relations. At her most utopian, she reimagined a divided society as a natural, virtually classless whole, marked by generational differences but bound together by mutual obligation and example, much as her ideal family was. Nevertheless, this vision was also not, any more than that of her predecessors, wholly egalitarian; rather, Ferber legitimated subordination in new forms.[8] If "shopgirls" encoded the protective approach that O. Henry often reinforced, Ferber's capitalized "Little People" suggests a maternalistic denomination, akin to a name given to children—supposedly spontaneous, unpretentious, yet also implicitly in need of care and supervision. Ferber's fiction, though seemingly honoring humble folk, just as frequently vacillated into representing *un*common commoners, recurrently a mother figure whose achievement radiated out to the Little People as a silent but powerful example.

For this last reason Ferber should hardly be taken as a simple representative of the urban salesforce O. Henry protected but, rather, as an instance of how his languages of class were taken, at least publicly, in a much less pluralistic, even more sentimental, and ultimately much more hubristically Main Street direction. In their public presentation, Ferber's denomination of "Little People" and her mythology of radiant leadership were reciprocal, mutually reinforcing social vocabularies. Late in her career, Ferber—and many of her readers among the intelligentsia—claimed to feel as if they had outgrown the middle class altogether. Yet again, these languages were also interdependent in often deeply conflicted ways, each the product of a split class and a familial identification Ferber never really resolved. Taken as a whole, Ferber's fiction hardly presents such transcendence of class. Shifting back and forth between two positions, between "schoolgirly" adoration of maternal power and "sociologic" depiction of clerical disappointment, her work represents the class conflict that her public persona often denied.

| | |

One of the more striking discoveries in a much-debated book, Richard Sennett and Jonathan Cobb's *The Hidden Injuries of Class* (1972), concerned recent perceptions of the status of selected occupations. In contrast to what republican discourse might dictate, in one national survey what we would now call "service" jobs actually ranked lower in desirability than manual jobs: a bartender below a coal miner, a store clerk below a carpenter. This was because, Cobb and Sennett reasoned, service employment was perceived as more dependent upon the whims of a larger number of people. "Dependence," that is, was not only a binary term set against "independence," or a veiled term for loss of self (as with O. Henry), but a term that denoted dependence on the customer as well as the boss. This added dimension introduces what Susan Porter Benson has identified as the "triangular" situation of a sales or service employee. These employees are not only asked to be part of a corporate identity but to be sympathetic to their patrons, identify with buyers' wants, put themselves in the shoes of customers (that is, before selling them a new pair). In such a triad, dependence thus entails more than simply robotic corporate loyalty; it also means participation in a multifaceted emotional economy. Hence the word "service"—the modern technocratic zeal for the "service economy" (and its junk jobs) notwithstanding—suits the situation much more effectively than "dependence." At the turn of the century, "service" itself evoked many meanings: sacrifice to others (often legitimated by Christianity), servitude in the sense of slavery, and associations with domestic service—still, even at this time, the largest female occupation in America.[9] Of course, then as now, these early sales and service jobs were occupied disproportionately by women.

Historians are only now taking into account these feminized vocations. In earlier histories, many of the metaphors used to describe the supposed psychological profile of these service strata had been bound to a male frame of reference, measuring a presumed declension from independence to dependence, from ownership to employeehood, or property holding to propertylessness. For women, these trade-offs are not only highly schematic and reductive, they may be exactly backwards. (For women like Progressive-era department-store employees, most of whom came from working-class backgrounds, they may be meaningless.)[10] Conversely, not all of these themes address what concerned turn-of-the-century women themselves. Thanks to the work of newer historians, another range of issues has come into play (themes struck by writers like Ferber): conflicts over dress in the workplace, the double-edged experience of spinsterhood and removal from domesticity, gender conflict on the sales floor. These matters can no longer be seen as inconsequential but, rather, a set of concerns about the emotional economy of work which were implicitly bound up in women workers' power, autonomy, and social status.[11]

Benson's work on department-store saleswomen from 1890 to 1940 provides a detailed portrait that revises the more familiar and one-dimensional republican jeremiad. In department stores during this era, well over half (and occasionally up to 90 percent) of salespeople were white women, predominantly native born, generally older than in other occupations women took up, but not so different in marital status as one might expect (the exception being shopgirls in small establishments). In all likelihood they lived away from home with greater frequency than other female workers even before 1920 (though the evidence is thin); however, even living outside the home did not necessarily put them outside the family (and family wage) network. They were paid approximately half the wage of their male counterparts; the six- or eight-dollar weekly wage quoted by O. Henry was not uncommon for saleswomen as late as 1910. Yet wages for saleswomen tended to be higher than in other women's jobs (excepting management), and their employment was steadier as long as they became regular employees (not part-timers). In the first part of the century, though turnover rates were probably still high, saleswomen also tended increasingly to remain with their firms or occupations longer than women in other fields.

What Benson calls this "patchwork" (181) of social parameters was accentuated by the wide range of work conditions and opportunities available to women in department-store retailing. With fatigue, tedium, and even possibly recourse to prostitution at one end, and glamour and financial security at another, Benson aptly dubs saleswork (in terms quite relevant to Ferber) a "Cinderella" (181) occupation. As Progressive-era social surveys demonstrated, saleswork provided everything from a life of continuous bare subsistence to one of dramatic transformations into relative autonomy and upper-middle-class status.[12] The status value of saleswomen's work, and thus much of their class standing, was itself contested terrain on the shop floor. After 1890, management emphasized replacing what was derogatorily referred to as the "blowsy" gum-chewing "shopgirl" (130), associated with lower-class employees who might offend customers and damage the store's image, with a "refined" saleswoman of the "better sort." This woman would think of herself as a professional (John Wannamaker refused to have his employees called "shopgirls" or "help" [155]), and she would become well versed in the consuming tastes of her clientele. Encouraged by store discounts for employees, she would beautify herself with the goods she sold, keep files on her regular clients, and learn the art of suggesting an ancillary purchase to fill out a wardrobe (148). In a real sense, imaginatively becoming the consumer, and yet also being able to manipulate him or her, became the store imperative. (Salesgirls called the customer, at times, "Our

Friend the Enemy.") The Cinderella trope, therefore, took on unusual explanatory power. The label reflected a struggle within the saleswoman's class identity, a contest between the mundane drudgery of the job and these new directives that management marketed, to her, as tickets to success. According to Benson, saleswomen often found real job fulfillment, took pride in their sales skills, basked in the glow of the consumer goods with which their jobs associated them. At the same time, female activists on the sales floor resisted separate employee entrances that differentiated them from customers, fought over uniforms and the hierarchies of the store, argued over efficiency and incentive programs that undermined employee solidarity. But by and large, it is the effort to remake the salesgirl that should demand attention here. Within the job culture itself, the Wannamaker style of advice did not fall upon passive workers but upon saleswomen with their own cultural coordinates who implemented often-impractical bits of wisdom in the friction-filled world of sales.

The recent work of sociologist Arlie Cameron Hochschild is especially revealing about the actual character of saleswork, labor she defines as work in which the *emotional style of the service* is part of the service itself.[13] In a study focusing on airline stewardesses (it will help to think of Macy's as a version of the friendly skies), Hochschild demonstrates the severe pressure often placed on women who work in jobs where a premium is put on a friendly and comforting appearance, on self-beautification, on sustaining a smile that does not look robotic. (Notably, contrary to some of our mid-century sociology on the organization man, "going robot" [129] is a term used by sales employees to designate turning off the charm the job demands.) Hochschild cites studies that show, in particular, that women are socialized to suit themselves to such work—to "react to subordination by making defensive use of sexual beauty, charm, and relational skills" (164), as opposed to males, who often rebound with aggression. Usually, however, the particular defensive mode is anticipated by the corporate loyalty code which anoints job performance as professionalism, often by linking it to the larger sales image of a particular establishment (e.g., Macy's likes sharp dressers, Bonwitt's elegant saleswomen). The variation in styles can, obviously, seriously affect the emotional economy initiated in a sale, yet across the board, whether with Benson's saleswomen or Hochschild's airline stewardesses, employees are enjoined to size up—which often means identify with—the style of the customer as a first imaginative step.

But only as a first step. On the one hand, Benson shows that her saleswomen could take pride in this sizing up, particularly in being able to identify the class position of a customer. Benson's *Counter Cultures* lists a multitude of defensive strategies that saleswomen subsequently engaged in: flattery to the homely, making themselves look pathetic to the Lady Bountiful customer, even feigning indifference to lower-class customers deemed unworthy of the store. These strategies swiftly became a source of in-house wisdom—working tools, as it were, even sources of employees' mutual amusement (as they would be for Ferber and her mother).[14] Yet on the other hand, such strategies come quite close to what Hochschild calls "deep acting" (33), a strategic distancing from one's own emotions followed by "emotional transmutation," acting out an imagined scenario in order to suppress one's first reaction and transmit a more effective sales persona. In fact, a sales establishment does not have to offer modern personnel training in order to develop its own ritualized initiations into its particular style of emotional transmutation. Just as medical interns are led to autopsies to learn detachment around the body, or rookie cops assigned to traffic duty to learn patience with modern street life, young saleswomen in the Progressive era were often given the toughest counter in the department store. (This analysis might well help one reexamine O. Henry's portraiture of the hard and self-assured shopgirl who distrusts the pitches she receives in her love life.)[15] What Hochschild's research suggests is that a mixture of a glowing countenance (beautified in the hard work of self-maintenance), and yet a hard-boiled interior, was part of a service employee's make-up: offering (and sometimes participating in) the glow and romance of consumption, and yet internally maintaining a core of disbelief in the performance being carried out.

Of course, such performances can be self-defeating, let alone simply draining, for the employee herself. Fears of personal fraudulence are commonplace in the sales economy, as is diminishing self-esteem when "sell yourself" seems only a charge to be selling something that is really the creation of the company or the fantasy of a client. A woman's pressures to beautify herself, especially for a calling like department-store retailing, can also become a threat as time passes. One thinks, as well, of the Marcel Marceau routine in which a smiling mask cannot be removed; the performance cannot be shut down in personal situations where we need our original emotional reactions, as Hochschild says, as clues to how the world works from our point of view (31, 85). Perhaps the most telling syndrome is not so much the masking of a "true" self, as the republican telos would describe it, but the tendency of a salesperson to imaginatively construct a "real self" hypothetically behind the performance, but a self that is somehow remote and vacant (34). Given these risks, one should also not overlook the manifold external social conflicts that a strong service personality (with its premiums on dress, voice, and radiance) was forced to cope with: the unpredictable client, the insubordinate employee, the boss.

For women like those Ferber represented, this emotional economy is complicated by gender coding that comes with service work. Within service jobs, of course, there is a pervasive rhetoric that reconstructs the sales or service arena as if it is another "home" to both the employee and to the customer (Hochschild, 105–7). Benson reports, for example, that at Filene's in the 1910s and 1920s, the store manager and counselor were known as "Dad" and "Mother" respectively (142) and that such denominations were characteristic of the new department-store paternalism. However—leaving aside the fact that "homey" or "homely" is a term perhaps not exotic enough for department-store saleswork, as Ferber was to suggest—this paternalistic discourse rarely succeeds in masking its contradictions. In fact, as Hochschild points out, many women experience a conflict between such an image of nurturing motherhood and the requisite cool, professional smiles of the workplace. Women are often given contradictory signals by both employer and customer about the appropriateness of their gender to the work they are performing and vice versa: stewardesses, for example, are often asked by customers when they plan to have children, even though airlines once prohibited their marrying, in part because companies assumed customers preferred the single image (come fly with me). Employees can be shuttled back and forth between male and female customers, between expectations of deferentiality from customers and their own need to assert authority, sometimes to control the sale, be professional in their own eyes.

Moreover, what is striking is how such variables appearing with the conflicts of the quotidian culture of the salesgirl—over her class status, over identifying with her customers or her workmates, over affecting homey motherhood or slick saleswomanship—seem analogous to the struggles evident in Edna Ferber's fiction. But they exist not just within her characters but in Ferber's own idiom of authorship. Ferber wrestled over the engendering of her own vocation, over identification with her fictional "sisters under the skin," over pleasing an audience that preferred a commoditized personality (her Emma McChesney persona) to what she thought of as another "real" writerly self. And this is not merely a matter of fruitful analogies;

rather, Ferber seems to have consciously inscribed the sales triangle into her social practice as a writer. Thus it followed directly that her fables would allegorize class struggle, harmony, and hegemony in a witty, commercial key. Yet less obvious is how, given Ferber's own experience and her mother's, such a key came to be struck in the first place.

| | |

Ferber's own sense of her early life is recoverable primarily through her first memoir, *A Peculiar Treasure* (1939). From a critic's standpoint, the book is aptly named.[16] A mixture of witty anecdotes, theatrical self-promotion, and memory occluded by unresolved conflicts in her family, the memoir (oddly, like Ferber's surviving letters), at times affecting a brisk, upbeat style, makes almost no mention of close personal friendships, leaves anger and disappointment between the lines. Ferber admits to being uncomfortable with the business of autobiographical "soul baring" (5). Nonetheless, certain disappointments—identifiable hidden injuries of her class standing—do emerge out of a pattern of having replaced modest female independence in a real life with fables of an imagined one. Born in Michigan in 1885 to middle-class Hungarian Jews, Ferber had grown up in an environment of declining entrepreneurial fortunes. She had been forced out into the working world as a teenager, first working as a reporter and then, having been ignominiously returned home, to work as a sales clerk under her mother's domineering eye. In this subordinated position, she had begun her imaginative self-authorization as a patron of the "Little People" to whom she felt akin—but, paradoxically, by mimicking her mother's power.

Perhaps surprisingly for a writer so commonly associated with Americanization, Ferber's Jewish heritage pervades her first autobiography (written with one eye on the rise of Hitler). Though she remembered the nurturing that had occurred in the ethnic community within Appleton, Wisconsin, and in her earlier childhood (in small towns like Ottumwa, Iowa), Ferber's family had been excluded and even ostracized by the mainstream, set back upon its own resources.[17] Going out of her way in her memoirs to say that she had not been an attractive girl, as in her fiction, Edna employed the word "homely," as if to imply the radius of the family tether (89). In rather conventional Victorian middle-class terms, no doubt accentuated by the threatening world without, the Ferbers thought of the home as a staging area for the larger world. As a child Edna had a flair for childhood acting and for oratory, created parlor theatricals, and gave prize-winning speeches at school. Her childhood dream was to be an actress. Somewhat like Sinclair Lewis, she had also been an inveterate interviewer and mimic from childhood on; she would later befriend Lewis in New York (Frederick A. Stokes, where he worked, was her first publisher), where they would often regale each other with comic impersonations of ethnic working-class Americans. Even as an adult, Ferber would speak aloud as she wrote, particularly when depicting slang or ethnic dialogue (167).[18] Partly to negotiate her outsider status, Ferber seemed drawn, like Lewis, to a pattern of self-dramatization, imagining her way into the world beyond the family's domain. When she later admitted to being stage-struck all her life—she said, as a playwright, "I think and act foolishly, without caution, like a person in love" (249)—she was referring to a lifelong imaginative strategy that carried over into her own literary professionalism.

Participation in gentile or mainstream culture was thus a loaded issue right from childhood. For her father Jacob, the social mechanism for assimilation had been a series of commercial dry-goods stores called, in succession, "Ferber's Bazaar" and the "My Store" (35, 154). Jacob's prosaic and patriarchal names for his establishments, which his daughter saw as pitiful gestures in a hostile world (154), seem to have had at least two meanings: to equate family and corporation, as in an older shopkeeper's usage; to set off his personal domain against a more modern and specialized world. As if invoking the antiquarian entrepreneurial upbringing planned by her father, as an adult Ferber would describe her Judaism as the source of a "Puritan" conscience; she would name one patriarchal character Issac Thrift. To Edna her father was "Old" world in both an ethnic and middle-class sense.

In part due to the very fact that his business was rooted in sales, Jacob's strategy proved a precarious one. The Ferbers' family business had foundered early on. When Edna was just a young girl, an employee in her father's store had been accused of "systematic theft" (her phrase), and then he had sued Jacob for slander and won a large settlement (49). Ferber's memory of this episode was murky; by 1939, she remembered the trial only as an "ogre" or "demon in the house" and being surrounded by "endless talk"—all of which, she said, gave her a lifelong fear of being sued (49). The family tended to repress the story, referring to it ominously as "The Trial" or "The Lawsuit"; they believed that the gentiles of the town had reversed pivotal testimony against Jacob Ferber and thus swayed the case. The judgment against Ferber's father subsequently broke the family's resources, and Jacob, already ill and growing blind, had allegedly been beaten by the plaintiff's family on the way home from work. The family business nearly folded, but Ferber's mother Julia took over the store (with "a kind of fury," Edna recalled [93]) and became the dominant figure in her daughter's life.[19]

The meaning of this event is obviously vital, but partly obscured. Edna's ogre and demon imagery, of people talking without her knowing what they meant, may well evoke a child's anxieties of encroachment from the outside, the potential unseating of family authority and security. Such an episode could not help but raise issues around the authority of the store as a private kingdom. As with O. Henry's trial, the Ferbers' suit centered upon both the issue of employee theft and the larger equation of character in the public community (slander). Yet, while the outcome of Jacob's trial was practically identical to Will Porter's embezzlement trial—Jacob Ferber's over-the-counter value had proved empty, and thus he had been bankrupted—the determination of the court was quite different. In the Ferbers' case, an employee had been vindicated—suggesting that the power of *this* family corporation was fragile, subject to challenge. Meanwhile, even more than with O. Henry, Edna had the repercussions of her father's failed economic status passed on to her directly. In a twist reminiscent of an O. Henry tale, because of an employee's rebellion, the daughter found herself made into an employee. Instead of going to Northwestern University after graduating from high school, Edna was forced to forgo her acting plans and to take up newspaperwork on the *Appleton Crescent* and then the *Milwaukee Journal*.

Rather than immediately apprenticing in O. Henry's Sunday-extravaganza semifiction, however, Ferber became a beat reporter. In later years, she liked to tell friends, "I was once a newspaper man myself" (109), proudly alluding, in part, to the modest independence she had attained. But as a young woman this changed status or new independence contained mixed cultural messages. Reporting also seemed to make her prematurely old and hard-boiled, even (in her terms) masculine. She later remembered that she would accompany an "occasional beau" to the park for dinner, but she was never swept away, because the "boys at the *Journal* office, wise, witty, hard-bitten, informed, had spoiled my taste" (147). As her joke about newspaper manhood suggests, what was being boiled away was Ferber's middle-class, female socialization as well as her childhood. ("I'm spoiled for sewing bees and church sociables and afternoon bridge," one of her earliest newspaper protagonists says.)[20] To an extent, this aging process was also intrinsic to reporting itself, where the common professional personality presented itself as debunked of illusions. As Ferber recalled, "[t]he alumni of this school [journalism] usually are alert, laconic, devastatingly observant, debunked and astringent. They are, too—paradoxically enough—likely to be at once hard-boiled and sentimental. The career of a newspaper reporter does not make for erudition, but *through it one acquires a storehouse of practical and psychological knowledge,* and a ghastly gift of telling the sham from the real, of being able to read and classify the human face, on or off guard" (110; emphasis mine). For the rapidly maturing Ferber, who had left "My Store," here was her own store/house of urban lore that she would draw upon, later, for literary purposes. Yet even this legacy was ambiguous; here, the gift of debunking is described as a "ghastly" talent, a classifying and perhaps invasive tool—another peculiar treasure.[21]

Like many reporters, Ferber was parceled out to beats that were laid out by the new rationalized assignment system that placed reporters in regular monitoring of the organs of government: police stations, courthouses, hospitals, morgues. Like other reporters, she seems to have relied on out-of-the-way city dwellers as sources of information, yet Ferber was not as interested in the criminal underside—that is, in the melodramatic exposure of urban ills—as much as in the lives of people who were the go-betweens or synapses within the larger brain of city life. These were her first "Little People"—those who helped her do her job. Her debt is captured in one fictional description of a woman reporter: "She ranged the city . . . for her stuff," Ferber would write. "Her friends were firemen and policemen, newsboys and elevator starters; movie ticket-sellers, newsstand girls, hotel clerks, lunchroom waitresses, manicures, taxi-drivers, street-sweepers, doormen . . . all that vast stratum of submerged servers over whom the flood of humanity sweeps in a careless torrent leaving no one knows what sediment of rich knowledge."[22] As a writer of fiction, Ferber would describe herself as "the indefatigable mole," the author who favored digging into the subterranean levels of the city. Clearly, however much it made one into a mole, journalism did not precisely offer membership in the classes she wrote about; she was still a spectator. True, Ferber speaks of the "submerged servers" of the service economy as friends who may well have reminded her of her personal loneliness as much as helping to assuage it, but her identification is mixed. On the one hand, she partly identifies with this stratum—interestingly, with their animosity for those "careless" (and cosmopolitan) figures above them socially. She sympathizes with the server's dependence on the whims of the served. On this side, her sympathy with the homely is also self-reflexive; her Little People, too, were workers and yet onlookers, those who knew the awkwardness behind smiling faces, the loneliness of the seemingly charismatic salesman, the shallowness of the city's glittering display. In another sense, however, Ferber sees these servers as a sedimentary deposit of general human knowledge (with "humanity" above them), ignored by those they serve. In this sense, they are not entirely equivalent to the mole who digs her way through and around them. Ferber is among them, nearly of them—but not quite.

Ferber did not sustain this apprenticeship as urban mole for very long. One evening in her Milwaukee boardinghouse room—"right out of an O. Henry story" (146)—she fainted dead away and subsequently had to return home. She later said that, in living the boardinghouse and newspaper-beat existence, she had neglected proper meals and personal care (a curiously homely diagnosis). Yet even in this explanation, there were other problems hinted at: "[T]he truth was that I was pressing too hard; I ate meals improperly balanced and at irregular hours; I was doing man's work; the red corpuscles were losing in the fight against the white. I had no ambition toward a career as an independent writer. But I wanted, somehow, to get together ten thousand dollars. . . . But the little plan was temporarily sidetracked (and, curiously enough, eventually achieved) through the fact that I quietly fainted one morning when I was dressing to go to the office" (151–52). Whatever the true roots of this collapse were, Ferber's setback in the city meant she had to go home.[23]

Ferber's return home puts her subsequent sponsorship of homely heroines—those who stayed on and toughed it out, who suffered in boardinghouses—in a complicated light. From this point on, Ferber necessarily called upon her theatrical skills, and her memory, as much as her investigative talents. Her impulse to write fiction began, she said, when her family pulled out an old typewriter. She later said she had found herself strangely reassured by the feeling of the keys, and twenty-five years later, she still remembered "the broken-down old typewriter grinning up at me with all its time-stained teeth" (154). She implied that the typewriter functioned both as a reflection of her own broken-down status and as a reminder of her newspaper days—even, it seems, as an embodiment of the smiles of those time-stained and mature, debunked journalists she had so admired. Ferber in fact always wrote on a typewriter; her oral style of dictation (and romantic self-envisionment) from childhood soon merged with this residual sign of her premature adulthood. This blending of modes was consonant with her own self-description as a writer, mixing fairy-tale fables with journalistic and sociologic fact.

Not all of her sense of the trials of Little People, however, derived from imaginative flights. Right through Edna's early success in representing the new woman out in the world of sales, she lived at home under her mother's wing—as a part-time salesclerk. She had been returned to child status and to that of a part-time employee. Even later in life, Ferber retained grim memories of her new subjection. "Sometimes," she recalled, "when I have a nightmare, I dream that it is Christmas time at the store, the aisles are packed and feverish, drafts of icy Wisconsin air stream through the constantly opening front door, and I am saying to a mill girl or to some townswomen, 'What can I show you?'" (*PT,* 94).

Her writing, meanwhile, took on the aura of a covert rebellion, a mixture of self-help, anger, and even emulation of her mother's power. Julia Ferber, who had taken over Jacob's store upon his death, referred to her daughter's writing as "Edna's typewriting," and by Edna's account subverted it in a multitude of ways (155). *A Peculiar Treasure* hardly hides the fact that Ferber's mother envied her writing skill, kept her from male suitors, called her "my baby" until she was into her thirties (164–65). The memoir also speaks repeatedly about Edna weathering interruptions while she lugged her typewriter from room to room: "Somewhere in the midst of a difficult paragraph," her mother would slide in, rummage around for a dress, break in with a "running stream of comment and instruction" before going out on a sales run (167). Ferber's first novel, *Dawn O'Hara,* is even dedicated to "My Dear Mother / who frequently interrupts / and To / My Sister Fannie / who says 'Sh-sh-sh!' outside my / door." The typewriter—notably, the technological form associated with so many clerical women in these years—was thus converted from a sign of her declension and failure into a subversive tool of ambivalent daughterly rebellion—of "sisters" who resisted their mother's role as family boss.[24] Yet a theatrical child's attempts at authoring often involves introjecting a parent's style of authority as well; Ferber's conflict over her gender and class seems to have involved just such a pattern.

Whatever the full psychological basis of Ferber's story—again her memories are theatrical and submerged—what is of primary concern here is how the growing generational struggle (eventually Edna's dominant formal pattern) developed on conflicting class values. Her class inquiry was traversed by conflicting patterns—the patterns of familial subordination and yet the security of middle-class domesticity—into which she had been returned. Ferber was both employee and daughter, but also the boss's daughter, able to devote her free time to writing. Consequently, her fictive investigations—or rather, fairy-tale ruminations—on the role of the sales personality and the meaning of service took on tortured, self-reflexive dimensions, shuttling back and forth among several points of identification and patronage.

In short, Ferber both learned and rebelled under her mother's energetic family sacrifice. On the learning side, Julia Ferber, the daughter of established bankers and merchants from Chicago, had become a living example of female success in sales because of a highly charged, magnetic personality. Edna remembered taking in the "atmosphere without being conscious of it" (95) like a "sponge," while her mother warded off the bank, bartered goods with farm women, mischievously joshed with the high-society customers who bragged about their social exploits. Julia kept a journal (which her daughter later read) that interspersed commercial details with personal laments about her "burdens" and her exhaustion in the work her daughter often saw as humiliating, degrading servitude. Even given those difficulties, Edna also clearly absorbed all the sales wisdom her mother exhibited: "Rather pitiful little tricks," the daughter recalled, "and [yet] touchingly desperate . . . legitimate" (96). Edna learned such tricks better than she realized; in her public professions, her writer's vocation would be marked by stout middle-class values: pride in work and more work, in inventive "gadgetry," in her ability to keep the pot boiling.[25]

However, this infusion of her mother's tricky, "economical" being also had its negative aspects—again, as it were, the underside of the class identity that Julia *herself* had chosen to serve her own ends. Such Machiavellian capability in defending the family store from the threatening outer, gentile world also had its colder, authoritarian side: "iron" and "astringent" were Edna's words for this aspect of her mother's enterprise. Julia often emerges from Edna's memory not only as capable but so bent upon her success as to suffocate her children, a "machine" in which radiance has become Hochschild's "deep acting." Obviously, such radiance also lorded over Edna's own professionalism. Even after her success, Edna remembered being "obsessed by a fear that the gift of writing might be snatched from me any day, leaving me ragged and shivering like Cinderella" (182), another daughter and near-spinster who returns home after the ball. For years, this many-sided conflict would emerge in a strikingly polarized literary idiom that would leave an ambiguous residue in Ferber's audiences. She would vacillate between heartfelt identification with homely Little People who could not reach such success (or privately rejected it) and the powerful romance of a woman who blended domesticity and sales in a radiant rationale for a new American class system.

| | |

Buttered Side Down, Ferber's first short-story collection, presented a dozen short tales, principally about clerks, sales "girls," and working women in the city. Following O. Henry's example, her tales usually begin by offering a folksy, commonsensical voice, brisk and self-assured about what it does know and blasé about what it does not. Readers were enjoined by direct address, by solicitations of their own knowledge—and, as well, insider's dope about the business of story-writing. "Maymeys from Cuba" offers these asides in its exposition:

> There is nothing new in this. It has all been done before. But tell me, what is new? Does the aspiring and perspiring summer vaudeville artist flatter himself that his stuff is going big? Then does the stout man with the oyster-colored eyelids in the first row, left, turn his bullet head on his fat-creased neck to remark huskily to his companion:
>
> "The hook for him. R-r-r-rotten! That last one was an old Weber'n Fields' gag. They discarded it back in '91. . . ."
>
> The Blasé Reader flips the pages between his fingers, yawns, stretches, and remarks to his wife:
>
> "That's a clean lift from Kipling—or is it Conan Doyle? . . ."
>
> Even with this preparation I hesitate to confess that this is the story of a hungry girl in the big city. Well, now, wait a minute. (121–22)

Explicitly identifying her prose with colloquial speech—and even dialogue itself with mimicry the reader would recognize—Ferber presents her writing as a "pitch" both for the reader's attention and his or her sentiment. By overdoing the confession of formula writing, Ferber pleas for the realism of her stories.

Naturally enough, Ferber had her own terms for the competing voices within her narrative persona. On the one hand, she said, she could be "sentimental and schoolgirly" (158), as in the Emma McChesney series. At her more mature moments—the side represented by this volume, she said—Ferber claimed she could be "astringent" and "economical," words she also associated with her mother. (Sometimes, Ferber later said, it was as though individual works had been written by "two distinct people." [158].) Generally, she couched this latter strategy, her preference between the two, in what she called a "sociologic" rationale, by which she seems to have meant, primarily, a style of narrative self-effacement—delving, molding, like the journalistic mole.[26] "It has always seemed to me that a writer of fiction should work almost as does a chemist," Ferber proclaimed, "That [the writer] himself should be the substance and the subject of the experiment has seemed to me akin to the case of the strange insect that eats itself for nourishment" (4). Believing that a writing style should be "impossible of sex determination" (172), she even took pride in the fact that she was repeatedly mistaken for a man writing under a female pseudonym.

If in personal terms Ferber suppressed the schoolgirly, autobiographical elements of her fiction in favor of older masculine toughness, in genre terms she balanced fairy-tale expectations against her journalistic gifts. Her titles often propose a fablelike expectation, while her exposition seems nearly Aesopian, aphoristic; what often follows in the plot, however, is matter-of-factuality. O. Henry was thus an appropriate mentor, as Ferber associated his samples with a "hard, tough" storehouse of ironic, deflationary narratives. Ferber also employed the episodic tale for purposes of social generalization, much as O. Henry had. She dubbed her homely protagonists with onomatopoeic, Dickensian names vaguely resonant of their social position or their comic desires toward cosmopolitan prettification—Pearlie, Millie, Gussie—while employing ethnic denominations (like Scotch) to play off stereotypical associations (like thrift). Much like O. Henry's tales, Ferber's experiments ran social humor through a fable structure that was available to moralization or snapper endings; yet her own choice of a fairy-tale idiom, with its rhetoric of totemic incantation, saving princes, and magical transformations, was especially apt for the Cinderella world of the salesgirls she represented. Some of her tales had titles—like "The Frog and the Puddle"—that presented themselves as grimmer than Grimm, episodes with Gerties and Gussies never transformed into princesses.[27] As her foreword to *Buttered Side Down* promised, she hoped to "stop, just short" of the familiar "they lived happily ever after" of the "Cinderella" or "Puss'n Boots" formula with simply: "*And so they lived.*"

Initially, Ferber's own setback seems to have made her skeptical of the Cinderella promises modern employments held for personal, female transformation. Even if she did often pull a sentimental heartstring during an otherwise homely plot line, Ferber did usually "stop, just short" of the happy ending, again preferring to emphasize the downbeat. Many of her tales survey that element of individual accounting and shallow horizons in which O. Henry had specialized: the small tragedies of a young girl finding a prematurely grey hair, or finding a hole in her stocking after floorwalking all day. Her characters are made to seem pathetic by their fruitless attachments to the totemic disciplines of a prudential ethos—brushing their hair a hundred strokes a night, saving pennies, mending their own clothes—so undercut by the city's extravagant rhetoric of personality and display. Meanwhile, her stories adroitly play off not just material deprivation, but the multiple ideological allegiances pulling upon the female worker: domestic responsibility, the pressures of impression management at work, the desires provoked by proximity to goods. "The Frog and the Puddle" retells the dreary evening of a Wisconsin-born clerk for a Chicago "gents' glove department" who weeps in a boardinghouse room, a room that has been split in two by a "flimsy partition . . . slicing the room in twain and doubling its rental."[28] Ferber highlights this young woman's need to beautify herself for her leisure time, ironically at the end of a day on which a floorwalker has gotten fresh. In "Maymeys from Cuba," a Scotch store clerk has been let go and now wanders the city streets, begging, mesmerized by store window displays, feeding her hunger by devouring department-store food samples. Finally she faints while trying to pilfer a scone. "There are people who will tell you that no girl possessing a grain of common sense and a little nerve need go hungry, no matter how great the city," Ferber writes. "Don't you believe them" (127). "Try it," she dares. "Plant yourself, penniless, in the middle of State Street on a busy day, dive into the howling, scrambling, pushing maelstrom . . . and see what you'll get out of it, provided you have the courage" (130).

One cannot read such O. Henryesque appeals—which read, let it be said, so much more personally, like a child's retort to a parent—without recalling Ferber's own past discouragement. Yet this particular one also helps clarify the relationship of her writerly "invisible arm chair" (itself a fairy-tale fantasy) to that first struggle. As an author, Ferber apparently felt she could turn her onlooker status into a virtue and recoup the sense of having been submerged in the city. Similarly, her stories attempt to remember what it was like to be inside desire and yet also admit that she is out of it now as a writer. Commonly, her texts use both sentimental pathos and sociologic distance in an almost rocker-arm motion, reading into a character's desire and then emphasizing the glistening surfaces, lights, situations her female character will not be permitted to enter. Of her Scottish clerk, Ferber writes: "To her the world seemed composed of one huge, glittering restaurant, with myriads of windows through which one caught maddening glimpses of ketchup bottles, and nickel coffee heaters, and piles of doughnuts, and scurrying waiters in white, and people critically studying menu cards" (129).[29] Ferber's women, even when they rise, are rather consistently shut out from the city's promises of higher status. In fact, in *Buttered Side Down,* one sees Ferber cobbling together her fairy tales into a collection, if not exactly a cycle. In Benson's terms, she is pondering a patchwork of possibilities: clerical or saleswomen who fail; the submerged servers who, though placed in jobs, are subordinated and thus shut out from their dreams of rising; and finally, the successful (and often masculinized) women who, Ferber observes, have missed out on the domestic side of life. Across this quilt, there is a persistent thread of loneliness, a sense that women come up short no matter how they piece together their lives and duties.

In perhaps Ferber's most revealing story, "The Kitchen Side of the Door," she attempts to adopt the point of view of her submerged servers. Here it is the point of view of a "kitchen checker" named Gussie Fink, whose job is to check waiters' trays before they head out to a hotel restaurant—as the story opens, on New Year's Eve. Gussie goes about the prosaic business of totaling up menu prices (in order to prevent some waiters from cheating, hiding tips, or undercharging) with the "divine" immaculateness of a "goddess" (79–80). However, in being moved over to the business of checking drinks—what is called the "Headache" department—Gussie is a figure explicitly identified as a worker promoted (notably, via a homely version of scientific management) to oversight of ("finking on") other workers—thus her newly "middle" status is striking. She is middle in her own desires as well. Her "maddening glimpses" of the restaurant and its glamorous customers are through the swinging doors of the kitchen. From the start, of course, one notes the ambivalence in those glimpses: the tale begins by dwelling on the vapid frivolousness of the New Year's revellers whom Gussie can occasionally see, men with phony Van Dyke beards, "respectable" (78) women who kiss each other's husbands, a "forelady" (78) who behaves like an actress out on the town. This ambivalence, in turn, is transposed to Gussie's worries about Heiny, a boyfriend who—as the result of a waiters' strike (82)—has been promoted to waiter and thus out to the other side of the door. Thus, Ferber's fairy-tale plot rather quickly establishes its social frame of reference. The distrust by the submerged servers of those they serve evolves into an ambivalence about their own social ambitions to rise. Heiny has been renamed "Henri," and thus mysteriously approaches membership in the Cinderella world of phony beards and ostentation.

Though Ferber employs a rather threadbare formula—boy, as it were, promoted above girl—her fable instructs primarily by reaffirming the doubts Gussie initially feels about the romance that exists beyond the door, where Heiny has gone. In a crucial turn of the plot, Gussie is herself moved out beyond the door and, now there, is able to witness the ignominies (from those non-Puritan Van Dykes) to which Heiny's promotion has actually subjected him. The revels of society are now described as "sordid and bacchanalian" and "poisonous," and Heiny proves to be as disgusted as she is. Intriguingly, both Ferber and Heiny respond by identifying successful "waiting" with the suppression of emotion (93). But not for long; when Heiny protests that a besotted woman (who, notably, has fainted) is not "fit" for Gussie to touch, the circle is closed; boy and girl agree to retire to "Joey's" for coffee and a ham on rye. On the way out, the reunited couple pays homage and "Happy New Year" to the scrubwoman Tillie who cleans up after the mess.[30] In a rather plain class allegory, Ferber's characters realign themselves with hand and not head (aches)—with the homeliness of toil and the kitchen side of the class door. Asking herself why they now feel consoled, Ferber says: "[P]erhaps, for much the same reason we rejoice in the wholesome, safe, reassuring feel of the gray woolen blanket on our bed when we wake from a horrid dream" (100–101). In awakening to the value of the wholesome, Cinderella kicks off her glass slippers and picks up a broom again. In place of the transformations that the movement from manual labor to service claims to provide (Heiny to Henri), Ferber implies one can best find home in the security and dignity of putatively more honest toil.

Or is it in knowing one's place? Despite her rhetorical dismissals of cosmopolitanism, Ferber's tales also demonstrate a desire to transcend the littleness they so fervently patronize. For one thing, Ferber has hardly effaced herself in her narrative voice. On the contrary, such humble plots are accompanied by an active, even hubristic narrative persona, one who sees through social facades from the start. Moreover, there are signs of Ferber's own self-authorization. It was not merely that, like O. Henry, she took her reader in with asides, jokes, or polemics about what magazines usually offered—after all, part of a long-recognized by-play between satire and "reality effects"—rather, the point is that these asides are, as often as not, directed at herself as much as her reader. "What She Wore," for example, begins: "Somewhere in your story you must pause to describe your heroine's costume. It is a ticklish task. The average reader likes his heroine well dressed" (38). "Maymeys from Cuba" pauses to admit the "story of a hungry girl in a big city" has been done by "every scribbler from tyro to best seller expert" (122). In O. Henry's tales, these are asides to the reader; in Ferber's they are closer to interior monologue. In other words, in these moments the reader sees the writer's side of the fairy-tale door; in the writing, they help create a narrator who is already an author by an act of will. Rather amazingly, the narrator of Ferber's very first tale, "The Homely Heroine," begins right off by saying that she, already a recognized author, had been accosted by a shopgirl who had complained that there were no homely heroines in conventional fiction. Another early tale, "Sun Dried," similarly tells the tale of a writer already in New York City, who accidentally meets an editor who tells her to write what she knows and not the "slop" of romance and New York (207). What one finds, in short, is Ferber empowering herself as an author as she writes; she literally envisions herself into clever O. Henryesque authorship by patronizing the humble. The process is reciprocal.

Even "The Homely Heroine," a kind of prospectus for Ferber's entire project, contains some of this ambiguity about class patronage. In this story, Ferber explicitly built upon her journalistic notion that servers are repositories of a generalized knowledge of human nature, not "blowsy" sentimental heroines but wise and alert. They become, at first, objects of emulation for the literary vocation itself. "In our town," Ferber writes, "the clerks are not the pert and gum-chewing young persons that story-writers are wont to describe. . . . They know us all by our first names, and our lives are as *an open book* to them" (177–78; emphasis added). So this narrator-author, or so she says, writes an internal story about Pearlie Schultz, an overweight and unattractive stenographer with whom salesmen never flirt. In this inset narrative, Pearlie maneuvers a late-night kiss out of an engaged yet lonely drummer after serving him a supper—a kiss that sends the town gossips going, but that gives Pearlie a kind of sad, secret wisdom that puts her above those gossips on the town's social ladder. The internal self-reflexiveness of Pearlie's tale soon becomes evident. Ferber's narrator-author is in a remarkably parallel situation; in a self-consciously applied analogy, Ferber's author claims to have been rejected over and again by editors, because her heroines are not beautiful enough. It would seem that the author and stenographer's orbits are potentially concentric, even a shared sisterhood of risks being broached, but the tale, rather pointedly, defers this possibility with a hard-boiled ironic ending. At the end of the frame plot of "The Homely Heroine," the "author's" own salesgirl reader complains that the tale of Pearlie did not end in marriage.[31] The "author's" own consumer-audience wants another set of goods, closer to the sentimental frame of the past; Ferber herself, the "author," prefers the inset, the Pearlies in the rough, and thus the potential for sisterhood with the salesgirl is thwarted. At best, the tough irony of the tale suggests, Ferber can only patronize her servers from across the counter.

| | |

To an extent, Ferber's patronage of Little People was both supported and undercut by her own self-authorization. It was a contradiction that would not go away. On the one hand, throughout her career, Ferber ingeniously analogized her own vocation to the particular pressures of sales and clerical work for women: for instance, having to "beautify" her characters to receive "advances" from editors, or having to resist the temptation to create closure through the fictional device of marriage. (In time, there came the desire to be one's "real self" over the Edna Ferber her buyers expected.) Ferber had herself, most recently, returned to part-time clerking. On the other hand, Ferber as author prefers, even in "The Homely Heroine," to present herself as a patron whose sentimental identification with servers now comes from being across the counter. Paradoxically, but perhaps not surprisingly, right after having returned to her mother's orbit, Ferber projected herself, almost theatrically, away from the habitat to which she had been consigned. She now gravitated increasingly to the representation of more managerial white collar females, employees who mastered sales work and found a home there. *Buttered Side Down* contains only one such character, a twenty-year veteran of clerking in corset sales, tough and capable, so accustomed to luxuries that she would not forgo her salary by getting married. ("Gabie," she tells her boyfriend, "I could have married any man I pleased. But I was what they call capable. . . . I worked my way up, alone. I'm used to it. I like the excitement down at the store" [109].) In a short time, of course, Ferber created Emma McChesney, the woman who had mastered a man's world.

To deepen her examination of the successful white collar woman was to confront the burden of the example of Julia Ferber—who was now, the author freely admitted, her only available source of information on the sales life (175) and the source of her first McChesney story (172).[32] No doubt this appropriation, in essence moling beneath one's parent, had its own trials. One can only imagine Edna's reaction when, as she began to create her most successful character, her mother—now having moved the family to Chicago, where she began managing real-estate investments—took to calling herself "Julia McFerber." Initially Edna seems to have silenced her own doubts, retuned her narrative voice to schoolgirly mimicry of her mother's sales energy, and thus articulated a much more upbeat social fable. Emma McChesney, for example, says she sees life "as a great universal scheme too mighty to comprehend—a scheme that always worked itself out in some miraculous way." Full of inspiration and transformation, this cycle of stories constituted, in many respects, business fairy tales of will, personality—Victorian female "faculty" that had become white collar "capability."[33] Ferber describes Emma preparing for a trip as follows:

> In the next forty-eight hours, Mrs. McChesney performed a series of mental and physical calisthenics that would have landed an ordinary woman in a sanatorium. She cleaned up with the thoroughness and dispatch of a housewife who, before going to the seashore, forgets not instructions to the iceman, the milkman, the janitor, and the maid. She surveyed her territory, behind and before, as a general studies troops and countryside before going into battle; she foresaw factory emergencies, dictated office policies, made sure of staff organization like the business woman she was. Out in the stockroom, under her supervision, there was scientifically packed into sample-trunks and cases a line of Featherloom skirts and knickers calculated to dazzle Brazil and entrance Argentina. And into her own personal trunk there went a wardrobe, each article of which was a garment with a purpose. Emma McChesney knew the value of a smartly tailored suit in a business argument. (13–14)

Edna's successful self-authoring, of course, had paved the way for such a personification of positive thinking, domesticity gone Dale Carnegie. But what in *Buttered Side Down* had been the lively, separate voice of an authorial persona was now submerged in the practical encomiums and sunny example of Emma herself. When Emma speaks, employees (and readers) listen.

A sign of Ferber's stylistic reformation lies in the fact that Emma McChesney's personal history is always in the past. To use the colloquial phrase, sales is quite literally her life. A divorcée who has worked her way up to sales roadwork and then to office management in the fashion business, largely to support her son, Emma is a physically attractive, radiant, and yet internally tough worker with all the popular ingredients for modern success. If anything, she seems to have bypassed the corporate shoptalk about steadiness and loyalty, leaping ahead magically to upper-echelon personality management. Emma knows the value of dressing for success, of a winning smile, of a "sincerity" that is one-quarter bunk—all of the prescriptions developing in the "personal magnetism" vogue of these years. As a result of her climb, Emma is capable at all levels of the business—from cutting to advertising—but she is particularly at home in sales. She knows that the key to success is to "cater to the personality" of the buyer (16), and she is hardly above a bit of flattery, an artful maneuver, even cutting her competition off at the pass. At the core was a Hobbesian sensibility to rival Carnegie; slipping a small bribe to a South American official, Emma sees money as "the Esperanto of the nations, the universal language" (31).[34] To Emma, business sense came as the "field flower" of experience, far better than the "hot-house plant" of logic and guesswork (11). Eventually she marries her boss and business partner, signifying the final closure of self and corporation. Her husband is named, fittingly enough, T. A. Buck.

Given such a name, and such occasionally dark humor, one has to consider how much Ferber herself was really invested in this refashioned social fairy tale, a shareholder in what this collection called *Emma McChesney & Co.* There may well have been a certain "staginess" to what Ferber later called, derogatorily, her "romances." In these fairy tales, business life seems restored, if not to prelapsarian entrepreneurial innocence, to humorously overdrawn, folktale proportions. Some intellectuals may have read Emma McChesney as a parody, testifying to a potential double-take over Ferber's irony.

Yet this distance could not fully obscure the risks of what was essentially introjection of her mother's example; in a few years, Edna herself would join the Market Association of America. Even on their own terms, despite their heralding of experience, such stories may be not merely instances of taking on a role and overplaying it but, rather, exercises in self-management, impressions of success learned at one remove. Meanwhile, a rather strident normalcy now entered Ferber's portraits of middle Americanness that suggests they were heartfelt. It was not only that, as other literary Main Streeters would, Ferber now began to lapse into a provincial nostalgia and hubris about common folk and the Midwest, about people who ostensibly were less "gussied" than their New York counterparts. Rather, it was that Ferber's appreciation for the commonplace or the prosaic slid easily into an uncritical praise for middle-class normality, not for its core of articulated values, but simply because of its normativeness. Musing about the small towns she had passed through as a saleswoman, Emma McChesney remarks about the "real" people there: "I've been peeking in at their windows for ten years, and I've learned that it is in these towns that folks really live. The difference between life here and life in New York is the difference between area and depth. . . . In New York, they live by the mile, and here they live by the cubic foot. Well, I'd rather have one juicy, thick club-steak than a whole platterful of quarter-inch" (111). One notes, of course, that Ferber's own identification had shifted from grey servers to blue business suits, from slices of buttered toast to club steak. Yet perhaps the more telling point is that Ferber's affection for the "real people" now seems like an agglomeration of hollow consumer choices: blue serge, roast beef, a depth that is revered but seldom represented.

As the dinner menu conceit above suggests, Emma McChesney's own independence was contained by elements that kept her securely within the horizons of middle-class domesticity. The necessity of providing for her son, for example (even as it removed her temporarily from the possibility of a romantic encounter), sanctioned Emma's having entered the workforce. Emma was placed resolutely in a "woman's business," established in the Featherloom Undergarment Company, thus staying securely within a conventionally feminized province. As the earlier quotation about packing demonstrates, Ferber justifies Emma's office experience on the grounds that efficient housekeeping made effective business skills—and vice versa. Much as turn-of-the-century salesgirls were actually encouraged to apply their domestic know-how to a sale, Emma converts her fashion sense to business sensibility—even to equating fashion with intelligence at large. (She had "a weakness for smart shoes," Ferber writes, "Hers were what might be called intelligent-looking feet" [194].) Ultimately, Emma is described, again quite compatibly with the middle-class sentimental tradition, as a molder of men—her son and, ultimately, T. A. Buck himself.

This adroit combination of masculine and feminine attributes in what contemporaries dubbed Ferber's "Bull Moose heroine" probably contributed heartily to Emma's success with audiences at *The American Magazine*, *Women's Home Companion*, and elsewhere. If O. Henry's artifice took hold in the believe-it-or-not world of the Sunday *World*, Ferber's aphoristic fables ran increasingly in those "practical" home magazines that had staked out middle-class domesticity as a refuge from muckraking and "highbrow" debate. Ads and stories concurrently running with Ferber's later serializations in the *Women's Home Companion* indicate that the audience projected included both housewives and working women,[35] but as even this popular context indicates, there was more here than Cinderella reborn as Charles Schwab. Ferber's vision elaborated itself into a prospectus not just for female, white collar legitimacy but for the hegemony of managerial maternalism. Again, her own behind-the-door rebelliousness, her fantasies of sisterhood, worked to her imaginative advantage for a time; "romancing" (in the sense of imaginatively "entertaining") Emma McChesney meant, for Ferber, somehow answering those internal, more sisterly voices that questioned such a heroine's legitimacy.

This contest was most apparent in "Sisters Under Their Skin," a story about the visit of female upper-class reformers to Emma's shop in order to lecture her working girls on proper dress. At the start of the tale, even beyond O. Henry's denials of class labelling, Ferber places herself resolutely against the entire notion that America was divided into distinct classes. She begins by displacing the residual nineteenth-century melodramatic idiom of "working girls" and "society women," so evident in a text such as Dorothy Richardson's *The Long Day*.[36] Ferber's denial, however, is framed even more broadly and is pointedly a defense of Emma's class leadership:

> Women who know the joys and sorrows of a pay envelope do not speak of girls who work as Working Girls. Neither do they use the term Laboring Class, as one would speak of a distinct and separate race, like the Ethiopian. . . .
>
> Perhaps this explained why every machine-girl in the big, bright shop back of the offices raised adoring eyes when Emma entered the workroom. Italian, German, Hungarian, Russian—they lifted their faces towards this source of love and sympathetic understanding as naturally as a plant turns its leaves towards the sun. They glowed under her praise; they confided to her their troubles; they came to her with their joys—and they copied her clothes. (178–79)

At first glance this might seem a stance traceable to the republican heritage witnessed by Tocqueville and others, modified only moderately to accommodate a new ethnic pluralism. Yet there was something else fantasized here. The normative is now mobilized into the argument that, beneath such polemical labels as "working girl" or "manager," there were in fact no significant classes at all. A corollary, in turn, was that "politics" was, in and of itself, an alien threat to this "natural" domain—here, an office polis akin to a family. Ferber, moreover, implements this maternalism without so much as a nod toward the Bread and Roses Strike, the Triangle Fire, much less the corset-workers' strike in her own birthplace, Kalamazoo.[37]

This remarkable development goes well beyond O. Henry's protectivist chivalry; in fact her idiom now runs counter to many of his intentions. O. Henry often protested the neglect and exploitation of a landlord or a shop manager, but here, in but a few years after *Buttered Side Down,* managerial hegemony is quite literally "naturalized," as leadership becomes the result of a kind of social photosynthesis in which poverty-ridden girls look up to the radiant and maternal Emma. Meanwhile, between employer and employee, the story relates, there is a broadly based social solidarity, a "sisterhood" that transcends the condescension represented by intrusive "reformers." The story's plot line bears this vision out, as the "movers," ugly and drab upper-class women ("What Ida Tarbell calls 'Restless Women,'" Emma remarks [190]) learn a lesson of their own from the shopgirls' adoration and Emma's transposition of domestic skills to the workplace. She has those reformers watch her at work—doing what she calls "bringing a new skirt into the world. I thought you might like to be in at the birth"—and then has a pretty shopgirl tell them a thing or two about how to dress. Obviously, the "new skirt" is the woman that Emma represents and that the shopgirl, the story tells us, longs to be. By collapsing the biological and the managerial (the sun/the manager) in resonantly female terms (the labor of birth/the labor of production), Emma offers a vision of progress based on sorority, empathy, and the upward mobility of the office—the merit of work and the loyalty of fashioning oneself on one's superior "mothers." Moreover, in a politics that her magazine editors no doubt appreciated, her vision is offered as a preferred avenue to the class divisiveness now supposedly created by meddling investigative reformers; women, by knowing how to "make" a skirt, know better how to dress themselves in one. One can hardly imagine a more adroit reenactment of the Alger myth, remobilized, supposedly as a prescription for social harmony, to suit a society based in consumerism and managerialism. This self-baptism of Emma's maternal rule was not "sociologic" so much as it was sacramental; the reader is present at the birth, and her "girls" need not testify.[38]

| | |

The idiom described above is prototypical of the fantasy of American regeneration at the heart of Ferber's subsequent romances. In *So Big*, for example, she created the story of a midwestern farm widow who revitalizes her husband's acreage on behalf of her son—very much the social plot that Emma McChesney had epitomized. If her new heroine, Selina DeJong, is a more rural, nostalgic version of Emma, her determined "jaw" and farm know-how (Ferber, in a sense, went even further Main Street in this decade) are in place to play against a younger generation—including her own son—who cannot see the "beauty" and "self-expression" (298) of hard toil (347). Ferber now invoked icons of nineteenth-century republican virtue—Abraham Lincoln (297), Louisa May Alcott's Jo (182)—to warn against the more "gilded" path of monetary success represented by Selina's indifferent son (358). Now, the disillusionment of the postwar years is dismissed as an "excuse for abandoning the normal" (285). (Notably, when Selina visits an urban office, the young female office workers [309] respond to her intuitively.) To be sure, it was predominantly this message to which most of her professional reviewers in the 1920s responded—including, apparently, the Pulitzer Prize committees looking for that "wholesome" reinforcing of "American" values.[39] And though Ferber's *Women's Home Companion* audience was probably suburban and white collar, the rural readers who wrote to the magazine also praised her work.[40] Meanwhile, Ferber became so identified with her "Bull Moose" heroines that she was able to preach her case widely, as an expert on modern class relations. Teddy Roosevelt himself commended Emma McChesney for the "way in which [she] solves her social problems."[41]

But by the same token, the daughter's vision was not quite her mother's, and Ferber privately began to chafe under her own popularity, particularly her identification with narrowly conceived entrepreneurial values. She had reacted adversely when a cosmopolitan magazine (probably *Vanity Fair*) said she was keeping Emma McChesney alive with "injections of black ink" (174)—a suggestion, perhaps, pointing to her own creation, in Emma McChesney & Co., of a "storehouse" that now simply could run itself. Ferber began to resent her identification with Emma—her "real self" lost in her acting, her desires in her "gadgetry"—and had abruptly dropped the series.[42] But the rural garb of her subsequent Main Streeting can be deceiving. To be sure, Edna's paeans to "hard toil" and normality contained rather traditional middle-class invocations of American self-help, a new-middle-class mythology cloaked in the old. But a tale like "Sisters Under Their Skin," as Roosevelt's endorsement suggests, was also read in a more modern, Progressive light. Even the Pulitzer Prize might well have reflected a response to her "reformist" dimension: the side that suggested Ferber's mythology was not merely an "inner"-directed fable for middle managers, but a broader rationale for class relations generally.[43] Many contemporary reviews reveal that Ferber's sometimes ironic, often flippant tone (her theatrical role-playing) made her seem modestly rebellious to many readers, provoking changes in how the "humble" life was to be perceived. Thus, despite their "homely" appearance, Ferber's maternal heroines could also be—and, in fact, were—read as exemplars of nonconformist self-expression and professional vocation, set against the "rubber-stamp" and "gilded" path the middle-class might take if it devoted itself only to monetary gain.[44] Ferber's *The Girls* (1921)—which she described as her first "mature" work—set the pattern. Slowly distancing itself from the conventional values of the Victorian middle class—thrift, work discipline, and female "service" through sacrifice—Ferber's first "big" book tried to emphasize how a "new skirt" might well be born out of the dessicated shell of that class.

Her entertainment of middle-class life now expanded to fill a much bigger, historical stage. No longer economical in the O. Henryesque sense, *The Girls* was an epic that surveyed female identity from the Civil War to World War I, centering its plot on changing cultural notions of middle-class spinsterhood. The book told the story of three generations of Chicago-based aunts and nieces, all spinsters, given progressively more modern (and more masculine) names: Charlotte, Lottie, and Charley. Charlotte is the quintessential Victorian spinster, who early on lost her lover in the Civil War; her brother is the patriarch Issac Thrift, a W.A.S.P. of stern upbringing whose name and tastes identify him squarely with the prudential ethos and its "calvinistic" (51) antecedents. Full of encomiums about idle hands, saving, and hard work, Thrift is a New York emigré who moves into Chicago real estate and then passes on his business to his daughter Carrie (Lottie's mother), who is left to tend to things when her own husband deserts her. After years of struggle involving failed romances and a gradual loosening of Carrie's power, Lottie achieves her own independence. She travels to do war work in France and returns home with a war orphan; when her own mother finally expires because of the shock of this and other rebellions, Lottie reveals that the child is her own, the result of an affair with a soldier who had died only three days after leaving her in Paris (thus reiterating, in new terms, Charlotte's Civil War sacrifice).

Ferber never fully clarified how she had come up with the intergenerational novel as her trademark form. The serial form of Emma McChesney—establishing her own "trademark" *in* the market itself—obviously had introduced Ferber to the idea of a more continuous story line. She may well have been contemplating a "counter-Russian" novel as well. During the height of her popularity in the 1920s, she complained that Americans should overcome their "inferiority complex" regarding Europe and recognize that America had "color, and romance, and glow, and vivacity, and depth all the way from Maine to Manilla." As she reconstructed her own enterprise, she described it in these terms: "Chicago writers talked a great deal about The Russians," she wrote, "American writers emulated the Russian writers' style, they adopted their pessimistic philosophy. This seemed to me as absurd as to exchange caviar and vodka for cider and pumpkin pie. . . . Here in America, I thought, there was lightness, buoyance, and an electric quality in the air. . . . Here was a new fresh country. Why not write in American?" (181–82). Not surprisingly, when George Horace Lorimer conceived the idea of extending work on behalf of The National War Savings Committee to the postwar period—running stories and articles in the *Post* to preach that "thrift means right living, peace of mind and, finally, opportunity to get ahead in the world"—he approached Ferber.[45] In public, at least, her "writing in American" now acted as a buffer against postwar intellectual disillusionment (and, covertly, bolshevism), as a source of middle-class regeneration, as an idiom of national renewal.

These intentions aside, it was clear that, most of all, Ferber now did have a kind of cycle for her fairy tales of gender and class. In so many respects, it seems that she had found a form suited to the patchwork of women's experience in and outside the service economy, and her normally astringent wit ranged across a broader canvas, in a way that—intentionally or not—recalls the discursive, intersubjective variations of the nineteenth-century women writers to whom she would covertly refer. Writers like Harriet Beecher Stowe, Sarah Orne Jewett, and Louisa May Alcott had favored a dictated, colloquial novel littered with direct address to include the reader, asides taking up various matters, random interjections into public debate under the guise of homiletic. The form derived from the necessarily porous condition of women's lives, so open by necessity to other duties and interruptions. Among these women, writing was sometimes conceived as "patchwork" or chains of "love and dependence" turned to narrative, emphasizing the reiterative pattern to a female existence based in recurrent stages of nurturance, loss, and only guarded independence. (Aunt Charlotte is, in fact, identified with patchwork, as "a renowned work of art" [47].)[46] Even Ferber's title, *The Girls,* was loaded with interlacing patterns. The "Girls" could have been another story of nobodies or everywomen; it could refer to the generation of office workers who emerged in these years, or it could refer to female persons infantalized by gender and kept on the margins. Conversely, it could refer to freedoms achieved by women no longer imprisoned on the pedestal by their designation as "ladies."

The remarkable thing about Ferber's new-middle-class allegory is that it is an exploration of all these things. In fact, the maternal photosynthesis of "Sisters Under Their Skin" has been considerably recast. In contrast to the virtually one-way sign implicit in Emma McChesney's Main Street, what the reader sees in *The Girls* is not merely a handing down but a mutual exchange of experience across the generations which produces a different variety of "birth" for each character. Weaving an elaborate tale full of parallels and coincidences across the generations, Ferber centered her epic on marginal women whose lives were maimed or deflected by male adventurism, selfishness, even abandonment. As in *Buttered Side Down,* Ferber returned to presenting a range of females, but she now pieced them together in a single narrative: older spinsters, based in and entrapped by ideals of family sacrifice, who now fear their lives have been a waste; self-made middle-class mothers, forced into the marketplace by male abandonment, who fear their daughters' independence and frivolity; younger, Progressive-era women who experience more freedom in the marketplace and yet often find only loneliness and drudgery there. Even though Ferber's sense of time is not eschatological (to use Jane Tompkins's term), the life crises facing different generations are markedly reiterative. The difference now—in a history itself made moderate and middle—is that pure reiteration (stasis in history) is a trap, a threat.

At the center of this broad canvas is, not surprisingly, the relation between Mother and Daughter: Carrie, a figure clearly based on Julia Ferber, and her daughter Lottie. At the outset, Carrie is nearly omnipotent and even admirable for her drive, a Victorian abandoned woman turning her rage to managerial energy. Nonetheless, this maternal figure is now stripped of her capable exterior to reveal an essentially Machiavellian, manipulative core. Carrie is undercut as a woman who has replaced a man and simply duplicated his faults. Almost a descendent of a character like Mrs. Marvyn in Stowe's *The Minister's Wooing,* she possesses "the mathematical and legal-thinking type of brain" (52); an Emma McChesney without charisma, Carrie overprotects her daughter, introduces Lottie as her "baby" (79) but gradually grows old, brittle, too demanding. She "worked like a man," Ferber writes, "ruled the roost, was as ruthless as a man. She was neither a good housekeeper nor marketer, but something perverse in her made her insist . . . perhaps . . . a colossal egotism and a petty love of power" (64). (Carrie, incidentally, was the character Mencken seized upon as his prototypical *Americanus.*)[47] Ferber explicitly identifies the threat that Mother will make Daughter (Lottie) into a version of her own sister—into Charlotte, the spinster aunt.

Yet Lottie is not simply a daughter in rebellion but a transitional figure, caught between her mother's managerial conception of being modern and the explorations of a younger generation on their way up, currently working as salesgirls. Lottie is the figure at the crossroads, not only chronologically, but sociologically, at the center of Ferber's own split identification around the issue of class. At the other end of the spectrum is the eighteen-year old, Charley, so named because her parents had wanted a boy.[48] She is described (after Ferber alludes to both Freud and Havelock Ellis) as "a young woman who belonged to the modern school that despises sentiment and . . . to whom rebellion is a normal state; clear-eyed, remorseless, honest, fearless, terrifying; the first woman since Eve to tell the truth and face the consequences" (128). Charley is an icon of "self-expression"—there is "no higher duty," she insists (187)—and she ridicules Lottie as just another instance of "The Family Sacrifice" (126–27). To her, Charlotte had been sacrificed on the altar of "service"—notably, in the old sense of the word—to the family. At one level, Charley seems little more than a device for inaugurating Lottie's rematuration. Her rebellious spirit seems to conspire with Charlotte's own sense of tragedy (becoming identified as a permanent "maiden" [45] by having been a Civil War nurse), converging on Lottie's sense of self, catalyzing the struggle with Carrie.

The intriguing problem, however, is that Charley's rebelliousness looks very much as though it will eventually accommodate itself to her culture's corporate design. Taking classes in merchandising and business efficiency, Charley begins as Carrie's version of the modern salesperson, elevated from gum-chewing "shopgirl" status.[49] Rather pointedly, Lottie feels that Charley's generation is too given over to "impulse" (127); within all the talk about "self-expression" and getting ahead, she detects a note of "ruthlessness" (226) that does not seem so different from Carrie's. "You kids today are so sure of yourselves," she says. "I wonder if your method is going to work out any better than ours" (222–23). Crucially, it is the novel's aversion to this risk of male, and class, recapitulation that alters Charley's plans, and this repulsion begins, importantly, as Charley discovers the limits of her own notions of service. Discussing Charley's work as a salesclerk, Ferber says: "She never called it a career. She spoke of it as 'a job.'" (134). Using a cultural keyword Sinclair Lewis and Sherwood Anderson would investigate, Ferber implies that Charley sees her work not the taproot of selfhood but simply a means to an end, which means then, that it is not service at all. A career, Charley feels, is too consuming; she turns to business education to side-step the drudgery and isolation involved in years of apprenticeship (135–36). Thus, though she argues confidently that business should be a "profession" rather than the "rough and tumble game" of the past, she realizes before long that too little has changed.

Before long, Ferber herself turns to Dickensian dismantling of modern business employment. At one juncture, Charley relates her encounter with an "Ever Upward Club" of women workers at her store: "I couldn't think of anything but Oliver Twist and . . . Bumble. Then this girl told us about the values of games and the Spirit of Play, and how we should leap and run about . . . having previously walked eleven thousand miles in your department. . . . 'The romance of business?' Ha!" (229–30). Charley instead runs off to join the ballet, not wanting the "hard finish" (346) that still comes with "plodding away" (347) towards business success. In a fairy-tale finish for this character, *The Girls* catapults Charley onto the stage, a place where she can give vent to her theatrical side. Such a "schoolgirly" option as Charley chooses was not, however, the actual locus of value in the novel—as her disdain for toil suggests. Ferber put her stock in another version of "middle" status: one that synthesized the desire for independence from domesticity yet reinforced the "service" ideal. Far from endorsing sheer Main Street normalcy, *The Girls* tried to mediate between middle-class values of different eras. This was the garb in which her class vocabulary was made to look fashioned from without.

Lottie—the "middle" generation—becomes the conduit for Ferber's proposed resolution. Originally, her world is one of spiritual jilting, failed attempts at freedom; she is very nearly, as Charley sees, a casualty of the civil war between the genders, a frozen adolescent. Yet "[i]n spite of objections," Ferber writes, "Lottie made sporadic attempts to mingle in the stream of life that was flowing so swiftly past her—this new life of service and self-expression into which women were entering" (86). In this vein, Ferber further develops the idea that modern women (like Charley) are passing by the older value of service without measuring its real value. Not that the book does not present the internal debate. "We've all gone in for suffrage, and bleeding Belgium, and no petticoats, and uplift work," one member of Lottie's Reader's Club complains, "and we think we're modern. Well, we're not. We're a past generation. We're the unselfish softies. Watch the eighteen-year olds. They've got the method. They're not afraid" (111). Lottie, however, will not succumb to this seductive logic; she wants, somehow, to find a place for service not couched in domesticity (Charlotte's sacrifice), managerial ruthlessness (Carrie's), or mere self-expression (Charley's motto). The alphabetical thread in Ferber's patchwork is now revealed as the real pattern, the true reiteration Lottie wants most to resist.

Lottie's negotiation first comes, aptly enough, in a trial scene: specifically, a "Girl's Court" to which Lottie comes as a spectator and, like so many O. Henry city characters, instead finds herself. She has been invited there by one of the independent newspaper women she admires (whose method was "moling" among average Americans, but only as a sediment to be mined). That it is a "Girls" court pointedly invokes Ferber's title: "In the ante-room red-eyed girls and shawled mothers were watching the closed door in mingled patience and fear. Girls. Sullen girls, bold girls, frightened girls. Girls who had never heard of the Ten Commandments and who had broken most of them. Girls who had not waited for the apple of life to drop ripe into their laps but had twisted it off the tree and bitten deep into the fruit and found the taste of gall in their mouths. . . . Girls who had rehearsed their roles, prepared for stern justice in uniform. Girls who bristled with resentment against life, against law, against maternal authority" (190).

Ferber's family court is itself a patchwork of female designs—knowledge-gathering, role-playing, outright rebellion, all of which usually end in bitterness. Fittingly enough, at issue on this day is a custody suit between an immigrant mother and daughter. Ferber portrays Lottie's dawning self-recognition as she identifies with the younger girl in the dispute, seeing "New America and the Old World, out of sympathy with each other, uncomprehending, resentful" (190). As her first act of protest, Lottie brings the girl home as a boarder, thereby incorporating the maternal rationale, yet helping the girl achieve financial independence from her own mother. In passing through this rite of service, Lottie prepares her own departure from the thread of maternal (and old-middle-class) power.

Although Lottie's belated motherhood is not far from a "fairy-tale" outcome in itself, it is certainly a big step away from old-middle-class spinsterhood.[50] But most important to Ferber, Lottie's choice is not simply "self-expression" unloosened. Rather, it is a blend of service and self-expression, an independence achieved through the patronage of "working girls." In Paris, Lottie learned of "freedom. Not license—freedom. Ordinary freedom of will, or intellect, or action" (372). In giving birth to her own daughter, a real birth that displaces Emma McChesney's mechanical one, Lottie not only breaks the chain of childlessness but she continues an unfinished quest of middle-class womanhood itself. Of the baby, the original family spinster Charlotte pronounces: "Perhaps she'll be the one to work out what we haven't done—we Thrift girls. She's got a job ahead of her. A job" (374).[51] Now Charley's derogated terminology of routine (the job) is recouped to stand for a larger mission blending service and personal independence, not only in a new-middle-class mythology, but in a rationale for class relations as well.

Ultimately, then, there may be something misleading about situating Ferber in a continuing tradition of nineteenth-century female authorship. It would be easy to see novels like *The Girls,* or *So Big,* as simply a secular working out of the ideology so apparent in a text like Louisa May Alcott's *Work.* Alcott's intersubjective novel, which follows a "girl" named Christie through several menial employments, then nursing, then marriage and motherhood—and finally into organizing working women—transposes the ideal of Christian service and sacrifice into a chain of interdependence among women across the classes. However, if Alcott's Christie learns humility by passing through her culture's "underground railroad" of servants and slaves—and, if Alcott herself learned it, by supporting her own family wage system through her writing—Edna Ferber's career proceeded primarily by sanctioning such "servers" but ultimately distancing herself from them. Her work developed instead by a difficult process of identification with, and finally revision of, one of her class's dominant idioms: establishing a trademark, disclaiming despair as a crime against normalcy, literally "bucking up" with theatrical self-development. Finally, that trademarked patronage of working women allowed her moderate independence from the strata she patronized so publicly.

It is easy to take this patronage at face value, to read only Ferber's assertion of the working woman's dignity and rights, and to pass over how the white collar perimeter circumscribed even these values. But it is revealing to examine how Ferber's vocabulary worked on a specific social occasion. In August of 1918, Ferber made a visit to Minneapolis, Minnesota, a guest of local civic groups; later she referred to the main event of this visit blithely, if obliquely, in her letters as her lecture to "eight thousand woikin' goils." Ferber arrived on August 24 as a guest speaker for the Minneapolis "Girls' Liberty League," where she joined a celebratory weekend of marches, sporting competitions and picnics, exhibitions of dance and military drill, which included thousands of young women. Hailed in the local press as the creator of Emma McChesney, Ferber reviewed the parade, handed out medals, and made a speech. Obviously thinking of the novel *The Girls* and explicitly drawing upon her recent essay on the "Joy of the Job," Ferber proclaimed to the crowd:

> In my opinion the Girls' Liberty league is the greatest organization brought forth by the war.
>
> I am glad to hear that nearly all the girls of the Liberty league are working girls. The war has made the working girl not only necessary but fashionable. Any woman who hasn't a job today is looked down upon; she is out of the running. When the war is over, and the world becomes calm again, and order has come out of chaos, there will be written on the asset side of the ledger of the United States item one: "A working habit, belonging to all American women; value, priceless."[52]

From one perspective, Ferber was bringing "order" and meaning to the chaos of wartime. She was asserting women's right to work; invoking the prosaic balance sheet of her popular heroine, she enjoined her audience to think of the older term, "working girl," now as a "fashionable" term of praise, on the credit side of the American column. As in *The Girls,* she illuminated parts of the social fabric—here, the realm of women, the homefront, the realm of work—still too often overlooked in our histories. To a few critics even today, this kind of speech demonstrated that Ferber was "extolling what she considered the very foundation of American society, the working class."[53]

On this particular social occasion, however, a different (and less consensual) reading seems more plausible than the one that a sheerly discursive or ideological decoding can describe. The Girls' Liberty League of Minneapolis was formed as the junior branch of the War Camp Community Service, a volunteer effort established at the request of the secretaries of war and the navy. Set up through local churches, recreation groups, and civic leaders, the W.C.C.S. was designed to provide a "good time, in decent, normal, manly, healthful, independent fashion" for soldiers away from home, stuck in military camps before shipping out—support, as one article put it, for "Private John Smith" whose morale might be slipping. If the cultural metaphor of John Smith represented a rewriting of social differences, even the W.C.C.S.'s supporters could not entirely erase persisting inequalities. As *Good Housekeeping* announced in endorsing the plan, these camps would allow soldiers to "have the right kind of girls" instead of the "wrong ones," who led to "disease, evil, and the defeat of our armies." (Not surprisingly, separate social clubs were set up for "coloreds.") The camps would take a soldier from farther down on the "social scale," having supposedly come "from a home where the father was worthless and the mother shiftless and dirty," and make him "fit for the better sort of home" by seeing "respectable ones"; it would also keep working girls from roaming "aimlessly" on the streets looking for such men. The Girls' Liberty League auxiliary surely aided in this function: sewing or canning for the war effort, organizing chapters by trade around local factories which vied for prizes—a few, by working over lunch, overtime, on Saturdays—when they were not running through marching drills.[54] Such patriotic "wholesomeness" was hardly value-neutral in the local politics of Minneapolis, where local socialists, radical unionists, and academics, drawing upon the resistance of many local German-Americans, had been labeled disloyal, harrassed, and even jailed for opposing the war. Though local trade unions loyally supported the war effort, the belated war support from their hero, socialist Mayor Thomas Van Lear, meant that he would be defeated for reelection the following November. Nor was Ferber's depiction of the war's effect on working women, or her prophecy, particularly accurate. A few months later, the telephone girls in Minneapolis who had contributed to the patriotic leagues were on strike for decent wages.[55]

By any lights, this small episode suggests one particularly divided interpretive community within which Ferber's updated class language, her notions of her own "job," and her contribution to the implied class iconography of Main Street took hold. To be sure, there were more back alleys to Ferber than the "Main Streeting" she so readily claimed as her storefront. By progressing from the imaginative "reader"/shopgirl to that Pulitzer-Prize-winning Lady Bountiful of the Little People, she had marketed, indeed embodied, a Cinderella story in which the clock struck twelve but only the coachmen turned back into mice. Like so many of her white collar peers engaged in disseminating the practical, commonsensical idioms of the sales economy, she wrote affectingly, theatrically, about the homeliness of toil even as she lunched at the Algonquin. Ferber's claim to represent Little People and yet transcend them had widespread appeal among her more cosmopolitan or reformist readers, but more commonplace readers did not, in fact, always embrace her. Privately she would feel stranded between audiences. Late in her career, Ferber would complain that the sum effect of her theatrical projections had only been to exclude her from warm welcome among the regions, and the people, she had depicted. In the mid-thirties, she complained that the United States was "closing in on [her] like Poe's prison walls." Regional readers disputed her factual claims, missed her irony, saw her only as a romancer. In short, they saw only her deep acting and denied her private claim to stand outside the middle-class matriarchs she represented.[56] Privately, Ferber probably had more in common with her readers' own doubts and self-denigration than her hubristic moments ever acknowledged. In a tough irony even she may never have fully grasped, Edna Ferber repaid Main Street many times over for the service, and the sacrifice, Julia had performed. Yet like her mother, behind the patchwork career, she became a worker that few customers really knew.

Part II Professions and the Public

Three

Representing the Average

The Making of Robert Grant

The better the novel, indeed, the more the [protagonist] approaches Everyman, and the more the background overshadows him.

—H. L. Mencken

By the 1920s, Edna Ferber had created a modern iconography of class relations that seemed familiar and new all at once. In novels like *So Big,* she made new white collar managerialism look like nineteenth-century civic republicanism reborn. Like O. Henry's cracker-barrel style, Ferber's mixture of old and new drew upon the storehouse of commercial and entrepreneurial know-how readily familiar to so many of her readers. Even *The Girls,* which rewrote the history of modern womanhood as the evolution of sacrifice, self-expression, and service ideologies, operated within a middle-class perimeter of self-development—a rather familiar strategy to middling readers raised on Alger. Ferber's most popular heroines were women whose social construction was predicated on the upwardly mobile, inventive, energetic "man on the make" ethos associated with middle classes since at least the Jacksonian era. As C. Wright Mills would discern decades later, the "little people" mythos retained its entrepreneurial garb long into the era of large-scale corporate organization.[1] A character like Emma McChesney may have eased this historic transition by making her social leadership seem not only traditional but natural, earned—a product of cultural common sense. Like other versions of American pastoralism, Ferber's Main Streeting thus not only reaffirmed and refashioned middling republican values, but, more to the point, it exemplified a form of power. In a sense Ferber created tutorial fables of authority by mythologizing matters of social deference, the currency in which power is often invisibly circulated. Moreover, like O. Henry's voice, Ferber's own narrative tokens of commonsensicality—sedimentary layers of aphorism, loving glimpses of shared fashion details, folksy colloquial speech that affirmed the American social family—made her seem on a plane with the Little People she patronized. Warm, homely, domestic icons littered her fables of class, enjoining readerly participation in her books, even safety in their possession. Her works therefore presented themselves not just as arguments for Main Street commonality but as examples of it. Her prose style, built upon speech, fashioned commonsensicality simply by exhibiting or modeling a way to talk about the world, by becoming axiomatic for her readership of "*Everybody's*."

And yet, whatever solace or modeling this mythos of "little people" provided modern white collar Americans, it was hardly the entire story. In the turn-of-the-century years, another group of white collar Americans was staking out a different ground for middling authority—that of modern professionalism. Nurtured in the modern university, growing with the specialization of knowledge and the extension of technical expertise, validated by elaborate systems of credentials and corporate support, these modern professionals have often, in recent scholarship, been identified with what it means to be new middle class itself.[2] Perhaps most important, the social vocabularies these professionals brought with them generated a rival form of social leadership—even competing models of how authority itself should operate—to challenge the commercial commonsensicality writers like O. Henry and Ferber favored. Whether in law, social science, medicine, or social work, modern white collar professionals have been linked especially to the redrafting of liberalism within Progressive reform movements. This linkage—and its relationship to two modern forms of literary authority—is the subject of the next two chapters.

Throughout these years, as political leaders like Theodore Roosevelt were dismissing the older idea that classes even existed "on this side of the water," political matters like popular sovereignty, majority rule, and local representation were under reexamination as well.[3] (In this sense, Roosevelt's endorsement of both O. Henry and Ferber certainly bears noticing.) Across the political spectrum, this reconsideration often emerged within a mass-cultural vocabulary. Dismissing the partisan and class-conscious languages of the past, modern liberals now argued that voters were to be understood in terms of their daily work in large, bureaucratic structures, in the subjection of their taste and reading habits to mass magazines and newspapers, in terms of their resistance to new, university-trained modes of professional expertise. Moreover, even Ferber's sense that heightened consumer longings essentially vitiated the social conflicts of the past—that subordinate workers more often looked up to their (assumed) social superiors' affluence with envy—was a rather common refrain among the social thinkers of her day (in the work of Simon Patten, Thorstein Veblen, and Walter Lippmann, to name just a few). American voters were thus to be viewed not in terms of the polarized, conflict-ridden Victorian society of "classes and masses" but as a mass of typically routinized, dependent, and commercially standardized middle Americans under the often-damaging sway of media culture.[4] Professional authority became axiomatic within modern liberalism as the only legitimate force capable of meeting this new electorate.

The association of literary realism and naturalism with this "ferment of reform" has been a standby theme in both conventional and more iconoclastic criticism. To be sure, an understanding of turn-of-the-century writers' *literary* professionalism—their increasing engagement (and friction) with the mass literary marketplace—is clearer than a decade ago. So too is the sense of writers' fascination with professions like engineering or medicine, or with technocratic liberalism itself. Many authors in this era employed the language of professionalism—of service, of responsibility to their public, even of democratic obligation—to negotiate their own involvement in the writing market. Yet paradoxically, more is known about writers as literary professionals than about their standing in any wider professional class.[5] More specifically, writers' imbrication in the specific manner and modes of turn-of-the-century professional expertise—in essence, the forms in which professional legitimacy was naturalized, made into a broader cultural vocabulary—has remained unexplored. To an extent, even the frequently provocative forays of discourse theory, which all too often simply declare the equivalence of language and power, leave the particulars of power unexamined (what kind of power, exercised by whom, submitted to or resisted by whom).[6] The exceptions to this general rule are those critical studies—by Elizabeth Deeds Ermarth, June Howard, and Richard Brodhead, among others—who have tried to link matters of narrative structure and readerly engagement to prevailing practices of power. These studies have suggested that any power that resides in a text derives not just from what it argues, or even (as with O. Henry or Ferber) how it models an axiomatic vocabulary, but rather, how readers are directed to read themselves into the cultural space of a text. Whether by enlisting consensus through perspectival realism, fashioning a spectatorial narrator, or engaging intimate readerly exchanges, texts may well encode and even discipline particular and local forms of authority into implied, and perhaps actual, readers.[7]

To follow the lead of these critics and retrace this particular confluence of the revision of liberalism and realistic literary representation, the overlooked career of Bostonian Robert Grant (1852–1940) bears examination. Admittedly, Grant—altogether marginal in terms of current understanding of literary realism—at first looks extremely provincial and Victorian, hardly worthy of reconstruction. Early in his career, Grant worked hard to establish himself as Boston's and Cambridge's unofficial (doggerel) poet laureate of Mugwump culture; in the 1880s and 1890s, he wrote a series of rather dreary upper-class novels that hardly anyone reads today. Even his best-known novel, *Unleavened Bread* (1900), seems to be rife with elitism and Brahmin nostalgia. The novel satirizes a midwestern arriviste named Selma White who ascends the national social and political ladder by successive marriages (and divorces): to a hardware man, an eastern architect named Wilbur Littleton, and finally to a corrupt senator-elect. The book has been read, consequently, in Brahmin lights: as a satire of social climbing, a direct assault on the new woman of its day, or as Grant's Victorian protest against the decay of the institution of marriage.[8]

Nonetheless, this portrait of a provincial Brahmin reactionary misconstrues Grant's other, more modern dimensions—suggested by the fact that *Unleavened Bread* was a national best-seller in 1900. As Edith Wharton and other writers realized, *Unleavened Bread* (along with Howells's *A Modern Instance*) pioneered the part of the modern Main Street tradition that many admired. Whereas Grant's early novels present interclass allegories about an American society polarized by ethnic conflict and leisure-class paralysis, *Unleavened Bread* centers instead on a middle-cultural personification of the modern American electorate. Selma White embodied what Grant in one essay called "a certain kind of American," the believer in "average opinion"; she exhibited "an indirect form of patriotic negation under the shadow of which low comedians and leading villains" of American politics "could ply their trade comparatively unmolested."[9] Blinded by her 100 percent Americanism, hostile to professional authority, new middle class and middlebrow to the core, Selma White personified what Grant saw as an American citizenry without the "leaven" of high culture; she was, in Grant's words, "hard, flat, and half-baked" (221).

It was Grant's representation of an "unbaked" electorate which had an even more seminal role in American liberalism at large. As critics have long known, Herbert Croly, often regarded as the principal theorist of the dawning Progressive movement, credited Grant's satiric novel as his inspiration for *The Promise of American Life* (1909). Particularly in Grant's portrait of the struggling professional architect Littleton, Croly found an illuminating allegory about the tensions between the Jeffersonian egalitarian tradition and the new demands of specialized intellectual disciplines that universities were now producing. He praised Grant for having "ingeniously wrought out the contradiction subsisting between certain aspects of the American democratic tradition and the methods and aspirations which dominate contemporary American intellectual work." Doing the seminal work of redrawing the imaginative canvas of liberalism, Grant's career thus makes a connection between two reciprocal cultural projects: the representation of a muddled, culturally homogenized constituency and the growing legitimation of professional authority.[10] Again, the contesting of middle-class mythologies between writers like Grant and Ferber is telling. What critics have commonly seen as a cultural divide in this period, between debunkers and the booboisie, or between intellectual and white collar culture, actually represented a largely internicine struggle within middle classes to define the style of their cultural legitimacy. Indeed, in taking stock of commercial Main Street as his antagonist, Grant's career internalizes this very struggle. To turn to such a writer (and subsequently, to Elmer Rice) is to engage a very different strand of cultural "averaging" that was taking hold at the turn of the century—what might be described as the "high republicanism" of professional and cosmopolitan strata which competed with the commercial Main Street mythology. To Grant Selma White is the self-same middle-class heroine that writers like Edna Ferber would enshrine.

Consequently, what follows is a biographical retracing of Grant *in* his locality and his class, particularly his apprenticeship within the growing liberal veneration of professional expertise. This is not a matter of simply tracing analogous social practices or homologies, or "punning" from one discourse to another. Rather my argument, again following current thinking on realist poets, is that *Unleavened Bread*'s narrative style demonstrates, in literary terms, a central American refashioning of political representation that Grant introjected from his professional legal training.[11] The narrative design of *Unleavened Bread* incorporates Grant's political denigration of "government by the average" into the traditional novel of manners. There, in contrast to the direct mimesis and consensual realism commonly associated with the form, Selma White is actually represented through a central, paraphrastic presence that seems intent upon rephrasing her intentions, her actions, and her will. In these moments, the reader finds a narrative voice remarkably reempowered, which has internalized the changing rationale of liberal governance itself. In this sense, Grant is by no means a marginal figure.

The beauty of Grant's method, for its admirers, was that this voice avoided looking like "governance" at all. As Edith Wharton—a writer who embraced professionalism over the drift of upper-class leisure—testified in a personal note praising *Unleavened Bread:* "There is, of course, no recipe for writing a good novel . . . but I am so great a believer in the objective attitude that I have specially enjoyed the successful use you have made of it; your consistent abstinence from comment, explanation and partisanship, and your confidence in the reader's ability to draw his own conclusions." Not only did Wharton, in creating personifications of Middle America like Undine Spragg, learn well from Grant.[12] She intuitively recognized how Grant's satirical style covertly transposed a class-cultural ethos of discipline, explicit moral evaluation, and self-restraint to a new nonpartisan style of liberal authority that, as in Progressive political practice, acts as if its "objective" judgement will "enlist" the reader's (voter's) consent.

| | |

If the trials of dependence, in all its fluid meanings, are commonly associated with the lower, more bureaucratized white collar strata, the theme of professionalism has dominated the upper and relatively more autonomous levels. Indeed, the tension between these two themes has often been at the root of disputes about the new middle class and its coherence, political character, and historical destiny. Among historians concerned with political authority at the turn of the century, however, the professional theme has dominated more recent scholarship. This scholarship has taken two interrelated paths. On the one hand, the so-called organizational hypothesis for late-Victorian and Progressive America—set forth in the work of Samuel Hays, Robert Wiebe, Burton Bledstein, Thomas Haskell, and many others—

links professionalism, scientific management, and nonpartisan reform in hypothesizing the dawning cultural leadership of the new middle classes.[13] Meanwhile, further on the left, Barbara and John Ehrenreich have hypothesized the emergence of a professional-managerial class ("P.M.C."), which mediates between labor and capital. To date, historians have been somewhat more hospitable to the first formulation than the second; nevertheless, both hypotheses have ramifications for the prevailing notions of authority in Progressive-era liberalism at large. Indeed, historians have perhaps not fully appreciated how much the languages of middle-class "awareness"—which, as Anthony Giddens suggests, work to deny the reality of classes themselves—were constitutional in this liberal redrafting of authority.[14]

How contemporaries perceived "middle" classes is a large part of the story. Burton Bledstein has shown the way by tracing the linguistic usage of "middle class" and its sustaining institutional cultures in the Gilded Age. As Bledstein points out, in the eighteenth century professionals (and entrepreneurs) were commonly grouped with farmers and mechanics in the middling ranks. Over the course of the nineteenth century, however, the man on the make—the mobile middling, professedly egalitarian figure embodied in Jacksonian ideology—gradually gave way to a more professionalized and hierarchical prototype of class thinking. Of course, much as in conventional recounting of success mythology, historians tracing the linguistic usages of "middle class" have too often emphasized a uniform and linear narrative. (Such terms may not reflect unmediated class consciousness, but operate defensively, draw borders where borders threaten to collapse.) In all likelihood, "middle class" itself was contested among commercial and professional elites. As Bledstein shows, the first dictionary definition of "middle class" appeared in the Mugwump *Century* American (1889) as "that class of the people which is socially and conventionally intermediate between the aristocratic class, or nobility, and the laboring class; the untitled community of well-born or wealthy people" (13). Set between classes and masses, between titles and the life of labor, even this definition seems in search of a common ground.

In search of the unstable commodity of social legitimacy, the middling Americans traced by Bledstein emerged from the specialization of labor and sought out new spaces in the educational and occupational ladder. Professional white collar life now became rooted in the idea of career, in graded occupational advancement through a lifetime (111). Among these strata, a life was, as Bledstein puts it, mapped out in "measured mobility," marked by discipline and the acquisition of specialized training. For Bledstein's professionals, the pivotal institution was the modern research university; its seminal idiom was science. "Science as a source for professional authority transcended the favoritism of politics, the corruption of personality, and the exclusiveness of partisanship" (90).

This model of authority, meanwhile, infused social reform movements and modern class relations. In the mid-1970s, Hays, Wiebe, and scholars like Roy Lubove emphasized how these newly professionalized elites, at the turn of the century, played an important role in refashioning American authority. Quite often, historians have positioned such professionals as foils to clerical nobodies and Victorian moralists alike. Professionals provided strategic coherence, Wiebe wrote, at a point when American society was passing beyond the "island communities" of mid-century and integrating into an interlocking national marketplace. Haskell likewise emphasized how the unconscious recognition of the constitution of social life—which had moved irrevocably towards market "interdependence"—spurred reform efforts; professionals offered their specialized knowledge to a public baffled by the increasingly remote causes of late-industrial social ills. Men like the founders of the American Social Science Association now formed various professional communities of inquiry, ushering in curricular reform, new means of certification, and internal policing. For instance, in the mid-nineteenth century, lawyers had customarily been trained under an apprenticeship system, reading law under the tutelage of an established attorney who would then recommend his student to the local bar. Clients were then acquired through courtroom practice. Early on, high republican ideology had stressed the importance of an "open" profession, and even Harvard Law School, before 1870, only required good moral character for its (male) applicants. In the 1870s, however, legal elites began organizing city and state bar associations (capped in 1878 by the American Bar Association), and legal education nationally was "Harvardized" by the example of Charles Eliot and the first Harvard Law School dean, Christopher Columbus Langdell. By the second decade after 1900, there would be forty-eight state bar associations; standardized bar exams would be the norm; professionals earned advanced degrees not by apprenticeship, but by studying instances of judicial opinion (case law). A similar pattern was followed in other fields. Such professionalism provided nonpartisan technical solutions for what Wiebe repeatedly called the "distended" national society—a theme chroniclers of the "P.M.C."

have echoed. As Barbara Ehrenreich has put it, through professionalization, the middle class gained "purchase on an increasingly uncertain world."[15]

At the center of these hypotheses is the revolution in values created by the leadership of these strata: a reliance on scientific method and casework rather than precedent or fixed laws; a preference for social accounting of human behavior rather than resorting to the intricate discriminations of Victorian moral standards; a renewed emphasis on bureaucratic standards like efficiency in place of partisan loyalties. Haskell emphasized the major intellectual reorientation produced by professional authority, a shift towards organic and "interdependent" (14–15) social thinking. Consequently, the historical portrait of professionalization has been linked, almost invariably, to a redefinition of American political authority within the liberal mainstream, a redefinition that culminated in Progressivism. In a step by step progression—from the New York Bar Association that resisted Boss Tweed, to the Mugwump lawyers in Massachusetts reform, to the professional social workers, medical experts, health reformers, and others who sponsored Progressive legislation—the upsurgence of professionalism, and the cultural paradigm shift outlined above, have been linked to the development of the nonpartisan, Progressive agenda. As Bledstein summarizes when speaking of Harvard's Eliot: "Ideological spokesmen for the American university such as Eliot justified the institution in terms of the nonpartisan professional class it would create. Democracy, according to Eliot, meant rule by merit—never equality. And merit belonged to those individuals who disciplined themselves to *acquire authority* by concentrating on a single object . . . without a university to select its leadership and cultivate special mental habits necessary in every special endeavor, American society was courting disaster" (322–23; emphasis added).

There are two fundamental planks to Eliot's program here, both related to class affiliation and how authority is conceived. First, a rather subtle self-definition: authority for professionals was acquired not just by specialization but by a heroic act of concentration, a "singling" of oneself out of the mass—cultivating special habits and securing a field. (Wiebe emphasized [129] how the "identifying act" of professional affiliation was itself something that contributed to the weakening of partisan commitments.) This relates directly, of course, to the second part of Eliot's program: the reconceiving of democratic sovereignty, the rewriting of high republican ideology to suit a culture conceived as a meritocracy. As Asa Briggs has pointed out, in classic texts like James Mill's *Essay on Government*, the "middle rank" *had* commonly been referred to as the most virtuous part of the community; this idea provided a foundation for much of "middling" American republicanism, a philosophy writers like O. Henry still retained (while sustaining a healthy distrust of professionals). Here, however, ever so subtly, the social middle was being legitimized by professional education, with the *un*-educated (or Emma McChesney's "field-flower of experience") being denigrated.

Considered in terms of positing "professionalism" against "the public," this act of self-definition and separation (the self and other of technocratic liberalism) is more familiar. Historians like Charles Forcey, Michael McGerr, James Kloppenberg, and others have made clear that disillusionment with classical democratic representation was not merely a consequence of the wreckage of World War I—critics like H. L. Mencken and Walter Lippmann had ridiculed liberal ideas well before the war. Moreover, as McGerr has shown, the distrust of pure political representation (as pure, that is, as white men of property chose to make it) had been a significant component of liberalism since the 1870s. Against a backdrop of declining presidential voter turnouts—from nearly 77 percent in the 1870s to nearly 50 in the 1920s—recurrent complaints had emerged from the northern gentry regarding the "vanishing voter," dull elections, and unqualified party nominees. In the 1870s and 1880s, northern liberals began to assail what they termed "pure democracy," to argue that the vote was a trust or a contract rather than a natural right, and even to reconsider property requirements for voting. When such rollback strategies proved impractical, northern liberals had turned instead to causes like civil service and ballot reform, to public education, and particularly to urging voters away from the military models of partisanship to nonpartisan, "independent" campaigns. (To use one distinction McGerr emphasizes, campaigns aimed at making voters ask why they should vote with their party rather than why they should not.) Moreover, even those who advanced the organizational hypothesis have long maintained that the Progressive era's seemingly inflated notion of "the public" contained within it a covert devaluation of democratic participation in deference to managerial politics. As Eugene Leach has best demonstrated, from Progressivism to the more technocratic theories of the 1930s, liberal theory was predicated on the public's mass malleability in the face of technocratic expertise. Liberal thought turned decisively toward conceptualizing an "average," or typical, or microcosmic citizen whose mind was often made up of headlines and mail-order self-help, saturated with cultural icons like *The Saturday Evening Post.* The rethinking of political authority was bound up in a reciprocal estrangement of "professional" and "mass" culture. As voters were viewed as increasingly "independent" and "middle" class, their loss of "reason" was rewritten as an unfortunate desire for cultural normativeness—merely being "average." Modern liberal theorists effectively redrafted the "minds" of voters as a collage of headlines, impulse buying, consumer whim, cluttered with those things professionals could supposedly rise above.

I cannot hope to sort out the differences among the many theorists of professionalism, evaluate its coherence as a class concept, or sum up its overall usefulness for understanding Progressive reform. Yet in retrospect, it should be clear that this one-dimensional portrait of a self-conscious, coherent professional class (much less "new middle class") of the organizational hypothesis has been overstated; even specialists in these areas have now begun to gravitate to seeing contradictory class locations among professionals and a pluralist base—a collage of rather diverse social languages—in Progressivism per se. There are good reasons for this newer, polyphonic emphasis, as well as the revived interest in the inner life not accounted for by professionalism's professing.[16] There is little disagreement about the fact that, as Martin Oppenheimer puts it, the growth of the professions is "widely assumed to be a major index of industrial development" (133). There are, however, drastic discontinuities in the class experience of professions: differences between those devoted to applied and basic research; between traditional occupations with medieval roots and newer professions like engineering or business management; differences caused by the routinization of some professional skills under progressive management and technological change. Even the customary criteria of a "profession"—a relatively autonomous service occupation that involves high degrees of training, education, and the acquiring of credentials within a specialized community of inquiry—provide little coherence when the term is applied so promiscuously (sanitation engineer, beauty consultant, funeral director). In modern usage, as Laurence Veysey has observed, at its most general, a "professional" can simply mean someone who gets paid to work (e.g., professional musician)—or worse yet, "professional" can be a derogatory term (e.g., "professional" politician).[17] Even if one's view is confined to the turn of the century, it also seems clear that the supposedly mushrooming figures for a new middle class depend disproportionately for growth in the lower ranges. In real numbers, for instance, the number of American lawyers grew from about 108,000 in 1900 to 123,000 in 1920—that is, at a slower rate than that of employed persons as a whole (46 percent)—while bank tellers easily outran that pace (235,000 to 1,323,000), as did nurses (12,000 to 149,000), and stenographers, typists, and secretaries (134,000 to 786,000). Over a longer period, from 1870, the difference in growth might well be more striking.[18] The paradox, of course, is that, though highly aggressive in this period, professions also seized "purchase" by continuing to restrict access to their membership. Consequently, in returning to the issue the contesting of middle-classness, what these statistics may well reveal is that this was a class, or class-in-formation, that was (to twist Wiebe's formulation) itself rather continuously being distended among its contradictory white collar positions—a pattern that may be continuing today.

It is possible to recover some of the precariousness and incoherence of new-middle-class life if one sees that the traditionally unstable escalators of middle-class mobility could have, in a sense, been internalized to the domain of professional strata. Becoming a professional did not mean leaving behind the socialization (and advantages) of local or familiar elites, but it did mean—as the class moved to more structured, progressive, career-oriented criteria—passing a series of sequential hurdles, technical requirements, often national standards. Here, perhaps, one should not lose sight of the restricted access to professionalism in order to see the sustained, and perhaps increased, pressures of life in a hierarchical, meritocratic system—in, as Eliot would have it, separating oneself from the run of the mill. In this regard, it is worth noting a particular dislocation in the word "average" throughout the nineteenth century, as applied to persons—a dislocation retained even today. Of course, "average" is currently recognized as a statistical term, "the result of taking an average." Yet "average" in the nineteenth century figured in another sense: as the antithesis of the "exceptional," as the "average" citizen who has not received the benefits of culture. Life in a meritocratic system produced pressures—a tautly edged linguistic and occupational landscape of progressive hurdles (bar exam, private practice, partnership)—now so much a part of professional life that it is taken for granted. Even today, as Ehrenreich has observed in strikingly commercial terms, the professional retains a "fear of falling," of losing the "discipline and will" necessary to sustain one's membership in a class in which knowledge is "capital."[19]

There are any number of other reasons for this internal precariousness to turn-of-the-century professional experience and authority. Even individual professions, in this era, did not simply coalesce into homogeneous occupations; rather, they retained vestiges of aristocratic privilege, ethnocentrism, and other class markings. Lawyering in Massachusetts, for instance, had long been a three-tiered profession, with upper echelons intermarrying among the Boston or Cambridge elite, while others struggled at the bottom merely to make a living; "good moral character" for Harvard applicants was obviously inflected by class, race, gender, and ethnicity. Individual professions like journalism also frequently divided over the meaning of professionalism (reflecting a guild, clerical, or market orientation) as it was shaped by these inflections.[20] Moreover, the simple assertion of professional authority was no guarantee for success, nor for autonomy, nor for public acceptance. Professionalization can often simply result in greater incorporation into bureaucracies and management practices.

The difference between "profession" and actual success shows how professionalism itself is often founded on a rather slippery linguistic claim. Professionals are unduly dependent upon language, not only in defining a specialized community of inquiry, but in acquiring legitimacy from their clients. Unlike skilled laborers, whose products allegedly speak for themselves, professionals must legitimate their own skill through persuasion. Sociologists still rely on the earliest, taproot meaning to distinguish professionalism—that is, to "profess" competence—yet this only begins to suggest the problem. As critics have pointed out, this root opens the definition up to nearly everyone in twentieth-century America. As JoAnne Brown demonstrates, professional languages often exhibit noticeable anxiety. Not atypically, professional languages feed off the legitimacy of other, more accepted professions or trades: feeding off ministry, clients become "laymen"; feeding off chemistry, law libraries become "laboratories."[21] Surely Charles W. Eliot would have thought of himself as a professional, as did Dean Langdell—but so again did pharmacists like O. Henry, or real-estate salesmen like George Babbitt. (The term "professional," in other words, was seized by commercial elites as well.) In fact, it is striking how much antagonism some professionals expend upon others who profess rival forms of expertise.

This linguistic slippage, however, only points to the precarious situation of professionals in the interdependent society that Wiebe and others described. Paradoxically, as Brown has pointed out, "[t]he increased specialization, bureaucracy, geographic mobility, disruption of community and division of labor that characterize much modern work also exacerbates the communication problem between practitioners and their clientele, and multiplies the occasions for expressing competence" (37). Not uncommonly, a tension develops within the profession between sustaining one's technical authority and popularizing it; during the Progressive era, the selling of expertise illuminated this problem. Set within the market economy, professionals may well experience instability in marking off their profession not only from corporate practice but from that of mere charlatanism, in seizing upon their specialized knowledge as a means of self-justification rather than helping a client.[22] If, as some more radical theorists of professionalism suggest, professional service often means "servicing" one's class, then professionalism certainly did find itself within the unstable economy of the triangular sales relationship. If anything, since selling is usually denigrated in professional ideologies, identification with one's client becomes all the more tortured. Clients, after all, are usually laymen lacking the specialized knowledge that one achieves, yet they are the source of one's livelihood, the people whom one ostensibly serves.

These rather uneasy parameters have much to do with the anxiety of white collar professionalism—indeed, with the rethinking of liberal authority as it played itself out in Robert Grant's career. Its consequences for the subtexts of representation, in fiction or cultural criticism, were profound. Fears of "proletarianization," as Marxian critics have suggested, may well have filtered into the fears of the collective unconsciousness of this era, yet just as frequently the domain of such fears was confined to a fall into normalcy or mere commercialism, into dependence or stagnation, out of expertise, yet still within the loose boundaries of the middle class itself.[23] This more internal struggle was, furthermore, played out in liberal theory, in how it conceived the citizens it hoped to manage. A far more telling "other" for class mythology than the proletarian brute, Robert Grant's mythology suggests, was the threat of being merely average. That personification of averageness could hover uneasily between the envisioned "face" of a client (or citizen) and a lapsed image of one's own fragile claim to authority.

| | |

As much as W. D. Howells seems securely fixed at the center of nineteenth-century American realism, his Bostonian contemporary Judge Robert Grant seems permanently exiled to the margins. At times, it almost seems as though the sardonic jurist preferred it that way. At several junctures in his career, Grant—born a banker's son with prestigious New England ancestry, raised on Beacon Hill, educated for a decade at Harvard (B.A., 1873; Ph.D., 1876; LL.B., 1879)—self-consciously positioned himself for posterity as Howells's Brahmin foil. Cloistered in the culture of Whiggery and Unitarianism, flooded with childhood memories of "the rebellion" and Lincoln's assassination, trained in history by Henry Adams, Grant nonetheless seems to have carved out the role of Mugwump gadfly. As a *Harvard Lampoon* contributor, the collegiate satirist parodied Howells's *A Chance Acquaintance* (1873) with a farce entitled "An Accidental Pick-Up"; after graduation, he ran his Mugwump parable *An Average Man* (1884) in *The Century*, shortly after *A Modern Instance* (1883) was serialized there. Years later, he penned *The Chippendales* (1909) as the belated Brahmin rejoinder to *The Rise of Silas Lapham* (1885). Nevertheless, Grant's strategy of rebutting the more successful Howells seems to have paid few dividends. Today, he is remembered, if at all, as a "jaundiced" proper Bostonian, at best an "amiable" satirist, at worst a shallow elitist "without a trace of moral perception." Still fewer recall his career as a Massachusetts probate judge—and even here, if only to resurrect his less-than-heroic role in upholding, as part of a gubernatorial advisory committee, the conviction of Sacco and Vanzetti just prior to their execution in 1927. Many of Grant's early books were self-conscious, interclass Brahmin parables, with coded names or phrases his Boston cohorts were liable to identify. In those days, his home-grown political affiliations were often an unappetizing blend of virulent ethnocentrism, antifeminism, and Anglo-Saxon sword-waving. In a poem delivered before Harvard's Phi Beta Kappa Society in 1883, for instance, he fancied the return of the ghost of "Yankee Doodle" in order to mourn the sight of "New England's valleys / A teemin' with O'Donahues, / O'Briens, an' O'Malley's." Grant compared his cohorts to the "august patricians" of Rome, swamped by the "hordes" of Gaul, a mob led by a statehouse boss who believed that "it is statesmanlike . . . to instergate the masses / into hostility agin / The eddicated classes."[24] It is little wonder that when writing a recommendation for Grant shortly after graduation, Charles Eliot Norton had simply written: Grant is "one of us."[25]

In part, the image of Grant as marginal and backward-looking persists because of the rather consoling contours literary historians have often fashioned around turn-of-the-century liberalism, the political ferment with which the realist movement has long been associated. In the 1890s, Grant seemed to divorce himself from the cardinal egalitarian doctrine of direct political representation—which he now dismissed as "government by the average"—and argued instead for government by those who "represent[ed] the best morals and brains of the community."[26] For many modern critics, Howells's more democratic sentiments, however guarded, project a far more reassuring linkage between aesthetics and politics. Yet even as Howells's realist program, as Amy Kaplan has so adroitly shown, embodied an aesthetic of the common, a moral invocation of a democratic communal consensus based in "men and women as they are," it was also designed to hold the line against the underworld of urban disorder. The centrality of Howells's Altrurianism to American liberalism can certainly be overstated; as the nineties progressed, Howells often felt marooned in America[27]; in contrast, Robert Grant's stock was on the rise.

Furthermore, Grant's reputation as a reactionary is partly a residual image left by consensus historiography. Following Richard Hofstadter's *Age of Reform* (1955), historians portrayed Mugwumps such as Grant as well-to-do, conservative idealists fretting over the decline of high republican character and their own social standing. More recently, however, historians have attempted to transcend the conservative/liberal dichotomy by emphasizing the Mugwumps' cosmopolitan and professional dimension. Mugwumps were not, for instance, simply gentlemen of leisure. As Gerald McFarland has shown, they were more often highly educated urban professionals (often, like Grant, lawyers) and businessmen; compared with Republican stalwarts, they tended to be younger, less likely to be war veterans, and less likely to be millionaires. Taking shape in the formation of the Massachusetts Reform Club in 1882, the young man's radical wing of Mugwumpery was made up overwhelmingly of Harvard graduates, often lawyers who combined faith in the legalistic, rationalistic, and independent idiom of the Founding Fathers with a decided fatalism about character and social leveling. Anxious about what they saw as the degeneration of republican virtue in a sea of affluence, they saw themselves as civic stewards who resisted party pragmatism and discipline. Theirs was a nostalgia for the free-thinking voter and "free" workplace. When in power in Massachusetts, the Mugwump zeal for independent voting, free trade and tariff reform, and civil service also pitted them against the growing Populist movement which would shatter Democratic unity in the 1890s. Mugwumps sponsored reforms that loosened both partisan and boss control (for example, the secret ballot and the removal of the poll tax) and anticipated the Progressive zeal for economic regulation.[28] In Massachusetts, Mugwumpery reached its apogee in the governorship (1890–93) of Reform Democrat William Russell.

Young men of Grant's generation naturally settled on Russell as their hero. The son of a war-horse Democrat, Harvard class of 1877, lawyer, Cambridge councilman and mayor, Russell epitomized what Harvard's Charles W. Eliot praised as government "satisfactory to the friends of pure politics and good order." Anticipating Progressivism, Russell established new programs of labor arbitration and embraced the Boston urban transit and park systems; moreover, he provided an example of class mediation by managing (albeit temporarily) to please both the Cambridge elite and recent Irish immigrants. For instance, he became committed to Irish Home Rule and opposed a Cambridge antisaloon ordinance in 1886; he backed a shorter work week for women and children and sponsored regulations regarding safety and health inspection, employee intimidation, and employer liability. Grant, who bolted Blaine in 1884 (175), epitomized the young Mugwumps drawn to this example. In his autobiography *Fourscore* (1934), Grant eulogized Russell as the personal embodiment of the role that politics could play in mediating class conflict. "He combined more admirably than any man I ever knew the personable sophistication of a man of affairs with an absolutely spontaneous faith in democracy . . . he seemed not only tolerant," Grant wrote condescendingly, "of the whole kettle of fish, but enamored of it" (190). Grant also stated that Russell would have been president if not for his untimely death in 1893.[29]

Grant, however, took time to live up to this example. In a minor way, it is suggestive that, when he remembered a family celebration of George Washington's birthday from his boyhood, he recalled hiding upstairs and secretly feasting on bonbons (50–51). Until he went to law school, Grant vacillated between indifference and outright prankishness regarding his high republican duty, extending his boyhood in collegiate highjinks—"Yankee" doodling. Grant's father had preached a stoic republicanism, disapproving of financial speculation, sending Robert to public school to mix with the other ranks, but at Harvard, Robert preferred the *Lampoon* and the ongoing athletic revival, later admitting that he had not been interested in his studies "beyond maintaining a respectable average in the middle of [his] class" (77). (When one looks through Grant's private records, one discovers that "average" is a word that he applied to himself in his early years; likewise, "underdone" or "half-baked" was first applied by reviewers to the collegians of his early novel, *An Average Man*.)[30] The young undergraduate also exhibited a fondness for pranks that he later said was mistaken for "indifference" by the faculty (85); he was even publicly admonished at a faculty meeting for having skipped mandatory prayer twenty-two times. In one of his few extant college letters, this one to Henry Wadsworth Longfellow, Grant also seems desperate about the future. Admitting to being "in the midst of the doubts and perplexities that I suppose always attend young men," Grant confesses that he has "no taste for law or business or for any other profession" but realizes he must have "some specialty," some "drier pursuit" to support his literary side.[31]

Underneath the varied pattern of ennui, frivolity, and hand-wringing was a clear desire for authority. Looking back on these years for *Scribner's* in 1897, Grant could only quote wistfully from Emerson's "Days" and refer to himself and his classmates as mere "boys" (S, 565). Such a feeling of perpetual juvenility resulted partly from Grant's generational burden. When the cornerstone of Memorial Hall had been placed in October, 1870, Grant remembered the envy he and his classmates felt for the noble deeds and great purposes signified by the Civil War and the "grand generation" that had passed away, the feeling that "we had been deprived by fate of an opportunity" (S, 565).[32] "In my generation," Grant admitted, "there was no phrase more invidious in the moral category than the reproach of not being 'serious-minded,'" yet Robert felt himself hounded with just such a label (121). One of the more serious "pranks" of which Grant was accused—unjustly, he claimed (86)—involved placing a small explosive charge in Harvard's Stoughton Hall. Subsequently, Grant was subject to fits of despondency that he offset by perpetuating such highjinks. For several years he vacillated, seemingly unsuited for the competitive pressures of litigation. Easily unsettled by disputation, his first law partnership dissolved, and he became "as regards location more or less of a rolling stone for several years" (124–25). His condition was hardly helped when his father Patrick failed by overextending himself in a commodity transaction, making him dependent upon Robert until his death.[33]

Nonetheless, it is significant that Grant—in the coded high republican language his Mugwump colleagues would have recognized—would later credit the "leaven" of Eliot's administration (S, 564) in gradually making him "earnest." For all his Brahmin anxiety, he went on to become Harvard's first Ph.D. in English, then to be professionally trained (rather than serving as a legal apprentice) at Harvard's Law School under the newly installed case-method system of Christopher Columbus Langdell and James Barr Ames. Under this system, law students, rather than memorizing classical legal principles from lectures, applied a scientific method to a collection of case precedents which they presented in class. Central to this method was applying scientific reasoning. According to Langdell and Eliot, law was unequivocally a "science"; libraries were akin to laboratories for "chemists and physicists"; cases were now the primary data. Harvard graduates would therefore learn to "classify the cases, to distinguish like from unlike despite superficial similarity, to reject as useless opinions which were ill-reasoned, based on bad logic, and hence were flawed specimens, unsuitable for generalization." The case-study procedure provided a synthesis for Grant, at that point divided between scholarly and practical pursuits; not coincidentally it provided Mugwump ideology (the scholar in politics) in microcosm. In time, this style of reasoning, sometimes called "judicial scientism," would prove essential to Grant's literary idiom.[34]

First, however, scholarly law gave Grant a vocation. This new idiom adapted itself especially well to the growing liberal strategy of commission-style governance that Mugwumps inaugurated. Grant climbed a ladder of local appointments: as Mayor Samuel Green's private secretary, as water commissioner (1888), and (from Russell) as judge of Probate and Insolvency for Suffolk County (1893), the post he held during and after writing *Unleavened Bread.* Though questions were raised, in the last appointment, about the suitability of a literary satirist for judicial decision-making, Grant clearly had found a home.[35] In contrast to his water commissioner post—in which Grant had been embroiled in a local water-rights war—judicial scientism apparently answered his needs for professional authority while not requiring the active interventionist style that so unsettled him. Grant said his new judgeship took him "out of the whirlpool of competitive court practices" and made him an "umpire in a continual panorama" of contemporary issues—vocational metaphors nearly identical to those he would use to describe the narrative voice of his novels.

Though Grant naturally denied readapting specific details from legal cases for literary purposes, he admitted that his court experience "unconsciously permeated" (227) his fiction. Reviewing his post in *Fourscore,* Grant mainly remembered the court's "atmosphere of perplexities" (238), where his authority was often challenged by bureaucratic red tape and legal chicanery. Probate decisions were, he said, easily overruled by the Massachusetts Supreme Judicial Court, often entangled in petty local rivalries, or mired in sheer contentiousness, but the method suited Grant's training quite well. In one instance, Grant recited a poem for a bar association dinner as "an accurate recital of the multifarious activities" involved in probate (244). After lightly satirizing the Godlike power of a judge to rule on litigants' sins, Grant then delivered a description that counterpointed judicial demeanor and litigants' crimes:

> Patient he sits while year by year
> Old women whisper in his ear.
> All sorts of skeletons he knows . . .
> He may not lay his bosom bare;
> He turns the key and keeps them there.
> . . . if the lawyers compromise,
> He knows the fees and gently sighs.
> . . . He construes the obscure devise
> And shows the difference which lies
> Twixt Tweedledum and Tweedledee,
> Which it is sometimes hard to see.
> . . . Thus equity corrects the flaw
> Which justice finds in common law. (245)

Even in this self-satirical doggerel, there was an implied vocational method: a reticent judicial style that nonetheless corrected "common law" by applying its own reasoning to the ill-formed maneuverings of "parties." Here was a jurist whose sober demeanor played off against contentious litigants and lawyers; it is the case-method as judgeship. Similarly, when describing the "Perils of Will-Making" for *Scribner's* years later, the judge would describe his role as an expert mediator who injected logic back into legal disputation. The business of modern probate courts, Grant said, was largely to compensate for the "well-meant but inept looseness of those who make wills," by applying a common-sense reconstruction of the intentions of those makers, rather than relying solely on legal doctrine. In other words, Grant as judge could, like an author of others' texts or "will," rewrite them to achieve "justice."[36]

| | |

Grant's literary and judicial maturation can be traced through his novels of the 1880s, his juvenile book *Jack Hall,* and finally *Unleavened Bread* itself. His early fiction was both class-conscious and self-reflexive, relentlessly allegorizing class polarities into contests of lower and higher natures, European and American democracies, French and English roots of republicanism. Consequently plot was their dominant formal feature, didacticism the inevitable byproduct. However, the choice of medium (like Pulitzer's *World* or Ferber's magazines) should also not be overlooked. That Grant once resorted, as Henry Adams did, to the privacy of the anonymous novel is not unrevealing; his early books are training narratives, coded for Grant's close circle of elite readers.[37] Yet over time, Grant worked his way into a decidedly more modern and public idiom. What was originally didactic moralism and speechifying by author-surrogates dissipates into an implied juxtaposition of a recessed narrator and a garrulous antiprotagonist like Selma White.

An Average Man (1884) was one of Grant's most explicitly personal allegories. The novel follows a pair of upper-class Bostonians, Harvard Law School graduates Arthur Remington and Woodbury Stoughton (not unlike the psychic doubles Ben Halleck and Bartley Hubbard), into Mugwump politics—the reader discovers that they are "young scratchers," meaning that they are so disdainful of party discipline that they disavow even Republican nominees.[38] Yet, as in *A Modern Instance,* these two college friends take drastically different paths. Remington remains a scratcher, cultivates a lean, genteel, Christian poverty, and searches for what he calls "a power somewhere, transcending human thought, which draws our spirit upwards" (249). Stoughton, however, takes on foreign tastes and habits, succumbing to indulgence and greed; ultimately, he subverts the reform cause by bolting back to his party and selling out to a municipal utility. The book closes with an ominous image of a tidal wave of "mob" democracy, a reaction against Stoughton's corruption.[39] The rather familiar note of Emersonian self-culture as the patrician response to mobocracy would hardly surprise those who continue to paint a defensive posture of Mugwumpery.

By contrast, Grant's anonymously published novel *Face to Face* (1886) begins to offer a more forward-looking allegory. A mixture of a story concerning two socially crossed lovers—a female English aristocrat with republican ideals and a Beacon Hill Harvard graduate feigning English peerage—this novel was Grant's attempt to work through his class's mission in personal and political terms. The first part of the novel is a modified comedy of manners. Evelyn Pimlico, born of "staunch Tories," comes to America to escape the marriage market of England; however, as soon as she arrives, she is shuttled off to the Newport season, where (in her words) the republican promise of American life is being "lulled to sleep" by "the twin narcotics of luxury and conservatism." At various contrived points, her path crosses that of Ernest Clay, who, despite the origins his name implies (his father has died at Antietam), has drifted into his millions, lacking a vocation, becoming what Grant calls "one of the immaculate young exquisites who float from ball-room to ball-room on the saccharine atmosphere of feminine flattery" (46). Evelyn's democratic utopianism, for all its naïveté, nonetheless inspires Clay's earnest impulses; he has already suspected that "breeding and luxury" have made "us all mere machines—conservative is the euphemistic term." What follows is a reciprocal exchange of ideals. Evelyn sees in Ernest "something better than primitive heroics" of her western fantasies; she in turn inspires both his love and his seriousness, hoping that "the leisure class" can "make good the expectations of those who sleep in the churchyard" (178). Both agree that the "so-called leisure class in the world really have the power to affect civilization more significantly than any other" (179).

For a time, however, this love match must be delayed, as Evelyn, striking out on her own, inherits a factory on the Hudson River, immediately adjacent to one in which Clay owns stock. As was so much the case in what labor historians term the "Great Upheaval" of 1886, there is an ongoing series of industrial strikes (there were over seven hundred in Massachusetts in 1886 alone), and Evelyn is drawn to a socialist workers' advocate named Andrew DeVito, an illegitimate Italian-American. DeVito is uplifted by Evelyn's idealism, agreeing to make industrial peace and work as her plant superintendent; at one point, in fact, he brashly kisses her as he works at her side. Thus when Clay abruptly proposes, Evelyn defers to her alliance with DeVito, resisting the "social suicide" that marriage to Clay seems to offer (279). Her humanitarian sentimentalism falls short, however, as the pressure of the business competition undermine her cottage-filled factory village. DeVito again presses his socialist and romantic cause, but the day is really saved when Clay returns, literally deus cum machina, with a patented electrical device that will reduce production costs. Clay, you see, has abandoned his conservative affluence and studied to become an engineer. Moreover, he has risen to his class responsibilities. When another strike ensues—starting a fire at a plant not favored by Clay's invention—DeVito subsequently martyrs himself in the conflagration, inspired by Clay's manly efforts not to desert a servant threatened by an unruly crowd. Clay and Evelyn are left to face the future together.

Even though Grant's finale, like his title, reinforces the Brahmin notion of character and the mythology of face-to-face personal relations, it is the intervention of a decidedly modernized professional class that saves the day—not the propertied bourgeois, nor the idle conservative. Rehabilitating the Emersonian theme, in fact, even allows greater class differentiation. At one point Evelyn lashes out at DeVito, "And what have you other men and women, as you call the laboring classes . . . ever done to promote that progress? Haven't you, rather, ever since the world began been a clog to us by your ignorance and brutality and indolence? . . . Are you fit to govern yourselves?" (340). The ending simply reinforces the fatalistic underside of Grant's Mugwumpery; DeVito cannot really triumph over his character, strikes will no doubt continue, but the example of the professional class might at least delay the apocalypse of class warfare.[40]

By the time of the appearance of Grant's juvenile novel, *Jack Hall or The School Days of an American Boy* (1888), this clarion call had thoroughly synthesized Brahmin and professional values; moreover, Grant separates leadership from money and property almost completely. His novel centers on a school called Utopia that is run by a Ph.D. named John Meredith who emphasizes honesty, seriousness, and manly scholarship. In an obviously autobiographical reference, Utopia is cast as the answer to a young man's wavering character. Jack Hall, a Civil War casualty's son who longs for his father's heroism, has been deemed "incorrigibly idle" (166) and has a reputation for reckless mischief and pilfering sweets (113). At Utopia Jack receives poor academic reports and falls under the influence of a mischievous crowd that flouts all the rules, led by childhood chum Bill French. As his name implies, French epitomizes a libertine distortion of America's egalitarian legacy; he heads up a "secret society" supposedly devoted to securing "to free-born American citizens the enjoyment of their natural liberties" (261). At the crisis of the story, this gang, Jack included, blows up a campus building.

The last third of the book is devoted to Jack's rehabilitation, stimulated mainly by Meredith's regime. The first step comes when he tells the truth regarding the bombing and resolves to shape up. His lessons seem to be couched in the example of the past. Meredith's warning about the "kernel of deceit" that is at the heart of "national ruin" sounds much like John Hall's premium on truthfulness, much as the school's banishment of hazing seems democratic. But if Jack's father had preached truth and equality achieved by social mixing, Meredith instead preaches a reclusive, almost ascetic regimen that allows one the loneliness of triumph; truth in his lexicon is not the outcome of pluralistic struggle but the achievement of exceptional men, what Eliot called "concentration" on that "single" pursuit.[41] One of Jack's friends, Hazeltine, is the baseball player, a team player; Jack saves him from such a fantasy, however, by getting him a position with a western railroad. Jack, created by the author who saw judging as akin to being an "umpire," is drawn instead to the single racing scull. In this final movement, Jack submits himself first to a period of atonement that is, particularly for a boy's book, remarkably severe: the distrust (psychological hazing) of his peers; corporal punishment by a Latin teacher; an endless battle with his own lazy mind and character. What Jack finally develops is a "love of reading and interest in refined thought" (338); professional self-culture is the agency of his rehabilitation. If Bill French becomes the dandy, Jack overcomes his fallen state by application of mind and body; diligence is necessary because God-given talents are handed out unequally. Within Grant's considerably remodeled Utopia, egalitarian deceptions give way to a belief in the disciplines of culture and character which separate Jack from the run of the mill—even allowing him to beat Meredith in a final sculling race. Jack defeats his uncultured side, his "Stoughton" rebellion, and his averageness all in one effort. Grant observes of Jack's reformation: "We often hear it said that the chief benefit of school or college is the effect on character. Very good; but surely it is no error to maintain that the character of the boy untrained to use his mind intelligently is not highly to be extolled. . . . We need today the services of keen, disciplined minds in active life, and in its quiet walks those who love learning for her own sake, and are ready to devote patient days to the pursuit of ripe scholarship"(233).

Though high republican character is not abandoned here, its Emersonian vein is tapped as the prerequisite to a professional ethos—what Herbert Croly will call "faithful and fearless work."[42] "[L]ove of reading and interest in refined thought" (338) now combine with the "disciplines" that are identified with the "East," which "manage" the easy-going egalitarianism of the West (Hazeltine). Jack, by overcoming his own averageness (his "Stoughton" rebelliousness, his libertine side), is all the more effective as a reformer/rewriter of others' will. Jack's management of Hazeltine's intentions forecasts the method Grant himself would soon discover in his appointment as probate judge. This is, to return to *Unleavened Bread*'s terms, how he is "baked."

| | |

Grant's accounts of *Unleavened Bread*'s genesis alluded both to Selma White's private meaning (his own unbaked past) and his new judicial perspective. Though he admitted that he had evolved Selma "from the depths of

[his] inner consciousness," she was also part of a "panorama" seen "through a telescope from the roof of [his] mind" (*Fourscore,* 227–28). He directed that telescope beyond Boston's environs:

> Newspapers, books, and magazines had already familiarized me with a point of view that regarded a house embellished with scrolls, flourishes, and fancy glass, with a metal stag on the lawn or grass plot, as the acme of democratic culture. That Selma went with this establishment and would resent any challenge of its merit as unpatriotic snobbery was but the logical interpretation of the sort of woman springing up throughout the nation, but especially in the Middle West, whose complacent egoism was the medium for boundless aspirations. The United States was God's own country largely because of the women, whose fathers, husbands, and sons were so engrossed with business as to have merely a bowing acquaintance with the arts or nicer morals. . . . It must be remembered, too, that the period was 1890–1900, and not even the complacent "pleased to meet you" had come in, I think, as the hall mark of stereotyped amenity. (228)

The novel first follows Selma from her midwestern city Benham, as she marries the architect Wilbur Littleton, to the social whirl of New York; rebuffed by high society, she returns to Benham, now seeing it as "a growing, earnest city—a city throbbing with the best American spirit and energy" (249). Following Wilbur's death, she enters into local politics, remarrying the corrupt lawyer Lyons (who calls himself "An American of the Americans" [431]), boosting Benham and her husband by resisting professional expertise as an "insidious canker of exclusiveness" (276). For Grant, Selma typifies those "who because of their aspirations saw themselves qualified for any opportunity; who resented special knowledge of any kind as un-American" (SLL, 222). She is akin to a psychological negative of the mature Jack Hall; Grant's alternative titles were "The Unconscious Hypocrite" or simply "The Aspirant."[43]

Selma, therefore, partly embodies another of Grant's political allegories. Initially the wife of a simple hardware man, she epitomizes the promise of democracy to the easterner Littleton when he first visits Benham. As the architect remarks, she seems to stand for "'the true import of our American life . . . the elements of greatness in our every-day people'" (49).[44] Wilbur and his sister Pauline represent, conversely, "those who have devoted their lives to conscientious effort to discover truth" (372)—a clear-headed, ascetic devotion. This contrast sharpens as Selma grows suspicious of anything "aristocratic," including Wilbur (soon to be her second husband), viewing him as a hopeless plodder devoid of American get-up-and-go (177–78). Meanwhile Littleton, put off by Selma's consumerism, denies "the ability of the free-born American, with the overflowing purse, to indulge his newly acquired taste for gorgeous effects without professional assistance" (164). Littleton's untimely death does not sidetrack this theme as much as it reiterates it. Selma negates the expert advice of a doctor in caring for Wilbur on his deathbed. Wilbur's overworking on Selma's behalf is the cause of his decline; she wants something "energetic" done when what Wilbur needs clearly is rest (255–57). He dies from a strain on his heart; her leaven has been poison.

Yet if this novel seems didactic, *Unleavened Bread* is actually quite unlike Grant's earlier political fables. Concerns about class or ethnic conflict are noticeably absent; *Unleavened Bread* portrays its central antithesis (between Selma and the Littletons) as determined by knowledge and professional authority. Of course, Grant's Mugwump impulse is hardly erased; Littleton's disillusionment with Selma represents Grant's own "divorce" from America's original democratic promise. Yet there is an important change registered in Grant's voice. Instead of relying on a direct narrative voice, Grant prefers a "behind-the-scenes" or umpiring stance, even for his most sympathetic characters. For example, Pauline is described as thinking: "She, like Wilbur, had heard all her life of these interesting and inspiring beings [like Selma]; intense, marvelously capable, peerless, free-born creatures panoplied in chastity and endowed with congenital mental power and bodily charms, who were able to cook, educate children, control society and write literature in the course of the day's employment. The newspapers and popular opinion had given her to understand that these were the true Americans, and caused her to ask herself whether the circle to which she herself belonged was not retrograde from a nobler ideal" (172). Though this reasoning is, to Grant's mind, wholly mistaken—antithetical to his own reading of the American panorama quoted earlier—his narrator does not explicitly moralize. Rather, passages like this exemplify what Wharton saw as Grant's avoidance of partisanship; he seems content simply to repeat a popular notion nearly unedited—"popular opinion had given her to understand"—to create an appearance of judicious re-reasoning. The narrative style Grant chooses here is substantially a paraphrastic one; private thoughts and rationalizations are recast in a pointedly aloof tone that, often by counterpointing outlandish conclusions with its own "sobriety," achieves an understated irony. The text is dotted with phrases like "or rather the case should be stated thus" (26), or "so he thought of her" (44)—phrases not unlike what Grant would describe as the probate judge's reconstructions of litigants' "ineptly" executed intentions. Selma's consciousness is constructed almost entirely out of popular-cultural hearsay. By exercising this "nonpartisan" reconstruction, Grant nonetheless tilts his own narrative towards Wilbur's and Pauline's ascetic "truth-seeking." Negative characters are, conversely, identified with excess and self-satisfied delusion, often hanging themselves by their own narrative testimony.

It is important to see, however, that this paraphrastic idiom is not merely a device for siding with the Littletons, for it is proposed as the synthesis of the struggle over representation in the plot. The marriage of Selma and Littleton deteriorates culturally, morally, even religiously. Selma explains how her thrill at the Methodists' "Onward Christian Soldiers" reveals to her that her heart is "divided" from Wilbur's; he, the Unitarian, responds "you are utterly different from what I supposed" (229). If she can be compared to a garish electric light, he is likened to a fading poetic star (241), ineffective in influencing her actions. Their marriage does not result in divorce—as a Progressive reformer Grant worried over the increasing trend towards divorce on the grounds of incompatibility[45]—but, rather, in something more like a stalemate. Grant writes: "Having realized his mistake, [Wilbur] did not seek to flinch from the bitter truth. He saw clearly that . . . tender comradeship and mutual soul alliance were at an end. *At the same time his simple, direct conscience promptly indicated to him that it was his duty to recognize Selma's point of view and endeavor to satisfy it as far as he could without sacrifice of his own principles*" (231; emphasis added). The lines italicized above underline the parallel between Littleton's decision and the implied strategy of Grant's judicial narrative. Wilbur's self-description, echoing Grant's own, sounds as though he is recasting court testimony: hearing Selma's complaints, but holding to principle and precedent. Even given the psychological separation of Selma and Wilbur, Littleton's resolution echoes Grant's own strategy of "honoring" Selma's view without sacrificing an implied narrative dissent.

Elizabeth Deeds Ermarth, in her discussion of realism and implied notions of authority, states that in some instances the personified critical term of "the narrator" may even be misleading—despite the example of writers like O. Henry or Ferber. In other cases, Ermarth suggests something more impersonal can take place:

> The realist consensus that makes such power available depends upon the management—one might even say the administration—of distance. One must step back from particulars in order to grasp them. In ordinary usage we say that someone is "realistic" who is able to sift relevant from irrelevant considerations and so to act in a manner appropriate to the situation. While this "realism" can be seen as moral or political cynicism, a rejection of any fixed standards, in fact it implies a faith in some kind of rule according to which something can be judged irrelevant and would so be judged by anyone with the same perspective. The implication of realist technique is that proper distance will enable the subjective spectator or the subjective consciousness to see the multiple viewpoints and so to find the form of the whole in what looks from a closer vantage point like a discontinuous array of specific cases. Any move toward the margins of experience means accepting a distortion uncongenial to the realistic gambit.[46]

Ermarth's application of judicial conceits—laws, judging, cases—is entirely intentional and certainly pertinent here. Yet what is so striking in Grant's case load—in a way quite characteristic of the "Main Street" debunking style to follow him—is that "consensual" realism has been nearly abandoned in favor of a central, adjudicating, partly satiric voice, a cosmopolitan presence that acts, quite literally, as a "mediator." The result is a portrait, in Grant's terms, that can lay claim to both an "internal" and a "panoramic" point of view, to be both personal and impersonally judicial. In political terms, as well, Grant's paraphrastic idiom no longer suggests merely Mugwumpish didacticism, nor even much patrician benevolence. If his narrative style is akin to judicial renegotiation, Grant's politics reaffirm, aesthetically, "honoring" one's democratic constituents without necessarily admiring them. Thus *Unleavened Bread*'s literary form internalizes—is not merely "homologous" with—a rationale central to modern American liberalism. By refashioning his own narrative style, Grant's novel embodies that form of political expertise that works not by direct representation but by anticipating and reforming the intentions of fundamentally "irrational" voters.[47]

| | |

The narrative style presented above, for all its elitism, nonetheless represents the confident outcome of Grant's Mugwump-liberal apprenticeship. Yet the paradox was that this acquisition of professional authority coincided almost exactly with the disintegration of the reform cause of Grant's youth. It has long been recognized, in fact, that the finale of *Unleavened Bread* is partly based on an infamous event in Mugwump history, the so-called "West End" affair involving Grant's hero, William Russell. Just before Russell's inauguration, a Mugwump rebel, one George Fred Williams, arose in the state legislature to demand an investigation of the franchise bill involving the West End Railway Company in Boston. The franchise had granted special rights for an extension of an elevated railway to create the comprehensive system Russell favored. According to historian Geoffrey Blodgett, however, Williams's protest was greeted only lukewarmly by the Mugwump "regulars"—including Russell, who actually asked Williams to call off the fight. Naturally, then, a tremor shook the ranks when it was revealed that Russell himself—in a turn of events eerily forecast by *An Average Man*—had ties, albeit legitimate ones, to the main entrepreneurial backer of the system, Henry M. Whitney (who had spent tens of thousands of dollars to secure its charter). The controversy faded rather quickly (perhaps in a whitewash), but Williams, who would soon desert Mugwumpery for Populism, would eventually undercut Russell's apparently assured nomination for president by backing William Jennings Bryan. Williams returned to Boston feted by one of the mass political rallies that Grant so detested, as his early portrait of Stoughton demonstrated.[48] Although Grant makes no mention of Williams's revenge in his autobiography—referring only to Russell's untimely death—one has to wonder about the incursion of this episode into the otherwise judicious text of his best-selling novel. Perhaps because achieving his own putatively "nonpartisan" authority has been so dependent upon overcoming his own "averageness," Grant's literary idiom struggled to suppress a persistent anxiety about that authority's disintegrating, as the larger cause had, into the merely "average" corruption for which Selma White was the emblem. In certain ways the finale of the novel represents an ideological vulnerability of Grant's liberal strategy.[49]

The dark implications of West End clearly infuse the final third of *Unleavened Bread,* encompassing Selma's third marriage to the lawyer Lyons and his rise to a vacated senator's seat. Here Grant's technique turns to an even more bitter documentation of cultural "averageness." Once Littleton dies, Selma claims the mantle of cultural "steward" of Benham. Meanwhile Lyons, the "good fellow" whom Grant detests, invokes the rights of "plain people" to stonewall the "board of specialists" (283) who want to reform Benham's educational system along Progressive lines. Lyons arrays himself as "a friend and champion of the mass of the people—the plain and sovereign people, as he was apt to style them in public" (284). Grant continues to present average rationalization in paraphrase, but his tone is quite bitter; Lyons's "speeches were apt to cause those whom he addressed to feel that they were no common campaign utterances, but eloquent expressions of principle and conviction, clothed in memorable language, as, indeed, they were" (284). In private, of course, Lyons is an agent of corporations. As he receives his senatorial seat, Selma gazes out upon the Benham crowd, Grant writes, with a "seraph look, as though she were penetrating the future even into Paradise" (431). (This, incidentally, was the finale that made Howells "shudder" when it was subsequently dramatized.)[50]

This finale superficially seems to adapt the West End scandal, but Grant's rewriting of history is now positively carnivalesque. In *Unleavened Bread,* the character named Stringer recalls George Fred Williams's role, and his agitation challenges Lyons's ties to a utility, but the novel doubles back on both covert historical referents. The corrupt Lyons actually "dishonors" his earlier bribe (for selfish fears of exposure) in order to appear as the people's defender; by mimicking the rhetoric of his more populistic antagonists, Lyons survives.[51] It is Charles Russell's apparent surrogate—the man Grant so praised in memory—who stands on the balcony with Selma White.

Even more problematically, the end of the novel not only sets adrift any secure allegorical moorings but it also preemptively undercuts its potential hero. First of all, Governor-elect Lyons has been refashioned from an earlier appearance in the plot when he had arranged Selma's first divorce. He is described early in the novel as "a large, full-bodied man of thirty-five, with a fat, cleanly-shaven, cherubic countenance, an aspect of candor, and keen, solemn eyes." Though occasionally pontifical, "his general effect was that of a cross between a parson and a shrewd Yankee—a happy suggestion of righteous, plain, serious-mindedness, protected against the wiles of human society. . . . A certain class of people, notably the hard-headed, God-fearing, felt themselves safe in his hands" (85). While not overlooking Grant's irony here, one may especially recall this description when the potential hero, Stringer, is introduced:

> Stringer was, as he described himself, a man of the plain people. That is he was a lawyer with a denunciating voice, a keen mind, and a comprehensive grasp on language, who was still an attorney for plaintiffs, and whose ability had not yet been recognized by corporations or conserva-

> tive souls. He was where Lyons had been ten years before, but he had neither the urbanity, conciliatory tendencies, nor dignified, solid physical properties of the Governor . . . [various] socialistic spirits . . . applauded vigorously the thinly veiled allusions which Stringer made in debate to the luke-warm democracy of some of the party leaders. (415)

As a heroic figure, Stringer pales noticeably in contrast to earlier characters such as Remington in *An Average Man*, Ernest Clay, or the rehabilitated Jack Hall. (Littleton's death is thus an important imaginative benchmark in Grant's evolution.) Yet it is not merely that Grant cannot posit Stringer as the novel's last locus of manly character; rather, it is also that Stringer is described here as only Lyons minus ten years. A potential Bartley Hubbard lurks in every Ben Halleck. Grant cynically hints that the corporate and conservative forces will soon make Stringer over in their own image; in this corrosive vision, Stringer and Lyons are Remington become Stoughton, Jack Hall become Bill French, essentially Tweedledum and Tweedledee. Stringer exists not merely as a moralistic rebuke to Lyons, or even to "luke-warm party leaders," but as a sign of the corrosive irony that Grant himself can no longer subdue.

This character corrosion is emblematic, in fact, of Grant's overall undermining of the moral didacticism for which he is infamous. For all of Grant's attempts to manage a judicious tone, an overwhelming sense of sameness, even Orwellian reversal (the section representing Lyons's failure is titled "Success"), informs the closing of the novel. Lyons and Selma both acquire a Hubbardesque bodily girth and moral dryrot (195, 280), as each character's thought processes become virtually indistinguishable from the other's. In turn, both choose to represent—here, in Grant's most bitter parody of "average" representation—the middleness of Benham down to the smallest possible detail. That the Lyonses' rationalizations end in almost suffocating self-duplication is most apparent when they consider how their lifestyle will be perceived by their constituents:

> The problem was but another phase of that presented to [Lyons] by his evolution from a jury lawyer, whose hand and voice were against corporations, to the status of a richly paid chamber adviser to railroads and banking houses . . . but his mind eagerly welcomed a suggestion . . . [that the] idea that the people would prefer to see him as their representative living in a style consistent with the changes in manners and customs introduced by national prosperity, affording thereby an example of cor-

> rect and elevating stewardship of reasonable wealth . . . came to him as an illumination which dissipated his doubts. [329]

Here Lyons and Selma fashion what political theorists call a "descriptive likeness" of cultural mediocrity without actually reflecting their constituents' true interests.[52] To Grant, the Lyonses' double claim to be "average" and yet stewards confirms the moral duplicity of their new Jerusalem. Moral landmarks become invisible in Benham's cultural whiteout; Everyman is his (or her) background.

Robert Grant's legacy may be, therefore, something more ambiguous than the parochial moralism his aristocratic reputation implies. In Grant's confident moments, the reader feels the technocratic energy given modern liberalism by its professional strata; in Selma White, conversely, there are many traits associated with middle-American consciousness in the literary and political representation of coming years: hypocritical boosterism and patriotism, consumer excess, political inattentiveness and vacillation. Selma is professionalism's other—no wonder she, and characters like her, struck such a nerve. As are so many characters in Sinclair Lewis's novels, in Mencken's "The American" (1913–14), or Elmer Rice's "Mr. Zero" of *The Adding Machine* (1925), Selma is a vitriolic burlesque of "half-baked" and half-attentive citizens upon which elite styles of political stewardship—from the right or left—would often make their case. Meanwhile, Grant's style of recessed, satiric narration, suggesting panoramic familiarity with American norms and yet disengagement from them, would be reiterated as well—not because writers consciously followed his example, as Croly did, but because they often shared the internicine middle-class anxiety Grant represented. As Wharton observed, his prototype of Main Street, and of how it was to be written, was his contribution to a new form in which authority was disseminated, made legitimate—made to seem, as in Wilbur Littleton's resolve, that it was married to democratic principles when it was secretly divorced.

Furthermore, the finale of *Unleavened Bread* also reminds us that this "average" American was one upon whom such a course for professional stewardship would often founder. Grant's outlook was obviously vulnerable to fatalism and inertia as well as Progressive uplift. The undermining of moral and partisan polarities in Benham looked ahead to the claustrophobia the reader experiences in such towns as Lewis's Gopher Prairie or Zenith, where boosters and bohemians, Babbitts and reformers, are simply mirror images of each other.[53] At its most profound level, then, Grant's consciousness illustrates the process by which the cultural politics of non-partisanship and the pleasures of debunking, whether in the aftermath of West End or World War I, could collapse back into indifference and cynicism—a Tweedledum and Tweedledee reaction not so different from the one modern American voters would, in increasing numbers, themselves soon begin to experience. In this way, Grant represents a judgment not that far removed from the average.

Four

Elmer Rice

"A Sort of Common Denominator"

It is not book-learning that young men need, nor instruction about this and that, but a stiffening of the vertebrae. . . .

No man, who has endeavored to carry out an enterprise where many hands were needed, but has been well-nigh appalled at times by the imbecility of the average man—the inability or unwillingness to concentrate on a thing and do it.

—*Elbert Hubbard,* A Message to Garcia

The machine is a quite prosaic reality. It consists of human beings who wear clothes and live in houses, who can be named and described. They perform all the duties usually assigned to the Oversoul.

—*Walter Lippmann,* Public Opinion

In scene 5 of Elmer Rice's *The Adding Machine* (1923), the protagonist, Mr. Zero—the department-store accountant who has just been convicted of murdering his boss—has been placed in jail awaiting his execution. In the elaborate dramaturgy with which Rice would customarily be identified, Zero is staged in an oversized cell (with the bars suspiciously far apart), while devouring a gargantuan plate of ham and eggs—which is all he could think of when asked to order his last meal. Subsequently, a guide in a blue uniform enters, leading in a miscellaneous crowd to view the now-infamous criminal who has killed his boss when told he would be fired after twenty-five years of service:

GUIDE [*stopping in front of the cage*]. Now ladies and gentlemen, if you'll kindly step right this way! [*The crowd straggles up and forms a loose semi-circle around him.*] Step right up, please. A little closer so's everybody can hear. [*They move up closer.* ZERO *pays no attention whatever to them.*] This, ladies and gentlemen, is a very in-ter-est-in' specimen: the North American murderer, Genus homo sapiens, Habitat North America. [*A titter of excitement. They all crowd up around the cage.*]

. . . He has the opposable thumbs, the large cranial capacity, and the highly developed prefrontal areas which distinguish him from all other species.

YOUTH [*who has been taking notes*]. What areas did you say?

GUIDE [*grumpily*]. Pre-front-al areas. He learns by imitation and has a language which is said by some eminent philiologists to bear many striking resemblances to English.

BOY OF FOURTEEN. Pop, what's a philiologist?[1]

In several respects, this is a trademark scene for Rice. Here, he juxtaposes stark stagecraft of exaggerated scale with everyday American idioms, and seemingly innocent humor with a severe undercutting of human self-delusions (in this instance, the pride of homo sapiens in his skull shape). Meanwhile, in his dialogue, Rice relies on a hyperbolic form of cultural *vraisemblance*—an agglomeration of typical vernacular idioms from zoos, circus sideshows, museum exhibitions, and tourist traps—to inflate Zero's imprisonment into a mass-commercial spectacle. Rice continues such an exhibiting of his protagonist's imitative, imprisoned soul throughout the remainder of the play. The plot follows Zero, after his execution, from graveyard to the Elysian fields to heaven, and to the final scene, in which he is simply reincarnated back to earth for another adding-machine job.

In its collapsing of corporate and cosmological space, its exhibiting of Zero's self-convicting psyche, and its use of reiterative plotting to portray the claustrophobia of mass existence, *The Adding Machine* epitomizes a modern style of psychological representation—sometimes called "expressionist"—recurrently attached to white collar portraiture in the twentieth century. Critics have successfully recovered Rice's debt to German practitioners of this style, to the techniques by which, as the playwright wrote at the time, "we subordinate and even discard objective reality and seek to express the character in terms of his own inner life."[2] Years later, Arthur Miller would provisionally title his portrait of salesman Willy Loman (and design his stage sets) as "The Inside of His Head"; Kurt Vonnegut, Jr., would twist the corporate world of General Electric into the fantastic "Ghost Shirt" rebellion of Paul Proteus in *Player Piano* (1955); Joseph Heller, who admired

Rice in his youth, would collapse the corporate color wheel (the office mates White, Brown, Green, and so on) into the black-humor interior monologue of file-clerk-turned-executive Bob Slocum of *Something Happened* (1974). Traces of expressionist technique may be found even in seemingly sober sociological accounts. In the evocatively titled *White Collar*, C. Wright Mills himself argues that the social conditions around the modern "little man" that "concern us most border on the psychiatric." Mills says that white collar life might best be visualized as one "enormous file" or "incorporated brain"—images Rice himself would have applauded.[3]

In these ways, Rice stands as an often-unacknowledged pathfinder in social portraiture. And yet, even in his own day, the conjoining of satiric cultural verisimilitude to white collar literary fictions was not all that uncommon. As the "typical Americans" dominating so much of smart-set humor—Mencken's businessman *Americanus*, James Thurber's Walter Mitty, Sinclair Lewis's Babbitt, or the daydreaming stenographers of a story like Dorothy Parker's "The Cost of Living"—new-middle-class characters were habitually depicted as citizens whose very brains were suffused with mass culture. Even more than their working class counterparts, white collar Americans were conceived as characters whose "averageness" derived from the byplay between the routine of their office jobs and the daydreaming stimulated by movies, advertising, even shop windows. Even more than in O. Henry's romance-dreaming shopgirls, being middle class was linked to consumer fantasizing, and white collar citizens were coupled with submission to mass authorities outside themselves. Much more than the general term "expressionism," this contemporary form of social comedy identifies the focus of Rice's work: his interest in the subjective dimensions of social authority. Not authority as the exercise of power, but as cultural legitimation: how the subordination of the corporate employee was authorized by broader psychological, cultural, even metaphysical reasoning processes—a "machine" in which the employee's own beliefs became the Oversoul. At the time, Rice's term for his own method was not "expressionistic" but "metaphysical."[4]

Rice had first-hand experience with these forms of white collar legitimation because of his early training as a clerk and lawyer. If Robert Grant exemplifies Progressive-era professional anxiety from above, Rice suggests a confluence from below: a poor, third-generation German-American and Jew, an outsider even in his own neighborhood, who had tried to make his way up to the law through a clerical apprenticeship. Rice's angle on new-middle-class ideology was thus not on how power is administered from above, as with Grant, but how it is deferred to from below, how management is perceived and reinforced by a network of professional, popular, and even subconscious mass-cultural attitudes.[5] Grant's Harvard education allowed him to imagine a liberal posture serenely adjudicating the democratic will; Rice's clerical apprenticeship exposed him to the fact that professional ideals, in the corporate world, coexisted uneasily with bottom-line considerations. Even Rice's stagecraft is best understood as pivoting upon the internal conflicts of his class: conflicts between professional aspirations and commercial theatrics, dreams of sales efficiency and the drudgery of office discipline, business paternalism and a young employee's dreams of rebellion. What has so loosely been termed German Expressionism actually derives from Rice's persistent imbrication in quite homegrown new-middle-class conflicts. The playwright's repeated assertions that *The Adding Machine* was an instance of "automatic" writing or that it "came right out of [his own] unconscious" were perhaps evidence enough of his own personal stakes in the play's portrait of the white collar psyche.[6]

To date, these dimensions of Rice's life and art have not figured prominently in critical equations; rather, he has been seen either as a commercial dramatist or a theatrical adaptor of Mencken's guerrilla warfare on the "booboisie." There are merits to this second genealogy; Rice had enjoyed reading the *Smart Set* in the teens, and his social vocabulary often echoed Mencken's own.[7] But like the label "expressionist," the Menckenian debt is interesting primarily in what it leaves out. When Rice actually met Mencken, while working with Dorothy Parker on *Close Harmony* (1925), yet another exploration of an "average guy" who wants out of his middle-class routine, Rice found the sage of Baltimore strangely "adolescent"—and, in a word, reactionary—for Rice, like Robert Grant, was a liberal. At precisely the point when Mencken had abandoned his early Progressivism in the teens, Rice had declared himself a socialist; written a play on behalf of the National Child Labor Committee; marched in suffrage parades.[8] He even said that the betrayal of utopian ideals in World War I had only regenerated his commitments to social justice (143) in the twenties. In the 1930s, he would join a group of non-Communists supporting Communist party candidate Foster, write the strike drama *We the People* (1933), advise Harry Hopkins on the founding of the Federal Theatre Project, and resign over government interference with the Living Newspaper. American Civil Liberties Union advocate, N.A.A.C.P. supporter, vocal antifascist, and anti-McCarthyite: in a century renowned for radical political mood swings, it would be difficult to find an intellectual with more consistently liberal credentials. We need, therefore, to turn the familiar critical inquiry around, and ask why American liberals were suddenly so hospitable to an influence like Mencken's and, more generally, to white collar satire.

Such broad questions are not easily particularized. Rice's autobiographical vocabulary, so characteristic of the cosmopolitan avant-garde in these years, marks the meeting of energy and naïveté where "conservative," "Philistine," or "Puritan" could lump together all those who supposedly adhered to convention. We also lack extensive primary material on Rice's white collar apprenticeship. Yet an examination of his memories of office work, his own daydreaming there, can reconstruct how he built that self-fashioning vocabulary. These sources suggest three points: first, that Rice's dramaturgical linking of class and mass derived from developing pressures he felt within his own white collar life and ideology; second (as with Walter Lippmann, Floyd Dell, Sherwood Anderson, or Sinclair Lewis), that far more influential on Rice's class vocabulary than Mencken were the widely published essays of H. G. Wells, George Bernard Shaw, Graham Wallas, and other British Fabians; and third, that Rice's investigations of authority and legitimation directly affected the form of *The Adding Machine,* not just its subject matter. At one level, Rice's special contribution to the representation of the average white collar life—average, in his vocabulary, in the sense of mass, routine, run-of-the-mill—was an exploration of what keeps the mill worker running. At a deeper level, Rice tried to create dramaturgy that would gain access to the "political unconscious" of his audience, make them see themselves in Zero and then recoil in disgust.

Given such divergent sources and ambitious aims, there is little sense in resorting to the brittle, polemical reiterations of Rice's "subversive"—or, conversely "complicitous"—relation to corporate capitalism itself. The actual story is a messy business, and little is gained in debunking the so-called "lyrical left" of the past.[9] Rice's play may have performed rather ragged cultural work in its time; its competing strands of anger, rage, and laughter were derived, after all, from the world it proposed to represent. To be sure, Rice's "compounding" (his word) of genres and vernacular idioms drew upon conflicts deeply embedded within corporate and legal life, just as his dramaturgy reflected the discipline and commercial theatrics he witnessed in the white collar workplace. On the other hand, to document only this overlapping pattern would be to ignore a central claim of *The Adding Machine* itself: that it offered the potential solace of a position, a satirist's safe ground, beyond class and cultural prescription—outside the very forms of metaphysical and unconscious legitimation it described. Just as Robert Grant sought out judicial umpiring apart from the muddled "wills" of average citizens, Rice sought a similarly high ground—a territory both potentially empowering and limiting. Even as Rice's play is built from within the cage of corporate life, it also seems to promise that his audience, recognizing the joke, can be outside the bars looking in.

| | |

For details of Rice's life, critics have necessarily depended on his autobiography, *Minority Report* (1963), a book self-consciously cast in the upbeat liberalism of a man unafraid to take a minority position for a good cause. His loving mother, Rice said, had instilled in him "the belief that goodness is the goal humanity must strive to attain" (22) and a courage Rice's political career reflected. Even this memory, however, invokes minority in the sense of juvenility and loneliness, the pathos of a Dickensian protagonist transplanted to New York City. Like Dickens—a writer frequently mentioned in this memoir—Rice portrays his younger self as an imaginative, introverted, forlorn boy coming of age in a commercial city. Some of this loneliness was a by-product of being poor: mourning over a brother who had died young, being sent to a school outside his neighborhood, sleeping in the living room of a crowded railroad flat. Among the crowds and street gangs, Elmer was teased about his clumsiness and his bright-red hair; at twenty-one, and nearly six feet tall, he weighed only 130 pounds. Much of his loneliness was also a consequence of being trapped in a family undermined by commercial bickering and legal maneuvering. Rice's father, a second-generation German immigrant, had once been a bookkeeper and traveling salesman, but during Elmer's boyhood, he had progressively deteriorated from epilepsy. Embittered by a family business dispute (for years referring to a hated brother as "It"), Rice's father terrorized his son by being cynically uninterested in the world around him, epitomizing power that was exercised without real legitimacy. Elmer found his father physically repulsive, horrific in his willful ignorance and prejudice, and, of course, "I wanted to admire and respect him and was resentful because I could not" (63). From the climate of endless "worry, worry, worry," the playwright said he had learned "never to be dependent upon anyone" (53). Later, he would change his Jewish name—Elmer Leopold Reizenstein—for commercial recognizability, he said, and to reflect pride in his Americanization (164). In one turn of the pen, Rice seized his "new" middle-class professional name and rejected his father's "old" immigrant one.

This desire for independence placed Elmer on the trail of white collar status, paradoxically seeking modest personal autonomy through professionalism and yet scraping along in clerical positions to reach it. He sought first to fulfill his family's great expectations. In his adolescence, since it "had always been taken for granted that I was to become a businessman" (44), he was sent to the High School of Commerce in New York, a trade school that taught business arithmetic, double-entry bookkeeping, and stenography. Subsequently he worked in a law firm for a cousin-in-law of his mother, then as a claims investigator for a pair of middlemen jobbers, at seventy-five cents a day, handling complaints from customers and passing them on to his bosses. After being laid off in the Panic of 1907, disgusted and bored, he resolved never to go back to business. Instead, he began work as a file clerk and then as a legal clerk. While he apprenticed to the law, his firm paid his fees at New York Law School, from which he graduated cum laude in 1912. He then became a managing clerk at his cousin Moe's firm before resigning his position right after being admitted to the bar at age twenty-one (96).

What was it about commercial or legal clerking—and the young Rice himself—that caused this disaffection? Deploying a cliché that middle-class children often use to evoke the gap between maternal domestic care and the disciplines of employment, Rice's own explanation was that his mother's idealism had unsuited him for the "real world."[10] As he put it half a century later: "My emotional goals were self-improvement and social betterment, two aspects of one objective. I was profoundly influenced by the living example of my mother's goodness. . . . Thrust into the world, I was shocked to find in the conduct of most adults a lack of dignity and of integrity, and a disregard for the sensibilities and well-being of others. . . . It became apparent to me that most people found no satisfaction in their daily occupation, not only because they were economically exploited, but because they took no pride or joy in their work" (85). According to Rice, only political activism and play-writing allowed this idealism to find an outlet. In law school, he became a socialist during that movement's strongest American years and began taking extension courses in literature and sociology at Columbia.[11]

Nevertheless, *Minority Report* is spiced with substantive, novel-of-manners, Dickensian detailing of the clerical world itself. Rice said he prized his education in human passions revealed in divorce cases (where he had been a process server); he credited his training in precise legal prose yet lamented, as O. Henry and Grant had from different positions, the obfuscations of legal maneuvering that dulled such precision. At the law firm, in addition, Rice had first-hand exposure to a modern Gradgrindianism cast in an American, Progressive key. Cousin Moe was an apostle of Positive Thinking and the Progressive efficiency movement; he hung a sign in his outer office which warned that "[t]he fellow who says it can't be done is always interrupted by the fellow who's doing it." He gave Elmer a subscription to Elbert Hubbard's journal *The Philistine* and gave every staff member a copy of Hubbard's *A Message to Garcia*. Young Elmer, however, preferred the nightlife of vaudeville and the legitimate stage.

Rice may also have harbored dreams of rebellion, but if so they were filtered through a growing elitist lens. Even when he acquired relative independence and new "authority" (87) on the job, he was still unhappy. That his job lacked "creative" or "constructive" features now seemed what was "basically wrong with the world we live in" (87). Yet in his memoir, Rice actually seems undecided as to whether the source of friction on the job was his idealism or whether his moral reservations were more a product of immaturity. Even in the recollection quoted earlier about his emotional goals, one notices that self-improvement and dignity are implied ends, that clerical work is judged not on (Marxian or muckraking) criteria of economic exploitation but in spiritual (Shavian) terms. Rice seems to have been worried about matters of personal creativity and morale (as Lewis and Anderson would be), about sustaining belief in his job and his future plans. Rice admits to having developed a spectatorial attitude, a reflex of distancing himself from those around him. In German, the young man frequently referred to himself in the third person (as "der Elmer"); he daydreamed on the job; he tuned out the "meaningless chatter" of his family and his office.[12] In a similar vein, Rice admits that some of his disdain for office work was, in part, revulsion from its sexual banter, something his "behavioral puritanism" (57) could not countenance. This too is a rather consistent thread within the mature man's plays: an uneasiness with sexual byplay that romanticizes the drudgery of white collar subordination.[13]

These admissions of "adolescent" tendencies—the term was one of Rice's most pejorative labels—are perhaps not surprising, but psychological distance, diffidence, and lack of will were at the heart of Rice's developing vocabulary about white collar life. For instance, here is his account of working in the claims department—a daydream as much Edward Bellamy's as Walter Mitty's:

> At first I found my job rather exciting. . . . *I applied myself to mastering the mysteries and techniques of the business world.* I was fascinated by the great stocks of merchandise that filled the building. . . . I awaited the return of [the salesmen,] eager to see in the flesh mortals who were privileged to visit such exotic, romantic places. I saw myself as a proprietor one day of an establishment even more elaborate. . . The lower floor was somehow to contain a canal or winding rivulet, along which prospective customers would proceed by barge or canoe to inspect the merchandise tastefully displayed upon the banks.
>
> But, as the novelty wore off, it became apparent to me that I was engaged in a dull routine, in unpleasant surroundings, *among people with whom I felt no contact.* I wondered dismally if this was to be the pattern of my life. [55–56, emphasis added]

It is not only that Rice was subject to the commonplace mood swings of a twenty-year-old. Rather, it is that his original aspirations for independence were driven (as the river fantasy attests) by an attraction to business managers and glamorous salesmen, themselves examples of liberation from the routine of work to which the status of clerk consigned him. The fantasy above is based on avoiding contact with both customers and fellow employees, envisioning a work environment of nearly Elysian ease and human absence—a Bellamyesque dream if there ever was one. Rice *dreams* of a sales machine even as he recoils from the tedium of work.[14]

Within all of Rice's confessions, there were substantial sources of ambivalence: a desire to rise, offset by unease with the routine and the deference expected within the hierarchical mode of office life. Here, as well, the contrast with Grant's education in law is telling. The fact that Rice was apprenticing, having been twice delivered to a relative's care, is not insignificant: Rice's conflicts often centered upon personal treatment by his employers—as *The Adding Machine* testifies—the friction between their authority and their obligations (or pretense) of mutual sympathy and family nurturance. Even in his memory of his mother and the "real world," Rice implied a connection between the need for such nurturance and his own motivation, the will he needed to sustain clerical life. The connection was a natural one. Middle-class families, if they are functional, often nurture motivation to rise until ambition is naturalized; offices require such loyalty, as O. Henry and

Ferber saw, claiming to replicate families. Yet Rice saw how deeply corporate authority was, in fact, contingent not only on sustained deference but on a will to believe in the rightness of one's continuing subordination at work.

The new management styles Rice encountered were themselves couched in paternalistic rhetoric. Cousin Moe's Hubbardism, with its famous Roycroft "family," was a model of Progressive-era paternalism. *A Message to Garcia,* Hubbard's pamphlet essay that circulated in the millions in these years, was written explicitly to take the side of employers beset with clerical staffs who seemed indifferent to orders. Like Lorimer's *Letters from a Self-Made Merchant to His Son,* the tone of *Garcia* is very much one of a frustrated parent, but its own models for authority were military. Citing as his prototype the discipline exhibited by a soldier-messenger in the Spanish-American War, Hubbard complained that most clerks showed only an "incapacity for independent action," "an infirmity of the will," an "unwillingness" or "inability to concentrate on a thing and do it." As Eileen Boris has shown, this was a system highly conducive to strict supervision and authoritarianism.[15] Rice's memory stresses this contradiction between paternalism and corporate discipline. Remembering staff meetings and conferences, he said of his boss: "He pointed out the need for efficiency and teamwork, for putting more effort into the job, getting more results. After all, we were one big family, all interested in the common good. The force of all this was somehow lost upon the married men who were trying to support their own families on twenty-five dollars a week. Nothing was said about pay increases or participation in the firm's profits" (70). Both "mystery" and "mastery," Rice's terms for sales and proprietorship respectively, had evaporated; office work only replicated his father's arbitrary rule. Instead of glamorous employers and salesmen, Rice said, he now saw that business was full of "little men with fiery mustaches and tempers . . . always flitting about, finding fault with everyone." *Minority Report* casts Rice's departure from law as a release into art and activism; the more mundane cause was that he left to avoid being upbraided by cousin Moe for a minor error on the job (96).[16] It follows quite naturally that, for Zero, dignified treatment—"a square deal"—is a recurrent plea.

There is another strain in Rice's class experience that Zero's story expresses as well: an employee's secret desire for revenge upon the public facades, the "professions" of the law and its commercial underside. Because Rice's style germinated within matters of will and belief, this aspect of professionalism soon took on the aura of a family secret begging to be let out—

to be exhibited. Even when he returned, as a successful playwright, to view his former boss at work as a city magistrate, this desire remained. Viewing what he called the "petty" court, Rice says he saw "in miniature" a system of "behavior based upon antiquated, sterile and destructive concepts of guilt and punishment, sin and atonement, affront and vengeance" (169). Rice built his art upon insights provided by claims work, or by legal clerking—to apply Hubbard's conceit, by front-line work that involves seeing the passions, the cutting of corners, the personal antagonisms that office generals often deny. In Rice's stage effects, the audience is often asked to see through such professional facades, or asked to view such a profession utterly out of scale and proportion, as though Rice's stage represents revenge on those things bosses overinflate.[17]

Rice's distrust of professionalism's public image-making is also reflected by perhaps the most paradoxical note in *Minority Report:* his rejection of law as a form of theater, of melodrama. In particular, Rice saw litigation as acting, the pretense of realism. It may be obvious that the combination of Positive Thinking and boosterism in the office seemed counterfeit to such a self-conscious youth; in court, legal dramatics similarly obscured the real sources of a conflict. Of trials Rice recalled, "Often I was interested more in the behavior of some well-known trial lawyer than in the subject matter of the case, as one might go to see a star, no matter what the play. The analogy is close, for the conduct of a jury trial depends more upon the art of acting than upon the science of law. Frequently all the legal knowledge a trial lawyer needs is an acquaintance with the rules of evidence, which are fairly simple. The day is often won by obfuscation, trickery and histrionics . . . [such] incident[s] did not diminish my misgivings about the practice of law" (80–81). Rice's nostalgia for a science of law (as if recalling the Harvardized academic ethos) is telling here, and so is the suggestion that clients or juries should not have to be sold on a verdict; what Rice disdains is the mixing of professional and commercial theatrics—the Barnumization of law.[18] (In Rice's clerical daydream, we recall, customers are not sized up, played to, flattered.) Drama was not, then, merely an outlet for his submerged social idealism. Rather, "theater" involved a more complex transposition of his class experience, a turning of the theatrics of legal professionalism, and the Positive Thinking required of clerical subordination, against themselves.

His career had been developing for several years, of course, before *The Adding Machine,* but given the above, it is not surprising that he remembered the composition of this play as especially cathartic:

> I wrote until dawn, spent a few sleepless hours in bed, breakfasted, and immediately went back to work. I kept at it day after day, scarcely speaking, sometimes leaving in the middle of a meal to hurry to my desk. My family must have thought me demented. In a sense I was: moving about in a semitrance, driven by an irresistible compulsion. It was as close to automatic writing as anything I have known. . . .
>
> The play was written in the stylized, intensified form loosely known as expressionism, though I had hardly heard the term at the time. It was a compound of comedy, melodrama, fantasy, satire and polemics. The dialogue was unlike any I had written before: an attempt to reproduce authentic human speech.
>
> Not the least puzzling part of the cathartic effect that the writing of the play had upon me was the purging of my lingering antagonism toward my father. (189–91)

Rice's purging went beyond the merely personal, giving his play a striking class resonance as well. A "compound" of styles and emotions that now flowed out of him, *The Adding Machine* made a mockery of some of his class's most public professions. The play also involved a collaboration of public and private in another sense: it proposed to present an inner life and authentic human speech, but it created a character that was but a compound of second-hand culture, an employee whose subterranean life had been colonized by the outer formulae of mass existence. In Rice's self-pleading formula, the singular voice of a minority position was preferable to the mass cacophony in the mind of most white collar adults.

| | |

Rice's anxieties as a clerical employee—his bristling under corporate paternalism, his worries that professionalism was subject to commercial Barnumizing, his waning motivation and will—explain partly why, at this time, he was drawn to the writings of the British Fabians. It was no coincidence that, just as he was apprenticing to the law, he had made the "cataclysmic" discovery of Shaw and other Fabians, which "completely altered my life, my way of thinking, my mode of life—everything" (86). While not untouched by homegrown political thought, Rice found in Fabianism a new vocabulary for addressing his growing interest in the subjective dimensions of authority. As a young man, Rice said he had devoured Shaw's *Novels of My Nonage,* Fabian tracts by Wells, Besant, and Wallas (137), and more.[19] Fabian ideas did not serve, any more than expressionism, simply as fashionable rationales for innovations in stagecraft; nor did they sift into Rice's mind in Platonic purity. Rather, for Rice—as for Anderson and Lewis—Fabian wisdom was compatible with traditional middle-class vocabularies of self-help and the new styles of Positive Thinking that he encountered in the workplace. Rice's compounding of cultural styles created an engaged versatility, in part by demonstrating his familiarity with the colloquial vocabularies of the crowd. Much of his humor and dramatic energy can be traced to this skill. On the other hand, his theatrical adaption of the Fabians' vocabulary—particularly their strategy of social permeation—went to the heart of Rice's vocational ideology and the forms his plays used to instill their own authority.

As a model of political action, the British Fabian Society, founded in 1883 and modestly influential in English labor politics for over two decades, made inroads only into the margins of American life, its influence evident only among a few ethically and aesthetically oriented intellectuals.[20] Historians have generally discounted the impact of Fabianism's political ideology and stressed its romantic, bohemian appeal to the pre-World War I intelligentsia. Henry May argued in 1958, for instance, that socialist faiths such as Fabianism offered only a generalized cultural iconoclasm rather than any particular social or political agenda. Socialism generally was embraced, or so May's argument went, as part of the larger bohemian quest for the liberating life force enshrined by thinkers like Henri Bergson. Prewar radicals are reputed to have filtered Fabian practicality through romantic, optimistic, and antimaterialist lenses—as they did with so many European intellectual systems (Freudianism being the most obvious example). It is true that American reviewers preferred the utopianism of Wells to his programmatic side; likewise, American intellectuals were drawn more to Wells and Shaw, the literary and cultural iconoclasts of Fabianism—rather than, say, to more technical theorists like the Webbs. Conversely, the Fabians most drawn to American sources (such as Whitman, Thoreau, or Henry George), and those who did make American connections (like William Clarke), were those thinkers in the wing of the British movement more devoted to ethical culture.

By now, however, these truisms of American intellectual history need reexamination, given the changing perception of Fabianism in Britain itself. A more recent strand of British historiography, following the lead of E.J. Hobsbawm, has suggested that the ethical and aesthetic strain was actually quite central to the Fabian project. According to these historians, this strain explains why Fabianism's membership was overwhelmingly middle class, why it drew not only upon the old propertied middle classes but upon salaried white collar workers, people "rising through the interstices of the traditional social and economic structure of Victorian Britain, or anticipating a new structure"—citizens who often felt a particular "lack of fit" within the new bureaucratic and corporate society. Fabian propaganda was written with these sectors in mind, as the timing of Rice's attraction suggests. Unlike American Progressive texts, many of which continued the nineteenth-century idiom of representing a polarized society of plutocrats' invisible government and an urban underside, or which worked in moral, economic, and explicitly political vocabularies, Fabianism emphasized the pivotal social element of middling groups and couched its critique in a decisively cultural and psychological idiom. The romantic, voluntarist languages of spirit and will, historians have argued, addressed the "divided selves" of salaried sectors that were forced to bury their creative or ethical aspirations in increasingly routinized white collar jobs. As Shaw wrote, "extraordinary individuals" who found "no place" for themselves in "ordinary society" were often "tormented by a continual shortcoming in themselves" imposed by the intrinsically "false position" that society had put them in. The Fabian future provided the way out.[21]

The divided self, Fabianism hypothesized, was often created by high white collar aspirations and low, ongoing proletarianization—a split that especially threatened the worker's motivation. Dull routine and bureaucratic stagnation were constant themes in Fabian texts. As Graham Wallas wrote in *Human Nature in Politics* (1908):

> In literature and science as well as in commerce and industry the independent producer is dying out and the official is taking his place. We are nearly all of us officials now, bound during our working days, whether we write on a newspaper, or teach in a university, or keep accounts in a bank, by restrictions on our personal freedom in the interest of a larger organization. We are little influenced by that direct and obvious economic motive which drives a small shopkeeper or farmer or country solicitor to a desperate intensity of scheming how to outstrip his rivals or make more profit out of his employees. If we merely desire to do as little work and enjoy as much leisure as possible in our lives, we all find that it pays us to adopt that steady unanxious "stroke" which neither advances nor retards promotion.

Fabianism in this instance was tied directly to the problem of clerkhood, to organizational entropy. The growth of salaried status, in Wallas's view, had eroded the traditional self-correcting mechanisms, and the aggression, by which citizens (in his terms, "men") had ostensibly sought out their true interest in the past. Shaw, once a Dublin clerk himself, testified that the Fabians' appeal lay in the fact that they were among the first to tell the middle class honestly that "capitalism was reducing their own class to the condition of the proletariat." The day had passed, Shaw asserted, when tests like the "unshaven chin" and having done manual work for weekly wages were the only test of worker status: "the commercial clerk," in Shaw's words, was himself a "very miserable proletarian." Wells, despite his personal disagreements with the management of the Fabian Society, also showed a particular fascination for this struggle of will within what he termed the "salariat," those people he saw as ground between the millstones of capital and labor and supposedly "reduced" to salaried employees.[22]

Rice did not share this nostalgia for middle-class productivity or the small shopkeeper; nor was nineteenth-century American republicanism (any of its variants) as alive for him as for O. Henry, Ferber or Grant. The specific appeal of the Fabian platform for Rice—and its relevance to the portrait of Mr. Zero—becomes clearer when one takes cognizance of its psychological, cultural, and spiritual vocabulary. This point is brought home by looking more closely at Fabianism's rhetorical "other," its often-fatalistic image of that "average sensual citizen." In the organizational bureaucracies that *Human Nature* described above, human nature was itself being rewritten; liberal politics, Wallas reasoned, must adjust. Wallas argued that liberalism must take notice of the full meaning of mass existence and step away from more formal, rational, nineteenth-century models of political authority. In retrospect, it can be seen—especially by including Lippmann's application of his Harvard teacher Wallas's work in *Public Opinion* (1922)—that, for Fabians and their followers, mass existence combined several key elements of modern life. They believed that bureaucratic employees often lost their motivation to work; that mass symbol-making, as in the reading of newspapers, had replaced the traditional model of face-to-face democratic culture; and that, consequently, the public mind had to be conceived in a pragmatist model of a habit reformed by a stream of gathered impressions and impulses.

This revision of liberalism took two main forms. Paralleling Robert Grant's rethinking of classical representation, Wallas's book first attempted to modernize the crude Benthamite calculus of pleasure and pain by recognizing the more irrational dimensions of human nature. Deriving his view of modern consciousness largely from William James's *Principles of Psychology*—believing that "the most important political result" of Darwin's influence was "the extension of the idea of conduct" to include "the control of mental processes of which at present most men are either unconscious or unobservant"—Wallas hypothesized a citizenry bewildered by an "unending stream of sense impressions," possessing an "indifferent and half attentive" mind when it came to politics. Wallas's citizen-to-be-feared was "a tired householder reading the headlines and personal paragraphs . . . and half-consciously forming mental habits of mean suspicion or national arrogance." The analogies to primitive culture ran throughout Wallas's book; the more technological metaphors for describing the popular mind cannot disguise the critique formed of the place of reason in liberal theory. Citizens reputedly responded better to symbol-making, impulse, and superstition than to reasonable persuasion, Wallas said; their minds were like a "slow photographic plate" on which ideas could take vague form only through repetition.[23]

Secondly, such assumptions about the public mind had direct consequences for Fabian notions of political action—or rather, action that took a decidedly intellectual and cultural form. Under the leadership of middle- and upper-class intellectuals, the Fabians had articulated a gradualist and democratic alternative to revolutionary socialism, a vision more attuned to the British world of trade unions, wider suffrage, and a state that was no longer simply an instrument of propertied classes. Rather than emphasizing Marxian class struggle, Fabians had preferred the strategy of intensive research by the intelligentsia and the permeation of their ideas into existing political parties; they saw themselves, as A. M. McBriar and Stanley Pierson have put it, "as turning the unconscious tendency [of the people] into a conscious one," of permeating their creative leadership into what they called the "average sensual man." Discounting the polarized class model of Marxian thinking—often quite distrustful of proletarians themselves—Fabians instead emphasized the struggle of those middle members of society to convert the "steady unanxious stroke" of bureaucratic employment into real creativity. If they could be aroused to answer their ethical desires by political permeation, broader social changes would follow. Consequently, to Fabians the men "of no more than ordinary ability, struggling with one another for work in the overstocked professions" were the target of permeation itself. In Wells's hopeful moments, he believed that social redemption fell on the shoulders of such middle men. Even as he dissented from the Fabian center, for instance, Wells continued to emphasize the potentially strategic counterweight offered by the "creative and imagination-using professions" in the future.[24] This specific platform did indeed attract American thinkers. As Floyd Dell put it, Shaw and Wells offered an uplifting view of the future, and "it was *our* future."[25]

For many Fabians and even this most bohemian of American interpreters, the prospect of a citizenry without will implicitly argued for more technocratic guidance. Drawing upon the Anglo-American legal system, Wallas at times leaned toward a jury model of political organization, a sequestered, decision-making, professional civil service that would educate the public (along Fabian lines) as well as administer that public. (The similarity to Grant's Mugwumpery is perhaps self-evident.)[26] Walter Lippmann also directly applied the jury model to the notion of a news elite that would stand between government officials and the headline-saturated public. Following Wallas, Lippmann argued forcefully that it was simply "no longer possible" to "believe in the original dogma of democracy; that the knowledge needed for the management of human affairs comes up spontaneously from the human heart" (158). Instead, democratic theorists had to recognize that mass existence was polluted by the symbol-making and news management of often illegitimate powers, governed by men tantalized by "episodes, incidents, and eruptions" of news. Here again, newspapers were especially villainous: Lippmann lamented that the "mass is constantly exposed to suggestion. It reads not the news, but the news with an aura of suggestion about it, indicating the line of action to be taken. It hears reports, not objective as the facts are, but already stereotyped to a certain pattern of behavior. Thus the ostensible leader often finds that the real leader is a powerful newspaper proprietor" (155). Hence Lippmann's own proposal for an "entering wedge" of technocratic experts and "intelligence sections" (242) to manage public life.

There were serious inconsistencies in this platform, not the least of which was a certain envy of both the totalitarian discipline and the mass symbol-making liberals putatively disdained. Rice himself exhibited these contradictions, but for the moment, his application of these ideas to his inherited form—the theater—is worth examining. That application is perhaps best illustrated by looking into Shaw's "Quintessence of Ibsenism," an essay Rice cites nearly verbatim in a letter from 1922.[27] In this study, Shaw had portrayed Ibsen as one of those pioneers whose intellectual probity and nonconformity were so far beyond conventional audiences as to invite only horror from moralists. To Shaw, therefore, Ibsen's themes merely portrayed the very process the dramatist's own rebellion epitomized: the struggle of spontaneous human will to break free from the false ideas and masks of respectability. Shaw argued that Ibsen recognized that the will was the "prime motor" of human change, adding that faith in mere reason was "no longer the criterion of the sound mind" (22). Shaw said Ibsen was "on the side of the prophets in having devoted himself to showing that the spirit or *will* of Man is constantly outgrowing the *ideals* [emphasis mine], and that therefore thoughtless conformity to them is constantly producing results no less tragic than those which follow thoughtless violations of them. Thus the main effect of his plays is to keep before the public the importance of being always prepared to act immorally" (121–22).

Such iconoclastic words certainly must have spoken forcefully to the young former lawyer, former clerk, and author of *The Adding Machine*. And the juridical analogies so central to the Fabian revisions of classic liberalism also made their way into Shaw's speculations about drama. Shaw reasoned that the audience's conversion was effected by Ibsenian drama this way:

> There can be no question as to the effect likely to be produced on an individual by his conversion from the ordinary acceptance of current ideals as safe standards of conduct, to the vigilant open-mindedness of Ibsen. . . . Before conversion the individual anticipates nothing worse in the way of examination at the judgment bar of his conscience than such questions as, Have you kept the commandments? Have you obeyed the law? . . . Substitute for such a technical examination one in which the whole point to be settled is, Guilty or Not Guilty? one in which there is no more and no less respect for virginity than for incontinence, for subordination than for rebellion, for legality than for illegality . . . in short, for the standard qualities than for the standard faults, and immediately, instead of lowering the ethical standard . . . you raise it. (123–24)

It should be clear from the above that this goal of conversion—in the Ibsenian drama Shaw is advocating—is akin to seeing theater as a device for the Fabian strategy of permeation, whether through dialogue, open-ended conclusions (for which Rice argued in the teens), or even occasionally shocking the audience.[28] "Ibsen substituted a terrible art of sharpshooting at the audience," Shaw wrote, "trapping them, fencing with them, aiming always at the sorest spot in their consciences" (145); for mere trickery, he had substituted a "*forensic* technique of *recrimination,* disillusion, and *penetration* through ideals to the truth, with a free use of all the rhetorical and lyrical arts of the orator, the preacher, the *pleader,* and the rhapsodist" (146; emphasis mine).[29] Shaw's platform not only assumed the Fabians' average sensual man as audience; more covertly, he encoded professional terminology (in noticeably legal terms) quite compatible with an American middle-class vocabulary. Rice's aggressive assertion of control over the stage might therefore be seen, in part, as creating a cross-examination of his original white collar fate. Rice would certainly not be shy about such compounding of effects in expressionist form; *The Adding Machine* would make use of revolving platforms, vocalized thoughts, incongruous emotions, characters with numeric names, fantastic habitats like Elysia and Heaven itself. In the stage direction following Zero's murder of his boss, Rice asks that "every offstage effect of the theater" (14) be employed—a rather inclusive request.

What was more important here than such matters of stage management, or the specific example of Ibsen or Shaw's realism (from which Rice departed), was the ideological and cultural function Rice now ascribed to such theatrics. Of course, there are any number of roots for Rice's "automatic" knack for mass-cultural *vraisemblance:* his gift for mimicry, his stenographic skills, his admiration for "the shrewd representation of American speech and behavior" (*MR,* 200) by a range of popular playwrights whose work, by 1914–15, young Elmer was seeing about every five days.[30] Some of this skill may be credited to Rice's bilingual upbringing; in *The Adding Machine,* colloquial idioms are humorously literalized unbeknownst to their speakers. Even more telling than these gifts is how much theatricality itself had become metaphorical for Rice's thinking about modern white collar life. The form, that is, embodied much of Rice's own ambivalence: by his own definition, "expressing" himself involved oscillation between "mastery" and distance, between fantasy and cold realism, between a young immigrant's assimilation into professional, American, and commercial culture and his ultimate rejection of it. The pattern of shifting between a sense of white collar confinement and daydreaming that Rice attributed to himself, and ultimately to his *Adding Machine* protagonist, was even reminiscent of the behind-the-counter fantasies of an O. Henry hero. It is thus not surprising that Rice also remembers himself as an "assiduous" reader of O. Henry in his early years, or that his first publication was what he called an O. Henry imitation—a story, in fact, about being unable to distinguish between theater and life.[31] Ultimately, however, the connection may have been an even more serious one. In the murderous premise of *The Adding Machine,* itself the story of an accountant, Rice would violently literalize and burlesque the issue of an employee's role within the script of corporate metaphysics.

| | |

In analyzing *The Adding Machine,* critics have habitually resorted to the formal label of expressionism to describe Rice's interest in the subjective rather than the naturalistic parameters of Zero's social state. Yet Rice's aggressive manipulation of both Zero and the play's audience suggests a particular cast to that subjectivity—or, more precisely, Zero's seeming lack of agency. For while it is true that Zero does not lack humanity altogether, or at least a potential for will, the dominant mode of Rice's verisimilitude represents Zero almost wholly in overwritten cultural, and thus passive and normative, terms. Zero's consciousness is portrayed as a kind of mass unconscious made normative: a dream-life of mass culture made to dictate clerical desire. Conversely, only when this dominant, hyperbolic cultural inscription is withdrawn does Zero (or Mrs. Zero, or Daisy) achieve sympathy: when a character distances him- or herself from mass scripting of life. Otherwise, like Robert Grant in Benham, Rice assumes that mass culture, in effect, is the contested American citizen.

The Adding Machine also might easily be mistaken for a lament about technological determinism. Yet Rice is not much interested in literal machines, any more than he is in the arithmetic reformism of wages, rentals, or disposable income, as O. Henry had been. Rather, the machine—and such mathematics—are "figures" for a corporate and even cosmological entity.[32] Economics do play a contributing role here: that the blood on Zero's white collar—which Rice explicitly compares to the slave collar (59)—is argued by defense lawyers as "red ink" (21) certainly affirms the role of the bottom line, and Zero stabs his boss (off stage) through the heart with a bill file (21). Even so, Zero's crime is viewed more as a violation of office discipline, initially framed (reflecting Rice's experience) as revenge for not being as error-free as his paternal boss demanded.

Because of the boss's quick departure, one might not notice his essential paternalism: how he had offered store picnics (47), donated a women's room to the department store in his will (22), projected a genial personality on the one occasion when Zero had greeted him in the morning (23). In truth, the boss's brief appearance works quite strategically. First of all, Rice all but eliminates the direct representation of vertical class conflict; therefore—and this is crucial—Zero's "slave" status is seen not as what theorists of class call a "relational" category but something intrinsic to him. The soon-absent boss becomes a kind of nonpresence, a sign that Rice's interest is not in visible oppression but in the prison in Zero's own mind.[33] Likewise, in the final scenes in heaven, office manager Lieutenant Charles, perhaps a private echo of Hubbard's *Garcia,* barks out military puns (e.g., "cease firing" [55]), a reminder that strict discipline is at the heart of Zero's dependent status.

Moreover, Zero's dreams of rising above that dependence are undercut by a Shavian trap in the play's structure. Each scene, yet another stage in Zero's after(murder)life, is built upon a familiar plea: "If we only had another chance"—which, as each stage proceeds, Zero does. Yet because, as the character Shrdlu observes, Zero cannot distinguish between the imperative "do" or the choice-laden "may" (53), the sum total of his life is extremely unprogressive. As Rice explained to the Theatre Guild actors in the twenties:

> Zero, like nearly everyone else, believes himself to be misunderstood. Believing firmly in his own superiority he conceives himself as the victim of an injustice. . . . This egocentric view of the universe is, of course, largely unconscious. Consciously he accepts authority almost unquestioningly, although there is in his acceptance the suggestion of a note of truculence: the effect of exposure to the democratic dogma, the superstitious belief that "one man is as good as another." . . . This is the key to the Elysian Fields scene. It bewilders him to be thrust into a world in which right and wrong are purely subjective, in which conduct is motivated by desire, in which there is no authority to serve as a touchstone for one's acts. . . . In the world of the machine Zero is happy, or if not happy, at any rate, he is at ease. For in this world, there are no problems. Everything is safe, rigid, symmetrical, predictable, governed by simple mechanical principles. This is Zero's heaven: a steady job which one holds through eternity.[34]

A steady job, in a sense, where Zero is but a figure kept on the books.

Throughout the play, Rice toys with numbers: not only in Zero's numeric name and those of his neighbors, nor in the oversized numbers inscribed on his walls of his office and home. Zero cannot stop his mind from adding and subtracting, and he expresses a fondness for numbers in a revealing way: "Goddam them figgers! I can't forget 'em. They're funny things, them figgers. They look like people sometimes. The eights, see? Two dots for the eyes and a dot for the nose. An' a line. That's the mouth, see? An' there's others remind you of other things: but I can't talk about them, on account of there bein' ladies here" (22).

Rice is obviously interested in evoking what mid-century sociology would emphasize as the namelessness of bureaucratic impersonality, but more important here is Zero's equation of his own personhood with his mathematic "figuring." Rice was clearly applying his education in business mathematics here. The opening sequence at the office is a satire on double bookkeeping that suggests only cultural disfiguration. Seated back to back, lacking personal sympathy, Daisy and Zero are both adding up figures and (in vocalized thoughts) adding up their lives. Yet they, too, will soon turn into zero (life) sums, one a convicted murderer and the other a suicide. In a sense, because they do not see their common denominators (loneliness, desire for each other), the sum of their wisdom is not totaled; they are subjected, therefore, to the cruel mathematics of efficiency that amounts to self-erasure. That is, Rice is interested in how white collar subordination does not add up; he underscores both characters' psychological and metaphysical vacuity.

Not surprisingly, then, the play's wildly metaphysical second half, on to heaven and back again, is meant to vitiate or evacuate the teleological codes legitimating Zero's existence. Along the way, it is apparent that neither retribution nor redemption sanctions Zero's crime—or condemns it. Zero's sentencing is paralleled to that of the prostitute he betrayed by turning her in to the police. (Secretly, he envies her freedom, but he succumbs to the pressure of his own wife.) But the prostitute, rather than being reformed, is seen haunting the graveyard proposing to have sex with another customer (36). Likewise, Shrdlu, the mother-murderer to whom Zero is also paralleled, finds his own metaphysical compass demagnetized. Whatever his minister, Dr. Amaranth, says about Shrdlu's "sinful nature" (41), Shrdlu cannot even find his own mother in heaven. Neither earthly nor divine justice seems to conform to Zero's respectable moralism. All of creation is really a white collar purgatory—in the end, envisioned as a many-layered corporation that simply reassigns its personnel. The play's final scene, in which Zero is assigned to totaling up souls, presents a metaphysical antiaccounting, a striking off the books of the entire metaphysical justification not just for guilt, punishment, and sin but for moral determination, especially for dreams of "raises": the cosmic adding machine. If there is any connection to Zero's anger on Rice's part, it is that, in some sense, Rice has killed the ultimate Boss: God is referred to as the "they" (59) of corporate authority, the machine of Lippmann's Oversoul.

Zero is also portrayed as having sentenced himself by his own passivity and desire for respectability. The very essence of Zero's character is his willingness to have other "figurin'" or verdicts written onto his life without expressing his own will. At a superficial level, Rice seems to point to Zero's simple shallowness and even mental deficiency. Zero appears unable to hold information or resolve; lacking will, he snaps back to his own simple conventionalism. Perhaps his most recurrent complaint is "not having the guts" to do something—a lack of will that corners him into murder in the first place (22). Later, with Mrs. Zero, he keeps a scrapbook of his own trial; orders ham and eggs as his last meal; worries whether one is allowed to sit on the grass of the Elysian fields. And, of course, at the close of the play, he chooses his own slave status again, led on by the false image of "Hope" (61) that heaven provides. At the end, he cannot even remember his troubles, much less his previous lives as monkey and Egyptian slave; his consciousness is merely soiled and "washed" again by what Lieutenant Charles calls a "cosmic laundry" (57). His white collar is cleaned and sent back to earth.

Zero's zero-sum consciousness thus reveals the severe revision taking place within one modern liberal's hypothesizing of citizen potential. Hardly the Lockean blank slate, Zero is one whose consciousness is already marked by the tumbling and circularity of his mass life. Rice employs a number of techniques that create a feeling of being cluttered by sense impressions, impulses, half-baked ideas—a cultural normativeness verging on a claustrophobia to rival Sinclair Lewis's *Babbitt*. As with the merry-go-round that frames the murder scene (another figure for the cyclical, zero-sum metaphysics of the play), Rice relies upon verbal echoes and plot circularity, turning already trite conversations back upon themselves to invoke narrative claustrophobia. In monologues such as Mrs. Zero's in scene 1, "meaningless chatter" is repeated and blended into shopworn colloquialisms; the movie or story titles she refers to all sound suspiciously alike; her conversation (to which Zero is inattentive) repeats other conversations that repeat others. Scene 5 thus becomes a synecdoche; clerical existence is defined, even in its private moments, as a prison-house of mass language, a life whose very synapses are bound to mass cultural experience, with its mix of envious fascination (spectacle) and inattentiveness (passivity). Many dialogues are, in effect, monologues loaded with clichés that are unresponded to (Mrs.

Zero to Zero; Diana to Zero and back; Zero to his boss and back; even God's agents and Zero). No one is listened to; the stories have presumably been heard before; repetition follows anyway, since characters still desire to be heard. In the dinner party scene in scene 3, Rice even strings a dirty joke together, in a format that ends in an undelivered punchline (a blank, where Zero's line should be):

SIX [*sotto voce*]. Did you hear the one about the travelin' salesman?
FIVE. It seems this guy was in a sleeper.
FOUR. Goin' from Albany to San Diego.
THREE. And in the next berth was an old maid.
TWO. With a wooden leg.
ONE. Well, along about midnight— (18)

In other instances, Rice verbalizes characters' un-free association, their scripting by mass culture, implying how the objects of envy become—in a process central to Zero's crime—objects of revenge. Each character takes turn in "judging" (8) others; violence creeps into slang expressions like "shoot" (9). Meanwhile, cultural catchphrases are converted into self-damning indictments; Zero, stuck in the same job for twenty-five years, affirms his conformity by saying, "I'm on the level" (9) over and over again. When he is fired in his boss's plan to follow "efficiency experts" and replace Zero with an adding machine, Zero says colloquially: "You mean I'm canned?" (14).

In Rice's presentation, such colloquial idioms thus create a curiously double perspective. In one sense, they become testaments of humorous familiarity and liberal patronage, as they are for writers like O. Henry and Ferber. More frequently in this play, however, they are deployed as registers of Zero's primitive consciousness. They are quite akin to self-indicting testimony, unconscious confessions of submission to authority, confessions of attractions to taboos. Mrs. Zero's opening speech is revealing:

MRS. ZERO [*as she takes down her hair*]. I'm gettin' sick o' them Westerns. All them cowboys ridin' around an' foolin' with them ropes. I don't care nothin' about that. I'm sick of 'em. I don't see why they don't have more of them stories like *For Love's Sweet Sake*. I like them sweet little love stories. They're nice an' wholesome. Mrs. Twelve was sayin' to me only yesterday, "Mrs. Zero," says she, "what I like is one of them wholesome stories, with just a sweet, simple little love story." "You're right, Mrs. Twelve," I

> says. "That's what I like too." They're showin' too many Westerns at the Rosebud. I'm gettin' sick of them. I think we'll start goin' to the Peter Stuyvesant. They got a good bill there Wednesday night. There's a Chubby Delano comedy called *Sick*. Mrs. Twelve was tellin' me about it. (3)

Mrs. Zero's protest of the tedium in her life cannot be overlooked, or even the pathos of her longing for "wholesome" love. Yet what matters to Rice, as Lippmann had put it in *Public Opinion,* is the "line of action to be taken" (155) by a citizen whose consciousness is alternately saturated with mass fantasy and yet so bored that s/he thirsts for more. It is not that Mrs. Zero's or Mrs. Twelve's lives are "mass" in their identical scripting, nor in their second-hand nature, but that their passional lives have been set by a pattern of stimulus and response, so much so that any option they choose seems only a redundancy. Their lives repeat what their mass "script" has written out for them. For example:

> ZERO. Women make me sick. They're all alike. The judge gave her six months. I wonder what they do in the workhouse. Peel potatoes. I'll bet she's sore at me. Maybe she'll try to kill me when she gets out. I better be careful. Hello Girl Slays Betrayer. Jealous Wife Slays Rival. (7)
>
> . . . .
>
> DAISY. I wish I knew what to ask for. Girl Takes Mercury After All-Night Party. Woman in Ten-Story Death Leap. (9)

Not knowing what to ask for, these minds stray into fantasies of headlines—headlines that, in turn, become catalysts for how they act. Their private fantasies and dreams are rewritten into dreams of revenge or suicide; the headline penetrates consciousness, and then consciousness conspires to make another headline. (Headlines, indeed.)

Of course, that is the circular, dead-end, zero-sum effect of Zero's action: merely creating another headline. (For one thing, Rice compares Zero's crime to that of the proofreader Shrdlu, whose name echoes the typographical DNA at work in each character.) The habitual form of the headline is itself instructive, because of its own zero semantics. Usually a statement of a past action, rarely of causation or motivation, a headline is usually cast in a clipped syntax, a set of words fixed in time, "grabbing" or presented in "scare" quotes. This odd combination of violence and repetitiveness is itself evocative of *The Adding Machine*'s overall atmosphere. By the play's end, the action has resembled nothing so much as the color comic supplement read by the Fixer who arrives from the claims department to remit Zero to his execution. The Fixer reads, at the end of the scene, the comic strip of Mutt and Jeff—and, intriguingly, he totals up the black eyes given over and over again in the strip (35). Ultimately, as his scrapbook suggests, Zero's life literally becomes a "living newspaper."[35]

There are moments when Zero and Daisy seem to be so much creatures of mass timidity that they acquire pathos and humor. Such moments have led some analysts to discount the pessimism in Rice's play and maintain that it asserts a bedrock commitment to humane liberal values.[36] Much like O. Henry, Rice does expose the particular irony of the clerical accountant's own vulnerability to bottom-line mathematics. The back-to-back bookkeeping of Zero and Daisy, reflecting the disciplined, military impersonality of their lives, is reiterated as the jury files out after the trial; they leave, Rice notes, in the "double column" (25) of ledgers and armies. Rice's career, in its heartfelt commitment to free speech and minority rights, registers a legitimate anxiety about the arithmetic, "objective" accounting of citizen's happiness O. Henry saw.[37] This is a partial index of how far liberalism, in Rice's hands, has removed itself from materialist criteria (and naturalistic representation), yet the limits of his accounting of the public mind must be recognized. Rice's conjoining of class and mass culture, in turn, point to a trapdoor in his adaptation of Shavian stagecraft: a profound distrust of the public he hoped his plays would permeate. Like Grant's, Rice's politics founders on the very "averageness" it denominates.

This final paradox was apparent most of all in Rice's career-long lament about American audiences. From the mid-teens through the thirties, Rice complained about the "puerile," "imbecile," "feeble-minded" nature of the theater-going public that expected him to "administer vibrations to their spinal columns" and "lachrymal glands"—metaphors of the body politic that just as easily could have come from Mencken.[38] This audience had itself invited the "stained-glass window morality" of conventional drama that only provided "empty jokes and easy titillation of the senses, in prettified portrayals of the habits and foibles of their class." Even Rice's leftist vocabulary of the 1930s only extended this complaint by equating audiences with a decaying bourgeoisie. Even here, Rice maintained that "crowd psychology" limited the drama. The language of averaging, however, was intrinsic to his argument. "Whether it be from gregariousness or from the desire for self-preservation, the members of a crowd assume a uniformity of conduct, a sort of common denominator, which tends to be based upon instinct, conditioned reflexes, and acceptance of tradition rather than upon reason or deliberate choice . . . half-discarded tabus reassert themselves vigorously, and a norm of propriety and orthodoxy is established which is far below the habitual level of the more intelligent and more emancipated members of the group."[39]

To give Rice credit, he fully intended to make his audience witness its culture's own spectacles. Rice's stagecraft is meant to remove the audience to a space outside the bathos of normative life, project them into a clinical distance from clerical dependence not unlike the satirical, yet juridical position in Grant's fiction. In *The Adding Machine,* Rice performs a telling maneuver: he places Zero's jury on the stage in view of the audience; the audience is asked to view not only Zero at a second remove but to judge the jury itself.[40] If the audience begins with something like Zero's consciousness, it is meant to be driven away by being shocked with a compounding and burlesquing of its own moral and mass-cultural vocabularies. Rice's play does not offer merely a veneer of Menckenian skepticism, nor does it endorse Zero's crime, as some would have it, as an act of radical resistance.[41] Rather, the play works by making Zero so paradigmatic of an empty social life that Rice's implied audience is meant to recoil from, stand apart from, Zero's normativeness, his primitive desires for revenge, even his "meaningless chatter." Rice tries to turn his own subterranean rage into a force for what Shaw would have called "emancipation."

This distancing effect collaborates uneasily, however, with Rice's compounding of cultural vocabularies. The effect reinforces Rice's belief that Zero is intrinsically a slave, a view revealed in Lieutenant Charles's lines in the final scene:

ZERO. You mean to say I've been here before—before the last time, I mean?

CHARLES. Been here before! Why, you poor boob—you've been here thousands of times—fifty thousand at least.

ZERO [*suspiciously*]. How is it I don't remember nothin' about it?

CHARLES. Well—that's partly because you're stupid. But it's mostly because that's the way they fix it. [*Musingly.*] They're funny that way—every now and then they'll do something white like that—when you'd least expect it. I guess economy's at the bottom of it though. They figure that the souls would get worn out quicker if they remembered.

ZERO. And don't any of 'em remember?

CHARLES. Oh, some do. You see there's different types: there's the type that gets a little better each time it goes back—we just give them a wash and send them right through. Then there's another type—the type that gets a little worse each time. That's where you belong! . . . You weren't so bad as a monkey. Of course, you did just what all the other monkeys did. . . . Yes, sir, you weren't so bad then. But even in those days there must have been some bigger and brainier monkey that you kowtowed to. The mark of the slave was on you from the start. (57–58)

As Rice's complaints about commercial drama attest, Zero *is* the audience who will not learn. Exhibit Z could himself exemplify the contradictions in Rice's own case; in the prison scene, the audience that visits Zero's cell is disturbingly inattentive. As it turns out, scene 5 was the one scene excised from the original production of *The Adding Machine*—for considerations of length, it was said, but perhaps really because it cut too close to the bone.[42]

Even more problematically, a play like *The Adding Machine,* for all its humane aversion to the mathematics of the bottom line, ends up by confirming a fantasy of its own: that Elysian emancipation is available for those who simply choose it, who set down their ledgers and amuse themselves in what are called "profitless occupations" (53)—meaning, subversively but not very substantively, white collar life upside down. Creating his own imaginary Elysian margin, Rice imagines a space offstage from mass culture, a space from which the public and audience can be witness but remain apart—a fragile claim given the metaphysics of the play. Rice could adroitly mimic the compounding of popular idioms that saturated his denominated public, but he could not always survey that Elysian place outside respectability that his public was supposed to inhabit. Little wonder, then, that this liberal's literary idiom has seemed little different from Mencken's disdain.[43] This was not merely a shared weakness for rhetorical excess. The deeper point may be that, lacking faith in professional expertise, science, or even "efficiency," knowing personally the capacity of the employee to daydream, convinced that democratic equality was "dogma" or "superstition," Rice was deprived of any other position than the skepticism his debunking implicitly claimed. This was a problem similar to the threat of fatalism, of "white out," in *Unleavened Bread:* Rice's reliance on claustrophobic, vocalized thoughts by a set of characters who merely echo each other's headlines had crowded out any meaningful position outside his overweening cosmological corporation. If the verdict on the "average" American polity is severe, what is more striking is how Rice has forsaken thinking of politics at all.

This absence of a substantive external ground exposes another limitation of Rice's social vocabulary. Rice's vocabulary for theatrical authority is itself permeated with the languages he professed to disdain. Rice's theatrics certainly seemed to be based on summoning will in his audience, but they did so by making the sensual man, Rice's public, realize his inner desires by surprise, by polemic, even by shock. Because Rice felt drama was based, as Wallas assumed politics were, upon "instant apprehension" rather than rereading, Rice's dramaturgy easily slipped into a more aggressive strategy to achieve suitable permeation. This was not, then, the mere commercialism with which Rice has occasionally been charged but a formal attempt to reverse the Barnumizing of his class, to use its own terms in hyperbolic mockery. Here again, "radical" theater could share more than it knew with its "theatrical" middle-class world. Like Lippmann's news elite, who even today customarily *contribute* to the "manufacture of consent," Rice's model dramatist could easily degenerate into applying the seductive logic of the sound bite. "Hence the dramatist must find pat phrases," Rice said, "must make his points again and again, must shout when he might prefer to whisper, and substitute a search-light for a candle."[44] Rice at times goes beyond even Wallas's or Lippmann's model—for in his universe, even juries are tainted.

The cathartic, "automatic" writing of this play was obviously empowering for the playwright himself. Rice's life-long commitments to social justice and civil rights can hardly be explained away; today, when the domain of discourse theory seems to create cultural histories with no exit, we might recognize how Rice's seemingly "naive" cultural vocabulary made him virtually oblivious to public censure, valiant in the defense of free speech, and resilient in the isolation of minority positions. There are, indeed, occasions for shouting, for resisting the disciplinary silence a corporate culture forces upon its subordinates. Nevertheless, even in his valiant protests, Rice often remained within the perimeter of his white collar fictions, his protestations to the contrary. The entire universe of *The Adding Machine* (husband or wife, accountant or secretary) is effectively "white"-washed into a white collar universe; even God's employee, Lieutenant Charles, complains about his accounting job (62). Bound by what is seen in the prison of Zero's mind, the audience is necessarily left with blank spots, left to imagine the ground that the play itself marks as off limits. The early exit of the boss figure, Rice's inference that some men are born slaves, his depiction of office co-workers like Daisy as merely romantic enticements for Zero's diminished desire—all of this may have been the result of Rice's "metaphysical" approach. That approach may underestimate the resources for unplugging the machine, the way clerical workers might resist the "scripting" of their consciousness.[45] Perhaps most of all, Rice's play cannot disguise its antagonism to the "public" that it tries to permeate. Perhaps this is why the play has performed so much more successfully in revival than in its original seven-week run; over time, audiences may lose the sense of their own resemblance to Zero. This was also all too characteristic of Rice's "minority" politics as well: his repeated disputes with theatrical troupes, with political parties, with Harry Hopkins. Rice could often imagine Elysia, but he could not often imagine whom to bring along.[46]

As the "Lady from Dubuque" for *New Yorker* subscribers, the irrational citizen of *Public Opinion*, or the Babbitts or Mittys of cosmopolitan humor, supposedly normative, Main Street "others" had become axiomatic in a number of senses: as hypothesized audiences, as personifications of "national character," and, most of all, as rhetorical foils for the ragged self-fashioning of the cosmopolitan elite. In time, of course, even this cosmopolitan "radicalism" proved quite culturally soluble. Even Fabian articulation of rebellious creativity and will seemed to become, over time, nearly indistinguishable from the Algeristic veneration of initiative, personal progress, and self-help that the American middle classes had traditionally venerated. (Just as Elbert Hubbard lamented the lack of "vertebrae" among the clerical forces, Zero is deemed "spineless" [61] by the action of the play.) Even more to the point, the imagining of an Elysian space where all are free to choose, beyond the routine and perimeter drawn by the white collar, is itself a component of new-middle-class "awareness": the claim that class is no real boundary at all. At this deeper layer, *The Adding Machine* only extended what was originally an intraclass conflict infused with its own ragged emotions—cosmopolitan elitism, a son's anger, "front-line" clerical disdain—a nearly automatic headline of the common denominators in Rice's own white collar experience. Perhaps this is why, as with Sherwood Anderson and Sinclair Lewis, even the most adult of minority positions could, over time, begin to look like language of one's own class reincarnated.

Part III
Versions of the Job

Five

Sherwood Anderson and the Personality Market

We go, each of us, through the treadmill of our lives, caught and caged like little animals in some vast menagerie. . . . We become shrewd, careful, submerged in little things. . . . Under the night sky the suburbanite stands in the moonlight. He is hoeing his radishes and worrying because the laundry has torn one of his white collars.

—*Sherwood Anderson,* Marching Men

One of the more remarkable recoveries of recent years has been Sherwood Anderson's letters to Marietta D. Finley, particularly those written prior to *Winesburg, Ohio* (1919). Anderson and Finley met in the fall of 1914 at the Chicago Little Theater; in the twenty-year correspondence that followed, Anderson vowed to convey—and did—his "observations on life and manners," providing new insight into years that have often been obscured by Anderson's notorious myth-making and misrememberings.[1] But the Anderson who emerges is occasionally quite different from the expected—as, for example, in this sketch from November of 1916:

> I went home in the rain and the car was crowded. The workingmen with their sad brutal faces climbed aboard in droves. I stood among them breathing the air that reeked with the strong scent of their bodies. I thought that I had made too much money. In my pocket was a pouch filled with bills. I put down my hand past the shaking body of a fat man and felt of the pouch. I was a little ashamed. Not because I had money when others had none but because the possession of even $75 raises me a little into the lower middle-class. There is a kind of healthy desperation in the utter lack of money. Often I have tramped in utter poverty and misery

> through the streets and got something out of my misery. For a moment on the car I was sentimental regarding this matter and then I laughed. My mind checked back to the notion that has again and again saved me, living as I do altogether among men of business. Again I put my hand down past the fat man and touched the pouch. I patted it affectionately. As the car rattled along I had keen joy in thinking of myself as an outlaw. "I have stolen the money from a stupid world," I whispered to myself and was happy. (*LB*, 9)

Some aspects of Anderson's mature literary idiom are germinating here: the simple, colloquial phrasing cast in a confessional first person; the empathetic foray into secret lives and wishes; the potential of human colloquy and its tragic thwarting. Yet on another level, this bald reaffirmation of his middle-class membership jars with our general sense of Anderson, the intuitive writer who is reputed to have raised the cultural rhetoric of commonality to high art. When we read *Winesburg,* Edwin Fussell once wrote, it is because "there are few works of any age in which the artist and ordinary men are seen so well *as fitting together* in a complementary union." To H. L. Mencken, Anderson lifted the short story out of O. Henryesque trickery and the "sad farce that one glimpses from train windows" into "a higher and more spacious level," the "life of the microcosm." Such praise has, moreover, always reconfirmed Anderson's sense of himself as "trying to get at and understand a little the lives of so-called ordinary people."[2] In this early letter, however, he seems little more than a fellow (train) traveler; disaffiliation from what Anderson terms "brutal" beings undercuts the possibility of empathy.

Perhaps this was merely a temporary lapse, or Anderson's attempt to shock his bourgeois correspondent by a confession he knew was out of character. One should remember, as Clifford Geertz writes, that most cultural transcription of "others" approximates "experience-near" cognition, not communion. But at the very least the sketch suggests that in 1916 Anderson-the-writer was simultaneously Anderson-the-businessman, a man who had moved into the new middle class from his father's world of manual labor. After leaving Clyde, Ohio, in 1893, Anderson had been a day laborer in Chicago for nearly five years. Yet, like Elmer Rice, he also had attended a commercial academy, going to night school at the Lewis Institute to study new business mathematics from September to December of 1897. After the Spanish-American war, having returned to finish high school, Anderson had become an advertising copywriter for Crowell Publishing Company.

Then, between 1900 and 1905, he had written advice columns (in series such as "Rot and Reason" and "Business Types") for his company's trade organ, *Agricultural Advertising*, and other journals. In 1906, he had returned to Cleveland to establish a mail-order business and become president of the United Factories company. Even after his nervous breakdown in 1912, Anderson went back to being an ad writer for Taylor-Critchfield (eventually Long-Critchfield), and would stay there through the writing of *Winesburg*. Seven of the *Winesburg* stories were composed on the cheap print paper used in blocking out advertisements; most were written, moreover, nearly a year before the streetcar sketch that appears above.[3] His first two novels, *Windy McPherson's Son* (1916) and *Marching Men* (1917), revolved precisely around this formative social transformation: from handwork to headwork, the taking up of the white collar that now figured explicitly as a sign of new-middle-class status.

The relationship between Anderson's art and his advertising career has long intrigued biographers and critics. William A. Sutton, Ray Lewis White, and Karen-Elisabeth Mouscher have uncovered a wealth of detail about Anderson's early employment; Sutton especially has demonstrated how Anderson's early business writings constitute his first forays into human fellowship and how his desire to master both business and writing subjected him to severe personal pressure.[4] In nearly all of these accounts, however, "art" and "business" are dichotomized into generalized and oppositional terms, obscuring the interaction between Anderson's class thinking, the specific kind of work he did—ad writing, advice columns, and direct-mail promotion—and the evolution of his literary idiom. This critical tendency has its mirror image in those institutional histories of advertising, usually drawing on Sutton's work, that habitually cite Anderson as an instance of the frustrated writer worried over prostituting his art.[5] Fortunately T. J. Jackson Lears, our shrewdest cultural historian of turn-of-the-century advertising, has seen Anderson as exemplifying a much more tortured engagement between copywriting and modernist artistry. Lears emphasizes Anderson's recoil from what he called the "quick surface effects" and standardized charm of modern advertising; by implication Lears suggests that even the composition of *Winesburg, Ohio* bears an affinity to the daydreaming office life that suffuses so much white collar representation. Even for Lears, however, *Winesburg* persists as a resting place of emotional refuge, a world of grotesques left behind by the cosmopolitan consumer culture Anderson once helped to fashion.[6]

In one way or another, what follows is deeply indebted to all of the accounts above—as well as to the work of C. Wright Mills, Roland Marchand, and others.[7] Ultimately, however, I want to take my own account of Anderson in a different (and perhaps conflicting) direction: into his languages of class, his social and political affiliations, and finally, into the continuities between advertising and his fiction. And rather than seeing Anderson solely in terms of advertising, he should be viewed as part of a larger white collar universe, what Mills calls a "personality market" within which young men are recruited and made into agents of the market itself. Business was hardly the solitary formative influence on Anderson's art, as generations of scholars have made clear; nonetheless, the advertising profession's fantasies of social mastery, its no-nonsense business discourse, and even its arithmetic audience typologies left residual marks on Anderson's maturing literary idiom. In fact, as with Sinclair Lewis, a business apprenticeship generated in Anderson a tell-tale distrust of avant-garde pretensions, a desire to reform American letters from inside workaday office life. This desire—again, as with Lewis—was directed especially at reforming American naturalism. The result was a significant revision of Anderson's literary representations of class, even given his continuing disdain for office drudgery and subordination.

For Anderson and Lewis, the word "job"—perhaps their central cultural keyword of class—contained traces of this revision. Anderson, who had grown up plagued by his father's occupational declension, had been called "Jobby" by his fellow townspeople. Most interpreters, following the writer's lead, read this nickname as a sign of Anderson's youthful ambition, his willingness to work even if it meant skipping school, to rise up and leave his town; others have seen the term as evoking Anderson's nostalgic embrace of craftsmanship when his ambition wore off.[8] Yet a third interpretation seems just as likely. In Anderson's fictional towns, characters are commonly designated by a single vocation (baker, harness maker, banker); "Jobby," however, is a more generalized term, in all likelihood referring to the young boy's odd job standing, his makeshift occupational status. In this social position, Anderson could be temporarily everything and yet permanently nothing, a vocational orphan nonetheless blessed with horizontal mobility. This is in fact what one feels in *Winesburg*: a multiplicity of fixed states seen by a knowing and yet recently mobilized eye, a person familiar to these citizens, to their hands and minds, and yet who has himself moved on. What often happens is a momentary empathy that settles not on a fixed class but skips across and around multiple social typings, an empathy that replaces class categories with a pluralistic averaging and appeal to commonality. This is especially important when one recognizes that the word "job" (in the singular) is the honorific Anderson most commonly applied to his own writing. Even as he fantasized of Elysian fields of art, his literary practice remained marked by the office world that had shaped his cultural dream work.

| | |

Among the determinants that have often been ascribed to new-middle-class jobs, dependence (or service) and professionalism have habitually been linked to a third theme: the removal of white collar Americans from the ostensibly "hard" universe of artisan labor, manual work, and farm production. In contradistinction, it is often said, the new middle classes engage in work that is commercial or administrative, concerned with managing people and processing information, or in producing cultural symbols rather than material things. As *White Collar* puts it:

> In the case of the white-collar man, the alienation of the wage-worker from the products of his work is carried one step nearer to its Kafka-like completion. The salaried employee does not make anything. . . . No product of craftsmanship can be his to contemplate with pleasure. . . .
>
> In his work he often clashes with customer and superior, and must almost always be the standardized loser: he must smile and be personable . . . such traits as courtesy, helpfulness, and kindness, once intimate, are now part of the impersonal means of livelihood. Self-alienation is thus an accompaniment of his alienated labor. (xvi–xvii)

> The major shifts in occupations since the Civil War have assumed this industrial trend: as a proportion of the labor force, fewer individuals manipulate *things,* more handle *people* and *symbols.*
>
> This shift in needed skills is another way of describing the rise of the white-collar workers, for their characteristic skills involve the handling of paper and money and people. They are expert at dealing with people transiently and impersonally; they are masters of the commercial, professional, and technical relationship. . . . The one thing they do not do is live by making things; rather, they live off the social machineries that organize and coordinate the people who do make things. (65–66)

Given such striking imagery, it is not surprising that *White Collar* is still for many the locus classicus. The reiteration of Mills's three terms of differentiation for new-middle-class work—"people, paper, and symbols"—has become virtually totemic in some social science circles. More recently this trinity has been combined into what Jean-Christophe Agnew has termed "culturalist" work, the manipulation and improvisation of cultural symbols, technical knowledge, and social meanings within capitalist organization; to many, advertising is the quintessential culturalist work.[9] However, what *White Collar* itself has to say about culturalist production is largely between the lines. The book's main themes are salaried dependence, submission to authority, the enfeebling of middle-class American political will—and, importantly, the "self-alienated" (184) "personality market" of modern corporate life. It is necessary to extrapolate from these more central issues—tease out the musings implied by this final theme in particular—before turning (with the help of recent historians) to advertising itself. Then, to approach Anderson, we need to examine those languages of expertise that were idiomatic to advertising at the turn of the century.

To begin with, Mills's three distinguishing features for white collar work elaborate upon a popular, centuries-old distinction between manual and nonmanual labor. In nineteenth-century class languages, the distinction between "hand" and "head" work was commonplace, signifying a popularly understood gap between craftsmanship, manual labor, and farm work on the one hand and clerical, commercial, or professional employment on the other. As noted earlier, Stuart Blumin has documented a hardening along the manual-nonmanual fault line as early as the Jacksonian era: the physical separation and differentiation of work spaces; divergences of income, property-holding, and family organization; the growing white collar affiliations with the world of entrepreneurs.[10] The distinction was especially prominent within nineteenth-century republicanism, which was suffused with nostalgia for "honest toil" and the "respectable worker," as opposed to supposedly parasitic money-lenders, lawyers, and the like. In truth, a variety of terms—colloquial, intellectual, and political—were used to differentiate between middling, white collar work and agricultural or manual labor: terms like "white-handed" work, Thorstein Veblen's "instinct of workmanship" (applied conversely to craftsmanship), or the label "brainwork" often used by socialists.[11]

One should not underestimate the day-to-day power of colloquial distinctions, especially on those Americans seeking work. Even into the twentieth century, seemingly mundane considerations—like whether a given job would involve "light" or "heavy" work, whether one would be on one's feet or sitting down, whether one worked inside a building or out—no doubt affected the choices made by job seekers. The tendency among some social theorists to deconstruct these differences altogether is probably misguided. Nevertheless, there are limitations to applying any of these popular distinctions one-dimensionally or unilaterally. Even Blumin, who attempts to substantiate the empirical foundation for white and blue collar popular taxonomies, admits that linguistic shifts often reflect changing social experience only imperfectly. Nor is the customary "base" of social analysis so firm. With modern machinery replacing heavy work in industrial settings, the difference between mental and "hand" work commonly diminishes; conversely, the white collar label, coming into use in the Gilded Age, pointed to the growing regimentation of much *office* work. Similarly, one should hardly presume that those whom some blue collar workers still call "white shirts" (or "suits") represented a superior form of knowledge in turn-of-the-century work settings. Rather, as David Montgomery has shown, such labels reflect the colloquial recognition of a contest over social knowledge, particularly the challenge to worker control posed by Taylorism and other managerial efficiency movements.[12]

A uniform application of the handwork and headwork dichotomy also generates the problem of nostalgia, so evident in *White Collar* itself. As various analysts have shown, Mills's study is often dependent upon a myth of middle-class decline from the nineteenth-century golden age of entrepreneurship, craftsmanship, freedom, and even rationality. Mills's personal identification with this myth severely contains his discussion, often forcing him to underestimate the sources of affiliation, pride, or power white collar employees might have found in nonmanual work. In many moments Mills inherits, and in turn uncritically accepts, the often-inflated rhetoric of nineteenth-century republicanism. (As Blumin has shown, republican orators may actually have been responding to a perceived denigration of manual work at large in their society.) Mills's use of an artisanal telos, finally, may be inappropriate to an elite profession like advertising in these years. If lower-level clerical employees often did have working-class roots, it is unclear how many advertisers had farming or manual labor in their immediate memory, much less artisanship.[13]

Nevertheless, Mills is at his most nostalgic when thinking historically. In other moments—moments his more severe critics have often not appreciated—Mills actually delimits the force of his nostalgia on his psychological profile of modern white collar workers. In his chapters on the meanings of work, for instance, Mills explicitly disavows the popular rationales of nineteenth-century liberal economics, which he dismisses as a "soulless business, a harsh justification for the toiling grind of nineteenth century populations, and for the economic man, who was motivated in work by the money he earned" (217). In addition, even though he describes fully both the Calvinist and romantic-socialist justifications for artisanal work, Mills avers that he cannot know whether either ever had any historically verifiable communal impact. He even acknowledges that the imputed disappearance of such traditions, as much as it captures the "*psychological imagination of the historian*" (228; emphasis mine), may have little to do with the consciousness of modern white collar workers themselves. This is a contradiction that critical invocations of the artisanal Mills (or Anderson, for that matter) often overlook. As much as Mills emphasizes (and obviously identifies with) the romantic ethos of artisanal work—that "image of the complete product," its essentially "aesthetic" (221) nature—he admits that this nostalgic landmark may have little relevance for the cultural memory of modern employees.

In less obvious ways, as well, Mills's analysis is often not concerned with the familiar, primary alienation of labor—that is, the contrast with "hard" artisanship—as much as it is with a series of second-order effects generated by the bureaucratization of corporate work. "Second order," because Mills was struck not just by the modern proliferation of selling but by the standardization (and sales) of sales expertise. As Gillam and Agnew point out, Mills hoped to demystify his contemporaries' accounts of a managerial "revolution" by debunking corporate "management" as little more than a glorified rabbit warren of salesmen's clichés. This in itself shows how Mills is interested not just in selling but in the organization of knowledge, how standardized sales techniques served both as "training" and as the corporation's mode of internal self-congratulation (as it were, its inner smile). Mills's term "personality market," often taken merely as a synonym for the selling of a service personality, in fact referred to a larger circulatory process and organization of knowledge: the recruiting of new employees; the promotion of internal office morale; the standardizing of "direct" consumer contact in sales; the "personality" of advertising or public relations; and finally—and most importantly, for Anderson—the creation of standardized expertise, the marketing, of sales wisdom itself. For Mills, even salesmanship had been reified by incorporation; modern businesses had standardized and centralized sales techniques into pat, routinized "presentations" (180) and distributed this diluted form to lower-echelon employees. Sales executives (185) therefore "authorized" a second-remove expertise that to Mills only reinforced the self-alienated state of their dependent white collar employees. The "white collar" generates a new "faith."

Mills's interest in this particular phenomenon clarifies other aspects of Sherwood Anderson. He was not, in his formative phase, merely an advertiser or a bourgeois businessman; rather, he was at the very least an advertiser's advisor, or, more precisely, he was someone who circulated *around* the various positions of a personality market, working to sell sales technique, boost office morale, write reformist tracts, establish his own business, and then return to copywrite for others. Much of his understanding of white collar work, as well as the fellowship he tried to find there, can be traced to how he composed these multivalent "middle management" jobs. Moreover, as Barbara and John Ehrenreich have pointed out, this versatility of new-middle-class specializations also helps to understand professional-managerial Americans' fascination for Progressivism and technocratic socialism in this period. Anderson, who declared himself a socialist while in business, saw himself as a reformer from within corporate ranks—a modern, scientific "expert" who could both humanize and democratize the world of sales. Anderson's case, conversely, can aid in a revision of Mills—whose study was not only nostalgic but lacking in historical particularity. Mills did not take into account the office rationales, class idioms, and personal desires that might have shaped white collar awareness in a given period—or more simply, the kind of expertise particular white collar professions marketed. To Mills such rationales, as they were to someone like Elmer Rice, were merely the intellectual circuitry of "cheerful robots." Advertising per se was so routinized, so Kafkaesque, it apparently merited little investigation.

Thanks to recent historical writing, however, the languages and professional desires operating within advertising's conflicted class terrain are much more visible than forty or even ten years ago. The three decades after 1890 are now recognized as a significant breakthrough period in advertising history, as the one-office printer's-ink shops of the Gilded Age grew into highly bureaucratized agencies. As late as the 1880s, many advertisers had been essentially space brokers subsisting on the margins of the newspaper and magazine industries; their role was to purchase advertising space and resell it to manufacturers and merchandisers. A background in journalism was not uncommon. Even the largest postbellum agencies employed only a handful of people at a time; N. W. Ayer did not hire a full-time copywriter until 1892. By 1915, however, all of the larger agencies housed sales executives, staff writers, even a few art departments—and eclectically incorporated psychological expertise, market research, and imitations of modernist visual styles like impressionism.

With bureaucratic growth came many of the contradictions that *White Collar* describes. Advertisers' salaries, and at least their self-described prestige, soared; a decade after Anderson patted his purse, advertisers made an annual income roughly five times the national median and rarely strayed from their own agency's city. On the other hand, turnover rates were high—the restless horizontal mobility of Anderson and Sinclair Lewis was not at all atypical—and internal pay scales remained steep. Not surprisingly, advertising was habitually recognized as a young man's profession. Working for clients, advertisers were also routinely subjected to what Mills calls the "clashes" with—and the required "smiling" deference to—"customer and superior" (xvii). As Marchand has observed, this problem of deference took on additional dimensions, since copywriters were forced to appeal to clients, bosses, and target audiences, let alone themselves.[14] Little wonder the new scholarship, especially that of Lears, has been exposing the self-doubts beneath the often fantastic hubris of advertising's public professions in these years. In many respects, this scholarship is extending Mills's paradigm: documenting the elaborate cultural justifications (again, the "smiles") that rationalized the exploitative and internally contradictory practices of the sales-based corporate pyramid.

Some of the contradictions necessarily made their way into the competing professional languages traversing advertising during this era. The trade undertook sporadic efforts at professional organization and self-regulation: the organization of the American Association of Advertising Agencies, the "Truth in Advertising" movement of the teens, the periodic resuscitation of "Reason-Why" copy. What Lears and Marchand have documented as the "specter of Barnum" was a constant threat. At their most confident, advertisers envisioned themselves in missionary terms, a role Marchand captures from the early 1920s. As an agency pronouncement put it, "The product of advertising is something . . . powerful and commanding—it is *public opinion;* and in a democracy public opinion is the uncrowned king. . . . It is the advertising agency's business to write the speeches from the throne of that king; to help his subjects decide what they should eat and wear. . . . Archimedes asked for a lever long enough and strong enough to move the world. We have a suspicion that if he lived today he would apply for work in an agency" (Marchand, 31). Advertisers quite commonly saw themselves as uplifters and public educators, proselytizers for a more cosmopolitan standard of living. Some took literary inclinations (along with college education) as a sign of advertising's new professionalism and a way to differentiate themselves from clerical subordinates. As one *Printer's Ink* columnist remarked in 1909, "The advertising department is the creative, advanceguard, way-blazing part of a business, and cannot be run in the same repressive way that the purely clerical departments of the office are run" (Lears, "Some Versions," 356). Then as now, secret dreams of literary escape (like Anderson's) were actually the norm, as were complaints from copywriters about their stifled creativity.

On the other hand, doubts were persistent. To a competing group of advertisers, the encroaching "literariness" of high-cultural pretensions was a way for Barnum to enter through the back door. Claims of kinship to Shakespeare, Dickens, Stevenson, or Jack London were, among this camp, greeted with ridicule. Advertisers like Nathaniel C. Fowler, much as they vaunted initiative over being a mere "clock man," warned that "mere brilliancy is often dangerous" and that cheerfulness, helpfulness, and optimism were really what made an office run smoothly. Hubbardism, filtered through Dale Carnegie, still aimed for more efficient product control and employee accountability; today in advertising, clients are still called "accounts."[15] Even more fundamentally to these advertisers, an apprenticeship within business rooted the advertiser in the direct, no-nonsense face-to-face idioms of sales. To this school of thought, this training was far more important than any artisanal background, the pretensions of a man like Charles Austin Bates to "ad-smithery" notwithstanding. Plain-speaking adjustment to the "mass"—what one 1915 textbook advised as the injunction to the advertiser to "forget style, forget self, think of those readers that he wants to reach . . . the language that they can understand"—was also linked to an upbeat tone. Such commonsensical idioms—the desire to extinguish the literary aura of editing, the desire to speak "plainly" and directly to a hypothetical reader—dominated the thinking of such men as Cyrus Curtis, Edward Bok, and George Horace Lorimer. Curtis publications figured prominently in truth-in-advertising campaigns. In the teens, Cyrus Curtis, who had once recommended Claude Hopkins to Albert Lasker on the basis of a "no-nonsense" ad, would twice seek out Anderson: to write business fiction and to create a series on the American small town.[16]

The heart of this commonsensical style was that it proposed to be client, customer, and product centered. In the mid-teens, under the banner of Reason-Why, many advertisers moved from marketing "trade-character" logos—"Sunny Jim" for "Force Cereal," and the like—to the notion that ads succeeded if they embodied the honesty of the manufacturer, the salesman, or even the advertiser. According to Reason-Why advocate John E. Kennedy, an advertisement was a printed salesman; others, as Pope and Marchand show, argued that an ad-writer should think of himself as working side-to-side with an individual potential buyer. To be sure, Hubbardism was often the root of this demand. Ingersoll-Rand Company executive W. L. Saunders, for instance, told *Printer's Ink* readers in 1915 that advertising should not be left to a "man with a literary turn of mind" instead of a businessman who knew the product.[17] Yet, as Claude Hopkins put it, the real crux was that literary affectation could smack of an appeal from a "higher class" which could only arouse consumer resentment. Hopkins thus denigrated boasting, "fine language," dilettantism. "I am trying to show . . . how ordinary, how plebeian good advertising is. And how ordinary humanity counts. . . . The real people in advertising who I know are humble people. They came from humble people, and they know them" (29). At the heart of this ethic was certainly something that normalized the missionary rhetoric of word mastery: a class language that presented its sales persona as a commoner of democratic instincts and egalitarian sentiments, making direct access to marketed goods a mark of those sentiments. Anderson's magazine courtiers were more comfortable in this idiom—Anderson himself was already drawn to it—yet what is especially striking about his position is how he straddled the competing languages, and conceptions, of advertising's mission. In one position in the personality market, he would speak of "sales mastery"; in another, he would turn the hubris of advertisers on its head and argue that artistry was the property of every occupational endeavor, the common lot of every job.

This second, "commonsensical" idiom also drew upon an arithmetics that was both endemic to advertising and constitutional to Anderson's own literary "averaging." This is especially apparent in the class languages of Reason-Why. Take, for instance, this definition of advertising prose: "True 'Reason-Why' Copy is Logic," E. E. Calkins wrote, "plus persuasion, plus conviction, all woven into a certain simplicity of thought—predigested for the average mind, so that it is easier to *understand* than *misunderstand it*."[18] As Marchand notes, such phrases exemplify advertisers' "conceding" voice, or what some have called the "talking down" so evident even in Reason-Why. All true. But in some ways, the inclusion of the syntactical term "average" is as telling as whatever mental capacities are attributed to the consumer. On the one hand, "average" was a term of commonality, a plain-speaking recovery of the common denominator between manufacturer, advertiser, and consumer. But on another level, "averaging" spoke as well to the market-research typologies and tabulations that were habitually pegged to the target audiences of given magazines. The appeal to the "average" involved the imputed solvent power of the commodity itself to traverse region and class differences in the name of different citizen "types." As Calkins's *Modern Advertising* (1905) reveals, what one chapter dubs "The Mathematics of Advertising" was well under way in these years: the classifying, polling, and targeting of specific audiences along "professional," "leisure," or working-class lines, along the categories of the Census Bureau (which advertisers lobbied to do their work for them), or by habitual consumption patterns themselves. For someone like Hopkins, a "class of people" meant a marketing category, even an idiosyncratic one, as it often did for Anderson.[19]

These seemingly variable meanings of "average" were entirely compatible, largely because they alleviated the ambivalences of advertising writing itself. For example, historians have often debunked someone like Reason-Why advocate Hopkins, showing that, even as he appealed to "humble folk," he also could argue that people were like "sheep." Yet, the language of average taste served to erase this difference: "We judge things largely by others' impressions," Hopkins wrote, "by popular favor. We go with the crowd. So the most effective thing I have ever found in advertising is the trend of the crowd." Evoking the typical, individual consumer was equally compatible with the averaging of his or her needs: "Don't think of people in the mass," Hopkins said, "Think of a typical individual." One might then see a way to reread the missionary rhetoric a scholar like Marchand has recovered. To advertisers' ways of thinking, public opinion was king, the "average" monarch of their own market mathematics. This "averaging of needs" was, in turn, supposedly a mark of editors' and advertisers' common bond with readers. Marketers merely tapped into what Lorimer called "the great silent majority" of readers who otherwise would never state their preferences. Not surprisingly, like Calkins, Lorimer applied averaging's reversibility: paradoxically, he repeatedly affirmed his own membership in that "silent" (numeric) majority.[20]

In part, it is to their credit that current scholars, reversing the simple "rationalist" label applied to Reason-Why in the past, are reluctant to take either business ideology—the "literary" and professional side, or the language of "common sense"—at face value.[21] They have also uncovered the perplexities (Marchand, 31), the elitism, and the appeals to the buyer's "unconscious" lurking covertly in Reason-Why's appeal to common sense (or, for that matter, "horse sense," which actually invokes the skeptical context of horse-trading).[22] Marchand has shown that advertisers implicitly viewed themselves as "conceding" to plain folk; certainly a jarring note occurs when Hopkins says he writes for the "common people," like those that "work on my country place" (177). If, however, one recognizes that both modernist experimentation and plain-speaking were only competing literary styles within advertising (not one "fake" and one "plain"), and if the final object is Anderson's literary representation (and granted, it is not always), then one might well risk going beyond Mills's tendency to see such styles as merely concessions, rationalizations, or technocratic psychic circuitry. They could then be seen as systematic class languages that suffused Anderson's idiom and, gradually, his engagement with such prevailing literary genres as naturalism. Again, only hindsight (including Anderson's own) leads us to believe that the author of *Winesburg* was struggling beneath, or in spite of, the advertiser.

To be sure, the broader impact of advertising on American languages of class, mass, and commonality is beyond the scope of this study. Historians have fully documented any number of topics not broached here: advertising's attribution of magical properties to goods (usually for upward mobility), the profession's hypothesizing of a feminine or irrational public, the trade's ever-expanding dissemination of a cosmpolitan "standard" of living. The living manifestations of this new hegemony are, of course, often elusive, but in Anderson's particular case—his cognitive landscape of class and the voice he would use to represent it through his art—many traces of advertising's white collar domain and self-representation are quite visible. Anderson himself once said: "The advertising business is one that binds itself peculiarly to what I wanted to do in life. I do not understand why more novelists did not go into it" (*LB*, 82).

| | |

Sherwood Anderson's renowned ideological elusiveness is bound to frustrate anyone trying to situate him in his intellectual milieu. Early manuscripts have been lost; around the time of his mental breakdown, Anderson was subject to wild mood swings; later the author prevaricated and mythologized. The fact that the manuscripts of *Windy McPherson's Son* (1916) and *Marching Men* were composed by a self-admitted office daydreamer, on a Dictaphone, and typewritten by no doubt stunned secretaries (*RW*, 180–81) further clouds the picture. Little wonder that some critics, as if throwing up their hands, rely upon the simplified chronologies of Anderson's own memory and consequently puzzle over his smorgasbord of "Marxist," "totalitarian," modernist, humanistic, and romantic vocabularies in the teens—none of which seem to have anything to do with advertising.[23] Yet, the sheer clutter of Anderson's early intellectual life has often served to reinforce the implicit claim of *Winesburg*. Recoiling from the world of business, the argument goes, Anderson turned from slickness to native plain-speaking, from abstract ideas to humanity, from representation to life itself. Anderson's loss of ideological rigidity, his turn from the setting of Chicago to a small town, his affirmation of Winesburg's grotesques all come to the fore, while Anderson's commitments in the teens are erased, his prose made transparent again. Back into the prose equivalent of handwork, for Anderson's return to Winesburg is often described, by critics and the writer himself, as a turn from slick business wordsmithery to literary craft-consciousness.[24]

One cannot hope to reconstruct Anderson's agenda in the teens completely, nor would it be responsible simply to invert the story of Anderson's rejection of business. On the contrary, his ruminations on business often read like testimonials from *White Collar* or even *Death of a Salesman*, and in equally expressionistic terms: "rats that live in a great barn," "clocklike" men, "futile" dream following upon futile dream. As Lears discerns, Anderson rejected both the exploitation and the emotional malleability required of advertising work. Nonetheless, the fact is that Anderson's literary career did not involve a clear rupture or break with business into rebellion; there were years of vacillating morale, rebellion, and reengagement that extended through 1922. It is necessary to cast light on these shadowy years if only to see how the hopes he invested in business, paradoxically, shaped the forms in which even his dissent would emerge. Within the contemporary record and the business novel *Windy McPherson's Son*, a rather different Anderson can be discerned: one who envisioned ad-writing not merely as profit-taking but as human fellowship, high service, and even political leadership; who imbued his rhetoric of commonsensicality from the Reason-Why business idioms of his day; who felt crude "life" existed in offices and cities, not outside them.[25] Moreover, even as these rationales dissipated, they left ambiguous residues on his evolving literary idiom: a decreased sense of political urgency and class conflict; a recoiling from capitalism, and from hopes of reforming it; and an acknowledgement that accompanying his brotherhood with American grotesques was a sense of their fundamental inertness. These ideas did not drive Anderson out into "life" but toward revisions of prevailing literary forms, notably the genre of naturalism.

Anderson's periodic depressions in these years obviously had many causes, but as many of his problems stemmed from bureaucratic malaise as from advertising per se. As much as he fretted over his "dreadful smartness," his playing upon human weakness, his "plausibility" as a "word slinger," Anderson also spoke of the dull routine of office work, a sense of imprisonment, and "grey days." Of his business associates who were planning an ad campaign, he wrote, "We are after all nothing but grey thieves, rats that live in a great barn but the deadly monotony of the thing wearies me terribly." (*LB*, 55). Much of Anderson's unease stemmed from the haste and incompletion that often accompanied what *White Collar* calls the "web" of paperwork; here he occasionally echoed the sense of business as "busy-ness," much as W. D. Howells once had.[26] He spoke of "living in a city of the dead" (*RW*, 215), even of days on which he fantasized about pulling out a revolver and shooting his office mates (*LB*, 8). He wrote to Waldo Frank in 1919: "The queer notion that I am in a prison clings to me and my laugh at it all grows a bit bitter" (*RW*, 209).

Anderson also connected the sheer triviality of juggling accounts with the frenetic pace of the office. "In a business office such as ours," he wrote, "the mental conditions are at the very worst. Men are occupied with matters so trivial and so very unimportant that their minds run about in little crazy circles" (*RW*, 214). His letters to Marietta Finley are full of such complaints about steady work, about "writing in a frenzy" on "a remedy for curing diseases of hogs," about the confused jumbles of merchandise that ran through his head (*LB*, 30). Such complaints arose recurrently over Anderson's twenty-year business career, only becoming more visible in the late teens. "The life of every busy man who really gets into the game," he wrote in one of his essays from 1903, "is one everlasting, unceasing effort to catch up the broken strings of things, tie the ends and feel at last that there is something finished, something done. In this as is everything else worth while, no man really succeeds. A few clever, clocklike men appear to succeed, but they don't. . . . Enthusiasm follows enthusiasm in hot succession; dream follows dream; and the life's ambition to-day is left broken and torn on the Jericho road while we with eager eyes are tearing and scraping at the obstacles at some ever endless path." Here, Anderson called each day an "endless, heart-breaking mess . . . lapping always into the next day, the next month and the next year" (MM, 233–34). Such trivialities also brought the confinement of the subordination to client and boss which Mills would describe. "Did the fat man with the gruff voice want to sell coffee, plows, automobiles or phonographs?" Anderson queries. Later he asks: "Why do these men not discharge me?" and adds: "It is perhaps due to a terrible dullness that exists among them" (*LB*, 62).

Anderson's white collar discontent did not always stem from romantic or even artisanal longings. On the contrary, echoing the creative-clerical distinction that pervaded advertising—signifying the new-middle-class dissension I discuss in Chapter 3—what Anderson often feared was lapsing into clerical status. As he connected "brutishness" to labor and working-class consciousness, he associated "dullness" with clerical subordination, with losing his "creative" upper-middle position. "Wage slavery" rarely if ever enters his worries; rather, he fears office routinization bringing on the mental blankness that he associates with workers beneath him. In his fiction Anderson portrayed lower-level clerical positions as exemplary of buried ambition and emotional blankness. In *Windy McPherson's Son,* one character describes public schools as "musty beds in which old clerkliness lies asleep"; protagonist Sam McPherson envisions the city divided between the men who run things and "the clerks going on year after year on small salaries getting nowhere." As Blumin and Braverman have suggested, white and blue collar labels may well have negotiated the proletarianization that eroded the traditional prospects of the business clerk in this period. Anderson himself uses the French *employé* as both noun and adjective, to signify dependent status and even inconsequentiality; such characters often remain unnamed.[27]

Finally, Anderson's periods of depression were also characteristically linked to the exhaustion following bouts of uplift or Positive Thinking.[28] His early advice columns often took on the tone of self-exhortation. Anderson wrote that the most characteristic experience of business was to be tossed about by one's own vacillating morale; each crisis had to be turned into renewed energy for the next task. "Day after day, week after week, year after year," he wrote in 1903, "[the businessman] faces his own failures and yet believes down in the heart of him that he is in the greatest business on earth and that next year will set all straight and turn all his penny marbles into diamonds" (MM, 233–34). Importantly, Anderson's years in the office told him that his experience was far from atypical. On the contrary: "Nearly all of the qualities of the Americans of my time are embodied in me. My struggle, my ignorance, my years of futile work to meaningless ends—all these are American traits." He also remembered coaxing himself back: "I wept, I swore, I worked myself into new fits of enthusiasm concerning the thing I was doing" (*LB*, 27). Similarly, in a column called "Finding Our Work" (1903), he writes: "[I]n the great majority of cases, it isn't so much a question of finding your work as it is of finding yourself, your faith, your courage" (MM, 235). Like Rice and Lewis, Anderson seems especially focused on the necessity of summoning will and confidence to offset fears of clerical subordination, fears of falling into a sleepy, mass dream-life. Anderson's periodic crises, what Fabians identified as the double life forced upon the creative yet bureaucratized salariat, sent him looking for many sources of faith, and when he began in these years to call himself a socialist, in all likelihood he meant he was drawn to its middle-class, technocratic, and spiritual variants.[29] (Even later in life, Anderson took pains to distinguish himself from the "rough egalitarianism" of, say, Sandburg or even Whitman.)[30]

To Anderson this political foray was not at all inconsistent with his business career; rather, he had periodically addressed his doubts as a second-order expert and reformer within white collar work. His roles as advertising columnist and reader's advisor were ready-made for a mediating role. Anderson's plausible temperament quickly absorbed the service and professional ideals that ran through contemporary advertising debates. As early as 1905, he argued that, "with the growth of organizations and organization men," there arose the demand for a "great and needed profession" of the advertising man, whom he compared to a "business physician" who could cure the ills of the selling system. Such a figure would be "clean and with soul untainted by the lust of money," a "proud lover of his profession," and a "quick and sure judge of human nature." A "compromise between the corporation lawyer and the advertising man," Anderson's name for this figure was "The Sales Master."[31] Repeatedly, Anderson tried to stake out a high ground, not only above the malaise of clerical routinization, but the influence of seedy (unclean) drummers and survival-of-the-fittest advocates in business. In the teens, he labeled one of his own business experiments "Commercial

Democracy"—apparently a joint stock company among dealers, inspired by a magazine that would preach "my idea of altruism in manufacturing and retailing."[32]

Anderson's own second-order expertise was also, symptomatically, a mix of leveling colloquialism and high-minded reform of the sales transaction. As for Lorimer, Claude Hopkins, or Cyrus Curtis, Anderson disseminated his advice in a cracker-barrel, no-nonsense, face-to-face voice. In his ads, Anderson favored the Reason-Why style, spoke about truth and a "square deal," and said an ad was best if it was "well written, plain excellent stuff that tells the story in an earnest, convincing way and then stops" (*RW*, 108). His advice columns, meanwhile, ranged horizontally across "Business Types." These in-trade fables, modifying their advice format with humor, horse sense, and small-scale human oddities, were framed for a companionate reader who was a businessman himself. Anderson's taxonomies for business types, meanwhile, were not wholly idiosyncratic, though to achieve commonsensicality they reached for just that effect. Actually, Anderson's thought rotated on two axes: personality stereotypes (e.g., "The Good Fellow" or "The Discouraged Man"), and sales specializations in the personality market ("The Travelling Man" or "The Trimmer"). In other words, Anderson's usually cautionary tales criss-crossed between types too fixed in their occupations and figures who left the imprint of human eccentricity upon their jobs. Throughout, however, Anderson praised those who dealt honestly and genially with colleagues and customers; occasionally semi-autobiographical, his columns sometimes told of a young town boy who was learning his way amid the odd customs and perplexities of sales life. Anderson consistently praised humane, democratic sales transactions that exhibited honesty and cheerfulness in getting the job done; frequently he decried the lust for money (MM 246–47). One column told the story of competition for a job between a "hot" young up-and-comer, who makes "literature" (MM, 258) out of his ads, and a "cold" old drummer, who confesses he would rather be retiring on a park bench; neither gets the position (MM, 261). Another told the story of an ad man who admires the cursing of a simple train brakeman, yet says the man wastes his talent in a job where nobody will hear him "except maybe a few scared steers." The tale ends by saying the brakeman might "reform" and go into advertising; instead, he will remain "The Undeveloped Man" (MM, 249).

Anderson's business experiments in the teens attempted to put these ideas into practice; in the market, however, they lost much of their reformist tenor. As a roofing-tar manufacturer, Anderson followed the current sales wisdom of embodying his own personality as a trademark of reliability, a personal guarantee. As Sutton has discovered, Anderson devoted an entire page of his roofing catalogue to an autographed picture and a statement entitled "My Word to You," which promised: "As you and I may never meet face to face I give you my word now that what is written in this book is true in spirit and fact." Here, as well, is a sequence that Sutton finds "characteristic" of Anderson's advertising pitch as a whole:

> Just let us reason this matter out for a moment.
>
> The average jobber to live must make from 10 to 25 per cent on the goods he buys from the manufacturer.
>
> The average traveling man receives a salary of from $25.00 to $50.00 per week. . . .
>
> The average local dealer makes from 25 to 100 per cent on everything he passes over his counter.
>
> It costs us but a very few pennies to put this catalogue into your hands.
>
> For us the catalogue is jobber, traveler and dealer. It works for us and works so cheaply that there is no wonder we can give you a better quality of goods and still save money for you. (*RW*, 153)

Anderson pins his commercial democracy on the efficiency of direct mail. Trying to cut through to the buyer/reader with direct appeals, Anderson hopes to master and reform the market by a program of direct exchange founded on effective wordsmithery. Grounded in both Reason-Why and the more subtle averaging of human wants and capabilities, he proposes the catalogue, his *writing*, as a medium to displace traveler, dealer, and "jobber," a middleman.

At times, therefore, Anderson's program did not look particularly radical at all. As his novels suggest, Anderson's socialism was all too soluble with his creative business ideology. At its most positive moments of uplift, Anderson's program looked very much like the portrait of the social order put forth in something like Ferber's "Sisters Under Their Skin." Grounded in an aphoristic dismissal of social hierarchy, clean-mindedness that rose above petty political reforming, and reassertions of the core of human commonality, Anderson often ended up simply reaffirming the given structure of capitalism. In one essay, for example, he countered Henry George's assertion that employees could not be employers this way: "[O]ne good, clean-minded business man, who gets down to work cheerfully in the morning, who treats the people about him with kindness and consideration, who worries not about world politics, but faces the small ills of his day and the people about him, who tries to understand the janitor with his cap in his hand as well as the corporation manager and who sees the manhood in both, is probably doing more downright good than all of the canting moralists that ever breathed." Belittling "dismal prophets" like George, Anderson went on to add: "Every man is a unit in the nation and a unit in the firm."[33] Here the modern corporation was the model of democracy even more explicitly than with Emma McChesney. Anderson accepts the occupational ladder as both given and open; his discounting of moralists in the name of "understanding" reeks of its own paternalism. To understand how this program developed—how it left its mark, even as its vision disintegrated—it is necessary to turn to Anderson's fiction.

| | |

Anderson's first published novel, *Windy McPherson's Son,* shows the businessman-author trying to develop the different strands of his thought within the epic scale of naturalism. As if working from the script of David Graham Phillips's *The Great God Success* (1901), Frank Norris's *The Pit* (1903), or Theodore Dreiser's *The Financier* (1912), Anderson's book traces the rise and fall of a young Iowa boy turned industrial giant in the Chicago manufacturing world of the 1890s. From internal evidence, Anderson's genre choice seems completely intentional; as the novel's internal commentary acknowledges, naturalism had been so thoroughly popularized by the mid-teens that one of its habitual plot lines—the evolution of an industrial leader—had been literalized, to the point where such books began to be written by businessmen themselves (235). This blurring of boundaries between true-to-life fiction and melodramatic, autobiographical exposé, in such books as Chicago author Robert Herrick's *The Memoirs of an American Citizen* (1905) and Thomas Lawson's *Frenzied Finance* (1903), made naturalism seem well suited for Anderson's self-reflexive examination. His protagonist, Sam McPherson, a small-town newsboy who "dreamed of dollars" (65), is explicitly seen by his town as a typical Alger hero (17). Yet Anderson casts his businessman, as writers like Dreiser and Norris had, in the popular-naturalist synthesis of realistic detail and romantic "force," predation, and mastery.[34] Part "Norse marauder" (125) and part Spencerian ego, Sam evolves into a dominant American species, "the kind of man of whom America boasts before the world" (233).

At least in spots, Anderson mimicked the value-neutral posture symptomatic of Spencerian prose, which had rarely disguised the naturalists' covert fascination with force. Anderson's form also initially provided the framework of a polarized social landscape of industrial barons and the masses beneath them. Meanwhile, Anderson worked rather comfortably within naturalism's decidedly unromantic conflation of artistic and business temperaments. Especially like Dreiser, Anderson sees both "force" and the drive to order as coursing through both great art and great business foresight—through "vision" generally. The businessman's skills are compared to "the stroke also of the master painter, scientist, actor, singer, prizefighter" (113). With this intellectual framework came naturalism's formal apparatus as well. Through most of the book, naturalist poetics holds Anderson's plot to a linear, evolutionary course, while providing his narration with severe formal distance, even interludes to expound on plot turns as evolutionary "phenomena." In short, naturalism provided a form in which to portray social process as an organic whole; Sam McPherson is seen both as "genius" and genus, an American super-type paradigmatic of industrial evolution.

Yet the genre did not conform perfectly to Anderson's modified agenda nor to his own experience. After all, he was in business but no giant himself. In addition, as his title suggests, Anderson (like Lewis) seems more intent upon rescripting Darwinian naturalism from the vantage point of a new generation. His novel treats Chicago's rough-and-tumble years as a news item already familiar to his readers, already an historical phase gone by. Albeit interested in what distinguished the "developed" man from the brutish masses, Anderson also occasionally separates such a man from the popular image of "brute trader." In contrast, Anderson writes, the real leaders were "instead, men who thought and acted quickly and with a daring and audacity impossible to the average mind" (220). In truth, McPherson represents the dilemma faced by a middle-manager, wordsmith, and efficiency expert in being drawn into the familiar social plot line that naturalism had depicted. His fate, in turn, is pitted not so much against competing industrial barons as it is between classes, between his role as either capitalist hero or social uplifter, interpreter of the masses.

Consequently, Anderson's novel gradually turns into a cautionary tale about this in-between, middle status. About the temptation of the predatory role, Anderson is quite explicit, as when he breaks into the editorializing reminiscent of his advice columns:

> There may be business men in America who do not get what they can, who simply love power. One sees men here and there in banks, at the heads of great industrial trusts, in factories and in great mercantile houses of whom one would like to think thus. They are the men who one dreams have had an awakening, who have found themselves; they are the men hopeful thinkers try to recall again and again to the mind.
>
> To these men America is looking. It is asking them to keep the faith, to stand themselves up against the force of the brute trader, the dollar man, the man who with his one cunning wolf quality of acquisitiveness has too long ruled the business of the nation. (131)

While one cannot overlook the Positive Thinking saturating this passage, Anderson as businessman-author is not cautioning against power hunger itself but against its monetary debasement and its promotion of further social disorder. To Anderson, Sam, who does exhibit the wolf quality (130), is "sick." Before long, Sam sees what the narrator sees: "[t]he great forward movement in modern industry of which he had dreamed of being a part had for him turned out to be a huge meaningless gamble with loaded dice against a credulous public" (237). Anderson's cautionary moralism is not derived from the perspective of a suppressed artist in business but from a man who implicitly allies himself—intellectually and formally—with the controlling intelligences that can visualize the whole of industrial development, see it as a potential social good gone wrong.

Nor is *Windy McPherson's Son* informed, as a novel like *Dark Laughter* (1925) would be, by any significant republican or artisanal nostalgia—quite the contrary. Young Sam is instead propelled by his revulsion from his broken-down father, a Civil War veteran who has degenerated into a "windy," grotesque house painter and drunkard. In a telling episode at the start of the novel, Windy McPherson embarrasses himself and his son by failing to blow a bugle during a town gathering (24); later, Sam's boast is explicitly played off against "another Windy McPherson failing to blow his bugle before the waiting crowd" (233). Despite the book's dedication to Anderson's own hometown folks, Sam experiences considerable revulsion from the "endless sameness and uneventfulness" (75) of one town elder, the lives of gossiping newspaper readers, women who work with "only their fingers occupied" and live an existence of "unspeakable blankness" (102). Reversing artisanal categories, Sam's first real boss in sales is named Freedom, a man who becomes "proud as a father" (72–73) of Sam's growth. Meanwhile, his true mentor, an artist-turned-businessman named John Telfer, tells him not to settle for "the habit of small success" or to squander his word-slinging talents as a mere "village cut-up" (61)—in short, to be an undeveloped man. Instead, Telfer has a vision that projects Sam past town's horizons; it begins with a comparison to the town's dollar man, the banker:

> "I am not like banker Walker," [Telfer] declared. "He thinks of the growing corn in terms of fat steers . . . I think of it as something majestic . . . I think of a vast river of life. . . .
>
> "And then in the fall when the corn stands shocked I see another picture. Here and there in companies stand the armies of the corn. It puts a ring in my voice to look at them. 'These orderly armies has mankind brought out of chaos,' I say to myself. 'On a smoking black ball flung by the hand of God out of illimitable space has man stood up these armies to defend his home against the grim attacking armies of want.' " (57–58)

One cannot imagine a longer Darwinian view than this. And periodically, throughout his business career, Sam will call up this image of successful bugling, seeing a vision of Telfer again in the advertising man who can recite Poe, mold public opinion, and have the rich men of Chicago seek him out (121–23); he will fantasize about running factories, banks, railroads (130). Consequently, contrary to naturalism's more customary fears, the threat to Sam is not proletarianization; rather, it is having been propelled so violently away from his father's failure that he will become "only" a dollar man.

Meanwhile the dream of sales mastery, the novel seems to say initially, can be sustained—as if turned from its predatory evolution—with the transfusion of socialist ideals. Much like Sinclair Lewis or Floyd Dell (the latter having read the novel in manuscript), Anderson employs two relatively unnaturalistic devices—the "village atheist" (Telfer) and the "modern" marriage—to suffuse the once-Algeristic plot with socialist prophecy in a decidedly technocratic and service-oriented key. Socialist vocabularies collaborate with Anderson's investigation of what constitutes, in a capitalist culture, a developed or "realized man"; socialist ideals provide the moral backdrop for the mid-life crisis Sam begins to experience. However, such ideals have really been there all along. Early on, Telfer tells Sam that he is as "superior to the run of boys in the town" as his own colt is to the "farm horses that are hitched along Main Street on Saturday afternoons" (53). The reader discovers that the colt is named "Bellamy's Boy," following Telfer's affection for *Looking Backward* (52)—a book with its own militaristic ardor. Later, Sam is identified as anticipating the "modern idea of efficiency" (138) and seen, a Tayloresque hero, with watch in hand eliminating needless motion in the office (139). When he marries his boss's daughter, Sue Rainey, a marriage much like those Lewis would write about, Sam is introduced to the socialist ideals of service and uplift, which his wife associates with being "clean" in body and mind—a native nobility that, in particular, passes their vision on to a child. In Sam, Sue generates a new perception: "[T]o be simple, direct, and natural, like the trees or the beast of field, and then to have the native honesty of such a life illuminated and ennobled by a mutual intelligent purpose to make their young something finer. . . . In the shops and on the streets the hurrying men and women took on a new significance to him. He wondered what secret mighty purpose might be in their lives. . . . He looked at the girls and the women at work over the typewriting machines in the office, with questioning eyes, asking himself why they did not seek marriage openly and determinedly" (182–83). Such natural and "simple" imagery of "native honesty" melded with an essentially technocratic vision. Even in retrospect, Sam remembers "the thought that they were two very unusual and thoughtful people engaged upon a worthy and ennobling enterprise," a "vigorous, disciplined, new life" created by the "combined efficiency" (208) of their bodies and spirits. The really free men, Sam muses later, are the technicians, the inventors of the "wonders of mechanical progress" (231).[35]

Even when Sam leaves his business to recover this lost sense of purpose, much of his time is spent exploring these ideas of mutual adaptation to a natural order through discipline and efficient combination of interests. For Anderson—and even more so in his other novel from these years, *Marching Men*—this phase of *Windy McPherson's Son* seems to have performed as a quite literalized dream-work, the playing out of a working fantasy of applying his culturalist skills to more explicitly political action.[36] It is not only his insider's knowledge of business that makes him, potentially, more effective as a subversive but it is also a matter of the political ambidextrousness of his culturalist, wordsmith skills. In *Windy McPherson's Son,* when Sam drafts political speeches or conducts a direct-mail campaign on behalf of striking workers, he simply applies (as Anderson's roofing catalogue demonstrates) methods from his colleagues in advertising (280); in *Marching Men,* when a manufacturer is terrorized by a mass mobilized by Norman McGregor, another advertising man implicitly understands the ploy and is glad to see his boss uneasy (190). Albeit with socialist accents, Anderson aligns culturalist work with the functions of symbol-making in modern liberal ideology: to manufacture consent, avert capitalism's predatory tendencies, and mold the "average" mind.

However, as Anderson stretches this dream-work to near-incredulity, the fabric disintegrates altogether. McPherson runs up against his own ruthlessness; his predatory deterioration is forecast from those early days in sales when he saw "a little of Windy McPherson's grotesque pretentiousness" in every customer and learned to "take advantage of it" (72). It is emblematic of the novel's downturn that the McPhersons' child of the future dies at birth; potentially the son of Windy, will have no son himself. For Sam's internal struggle, predatory sickness is only part of the story; more subtly, Sam's corrosive business sense works against sentimental hopes for human betterment. He risks recapitulating a social bugling that is every bit as windy as his father's. A key break in the love plot comes when a cynical advertising colleague guys Sue's socialist crowd by mimicking its Positive Thinking (217). Even more tellingly, Sam is also separated from his wife's utopianism—and subsequently, from her—by his persistent skepticism about the credulous public mind, particularly that of the brutish workingman. As Anderson writes:

> To express his determination to continue being Sue's companion and partner, Sam during one winter taught a class of young men at a settlement house in the factory district of the west side. The class in his hands was unsuccessful. He found the young men heavy and stupid with fatigue after the day of labour in the shops and more inclined to fall asleep in their chairs, or wander away, one at a time, to loaf and smoke. . . .
>
> Once Sam heard a group of them talking of these women workers on a landing in a darkened stairway. The experience startled Sam and he dropped the class. . . .
>
> "Why should I love these men?" he asked himself. . . . "These heavy-featured young men are a part of the world as men have made it. Why this protest against their fate when we are all of us making more and more of them with every turn of the clock?" (214–15)

As fatalistic as this story seems, its "moral" (215) is recapitulated time and again through the rest of the novel (and on Anderson's own trolley). Sam sees only dullness and hypocrisy in tramps (266); a local minister tells him his parishioners dream only of a heavenly " 'city in the sky, a kind of glorified Dayton, Ohio' " (269) or retirement oasis. Where Sam once saw promise and dreamed about awakening social purpose, he now sees the "real" Americans as those "stunted or imperfectly developed bodies," those "who toil without hope of luxury and wealth" (244). As the book portrays Sam running his direct-mail strike campaign, the reader sees that he is always caught in the middle, between distrust of his intentions by both capital and labor. The former distrusts his labor sympathies; the latter, his slickness and managerialism. Sam's first exposure to political work is, in his words, emblematic of an "abortive" quality to life as a whole (262–63).

This abortive or atrophied middle state becomes idiomatic for Anderson's more complicated moral geography in *Winesburg, Ohio,* but in *Windy McPherson's Son,* Sam's atrophy begins to engender a stillborn social vision, doubts about public will that Anderson's advertising experience and his modified Fabianism may only have reinforced. Caught in a landscape of industrialized brutishness, bureaucratic blankness, and predatory disease, Sam very nearly exhausts his potential affiliations with all the vertical ranks of his social register. Though he embarks on a vagabonding journey to "find Truth"—turning instead to a horizontal strategy, fanning out across a range of occupations (bartender, day laborer, and so on)—he really has little place to go, given the fact that his bugling strikes up no responsive chorus. His political work, Anderson writes, constitutes his "first serious effort at anything like social service achieved through controlling or attempting to influence the public mind, for his was the type of mind that runs to the concrete, the actual" (263). He eventually decides that "at bottom [he] did not believe the people wanted reform. . . . The public mind was a thing too big, too complicated and inert for a vision or an ideal to get at and move deeply" (264). In short, Anderson's protagonist recoils from both "managing" a credulous public and hoping to uplift it; advertising and political mastery, direct mail and speech-writing, go down to defeat together. ("Dropping the class" thus becomes a synecdoche for this final movement.) In the end, Sam returns to his wife, taking three orphans back with him; embracing failure as a common lot, he can only hope to be "a truly humble man" who is "filled with human perplexities" (328). As a businessman intones in *Marching Men,* following a similarly "abortive" (199) political fantasy, " 'No man is big enough to grasp all of life. . . . It cannot be comprehended so. One has to realize that he lives in a patchwork of many lives and many impulses' " (222).[37]

Anderson's readers and critics will certainly seize upon those idiomatic phrases here—the "concrete, the actual," the "patchwork"—as harbingers of *Winesburg*'s design, but for the moment, it is important to examine the genealogy of such developing commitments. In the first place, in the closing moments of *Windy McPherson's Son*, Anderson turns against his own naturalist form. Paradoxically, both naturalism's rhetorical distance and Anderson's desire to see his business baron as a historical genus allowed the novel just this opportunity to backtrack. In one passage at mid-novel, he equates "bowing" before the romance of destiny and predatory mastery with being a "novelist" (191). Later, when Anderson acknowledges that current phenomenon of "captains of industry turned penmen, Caesars become ink-slingers" (235), both irony and self-accusation surface. Anderson now seems particularly cynical about how, in an echo of such authors' own predatory ills, they "bruited the story to an admiring world" (235). Finally, by the novel's end, naturalist exposé is directly connected to the disease it means to cure:

> As a matter of fact were not many writers and reformers unconsciously in league with the procurer, in that they treated vice and profligacy as something, at bottom, charming? . . .
>
> He thought of men like Zola who saw this side of life clearly and how he, as a young fellow in the city, had read the man . . . and had been helped by him. . . . And then there rose before him the leering face of a keeper of a second-hand book store in Cleveland who some weeks before had pushed across the counter to him a paper-covered copy of "Nana's Brother," saying with a smirk, "That's some sporty stuff."
>
> . . . His heart was bitter at the thought of men throwing the glamour of romance over the sordid, ugly things he had been seeing in that city and in every city he had known. (295–96)

In recoil from sales mastery, socialism, and now its initial literary form, Anderson's book virtually implodes: the very project of "throwing romance" and charm around predation even takes on an aura of self-castigation, as though chastising the attempt to "master" the reader's mind.[38] In narrative terms, instead of climaxing around the high melodrama of industrial confrontation, or conflict between the private life and political designs, the novel turns back upon its epic scope right at Sam's turn to vagabonding. Now it inserts a more episodic, ruminating form that attends to "little incidents" (293). It would be tempting to see Anderson's turn, as it so often has been, as a fall out of representation altogether, a turn towards "real" life and its intrinsically antiformal nature. In truth, it is more accurate to say that Anderson snapped back from naturalist idioms to his less grandiose, Reason-Why approach, his earlier preference for probing human perplexity, the tension between "job" and human desire, in isolated case studies. The difference now was that he had considerably less faith in reason, or in the why, or in reform.

Seen in this fashion, Anderson's resuscitation of his original business idiom—given his bouts of bureaucratic malaise—left him in something of a double bind. Paradoxically, as Anderson admitted to Finley, business writing might actually be bound "peculiarly" to "what [he] wanted to do" in his art, and Anderson retained his business ties to Long-Critchfield until 1922. Recommitting himself to life in smaller moments did not necessarily mean abandoning his job; on the contrary, throughout the teens Anderson expressed a sustained distrust of "pure" literariness and literary "sophistication" comparable only to Frank Norris's essays. Anderson's code words for his continuing attachment to office work were "American" and "crude" life. "I am thinking of American Art," he wrote to Finley in 1916. "It must remain crude to be American. The land is not sophisticated. As a man writes or works in any field of art endeavor he is likely to become less American. His very refinement stands in his way" (*LB*, 34–35). Privately, he ridiculed the notion that artists should have long hair or give up working for money (*LB*, 13): "Put the badge of a poet on a man and you crush the poetry in him" (*LB*, 28). Admitting he was "tarred" by the world, he insisted that "my only chance lies in staying in my own puddle here. I have got to live as the men right here in this office live. I have got to make my living as they do" (*LB*, 15).

Anderson's public statements actually differed very little from these self-deprecatory admissions. In an essay for the Chicago *Daily News* in 1917 entitled "Apology for Crudity," he aired his revised agenda. "To draw ourselves apart, to live in little groups and console ourselves with the thought that we are achieving something intellectually, is to get nowhere. By such a road we can only go on producing a literature that has nothing to do with life as it is lived in the United States" (*LB*, 334). To Finley, Anderson now reaffirmed his claim that the world was large enough for a horizontal spectrum of vocations that embodied the artistic calling in average lives: "In America we have so little come to understand the term artist that we set all artists aside, grouping them blindly into one mass . . . there are many kinds of artists, the small store keeping artist, the artist who keeps a little garden and produces say, imagist poems for the early spring market, the artist who is smart and sharp like, say, a Chicago advertising man, and writes stories for the Saturday Evening Post or like George Ade and Ring Lardner who is professionally funny for the Chicago Tribune" (*LB*, 13). This was certainly a "jobby" vision of the literary vocation and of the American class structure, entirely consonant with the "typicalities" and taxonomies of Anderson's business writing.

Anderson's platform now ran to separating himself from socialist action as well, an idea perhaps most clearly expressed in late 1916. In response to a letter from Upton Sinclair, who questioned the depth of his socialist commitment, Anderson said he still voted Socialist, yet added: "[B]ut if I thought the fact of my doing so set me apart in the way your letter suggests I'd quit in a hurry." "I do so want to see writers quit drawing themselves apart," he elaborated, "becoming socialist, or conservatives or whatnot. I want them to stay in life. I want them to be something of brother[s] to the poor brute who runs the sweatshop as well as to the equally unfortunate brutes who work for him" (*LB*, 33). In this way, Anderson saw industrialism as a force that damaged all involved—a more holistic view reminiscent of antebellum anxieties about slavery brutalizing the masters as much as the slaves. Again, in something of an "under the skin" maneuver reminiscent of Ferber, he still argues for human brotherhood based on this recognition. "Loving" and "understanding" replace exposing, molding, and changing.

Nevertheless, Anderson's embrace of the "concrete" brought with it an implicit acknowledgement of public inertness, of lives too much swept up by other's voices (town voices, advertising voices, political voices)—a negative awakening only too apparent in the disillusioning passage of Sam McPherson. In his "Apology for Crudity," Anderson says, "the artist must become . . . more like our fellows, more simple and real" (*LB*, 334), both of these laudatory terms carrying residues not just of a turn from "fixed" thought, but from ideas that told him matter was subject to the force of will. "I quit wanting to change people," Anderson later wrote, "I began more and more to want to understand rather than change" (*RW*, 176–77). Anderson's exploration of his class role did not disappear entirely; indeed, he remained intent upon distinguishing the "meaningful" or "developed" life from those that were not. Doing so, however, brought with it the subtle and often pathetic sense that, as Sam McPherson comes to feel, he is a "'result, not a cause'" (242).

| | |

Generations of criticism have established how Anderson's quest for literary models more suited to the short story form became quite eclectic in the late teens. It is useful to think of *Winesburg, Ohio* as a "patchwork" (though not in Ferber's sense) not just of stories but of genres. Rather than readapting a singular literary model, Anderson in all likelihood synthesized many sources: the regional pathos of Edgar Lee Masters's *Spoon River Anthology* (1915); the visual emblems and perspectival shifts of modernist painting (Whistler, for instance, is mentioned [113] in *Windy McPherson's Son*); the open "songs" of his own impressionistic poetry in *Mid-American Chants* (1918). As David D. Anderson has shown, Sherwood Anderson admired the language rhythms and shadow puppetry of Cloyd Head and Maurice Browne's drama, "The Grotesques" (1915), where he saw Fate personified as a puppeteer, "carelessly" waving about characters who were "half-human and half-artificial" into a procession of "various poses, the main incidents of their lives." Other influences have also been identified.[39]

This eclecticism, however, did have a core method. Anderson was propelled—as Rice and Lewis were—by a rejection of naturalistic forms toward more internal, psychological representation. Meanwhile, like these writers he relied upon cultural typification as a means of diagnosing the psyche of a putative national genus, the "prescriptive" cultural formula, the "outside" voices that penetrated even colloquial speech, as predicates of a typical American gestalt.[40] This paradoxical mixture of psychological individuation and cultural *vraisemblance*—in all likelihood, what Mencken saw when he called *Winesburg* an "anatomizing" diagnosis of "the microcosm"—also reflected these white collar writers' anxiety over the "deadness" of middle-class routine, over how different lives "added up" or stayed "undeveloped" in the crowd. To represent this paradoxical "microcosm," Anderson, Rice, and Lewis all employed an open, "collating" method of "collecting" normative speech patterns, daydreams, even folk tales of modern "mass" existence. (If Rice's term was "compounding," Anderson's word for his quest was finding "testaments.") In Anderson's case, typicality takes on such individuation that it is difficult to recognize his generalizing motive—especially in the case of his protagonist, George Willard.[41]

To achieve this compounding of commonality, the boundary between his fiction and his business life remained open. This fluid boundary (and Anderson's own vacillating opinions) often contributed to *Winesburg*'s formal balance, tension, even beauty. At the simplest level, his persistent interest in addressing his reader directly, and in "crudity" rather than a polished literary appearance, became the dominant impression *Winesburg*'s prose would make—even controlling how he conceived his audience in the first place. In his letters from the teens, Anderson readily acknowledged how he had shifted to the short-story form for the simple reason that it "fit better" (*RW*, 432) into his life—particularly, into the crevices of a life fragmented by the demands of work. Anderson later described the manuscript as having been written in a rooming house, "or in hotels as he travelled about, visiting clients of his employers" (*RW*, 435). In an essay, "From Chicago," in the *Seven Arts* (1917), Anderson articulated a vision of art as a transcription or collection of stories gathered from the fragmentary encounters of one's own life—even the imaginary transcription of others' private thoughts. Anderson envisions his artists, his subjects, and his audience as occupying interchangeable positions, becoming readers of each others' dream-scripts: for one such subject, "[t]o talk to the novelist was like talking aloud to herself" (a skill demonstrated by George Willard). More than a few of Anderson's imagined subjects are situated in stores or offices; moreover, Anderson occasionally implies that he himself is there, seated next to them, imagining their daydreams. Of one of his artists he wrote:

> He wants to tell the store manager of her [the woman talking to herself] and the little wiry man who has a desk next to his own. In the Wabash Avenue store there is a man who sits on a high stool. . . . Again and again I proclaim the richness of life that men miss. Have you not also walked in the street reconstructing the conversations, the meetings, the brief awkward moments through which you have passed?
>
> You were making literature then. In the actual moment you had been crude and awkward and so as you walked muttering you reconstructed the moment, made it more lovely, more live with meaning. (*LB*, 73)

Situating this reconstructive dream-work in Anderson's sales life does not mean to indicate that his art (in the hyperbole of postmodernism) was "contaminated" by commercialism; nor did he impose any simple ideological uniformity on his subjects—quite the contrary. Instead, Anderson attempted to create human commonality by connecting the dots of different dreamlives, by collecting what he calls a "testament"—"an inner story of struggle and failure" (*LB*, 81)—that echoed his own ongoing bouts of vacillating dream and morale. This process of reconstructing, overhearing, transcribing a blurred "inter-text" of his own and imagined thoughts is meant to involve *latitude* in the telling, as *Winesburg* does. Just as Anderson saw Head and Browne's grotesques as "motifs" who are "half-human and half-artificial," and who "begin to speak out of their lives, to burst into tiny rebellions" which the artist "controls with difficulty" (39), so too do Anderson's prose testaments provide, like biblical gospels, different versions of the same "common" experience of suffering and sporadic rebellion.[42]

In a more obvious way, returning to something closer to the column form gave his voice opportunities to expound even more variously than naturalism's design did. *Winesburg* contains various digressions concerning changes in modern womanhood, magazine reading, and avant-garde pretensions (92, 71). In return, Anderson implicitly connected the self-reflexiveness of this experiment to his earlier sales columns, indeed, to his own life. "Again I begin," he wrote with especially telling phrasing in "Chicago," "the endless game of jerking *my own life out of the shell that dies,* striving to breathe into it beauty and meaning" (*LB,* 81; emphasis mine). If *Windy McPherson's Son* splits in two upon Sam's departure from business, *Winesburg* turns the competing halves of that narrative into simultaneous narrative axes: Anderson's familiar, personal, linear narrative of a "jobby" young man coming of age, set against a patchwork of testaments, some of which (like the story of Jesse Bentley) Anderson culled from his days on the road.[43]

Even Winesburg the town is something of a social juncture—a place in which these testaments occur, a place through which and beyond which George Willard's trajectory extends. To the extent that Winesburg is a place at all, it is no refuge; in Anderson's languages of class, it is a middle landscape, not just geographically (as in Middle American), but a place between farm and city. Farm self-sufficiency is placed in the antebellum years (63–65); Anderson is still thinking, as in *Windy McPherson's Son,* in historical "stages" of evolution, matching three American genuses to three phases—farmers, Winesburgian elders, and then George Willard's generation.[44] Originally plotted along Wine Creek (105), growing in the roughly fifty-year time-frame of Anderson's storytelling into a "thriving town" and "burg," Winesburg is adjacent to farm land—principally berry, apple, and corn fields—and some of the farm crops still grow in vacant lots along sidewalks (60). However, these farm crops are thoroughly mass produced and marketed, as nameless boys, girls, men, and women (128) pick the crop that each day is taken by train to the city (33, 36), leaving only damaged fruit behind for the town. Meanwhile, city ambitions and dreams fill the young people's minds—especially those the city will pluck and take away on the train.

As Winesburg's agricultural base is quickly recessed into the background of Anderson's narrative, the reader visualizes the town's coordinates, slowly, through clues (and even, in some editions, maps): a small four-cornered grid framed by Buckeye Street and the railroad, traversed at right angles by Main Street—literally and psychologically the main artery of the town. Main Street itself signifies Anderson's organization of psychological space: a string of singular storefront facades, domiciles behind, alleys and shadowy outreaches beyond. Anderson's narrative, sustaining the two axes of his earlier business types, sees Winesburg's populace as male persons attached, in an entrepreneurial tradition, to their fixed vocation or store, *to* those storefronts: Banker White, Sinning's Hardware, the New Willard House. Only two stories (and their characters) are devoted to representing farmhands ("Hands" and "The Untold Lie"). The rest of Anderson's cast consists entirely of petty entrepreneurs, professionals, sales workers, and clerical employees; the women who marry or are born to such men; the young sons of such men (Anderson's third generation) who also do white collar work and hope to get to the city.[45] Though vocations are attached to the aura of petty merchandising, though seen in "occupational" rather than "class" terms per se, Anderson's common lot is a patchwork of the middle class, of service, commercial, and communications occupations. Though farmers and artisans are alluded to, none are directly represented; even Jesse Bentley is pointedly cast as an agribusinessman who manages several farms (97–98), and Wing Biddlebaum, a farm laborer, seems to be a case study in industrial culture.

Anderson's depiction of Biddlebaum in the opening tale, "Hands," has received so much useful interpretation that it seems little more could be said. Yet, because the story is often taken as a keynote of Anderson's putative nostalgia, and in particular for "hand work," Biddlebaum's social representation needs reexamining. The opening of the tale serves to establish Anderson's moral and psychological geography:

> Upon the half decayed veranda of a small frame house that stood near the edge of a ravine near the town of Winesburg, Ohio, a fat little old man walked nervously up and down. Across a long field that had been

> seeded for clover but that had produced only a dense crop of mustard weeds, he could see the public highway along which went a wagon filled with berry pickers returning from the fields. The berry pickers, youths and maidens, laughed and shouted boisterously. A boy clad in a blue shirt leaped from the wagon and attempted to drag after him one of the maidens, who screamed and protested shrilly. The feet of the boy in the road kicked up a cloud of dust that floated across the face of the departing sun. Over the long field came a thin girlish voice. "Oh, you Wing Biddlebaum, comb your hair, it's falling into your eyes," commanded the voice to the man, who was bald and whose nervous little hands fiddled about the bare white forehead as though arranging a mass of tangled locks. (27)

This opening obviously collapses social space into Biddlebaum's forehead—hence the expressionist label sometimes applied to Anderson—the disembodied voices and "locks" imprisoning his thoughts. But as critics have often not seen, Anderson also sets up the traversing patterns of young men kicking dust and an old man facing his declining years. True, Anderson establishes Wing as a thwarted, unrealized man amid the processes of industrial work—a man whose clover has turned to mustard seed—yet the reader also sees, rather uneasily, young (blue-shirted) workers more interested, as they are in *Windy McPherson's Son*, in random pleasure than sensitivity to Wing. Originally "grotesque" and yet made "more grotesque" (29) by his berry-picking fame, Wing is mocked by the town in being regarded, in the Dickensian sense, as only a "hand." After being banished by a homophobic Pennsylvania town, he has taken his last name from a "box of goods seen at a freight station" (33); his whole identity is summed up at the turning of the day, as the berry train rattles past his house at the story's close (33). If Winesburg is the middle landscape of a lapsed pastoral, a stagnated middle terrain, Wing is its unrealized shepherd.

However, for all of Anderson's animus against the industrial-commercial economy that imprisons, centralizes (32), and degrades Wing's energy, Anderson's own telos is in this instance not based in nostalgia for the self-sufficient farmer or even craftsmanship; rather, Wing's status is seen as a declension from teaching, from the power principle of expressiveness, from the "master" status (32) of uplifting or awakening dreams in others. In this sense, "Hands" evokes not manual labor alone, but caring and molding, leadership—as when Sam McPherson had a classroom "in his hands" (215). Notably, when Anderson does invoke a nostalgic telos, it is of a different and quite literary order: "Out of the dream Wing Biddlebaum made a picture for George Willard. In the picture men lived again in a kind of pastoral golden age. Across a green open country came clean-limbed young men, some afoot, some mounted upon horses. In crowds the young men came to gather about the feet of an old man who sat beneath a tree in a tiny garden and who talked to them" (30). In this "picture" Wing is seen, as critics have realized, as a lost Socrates—even, more covertly, a Christ made prematurely old. Anderson has merely downscaled his earlier premium on word mastery, on the "bugling" to troops of clean young men. George is seen, conversely, as a "medium" (33) for Wing's love and vision, medium in the sense of a mediator of master dream and future action. The drama between young and old thus becomes synoptic of Anderson's two narrative axes: Wing is a "testament," yet one whose voice is lost, subdued by his internalization of others' voices, the very crime he warns George against; his status is fixed. Conversely, George appears (as "Chicago" suggests) to Wing as if Wing is talking to himself, a restorative force that momentarily takes Wing's thoughts and releases them "like a fish returned to the brook by the fisherman" (28). George Willard's skill seems to recapitulate Anderson's implied claim about the potential of *Winesburg*'s prose testaments.

Given Wing's declined status, it is worth noticing how Winesburg's middle-industrial state, its Main Street malaise, plays across both Anderson's languages of class and his overall schema for the "economy" or market in which the town is positioned. Of course, much of Winesburgian loneliness, narrowness, and thwarted desire has nothing to do with these concerns; the town's coldness and "whiteness," exemplified by the plaster that a workman installs to forever bury George's legacy from his mother (232) or the "white sheet" (231) that finally settles over her body, have numerous causes. As much as Anderson testifies to the "sweetness" of "twisted apples" (38) in this lapsed garden, however, another part of him—the George Willard trajectory—sees Winesburgians as made doubly grotesque by their fixed positions in a larger economy. It is not only that human longings of all sorts strain against the "old" middle-class and clerical vocational typifications imposed upon his characters by their Main Street facades (a similarity to Ferber's *The Girls*)—teachers who fear unhearing students, preachers who cannot save souls, doctors who hide in their offices. Moreover, Anderson suggests the predilection of the personality market to pluck particularly fresh souls for removal to the city. This ironically doubles back upon Winesburgian fixity in the form of city "voices" that raise the remaining citizens' expectations and only further distort their fixed lives. In a circular fashion that reinvokes the problem at the heart of Anderson's first two novels, city bugling now calls to troops that cannot respond because of their deformed bodies.

The reader witnesses stray examples of this kind of encounter: the city alcoholic who tells Tom Hard's daughter, mysteriously and mystically, to be "Tandy" (145); city dweller Ned Crane's lapsed love affair with Alice Hindeman (113); Helen White's instructor in "cosmopolitan" airs of the city (238). Several of the figures most stimulating to George, good and bad, have all been somewhere else: Wing, Dr. Percival, Helen White. George himself is the child of a hotel, a "stream of people" (223) who are not residents; his encounters recapitulate those of his mother, when patrons made her unhappy and her father told her not to marry his clerk (225). Beyond these sparse moments of friction between city and burg, lies the more substantive account of Jesse Bentley's growing neurotic fantasy. Raised on an isolated, self-sufficient farm, Anderson's pioneer-turned-businessman develops his original paranoia about his neighbors from biblical texts, seeing "Philistines" gathering in the hills. But a second order development also occurs:

> In the last fifty years a vast change has taken place. . . . The coming of industrialism, attended by all the roar and rattle of affairs, the shrill cries of millions of new voices that have come among us from overseas, the going and coming of trains, the growth of cities, the building of the interurban car lines that weave in and out of towns and past farmhouses. . . . Books, badly imagined and written though they may be in the hurry of our times, are in every household, magazines circulate by the millions of copies, newspapers are everywhere. In our day a farmer standing by the stove in the store in his village has his mind filled to overflowing with the words of other men. . . . The farmer by the stove is brother to the men of the cities, and if you listen you will find him talking as glibly and as senselessly as the best city man of us all. (70–71)

Jesse formed the habit of reading newspapers and magazines. He invented a machine for the making of fence out of wire. Faintly he realized that the atmosphere of old times and places that he had always cultivated in his own mind was strange and foreign to the thing that was growing up in the minds of others. The beginning of the most materialistic age in the history of the world, when wars would be fought without patriotism, when men would forget God and only pay attention to moral standards,

> when the will to power would replace the will to serve and beauty would be well-nigh forgotten in the terrible headlong rush of mankind toward the acquiring of possessions, was telling its story to Jesse. (81)

As the story's ironic finale reveals—Jesse struck down by his grandson David's slingshot—Jesse himself has capitulated, been absorbed, by the process described above, made over into a middle Philistine. But the more telling point may be the circulatory exchange that occurs here: one of the reasons for Jesse's neuroticism is the system's own production of substitute "voices." To apply an idea from postcolonial criticism, Winesburg is not just a backwater, a place left behind, but an instance of "the development of underdevelopment." Anderson's "us all" includes narrator and reader as city dwellers already in the system. In addition, George Willard's trajectory suddenly becomes much more loaded, as the centripetal energies of this personality market threaten to undermine his own outward movement, make him into one of the "voices" who bugle to the Jesse Bentleys only to make their lives more grotesque. (Even Wing Biddlebaum, so often romanticized in critical readings, becomes another emblem of this risk; the touch of his hands aroused only distorted dreams in his student.)

Of course, this rather extraordinary threat has been contained by a recurrent critical insistence that George Willard is a kind of Stephen Hero figure, a portrait of the artist as a young man who will not enter this system. Certainly, for Anderson this autobiographical referent was probably very much in play. For worthwhile reasons, George has many of the narrative markings not only of an Anderson surrogate but a narrator surrogate: the narrator knows what is only said in George's presence; George and his family are virtually the only reiterated characters; George serves as a magical touchstone for others' expression, is called a potential "genius" (163), and implicitly apprentices to writing in his newspaper vocation. Artistry, or so the argument goes, will take him out of the circulatory system. As a claim that is particularly evocative of the New Criticism's agenda, *Winesburg, Ohio* becomes something like the proof of the pudding, the mode of artistic perception that proves George will separate himself from the circulatory exchange of thoughts and voices. As critics have been at pains to point out, many of George's "masters," even the essentially failed teachers, warn him against participation in that system. Kate Swift, who recognizes his "spark of genius," warns him not to become a "mere peddler of words" (163); Wing Biddlebaum tells him to "shut [his] ears to the roaring of the voices" and to dream (30); and, most importantly, Elizabeth Willard warns her son not to be "all words and smartness" (43), to preserve the thing that died in her. George's "departure" is read as not succumbing to the fate that is, as Enoch Robinson intuits, "hidden away" in the "elders" (170).

This account of George's exemption, however, may seem unduly dependent upon several assumptions. First, it depends upon George's departure to the city being unambiguous—which, in the circulatory exchange market it is not. George should be taken, initially at least, for what he is—an aspiring "jobby" boy—and Anderson underlines the fact that the reader does not know his fate even at the end of the book. Secondly, George does not hear or absorb many of the messages from his elders. George says of Wing Biddlebaum, as the young man leaves "perplexed and frightened" (31), "'There's something wrong, but I don't want to know what it is.'" Of Kate Swift, he says: "'I have missed something. I have missed something Kate Swift was trying to tell me'" (166). In a powerful twist upon the corn imagery of *Windy McPherson's Son,* Elizabeth Willard wants, with her secret love Dr. Reefy, to be able to "project herself out of the husk" (228) of her tired body, but calling out for her boy, she only greets Death as her lover (229). The reader must often intuit, with the narrator's assistance, much of what George has actually missed.

This is why George, critics have often argued, is implicitly linked to the reconstructions of such events made by Anderson's narrator-artist. And yet, in turn, even this would depend upon whether Anderson—or even, for argument's sake, Anderson's narrator—is the exempted "artist" this criticism presumes. There is considerable evidence, in the narrative alone, to indicate that he is not. For example, in the extended dismissal of artistic circles in "Loneliness"—incidentally, Anderson's favorite tale—Enoch Robinson makes the mistake of "playing" with realities in his advertising job or mouthing socialist opinions ("the advisability of the government's owning and operating the railroads" [172]). But these mistakes are cast as little different from the self-delusions of "pure" artists, who—like the bad novels filling Jesse Bentley's farmhouse—are described in terms suggesting narrowness and superficial talking:

> The room in which young Robinson lived in New York faced Washington Square and was long and narrow like a hallway. It is important to get that fixed in your mind. . . .
>
> And so into the room in the evening came young Enoch's friends. There was nothing particularly striking about them except that they were artists

> of the kind that talk. Everyone knows of the talking artists. Throughout all of the known history of the world they have gathered in rooms and talked. They talk of art and are passionately, almost feverishly, in earnest about it. They think it matters much more than it does. (168–69)

Meanwhile, much as in his public statements, Anderson seems intent not to "put the badge of the poet" on his narrator. Rather, in "Hands" and elsewhere, *Winesburg*'s narrator differentiates his own storytelling this way:

> The story of Wing Biddlebaum is a story of hands. Their restless activity, like unto the beating of the wings of an imprisoned bird, had given him his name. Some obscure poet of the town had thought of it. (28)
>
> . . . The story of Wing Biddlebaum's hands is worth a book in itself. Sympathetically set forth it would tap many strange, beautiful qualities in obscure men. It is a job for a poet. (29)
>
> . . . Perhaps our talking of [the hands] will arouse the poet. (31)
>
> . . . And yet that is but crudely stated. It needs the poet there. (31)

Generally, this byplay has been received as Anderson's self-deprecation, even a sly doppelgänger effect, yet this seems to skip over the preliminary and perhaps more central effect: to create a nonpoet persona, "crude" in expression, who writes not only spontaneously but also collaboratively with the more obscure "poets," the common citizens of the town.

The point here is not merely that *Winesburg*'s narrative prose is "colloquial," nor that Anderson's style is any less contrived than other literary styles—researchers have shown that Anderson revised extensively—but that Anderson's effect is one of commonality, equivalence, "crude" unrevised prose. Some of these effects may be seen in the following: "Joe [Welling] himself . . . was like a tiny volcano that lies silent for days and then suddenly spouts fire. No, he wasn't like that—he was like a man subject to fits" (103); and "Everything about [Wash Williams] was unclean. Even the whites of his eyes looked soiled. I go too fast. Not everything about Wash was unclean" (121). These effects, understandably, have been connected to Anderson's developing affiliations with modernism: Stein's "time of the composition" or Hemingway's writing degree zero. There is a powerful "surfacing" effect here, as Anderson's prose (here again a limitation of the "plain speech" model) becomes anything but transparent; lives are quite explicitly turning into "stories" or memories. But it is important to see that, in *Winesburg,* the antithesis of "crude" is a "smart" surfacing—as when Tom Willard paints his hotel "new and smart" (227), whitening the surface and polishing the facade. Anderson's desire is not to be "smart," not to have glib or polished answers to the riddles he portrays. Anderson's style works in the passages above to reinforce the impression of an undeveloped narrator, one distrustful of literary affect and slickness alike—not at all the "pure" artist the current body of criticism often supposes George will become. The sum effect is to cast a quite different horizon for George Willard's trajectory; as he projects outward, a powerfully retrospective, yet *still* crude, older voice is suggested, a voice that is still struggling for expression as all of the Winesburgians are. This complex of old and young consciousness is what *Winesburg* defines as the more "sophisticated" outcome of modern living. The proof may be in the pudding, but the "curing" is still in process; art is only one job among many.[46]

The full ramifications of this forceful containment of George's trajectory—the imposition of the circulatory personality market, Anderson's desire to present an "undeveloped" prose surface—are perhaps brought home most tellingly in the book's denouement, in the chapters "Sophistication" and "Departure." As George's mother passes away without projecting her dream onto him, George is entering a new phase, partly brought on by ruminating upon her death. He now exhibits a more tragic and sober sensibility—experiencing what Anderson calls the "older, more sophisticated thing" that "reflects and remembers" (240), balancing the young "animal" in George. Anderson describes this new maturity:

> Ghosts of old things creep into his consciousness; the voices outside of himself whisper a message concerning the limitations of life. From being quite sure of himself and his future he becomes not at all sure. If he be an imaginative boy a door is torn open and for the first time he looks out upon the world, seeing, as though they marched in procession before him, the countless figures of men who before his time have come out of nothingness into the world, lived their lives and again disappeared into nothingness. The sadness of sophistication has come to the boy. With a little gasp he sees himself as merely a leaf blown by the wind through the streets of his village. He knows that in spite of all the stout talk of his fellows he must live and die in uncertainty, a thing blown by the winds, a thing destined like corn to wilt in the sun. (234)

In this moment—albeit with the qualifications I have offered—George is drawn closer to his narrator; his outward trajectory is contained by his internalization of the narrator's reflecting, reconstructing voice. Yet like Anderson's white collar vacillation, this is quite pointedly a mood that shifts and dissipates. Anderson's acknowledgement of the struggle to repeatedly pull his life "out of the shell that dies" is worth bearing in mind. George continues to project outward from the "husk" of his town, yet he is now presented by a narrator knowing the mistakes he will make, knowing the corn will eventually wilt in the sun. In this way, the personality market—the cycles of crudeness and smartness—is partly accepted as a given, yet its effects are only temporarily neutralized by the retrospective desire of Anderson's business of art. George, after all, does depart for the city.

This mixed message underneath *Winesburg*'s finale is conveyed, again, by Anderson's spatial and psychological conflation in the book's elusively beautiful yet sober final passages:

> George glanced up and down the [train] car to be sure no one was looking, then took out his pocketbook and counted his money. His mind was occupied with a desire not to appear green. Almost the last words his father had said to him concerned the matter of his behavior when he got to the city. "Be a sharp one," Tom Willard had said. "Keep your eyes on your money. Be awake. That's the ticket. Don't let anyone think you're a greenhorn."
>
> After George counted his money he looked out of the window and was surprised to see that the train was still in Winesburg.
>
> The young man, going out of his town to meet the adventure of life, began to think but he did not think of anything very big or dramatic. Things like his mother's death, his departure from Winesburg, the uncertainty of his future life in the city, the serious and larger aspects of his life did not come into his mind.
>
> He thought of little things—Turk Smollet wheeling boards through the main street of his town in the morning, a tall woman, beautifully gowned, who had once stayed overnight at his father's hotel, Butch Wheeler the lamp lighter. . . .
>
> The young man's mind was carried away by his growing passion for dreams. One looking at him would not have thought him particularly sharp. With the recollection of little things occupying his mind he closed his eyes and leaned back in the car seat. He stayed that way for a long time

> and when he aroused himself and again looked out of the car window the town of Winesburg had disappeared and his life there had become but a background on which to paint the dreams of his manhood. (246–47)

The last lines here may seem pointedly belletristic, again suggesting that George's fate lies in the realm of art. The entire landscape of Winesburg seems to be transposing into emblems and symbols of memory and reconstruction. And yet, voices, emblems, and symbols might also fulfill the culturalist vocations that may await George Willard in the modern personality market. It is also important to see that George follows his father's advice—that like Anderson he pats his purse as he boards the train. Not unimportantly, George has already begun to daydream, to vacillate between the waking and dream-life, between child-past and white collar future. The reader may also notice that Anderson neutralizes the movement of the train, the central icon of the book's circulatory market, as if to undercut George's pilgrimage with the cycle of return implied by the natural iconography of the corn fields. Strikingly, where corn was, in *Windy McPherson's Son,* an army to be mobilized, Anderson now writes from the point of view of the corn itself, a commodity to be harvested or left behind.

In his more optative moods, of course, Anderson could still invoke the progressive vision of a developing literary elect.[47] In time, Anderson's more romantic and craft-conscious conceptions of the artist's role, if never losing the aura of the "job," would become much more prominent in his thinking. Much as Sinclair Lewis's representation of the commonplace would receive a varied cultural reading—hailed as an American Zola, cast in the "revolt from the village," and yet be patronized by such different figures as Mencken and George Horace Lorimer—Anderson was also quite able to glow in the iconoclastic lights of the Chicago Renaissance and Washington Square, even as his fiction covertly belittled such haunts.[48] In the prevailing intellectual rhetoric of America's supposed "coming-of-age," Anderson could easily convert his account of the George Willards, of the "class" who would provide cultural leadership, into heroic terms again. In a letter from 1920, Anderson had already begun to accentuate this side of his case when he said, "I want a body of healthy, young men and women to quit working . . . [and] to become intense individualists. Something of this kind must happen if we ever are to bring color and a flair into our modern life. Naturally I believe that the growth of such a class would do more than anything else to make this a better world to live in" (*RW,* 51).

This was not, apparently, Anderson's retrospective half. What he is describing is a "class" born out of the dead husk of the office world, a world of "clean" young men and women living out an "intense" individualism of youth.[49] In his more retrospective, prosaic, and cruder American voice, he retained senses, in *Winesburg,* of a more sober prospect: of a life that led in "crazy little circles," that blurred the boundaries between what was artistic and what was business desire, that turned the symbols and emblems forming in George Willard's mind toward a number of less hopeful social applications. Anderson's collecting idiom also reminds us of the typicality that underwrites George's quest for individuation; as Winesburg dissipates into memory, George is passing from the "sharpness" his father advises and from a visual sharpness, dissipating into the crowd. Like the puppeteer of Fate in Anderson's drama, the conductor on the train sees George as only one of thousands heading off to the city, to what Anderson calls "the uncertainty of his future life" there (246–47). In this way, George's quest for cultural power becomes "a commonplace enough incident" (246).

Six

Sinclair Lewis and the Passing of Capitalism

"He too considers the job a joke, but after several months at it, the joke begins to escape him. . . . He also discovers that his correspondents take him seriously. For the first time in his life, he is forced to examine the values by which he lives. This examination shows him that he is the victim of the joke and not its perpetrator."

—*Nathanael West,* Miss Lonelyhearts

In Chapter 8 of *Babbitt* (1922), Sinclair Lewis describes in excruciating detail the preparations—and the restive anxiety—surrounding George and Myra Babbitt's execution of a time-honored middle-class ritual: the dinner party. "Though he had been born in the village of Catawba," Lewis writes, "Babbitt had risen to that metropolitan social plane on which hosts have as many as four people at dinner without planning it for more than an evening or two."[1] But a dinner for twelve, Lewis adds, "staggered" even the Babbitts—they "studied, debated, and arbitrated the lists of guests" for two weeks; contradicting their support of prohibition, George sneaks across the tracks for a little gin. By the time the guests arrive, "including the inevitable late couple," a "great gray emptiness" (93) has already settled in his brain. After dinner, the men "leaned back on their heels, put their hands in their trouser pockets, and proclaimed their views with the booming profundity of a prospering male repeating a thoroughly hackneyed statement about a matter of which he knows nothing whatever" (95). So to liven things up, Babbitt introduces something mildly risqué:

> The women wriggled, and Babbitt was stirred to like naughtiness. "Say, folks, I wished I dared show you a book I borrowed from Doc Patten!"
>
> "Now, George! The idea!" Mrs. Babbitt warned him.
>
> "This book—racy isn't the word! It's some kind of an anthropological

> report about—about Customs, in the South Seas, and what it doesn't *say*! It's a book you can't buy. Verg, I'll lend it to you."
>
> "Me first!" insisted Eddie Swanson. "Sounds spicy!"
>
> Orville Jones announced, "Say, I head a Good One the other day about a coupla Swedes and their wives," and, in the best Jewish accent, he resolutely carried the Good One to a slightly disinfected ending. Gunch capped it. But the cocktails waned, the seekers dropped back into cautious reality.
>
> Chum Frink had recently been on a lecture-tour among the small towns, and he chuckled, "Awful good to get back to civilization! I certainly been seeing some hick towns! I mean—Course the folks there are the best on earth, but, gee whiz, those Main Street burgs are slow, and you fellows can't hardly appreciate what it means to be here with a bunch of live ones!" (98)

The novel is full of such self-defeating, entropic dialogue. And yet we also notice the resemblance of Lewis's *own* methods to the anthropology of the undiscussed book: itemizing of social customs and gestures; minute accounting of colloquial speech patterns; representation of a normative cultural hero testing out the borders of taboo before snapping back to "cautious reality"—all in a book Lewis originally planned as a day-in-the-life of an ad man.[2] Nor can one overlook how Lewis's own keyword, "Main Street," has already been absorbed in Zenith's vocabulary (its own non-"other"). Yet in an even more personal, if more light-hearted sense, Lewis also includes something like an insider's joke from his apprenticeship in book publicity. Babbitt and his neighbors are portrayed as potential readers—yet, as it turns out, superficial skimmers. If Doc Patten's unnamed anthropological study might have cured Zenith's ills, at least by challenging its cultural absolutism, the book's potential is negated by boosterism—converted, like the proverbial photographs of *National Geographic*, into middle-class pornography.

By and large, because Lewis has long been regarded as a journalistic, "externalizing," and even documentarian novelist of middle-class manners—a "diagnostic" debunker—such personal asides have long been discounted.[3] Ironically, New Critical formalism, which discredited the biographical fallacy, collaborated with Mark Schorer's encyclopedic and yet ultimately unsympathetic profile (1961) to discount Lewis's seriousness in the years prior to *Main Street*. Scholarly tracings of Lewis's apprenticeship all but omit his white collar experience in journalism and book publicity. Having severed one of this century's best-sellers from his own history and his institutional context, we have lost sight of a writer who tried to craft a popular mythology—a working fiction—for modern white collar life. Contemporary middle-class readers have often recognized Lewis's sensibility as "seismographic," but it is now nearly impossible to remember why.[4]

Part of the answer lies in reconstructing Lewis's imbrication in the white collar life Zenith came to represent. Lewis's style had as its crucible the experience of a young man apprenticing in culturalist work—intriguingly, in and around the marketing of reading itself. Later in life Lewis claimed that his literary Main Streeting had begun in a modest vocational crisis while still at Yale. Young Harry Lewis—the son of a methodical, parsimonious, stoical country doctor who virtually embodied the Protestant work ethic—had returned home during summer vacation:

> . . . and after two months of it, after two months of overhearing the villagers none too softly wonder, "Why don't Doc Lewis make Harry get a job on a farm instead of letting him sit around readin' and readin' a lot of fool histories and God knows what all?" I was converted to the faith that a good deal of this Neighborliness was a fake; that villages could be as inquisitorial as an army barracks. So in the third month of vacation, fifteen years before it was published, I began to write *Main Street*.
>
> But the title, then, was *The Village Virus*, and the chief character was not Carol Kennicott but Guy Pollack, the lawyer, whom I depicted as a learned, amiable, and ambitious young man (altogether, you see, in the image of Doc Lewis's youngest boy, Harry) who started practice in a prairie village and spiritually starved there.

Many critics still doubt this story,[5] but however mythic, the memory is nonetheless evocative of Lewis's larger cosmology: seeing "Main Street" as not just a regional background but as a representation of the risky vocational path of the middle class. Even in this memory, Main Street intersects with the avenues of Lewis's own class apprenticeship or, rather, threatens to detour him: into fraudulence, stagnation, subjection to an inquisitorial village surveillance. *Main Street* as a book, conversely, emerges as a text of self-inoculation against this potential virus.

Thus in Lewis's apprenticeship, there was more than the education of a satirist. As this memory implied, Lewis initially approached the purveying, promoting, and writing of books as serious "meaning-making" activity, arguing that literature provided nostrums for capitalism's afflictions and scripts for more progressive living. In short, he understood his work as culturalist mediation, as the promotion and dissemination of material that could have a constitutive role in shaping the white collar future. Lewis had occupied a strategic, middle "gatekeeping" position between the life scripts that "high culture" had taught him and what C. Wright Mills calls the "sanctions or justifications for the new routines we live," the white collar "plan of life" (xvi) as it took shape *around* him. Most of his apprentice fiction was directly concerned with white collar "jobs"; he wrote one novel, *The Trail of the Hawk* (1915), while commuting on the Long Island Railroad; he promoted authors especially concerned with prophesying and scripting a white collar future. It is Lewis's mediation or "management" of this confluence of "cultures"—literary and commercial—that is worth exploring.

Some of this exploration will necessarily involve recovering his job experience and his early fiction. Both fields are necessary, because at the heart of Lewis's ambitious idiom was an attempt to synthesize both high visionary prophecy—as with Rice and Anderson, imbibed largely from Fabian sources—with the more mundane realities of his own publicity training. One of the central paradoxes of his style—the combination of "paradigmatic" class mythologizing and an encyclopedic, discursive method—was a reflection of this synthesizing quest. Unlike Anderson, who negotiated white collar anxieties with Reason-Why plain-speaking, Lewis threw himself energetically into the stunts and new literary ploys of modern publicity culture. In turn, even the apparently documentary surfaces of *Babbitt* are not simply by-products of field work or "scientific" observation—though they make that claim. Rather, they are thick cultural descriptions layered with the thinner tissues of Lewis's own white collar apprenticeship: mixed layers of heartfelt myth and hyperbole, prophecy and publicity, sympathy and diabolism—in a sense, Dickens and the Dictaphone.[6]

The currently shallow sense of Lewis's method cannot entirely be blamed on the rigid categories of formalist criticism—even the map, say, of Mencken's misreading. Lewis himself often seized the "diagnostic" claim and spoke of Babbitt as a genus of a culture the author hoped to render extinct, dinner parties and all. Yet Babbitt might be better seen as similar to Robert Grant's Selma White, not just hypothesized in the negative image of technocratic liberalism, but concatenated there only after considerable personal struggle over class and mass within Lewis himself. Despite their appearance of Archimedean distance, Lewis's texts originated in the drama of will and entropy in white collar experience—an imbrication that is betrayed by a shared fear that the very tissues of one's being are suffused with the promotional culture being represented. That Sinclair Lewis and his art shared so much with his genus of modern capitalism is, itself, part of another inside joke—a joke that, like the one in the dinner scene, never really seems to get told.

| | |

If Anderson extended the literary skills of capitalism into his own "crude" art, there is an inverse white collar phenomenon in Lewis: a young literary man whose skills were incorporated into the marketing of books. After college, Lewis ranged uneasily across a variety of jobs, only gradually specializing in literary reviewing and publicity. Beginning in July of 1908, he worked as an editorial writer, telegraph editor, proofreader, and dramatic critic for the Waterloo, Iowa, *Daily Courier;* then, he became a night clerk and claims investigator for a charity relief organization in New York City. For several months following, he became a literary secretary in California, then a news rewriter for the San Francisco *Bulletin,* then a local wire editor for the Associated Press. During this period, he also wrote upbeat success serials for a leading "New Thought" periodical, *The Nautilus.* After being let go from the A.P. position, he worked for six months on the *Volta Review;* then he spent two years with Frederick A. Stokes, first as a fifteen-dollar-a-week manuscript reader, then in publicity. In October of 1912, he became an assistant editor for *Adventure Magazine,* and six months after that, he earned sixty dollars a week writing book reviews for a newspaper syndicate started by a former employee of the J. Walter Thompson advertising agency, W. E. Woodward. When the syndicate collapsed at the start of World War I, Lewis was hired as an editorial assistant and advertising manager by publisher George H. Doran, with whom he stayed until leaving office work for good in November of 1915.

What the young man gleaned from this seven-year skein has been, to date, far less clear. Neither Schorer's biography nor Lewis's own sardonic memoirs delineate any meaningful pattern or progress. Schorer, nonetheless, does help outline Lewis's original plan. While preparing for Yale at Oberlin College, Lewis had been drawn to "muscular" evangelical Christianity, joined the Student Volunteers, and for a time planned to be a missionary. (Even as his religious faith faded, Lewis's idiom would always mix the vocabularies of commercial and evangelical persuasion.) He had also supplemented his college costs with work on a New Haven newspaper, occasional clerking, and saleswork (including some time in the book section of a department store). At Yale, for a long period, Lewis had been undecided about his future. As early as 1904, he had contemplated leaving college and cogitated in his diary about "[l]aw, writing (& journalism), teaching (English, or history or philosophy or economics?)" (87), leaning towards the law. Like many restless undergraduates, he had both a strong desire to leave college and no idea what to do if he did. Ultimately, however, he settled on a plan to write fiction and to supplement his literary vocation with teaching or journalism. By his senior year, he had already hired his first literary agent.

This plan had a number of repercussions for how Lewis would approach his occupations and how, more generally, he would construct his white collar vocabulary. In the long term, Lewis approached literature as a profession, a business, a job; he only accelerated the entrepreneurial drive of his two principal literary mentors, Upton Sinclair and Jack London. Lewis's later denigration of inspiration, his insistence that young writers need most of all to "put seat of pants to seat of chair," reflect lessons well learned. Like Sherwood Anderson, Lewis would belittle avant-garde pretensions about the craft of writing.[7] But on the other hand, Lewis's decision not to depend solely on his writing, as both London and Sinclair had, but (like Robert Grant) to supplement it by ancillary vocations, left its mark as well. In part, this decision reflected Lewis's candid self-evaluation. The young man privately knew that his omnivorous tastes for reading, for going to plays, for travel, were built around a more conventional middle-class complex—even, as Schorer notes, aristocratic fantasies. (At one point, Lewis even mused wistfully about how Robert Browning's father, unlike his own, had provided an income from banking so the poet could ply the muse [121]). Lewis saw his work—and salaried work more generally—largely in terms of how it fulfilled such needs. Conversely, he approached his supplementary vocations as valuable insofar as they provided what Anderson would have called "testaments" for his main vocation. As late as 1908, he wrote about how the "priest, & *doctor,* & the reporter have of all men the best opportunity of gathering vital 'literary material'" (136). One of his characters refers to such a plan as becoming a "hyphenated" citizen, half in the "race" of office dwellers and half out.[8] With his long-term goal of authorship in sight, Lewis soon became ready to pick up at a moment's notice when the job at hand bored him; constantly restless, no strategy other than making himself into an author seemed to matter. This too left traces on Lewis's axiomatic term, the "job," which he used to invoke temporary, day-to-day employment—

an antithesis to "career." Settling into a permanent position, by contrast, Lewis associates with fixity, with "stolidity," even (in *Trail of the Hawk*) with turning "granite."[9]

Lewis first entered journalism to try to sustain this "hyphenated" strategy. In Waterloo, as Schorer writes, he was actually able to devote himself to detailed note-taking—grist for his fictional mill—during his off hours (143). Before long Lewis came face-to-face with the office rationalization that had overtaken reporting in these years. He began to complain about how little time he had left over for "outside" work (154). When he moved to San Francisco, where Hearst and others had revolutionized reporting, the problem did not disappear. Lewis seems not to have been drawn at all to the romance of investigative reporting. He seemed to prefer standing back from events, digesting them editorially; his own memoirs affirm the young collegian's fastidious recoil from the business of reportorial snooping. "From ten to four," he remembered of his California post, "we were supposed to go out and ask embarrassing questions of people who much preferred to be let alone" (*MFMS,* 92). Nor did city dwellers become, as they had for O. Henry or Ferber, sources of submerged class knowledge; to Lewis, their testimony was suffused with self-promotion and deception. He recalled one time when a hotel manager, looking for publicity, had puffed up the service by one of his bellboys. Lewis wrote up the lie—profiling the bellhop as a mixture of Dickens's Tiny Tim and a Horatio Alger hero, he said—and the story was reprinted all over newspaperdom (*MFMS,* 95–96).

Whether or not this story is apocryphal, it points out how misleading it is to designate Lewis as a "journalistic" author. If his naturalist mentors often envied the reporter's quest for "facts," heroically projecting themselves into the urban landscape of "classes" and "masses," Lewis (like Ferber) treats this style as very nearly passé. He is more likely to remember the humorous diversions of designing alliterative headlines or mimicking the bloated speechifying he had been assigned to cover. Lewis as a journalist is perhaps more properly understood as a re-write man. He used his encyclopedic and synthesizing skills to transpose the increasingly standardized words of "news" into comic prose and headlines (and, in a few years, into literary publicity). His subsequent A.P. work seems to suggest this developing synoptic and second-order reflex. A surviving worksheet enumerates Lewis's tasks with the bureau: cross-checking A.P. reports against daily newspapers to see what was missed; sorting and filing news stories to syndicated papers; watching for libellous and fake material. In many respects, Lewis was a "news manager," and years later he would say newspaper work was the "one basis" for success in publicity.[10] He was, in short, a "middle" manager who doubly distanced himself from his routine by mocking his own mediations and his news "informants."

Some of Lewis's doubts arose from the routinization of work; the worksheet illuminates what would become a constant refrain in Lewis's complaints about office life, a condition he subsumed under the term "wage slavery." Lewis did not, however, use this term in the Marxian sense—that is, to invoke the theft of labor—nor as the antithesis of what nineteenth-century journeymen would have called "personal independence," the freedom to think or act. Rather, he often envisioned the office in spatial terms, as territory or "clock" discipline to escape.

One daydreaming fragment reflects this vision:

> His life steady, busy, + unprogressive
> + routine as the office clock.
> Even the chief clerk was
> @ best an hour=hand, [garbled] was
> but a minute hand
>
> -
>
> The scientist in his study
> a meterograph
>
> ---
>
> + so on.

The word "job," in turn, signified subjugation to routine, to boredom, to time discipline—all veiled threats of permanent subordination. Though later, like Ferber, Lewis felt some residual attachment to a "backstairs" or subterranean world of "small" employees, even his romantic testimonials retained this anxiety. Later when he was writing his novel *The Job* (1917) out of this life, Lewis would inscribe one copy (to his wife) in Ferber's "so they lived" tone: "A world where the Goddess of Romance doffs her turquoise robe, her silver fillet & the tissue of dreams, to jerk on each morning, when the alarm clock sounds, a neat suit that doesn't show stains or grow shiny under the sleeves too quickly." That is, which doesn't show its sweat.[11]

As this anxiety persisted, however, it only propelled him upward. By the time Lewis had moved into literary syndication, he seemed to have found a mode of work better suited to his "hyphenated" strategy. For Woodward, Lewis wrote the lead review on syndicated book pages sent out to regional newspapers—as a surviving scrapbook attests, reviewing everything from fiction to biography to garden almanacs.[12] Yet Lewis was anything but a "Reason-Why" promoter; rather, under a variety of pseudonyms, he produced work that contemporaries identified as "stunts": folksy narrators like "The Village Doctor," mock "recipes" for reading, clever reviews in the form of rhymed verse or eye-grabbing typographical effects (like a review of a book called *Jam* in the shape of a jar.) Lewis blended literary authority and sales hyperbole, often by singling out a "major new author" on the horizon. Especially important here was the tone becoming idiomatic to Lewis's voice. Quite typically, his publicity prose created that "double-take" many analysts have identified as intrinsic to Barnumesque hyperbole: so overstated, that it implied a knowing wink that took its intended audience into its ploy. Advertising overstatement implicitly acknowledges that the rule of the game is to fool the reader, and it enjoins the reader to play along, a comrade in the con. Meanwhile, Lewis's publicity writing also purveyed status details in an energized "descriptive litany" for his readers, itemizing his authors' idiosyncrasies, their "messages," the profound words great writers attach to books. If not quite Umberto Eco's "lingering glance," consuming books nevertheless becomes luxurious, contagiously so. Typically, Lewis portrayed the proper reaction to a new novel as being swept up enthusiastically—to respond with zeal to its script for living.[13]

Lewis's subsequent work for Stokes and for Doran involved a toning down, but not a remarkable difference. Neither firm could claim the most aggressive promotion in these years. Following the reordering effected by international copyright in 1891, both houses—reflecting Lewis's own tastes—retrenched by firming up their list of British authors, since more aggressive firms often held the rights to American best-sellers. Stokes announced that these frenetic years had convinced publishers that "general" advertising strategies were not reliable in selling books and that new strategies had to be devised.[14] That Stokes and Doran hired Lewis is in itself suggestive of a rethinking in publicity work. In part echoing the truth-in-advertising arguments pervading advertising in the teens, relatively conservative book publishers were drawn to a publicity man who knew the "product" intimately, who saw no necessary contradiction between a love of literature and disseminating it with zeal. Even decades later, Alfred Harcourt—Lewis's editor at this time and later a collaborator on *Main Street*'s campaign—would employ this reasoning. On the one hand, Harcourt would say, an apprenticeship in sales taught knowledge of public taste first hand and developed "zeal for the cause of literature"; on the other hand, Harcourt—having little patience for market research—felt that advertising must be informed by a thorough knowledge of the author, the book, and its underlying purpose. The publicity employee was thus a "middle" man between sales and literary cultures. The growing consensus in the teens was that the "book-buying habit" was not secure among the general public and that book promotion needed to focus instead on "opinion makers," notably critics, discriminating booksellers, or influential community figures, and, in Doran's words, be more "impartial," professional, even academic.[15]

Lewis's surviving publicity work suggests that he may well have been pulled in contrary directions. This work is more conservative than with Woodward—in house, Lewis was called a "literary advisor"—using testimonials and early reviews of novels to promote further sales. Inverting his earlier training, Lewis referred to this publicity work as "planting," now creating notice *in* the newspapers. Doran's memoir makes it clear that Lewis was chief editor at the house, an "advisor" and manager of the literary field rolled into one. Doran later praised both Lewis's editorial intelligence and his ability to produce "literally reams of publicity stunts"; he was, Doran said, a "dynamo of energy and freshness of thought," "too intelligent" to be a mere solicitor of ads. Indeed, remnants of such "stunts" are still extant. A pamphlet survives which calls Will Levington Comfort's *Midstream* (1914) a "picture of the material life of a great adventurer, and a pure spiritual revelation" akin to the work of Wells, Bennett, Rousseau, or Twain. Much of Lewis's writing seems to work back and forth across his two forms of expertise—a double-take mixture of "serious" criticism and syndicated puffery. For instance, Lewis could discuss "romance" as a literary genre or employ the term as a sales category: "romance" as healing, escapist reading for the "Tired Business Man" which renewed his desire to go on working.[16]

Lewis's surviving personal assessments of this publicity phase often echo a professional's "service" vocabulary. If Schorer is right that the portrait of the Van Zile Corporation in *The Trail of the Hawk* is drawn on Stokes (223), then it is worth seeing how Lewis's hero, Carl Ericson, responds to the experience of marketing. (The novel is in fact dedicated to six of Lewis's colleagues in literary publishing, "Optimistic Rebels," including Alfred Harcourt.)[17] Ericson had been a flyer by profession, but he had scaled his work down to the marketing of a Touricar, a modern touring automobile. Carl's mind boosts itself, as Anderson's had, by invoking a spirit of practical service to modern life. "Because he was not office-broken," Lewis writes of his protagonist, "he did not worry about the risk of the new enterprise. The stupid details of affairs had, for him, a soul—the Adventure of Business. [All the details] made it interesting to overwork, and hypnotized Carl into a feeling of responsibility which was less spectacular than flying before thousands, but more in accordance with the spirit of the time and place" (213). Even if true freedom is associated with romantic "flights," the marketing of devices for others' freedom gives Carl a sense of responsibility and public service.

Though the acknowledgement of "stupid details" should not be overlooked, Lewis's zeal for literature made publishing seem quite worthwhile, an "optimistic rebellion" that could cure both the Village Virus and Tired Business Man's malaise. In the same spirit, while working at Doran, Lewis became one of the founding members of a club called the "Small Fry," composed of subordinate workers in publishing houses and headed up, notably, by that future middlebrow and O. Henry apostle, Christopher Morley. With Morley, Lewis helped plan a publisher-employee's luncheon club that would invite literary speakers and craft a newsletter to reform contemporary book publicity. The "Small Fry" offered what Schorer calls "plain descriptive accounts" (216) of books to offset the one-line grabbers of publicity prose and inflated testimonials. Morley's advocacy for this "reform" agenda, of course, soon became widely known in the trade. In his fable *Parnassus on Wheels* (1917), he would create the character of a traveling "Professor," a throwback to the country peddler, who traveled the countryside preaching the usefulness of good books to farmers.[18] Much as general advertisers utilized the language of "plain folk," Morley—the future proseltyzer for the Average Citizen—crafted his publisher surrogate as a "travelling missionary" (44) who offered "everlasting salvation" for the "little stunted minds" and lives of the village dwellers he met on the road. Protagonist Roger Mifflin, himself a fan of O. Henry, promotes books that "teach you how to live," and he sees himself not as one of those "mandarins of culture" who overlooks the "common folk" but as someone who gives the people "good, homely, honest stuff." In the sequels to this fable, Morley's protagonist lectures to a fresh young man from the "Grey Matter Advertising Agency" who needs to learn that books are "living advertisements" for themselves. The O. Henry modeling becomes all the more clear. Ensconced in what might well be an apothecary shop, Roger envisions books as curative potions: people need books for their idiosyncratic ills, he argues, but they just do not know they need them. Ads were therefore tied to books' "messages." Both Lewis's contemporary remarks on publishing and his memoirs are laced with the languages of evangelism, missionary work, and therapy; one of his reviewing pseudonyms, as mentioned earlier, was the "Village Doctor"—his own father rescripted in the garb of publicity's nostrums.[19]

In all, however, this mediation of commerce and culture was subject to contradictions. Woodward's syndicate service, for instance, provoked a challenge in 1914, when a bookseller wrote to *The Dial* to complain that a "hired corps" of New York publicity writers, "practically" in the pay of publishers whose advertising they solicited, were now using canned reviews to circumvent both local booksellers and the staffs of regional newspapers. Syndicate offerings presented themselves as local doctoring but in truth offered "tainted news." Woodward responded indignantly:

> With the possible exceptions of three or four of the big dailies that make a specialty of literary news, the book reviewing of the daily press is done by immature reporters, and people out of a job, and narrow-headed schoolteachers. . . . There are innumerable instances of absolutely worthless books being called "the book of the year," and so on, by reviewers of this stripe. . . . Then, we know of cases where really great books were ignored or dismissed with a line or two because the local reviewer had no literary standards or guides, and really had no idea of literature. Then, there are many cases of the morbidly perverse or immoral in literature being held up as wonderful and epoch-making productions because they happened to be handed out by the local editor to some long-haired extremist.

Even in Woodward's case against consumerism, one cannot overlook the middlebrow "reformist" claim to overcome the shallow one-liners of local criticism, to blend cultural "standards" and commerce, to avoid both amateurism and extremism—claims Lewis himself definitely internalized.[20]

Also, one cannot overlook the cosmopolitan hubris that was quite common to advertising at large. The fact was that Woodward's and Morley's prescriptions, the folkloric image of "Parnassus" come to the consumer notwithstanding, helped to centralize bookselling. In many ways, Woodward was running a book review wire service, and its puffery was always tied to pumping up a book by useful synopsis of the fundamentals: who is the author, what is his or her "message," can he or she "tell a story" (the answer is almost always yes). Even given Woodward's emphasis on professionalism and "impartiality," Lewis's publicity writing (under pseudonyms that hardly suggest professional aspirations) did go out under "Book of the Week" headlines, "Lively Paragraphs About Books," "Exciting Tales," or "Helpful Suggestions for Christmas Giving." Very few extant reviews offer negative remarks on books; publishers' names and prices are always dutifully noted. Indeed, his notices are full of bandwagon reasoning (everyone will be reading it, or "Books They're Talking About"), pleas to sentimentality and human tenderness, inflated "real-life" claims to documentarian authenticity. A blurring of the boundary in Lewis's mediation even extended to his own novel-writing. Lewis puffed books that he later tried to link his own novels to in other publicity campaigns; conversely, he clipped ads that quoted puffery he had authored, apparently seeing "name recognition" as advertising for his own career.[21]

These ambiguous dimensions to Lewis's work—creating a confluence between literary and commercial culture—were intrinsic to the kind of commodity he was servicing. As noted earlier, conservative publishers often claimed merely to tolerate the "stunts" of general advertising. And yet, in other lights, book publicity could seem like the quintessential commodity advertising. When Harcourt would say that a book was not like toothpaste, as much as commercial houses wanted it to be, he partly meant this as a lament: that is, that publishers were thereby forced to produce a new ad campaign every three days for a new title. Much of Lewis's recurrent energizing, and much of his sense of routinization, must be tied to this treadmill created by marketing the book commodity—the requirement that one must constantly drum up *new* stunts for each "message" and yet not be too "impractical" (that is, costly). (In one letter, Lewis calls a publicist a man "who every day has to try some new stunt in practical advertising.") "Stunts" could thus create a discernible devaluation on the only currency, words, which could meet this demand; intellectual clutter followed as well. Even Morley's fictional proselytizer admitted that the "life of a bookseller is very demoralizing to the intellect." Dipping into book after book, "[h]is mind gradually fills itself with miscellaneous flotsam, with superficial opinions, with a thousand half-knowledges" (101). Lewis's letters also express this fear.[22] This anxiety about intellectual devaluation combined, in turn, with Lewis's developing unease about how much of his "energy" was really his own.

As Doran attested, Lewis amazed his office peers with his vitality. In his early "New Thought" serials Lewis outwardly professed vim and vigor,[23] and yet, privately, his original plan to escape only grew in intensity. The result was not merely a sense of confinement but a fragmented outlook on the job itself. Doran claimed that Lewis was so content that the young man had told him he wanted to work in publishing forever; privately, however, Lewis referred to himself in a letter to Hamlin Garland as "stolidly and stodgily here on the job every day." (In publishing, Morley would note, "jobs" are the "overstocks of laggard titles" or the special house schemes that never move off the shelf.) To his wife, Lewis spoke about the absurdity of writing ad slogans and packaged lies. He referred to his desk at work as a "gray sea-mirrored dune"; to Grace he spoke of his short stories as "our key to freedom." In one letter, he said that he was glad neither he nor his wife wanted "a life-time of that strain, of fame mixed with duplex apartments and motor cars and the rare privilege of being allowed to eat lobster at midnight in company with three actors and a social climber."[24] No longer wanting to "climb" up the back stairs into the honeycombed space of modern bureaucratic life, his own vocational identification had begun to splinter. Being promoted seemed simply to risk being put in the position of motivating others in a tyrannical way. A better salary—again, in part because his class awareness was so pegged to a sense of how "jobs" met consumer needs—now looked like a boss's license to require him to work overtime.

Finally, this eerie, splintering effect of bureaucratic life extended into Lewis's sense of client relationships as well—that is, into his relationships with authors. As time passed, Doran noticed the emerging contradiction that Lewis himself had become a prominent young author for another house. To Doran, this may have raised the question of employee "loyalty," but Lewis saw it differently. He saw that he was now in the position of marketing some authors—and managing them—while *he* was in the position of being managed somewhere else. (Conversely, while at Doran, he would write to Harper's, as a fellow ad man, and tell them how to promote his own fiction.) One of Lewis's letters points to what amounts to a social hall of mirrors. After complaining to a correspondent about the ills of contemporary publishing-house reviewing, Lewis added:

> Of course it behooves a bright young man at the publishers to preserve a suave attitude of commendation toward all the Game; to belief that ALL is for the Best in this Best of All Possible Worlds. . . . And I'd by God rather have that attitude than to do nothing but go about table d'hotes and curse the revieweeers. Nevertheless, to you, whom I know tho I've never seen you, I'll admit that sometimes the American reception of books makes me so damned sore that I'd quit the novel game if I were not as stubborn as a

> mule. . . . Thank god I'm not dependent on my novels for a living—I can and do hold down a job, write pot-boilers. . . .
>
> You'll be amused at this outburst from a person who, nursing other Prom[inent] Y[oung] Authors along, daily hears just such outbursts from them and comforts them. . . . I'm going to mail this quick to you, and then tomorrow, when I'm again a wise young publisher, it'll be gone.[25]

The white collar contradictions running through this passage are hardly lessened by the fact that Lewis, in writing his own publicity, had contributed to clouding the very professional climate he claimed to reform. However much he attempted to combine high culture and commercial management, however much he compared his publicity work to nursing or other therapeutic skills, he also experienced the "double-take" of being on the other side of the memo, being a client for ministrations not unlike his own. The fact that the publicity writer cannot be separated from the young author in the letter above is very much to the point. In fact, though the letter lapses back on Lewis's ancillary strategy of using publishing as a fallback, he reverses his original claim; writing is now identified as the supplementary job, called "potboiling," and both fields are "games." In positioning him both as manager and (to coin a Lewisism) "managee," the office had begun to shape even the kind of "middle" class prophecy he was drawn to.

| | |

If Sherwood Anderson was an eclectic thinker, the young Sinclair Lewis was temperamentally an encyclopedic one—so much so that critics have generally assumed his early career lacked an intellectual rationale altogether. His life beyond the office seemed a tangle of loose ends. He had sojourned at Upton Sinclair's Helicon Hall, Greenwich Village, and Carmel's literary colony, yet satirized "Hobohemia" as he moved into publicity work; he shifted aimlessly from job to job, yet wrote those upbeat "New Thought" serials; he moved in and out of the Socialist party, and yet authored what critics have often dubbed "affirmative" novels about American business.[26] Lewis has therefore been variously described as a young writer "studying himself," a quixotic and faddish thinker lacking a "settled perspective or viewpoint," so much the "intellectual vagabond" that he was, in Schorer's estimate, practically "impervious" (181) to the main philosophical currents of the Innocent Rebellion. Critics have been recurrently perplexed not only by the apparent contradictions within Lewis's early thought but by the apparent discontinuity between his apprentice fiction and the work of the 1920s.[27] The early work has been dismissed as "frankly potboiling" (a charge Lewis later denied); as the forgotten poetic expression typical of a "lost" generation that was intellectually disillusioned by the war (a pose his fiction cannot easily support);[28] as a phase of "optimism" and "romance" that dissipated, mysteriously, into the pessimism and "dissent" of the 1920s. For one decade Lewis was called impervious to the intellectual ferment of his times; for the next he was its representative.[29]

If a consensus can be said to exist among these various interpretations, it is that the author's early socialism was a brief flirtation, a romantic optimism wholly inconsistent with his satiric calling, his business work, and his mature art. In point of fact, all these assumptions err by measuring Lewis by brittle and abstract notions of philosophical formalism, radicalism, or "realism"—thereby dismissing him as a shallow thinker or "journalist" (Schorer's charge in particular). At the very least, however—in light of Anderson's or Rice's affiliations in the teens—Lewis's intellectual interests should not appear as idiosyncratic as they once did. Simply put, like these writers Lewis was initially drawn to middle-class British socialism—most notably, in his case, to H. G. Wells—because Fabianism provided a cultural script quite readable in terms of his own life. Specifically, Fabian theory described not only a precise evolutionary moment for contemporary life—a "middle" and potentially stagnated historical phase between capitalism and socialism—but also predicted that the "creative" and technical members of the middle class could, of their own choosing, "will" this evolution along. To Lewis, Fabianism was not a static doctrine but a manner of flexible cultural explanation, discursive and impressionistic, prone to small detail and grand prophecy alike. Moreover, Lewis saw a connection between Fabianism's voluntaristic language and the popular American variants of "Positive Thinking" pervading his office life. In sum, Fabianism provided the substance of middle-class myth, serving to "synopsize" historical change, personal psychology, and even literary thought in a syncretic and even occasionally fantastic mode. It was a manner with room for dream and for doubt, romance and burlesque.

How Lewis proposed to map out his translation of a Fabian-inspired literary program is apparent in a little-regarded essay from 1914, a *Bookman* review he wrote entitled "Relation of the Novel to the Present Social Unrest: The Passing of Capitalism." Here, Lewis outlined what he considered the "biggest, vitalist current" in contemporary letters:

> . . . does it not by now seem that practically every writer—certainly in America and to some extent in England—who is gravely seeking to present the romance of actual life as it is today, must perforce show capitalism as a thing attacked, passing—whether the writer lament or rejoice or merely complain at that passing? Few of them have any very clear idea of how the passing is to occur; as to what is to take its place. And now more than ever, with the European war shaking all the belief of the International Socialists in their might, one wonders what and how and why and when. Yet there it is, in nearly every seeing writer of today—an attack on capitalism. (332)

Lewis demonstrated here much of Fabianism's own manner, exhibiting a vigorous and yet randomly digestive approach, synthesizing trends in fiction from across the Atlantic, the debate within socialism about whether the Great War was capitalism's last gasp, and the current American interest in "the romance of real life" in novels.[30] With equal flexibility, he took in the current vogue of literary naturalism, the works of the Greenwich Village crowd, and a mélange of lesser-known authors, some of whom were published by his own press. Like Anderson, Lewis seemed especially intent upon revising naturalism, as the prevailing American genre, from a new generational viewpoint infused with socialist reasoning and standards of efficiency. Gone, in Lewis's view, were both the "pure individualism" and the fatalistic invocations of "blind force" that infused late-Victorian Anglo-American fiction in a Howells or a Hardy (328). Instead, he found contemporary novelists aiming for a more "complete criticism of life today," placing "an individual's actions" against the background of an entire "People" demanding their rights (328–29).

But most naturalists, Lewis argued, seemed out of step with these changing times. Dreiser's *Financier* series—based, after all, upon events in the 1870s—appeared, to Lewis, to sympathize with Frank Cowperwood's power and individualism. Robert Herrick's Chicago novels Lewis found "earnest" but offering no "wider solution" other than old entrepreneurial initiative. Frank Norris's *The Pit* and *The Octopus*—the latter based upon the Mussel Slough affair of 1880—seemed to "take all the apparent injustice of the world as the necessary friction of progress," a view Lewis shrewdly saw was quite "comforting to the capitalist" himself.[31] Though Lewis admired the passion of naturalism, noting particularly its penetration into the "hearts of crushed men," he was himself on the lookout for fiction that would convey a more holistic view of the capitalist "system," would not romanticize but protest its irrationality and inefficiency, and that would offer answers in a more collective vein (332–33). Not surprisingly, then, Lewis reserved his greatest praise for H. G. Wells—the one good thing, Lewis said ironically, capitalism had produced. "Without ranting, without saying very much about Socialism," Lewis wrote, "Wells goes the whole journey and convicts Capitalism of puerile cruelty to most people, leaving in the reader's mind a strong feeling that men are about being done with leaving the conduct of things in general to little men in woolen undergarments who have made a fortune by the manufacture of injurious patent medicines. He leaves a strong desire to see men get together and act like men; [to] try seriously . . . to find out what is the matter with the economic system, and remedy it" (329).[32]

How Lewis arrived at this program has often been a mystery. Although Wells's influence is practically the sole serious debt Lewis scholarship acknowledges, even this is often trivialized as another phase in the young author's intellectual vagabonding and faddishness—a matter of borrowed themes or generalized sympathy for the British author's "romantic gaiety" or reformist "optimism."[33] Lewis's fascination was, however, of longer standing, staying power, and detail. In the first place, his fascination for Wells was layered (as Schorer grudgingly details) upon a developing curiosity about political alternatives going back to Oberlin, where the young aspiring missionary resisted the visiting lecturer Mark Hanna because he "represented . . . selfish & dominant capital"; to Yale, where he was called "Red" for his hair and his radical views; to Helicon Hall, where he also encountered New Thought advocates; to Carmel, where he befriended and worked for socialist and poet George Sterling. In 1911 Lewis joined the local New York chapter of the Socialist party, sometimes signed his letters (as Jack London had) "Yours for the Revolution," witnessed Emma Goldman and Theodore Dreiser debate anarchism (which Lewis felt needed to wait upon the achievement of economic equality).[34]

To admit that Lewis's commitment to social action or political work was not as strong as that of these advocates of revolutionary socialism is to miss the point. All along Lewis viewed these figures (like the naturalists some of them were) as members of an older, mentoring generation whose working-class radicalism smacked of bohemianism and mechinistic thinking. His private and public comments suggest he felt that Marxian socialism and anarchism were rapidly growing out of date. In the teens, Lewis found the obligatory Marx—probably *Capital*—to be a "dusty collection of terms" like the Bible, a dull treatise about profits, wages, and rents, an antiquated text concerned with only the materialist dimensions of modern culture and politics. When Lewis later recalled discovering *Mr. Polly*—what he called that "eternal story" of the "Little Man"—he cast that remembrance in an anecdote about squirming in a bohemian parlor while a young woman pressed Emma Goldman and anarchism upon him.[35] Lewis's interests, like Rice's and Anderson's, ran to the spiritual, psychological, and voluntaristic, and his faith was not based in a revolutionary working class.

In contrast, Wells's social accounts of the historic role to be played by the "creative and imagination-producing professions" obviously struck a chord. Wells's version of the future was based in a vision of class "deliquescence"—the degradation of the upper and lower classes into "functionless" and static entities (the Eloi and the Warlocks) and the development of a heterogeneous social "middle" that was different from the petty bourgeois class that preceded it. Though this intermediate group was a "molten mass" with a "vast, intricate confusion" of social functions and types, to Wells it was still the only "really living portion of the social organism," one that was currently distending and restratifying under technical advancement and education so as to develop "specific new groups" with more "distinctive characters and ideals." The "nucleus" of these new middle strata were mechanics, engineers, and medical experts who would join forces with a broader educated class to disseminate its scientific reason in society as a whole. Opposed to this cadre of experts and "capable men," Wells predicted, would be those who, in the "more or less necessary operations of organization, promotion, advertisement and trade," would cling to the degraded culture of the political and financial operator, Lewis's man in woolen undergarments.[36] For the time being, however, these competing elements "will be mingled confusedly together, passing into one another by insensible gradations," swept along by mechanical progress and hampered by outworn tradition. Wells's Spencerian synthesis of the "new republic" still lay in the future, but he also argued that, contrary to the predictions of Marx, the middle class was not really disappearing, nor should current middle-class citizens resist becoming absorbed into the salaried positions of large organizations. They should, instead of "remain[ing] disorganized and passive," become "intelligent and decisive" in averting Plutocracy in favor of Socialism, "whose opposition is the supreme social and political fact in the world at the present time."[37]

Up to a point, the critical commonplace that Lewis did little more than apply Wellsian "themes" to his apprentice novels is plausible; Martin Light's characterization of Lewis's art as "quixotic," even picaresque, seems especially on point. Wells had provided a ready-made rationale for the seeming vagabondage of Lewis's intellectual interests: his ridicule of anarchism and yet claims to socialist interests that extended through even *Babbitt;* his praise in "Relation of the Novel" for such forgotten novels as Comfort's *Midstream,* a wild and visionary tract about the quest for "will" and "world-consciousness"; even Lewis's interest in New Thought philosophy.[38] The New Thought advocates for whom Lewis wrote felt there was a recognizable continuity between technocratic socialism and the uplift of their own mind-cure techniques.[39] Wells's example, at first, seemed to invite merely discursiveness and utopian fantasy, and the connections to business life seem vague indeed. ("For a socialist," Carl Ericson remarks in his diary, "I certainly do despise the pee-pul's *taste*!")

Nonetheless, the "quixotic" or vagabonding label loses value precisely at this point: when Lewis's translation of Wells is depicted as sheer faddishness and not as an attempt to "re-script" the mundane details of his life. Even a romance like *Trail of the Hawk* demonstrated Lewis's belief that Wells's philosophy could be scripted in this way; the "Touricar" itself was, in short, a coming down to earth, to the terrain a "real" middle-class man might occupy. This is especially apparent in how Lewis represents the Fabian professor Frasier as he describes the philosophy of Wells and Shaw:

> "These men have perceived that this world is not a crazy-quilt of unrelated races, but a collection of human beings completely related, with all our interests—food and ambitions and the desire to play—absolutely in common; so that if we would take thought all together, and work together, as a football team does, we would start making a perfect world.
>
> That's what socialism . . . means. . . .
>
> The solution of labour's problem; increasing safety and decreasing hours of toil, and a way out for the unhappy consumer who is ground between labour and capital. A real democracy and the love of work that shall come when work is not relegated to wage slaves, but joyously shared in a community inclusive of the living beings of all nations." (81–82)

This is an extraordinarily rich passage for understanding Lewis's translation. First of all, Lewis identifies being "middle class" with consumerhood, with a "dependence" not just tied to the rationalization of work but to the world of goods. The essential meaning of being "middle," therefore, is that of marketing and consuming goods from which other "wage slaves" are excluded—

a position that makes one "unhappy." Here, one finds how inward-looking Lewis's middle-class vision really was.

Furthermore, Lewis seems interested in Wells's socialism partly because it negotiates this cultural convolution, assuring the "maker" and seller that his own consumerist needs—"food and ambitions and the desire to play"—are shared up and down the social hierarchy. Thus "working together," improving labor safety and advancing technical progress, which supposedly frees all persons from the regimentation of work, will create a more "joyous" and communal (even international) life. Thus, for Lewis, the "ad-venture" of the Touricar follows naturally. Carl places his faith in the ability of "creative" engineers and designers to incorporate freedom and world-consciousness into the decaying forms of capitalism, to replace "slavery" with freedom. This was a program very much in the gradualist vein and perhaps as close as Lewis gets to Anderson's dreams of sales mastery. Carl goes from "playing" to the crowd ("flying before thousands") to trying to serve it (213), and "with the love of a woman"—reminiscent of the McPhersons and an ingredient that "Relation of the Novel" also endorsed—Carl is able to overcome some of his doubts by an act of Positive Thinking. He retains his faith in his ability to incorporate "temperament" into capitalism; the novel ends with a new job "adventure," and the promise that Mr. and Mrs. Ericson will inject a little "madness" into the "Respectable." "How bully it is to be living," Carl concludes, "if you don't have to give up living in order to make a living" (384).

Beyond these problematic matters of self-scripting, Wells's influence also went beyond matters of social prophecy or ideology into instructions on literary form—particularly the "paradigmatic" Wells, who seemed to synopsize the "state" of a nation in the confused psyche of a Dickensian character.[40] Centering his method in studies of character, in what he called "study of the association and inter-reaction of individualized human beings, inspired by diversified motives, ruled by traditions, and swayed by the suggestions of a complex atmosphere," Wells collapsed cultural heterogeneity into a web of individual association, indecision, and conflicting motives. As Van Wyck Brooks realized, the protagonist of Wells's *History of Mr. Polly* is "not merely an individual, he is an emblem of the whole, he is society *in concreto*." Wells, Brooks saw, had an "uncanny" ability to telescope his view from "the very little to the very large," thus "elaborating a bridge—between the little world of dumb routine and the great world of spacious initiatives." Wells provided Lewis with a technique whereby, as the narrator of *Polly* says, one could "bridge the General and the Particular." Mr. Polly was a microcosm of the larger decay of capitalism. His life, Wells said, had no tragic scale, just a "slow, chronic process of consecutive small losses"; he "lived at variable speeds," "muddled and wrapped about and entangled like a creature born in the jungle who has never seen sea or sky." He was a symptom, Wells said, of the "collective dullness of our community."[41]

Wells's "paradigmatic" or synoptic mode worked in several dimensions. First, Wells's heroes tended to "outline" history (as the author's later efforts would), placing the self in a tight historical bind between capitalism and socialism. A large part of Wells's particular appeal in this country was that he, like other Fabians, placed American social development at center stage in the ongoing crisis of late industrial capitalism, rewriting the Old World/New World mythology in terms of a coming revolutionary change. But more to the point, by working in a syncretic, Darwinian mode, Wells tightened the analogy even further, collapsing the distance between national "species" and the individual psyche—and particularly, as Rice and Anderson might have said, collapsing both to a crisis of the will. Nearly every social problem "ha[d] at its core a psychological problem," Wells wrote, "one in which the idea of individuality is an essential factor." Middle-class hetereogeneity he diagnosed, perhaps a little loosely, as "strictly analogous to that strange mental disorder which is known to psychologists as multiple personality"; the common citizenry of Britain was like a confused man, "without clear aim; it does not know except in the vaguest terms what it wants to do; it has impulses; it has fancies." Protagonists thus became, as they would for Lewis, emblems of nationhood, the "new" republic trying to be born. Wells's analogizing of middle-class persons and state was thus reciprocal with his sense of historical change. Disavowing class struggle, Wells asserted that to him socialism was "no more and no less than the awakening of a collective consciousness in humanity, a collective will and a collective mind out of which finer individualities may arise."[42] This was an important twist; this final promise opened the door for a rhetoric of human commonality in what was otherwise a technocratic vision. In "Relation of the Novel" Lewis wrote that the Pollys of the world have a capacity for joy and beauty "at least as keen and subtle as yours or mine"; eventually, Polly discovers that "[if] the world does not please you, you can change it." The common man could be satirized but not abandoned; one's "diabolic intentions are veiled" (330) in the doubts of a character otherwise buried by the sedimentary layers of his own middle-class routine. "Without ranting, without saying very much about

Socialism," Lewis realized, Wells made "[t]he foolish haberdashery where Mr. Polly accumulated poverty and indigestion . . . frankly the symbol of all the State's activities." On the other hand, Wells was also "the discoverer of importance in the pettiest and drabbest character."[43] (This combination of "paradigmatic" and "diabolic" writing is especially relevant to the radically antithetical receptions Lewis would provoke.)

In Lewis's idiom, the novel became "high" naturalism made down-to-earth Touricar—both myth and fact. How he began to implement Wells's program is most apparent in Lewis's prosaically entitled book of 1917: *The Job,* subtitled *An American novel. The Job* told the story of a member of the disenfranchised old middle class, "an untrained, ambitious, thoroughly commonplace small-town girl" named Una Golden. Upon the death of her father, Una is forced to abandon village life for the dull routine of the urban salariat. Lewis made explicit his primary goal of modernizing the naturalistic rhetoric. To one reviewer, he had vowed to write a book about "the office *as I know it,* the office of real workers, without any of the romance of the Business Melodramas and Big Deals."[44] Lewis intentionally scaled down naturalistic proportions: Una attends a commercial college, lives in a boardinghouse and learns to take orders from her bosses. Initially, as with Wells or Lewis's publicity writing, romance is only a potential quality, a life force submerged in the quiet desperation lived by tired business people. Commuting to work on the El, Una sits across from a "well-bathed man with cynical eyes" (116) who fails to see the drama in her aspirations. The struggle, as Lewis saw it, was her entrapment in a world distorted by the profit motive and bureaucracy:

> There was a heroic side to this spectacle of steel trains charging at forty miles an hour beneath twenty-story buildings. The engineers had done their work well, made a great thought in steel and concrete. And then the business man and bureaucrats had made the great thought a curse. There was in the Subway all the romance which story-telling youth goes seeking. . . . But however striking these dramatic characters may be . . . they figure merely as an odor, a confusion, to the permanent serf of the Subway. . . . A long underground station, a catacomb with a cement platform, this was the chief feature of the city vista to the tired girl who waited there each morning. A clean space, but damp, stale, like the corridor to a prison—as indeed it was, since through it each morning Una entered the day's business life. (134)

Here was the Wellsian bridge between the General and the Particular. The setting symbolized a social and psychic "State," the individual (Una) was representative of a new class. Lewis intentionally lowers his eyes from naturalistic heights to explore a catacomb of wage slavery.

For a time, Una is wholly trapped. She is besieged by office triviality, by bosses who extort work and then take credit, by advertising schemes that "make something out of nothing" (224). The struggle for her spirit is encapsulated in the novel's love story. Una's dalliance with the cynical publicist Walter Babson, the closest thing the text offers to the young Sinclair Lewis, temporarily breaks off; in her despair, she is engulfed in a bad marriage to a salesman named Eddie Schwirtz, a character Lewis later described as a prototype of Babbitt. The soul of capitalism has temporarily fallen. Yet after dismal days of marriage (reminiscent of Dreiser's Carrie with the failing Hurstwood), Una finally acquires the will to break out of her life. She does so by effecting a kind of mind-cure. "Her whole point of view was changed," Lewis writes. "Instead of looking for the evils of the business world, she was desirous of seeing in it all the blessings she could." She is thus able to "rise above her own personal weariness" and see business's superiority to other "muddled worlds"; she "believed again, as in commercial college she had callowly believed, that business was beginning to see itself as communal, world-ruling, and beginning to be inspired to communal, kingly virtues and responsibility" (280). On the surface, Una acquires all the virtues of modern management: dressing for success, "sincerity," and successful conversion of the "energy of life" into a career in real estate and hotel management. Her exterior is a testimonial to Positive Thinking. Internally, however, she retains a "half-comprehended faith in a Fabian socialism," believing in an evolutionary process that would result in the "abolition of anarchic business competition, to the goal of a tolerable and beautiful life."[45] Not too surprisingly, Una is reunited with Walter Babson. A story by Lewis titled "Honestly—If Possible," printed in Lorimer's *Post* in 1916, ended much the same way. Here, a young real estate copywriter named Terry Ames is bored with office life and despairs of ever being able to write "honest" copy, but Terry's faith is restored when he falls in love with a female office worker. Together, they vow to turn things around.[46]

There were certainly many elements in Wells for Lewis to draw upon: a script not just for "optimism" but for describing contemporary social confusion; romantic energy but a decidedly technocratic vision; radical politics but cast in regenerative new-middle-class terms. Wells, in particular, shifted the grounds of liberalism so that the "mass" no longer referred to the working classes or even manual laborers but to an aggregation of middle-level occupations lacking the "capabilities" of experts. To Lewis this was the stuff of a modern class myth. On the other hand, it was almost as if Wells provided too many answers. Wells often seems nearly omnicompetent in Lewis's eyes—an instance of the "capable man" become Divine Literatus. Obviously sympathetic to Wells's expansive, discursive style, Lewis would often stuff the consciousness of relatively small-minded characters with a surfeit of issues. Meanwhile, Lewis inherited the decidedly clinical and non-egalitarian side of Wells, the technocratic envy beneath the spiritual rush,[47] rarely transcending the middle-class horizons of Wells's example. Though Lewis's novels would provide an encyclopedic compendia of "capable," creative, and yet troubled middle men—automobile marketers, hotel managers, real estate brokers, doctors, scientists, preachers—had he more patience for the "antiquarian" business of rents, wages, and profits, he might well have attended to the vertical and relational aspects of class conflict that were part of the "system" he said modern social fiction should describe.

Finally, although Lewis was relatively uninterested in the materialist dimensions of class, they had already become interested in him. Rather than "kingly" visions, even Carl Ericson occasionally sees another republic: one in which the "tyranny of nine to five is stronger, more insistent, in every department of life, than the most officious oligarchy. Inspectors can be bribed, judges softened, and recruiting sergeants evaded, but only the grace of God will turn 3:30 into 5:30." As E.J. Hobsbawm suggests, the salariat was a stratum with a "double-edged" social potential.[48] In the short stories written in these years, Lewis evolved a darker vision eventually at the heart of *Babbitt*. The Pollys and Wrenns, those timid birds of the fading order, failed to take up the cry of the future; instead, they adopted the modern crow of the advertiser and booster.

| | |

Lewis's early business stories, which usually ran either in the *Post* or the *Metropolitan* magazine, have not attracted much attention. (Schorer, for one, was at a loss as to whether he should take Lewis's apprentice work seriously.) Nor has the formalist tendency to affix broad generic categories—"romance" or "realism"—produced much analysis; these tales often juxtapose chivalric imagery, modern social burlesque, and futuristic socialist prophecy in the space of a few pages. Lewis's protagonists—usually publicity writers—were mildly appealing and yet pathetic figures, both boosters and disbelievers, spasmodically plotting revenge against a culture of their own making. In fact, the unsettled social subtext is telling: protagonists of these stories, and Lewis himself, are decidedly confused about how "serious" their work really is. The intellectual grounding of these tales reverberates with seismographic doubt. Crafted in both drab realism and hyperbolic diction, they work not as fables of class (like O. Henry's or Ferber's tales) or even dream-work (as with Anderson's novels); rather, they are exercises in a literary "double-take," giving voice to the sanctions of white collar life and yet so excessively overstating them that the prose often looks like self-burlesque.[49] The divided life of salaried work was not merely the subject of Lewis's white collar fictions; to a large extent, it was also their substance.

Even the more upbeat *Post* stories reveal that Lewis's youthful marriage of faiths was not only Positive Thinking, but positively wishful. Within the young writer himself the will was fading. The persistence of the Wellsian premise, but not the promise, is visible in a story called "Commutation: $9.17," no doubt drawn upon the days dragging between Port Washington and New York. Here Lewis tells the tale of a mean-spirited office manager named Whittier J. Small, a Long Islander whose defining characteristic is his absolute averageness. "His face was medium looking," Lewis writes. "He was medium sized. He was medium." Small's desire is to be well liked—in particular, to join locally prestigious social clubs. Like George Babbitt, later bracketed between the Dopplebraus and the McKelveys, Small is befriended by a mousy character named Percy Weather, but he longs to associate instead with one Cornelius Berry, a "man so accepted by smart society that he had once spent a week-end at Narraganset Pier—where the tide rises only seventeen minutes later than at Newport." Small finally devises a ruse to climb. When the commuter train switches from an express to a local, he leads a contingent of suburbanites who resist having their tickets rechecked; now a hero, he snubs Weather and sits alongside Berry. But when he aspires to yet another rung by repeating the same strategy, he is thrown off the train. Later, he is snubbed by friends, ridiculed at the club, loses his job—and, in final ignominy, loses his discount rate ($9.17) as a regular commuter. The protagonist ends the tale chastened, not nearly so mean-spirited in a new job. Although Lorimer might well have been pleased by this seeming endorsement of shrewder personnel management, Lewis's use of "commutation" obviously implied, more diabolically, that Small had barely avoided a permanent social sentencing—and imprisonment.[50]

This threat of entrapment appears again in "If I Were Boss," another apparently upbeat *Post* story. Here Lewis tells the tale of Charley McClure, an ambitious and good-hearted traveling salesman, a small-fry "echoing millions of underdogs everywhere," convinced that, if he were promoted, he would be both friendly and efficient. But when Charley does get his promotion, however, he begins to recognize the plight of the office manager under whom he had once rebelled. Lewis writes that, at twenty, "Charley had believed that bosses were a race of congenital fiends organized to keep young men from getting jobs in the first place, and making good on them in the second. Now he was equally sure that bright young men of his generation were organized to teach one another new ways of being unreliable and generally worthless." The final irony is evident when his immediate boss hires an up-and-coming salesman who makes proposals for improving office efficiency and gradually takes over some of Charley's territory. Later, Charley slides "into a strange vision, of which he wasn't even conscious. Standing motionless, his hands prosaically in his trouser pockets, he felt he had lost all individuality as Charley McClure; that he was only an indistinguishable part of the unknown force that drives pilgrimages." Lewis says Charley sees his office comrades as "all one person, confusedly carrying on some vast work that was to make a great world." Here, to be sure, is an echo of Wells's theology of collective will and world-consciousness; once again Lorimer would have liked this seeming invocation of business service. Yet Charley is actually motionless, his place in the evolutionary process described as an act of submission, of drift rather than mastery; he is "Boss" of very little. In another harbinger of *Babbitt,* Charley returns to face his son's complaint that his bosses generally will not let subordinates get ahead. Charley counsels his son to strive and succeed while, in the back of his mind, he plots ways to resist the upstart in his own office. At the microcosmic level—like Lewis's own experience in managing those "Prom. Y. Authors"—the evolutionary process looks suspiciously like a revolving door—which, incidentally, was invented around 1890 and installed in American buildings during these years.[51]

Part of the point may be that, contrary to Wells's predictions, the kind of work Lewis did only drew him closer, not to capable technical expertise, but to the superfluous sales culture Wells had described as the vestige of a decayed Plutocracy. But, for the moment, it is far more important to recognize the way that Lewis's introduction to the science of ad-writing seemed to acquaint him with the disturbing similarity between the therapy of mind-cures (including book-cures, even Wellsian-cures) and the before and after puffery of the modern advertisement. This ludicrous but disabling likeness also exposed how Positive Thinking, in a bureaucratic setting, often functioned simply as a superior's way of managing office morale and productivity. Revealingly, one of Lewis's fictional surrogates, real estate promoter Terry Ames of "Honestly—If Possible," had once been a fan of Positive Thinking, even purchasing a book titled *Punch the Buzzer on Yourself.* But soon Terry reflects that although it was a "chatty book," it "sneaked up behind you and yelled in your ear in fourteen-point italics. Yet all that it said was to be good and work hard and buy the other books by the same author." In other words, the Positive Thinking manual is revealed as merely advertising copy itself—for more book buying. Both *The Job*'s confident closing and that of this story masked the fact that Lewis had already resigned from Doran in November of 1915.[52]

For all of its scaled-down romanticism, what "Honestly—If Possible" really indicated, as the vacillation of the title suggested, was the splintering of Lewis's own faith. Hero Terry Ames is described as a bookish schoolboy who, most of all, is in search of a philosophy that can overcome the degradation and isolation he feels. A Wellsian "good clean life," he says, "sounds so simple in the books and works out so jaggedly in ordinary life." Privately, he even draws fictional sketches of a young hero who would "convert the office to truth, single-handed," an office Lancelot. Terry is seen, in fact, as a kind of O. Henry protagonist, singular and solitary and yet "one of the three hundred thousand" young men who ply their trade in the New York work force. Immersed in the smell of "paper and typewriter oil and eraser dust," he occupies a "below-stairs" world that is lorded over by a cynical and tyrannical boss. The city and office themselves are seen as both a desert and wilderness, a "thicket of useless industry," or (as in *The Job*) as a kind of Egyptian tomb dominated by grey and granite, blank and brooding, itself cryptic in its lack of answers. "Gloomed," in fact, is used to describe Terry's life. He is "facing the blankness of life as somberly as an anchorite in a parching desert cell. If he could only be heroic or tragic or criminal or anything that would make him feel things! Any sorrow rather than row on row of unchanging grey days. He wanted to do high, vague, generous things, and the city told him to attend strictly to his desk . . . You would have been amused—or touched or impatient or morally edified—to see Terry trying to find out what a good, clean life really meant in the case of a young man whose boss pompously encouraged him to write advertisements that were deliberate, careful, scientific lies" (28).

The alternative interpretations Lewis offered here (amusement, sympathy, skepticism, moral edification) reflect the salariat's hall of mirrors. Much as Anderson's white collar minds worry over voices echoing in their ears, Terry Ames's world—with its imperative "you," even the assonance of "sorrow" and "row upon row"—evokes a narrative echo chamber. This reverberation plays itself out in the plot. For instance, Terry's devilish cohort, the optimistic rebel Miss Bratt, offers him a better version of himself; though he fancies himself as a lost Galahad, he sees that "[h]er face was as serenely gallant as that of a boy crusader . . . so untiring, so incisively interested in her work." But, on the negative side, Terry sees another kind of reflection in the very work that he does. Mooning morosely over an ad he is writing, he tries to imagine his implied audience—the tired, cold, overworked man of northern climes—for the deliberate lies he is writing about Florida. He finally realizes, "That's me." The real impetus for Terry's desire to reform comes not just from love but from a correspondent who writes in and tells him the truth about the land he is selling.

Lewis's use of the imperative "you" may also mean to involve the reader in a kind of correspondence across the border of his fiction—the implied reader shares in this mirroring effect. In Lewis's use of the third person so very singular, we ("you") have access directly to Terry's thoughts, sharing (with the narrator) Terry's emotional variations, his indignation over (in a characteristic double-take) the boss's "jolly little way of influencing *you*" (emphasis mine). We/you become, in Nathanael West's words, the perpetrator and the victim of the lies Terry writes. Provisionally, this implication of the reader in the making and consuming of ads might be a way of making the reader recoil from the process. The fiction itself proposes to be like the reforming uplift Terry imagines, a desire to see the truth in the telling.

Nevertheless there are contradictions that contain whatever rebellion the story proposes. For one thing, Terry and Miss Bratt agree they cannot really forsake their middle-class standing. When Terry glooms over his wage slavery, he has a vision of the class beneath him: bums occupying a park bench—where Terry worries about becoming a "derelict" in spite of being "clean" and "efficient"—and the gum-chewing temporary girls who are hired on to do the company's "personal" letter writing campaign. Terry and the rebel Bratt agree that they could never descend to this level, that of "a day laborer." This is, in fact, what reinforces their resolve, one might say their realism, about staying on the white-handed job. Even their marriage is based upon the fact that, if one spouse is fired, the other can work; their needs as middle-class beings will continue to be met no matter how much they rebel. (In essence, they incorporate.) Even their support for truth in advertising hinges upon sustaining their consumer needs, no wonder they recommit themselves to the round of life (office work, domesticity, perhaps Florida retirement) that the story seems to debunk. The contradiction—"That's me"—lurks as the principal device of reconfining the tale's rebellion. Here was, in some ways, the return of the repressed "Tired Businessman" from Lewis's publicity writing.

In other ways Lewis's desire to scale down naturalistic scenarios had overshot the mark, forcing just such a containment back on his own fictive rebels. Just as he had reduced the drama of "Big Deals" to the petty intrigue of the office, the Fabian will became impoverished to simply the renewed energy of the office worker ready to face another day. "I guess there's nothing but petty victories in life," Terry Ames's girlfriend tells him, "that and the real big thing of going on fighting." Increasingly, Lewis's characters settle for lording over smaller and smaller territories—the office, the interior of a train, the social club—even as their sense of romance becomes eerily disproportionate to the trivial drama of their lives. Failed melodrama easily becomes farce; the quest for will becomes an ongoing mid-life crisis. Like Charley McClure, many of Lewis's protagonists now see life as repeating itself; they find themselves mocked by the will of younger subordinates and blocked by the intransigence of older superiors; their schemes boomerang back on them.[53] In their own middle-class habitat, they experience a white collar malaise approximating social claustrophobia. Yet what Lewis was really intent upon—in the more severe and diabolic stories in the *Metropolitan*—was a paradigmatic character who internalized the faith, doubt, and dissent of white collar justifications in his soul.

The original presentation of the Lancelot Todd stories in the *Metropolitan* magazine hinted, in a mock-serious way, at their autobiographical resonance. (The biographical referent, that is, is part of the publicity tease.) The first tale, "Snappy Display," appeared with a photograph of Lewis over a caption that said: "This author is at his best when his stories center around his lurid past." Throughout the series, the hand-drawn illustrations of Todd looked eerily like the author himself. Just as Lewis described himself to friends as "the George M. Cohan, the Billy Sunday, the Mary Pickford of modern fiction," he called Todd the "prophet of profits," the "bard of bacon," the "sweet singer of shotguns." In "Snappy Display," the reader learns that Todd, like Una Golden, was from a small town and had always displayed a skill for applying sharp words to make a sale. He applied the theology of the mind-cure, modeled himself on the Reverend J. Murray Sitz (the pastor of the Church of Modernity), and became an insatiable social climber. Though unmechanical by nature, Todd does "understand what the people need. They need to have their money kept in circulation, and Lancelot is the human circulation pump" ("Slip It to 'Em," 26). Meanwhile, descriptions of Todd's ad-writing reflect Lewis's own—here, where the publicity surrounding a book campaign is compared to patent-medicine cons: "[The promotional material] pointed out that Washington, Franklin, and Al Jolson had all read books, as boys. . . . There was a handsome picture of the seven books, redrawn from life—quite a long way from life. There were twelve testimonials from readers. . . . By a coincidence, six of the authors of these testimonials had previously gone on record as having been cured by Mother Nickerson's Home Tonic, for which Mr. Lancelot Todd conducted an advertising campaign" ("Slip It to 'Em," 26). There is little doubt whom the cure—what Lewis calls the "three-ring-circus style in literature"—is servicing. In one tale, Lewis describes Todd as someone who is "as talented in giving first aid to wounded corporations as he is in writing optimistic prose poems for the magazines"; he is not so much intent upon creating a higher standard of service as a "higher standard of living for himself."[54] Todd's motorized energy is, however, subject to perpetual backfire. In "Snappy Display," his attempt to enter high society, like Whittier Small's, falls short, this time because his reputation as an office tyrant is exposed by one of his subordinates.

"Jazz," subtitled "Lancelot Todd Vigorizes the House Organ," ends in a similarly emasculated fashion. Todd attempts to reinvigorate the house newsletter of the Universal Grocery Store by inspiring what the corporation president calls "espreedy core"—something different, the client says, from the "good old paternal employer stuff" of a decade earlier. Since clerks have been stirred up by "socialists and agitators and fool magazines"—always the publicity man, Lewis loved to include this puff for his own platform as an aside—the boss needs something full of pep and energy. "We want to make 'em forget their misery," Todd tells his copywriter. "And we want to fill 'em so full of ambition that they'll sell the counter and breakfast-food posters. . . . Efficiency and the Superman! Will-Power! The Soul Victorious! . . . Con and Concentration." To this end, Todd hires the erratic William

John Buckingham (fresh from *Thought Power* magazine), an alcoholic and a brilliant mimic of Boosterese.[55] But Buckingham works, in fact, in a subversive and diabolic way, by overplaying the "jazz" of the office organs. Under the pseudonym "Uncle Jerry Ginger," he writes the following philosophical pablum in typographical design not unlike Lewis's own:

> "We aren't satisfied with clerks that spend only eighteen hours a day in working or thinking about work. What are you doing with the other six hours? Huh? What's that? Sleeping? You remember what happened to Rip Van Winkle. He slept forty years, and all he had to show for it was a load of chin-alfalfa!" (52)

> "O r U gonna b a busy b, b, b?
> O r U gonna * or merely c, c, c?
> O g! the lazy js will cuss a big d——d!
> Kum kan the t-talk, boys, and in ur B-V-D,
> Y, work like 1, and get the $$ same as me?" (52)

Unfortunately for Todd, Buckingham fully exposes his diabolic intent at a house banquet and then pens a last editorial saying that "this glorious philosophy of hustle-jazz-pep" was just a ruse to keep them from asking for raises. "It sounds like heroic progress," Buckingham writes, but what it meant was grinding with little time for friends and family. Like Lewis, Buckingham ultimately quits; unlike Una Golden, he will probably not start up his own business.

In the character of Lancelot Todd, Lewis adhered to Wells's particularizing motive in representing the plight of capitalism, but rather than transcending that "state" by tapping will power, it is Mr. Polly's befuddlement that returns with a vengeance. Todd is repeatedly the victim of his own designs. In "Getting His Bit," he markets a "Khaki Komfort Trench Bench" as a war profiteer and later falsely claims veteran status; real veterans, however, kidnap him and force him to admit his lies under the threat of actual enlistment. In "Might and Millions," Todd acquires a series of self-help books that he rechristens the Will Power Library, for which he also claims authorship. But then he is accosted by an office stenographer who takes his prose wisdom to heart and threatens to undermine his office. He is forced to pay a charlatan mystic to cart her away, only to find the two are in cahoots. Finally, in "Slip It to 'Em," Todd takes to marketing the Vettura Six, an utterly worthless car (good for "impressing the family across the street," Lewis writes, but better without its engine), while he also courts a wealthy woman as a financial backer. In the middle of a storm, however, he is forced to drive the woman to a train station in the Vettura. Needless to say, the car disintegrates en route: like the system it symbolizes—unlike the Touricar—its periodic breakdown, to Lewis, was still predictable. Yet unlike earlier heroes, Todd cannot get out and effect repairs: he is trapped, in the rain, in the car itself. He is hardly "capable" of fixing the car.[56]

Of course, it was still several years yet to *Babbitt*. By the Lancelot Todd stories, however, the diabolic and paradigmatic aspects of Lewis's mature idiom were nearly in place. For the apprentice novelist, Lancelot Todd was a fitting name for his pivotal character; it seemed to mark the point at which romantic excess congealed into the rigor mortis of Plutocracy. ("I wonder," Carol Kennicott says of Gopher Prairie, "how much of the cement is made out of the tombstones of John Keatses?" [327]). The tomb that encases Babbitt, even in the language of the narrative, is the imprisoning fabric of the promotional culture Lewis knew so well.

| | |

In Lewis's mind, *Babbitt* was directly linked to the white collar fictions of the teens; as early as 1918, he had ruminated about "a novel about a travelling man—a man like Mr. [Eddie] Schwirtz in *The Job*." Originally Lewis planned to "make the whole novel 24 hours in [Babbitt's] life, from alarm clock to alarm clock," once again tying his fiction to the diurnal oscillation of dream periods that bracket the waking office life. Even though *Babbitt* was residually marked by the short-scene pulses of Lewis's earlier (and now largely forgotten) work, the novel is more ambitious, presenting what many contemporaries deemed a "documentarian"—or, to use the author's word, "sociologic"—appearance. A virtual compendium of Zenith's byways, its home and office life, its reading matter, its public oratory, its private love affairs, *Babbitt* seems overstuffed with the sheer artifactuality of the culture it proposes to represent. At its center is an "informant" ostensibly representing not only a class but a whole culture—a "middle" or "paradigmatic" personification of national averages come alive. Zenith's cultural likeness seems so "documentarian" that many readers have found it difficult to locate Lewis's own relationship to his text. Since mid-century, Lewis has repeatedly been termed a "diagnostic" writer, an Archimedean satirist debunking social ills with no declared solution in his texts.[57]

Of course, this socially claustrophobic "feel" to *Babbitt*—and its method of synopsizing a class figure into a cultural generalization—had many root causes. The evidence suggests, for one, that Lewis had been extending his earlier interests in anthropology; *Babbitt* works in a horizontal "ethnographic present," exhibiting in sequence the cultural functions (Home, Work, Play) of a normative cultural genus, his struggles with taboo and convention.[58] More substantially, Lewis had begun to mine his earlier white collar experience. Starting with *Babbitt,* he settled into what Schorer calls his signature composition method: "full biographies of all the leading characters; a 'field'—in this instance, real estate—to master; elaborately detailed maps of the setting, Zenith; floor plans and furnishings of houses; a complete scenario of the action, step by step" (314). Lewis's letters to Harcourt ask for advertising pamphlets, psychology manuals, and real estate materials to be incorporated into the text, materials he had known in New York.[59] All through his career, Lewis liked to do literary field work, gather research materials on the middle-class profession he was profiling, make exhaustive lists of objects in a given scene, interview or mimic his informants—doctors, manicurists, waiters, automobile salesmen. The "documentarian" feel was, in this sense, a by-product of Lewis's having turned his rewrite skills and promotional energy into his primary vocation. *Babbitt* is partly a work of imagination and partly, in the marketing sense, the product of literary work conceived as a "campaign."

Much in the novel does seem "sociologic" and documentarian. Like Winesburg, Babbitt's city is seen as a "middle" social burg, a stage of civilization (Lewis calls it the "Age of Pep" [183]) that claims to represent an evolutionary "zenith." Lewis's method, from the start, is to expose a paradigmatic citizen who discovers, in time, that he bears the "disquiet and illusion" of his office, his family, and even the streets of the town "in his own brain" (242). The novel opens with a contrast of scale and the narrative voice of a naturalist manqué that it rarely abandons; turning from the "heroic" towers of Zenith, the spires of Babbitt's faith, Lewis zeroes in on the empty being who inhabits them, the genus of publicity culture, the "modern business man" (11). A creature who, to use Lewis's construction, is only "capable"-seeming (8)—"to the eye, the perfect office-going executive" (26)—Babbitt occupies a world saturated with commodities and his own trivial habits. He is a man who regards the "changing from the brown suit to the grey" a "sensational event," whose sleep cycles create forgetfulness within which both resolution and dissatisfaction dissipate. Yet cycles and mood swings are part of Babbitt's psyche. Zenith's office building is described as his "pirate ship" where he feels himself a member of the "squirearchy" (30), a place of "clean newness" and "bustle" (31); in his down moods, it is a "vault, a steel chapel where laughing and loafing were raw sin" (31). If his office is a place of a "thousand nervous details" (37), unnerving dictation, and office mutinies, Babbitt himself is both "boss" and subject to "that approval of his employees to which an executive is always slave" (61). Like earlier protagonists, George Babbitt inhabits a world of puffery and self-confidence offered by preachers, New Thought advocates, and home-study courses in "Power and Prosperity in Public Speaking." He faithfully attends, and later rebels under, the sermons of "Mike Monday" and the brotherhood of boosterism.

In narrative terms, this litany of entropy is matched by Lewis's discursive convolutions. He accentuates the formal patterns of his short stories—plot reversals, entropic and repetitive dialogue, and bathetic undercutting of romance—which often serve to close down his own discursive elaboration, to create the appearance of clinical detachment despite his obvious hyperbole. Chivalric aspirations or romantic dreams are often merely the set-up before the punch line. But in many respects, these turnabouts are built into Lewis's social plot line. Babbitt, a normatively dishonest realtor, nonetheless lives in a speculation home; though an expert in consumer ploys, he and his family are constantly victimized by them. His children want consumer goods, and his office workers want raises; the dissenting "Bunch" is as cloying as the Good Citizens' League; thoughts and conversations are so standardized that it seems everyone already knows what everyone else will say.

This catalog of cultural norms and village viruses does seem clinical, "sociologic." Yet as descriptively plausible as these labels seem, none of them—any more than diagnostician or documentarian—really fits. In the first place, Lewis had hardly eliminated his characteristic social cures. In its overall plot outline, and its diabolic use of marginal figures (Seneca Doane or Babbitt's employee Stan Graff) to espouse socialist ideas, *Babbitt* reiterated most of Lewis's earlier platform. The novel's plot and its resolution would have been, to readers of Lewis's stories, quite familiar. For a time, George's sense of entrapment gives vent to a pattern of "veiled rebellions." He is subject to oscillations of will derived from his own disbelief in the ads he produces. Beset by a gnawing sense of entrapment, every day he tries to buck up his resolve and return to the office. His loss of Paul Riesling makes him vulnerable to the "virus of rebellion" in the air—momentarily drawn even to the defense of the socialist Doane—but before long he is forced to recant in public, to reaffirm a code in which he no longer believes. "[Babbitt] felt that he had been trapped," Lewis writes, "into the very net from which he had with such fury escaped and, supremest jest of all, had been made to rejoice in the trapping." All too tragically acquainted with his own limitations, Babbitt is now reduced to little more than rattling the cage he has built himself. Nonetheless, he receives consolation in that his son Ted, in the grammar of Wellsian vocabularies, wants to be a mechanic. Although George knows that he himself has "never done a single thing" he wanted to in his whole life, the son is told that Babbitt gets a "sneaking pleasure" out of the fact that Ted has asserted his will.[60] As in *Trail of the Hawk* or *The Job* (or even *Main Street*), Lewis continued to hope for a more capable future based on technical expertise, middle-class socialism, and an intellectual "world culture."[61] Like Wells, his utopian politics patronized the "little man"—his "authentic love" of neighborhood and clan, his love of wife and son, his "eternal human genius" for arriving at tolerable goals if through circuitous means (184). These are the "good little people," George sees in one vision, "comfortable, industrious, credulous" (258). To Lewis's mind, since he was only discussing a collective human potential this patronage was not at all inconsistent.[62]

If the "diagnostician" label only disguises Lewis's continuing ideological intention, the documentarian label obscures the novel's execution. Lewis's residually romantic class vocabulary hardly provides a locus for "objectivity" or scientific distance. His use of names like Frink or Pumphrey or Babbitt exemplify a diction closer to Dickens than to Darwin. Meanwhile, by using the imagery of romance and popular anthropology "straight," and then inside-out as burlesque, Lewis's own narrative perspective often shifts its intellectual ground. In some moments, for instance, Lewis uses the word "clan" to praise Babbitt's desire for fellowship and his "village" sensibility as a sign of the communal utopia he wants—as when, in his period of rebellion, he sees through social difference, arguing that Zenith's striking laborers " 'look just about like you and me' " (253). Lewis also uses the term "knight," as in his earlier work, to suggest the quality of personal heroism. But feudal motifs are used quite differently elsewhere:

> The little unknown people who inhabited the Reeves Building corridors —elevator-runners, starter, engineers, superintendent, and the doubtful-looking lame man who conducted the news and cigar stand—were in no way city-dwellers. They were rustics, living in a constricted valley, inter-

> ested only in one another and in The Building. Their Main Street was the entrance hall. . . . [Babbitt] Himself, he patronized the glittering Pompeian Barber Shop in the Hotel Thornleigh, and every time he passed the Reeves shop [in his own building]—ten times a day, a hundred times—he felt untrue to his own village.
>
> Now, as one of the squirearchy, greeted with honorable salutations by the villagers, he marched into his office. (30)

Here, as in the scant allusions to Nottingham (201), or Charles McKelvey's "baronial" status (158), Lewis uses the village motif to represent narrow-mindedness and (like Thorstein Veblen) residual feudalism, suggesting Zenith's atrophied social structure. Zenith is still mired, as Seneca Doane tells us, in Hobbesian "traditions of competition" and mutual squeezing, a suffocating clannishness (represented by the Good Citizens' League) to which Babbitt himself will become subject at the close of the book. Lewis employs his apparently "sociologic" imagery as a quite flexible, quite evaluative, and even "double-take" vocabulary that fuels something like a twin-cycled engine of sympathy and burlesque.

Like Lewis's class vocabulary, the text's actual "documentary" moments also seem double-edged. There are passages in *Babbitt* in which the narrator makes an evidential claim—a claim that his facts or episodes are meant to stand as actual proof of social conditions. In a rather characteristic moment in Chapter 19, when discussing a political "fix" made on Babbitt's behalf, Lewis writes, "Carbon copies of the correspondence are in the company's files, where they may be viewed by any public commission" (191). Here, Lewis echoes the rhetoric of muckraking, treats his fiction as if it is a nonfiction novel.[63] In other instances, rather than setting a scene—even portraying a town speech—he claims to be actually reprinting a newspaper account from Zenith's own *Advocate-Times* (148 ff.). This is what lends the book its documentarian appearance; Lewis prefers to recreate "artifacts" from Zenith's publicity culture, taking glee in rewriting newspaper stories, the ads for Babbitt's realty company, or Chum Fink's Zeeco campaign, much as he himself would have written them. In one instance, Lewis prints the entire typographical layout for Ted Babbitt's home-study pamphlets on "Power and Prosperity in Public Speaking" (66–67). In perhaps his most documentary ploy, he reprints one of Babbitt's daydreaming doodles. Repeatedly the reader is put in the ostensibly clinical position of seeing Zenith as a "habitat" (or more aptly, perhaps, a circular "orbit") through its documents, and it is difficult to discern the difference, quite often, between these documents' own hyperbole and Lewis's own "externalized" satire.

The fundamental difficulty is that both the diagnostic and documentarian claims serve, however unwittingly, to obscure Lewis's continuing indebtedness to the culture he means to debunk. To follow the familiar line of generations of critics to affirm Lewis's "mature" authorial status is to imply that Lewis has become, finally, the "capable man" *qua literatus*. We unwittingly capitulate, that is, to Wells's middle-class outline of history, the self-same ideological myth Lewis's white collar fictions lay claim to; his developed "art" removes him from the determinants of white collar life. (This affirms something like the "developed" voice that many critics have assumed narrates *Winesburg*.) It is not only that these labels reinforce an ostensibly "scientific" (or anthropological) character to Lewis's position, but they also mistake the particular character of his "collecting": the nature of his documents, how he portrays publicity culture itself, even how he accounts for the motivation of Zenith's inhabitants.

Babbitt's private doodle (in Chapter 13) suggests another side to Lewis's white collar fictionalizing. Even forgoing its potential similarity to Lewis's own office scribbles, this doodle—during which Babbitt is trying to pump himself up for a speech—partly underscores how difficult Lewis's task of transcription really is. To begin with, the doodle suggests Babbitt's lack of focus; he can enumerate only a flaccid claim to professionalism (which hinges on an unstable language claim), and then he runs out of steam. He daydreams about his "fairy girl," even as he figures the realtor's (7 percent) rate for a sale (thus undercutting the professionalism claimed). The numbers on the left, as does the # sign (which can double as a rebellious imprint), exist in limbo, and at the bottom right (as if a sum), are a row of zeroes, Babbitt's initials, and then an extended doodle on the word "real," as in "realtor." That the reader does not know what is "real" for Babbitt is the point and the problem, for the sum of Babbitt's life is suggested in its very constitution by the fabric of publicity. Most of the "documents" in *Babbitt* are not evidence of belief at all; rather, they are the surface effects of will and puffery, now become what Lewis calls evidence of how "the large national advertisers fix the surface of [Babbitt's] life" (78). In what Doane calls the "standardization of thought," Babbitt's beliefs are "lifeless things of commerce" (78) internalized. This is a culture that has absorbed its own rebellious dream-work and rescripted Babbitt's desire for its own ends.

This saturation of publicity creates insubstantiality and will-less-ness in

Zenith's documents and its characters. Lewis's portrait of Babbitt's publicity "brain" suggests real intimacy with its circuitry; the novel repeatedly describes publicity work as incorporated "art," as a matter of different literary "models" and genres (33), as built upon a necessarily "classifying" (115) mind full of reader typologies like Babbitt's "Real Ladies, Working Women, Old Cranks, and Fly Chickens" (104). Babbitt's conception of his own expertise, meanwhile, is presented in stoutly white collar terms, as a professionalism based upon a language claim; (much like "literary advisor") he is a "realtor," not just a real estate man. Babbitt imagines himself and his friends as "middle"-class men, moderate and republican, in a specifically historical sense: as a middle generation between his "Yankee" father-in-law, and figures like Noël Ryland, sales manager of the Zeeco, who is a Princeton graduate and the "extreme of frothiness" in his love of poetry and fancy dress (59). This, of course, is an unstable middle, a false center that the pervasiveness of publicity, Lewis's bracketing plots, and Babbitt's own Hobbesian underside serve to negate. Whether tracking through Babbitt's cycles of "boom" or "knock" or embracing his momentary, Wellsian recognition of human equality, the end result is a sense of social deliquescence in which everything is seen as hollow publicity rewriting: religion, reporting, even (most diabolically) puffing up one's own children to stick to the job. The conundrum surfaces in Babbitt's own office. Not only is Babbitt forced to discipline subordinates who could be his own children—his own Verona is a filing clerk, for instance—but Babbitt encourages Ted immediately after squashing Stan Graff. Irony of ironies, Babbitt's own stenographer rewrites the publicity that he "dictates" (32). Babbitt, who preaches what he does not practice, is only one instance of Lewis's zero sum "hollowing out" of his characters: Zenith's hall of mirrors has many other members. Production and consumption are so diabolically linked in Lewis's mind that Zenith is witness to a number of oxymoronic citizens: Kiplinsky, who wants to keep foreigners out (121); the Jewish comedian who tells anti-Semitic jokes (144); the reformers who, as in *Unleavened Bread,* are incorporated into the corporations they once muckraked (248). Each of these characters is trapped in a circulation pump, in what to Babbitt, and to Lewis, has become a closed personality market.

The very extensiveness of publicity's domain in the novel suggests why the familiar "externalizing" labels applied to Lewis—journalist, diagnostician, documentarian—are so misleading. Just as it becomes difficult to gauge what an "authentic" document of Babbitt's desire would be—a document free of publicity's scripting—it becomes difficult not to notice traces of that domain in Lewis's own literary ethnography. *Babbitt* works by the layering on of publicity "romance," reader typologies, and prose hyperbole—an accretion of cliché made over into characterization, popular sayings, or beliefs literally incarnated as people. Lewis seems to attempt to create "thick" cultural description out of the thin materials of his culture's dominant "banalities."[64] What is "cultural" in *Babbitt* is almost by definition hollowed out, like the dinner scene described earlier: books left unread, jokes left untold, self-serving distinctions about "civilization"—and a town—that is no place because it is everywhere. In Lewis's imagination, nearly everyone in Zenith is a carbon copy; even more fundamentally, they are seen in a language that is constituted, even in its moments of burlesque, by that characteristic "double-take" of publicity prose. *Babbitt* is surely a radical aesthetic experiment, yet one that Lewis only seems to fully "manage."

As one instance of the doubleness to *Babbitt*'s documentarian surfaces, note his descriptions of the commodity world itself. Early on, this description of the Babbitt commode appears: "Though the house was not large it had, like all houses on Floral Heights, an altogether royal bathroom of porcelain and glazed tile and metal sleek as silver. The towel-rack was a rod of clear glass set in nickel. The tub was long enough for a Prussian Guard, and above the set bowl was a sensational exhibit of tooth-brush holder, shaving-brush holder, soap-dish, sponge-dish, and medicine-cabinet, so glittering and so ingenious that they resembled an electrical instrument-board" (8). For some readers, Lewis's familiarity with the minute detailing of this habitat creates, as Virginia Woolf felt, astounding realism.[65] Yet an odd echo occurs in Lewis's satire of a similar passage from the *Advocate-Times*—a description of the McKelveys' home:

> . . . Set in its spacious lawns and landscaping, one of the notable sights crowning Royal Ridge, but merry and homelike despite its mighty stone walls and its vast rooms famed for their decoration. . . . The wide hall is so generous in its proportions that it made a perfect ballroom, its hardwood floor reflecting the charming pageant above its polished surface. Even the delights of dancing paled before the alluring opportunities for tete-a-tetes that invited the soul to loaf in the long library before the baronial fireplace, or in the drawing-room with its deep comfy armchairs, its shaded lamps, just made for a sly whisper of pretty nothings. (21)

The point is not merely that what *Babbitt* calls the "best urban journalistic style" of Zenith (21) contains clues for Lewis's own diabolic dissent—a baronial entrance hall big enough for a dance—or even that this column eviscerates the Floral Heights difference in Royal Ridge's "second-hand," aristocratic pretensions. Rather, it is that *both* of the passages contain the "descriptive litanies" of publicity writing; their difference is largely a matter of an inversion of tone, of how much Lewis has mocked his own prior expertise. Is the tone of "glittering" or "ingenious" (8) in the first passage sarcastic or not? The text makes it impossible to tell; it is not a matter of aesthetic discernment, as so many of Lewis's analysts want to believe.

This "double-take" problem extends to Lewis's depiction of characters' private motivations. Babbitt's "authentic" love and affection for his family and clan are repeatedly undercut by exposures to what Lewis still saw as a village "virus." Now, even reading itself is described as a "drug," not a curative potion (18). If George authors ads in the morning, Myra reads them in the evening (21). Most conversations in the outer, public world become stale reiterations of newspaper editorials, promotion, or ads; even friendly neighborliness, such as Babbitt's exchange with his car mechanic, become subject to doubt, as Babbitt drives away puffed up by merely good salesmanship (27). At some points Lewis simply "coordinates" (39, 170) Babbitt's opinions, meaning that he synopsizes him into a "typical" set of views.

The problem deepens, subsequently, when the reader finally gains access to these characters' private imaginings. Occasionally, of course, the despair they share with Babbitt is visible behind the production of puffery: the lament of Paul Reisling (a man, like Sherwood Anderson, in roofing tar); Chum Frink's drinking episode; the complaints of Stan Graff; even Tanis Judique's self-doubt. Zenith may punish Babbitt's public doubt because he ventures to imagine, and say outright, that the emperor has no clothes. But it is also evident that Lewis is himself remarkably guarded about revealing private thoughts, even doing something of a double-take in depicting them. Repeatedly, Lewis writes that Babbitt—even in his moments of resolve—"pictured himself as" (302) one thing or "honestly believed" (128) something else; to Lewis's eyes, Babbitt's brain has been rather thoroughly whitewashed. At one point, Lewis even writes, "It is not known whether he [Babbitt] enjoyed his sleeping-porch because of the fresh air or because it was the standard thing to have a sleeping-porch" (80), as if Babbitt were a real informant who could otherwise be asked. In all of these instances,

Lewis's documentarian veneer threatens to become all that Babbitt is. Conversely, Lewis's text dead-ends at blank invocations of the romantic and "real" life that Zenith could possess—as, for instance, that the "only" problem with the Babbitt house was that it was not a "home" (16), that it contained "no signs" of people having loved and lived there. But, of course, they have, and Lewis has shown it to be so. Lewis's hyperbolic invocations of authenticity constantly threaten to collapse into puffed up claims, into the rhetorical zone he professes to disdain. His edgy imbrication is perhaps no better suggested than by his "carbon copy" claim in Chapter 19, for here is a claim so very typical of publicity culture itself, where ads claim an authoritative study "in their files" that the consumer can examine simply by writing in. In short, it is an advertising testimonial.

As such a self-publicizing passage suggests, this pattern invades Lewis's social advocacy. Ultimately Lewis's evisceration of motivation and documentation make it difficult to reconceive "freedom" in anything but publicity culture's terms. (Perhaps this is why critics still overlook Lewis's curative prescriptions.) Repeatedly, his images of romantic escape, like Babbitt's imagined "Fairy Girl" or the exotically embodied "Tanis," forever populate Babbitt's fantasy life—and Zenith's commercial being. Lewis seems to recognize that this language of romance has been incorporated into, say, the "Pompeian Barber Shop," into Eunice Littlefield's movie dreams, or into the home-study courses Ted reads. The difficulty is that Lewis may not fully recognize that this incorporation undercuts his articulation of or longing for a "world elsewhere" outside the suffocating habitat of Zenith; he is unaware that his own dreams have been colonized. This imbrication is best exemplified by yet another poetic invocation of the automobile, this time authored by Chum Frink in a pointedly "highbrow" manner:

> The long white trail is calling—calling—and it's over the hills and far away for every man or woman that has red blood in his veins and on his lips the ancient song of the buccaneers. It's away with dull drudging, and a fig for care . . . it's Life for you and me! This great new truth the makers of the Zeeco Car have considered as much as price and style. It's fleet as the antelope. . . . Class breathes in every line. Listen, brother! You'll never know what the high art of hiking is til you TRY LIFE'S ZIPPINGEST ZEST—THE ZEECO! (101)

As Babbitt sees later, Chum Frink thinks of himself as a John Keats buried in cement [220]; six years earlier, however, this could have been written by Carl Ericson or Lewis himself. It certainly matters which social logos—technical or aesthetic—Lewis is finally laying claim to. Despite the fact that Ted Babbitt hopes to become a mechanic—and much like his namesake, Theodore Roosevelt, regenerate the culture of his class—Lewis's covert identification is still unresolved: splintered between makers and consumers, middle masters of symbols and makers of things, "little people" and capable men.[66]

One can only speculate on whether these rather eerie redundancies of publicity culture were recognized by Lewis's readers. Lewis's white collar fictions became so culturally soluble that little of their inner turmoil reached the surface of debate. Sales of *Babbitt* eventually outdistanced those of even *Main Street* (1920), and in a few years, "Babbitt" would enter the American vernacular—or rather, its image would, as readers responded to a "type" that *Babbitt*'s own publicity, including that by Mencken, had created (and reified). For some, like Lancelot Todd before him, Babbitt offered a shock of recognition; for other readers the reflex of denial and distance prevailed. Contrary to the realization that strikes Terry Ames as he looks down at his ad, *Babbitt* was a text that could allow many a middle-class reader to say: "Not me." Although the response of professional reviewers (Lewis's peers) and businessmen (Lewis's former peers) was predictably heterogeneous, few disputed the more subtle assumptions that a cultural norm had been located, "little people" identified, an "average" American denominated.[67] At these levels, represented in the brisk languages that themselves fixed only the surface of white collar life and its most shallow dreams of freedom, "Babbitt" became that most exchangeable of cultural coinages: familiar, smooth-worn, easily circulated yet easily discounted—its surface dulled so it could not always reflect.

Afterword

Within the White Collar Perimeter

Carl Becker has called attention to the presence of such quietly omnipresent little keys to every era: "If we would discover the little backstairs door," he says, "that for any age serves as the secret entranceway to knowledge, we will do well to look for certain unobtrusive words with uncertain meanings that are permitted to slip off the tongue or the pen without fear and without research; words which, having from constant repetition lost their metaphorical significance, are unconsciously mistaken for objective realities. . . ." Around these magic words, assumptions grow up which are regarded as so much "of course" as hardly to require proof; they are passed readily from hand to hand like smooth-worn coins.

—*Robert Lynd,* Knowledge for What?

Culture is ordinary: that is the first fact.

—*Raymond Williams, "Culture is Ordinary"*

This study of literary and material white collar fictions has dealt with the commerce between a set of social conditions, class parameters, and social vocabularies constituting an influential body of modern literary representation. My main goal has been to restore the determinants of white collar experience and ideology to turn-of-the-century writing that often denied their presence—and to track the consequences of class for matters of form, audience, and social portraiture. As conflict-ridden as this body of representation was in its own era, one nonetheless sees its residual traces—Carl Becker's "unobtrusive words" that stand in for objective social conditions—surviving in the popular culture of today.

Upper-level corporate employees are still sentimentally dubbed the Bob Cratchit "little people" at the whims of their Scrooge-like bosses; sweater-clad, den-dwelling, bespectacled suburbanites are still identified as "average guy" models for television and telepoliticians alike. In the film *Working Girl,* which appeared at the end of the 1980s, a New York secretary—who rides the Staten Island ferry to work and falls in love with her boss's client, causing a series of mistaken identities—once again became a focal point for a film fantasy of populist revenge and upward mobility. One sees changes since mid-century as well: the fixing of "Middle American" to conservative white and blue collar workers, "Main Street" applied to the middling constituents of the Republican party, the disappearance of "John Doe" as a name too plebian for the credit card advertisements of the 1980s. It would hardly be a surprise if my historical reconstruction of such social keywords and vocabularies has been subject to errors of presentism or hindsight. This is an occupational hazard of writing literary or cultural history: inevitably the horizons of the present become part of one's own past, and vice versa.[1]

If so many readers did find common sense and "human nature" in O. Henry, or science and nonpartisanship in Robert Grant, the "cultural work" performed by such writers may well have been considerable. The cultural power of popular literature, as Jane Tompkins and Philip Fisher have suggested, often derives from its "tapping into a storehouse of commonly held assumptions, reproducing what is already there in typical and familiar form," becoming "obvious and unrecoverable because it has become part of the habit structure of everyday perception."[2] O. Henry's commonsensical idiom, Ferber's Cinderella tales, Rice's automatic venting of mass consciousness, Lewis's redrafting of publicity copy in *Babbitt*—these varieties of cultural *vraisemblance*—all managed, in different ways, to tap into circuits of cognitive power. Moreover, writers drew upon a storehouse of everyday *social* practices within the workaday world of white collar life: the wisdom of over-the-counter tactics, the "umpiring" of probate court, the "wink" of publicity. White collar literary fictions, even at their most fantastic, performed the ideological work of affirming and ordering the social landscape, of foiling social "inferiors" and setting boundaries. White collar anxiety was "tested out," middle-class utopia(s) surveyed. Literary works, it should be realized by now, are not the means by which a given character's class standing might be "objectively" determined; rather, they often serve to set a social perimeter, to contain, label, or cordon off available social "characters" and types.

Naturally, even this setting of perimeters is not the whole story. Cultural "work" implies something more than the reciprocating, essentially ideational functions that this study has emphasized. Like "cultural materialism," cultural "work" is meant to conjoin a text's cognitive map—its system of meaning and value—with the material and behavioral practices of specific audiences. Thus my turn to "local occasions" like O. Henry's memorialization, Grant and the West End affair, Ferber and Minneapolis labor after the war. As I have suggested, this juxtaposition can provide a necessary corrective to the idealism to which merely discursive decoding is vulnerable. These are, in some sense, occasions where "contests" in texts become publicly settled, where the "scrimmaging" of stories actually enters the social playing field.[3] On the other hand, anyone working in this line of inquiry soon becomes aware that we cannot always recover even generalized reader-responses from the past; that such responses are usually accented by class, gender, and other social factors; that our post-New-Critical predilections for text-centered analysis cannot simply be written out of our historical criticism in the name of what "average" readers interpreted. The problem of historical hindsight also looms large in critical reconstructions of a consensus putatively being fashioned in a literary work. For these and other reasons, I have emphasized merely the "solubility" of this writing, the open borders these literary fictions created with their audiences within and beyond a common class perimeter.

"Cultural work" itself may better be viewed as an umbrella term, a rubric under which varieties of different work have been undertaken—including (as Fisher emphasizes particularly) the reassembling of conventional assumptions into new social "facts." No singular term—cultural work, "dream-work," and other rival notions—can encompass all of the functions that literary fictions perform. A specific variety of cultural work may be orchestrated within a given perimeter that a literary historian may have reconstructed (like class), but it is hardly restricted to it. By trying to trace three different strategies of power—O. Henry and Ferber's modeling an axiomatic vocabulary, the ordering of narrative space and perspective by Grant and Rice, and the scripting of a white collar life by Anderson and Lewis—I have also tried to sketch out a vocabulary for differentiating forms of power so as not to create too uniform or inflated a portrait of the work their texts may actually have done.

Even within the white collar perimeter, one finds illustrations of this differentiated spectrum of cultural power. Robert Grant's early fiction, particularly his juvenile novels, come closest to what critics have called a "training narrative" function—in this case for his Mugwump cohort.[4] By occasionally choosing anonymity, yet peppering his fiction with precisely coded Cambridge allusions, Grant clearly had a recipe for how the Brahmin version of the new middle class would be "baked." (And Croly testifies that Grant's tutoring worked.) Similarly, the apprentice fiction of Lewis and Anderson—again, associated with the social aspirations of upper white collar strata—seems drawn to this disciplinary or hortatory work, trying to script the business of living for readers like themselves in offices and corporations. Much as Ferber ingested her mother's "deep acting," both Anderson and Lewis ventured modern versions of the "developed" or capable upper white collar male. But in other ways, novels like *Windy McPherson's Son* or *The Trail of the Hawk* or *The Girls* are tied as well to "ad-venturing," to imaginative forays *prior* to, and perhaps *in absence of,* the implementation of such designs in the nonsymbolic realm. Splintered social identifications—even the wild oscillation between fantasies of sales mastery to parables of wage slavery—often undercut any tangible prescriptive design on readers. In this sense the undeveloped narrator of *Winesburg* and the uneasy "you" of a story like "Honestly—If Possible" may be paralleled; each registers the wavering hopes Anderson and Lewis ultimately invested in white collar power, literary or nonliterary. Even farther along the spectrum of genres—the degrees of solubility—the fables of O. Henry and the early Ferber are conceived as gimmicky, even temporary palliatives for nagging social ills. Their fables were potions prescribed to alleviate the strains of more tangible forms of accountability in the modern workplace and were not always designed to create new forms of "discipline" themselves. These tales, designed originally for the Sunday paper or the weekly parlor magazine, have a reader in mind who will muse along with their hard-boiled narrator—hardly a disciplinary project on the order of, say, nineteenth-century evangelical fiction. If genres are, in part, codified forms or stockpiles of social knowledge, we must recognize that they are often, as well, different ways to think (and talk) about class—containing flippant, dismissive, or contrary attitudes toward class leadership, surreptitious revenge fantasies against bosses, carnivalesque overturnings of capitalist social formations—ways of thinking not always reducible to a single literary convention or utopian desire. Writers like Ferber and Lewis—albeit unwittingly—often created a kind of double-take in their fiction: irony that allowed readers to wink at their fictions of mastery, dismiss them, or swallow them whole. Given such variation, the hopeful critical notion that there is a fixed or "fine power of culture"—a capacity to "fill brains . . . so they are alike in fine detail"—may represent only a utopia (and normative bias) inhabiting the writing of cultural history itself.[5]

Cultural work also takes place within the power of social institutions that have their own educative agenda. Here, I have attempted to view O. Henry in light of the new journalism's reformation of "classes" into masses, Grant in terms of the Republican party, and Ferber in light of the Pulitzer Prize complex that favored "wholesome" novels about midwestern American citizens. Even more locally, we see institutional sponsorship of varied kinds: O. Henry knighted by New York clerical unions, Ferber enlisted by the War Camp Community Service. My biographical approach may not have always illuminated all the dimensions of such local occasions of sponsorship—Nicholas Murray Butler's affirmation of a singular "American" type, for instance, in the context of ongoing immigration restriction debates. These different forms of "sponsorship" were "acts" with consequences beyond the symbolic. A counterexample is offered, however, by O. Henry's legacy, which was marked by shifting patronage and appropriation—from his publishing memorializers, to clerical unions, to the smart set of New York, to Russian formalists, to Ronald Reagan. To his supporters, this mass patronage is a sign of his universality; to me, it is a sign that one of the risks of axiomatic, "soluble" power is that it can lend ideological sanction to very different social edifices. We should not collapse the patronage, say, of a Butler or a Lorimer or a Cyrus Curtis into ideological agreement with a given writer; literary relationships themselves have structure. Lewis, for example, knew quite well what a *Post* formula story was, but his fictions actually vacillated between low-capitalist romance and more diabolic revenge—a struggle Lorimer doubtless never saw. As with other forms of labor in our society, a text's (cultural) work is not simply its own.

To be sure, there are common denominators in these writers' social vocabularies. On the whole, these writers exhibited a common effort to transpose the dichotomous or polarized social vocabularies of the past—"classes" and "masses," upper and lower "halves," "working girl" as a label of lower-class standing—into more horizontal or "paradigmatic" middle-class figuration. They were characteristically uncomfortable with fixed class or even occupational labels; conversely, in their work, we often feel a narrowing of imaginative ranks, in which other class types—Andrew DeVito, the silent sisters of Emma McChesney's shop, the farm laborers of Winesburg, the striking workers with whom Babbitt momentarily empathizes (but whose voices we do not hear)—are diminished in perspective. Drawing upon the storehouse of arithmetic typologies and client strategies of census-taking, personnel management, market research, law, even sales itself, these writers often collaborated in seeing the middle class as a cultural middle—as a "typical" American—and seeing class itself as a heterogeneous, idiosyncratic, horizontal ranking of occupations. In some moments, their "typical" Americans (with whom they identified) were seen as common denominators of nationhood itself.[6] Even the Archimedean fantasy of writers like Grant or Rice tends to position writer and reader outside Americans conceived en masse, as a public whose will and opinion is visualized monolithically, personified by what it reads. The writers in this study certainly performed significant groundwork for the varieties of white collar representation to follow: O. Henry for writers like Christopher Morley, whose *Kitty Foyle* made its way to Hollywood; Rice for Arthur Miller and Joseph Heller; a book like *Babbitt* for Kurt Vonnegut, Jr.'s *Player Piano*. And as her own quick absorption into Hollywood suggests, Ferber's sequence of regional, intergenerational epics—most of them about underdog, Lincolnesque folk succeeding after a long struggle in the modern business arena—no doubt set a pattern for innumerable popular novelists who are romancing American capitalism even today. Albeit with considerable variety, these were some of the ways in which what began (to return to Harry Braverman's distinction again) as the "short-term relative expression" of underlying class attitudes acquired literary longevity and greater popular diffusion.

This diffusion did not, however, constitute an ideological fait accompli for the cultural consciousness of mid-century Americans. To say so would be merely to reimpose the label "middle class" as a uncontested historical term, even to under-read the testimony of the white collar writers in this book. A writer like Sinclair Lewis, for instance, in his figuration of the office building as a modern feudal fortress, hardly equates mass-*cultural* standardization with actual classlessness. Lewis's normative, popular anthropology does tend to eviscerate social distinctions across Zenith's habitat—making Babbitt, Chum Frink, and everyone else the same species; he does, perhaps fatally, view Babbitt as constituted by the banalities of mass publicity. Nevertheless, he still sees Babbitt as a small player in a powerful, national, if internally pained, Plutocracy.

Moreover, these white collar literary fictions reaffirm the persistence of internal friction within the middle class itself. Although several historians posit this period as a concatenating phase for professional-managerial strata, these literary representations actually point to considerable friction between professional, technical values and commercial iconography—between the cultural vocabularies, as it were, within which new-middle-class authority would be phrased. Ferber's Selina DeJong might well be Robert Grant's Selma White. A writer like Ferber generates a folksy, commonsensical idiom that discounts meddling experts and claims the commercial authority of Main Street. For Grant such hypothesized average Americans represent a threat to taste, professional expertise, even liberal governance. Of course, it is intriguing that this idiomatic variation masked strikingly common social ends—another sign of a dispute that was merely internicine. (If Ferber's "just folks" idiom explicitly legitimated a modern form of paternalism, Grant's judicial manner also inspired Hamiltonian means; in fact, he views the limited capacities of "average people" as a precondition that legitimates such new forms of governance.) Nevertheless, the friction implied here was substantial—disagreement not only over *who* governs but in which realms such governance is tutored (the office, the home, the professional school). Meanwhile, an ongoing white collar division between "creative" (professional and managerial) and clerical strata was extended by the literary ideology of many of these writers, their patronage of "little people" or "the job" notwithstanding. If an author like O. Henry tries to reincorporate clerks or working girls into a common social family, even to endorse the clear-sightedness and practicality of working men and women *against* professionals and managers, others—Ferber, Grant, Rice, Anderson, and Lewis—bear traces of upper-strata segmenting themselves from "wage slaves," mere clerks, or temporary employees. Such internal differentiations are not inconsequential: a number of these writers—Grant, Ferber, even the early Anderson—quite explicitly hope to reform white collar habits in order to participate in new versions of ruling. Even Babbitt, for all his honorable clan feeling, has his Hobbesian radar intact and fantasizes about Theodore Roosevelt Babbitt's more capable future.

Finally, even given doubts like Edith Wharton's, the perimeter I have traced within white collar literary fictions hardly means that they are all somehow rendered inadequate as literature. Class is too often employed as a disqualifying term, as if we can imagine a literary vision wholly unmarked by it. Within the white collar field of representation, there was plenty of room for suffering and conflict, self-examination and doubt, humor and rage—the drama productive, again contra Wharton, of "great [literary] arguments."[7] Moreover, how the literary historian encounters (or debunks) such cultural work, such internicine class disputes, or such fantasies of power is a notoriously difficult task—let alone when writing about one's own class. History is always messier and more personal than representation; however much one discounts a given power urge, or scoffs at a plea to commonality or utopia, the fact is that most interpretive ideologies, even ostensibly democratic ones, have marks of both.[8] But this common perimeter need not be a simple disadvantage; rather, it may allow us, drawing from our own histories, disappointments, and personal investments, to see how some of the axiomatic assumptions of "middle-class awareness" are not sheer mystifications, nor socially omnipotent, nor fixed, but cobbled together by personal desire, networks of representation, and persisting conditions of inequality.

To be sure, the conflation of "average," "middle-class," and white collar status constituted one of turn-of-the-century America's central mythological constructions. At its core—as critics as different as Georg Lukács, Anthony Giddens, Stuart Blumin, or C. Wright Mills have complained—was the often-confounding paradox of "middle-class" awareness: the cognitive perimeter that acknowledges its own class affinities but denies the reality of classes as a whole. White collar Americans often express allegiance to the language of bourgeois individualism (or "the little man") in a society whose structure long ago contradicted it.[9] Yet in part to counter this tendency to unveil social fictions rather than explore their construction, I want to turn, finally, to one of Mills's contemporaries, Robert Lynd. Lynd, as the co-author of *Middletown* (1929) and *Middletown in Transition* (1937), was certainly familiar with the social vocabularies discussed in this book; in temperament and outlook, he surely shares more with Robert Grant than, say, Edna Ferber. While accepting Carl Becker's central formulation (quoted in the epigraph to this chapter) about the "magic" and yet "unobtrusive" words that pass for common sense in a culture—agreeing that citizens employ such terms as "gap closers to smooth the way before their feet"—Lynd reminds us that such terms should not be seen too narrowly:

> As one begins to list the assumptions by which we Americans live, one runs at once into a large measure of contradiction and resulting ambivalence. This derives from the fact that these overlapping assumptions have developed in different eras and that they tend to be carried over uncritically into new situations.

> . . . These contradictions among assumptions derive also from the fact that the things the mass of human beings basically crave as human beings as they live along together are often overlaid by, and not infrequently distorted by, the cumulating emphases that a culture may take on under circumstances of rapid change or under various kinds of class control. In these cases the culture may carry along side by side both assertions: the one reflecting deep needs close to the heart's desire and the other heavily authorized by class or other authority.[10]

In part, Lynd's point is that any given axiomatic value in a culture should not be seen—by readers or historians—in univocal terms. Rather, such assumptions (and their contradictions) often derive from an overlapping of hegemonic authority, the dominance of a given class (not always the same thing)—and finally the reservoir of human needs, experience, and common meanings within what Raymond Williams eloquently calls "ordinary" culture.[11] This might lead us to mollify the reaction, or at least temper the disdain, that follows upon the opinion polls in which so many Americans do indeed frequently resort to the term "middle class" to describe themselves. Perhaps they are not providing an indication of an actual median (much less class) position—the sociologist's dream—nor of some putative false consciousness we might easily debunk. The white collar fictions herein suggest that these Americans may be testifying to other views: how they have reconceived their wants in terms of ordinary concerns about job dignity, about securing human chances in a chancy world; how they perceive themselves as occupying a potentially mobile position in a gradated society but cannot clearly or honestly identify themselves with unmediated power or powerlessness in it; how they recognize inequality as a persisting feature of their society and try to reaffirm their democratic resistance to that inequality by disdaining "upper" or "lower" class labels.

These views may well be contradictory—testifying, perhaps, to circumscribed dignity, internalized paternalism, diminished expectations—but the desire for dignity and "entitlement" is there. Upon local or national occasions—attenuated, reinforced, or resisted—such testimony suggests the mixed potential inhering within many a white collar fiction and the cultural work it may do. Its work on other social occasions is the work of histories still ahead of us.

Notes

Abbreviations

Periodicals

Advocate	*Retail Clerks' International Protective Association Advocate*
LHJ	*The Ladies' Home Journal*
LGW	*Ladies' Garment Worker*
PW	*Publisher's Weekly*
SEP	*The Saturday Evening Post*
WHC	*Women's Home Companion*

Manuscript Collections

(BLY)	Collection of American Literature, Beinecke Rare Book and Manuscript Library, Yale University, New Haven, Connecticut
(CSC)	Charles Scribner Collection, Firestone Library, Princeton University, Princeton, New Jersey
(EFC)	Edna Ferber Collection, The State Historical Society of Wisconsin, Madison, Wisconsin
(ERC)	Elmer Rice Collection, Harry Ransom Humanities Research Center, University of Texas at Austin, Austin, Texas
(FSP)	Firestone Library, Princeton University, Princeton, New Jersey
(GHM)	O. Henry Collection, Greensboro Historical Museum and Library, Greensboro, North Carolina
(GPL)	O. Henry Collection, Greensboro Public Library, Greensboro, North Carolina
(HUH)	Houghton Library, Harvard University, Cambridge, Massachusetts
(RGC)	Robert Grant Collection, Houghton Library, Harvard University, Cambridge, Massachusetts
(SLC)	Sinclair Lewis Collection, Beinecke Rare Book and Manuscript Library, Yale University, New Haven, Connecticut

Introduction: Representing Main Street

1. C. Wright Mills, *White Collar,* ix.

2. For a witty exposition of American "embarrassment" about the topic of class, see Paul Fussell, *Class.* As Fussell notes, Americans overwhelmingly prefer (as sur-

veys from the late 1930s onward have shown) to identify themselves as "middle class" (38)—in some surveys, upwards of 80 percent of respondents. See also Stanislaw Ossowski, *Class Structure in the Social Consciousness,* esp. 103–6, and Benjamin DeMott, *The Imperial Middle,* esp. 111–25.

3. Vernon Parrington, comparing *Babbitt* to Mencken's *boobus Americanus,* in *The Beginnings of Critical Realism in America, 1860–1920,* 363; Alfred Kazin, *On Native Grounds,* 222. Even a relatively hostile critic, and one who recognized the class dimensions of Lewis's portraiture, called him "American to the core" and "the most American of American writers." V. F. Calverton in *The Liberation of American Literature,* 33, 38, 433.

4. Anthony Giddens, on this paradox of "class awareness," in *The Class Structure of the Advanced Societies,* 111: "[I]n so far as class is a structurated phenomenon, there will tend to exist a common awareness and acceptance of similar attitudes and beliefs, linked to a common style of life . . . 'Class awareness,' as I use the term here, does *not* involve a recognition that these attitudes signify a particular class affiliation, or the recognition that there exist other classes . . . class awareness may take the form of *a denial of the existence or reality of classes.* Thus the class awareness of the middle class . . . is of this order." If we take Giddens to be referring to a struggle between what a class recognizes and what it denies, this is the sense in which I will adopt his notion of "class awareness." For a recent application of Giddens's ideas to an earlier period, see Stuart M. Blumin, *The Emergence of the Middle Class.*

5. See esp. June Howard, *Form and History in American Literary Naturalism;* Amy Kaplan, *The Social Construction of American Realism;* Walter Benn Michaels, *The Gold Standard and the Logic of Naturalism;* and Daniel Borus, *Writing Realism.* For Raymond Williams on "residual" and "emergent," see his "Base and Superstructure in Marxist Cultural Theory," in *Problems in Materialism and Culture,* 40–42.

6. Stephen Greenblatt, "Murdering Peasants," 16. Clifford and Marcus, introduction to *Writing Culture,* 7. Harry Braverman, *Labor and Monopoly Capital,* referring to the "dynamic complex of moods and sentiments affected by circumstances . . . [which] draw upon and give expression to the underlying reservoir of class attitudes" (29–30).

7. Jürgen Kocka points out that the ethnic make-up of white collar employees (and trade union leadership) at the turn of the century was distinctly more indigenous than among manual workers, in part due to the language needs of such employment—and, doubtless, the prejudices of customers with whom white collar workers often had direct contact. Jürgen Kocka, *White Collar Workers in America, 1890–1940,* 71–73. See also Sharon Strom, "We're No Kitty Foyles," 206–34.

8. As opposed to "discourse," which often implies a systemic, regularized, even disciplinary relationship between knowledge and power, by "idiom" I mean to capture the feel and flexibility of colloquial and nonsystematic thought.

9. Jonathan Culler, drawing upon Roland Barthes's *S/Z,* defines this verisimilitude as the drawing upon a "shared knowledge" in a culture, a range of typifications that are recognized as "generalizations" of cultural norms. In Culler's account, this is akin to drawing upon "manuals" of popular culture—something, as we shall see,

Sinclair Lewis literally did—to constitute character and action; it is fundamental to what has often been called naturalization. *Structuralist Poetics,* 141–42.

10. For useful overviews of this literature, see Martin Oppenheimer, *White Collar Politics;* Peter Stearns, "The Middle Class: Toward a Precise Definition."

11. "Real" figures of selected occupations also show considerable growth: bank tellers (like O. Henry) rose from 235,000 in 1900 to 1.3 million twenty years later; real estate agents (like George Babbitt) from 34,000 to 89,000; male store salespersons and clerks from 232,000 to nearly 1.7 million. Naturally, available statistical counts are marred by conflation of categories, disagreement over them, by inflations of titles and configurations that, in themselves, represent assumptions about class structure. I have drawn my statistics from two recognized sources, resolving discrepancies where possible: Alba M. Edwards, *Population: Comparative Occupation Statistics for the United States, 1870 to 1940,* and *Historical Statistics of the United States, Colonial Times to 1970,* Part I.

12. Quotations from Arno J. Mayer, "The Lower Middle Class as a Historical Problem," 409.

13. On the above, see Paul E. Johnson, *A Shopkeeper's Millenium;* Mary P. Ryan, *Cradle of the Middle Class;* Blumin, *Emergence of the Middle Class;* and Sean Wilentz, *Chants Democratic.* See also John Gilkeson, *Middle-Class Providence, 1820–1940.*

14. On class and culture in the nineteenth century, see Karen Halttunen, *Confidence Men and Painted Women;* Christine Stansell, *City of Women;* Charles E. Rosenberg, "Sexuality, Class and Role in 19th Century America"; Eliot Gorn, *The Manly Art;* John Tomsich, *A Genteel Endeavor;* and Michael Denning, *Mechanic Accents.* Burton J. Bledstein, *The Culture of Professionalism,* points out (8) that the first *O.E.D.* definition of "middle class" in the singular comes from 1812 but that the first American definition comes decades later (see my Chapter 3); see also Asa Briggs, "The Language of 'Class' in Early Nineteenth Century England," 43–73. On the literary front, see Alan Trachtenberg, *Incorporation of America,* 10–39, and Kaplan, *Social Construction of American Realism,* 44–65.

15. This point modifies what some critics in the Marxian tradition commonly refer to as the "contradictory class locations" of white collar work. For examples of this viewpoint, see esp. Oppenheimer, 7–9, and Erik Olin Wright, *Class, Crisis and the State,* 61–87. My modification is that what is contested is middle-classness itself, not that—in the more orthodox Marxian formulation—white collar occupations exist among or between more "authentic" class positions.

16. For a superb analysis of Mills's work, see Richard Gillam, "*White Collar* from Start to Finish." Gillam also mentions Richard Hofstadter's sense of the expressionist hyperbole (18) of *White Collar.*

17. For the idea of "middle class" as a heuristic term, see Stearns, 380. I mean to apply "heuristic" here to further exploration of these middle classes, not to question their material existence; cf. Ossowski, *passim,* on this point. Like Mills, I also resort occasionally to "new middle classes" (in the plural) to represent the contestation of this label, indeed the internal fracturing, distension, and self-differentiation that is part of middle-class history. See also Giddens, 182 and 192, and Robert K.

Shaeffer, "A Critique of the 'New Class' Theorists." By emphasizing the cultural dimensions, however, I am turning my eye away from the technical occupations such as shop management or engineering. On these dimensions, see David Montgomery, "White Shirts and Superior Intelligence," 214. See also Norris W. Yates, *The American Humorist,* 38, on the "Little Man." On the emergence of "white collar," see Blumin, *Emergence of the Middle Class,* note 104, p. 386. For language changes generally, see Bledstein, *Culture of Professionalism,* 8–45.

18. To follow suit, one would then select only "images" of supposedly verifiable white collar citizens in given works of fiction, a standard but reductive ploy in many a cultural history. We will simplify the processes at hand if we fail to see that within white collar idioms, middle-class values were extended to embrace "average" citizens not necessarily identified with white collar occupations; again, this is a book about representations *of and by* white collar Americans. Thus, in the chapters that follow, I discuss characters like O. Henry's Lou and Nancy in "The Trimmed Lamp," Selma White in *Unleavened Bread,* or Lewis's Babbitt (who is a boss and owner), who are seen through the lens marked by white collar idioms.

19. On "passive" cultural models, see Robert Williams, "Base and Superstructure in Marxist Cultural Theory," in *Problems in Materialism and Culture,* 34–35. See also Cathy Davidson, *Revolution and the Word,* 260–62; Lloyd S. Kramer, "Literature, Criticism, and Historical Imagination," 97–128; Denning, 3. See also Hans Robert Jauss, "Literary History as a Challenge to Literary Theory," 3–45. On the idea of serial novels as "a real way of day dreaming," see Antonio Gramsci, *Selections from Cultural Writings,* 349.

20. On my use of "determination" and "determinants" in this study, see Raymond Williams, *Marxism and Literature,* 83–89. Marxian critics, it should be pointed out, often use "dependence" as a dialectic or reciprocal term, suggesting the interdependence (or "asymetrical" reciprocity) *between* classes: each class needs the other, but their interests are mutually exclusive and their power not equal. See Giddens, 29. For the discussion of my three determinants I have relied especially on Kocka; Margery W. Davies, *Woman's Place is at the Typewriter;* Blumin, *Emergence of the Middle Class;* Alfred D. Chandler, *The Visible Hand;* Braverman; Barbara Gerson, *All the Livelong Day;* Barbara Ehrenreich and John Ehrenreich, "The Professional-Managerial Class"; and Jean-Christophe Agnew, "A Touch of Class," 59–72. Giddens lists three sources of "proximate" class structuration: the division of labor, relationships of authority, and "distributive groupings" around common consumption patterns; necessarily, I neglect the last category. Oliver Zunn's *Making America Corporate 1877–1920* (Chicago: University of Chicago Press, 1990) appeared too recently to be incorporated into this study.

21. For relevant discussions here, see Robert H. Wiebe, *The Search for Order;* Eugene E. Leach, "Mastering the Crowd: Collective Behavior and Mass Society in American Social Thought, 1917–1939"; Daniel Horowitz, "Frugality or Comfort: Middle-Class Styles of Life in the Early Twentieth Century"; Michael McGerr, *The Decline of Popular Politics;* Robert Westbrook, "Politics as Consumption," 145–63;

and James T. Kloppenberg, *Uncertain Victory*. See also Robert S. Lynd, *Knowledge for What?*, 103–5.

22. For a good definition of "culturalist" work, see Agnew, p. 72. The seminal essay to which Agnew refers is Ehrenreich and Ehrenreich, "The Professional-Managerial Class." See also Kocka's working definitions, 12, and Giddens, 182.

23. On "micro-foundation," see Borus, 187; for a contrasting view, see Wai-chee Dimock's formulations in "Slippery Connections," 131.

24. Resistances, in truth, cut both ways: new social historians frequently dismiss fictional, artistic, or mass-cultural representations as mystifications or romantic distortions of an empirical reality. See, for instance, the comments of Susan Porter Benson in her otherwise insightful *Counter Cultures,* 214–15. E. P. Thompson on "idealism," *The Poverty of Theory and Other Essays,* esp. 196–201. For a recent Marxian rebuttal to the "languages of class" scholarship, see Bryan D. Palmer, *Descent into Discourse,* esp. pp. 120–45. I analyze new historical criticism from a different perspective in "Containing Multitudes: Realism, Historicism, American Studies."

25. Clifford Geertz, "Thick Description," 30.

26. These critical paradigms were established in the twenties and refined only moderately at mid-century. See Carl Van Doren, *Contemporary American Novelists, 1900–1920,* 146–56, 161–64; Van Doren, *The American Novel, 1789–1940,* 294 ff; Parrington, *The Beginnings of Critical Realism,* 363–73; Frederick J. Hoffman, *The Twenties,* 304–70; Kazin, 209–23; and Anthony Channell Hilfer, *The Revolt from the Village, 1915–1930.*

27. Lewis objected to the "revolt from the village" hypothesis when Carl Van Doren first proposed it in *The Nation* in the early twenties. As the critic later admitted in his autobiography *Three Worlds,* he had woven his "revolt" banner quite self-consciously out of threads from his own village past, and he did so having read only a fraction (one novel) of Lewis's early work. On such holistic theories in history, see esp. Robert Berkhofer, "Clio and the Culture Concept," and Dominick La Capra, *History and Criticism.* On "horizons," see Jauss, 3–45.

28. See George Soule, "The *Saturday Evening Post,*" *New Republic* 1 (23 Jan. 1915): 29, and "Main Street in Fiction," *New Republic* 25 (12 Jan. 1921): 25; William Allen White, "Splitting Fiction," *New Republic* 30 (12 April 1922): 30, and "Clean Fiction," *The Bookman* 62 (Oct. 1925): 115–16; Robert Littell, "The Great American Novel," *New Republic* 43 (15 July 1925): 43; and "The Great American Novel," *The Bookman,* 56 (March 1927): 3–4.

29. Cf. Bledstein, *Culture of Professionalism,* 40. In the story Bledstein cites, Ade writes: "Theoretically, at least, there are no classes in Chicago. But the 'middle class' means all those persons who are respectably in the background, who work either with hand or brain, who are neither poverty-stricken nor offensively rich, and who are not held down by the arbitrary laws governing that mysterious part of the community known as society." "The Advantage of Being 'Middle Class,'" in *Chicago Stories,* 75.

30. For but a few examples of the "national character" debate, see the list provided

by George Perry Morris, "Is the American Character Declining?," *The World's Work* 5 (Nov. 1902): 2775–78.

31. On O. Henry's influence see Carl R. Dolmetsch, *The Smart Set,* 16; Dale Kramer, *Ross and The New Yorker,* 12–13, 87–88, 206; James Thurber, *The Years With Ross,* 76–78; Charles Hanson Towne, *Adventures in Editing,* 90; and Douglas Stenerson, "Short-Story Writing: A Neglected Phase of Mencken's Literary Apprenticeship," *Menckeniana* 30 (Summer 1969): 8–13. See also "The Curse of Cleverness As a Fault of Our Newest Writers," *Current Opinion* 62 (Jan. 1917): 49–50. On Mencken's critical preferences for novels of "typical Americans," see William H. Nolte, *Henry L. Mencken: Literary Critic,* 75. On film, see Lary May, *Screening Out the Past,* 97–103; Richard Schickel, *Harold Lloyd: The Shape of Laughter,* 20, 35–36, 48, 73. Lloyd thought of his younger self as a "Tom Sawyer" type, the character who always ended up with his eye on the clock. With some adroit promotion of his own (including a national blitz begun in the *SEP*), Lloyd became one of the wealthiest men in show business in the twenties. On Williams, see esp. Edward Sorel, "The World of Gluyas Williams," 50–57.

32. On the modern intelligentsia's lament, see Mary Kolars, "Some Modern Periodicals," *Catholic World* 116 (March 1923): 781–89. See also Loren H. B. Knox, "Our Lost Individuality," *Atlantic* 104 (Dec. 1909): 818–24.

33. Cf. Christopher P. Wilson, *The Labor of Words,* 74. My sources here are Alice P. Hackett, *Seventy Years of Best Sellers, 1895–1965;* Irving Harlow Hart, "Fiction Fashions from 1925 to 1926," *PW* 111 (5 Feb. 1927): 473–77, "Best Sellers in Fiction During the First Quarter of the Twentieth Century," *PW* 107 (14 Feb. 1925): 525–27, and "The Most Popular Authors of Fiction Between 1900 and 1925," *PW* 107 (21 Feb. 1925): 619–22. See also "Twenty-five Years of 'Best-Sellers,'" *Current Opinion* 78 (April 1925): 424, and "A Quarter-Century of Best Sellers," *Outlook* 139 (15 April 1925): 564–65. For an interesting discussion of class which identified the new interest in employee relations, see Louise Mausell Field, "Social Relations in the Modern Novel," *Forum* 53 (Feb. 1915): 244–50.

34. Cf. Wilson, *Labor of Words,* 74.

35. On the O. Henry award, see Fred Lewis Pattee, *Side-Lights on American Literature,* 3–55, and *The Development of the American Short Story,* 372–73. The prize is discussed in Society of Arts and Sciences, *O. Henry Memorial Award Prize Stories,* vii–xvii. Stuart Sherman, Hamlin Garland, and William Allen White—all Pulitzer Prize board members—at one time or another were on the O. Henry Award Honorary Committee. For a defense of O. Henry against Pattee, see the editorial "Journalization," *New York Times Book Review,* 8 April 1917, 128. For O. Henry's sales figures and reception, see Pattee, *Side-Lights,* 3–10.

36. Nicholas Murray Butler, *The American As He Is,* 30, 58. See also W. J. Stuckey, *The Pulitzer Prize Novels;* Robert Morss Lovett, "Pulitzer Prize," *New Republic,* 11 Sept. 1929, 100–101, and "Sinclair Lewis's Gesture," *New Republic,* 19 May 1926, 397. In all likelihood, Grant sided with critics like Lovett who successfully chose *Main Street* in 1921, only to be overridden by Butler. For Grant's praise of the novel, see his *Fourscore,* 260, 383. On Howells as "dean," see also my "Markets and Fictions."

37. I have discussed these trends more fully in "The Rhetoric of Consumption," 39–64, and *The Labor of Words.*

38. Dwyer as quoted in Zona Gale, "Editors of the Younger Generation," *The Critic* 44 (April 1904): 319. See "A Blot on Our American Life," *LHJ* 12 (July 1895): 14; "At Home with the Editor," *LHJ* 12 (March 1895): 12; "Where American Life Really Exists," *LHJ* 12 (Oct. 1895): 14.

39. See Burton Rascoe, *We Were Interrupted,* 84–87, and "Rhetoric of Consumption," 44.

40. Typical commentary on the *Post* can be found in George Soule, "Magazines and Democrats," *New Republic,* 1 (21 Aug. 1915): 78–79. Here, Soule describes "standardization" as a trend of his time, arguing that it is due to anticipating audiences who live by formulae themselves. To Soule—who worked with Sinclair Lewis on the Woodward syndicate, discussed in Chapter 6, and shared many of Lewis's views on the literary profession—this was a civilization in which "the average must be intolerant of the exceptional." Earlier, in "The *Saturday Evening Post,*" Soule had identified his target more directly, saying the fiction produced by Lorimer was akin to "merely a depiction of the average by the average for the average."

41. In our best account of Lorimer, *Creating America,* Jan Cohn makes two important points. First, "American" was Lorimer's totem word—the label with which he praised anything within his normative domain—and "socialism" was one of its antonyms (152). "American" often stood in for the modern businessman himself. Secondly, Cohn points out that, by "businessmen," Lorimer meant "something a good deal more inclusive": the professions, drummers, clerks (31)—as well as the "average American," a category broad enough to include even the small entrepreneur. See Cohn, 30–32. This kind of rhetorical conflation was highly characteristic of the Main Street style itself. In 1908, as well, the *Post* also announced explicitly that it was "not for men only" (Cohn, 65).

42. Most evocative of the style Lorimer engineered were his color covers, boldly resisting what he called the "bizarre and Bolshevistic" invocations of modernism, expressing instead what one enthusiast called "the mirror of average America," ordinary Americans frozen in a "just folks" moment with whom the viewer was often asked to identify. "Gossip," *SEP* 179 (25 Aug. 1906): 14. On "mirror of average America," see John Tebbel, *George Horace Lorimer and the Saturday Evening Post,* 108.

43. "The Editorial Desk," *LHJ* 7 (Feb. 1890): 8. In October of 1891, under "In Literary Circles," p. 18, Bok says: "Strike for the heart first, then reach up to the head." He described his own magazine as a "messenger of contentment to the heart and entertainment to the mind," *LHJ* 10 (Nov. 1893): 12. Ruth Ashmore, "What Shall a Girl Read?," *LHJ* 11 (Dec. 1893): 20, says a good novel is one "written in good English, tells an interesting story, has a distinct plot, and ends happily." Compare also the *SEP* editorial, "The Pessimism of Herbert Spencer," *SEP,* 176 (6 Feb. 1904): 12. See also Tebbel, 18, 47–48, 108, 147; "The Plain American," *SEP* 176 (23 Jan. 1904): 14; John B. Kennedy, "Nothing Succeeds Like Common Sense," *Collier's* 78 (27 Nov. 1926): 8, 47–48; Irvin S. Cobb, "George Horace Lorimer, Original Easy Boss," *Bookman* 48 (Dec. 1918): 389–94; and Walter Tittle, "The Editor of the *Satur-*

day Evening Post," *The World's Work* 55 (Jan. 1928): 302–7. Editorials quoted here include *SEP* 176 (30 Jan. 1904): 14; *SEP* 173 (23 Sept. 1900): 12. For another instance of Lorimer's counseling of patience, see "Sore Heads and Swelled Heads," *SEP* 176 (5 March 1904): 12. For different views, see Paul A. Carter, "Horatio Alger Doesn't Live Here Anymore," 145–61, and Warren Susman, "'Personality' and the Making of Twentieth-Century Culture," 212–26.

44. This was actually a misquote on Wharton's part—or perhaps on the part of Van Wyck Brooks, her source (652); Howells had responded to James that "we have the whole of human life remaining, and a social structure presenting the only fresh and novel opportunities left to fiction." See this review, reprinted in *W. D. Howells as Critic,* 54. Edith Wharton, "The Great American Novel," 646–656. Further citations in text. Contrast Edna Ferber's "There There My Precious," *Bookman* 64 (Dec. 1926): 443–44.

45. Stuart M. Blumin, "Explaining the New Metropolis." Drawing upon systematic samples of newspapers (including workingmen's papers), magazines, autobiographies, and other publications, Blumin finds "discussions of social polarization appear with increasing frequency . . . [in] the second half of the [nineteenth] century" (309); see also *Emergence of the Middle Class,* 285–90. Ossowski also points out that "dichotomous" metaphors of the class structure are less prominent on the American scene in the twentieth century, displaced by what he calls "gradation" and "functionalist" schemes; see also his chapter on American "non-egalitarian classlessness" (100–18). Cf. DeMott, 41–54. For another account of nineteenth-century polarized vocabularies, see also Charles H. Page, *Class and American Sociology,* 47, 95, 128–35. For good instances of this polarized idiom, one thinks of Jacob Riis's *How the Other Half Lives* (1890); Stephen Crane's paired "Experiments" in "Misery" and "Luxury" (1894); or a novel like *Sister Carrie* (1900), which posits two possible social paths for an urban newcomer. For contemporary editorial examples, see E. L. Godkin, "Social Classes in the Republic," *Atlantic,* 78 (Dec. 1896): 721–28, or Saul Beaumont, "The Class Struggle of To-Day," *Arena,* 40 (Nov. 1908): 453–58. By way of contrast, see Robert Rives La Monte, "The American Middle Class," *Arena,* 39 (April 1905): 436–39; and "The Middle Class Again," *Independent,* 27 Sept. 1900, 2342–44.

46. For a helpful discussion of this vernacular style, see Howard W. Webb, Jr., "The Development of a Style: The Lardner Idiom," 482–92.

47. Crozier, 1.

48. Cf. Robert L. Martin, *H. L. Mencken and the Debunkers.* See also Kazin, 220, and Virginia Woolf, "American Fiction," *Saturday Review of Literature,* 1 Aug. 1925, 1–3, which praises the realism of Lewis, Anderson, and Ring Lardner. Such claims appear, albeit more covertly, in critical characterizations of literary talents as based in mime or even eavesdropping (cf. Martin, 119–20, or Kazin, 210); as "naive" or "intuitive" (Kazin, 214–15); as derived (in largely unsubstantiated ways) from transcription of "oral" testimony. For the argument about structural lapses, see Stuart P. Sherman, *Points of View,* 22, 151–70, 187–219. I am indebted, however, to Sherman's use of "synoptic" to describe Lewis's "averaging" technique. T. W. Adorno, "Veblen's Attack on Culture," 73–94.

49. Cf. Antony H. Harrison, "Reception Theory and the New Historicism," 163–80.

50. Terry Eagleton has put this in rather schematic formulation: that the "literary mode of production" (LMP) is rarely if ever broached as related to, much less a component of, the "general mode of production" (GMP). Terry Eagleton, "Towards a Materialist Criticism," in *Criticism and Ideology,* 44–53. By "contiguity" or "imbrication" I mean something more than simply analogous social practices or "homologies"; I mean actual structural bordering and overlapping that, while not complete or continuous, was hardly unsystematic.

51. E. P. Thompson, *The Making of the English Working Class,* 9.

52. Kazin on the fate of Lewis and Anderson, 220. Philip Fisher, *Hard Facts,* 3–9; T. J. Jackson Lears, "The Concept of Cultural Hegemony: Problems and Possibilities," 589–90. See also Jane P. Tompkins, *Sensational Designs,* 156.

53. "Cement" quote in Mayer, 425.

54. Becker as quoted in Lynd, *Knowledge for What?,* 57. Afterword epigraph from this page as well. See also Lynd's discussion of "little man" nostalgia, 78; cf. Mills, x–xiii.

Chapter 1. Over the Counter: O. Henry and the Loyal Employee

1. The photograph, with the caption "'The Four Million' on Parade," appears in the 1920 Doubleday, Page edition.

2. William Saroyan, "O What a Man Was O. Henry."

3. See esp. Robert H. Davis and Arthur Butler Maurice, *The Caliph of Bagdad,* 374–79. The authors also conducted a survey of ten authors, asking them to list their ten favorite O. Henry stories. In the end, sixty-two different stories made the top one hundred stories.

4. See, for example, the following limerick composed by Porter:

> A good natured young Dr. named Beall
> Was quite pleased when his patients got well
> When they did not do so
> He would blame the drug-sto'
> And say "drugs is now made for to sell."

The manuscript for the above, as well as additional sketches and limericks, are currently kept in (GHM).

5. On the druggist name, see Eli Oettinger file (GHM). This is only one of several theories about Porter's use of "O. Henry." The poem by Morley is in O. Henry, *Waifs and Strays,* 230. For Lorimer's affection for O. Henry, see Tebbel, *George Horace Lorimer,* 69–70.

6. Generalizations derived from surveying reviews listed in *O. Henry Papers*—essentially a memorial pamphlet in (GPL). On the vagabonding form of realism see Raymond Williams, *The Long Revolution,* 276.

7. See, for instance, Vachel Lindsay, "The Knight in Disguise," in O. Henry, *Waifs and Strays,* 169–70, or Upton Sinclair's *Bill Porter,* 58. Hackett as quoted in *Waifs*

and Strays, 274. Here and elsewhere in turn-of-the-century usage, "clerks" referred to employees in both clerical and saleswork, e.g., in department stores. I have followed this contemporary usage. On the Henry James comparison, see Seth Moyle, *My Friend O. Henry,* 16.

8. Cindy Sondik Aron, *Ladies and Gentlemen of the Civil Service,* 39.

9. Harry Braverman, *Labor and Monopoly Capital,* 297.

10. Albert Shaw, *The Outlook for the Average Man,* 15. On Shaw's reception, see Donald Meyer, *The Positive Thinkers,* 163–64. Historians have often tended to synthesize success advice into singular, common norms. I suspect that these advice manuals were tracked and class inflected for lower- or upper-echelon white collar workers. "Personal Magnetism" or "creativity" were, for example, associated more commonly with advertising work or public relations. But since "clerking" referred both to in-house work like accounting and to sales, there was considerable overlap in advice. In the teens, for instance, the *Advocate* ran Orison Swett Marden, poems like Ella Wheeler Wilcox's "Be Not Content," and a long series on "Clerkology" by George E. B. Putnam which emphasized prudential values. See also Warren Susman, "'Personality' and the Making of Twentieth-Century Culture," 221–25. On these academies, see Margery W. Davies, *Woman's Place is at the Typewriter,* 73.

11. Arlie Cameron Hochschild pictures the problem facing service workers as "How can I feel really identified with my work role and with the company without being fused with them?" *The Managed Heart,* 132.

12. Robert H. Wiebe, *The Search for Order,* 14. On earlier meanings of personal "independence" within artisan culture, see Sean Wilentz, *Chants Democratic,* 92; clerical journal quoted is *Advocate* 15 (Feb. 1908): 15; cf. Jürgen Kocka, *White Collar Workers in America,* 76.

13. See E. P. Thompson, *Making of the English Working Class,* 9. On living conditions, see Kocka, 80–83. Kocka also (87) mentions a union survey that reported more than half of its members saw their job as transitional. On gender roles in the workplace, see Judith Smith, "The 'New Woman' Knows How to Type"; on marriages, see Ileen DeVault, *Sons and Daughters of Labor,* 160–68.

14. Blumin infers middle-class "awareness" (*Emergence of the Middle Class,* 290–97) by the *absence* of its representation in the discourse of the day—a somewhat difficult case to verify. Contemporaries, Blumin and David Montgomery tell us, still frequently pictured a society polarized between plutocrat and poor, and they referred to working classes in the plural. O. Henry, in fact, occasionally presumes a public, conventional attitude of a two-tiered society, if only to undermine that attitude. For instance, in a 15 Dec. 1895 Post-Script, O. Henry began a conventional story with a "great city" with "sharp contrasts of wealth and poverty," but the contrast is undercut, whimsically, when a couple shivering in the cold outside a party is revealed to be simply waiting for the next dance. Typescript (GHM). See also David Montgomery, *Beyond Equality,* 29–44.

15. On the R.C.I.P.A., see Kocka, 58. On wages, compare the statistics cited by Kocka, 77, and the source Michel Crozier cites (13) in *World of the Office Worker.*

16. See Kocka, 125–26; compare Crozier, *passim.*

17. See Meyer, 133, and Ayer quoted in Davies, 42. Historians have begun to reconsider, of course, how much Alger represented "middling" interests to begin with. See Michael Denning, *Mechanic Accents,* 170–71.

18. Edward Bok, *Successward,* 18, 43, 57.

19. George Horace Lorimer, *Letters from a Self-Made Merchant to His Son,* 58, 88, 163–64; Kocka, 87–89. It is also intriguing that Lorimer, like O. Henry and Ferber, had actually failed at being a loyal employee. Lorimer had been dismissed from Armour & Co.—another bastion of modern personality management. In the pages of Bok's *Ladies' Home Journal,* meanwhile, the American wife was counseled not to be Sarah Hale's "guiding" moral influence, but an aide-de-camp for her husband, efficient in accounting and home budgeting; Bok, in other words, made the wife the loyal employee of the family. See my "Rhetoric of Consumption," 53–55. For a good sampling of one clerical union's thinking, see Harvey H. Woolfolk, "Relations Between Employer and Employee," *Advocate* 15 (Jan. 1908): 16; "Confidence," *Advocate* 15 (Nov. 1908): 24; and "Booster One's Self," same issue, 22, 24.

20. In its more aggressive phase after 1907, the R.C.I.P.A. tried to exclude any salaried employee who accepted or owned stock worth more than five hundred dollars in their own company. Kocka, 61.

21. Historians of success literature might do well to recognize, as sociologists like Michel Crozier have, that just because corporations asked for loyalty does not mean they got it. In fact, strategies of "retreat" and disaffiliation, precisely the coping mechanisms that I will argue O. Henry appealed to, are quite common in modern white collar work. See also David E. Nye, *Image Worlds.* Nye also argues (95) that, while corporations were concerned with disrupting the solidarity of blue collar workers, the threat from white collar employees was a lack of integration; in response G.E. promoted its own "tribalism."

22. See, for instance, John Kasson, *Amusing the Million,* and Lary May, *Screening Out the Past,* 43–59.

23. Adrian Forty, *Objects of Desire,* 124–27, 138; Braverman, 304.

24. O. Henry himself parodied internal accounting in a Post script column called "The Cynic"; see *Post scripts,* 141:

JUNIOR PARTNER: Here's an honest firm! Sharp and Simpson sent us a check for $50 in addition to their monthly account, to cover the difference in price of a higher grade of goods shipped them last time by mistake.

SENIOR PARTNER: Did they give us another order?

JUNIOR PARTNER: Yes! The largest they have ever made.

SENIOR PARTNER: Ship 'em C.O.D.

25. See the transcript of a letter to Mrs. Roach, n.d., written from the Ohio Penitentiary (FSP): "in spite of the jury's verdict I am absolutely innocent." Perhaps the most egregious mystification is Stephen Leacock's: "A certain cruel experience of his earlier days—tragic, unmerited and not here to be recorded." "Bagdad on the Subway," a pamphlet essay published in *Essays and Literary Studies,* 21. See also Carl Van Doren, "O. Henry."

26. Typescript, apparently prepared by Joseph Katz (GHM), 24 May 1896.

27. Biographical information culled from various sources, where noted. In order of general reliability: Gerald Langford, *Alias O. Henry;* Marilyn McAdams Silbey, "Austin's First National and the Errant Teller"; Cathleen Pike, *O. Henry in North Carolina.* Contemporary sources include George McAdam, "O. Henry's Only Autobiography," in the *O. Henry Papers* in (GPL); Arthur W. Page, "Little Pictures of O. Henry," in (GPL); C. Alphonso Smith, *O. Henry;* Carl Goerch, "O. Henry's Brother Lives in Ayden" in (GPL); Moyle; Davis and Maurice; William Wash Williams, *The Quiet Lodger of Irving Place.*

28. Porter's family often denied that the invention was a perpetual motion machine. See the letter from Shirley Porter to Mrs. Caroline Coffin Thornton, 15 Dec. 1936 (GHM). "Monkey" quote and self-description in Will Porter to Sarah Coleman Porter, July 15, n.d. (GHM).

29. On "agony," see Langford, 15; C. Alphonso Smith, 92; Moyle, 16. See also Pike, 10, and Porter to "My Dear Doctor," 27 Feb. 1884 (GPL), and Letter to Mrs. Hall, 13 March [1883-4?] (GPL). Various tales play off the saving power of the doctor; see for instance "The Skylight Room." Clerical unions often singled out the drug clerk as the most dependent kind of employee, in part because he was expected to work seven days a week. See the cartoon of "The Drug Store Slave," *Advocate* 15 (July 1908): 22, and "Drug Clerks to the Front," same issue, 25; also 15 (Aug. 1908), editorial section: 14.

30. On the requisite attributes for white collar appearance, see Aron, 17. On Porter's demeanor, see Arthur Page, 31. On his politics, Langford (253) finds *Rolling Stone* "without a consistent political attitude," but he does note that columns regularly ridiculed populism and socialists; on Porter's character in Austin, see Page, 31. See also Frank Luther Mott, *A History of American Magazines,* 4: 665–70.

31. Cf. Aron, 31.

32. On the impasse, see Langford, 71. On "technical" matters, see the letter to Mrs. Roach, n.d., transcript in (FSP). The specific charges involved the embezzeling of about $845; a federal bank examiner testified that he found about fifty separate instances in which Porter "unquestionably" diverted funds for his private use—probably in siphoning off petty cash. The main charges concerned Porter's failure to credit bank drafts, one from a Singer Sewing Machine man, another from a neighboring bank. Porter himself claimed that though he was technically responsible for the shortages, he did not take the money (Langford, 121).

33. On the changing bank practices before and after O. Henry's trial, see Silbey, 478–506. A character in "Blind Man's Holiday," who has gambled with his employer's money and been falsely accused of a simultaneous theft from a vault, says: "It is not in the unjust accusation . . . that my burden lies, but in the knowledge that from the moment I had taken the first dollar of the firm's money I was a criminal." *The Complete Works of O. Henry,* 1226. All citations in text of O. Henry's tales from this collection.

34. On the prison scene, see Porter to Mrs. Roach, 18 May 1898 (FSP). See David Rothman on prison composition and hard labor in *The Discovery of the Asylum,* 253. Observer quoted in Langford, 134. See also the transcripts of letters to Mrs. Roach

(FSP), and Porter to Mrs. Roach, 16 Dec. [1898?] and 5 Nov. 1900 (HUH). As noted earlier, the dropping of the final "e" in "employee" was common in contemporary usage.

35. O. Henry is frequently termed an urban local colorist. And yet, in his only interview, O. Henry said his stories were not at all dependent on the "local color" of New York but could be about "Main Street" (*his* word) anywhere. *O. Henry Papers,* 21. And in the musical entitled "Lo" composed by O. Henry and Franklin P. Adams, the song "Little Old Main Street," included the following lyrics:

> Singers may boast about Broadway,
> And they most gen'rally do;
> Spring all that flower *fluff* on the Bowery,
> Take it, I'll stake it to you,
>
> Call me a yap if you care to,
> Say I'm a rube or a shine,
> But give me the street that has got 'em all beat;
> Little old Main Street for mine. [GHM]

36. Fred Lewis Pattee, *Side-Lights,* 360–64. For the label "pseudo-realist," see Werner Berthoff, *The Ferment of Realism,* 32–33; Jesse Bier, *The Rise and Fall of American Humor,* 198, on the "corruption" of O. Henry's art; even Langford, 214. Cf. Denning on the dime novel, 201. O. Henry's style was also the foil for "serious" art in Cleanth Brooks, Jr., and Robert Penn Warren, *Understanding Fiction,* 114–18. Contrast, however, Van Wyck Brooks, *The Confident Years, 1885–1915,* 271–82.

37. On being given story copy, see Davis and Maurice, 201–4; on "ordered up" tales, see William Wash Williams, 25. On "attractive" material, see George P. Juergens, *Joseph Pulitzer and The New York World,* 57–83.

38. Obituary in the *New York World,* 7 June 1910, 8, emphasis mine. Direct allusions to cracker-barrel stories on O. Henry's part are rare, but a letter to his daughter Margaret, 8 July 1898 (GHM), mentions Uncle Remus; doubtless he was familiar with many other writers, like Bill Nye, who had already been running in the *World.* On potions, see J. Worth Estes, "The Pharmacology of Nineteenth Century Patent Medicines."

39. Clifford Geertz, "Common Sense as a Cultural System," in *Local Knowledge,* 73–93.

40. For evidence of how this mimicry drew upon the legal language Porter had to master in his own white collar employment, see Porter to (Dr. H. B. Marley), 9 Oct. 1890 (GHM).

41. See Porter to the editors of *Ainslee's,* 1 Dec. [n.d.] (BLY, xerox in GHM) in which O. Henry wrote: "I compose with greater ease on unruled paper and Fridays. . . . My favorite authors are Carolyn and Artesia Wells. . . . Favorite flower? self raising."

42. On strong drink, see Langford, 233. For "bread and butter," see Porter to Alphonso Smith, 24 Feb. 1908 (FSP).

43. Park as cited in Juergens, note p. 59. Dan Schiller, *Objectivity and the News,* 48, 70–71. Pulitzer memo from 1910 on "classes and masses," Juergens, 32. Soviet critics have often been ambivalent about O. Henry's erasure of class difference and polarization. After 1937 he was resurrected as a writer *protesting* the "arithmetical mean" approach to the ordinary American. See Deming Brown, *Soviet Attitudes Toward American Writing,* 230–38.

44. George Jean Nathan quoting O. Henry in *Waifs and Strays,* 224.

45. This is the Sunday, 6 Dec. 1903 issue.

46. That O. Henry did not appear in the *World*'s more "cosmopolitan" *Metropolitan* section is worth noting, given O. Henry's eventual appropriation by the "smart set." See Carl R. Dolmetsch, *The Smart Set,* 16.

47. See also Vachel Lindsay's tribute: "The Knight in Disguise," which described O. Henry's characters: "They overact each part. But at the height/ Of banter and of canter, and delight/ The masks fall off for one queer instant there/ And show real faces, faces full of care/ And desperate longing." *Waifs and Strays,* 223. O. Henry himself talked about sustaining an "honest human view"; see Langford, 231.

48. Cf. Fredric Jameson's comments on the function of narrative to "square its circles," in *The Political Unconscious,* 83.

49. On the six tales, see C. Alphonso Smith, 221. Theodore Roosevelt quoted in Langford, 174.

50. As quoted in *Waifs and Strays,* 251. This famous quote was engraved on many a memorial plaque.

51. In its own time, "shopgirl" was a term fought over by both managers and the women who were in sales. See Susan Porter Benson, *Counter Cultures,* 24, 141, 145. For historians' distrust of the sentimental figure of victim, see Benson, 25, 215.

52. For a different perspective on this shop-window fascination, see Stuart H. Culver, "What Mannikins Want," esp. note 15, p. 114–15.

53. Aside from the common colloquial term—don't "buy" it—we should notice that a "line" is often a line of goods a drummer might bring to a store.

54. The *World*'s logo, a glowing Statue of Liberty between "old" and "new" halves of the globe, captured this duality: the aristocracy and decay of Europe holding both fascination and dread.

55. Several of my colleagues at Boston College, particularly Professor Dayton Haskin, have pointed out the extensive allusions to biblical pre-texts in "The Trimmed Lamp"—suggesting another important Sunday form of reading the newspaper supplanted. This tale, I have been told, primarily adapts (or "copies," like Nancy) Matthew 25: 1–13, the story of five "foolish" and five "wise" virgins awaiting the bridegroom (among other biblical stories). Intriguingly, however, if the biblical story seems to underwrite traditional domesticity, frugality, and future-mindedness, O. Henry has transposed these prudential qualities to sales mastery, clear-eyed urbanity, and disciplined consuming.

56. The tale reprinted was "The Unfinished Story," in *Advocate* 17 (Nov. 1910): 16–18; it was praised in the editorial section, 23. For a fine reading of the "Knight"

image in an earlier period, see Denning, 176–78. Department-store figures from *LGW* 4 (July 1913): 19.

57. Reagan tribute in (GHM), 15 March 1985. On the relevance of the "average American" iconography to presidential styles, see Steven Stark, "A perfectly average American," 13.

58. Sheldon Wolin, "What Revolutionary Action Means Today," 23.

59. On this point, see Howard Horwitz, "The Standard Oil Trust as Emersonian Hero," esp. 118.

60. See esp. the letters from Porter to Witter Bynner and Robert Davis (HUH). In a 1907 letter to his daughter Margaret, 3 Jan. (GHM) as well, Porter revealed that certain stories had been announced in the magazines before he had finished writing them.

61. As quoted in Langford, 224. See also the passage in "Sociology in Serge and Straw": "all of life, as we know it, moves in little, unavailing circles. More justly than to anything else, it can be likened to the game of baseball. . . . If we earn a run (in life we call it success) we get back to the home plate and sit on a bench. If we are thrown out [notice: not strike out], we walk back to the home plate—and sit upon a bench. . . . When you reach the end of your career, just take down the sign 'Goal' and look at the other side of it. You will find 'Beginning Point' there. It has been reversed while you were going around the track" (1139).

Chapter 2. The Submerged Server: Edna Ferber

1. From her memoir, *A Peculiar Treasure,* 171. Hereafter cited as *PT*. All biographical page citations in text are from this source. See also Mary Rose Shaughnessey, *Women and Success in American Society in the Works of Edna Ferber;* Julie Goldsmith Gilbert, *Ferber;* and the entry by Carolyn Heilbrun in *Notable American Women*. *Everybody's* had run series on working women, and stories by O. Henry galore; later it would run a crusade against "tainted fiction." See Frank Luther Mott, *A History of American Magazines,* 5:72–87.

2. In the teens and twenties, Ferber became one of America's most sought-after short-story writers; in 1928, she received what she said was the largest single check yet written by Doubleday & Page for a six month sale (*PT,* 120). Cf. Shaughnessey, 11–12. For contemporary comparisons with O. Henry, see "The Imitative School," *Bookman* 35 (May 1912): 225–27, and "The Literary Spotlight," *Bookman* 54 (Jan. 1922): 434–39.

3. William Allen White, "Edna Ferber," *The World's Work* 59 (June 1930): 36–38, 90, and his "Splitting Fiction," *New Republic* 12 April 1922, 22–26; Louis Bromfield, "Edna Ferber," *Saturday Review of Literature* 12 (15 June 1935): 11; and Grant Overton, "The Social Critic in Edna Ferber," *Bookman* 64 (Oct. 1926): 138–43.

4. *PT,* 35. See also Ferber, "Midwestern, Middle-Class Me," as cited in Gilbert, 398. On the Main Street craze, see Wharton, "The Great American Novel." Wharton

herself found *So Big* "thick and inconclusive"; see R. W. B. Lewis, *Edith Wharton,* 443.

5. For one Alcott allusion, see Ferber, *So Big,* 182. In her memoir, Ferber mentions (among, let it be said, many other authors) having read "*all* of Louisa Alcott" (*PT,* 36, emphasis mine), as if to single her out for special attention. This could not have meant, of course, the recently recovered "thrillers" Alcott wrote under the pseudonym A. M. Barnard.

6. On Victorian careers, see Mary Kelley, *Private Woman, Public Stage.* Of necessity here I will conflate the varieties of expression within (and critical disputes concerning) this tradition. Cf. Kelley; Jane P. Tompkins, *Sensational Designs;* Ann Douglas, *The Feminization of American Culture;* and Richard Brodhead, "Sparing the Rod: Discipline and Fiction in Antebellum America," 67–96. See also Mary Ryan, *Cradle of the Middle Class,* on Forrester in Utica, 58.

7. For a typical example, see Laura Jean Libbey, *A Dangerous Flirtation.* This is quite clearly a cautionary Cinderella tale, beginning with the ill-fated encounter of a Newport gentleman with one Ida May, a telegraph operator whom he mistakes for one of his own class. After their wedding ceremony is deemed invalid—and he abandons her—the "dear reader" (97) is exposed to a litany of "awful woe" (129): a lost infant, Ida's expulsion from a cotton mill, her stay in a sanitorium, and finally what Libbey calls "this woman's heritage, this dower of passion and sorrow, called love, changing the world into a golden dream" (208). Cf. Michael Denning, *Mechanic Accents,* 197–200.

8. Cf. my "Tempests and Teapots."

9. Richard Sennett and Jonathan Cobb, *The Hidden Injuries of Class,* 221–25, 235–36; see also the discussion in Arlie Cameron Hochschild, *The Managed Heart,* 171. See also Susan Porter Benson, *Counter Cultures,* 125. On domestic work, see Thomas Dublin, *Women at Work,* 13. The *O.E.D.,* 15:37, lists "service" as "Provision (of labour, material appliances, etc.) for carrying out of some work for which there is a constant public demand" from 1853, and "The section of the economy that supplies needs of the consumer but produces no tangible goods," from 1936.

10. See esp. the work of Margery W. Davies, *Woman's Place Is at the Typewriter;* Benson; Jürgen Kocka, *White Collar Workers in America;* Judith Smith, "The 'New Woman' Knows How to Type." On class backgrounds, see Ileen DeVault, *Sons and Daughters,* table 10, p. 79 and pp. 174–5.

11. This does not, one must add, prevent some social historians from discounting "literary" evidence and seeing a writer like Ferber as purely a romanticist; compare for example, Benson, 215.

12. Benson, 181. See the surveys on wages she cites, 134–35; cf. DeVault, 51–52.

13. Hochschild, 5. All further citations in text.

14. For some examples of this kind of wisdom, see the following: Emil Mock, "A Successful Clerk and How to Become One," *Advocate* 15 (Jan. 1908): 29; C. MacA. Willcox, "The Department Store Man," *Advocate* 15 (Feb. 1908): 33; and "Dreamy Girl Not In It," *Advocate* 15 (March 1908): 36.

15. Benson, 263. Fiction in union journals often emphasized a cool, calm heroine who stood up for her rights. See, for example, "Mr. Skinner Climbs Down: A Story

of a Girl's Strike and its Success," *LGW* 4 (Feb. 1913): 17–19. As noted earlier, this union also discouraged romantic reading; see Pauline Newman, "When You Have Time to Read," *LGW* 4 (June 1913): 34: "Don't read books that take you into a fairy land and introduce you to a Prince who falls in love with you. You are wasting time reading such books."

16. Ferber actually chose the title to allude to her ethnic heritage; see *PT*, 258.

17. On Ferber's ethnic dimension, see Stephen P. Horowitz and Mirriam J. Landsman, "The Americanization of Edna."

18. In *PT*, 192, Ferber described their banter this way: "Together we would go gesticulating and jabbering along the New York streets . . . . He and I had built up two characters which we always assumed when together. Red [Lewis] was Gus, the janitor of a mythical office building, and I was Tillie, the scrubwoman. We talked in a bad German dialect, faintly Weber-and-Fieldsian, and not very funny except to us." See also the letters from Ferber to Lewis, 29 March [1914], and another [n.d.] addressed to "Very Young Man At the Publishers' Office" (BLY), in which Ferber uses these names.

19. Cf. Gilbert, 431.

20. Cf. Ferber's comments on the "immense professionalism" (*PT*, 119) of female journalists and "a certain masculine type of woman, enormously efficient" (*PT*, 192)—the literary agent Flora Mai Holly, also Lewis's first agent. Sewing bees reference in *Dawn O'Hara*, 50.

21. "Objectivity" and "hard-boiledness"—or rather, the suppression of emotional reactions—as Ferber was learning, were the requirements of reporting. The crucial scene in *The Girls*, as I will show below, appears in a police court; Lottie herself is counseled by a reporter. Cf. Hochschild, 31.

22. Ferber, *The Girls*, 194. All further citations in text.

23. Ferber never clarified what her "little plan" for ten thousand dollars meant to address, and it is impossible to diagnose a letdown that was probably psychological in origin. Ferber recalled that "I wept at the slightest provocation" (*PT*, 153). Compare Gilbert, 422.

24. Edna's memories of Julia are decidedly mixed: loving, envious, even occasionally prone to matricidal undertones. I say matricidal, because Ferber speaks jokingly about "killing off" her mother in her novel *Fanny Herself* (*PT*, 223).

25. Gilbert also refers (425) to this journal that Julia Ferber kept from 1900 to 1910; and Ferber herself alludes to it in *PT*, 31–32, 54. Unfortunately, the trail to this document has recently dried up. See Ferber on the importance of "work and more work" (*PT*, 13), on gadgetry and her "little stories" (*PT*, 11), and on the Native American name of her birthplace, Kalamazoo, meaning "boiling pot" (*PT*, 15).

26. Contemporaries often equated "sociologic" with what we now call "naturalistic." See Randolph Bourne, "Sociologic Fiction," 511–14. Lewis also used this term.

27. On the oscillating apprehension that a child brings to fairy tales—believing in their psychological truth yet denying their factuality—see Bruno Bettleheim, *The Uses of Enchantment*, 31–34. It is interesting that Ferber, as my epigraph suggests, partly wanted to discount the evasion of marital bliss in the fairy tale form. Bettle-

heim also demonstrates (253) that the name "Cinderella" was implicitly associated with lower-class labor. For Ferber's identification of her own writing as a "Cinderella" profession, see *PT,* 182.

28. *Buttered Side Down,* 6. All further citations in text.

29. Cf. Kocka, 79, and the sources cited in my note 5, Chapter 4.

30. This is a good instance of how what I have been calling "white collar fictions" used the Main Street vocabulary to ingest other classes—here, a manual worker—into their horizons, if only to finally discount them. A parallel today is the tendency to use "middle American" to synopsize a vague social center that mixes blue and white collar work, supposedly the "majority" experience of America. See, for instance, Robert Coles, *The Middle Americans.*

31. One *WHC* letter did ask for just this device of closure in relation to *So Big;* see note 40 below.

32. In *PT,* 272, Ferber bragged about being able to project herself into anything that interested her, even if she knew nothing about it from her own experience.

33. "Scheme" quote from *Emma McChesney & Co.,* 208–9. All further citations from this volume in the series.

34. The best sources on this vogue are Warren Susman, "'Personality' and the Making of Twentieth-Century Culture," and Donald Meyer, *The Positive Thinkers,* 117–94. On the Hobbesian side of Carnegie, see Meyer, 187–88. One might also notice the decidedly expansionist side to Ferber's hubris, as in her seeing of "America" from "Maine to Manilla," cited below.

35. Fact about Marketing Association cited in Arnold Patrick, "Getting into Six Figures: Edna Ferber," *Bookman* 60 (April 1925): 167. On the Bull Moose label, see the caption to the review of *Roast Beef, Medium* in *Current Opinion* 54 (June 1913): 491. See also Theodore Roosevelt to Edna Ferber, 14 April 1913, and 15 April 1918, Box 1, Folder 1 (EFC). Gilbert quotes an interview with Ferber from 1915, in which she says there is "nothing so thoroughly domestic as the successful business woman" (400). Here Ferber also complained about "Feminists" who could not make a shirt or wear it properly. For the concurrent articles, see "Extra Cash After Office Hours," *WHC* 51 (Jan. 1924): 76—the same issue promoting Ferber's *So Big;* "The Office Housekeeper," *WHC* 51 (Feb. 1924): 79, or a "Pin-Money Club," *WHC* 51 (Feb. 1924): 135. Editorially, under "Who's Who in This Issue" (76), the *WHC* called *So Big* a "dramatic study of American life and ideals and of a woman of extraordinarily vivid personality."

36. On such reform efforts in the workplace, see Benson, 134. Compare also Dorothy Richardson's application (*The Long Day*) of "working girls" to anyone female (including herself) who received a wage, including the better-paying job of stenographer (267–68). This corresponds with some current research (see Blumin, *Emergence of the Middle Class,* 292–93), which suggests the parents of clerical workers did not always see their children moving to nonmanual work as a change in class status, but compare Richardson's account of work conditions in an underwear factory, 203. See also Richardson's call for "wholesome" romance, 300–01.

37. The Triangle Company was itself a "family affair," Pauline Newman of the

International Ladies Garment Union wrote: "all relatives of the owner running the place, watching to see that you did your work, watching when you went to the toilet." On the day of the infamous fire, employers had locked the employees (mostly women) in the building; since doors opened inward, many could not escape. See Newman as quoted in Barbara Mayer Wertheimer, *We Were There,* 294, and Leon Stein, *Out of the Sweatshop.* I am indebted to an unpublished paper by Nancy Palmer for this information. On the Bread and Roses strike, see Ardis Cameron, "Bread and Roses Revisited: Women's Culture and Working-Class Activism in the Lawrence Strike of 1912," 42–61. See also "The Strike of Corset Workers at Kalamazoo," *LGW* 3 (April 1912): 4–8.

38. "Skirt," of course, was also a term for females in this period; Ferber doubtless employs it here as a pun. Benson's word for this use of the commodity as a form of identification is "commoditized" sisterhood; see pp. 227–82. In "Civilized Clothes," *LGW* 3 (March 1912): 12–13, Gertrude Barnum took a strikingly different view: that what was really uncivilized about women's clothes were (a) "the hidden harnesses and conspicuous stilts which cause internal and external injuries," and (b) "the conditions under which our clothes are made." In the Kalamazoo strike, according to the *LGW*, six hundred strikers (most of them women) wanted reduction of working hours from fifty-nine to fifty-four hours per week, and a minimum wage of seven dollars per week. One Michigan Federation of Labor investigator found a girl who worked, after employer deductions, 35 hours for $1.89.

39. Ferber was also privately asked to be on the Pulitzer committee; see her letter to William Lyons Phelps, 27 Nov. 1935 (BLY). See also her "Our Beautiful Young Idiots," *Literary Digest,* 3 Oct. 1931, 18–19, for her criticism of Jazz Age youth.

40. Some of these "folk," it should be noted, verified White and Bromfield's sense of Ferber's patronage. The *Woman's Home Companion* ran several letters like the one from Mrs. L.C., of Tennessee, praising Selina, Ferber's main character in the *WHC*-serialized *So Big:* "It is so understandable even to one of limited education like me. I just live it, feel it. . . . I am a farm woman," *WHC* 51 (March 1924): 152; see also letter from "F.J.F., Georgia" in June 1924 issue (148), which praises Selina as "the most wholesome, cleanest, most interesting, truest-to-life story I've read." Compare the fan letter from Abe Rosen, 12 Dec. 1917, Box 1, Folder 1 (EFC).

41. Roosevelt as paraphrased, I would guess, in the *Current Opinion* review.

42. When Doubleday ads compared *The Girls* to the McChesney series ("If you liked Emma McChesney," etc.), Ferber flew into a rage (*PT,* 265) at the implied comparison. Even by this second volume, *Emma McChesney & Co.,* the formula was clearly playing itself out; the last chapter is called "An Étude for Emma."

43. W.J. Stuckey points out that Stuart Sherman, a regular Pulitzer juror, had especially favored the "service of work" (*The Pulitzer Prize Novels,* 18) for the ills of the middle-class young; that nearly all jurors favored "wholesome," panoramic texts; that William Lyons Phelps praised *So Big* as "purely American" (48). For an earlier endorsement of Ferber by William Allen White in an article claiming popularity was the key factor in taste, see his "Splitting Fiction," *New Republic* 30 (12 April 1922): 22–26.

44. No less an iconoclast than H. L. Mencken praised *The Girls* as an "A-No. 1 piece of work"; critic Grant Overton detected in her work a "contempt for [the] correctly patterned existences"; even William Allen White declared that Ferber separated herself from a "moron" (36) middle class. See also *PT,* 216–18, and Mencken to Ferber, [30 Sept. 1921], Box 1, Folder 1 (EFC). This letter says that his review is in the *Baltimore Sun,* Saturday edition of the week of October 4, 1921.

45. On Maine to Manilla, see Ferber, "No Apologies for American Art," *Bookman* 52 (Nov. 1920): 219–20. Not unimportantly, here, Ferber also praised Willa Cather's *My Antonia* as a book she admired, one which worked in the vein she was tapping. See esp. Book III's depiction of the small village, Black Hawk, in which Antonia and other "hired girls" work. Lorimer to Ferber, 3 July 1918, Box 1, Folder 1 (EFC).

46. Cf. Elizabeth Ammons's discussion of the "web" narrative, "Going in Circles," 83–92. On the intersubjective links in women's culture, see, Carol Smith-Rosenberg, "The Female World of Love and Ritual," 53–76.

47. Mencken to Ferber, 30 Sept. 1921, Box 1, Folder 2 (EFC).

48. So had Ferber's; see *PT,* 14.

49. See the O. Henry allusion here, *The Girls,* 226.

50. Ferber herself, the prosodist of Americanization, was actually prevented by doing this war work—held, stateside—by the fact of her "German" background. See *PT,* 237–38.

51. My chapters on Anderson and Lewis discuss this investment in children; here *The Girls*'s ending very much anticipates that of *Babbitt,* as discussed in Chapter 6.

52. Ferber refers to this visit as a lecture to "woikin' goils" in a letter to William Allen White, 23 Aug. 1918, Box 1, Folder 1 (EFC). Ferber's speech quoted in *Minneapolis Sunday Tribune,* 25 Aug. 1918, 8.

53. Horowitz and Landsman, 77.

54. "The Girls' Liberty League," *St. Nicholas* 46 (Nov. 1918): 27–29; Margaret Widdener, "W. C. C. S.," *Good Housekeeping,* 67 (Sept. 1918): 25–27, 105; Samuel Hopkins Adams, "Private Smith is Cordially Invited," *World's Work* 36 (Sept. 1918): 528–37; War Camp Community Service, *A Retrospect.*

55. On the "patriotic" demand that women should return to the home—resulting in the fact that, by 1920, women made up a smaller percentage of the labor force than they had in 1910—see David M. Kennedy, *Over Here,* 285. On the local telephone strike, see *Minneapolis Labor Review,* 22 Nov. 1918. On trade union support, see the reprint of Samuel Gompers's "All Must Make Increased Sacrifices to Win the War," *Minneapolis Labor Review,* 30 Aug. 1918, and "Save the City for Labor," *Minneapolis Labor Review,* 25 Oct. 1918. On the election results, see "Election Analysis Reveals Facts," *Minneapolis Labor Review,* 15 Nov. 1918. The year 1918 also saw the founding of Minnesota's Farm-Labor party, concatenated by this same conflict. See Millard L. Gieske, *Minnesota Farmer-Laborism.*

56. Ferber complained, albeit disingenuously, that her popular audience read her only as a romance writer, missing her irony and even her "hate" for the "fine flower[s] of American womanhood" she depicted. See her letter to William Lyons Phelps, 25 March 1930 (BLY): "I'm happy to learn that you liked *CIMARRON.* My experience

with it, after publication, has been devastating. I mean that I wrote—or thought I wrote—a book about one amazing phase of American life, colored with irony. Its whole intent was, for that matter, ironic." On "Poe's prison walls," see her letter to Phelps, 6 Sept. 1934 (BLY), and the article "The Way of a Novelist," *Literary Digest,* 5 Dec. 1931, 14, which discusses a Connecticut town's negative reaction to *American Beauty* (1931).

Chapter 3. Representing the Average: The Making of Robert Grant

1. Mencken as cited in William H. Nolte, *Henry L. Mencken: Literary Critic,* 75. On the "man on the make" ethos, see Burton J. Bledstein, *Culture of Professionalism,* 11. On the "little man," see C. Wright Mills, *White Collar,* 35–36.

2. Best known here is Robert H. Wiebe's usage in *The Search for Order.*

3. Roosevelt as quoted in T. J. Jackson Lears, "From Salvation to Self-Realization," 5.

4. On these aspects of liberal theory, cf. Eugene E. Leach, "Mastering the Crowd"; Michael McGerr, *The Decline of Popular Politics;* Robert Westbrook, "Politics as Consumption"; and esp. James T. Kloppenberg, *Uncertain Victory,* 267–77. The first effort at a mathematical averaging of a "middle" citizen from government census statistics which I have found is in Joseph Jacobs, "The Middle American," *The American Magazine* 63 (March 1907), 522–26.

5. On writers and professional ideology, see Amy Kaplan, *The Social Construction of American Realism;* Daniel Borus, *Writing Realism;* June Howard, *Form and History in American Literary Naturalism,* 125–26; Elizabeth Ammons, "The Engineer as Cultural Hero and Willa Cather's First Novel, *Alexander's Bridge*"; and Cecilia Tichi, *Shifting Gears.*

6. The driving theoretical force for this application is, of course, Michel Foucault; see esp. Mark Seltzer, "The Naturalist Machine," and Walter Benn Michaels, *The Gold Standard and the Logic of Naturalism,* esp. 177. Comparable in this respect is Tichi's assertion that the literary works she studies are not "about machines. Their fiction and poetry, instead, *is* the machine" (16). While it is certainly true that writers and texts often envied technological regularity, this critical equation might be said to romanticize machines themselves—which produce not just regularity but noise, waste, human injury, and human subjection. Even our best critics may be reading machines through the clean lines that naturalism and modernism have imposed upon them.

7. My account in the following draws especially from Elizabeth Deeds Ermarth, *Realism and Consensus in the English Novel,* esp. 35–38, on the "jury" narrative; see also Howard on the "spectator" in naturalism, 105, and Brodhead, "Sparing the Rod."

8. See the interpretations of Robert Grant in Grant C. Knight, *The Strenuous Age in American Literature,* 36; Werner Berthoff, *The Ferment of Realism,* 132–33; Gordon Milne, *The Sense of Society,* 107–09; Frank Bergman, *Robert Grant;* and Sam Bass Warner, Jr., *The Province of Reason,* 5–20.

9. On Grant's role in creating "Main Street" fiction, see Wharton, "The Great

American Novel," 646–56, and her *A Backward Glance,* 147–48; Van Wyck Brooks, *New England,* 44; and Walter F. Taylor, *The Economic Novel in America,* 88. On "average opinion," see Grant, "To a Political Optimist," in *Search-Light Letters,* 214–15, 232; hereafter cited as SLL.

10. Cf. Kloppenberg, 313 and note 36, p. 489; David W. Levy, *Herbert Croly of the New Republic,* 119; Herbert Croly, "Why I Wrote My Latest Book: My Aim in 'The Promise of American Life,'" *The World's Work* 20 (June 1910): 13086; and *The Promise of American Life,* esp. 329, 427. Aside from the sources already mentioned, see also the discussion of expertise in the new liberalism in Charles Forcey, *The Crossroads of Liberalism,* and Carl Schorske, *Fin de Siécle Vienna,* esp. 5. On the reciprocity of these two critiques within one instance of Progressive "debunking," see esp. T. W. Adorno, "Veblen's Attack on Culture."

11. Cf. Hannah Fenichel Pitkin, *Representation,* esp. 10–21; compare Grant, SLL, 215–16.

12. Wharton quoted in *Fourscore,* 223.

13. Under this rubric, see Wiebe; Thomas L. Haskell, *The Emergence of Professional Social Science;* Bledstein, *The Culture of Professionalism;* Maxwell H. Bloomfield, "Law," 33–49. For updated views, see Bledstein, "Discussing Terms," 1–15; Don S. Kirschner, "'Publicity Properly Applied,'" 65–78; and JoAnne Brown, "Professional Languages," 33–51.

14. Barbara Ehrenreich and John Ehrenreich, "Professional-Managerial Class," 12–18. This model is formulated, in part, by removing clerical strata into a "white-collar working class" and emphasizing the managerial dimensions of professional work. Walker's volume in which this essay appears contains useful criticisms of this model; see also Jean-Christophe Agnew, "A Touch of Class," 70–72.

15. See Jonathan Lurie, *Law and the Nation, 1865–1912,* 44–52, and Bloomfield, 35–43. Barbara Ehrenreich in her *Fear of Falling,* 80.

16. On the social languages of Progressivism, see esp. Daniel T. Rodgers, "In Search of Progressivism," esp. 118. For the new emphasis in Bledstein's work, see his "Discussing Terms," 10.

17. Laurence Veysey also offers a fuller critique of the connection between university culture and professionalism—and, notably, Bledstein's case. See Veysey, "Higher Education," 15–32.

18. Cf. *Historical Statistics,* 140–45; Alba M. Edwards, *Population,* Table 8. Bledstein reasons in *The Culture of Professionalism* that the "professional class" rose from 2.6 percent in 1870 to 4.1 percent in 1900, whereas clerical occupations rose from .6 percent in 1870 to 2.5 percent in 1900, to 4.6 percent in 1910. Stuart Blumin (*Emergence of the Middle Class,* 313) says the number of office workers increased nine-fold in the last thirty years of the century.

19. On the role of "average" in liberal theory, see for instance one of the works to which the *O.E.D.* refers, J. S. Mill, *On Liberty, Representative Government, and the Subjection of Women,* 82, 85, 156, 197. Cf. also Ehrenreich, *Fear of Falling,* esp. 80.

20. On the legal profession, see Bloomfield, 36. On professionalism in journalism, see Michael Schudson, *Discovering the News,* 77–87, and my *Labor of Words,* 20–24.

21. On the profession of competence, compare Hughes in Haskell, note 4, p. 28, with Brown's discussion.

22. On the selling of expertise, see esp. Kirschner. For an illuminating discussion of the problem of "Barnumism" in relation to the turn-of-the-century advertisers, see T. J. Jackson Lears, "Some Versions of Fantasy," 349–405.

23. On the proletarian "other," see esp. Howard, 70–141.

24. Grant, *Yankee Doodle,* 15, 22–23. In a poem from 1898, Grant also wrote: "Dewey's triumph on the flood / Thrills the Anglo Saxon blood;/ And our kindred pulses stir/ At the deeds of Kitchener." Letter to Barrett Wendell, 4 Nov. 1898 (RGC).

25. See also the poem-parody in Grant's Scrapbooks, 1889 (RGC). On "An Accidental Pick-Up," see Grant, *Fourscore,* 113–16. All further citations of biographical material are to this last source, except where noted. Quotations from interpretations of Grant in Knight, 36; Berthoff, 132–33; Milne, 107–9. For Grant's version of the events surrounding Sacco and Vanzetti, see *Fourscore,* 351–74. Letter from Norton mentioned in Grant to C. E. Norton, 16 Nov. 1907, (RGC).

26. Grant, SLL, 214–15, 232.

27. Amy Kaplan first developed her ideas in "'The Knowledge of the Line'"; see esp. 70. On Howells in the 1890s, see my "Markets and Fictions," 4.

28. Throughout this discussion of Mugwumpery, I have relied upon Gerald W. McFarland, *Mugwumps, Morals, and Politics, 1884–1920,* esp. 5–51, and Geoffrey Blodgett, *The Gentle Reformers.* On Massachusetts reforms, see Blodgett, 114–37, 173–239.

29. On Russell, see Blodgett, 87–112. Barrett Wendell's eulogy of Russell stressed the same virtue; Russell epitomized "how classes and masses alike realize the transcendent value of an interpreter." As cited in Blodgett, 214.

30. Much like Howells's fiction, Grant's novels—as discussed below—are littered with "doubles" or alter ego characters who represent, alternatively, either cynical disgust with republican virtue or ascetic, heroic embrace of its mission: Remington/ Stoughton, Bill French/Jack Hall. "Yankee Doodle," as I have implied, was in all likelihood an oxymoron. Suggestively, even the title *Unleavened Bread* slips into such a "doubling" effect—since, as Grant acknowledged his error, the "leaven" of the Pharisees was actually an "evil process" (*Fourscore,* 221). See also Grant, "Harvard in the 1870s," *Scribner's* 21 (May 1897): 564–565. Cited in text as S. On "half-baked," see Scrapbooks, I, 6 (RGC).

31. Grant to Henry Wadsworth Longfellow, 18 Nov. 1874 (RGC). On Grant and professionalism, see also Grant to Charles Scribner, 29 Feb. 1896 (CSC).

32. The epigraph to *Face to Face* comes from Lowell's Commemoration Ode: "Is earth too poor to give us/ Something to live for here that shall outlive us?"

33. On Grant's disguising his Yankee anxiety under the gaiety of social doodling, see his remarks on his father's troubles, *Fourscore,* 158.

34. Langdell as quoted in Lurie, 50. Cf. also Lurie's discussion of the implied "judicial supremacy" here (51–52). Langdell on libraries in Bloomfield, 41–42. In his own review of the system in *Bench and Bar in Massachusetts, 1889–1929,* Grant wrote that "Langdell's innovation was regarded with distrust at first, except by the

best students" (106); under Ames, Grant says in *Fourscore,* "many of us soon discovered that the balm for not being able to reason soundly in open class without warning could not be wholly laid on diffidence" (112). Ames, in turn, was a significant appointment, because he had not yet practiced law, thus representing the new "scholarly" emphasis at Harvard Law School.

35. See the negative press clippings in Scrapbooks, I, 39, 40, (RGC). Notably, one person coming to Grant's defense (*Fourscore,* 192) was George Fred Williams (discussed below in relation to the West End controversy).

36. See Grant, "Perils of Will-Making."

37. Typical here were Grant's veiled references to the Stoughton Hall incident. In *Jack Hall,* this is invoked by the bombing of a tool shed (see below); in *An Average Man,* the evil foil to Mugwump reform is named "Stoughton."

38. See esp. McGerr, 57, on the relevance of this movement to northern liberalism's development.

39. Grant, *An Average Man.* In Howells's *A Modern Instance,* Bartley Hubbard's collapse is tied to the election of 1876, where Hubbard uses the stalwart republican Ben Halleck's money, ironically, to bet on "the reformer" Tilden. Grant clearly means to point out the political consequences of not resisting the Stoughton/Hubbard breed.

40. For the number of Massachusetts strikes, see Blodgett, 129. Quotations from *Face to Face.* On the publication of Grant's novel anonymously, see Grant to Charles Scribner, 6 April 1886 (CSC).

41. In this respect it is worth noting that, at the start of *Fourscore,* Grant pauses to explain that his father's name, "Patrick Grant," often meant that he was mistaken for an Irishman; of course it was Patrick who sent Robert to public school.

42. Croly, *Promise*, 431.

43. See Grant to Charles Scribner, 13 July 1899 (CSC).

44. This and all further citations from *Unleavened Bread* in text.

45. For Grant's advocacy of an Interstate Marriage and Divorce Law that he explicitly compared to Progressive regulation of Interstate Commerce, see his "Marriage and Divorce."

46. Ermarth, 35.

47. On this particular aspect of modern liberalism, see esp. McGerr; Westbrook; and Leach, esp. 102–3.

48. Cf. Blodgett, 109–12, 201.

49. Cf. the suggestive essay by Richard Wightman Fox on another critic of middle Americanness: "Epitaph for Middletown," in Fox and Lears, *Culture of Consumption,* 101–41.

50. Howells, "The Recent Dramatic Season," *North American Review* 172 (March 1901): 475–77. Grant also mentions a letter from Howells praising the novel; see Grant to Charles Scribner, 31 May 1900 (CSC).

51. Contrast the decidedly more moralistic finale of Hamlin Garland's *A Member of the Third House,* also modeled (cf. Blodgett, 217) on the West End affair. For Grant's dim view of Garland, see Grant to Charles Scribner, 29 Feb. 1896 (CSC).

52. On the concept of descriptive likeness, see Pitkin, 10.

53. In fact, as a Pulitzer Prize Board judge, Grant in all likelihood lobbied for both *Main Street* and *Babbitt*. Cf. *Fourscore,* esp. 260, 383.

Chapter 4. Elmer Rice: "A Sort of Common Denominator"

1. The version of *The Adding Machine* cited is reprinted in Elmer Rice, *3 Plays*. For convenience's sake, I have cited page numbers only in text; these lines are from 25–26.

2. Elmer Rice, Typescript entitled "Notes on Characters," given to the actors first performing *The Adding Machine* (ERC). A French version of this guide is apparently in print: "Zero et Shrdlu," *Masques, Cahiers d'Art Dramatique*. Contemporary reviewers immediately identified *The Adding Machine* as an expressionist play; see the reviews of Ludwig Lewisohn in the *Nation* 116 (4 April 1923): 399, and Stark Young in the *New Republic* 34 (4 April 1923): 164–65. See also William Elwood, "An Interview with Elmer Rice on Expressionism," 1–7. For Rice's attempts to differentiate his methods from expressionism upon the heels of the play's production, see Elmer Rice, "To the Dramatic Editor," 2, and Rice to Percival Wilde, 29 May 1931 (ERC).

3. My first knowledge of Heller's early reading of Rice came from reading Marshall Toman, "Nonsense and Sensibility." On "The Inside of His Head," see Arthur Miller, *Theater Essays of Arthur Miller,* 135. On Mills's expressionist leanings, see Richard Hofstadter as quoted in Richard Gillam, "*White Collar* from Start to Finish," 18. On the "file" or "brain" images, see Mills, *White Collar,* xx, 189. Rice's *The Subway* presents an office as a huge filing cabinet.

4. Rice offered this definition of his alternate term: "[t]he author attempts not so much to depict events faithfully as to convey to the spectator what seems to him their inner significance. To achieve this end the dramatist often finds it expedient to depart entirely from objective reality and to employ symbols, condensations, and a dozen devices which, to the conservative, must seem arbitrarily fantastic." "To the Dramatic Editor," 2.

5. In current discussion, "mass culture" normally is restricted to the effects of modern media. For this chapter, I would like to resurrect its fuller sense: as including the "mass" existence of modern bureaucratic employment, the disintegration of family authority, and participation in media-made, consumer fantasy. On this complex, see Christopher Lasch, *The Culture of Narcissism,* 176–86, which includes a discussion of Heller's novel. On shopwindow gazing, see Stuart H. Culver, "What Mannikins Want," and Rachael Bowlby, *Just Looking*. It should be noticed, however, that Dreiser uses a residual nineteenth-century vocabulary to describe Carrie as of "the middle American class"—as a "rural" middle class for whom the "destiny" of the shopgirl represents a decline; compare Stuart Blumin, *Emergence of the Middle Class,* 245. Carrie's father is described as a "miller" in a "flour-dusted . . . suit"; see 8, 19, 140.

6. This notion of "automatic" writing was not hindsight from the date of his autobiography—*Minority Report,* hereafter cited as *MR*. (All biographical citations in text

from this source). See the letter to Frank Harris written upon finishing the play, *MR*, 190. In another letter from 1930, Rice said he conceptualized all his plays as successive summaries of his own "psychic states," a "further sloughing off of the complexes and maladjustments that were the heritage of a thwarted childhood." Letter to Barrett H. Clark, 11 March 1930 (BLY). Rice also made this claim in his own selection of *The Adding Machine* for Whit Burnet, ed. *This Is My Best*, 459–60. Here, as well, he added that this "automatic" quality meant that he had "very little control" over the material of the play. His recurrent references to "automatic writing" suggest some familiarity with William James's pragmatism, perhaps learned from John Dewey at Columbia.

7. For critical arguments in this vein, see Frank Durham, *Elmer Rice*, 51, and Jules Chametzky, "Elmer Rice, Liberation, and the Great Ethnic Question," 98. Compare *MR*, 92. Rice's instructions in "Notes on Characters" refer extensively to Zero's "repressed sexuality" and "the blight of Puritan morality." Biographical information also drawn from Anthony F. R. Palmieri, *Elmer Rice: A Playwright's Vision of America*. Rice also credited (*MR*, 198) the example of Theodore Dreiser's *Plays of the Natural and the Supernatural*, dramatized in 1916, which anticipated the metaphysical flights of *The Adding Machine* and even the street scenes of Rice's later plays.

8. See *MR*, 206. For a good account of Mencken's early Progressivism, see Martin, *Debunkers*, 62, and esp. 72 on Mencken's reading of Lippmann. One should also note, however, that Rice says he never joined the Socialist party nor finished anything by Marx—ever (*MR*, 100, 138).

9. Cf. my "Broadway Nights," esp. 24–25. The appeal of a tone of a "higher, sadder wisdom" for historians is well discussed in Kramer, "Literature, Criticism, and Historical Imagination," 105.

10. This long-standing middle-class cliché disguises the historical role of family discipline in creating self-sufficiency. On this role, see esp. Mary P. Ryan, *Cradle of the Middle Class*, 145–85. Chametzky's essay is our best account of Rice's Jewish background.

11. Notably, Rice took courses not only from Dewey but from Franklin Giddings in sociology and Charles Beard in history during the teens.

12. For all that he says about the maternal taproot of his liberalism, Rice also admits, "I often am guilty of the very petulance and ungraciousness to which I objected in my father" (64). "To mitigate the excruciating tedium" and the "meaningless chatter" of home, he said, "I developed the art of not listening" (64). In Shavian usage, "idealist" was a pejorative term denoting a mind too prone to unpragmatic abstractions; see George Bernard Shaw, "The Quintessence of Ibsenism," in *Major Critical Essays*. All further citations from this source in text. This edition contains the edition of "Quintessence" from 1922, the year in which Rice quoted it; the earlier American edition (New York: Brentano's, 1910) alters the wording of these passages somewhat. As a playwright, Rice would spend as much time watching the audience as the play itself. "A box office," he writes, "is an excellent place to study human conduct: a diversity of individuals displaying varying degrees of truculence, timidity, suspicion, cajolery and confusion" (*MR*, 124).

13. One of the most troubling aspects of *The Adding Machine* is the gradual conversion of the "human" Daisy DeVore, potentially a love interest for Zero, into a new figure called "Hope," a female icon that merely keeps Zero running. This character, too, is a compounding of mythological icons: her full name is Daisy Diana Dorothea DeVore.

14. As another sign of how Rice was drawn into Moe's influence, Elmer was momentarily drawn to Christian Science as well; see *MR,* 84. For one of the best accounts of Bellamy's relation to Progressivism's fantasy life, see John F. Kasson, *Civilizing the Machine,* 189–202.

15. Cf. my discussion of military models for the management of newspaperwork in *Labor of Words,* 29. Cf. Eileen Boris, *Art and Labor,* 149–50. Hubbard's *Message to Garcia* was circulated by railroad publicist George H. Daniels in a "Four-Track Series" for the New York Central Railroad; quotation from this pamphlet (n.p: George H. Daniels, 1900), 4–6. For Hubbard's self-description, see his "A Village Industry," *Wisdom* 1 (Aug. 1907), 255–66.

16. The similarities to Arthur Miller are perhaps obvious here. See esp. the account in Daniel Walden, "Miller's Roots and His Moral Dilemma: or, Continuity from Brooklyn to *Salesman,*" 189–95. Rice also implicitly credits John Galsworthy's *Justice* as a source for *The Adding Machine;* in this play, a "fumbling little clerk . . . is crushed beneath the 'chariot wheels of justice'" (*MR,* 145) for passing a bad check.

17. In his first play, the commercial melodrama *On Trial,* Rice dramatized such a facade in staging a trial in reverse: by presenting its verdict to the audience first and then "flashing back" through time to reveal the quite different commission of the crime. This play is reprinted in Rice, *Seven Plays.*

18. Cf. T. J. Jackson Lears's account of similar tensions in advertising, in "Some Versions of Fantasy." Contrast also Edna Ferber's incorporation of the "trickery" of her mother's saleswork.

19. In his essay "Sex in the Modern Theatre," 665–73, Rice found even Shaw too conventional—"all talk." See esp. 672.

20. See esp. Boris, 149–58, and Peter Weiler, "William Clarke," 77–108; see also 90, note 54, on Clarke's job complaints.

21. E. J. Hobsbawm, "Fabianism Reconsidered," 250–271; quote from 257. See also Stanley Pierson, *British Socialists;* Ian Britain, *Fabianism and Culture;* and Wieler, 93. For my own critique of May, see "Coming to Terms with *The End of American Innocence,*" *American Intellectual History Newsletter* 12 (Nov. 1990), 33–37. Cf. also Martin J. Wiener, *Between Two Worlds.*

22. Graham Wallas, on officials in *Human Nature in Politics,* 280. Shaw, "The Fabian Society," 158. Notably, Wallas's critique of the Benthamite calculus aimed at turning liberalism away from "crude" definitions of the "average" citizen, arrived at by quantitative measurement; see 148, 178–79. Wallas also discounted the vocabulary of "class war"; see 193. On Wells, see my discussion in Chapter 6.

23. Wallas, 48–49, 83, 115, 131, 136–37, 198, 280; see also 64–65 on newspapers, 223 on the jury system, 262, 276 on civil service.

24. Quotes on permeation from A. M. McBriar, *Fabian Socialism and English Poli-*

tics, 65–68; Pierson, 95. Shaw on the professions, "The Fabian Society," 158. On Wells's view of the professions, see Norman MacKenzie and Jeanne MacKenzie, *The Fabians,* 250; Pierson, 306.

25. Margaret Cole, *The Story of Fabian Socialism;* Henry May, *The End of American Innocence,* 179, 230–32; Floyd Dell, *Intellectual Vagabondage.*

26. Cf. my use of Ermarth's work on the jury form of novelistic realism, 123–24. Fabians like Wallas, of course, worried that civil service workers could themselves be subject to bureaucratic inertia. Subsequent quotes in text from *Public Opinion.*

27. See his letter to the editor, "The Public Censorship," *New York Times,* 29 Jan. 1922, sec. 6, 1.

28. See Elmer L. Reizenstein, "Some Lame and Impotent Conclusions," 6.

29. Cf. J. Percy Smith, *The Unrepentant Pilgrim,* 212, and the argument about Shaw's "double effect" in Martin Meisel, "Shaw and Revolution," 106–34.

30. On the affiliations between Jewish-American backgrounds and later "black humor" styles, see Sanford Pinsker, *The Schlemiel as Metaphor,* and Melvin J. Friedman, "Something Jewish Happened," 196–204. On Miller's job experience and his ethnic background, see Walden, pp. 189–95. Number of plays per week cited in Rice's letter, "Elmer Rice Joins the Disenchanted," *New York Times,* 13 March 1966, letter to the editor (BLY).

31. Rice says this contribution was entitled "The Fires of Thespis" and submitted to Munsey's *Argosy,* May 1913; other bibliographies list it as "Out of the Movies." *MR* remembers the plot exploring the permeable boundary between theater and life: "An actor, long unemployed, gets a good part in a Broadway production. On the opening night, in the big scene of the play, his wife, anxious to have him find a missing document, shouts to him from her balcony seat that the paper is hidden in the fireplace. He rejoins the ranks of the unemployed" (94).

32. Adrian Forty (*Objects of Desire*) cites W. H. Leffingwell as praising the dictaphone for eliminating the "human factor element which often intrudes itself between dictator and stenographer" (137).

33. Rice's "Notes on Characters" (ERC) speaks of the relationship this way: "He and the boss scarcely move in the same world. In fact, to [Zero] the boss is scarcely a personality at all. He is an institution, one of the conditions of Zero's life."

34. "Notes on Characters" (ERC).

35. My colleague, Richard Schrader, drew my attention to Shrdlu's name, which is the crosswise line of keys on a typesetter's keyboard. These letters are typed out to indicate that a line should be reset—yet another reincarnation motif in the play. See also R. A. Weaver, "*The Adding Machine:* Exemplar of the Ludicrous." Rice also comments on newspapers in his "Notes on Characters." For his later interest in the Living Newspaper, see Palmieri, 17.

36. Chametzky, for one, finds Rice's Menckenesque sensibility "superficial" and belied by Rice's "witty, bedrock commitment to living and human values." See also Durham, 41.

37. Cf. Sheldon Wolin, "What Revolutionary Action Means Today," 23–24.

38. These quotes on the public from Rice, "Some Lame. . . ," 6. Compare Mencken's

remark that the American "thinks with his nerve ends, his liver and his lachrymal ducts, and only revises and regrets with his cerebellum." "The American," *Smart Set* 40 (June 1913): 91.

39. Rice also maintained that audiences represented a level of intelligence that, in an echo of *The New Yorker*'s motto, "is somewhat above that of a feeble-minded Kansas housewife of the 1870s." In 1922, citing Shaw's "Quintessence of Ibsenism," Rice resisted plans for a censorship board over the theater which threatened to stifle the "pioneer" and deliver "the creative artist into the hands of those who distrust freedom and to whom heterodoxy is anathema." These are nearly direct quotations from Shaw. Rice, "To the Dramatic Editor," 2. In Hollywood, Rice recalled Samuel Goldwyn's standard: "Yes, but will Lizzie like it?" (*MR,* 185). See also Rice, "Towards an Adult Theatre," 5, 18; on class foibles, Rice, introduction to *Other Plays & Not for Children,* 7–22; Rice, "Sex in the Modern Theatre." On Rice's later disillusionment, see "Mr. Rice States His Case," *New York Times,* 12 Feb. 1933, Sec. 9, p. 3.

40. Rice may have anticipated, as the lawyers for San Francisco's Dan White apparently did, that jurors and audience members might empathize with revenge upon a boss; even this plea, however, is followed immediately by Zero's confession that, after reading about southern lynchings, he felt like shooting a black man who crowded him in a subway (24).

41. Contrast the reading of Robert Hogan, *The Independence of Elmer Rice,* 13.

42. On the excision of scene 5, see Burnett, *This is My Best*, 459–60.

43. Cf. Hazel Carby's discussion of patronage of the "folk" in *Reconstructing Womanhood,* 164.

44. Rice, *Other Plays,* 21.

45. Cf. Sharon Strom, "We're No Kitty Foyles," pp. 206–7, and Lizabeth Cohen, "Encountering Mass Culture at the Grassroots." In this respect, Rice's reading of mass culture is similar to middle-class anxieties about dime-novel reading; on the utopian desire possibly there, see Michael Denning, *Mechanic Accents,* 201–13.

46. On this matter of the play's reception, see *MR,* 198–99. Ludwig Lewisohn warned *Nation* readers in 1923, "Mr. Rice's vision of the world may infuriate you. There were people behind me at the Garrick who first grumbled and then cursed politely." Stark Young, similarly, says the "public tends to resist [the expressionist style], to jeer or strain away from it, to suspect it of some decadent evil," but Young also suggested Rice had blended in commercial appeal, bringing his play "smartly to the market" (Review of *The Adding Machine,* 165).

Chapter 5. Sherwood Anderson and the Personality Market

1. Sherwood Anderson, *Letters to Bab,* 8. This collection also reprints other Anderson letters, and a few essays. For convenience's sake, all further citations will be *LB.* Most of the letters I cite will be from 1916 or 1917, except where noted.

2. Edwin Fussell, "*Winesburg, Ohio,*" 109; H. L. Mencken as quoted in Ray Lewis White, "Mencken's Lost Review of *Winesburg, Ohio.*" Mencken's review was in the

28 June 1919 *Chicago American*. See also Virginia Woolf, "American Fiction," 1–3, on Anderson and Lewis. On "ordinary people," see Anderson's letter of 19 Dec. 1938 to Daniel Lerner, quoted in William A. Sutton, *The Road to Winesburg*, 160–61. Since the factual bases of Anderson's life are often in dispute, I have cited information drawn from this source, in text, as *RW*.

The views expressed by Fussell and Mencken are in many ways still the prevailing point of view, exemplified by such essays as David D. Anderson, "Sherwood Anderson's Moments of Insight." This fine essay nonetheless emphasizes Anderson's movement "beyond his own experience into an intuitive perception of the experiences of others" (157). *Winesburg*, Anderson asserts, is not about "social structure"; "[r]ather he was writing about people . . . to discover them as individuals" (158). See also *Winesburg, Ohio: New Essays*, edited by John Crowley, forthcoming from Cambridge University Press. Crowley has graciously allowed me to read a draft of his Introduction.

3. Clifford Geertz, "From the Native's Point of View," *Local Knowledge*, 55–70. William L. Phillips, "How Sherwood Anderson Wrote *Winesburg, Ohio*."

4. *RW*, 124. Anderson also saw that the desire to succeed as a writer could be just as tyrannical a "master" as more common versions of the middle-class American dream. He wrote in 1917: "There is something terrible in this madness for the created thing, so universal here in America. I am sick at heart when I realize what a grip it has on me, too" (*LB*, 51). Sutton emphasizes Anderson's fears of losing his "boyishness" and becoming middle-aged; see *RW*, 124–25. For a helpful survey that also reprints Anderson's early columns, see Karen-Elisabeth Mouscher, "Sherwood Anderson: The Early Advertising Years."

5. See, for instance, Daniel Pope, *The Making of Modern Advertising*, 180–81.

6. T. J. Jackson Lears, "Uneasy Courtship," 142–43. Lears's work-in-progress has surfaced in a number of sterling essays: see also, among others, his "From Salvation to Self-Realization," 1–38, and "Some Versions of Fantasy."

7. I have relied throughout on Roland Marchand, *Advertising the American Dream*, and Stephen Fox, *The Mirror Makers*. Seminal also to Lears's, Marchand's, and my understanding of advertising is Raymond Williams's essay, "Advertising: The Magic System," in *Problems in Materialism and Culture*, 170–195.

8. Contrast the discussion in Thomas Reed West, *Flesh of Steel*, 21–34.

9. Jean-Christophe Agnew, "A Touch of Class," 70. For a full discussion of the "P.M.C." hypothesis, see the essays in Pat Walker, ed. *Between Labor and Capital*, and Martin Oppenheimer's summary of its weak points in *White Collar Politics*, 61–63.

10. Stuart Blumin, *Emergence of the Middle Class*, 121. Rodgers, in "Upstairs, Downstairs," has pointed out that Blumin's analysis suffers from a reimposition of census labels to matters of "consciousness" and class relations. While I do not share Rodgers's apparent sense that class can only be understood "vertically" or relationally, rather than as a horizontal (and variegated) class culture, Blumin's study does neglect this aspect of class conflict.

11. Charles Page, in *Class and American Sociology*, details late Victorian and Progressive usage, much of it retaining the "two-class" map of classes and masses. For

contemporary commentary, see E. L. Godkin, "Social Classes in the Republic," *Atlantic* 78 (Dec. 1896): 721–28; Saul Beaumont, "The Class Struggle of To-day," *Arena* 40 (Nov. 1908): 453–58; Robert Rives La Monte, "The American Middle Class," *Arena* 39 (April 1908): 436–39; and "The Middle Class Again," *Independent* 52 (27 Sept. 1900): 2342–44. See also John Corbin, *The Return of the Middle Class,* and Alfred M. Bingham, *Insurgent America.*

12. David Montgomery, "White Shirts and Superior Intelligence," 224, 231, 240. See also Harry Braverman, *Labor and Monopoly Capital,* 293–98; and Blumin, *Emergence of the Middle Class,* 290–97.

13. See Blumin, *Emergence of the Middle Class,* 121 ff. Mills's often-uniform narrative, as Gillam has pointed out especially well, only suggests his surprising affiliations with mid-century Parsonian sociology, consensus history and national character portraiture. Cf. Richard Gillam, "*White Collar* from Start to Finish," 11–12.

14. See Pope, 119–20, 139, and Marchand, 37–38. It is worth noting that advertising scion Claude C. Hopkins said he never had a client become a friend; see his *My Life in Advertising & Scientific Advertising,* 104.

15. Nathaniel C. Fowler, Jr., *Grasping Opportunity,* 14 ff.

16. Bates in Fox, *Mirror Makers,* 37; textbook quoted in Pope, 243. See also my "The Rhetoric of Consumption," 47–50. On Lasker, see John Gunther, *Taken at the Flood,* esp. 68–69.

17. Kennedy on ads, as quoted in Fox, *Mirror Makers,* 50; Marchand, 10–12; "The Value of Advertising Is the Value of the Man Back of It," *Printer's Ink* 91 (15 April 1915): 76, 78–80, 82. This trade magazine cited hereafter as *PI.*

18. Calkins as quoted in Fox, *Mirror Makers,* 50. It is also telling that this conceptualizing of the advertising audience, which Marchand discusses brilliantly, was often conceived as Rice conceived Mr. Zero: as a reader of *True Story* magazines, gossippy newspapers, and the like. See also the *PI* editorial, "Losing the Grasp of One's Audience," *PI* 89 (5 Nov. 1914): 73–74.

19. See E. E. Calkins, *Modern Advertising,* 291, 285. For example, Calkins said a "general" appeal often would not work. Instead, "an offer limited to a certain class of people is far more effective than a general offer. For instance, an offer limited to veterans of the war. Or to members of a lodge or sect. Or to executives" (245).

20. Hopkins, 119, 224; Calkins, 289. The founder of market research began in the Curtis magazines: Charles Parlin, who often ended his speeches with the declaration that "the consumer is king." See Wroe Anderson, "Charles Coolidge Parlin," *Journal of Marketing* 21 (July 1956): 1–2. For early explorations, see F. H. Little, "The Way to Better Advertising," *PI* 89 (10 Dec. 1914): 10, 12; for a later development of this approach, see also Percival White, *Advertising Research,* for its discussion of averages and medians, 82–83, esp. 228, and "The Average Consumer," 249–50, which White sees not as a by-product of psychological reasoning but statistical research. See also the *PI* editorial, 22 Nov. 1899, 35, as cited in Merle Curti, "The Changing Concept of 'Human Nature' in the Literature of American Advertising."

21. For earlier scholarship, see Curti, 335–57.

22. In another direction entirely, see Richard W. Pollay, "The Subsiding Sizzle,"

24–37. Through content analysis, Pollay argues that nearly two-thirds of surveyed ads employed a "straight pitch" from 1900 to 1910 and "presented assertions where logical induction and deduction would lead to a product preference." Even in the 1920s, Pollay sees only 8 percent of the surveyed ads trying to create "an awareness of negative conditions that product consumption would help avoid." Pollay's research implicitly challenges the periodization of Lears in particular; such content analysis, however, is always open to interpretation.

23. For one attempt to sort out *Marching Men*, see John Ditsky, "Sherwood Anderson's *Marching Men*: Unnatural Disorder and the Art of Force." *Marching Men*, which includes many of Anderson's early essays, cited hereafter as *MM*.

24. See Anderson's self-description in "The New Note: 1913," 13; cf. Alfred Kazin's likening of Anderson, in *On Native Grounds*, to "artisans who worked by sudden visions" (215).

25. In one of his essays called "A Writer's Conception of Realism," Anderson, in fact, insisted that all the character types in *Winesburg* were not drawn from small-town life but imagined (in an O. Henryesque way) from neighbors in his own city boardinghouse. As reprinted in *The Sherwood Anderson Reader*; see 345. For a fine reading of the mythical dimensions of Anderson's memoirs, see John Crowley, "The Education of Sherwood Anderson," 185–201.

26. See my "Markets and Fictions," p. 11.

27. Edition cited is University of Chicago Press, 1965; these quotes from pp. 66–67. All further citations in the text are from this edition. "Employé" used as an adjective on p. 227. Cf. Blumin, *Emergence of the Middle Class*, note 104, p. 386, and Braverman, 298.

28. In *MM* (204), Anderson's protagonist compares his own work to that of Mary Baker Eddy. Anderson declared to Finley that "[i]n a way the whole big message of my life is bound up into that volume" (*RW*, 271).

29. Criticism of Anderson has suffered by an inability to distinguish among the socialist faiths of the prewar years. For many critics it has seemed unclear how "radical" politics aligned with his business vocation (cf. *RW*, 371–73, or Ditsky, 113–14). We do know, however, that he first penned a (now lost) pamphlet entitled *Why I Am a Socialist* [191?] in Elyria and that certain Ohioans remembered his defending George Bernard Shaw in literary circles; we also know he spoke of himself as a socialist until at least 1916, even though he criticized the Socialist party's position on the war. (See *RW*, 127, and the letter to Sinclair in *LB*, cited in the following). Anderson the businessman was drawn to a managerial style of politics; one of his longest orations on "order" in the letters to Finley, for instance, praised the construction of the Chicago Municipal Pier, which he said had "got itself built in spite of petty politics and small minded men" (*LB*, 12–13).

30. See *RW*, 371–72.

31. *RW*, 112–20. Anderson remembers, in a letter of 14 Sept. 1938, "There was a good deal of talk about the nobility of business. . . . The word *service* had begun to be used. I went in enthusiastically" (*RW*, 139). Compare Barbara Ehrenreich and

John Ehrenreich, "The Professional-Managerial Class," 22–25, 30–41, and Lears's comments on the physician model in advertising, "Some Versions," 366.

32. See *RW*, 172. Anderson's former wife Cornelia also connected this project directly to their mutual interest in socialism; see *RW*, note 43, p. 201.

33. *RW*, 110–11. On Anderson's reader, contrast Mouscher, 36.

34. On this synthesis, see my *Labor of Words*, 198–99.

35. Contrast Lears, "Uneasy Courtship," 134, 143.

36. The fruitful concept of "dream-work" is often employed to uncover an ideological subtext, or utopian desire, beneath the rhetorical disguise of a given literary convention; see esp. Michael Denning, *Mechanic Accents*, 81. The limitation of this interpretive ploy is, obviously, that almost any disguise can be so converted—because dreams have no discursive regularity, no "laws." See my "Containing Multitudes," 484–85. Here by "literalized" I mean the text's ideological fantasy is exhibited *in* the apparent plot.

37. In fact, the ending of *Windy McPherson's Son* was argued over by Anderson's publishers; see *RW*, 352, 365.

38. See my discussion of Jack London in "American Naturalism and the Problem of Sincerity."

39. David Anderson, "Sherwood Anderson's Grotesques and Modern American Fiction"; see also Sherwood Anderson's review in the *Little Review*, 2 (Dec. 1915): 38–40. Next citation will appear in the text.

40. Describing Willy Loman, Arthur Miller once said: "It is the tragedy of a man who did believe that he alone was not meeting the qualifications laid down for mankind by those clean-shaven frontiersman who inhabit the peaks of broadcasting and advertising offices. From those forests of canned goods, high up near the sky, he heard the thundering command to succeed." *Theater Essays*, 15.

41. In formal terms, *Winesburg* is perhaps most similar in this way to a book like Sarah Orne Jewett's *Country of the Pointed Firs*, or to Willa Cather's *My Antonia;* compare Jim Burden's rumination on his and Antonia's trajectory in Cather's final chapter.

42. Beyond the biblical cadences and rhetoric that Anderson employs in *Winesburg*, certain stories are pointedly tied to different testaments of Christ's suffering or other biblical stories: "Hands," Jesse Bentley's reiteration of David and Goliath, even Dr. Percival's ranting about "everyone in the world is Christ and they are all crucified" (57). This is perhaps why, in *Windy McPherson's Son*, Anderson refers to his philosophy as the "Christian" philosophy of "failure," or why Anderson called Jesus the "master artist" (*LB*, 51). All further citations from *Winesburg, Ohio* appear in the text.

43. On the sources of this story in Anderson's sales life, see Robert H. Sykes, "The Identity of Anderson's Fanatical Farmer."

44. Waldo Frank's fascination for *Winesburg* is well known; for a framework similar to Anderson's, see his "Land of the Pioneer."

45. Since this might seem an extravagant claim about the class boundaries of

Anderson's perspective, let me offer a rough list: two doctors, one schoolteacher, hotel keeper, saloon keeper, two druggists and their clerks; bankers, a "vehicle merchant," a Standard Oil agent, cider mill operator, telegraph operator, Reverend, night watchman, advertising man, bookkeeper—and so forth. These are the men. Elizabeth Willard is a former actress and now a hotel keeper; Virginia Rich goes into stenography; Kate Swift is a teacher; Alice Hindeman, Louise Trunion, Belle Carpenter all are courted by middle-class men. Of the younger generation, aside from George Willard and Helen White, there is Ned Currie, also a reporter, and Elmer Cowley, a junior member of the store in which he works. After Biddlebaum, the two named farm workers are Ray Pearson and Hal Winters.

46. This "curing" obviously applies to the composition of *Winesburg* itself. Though Anderson liked to portray his intentions as creating a *bildungsroman,* in fact (as William L. Phillips has shown), the concatenizing stories "Death," "Sophistication," and "Departure" were composed at the final stages; it is unlikely, as Crowley concludes (in his forthcoming introduction), that Anderson had this plan in mind from the outset.

47. See Sutton's discussion of Anderson's longing for "Elsinore" in *RW,* 192. Cf. my discussion of Elmer Rice's Elysium in Chapter 4.

48. How Anderson was "constructed" by the *Seven Arts* contingent—and by William Lyon Phelps, Burton Rascoe, and others so vital to writers like Ferber—is well discussed in Crowley, "Introduction" to *Winesburg, Ohio: New Essays.* See also Walter Rideout's discussion of Anderson's fluctuating reputation, in "Sherwood Anderson," 11.

49. On this cultural program, see Christopher Lasch, *The New Radicalism in America,* esp. the chapter on Randolph Bourne, 69–103.

Chapter 6. Sinclair Lewis and the Passing of Capitalism

1. Sinclair Lewis, *Babbitt,* 90–98.

2. On the *Babbitt* plan, see Mark Schorer, *Sinclair Lewis: An American Life,* 268, 298. Cf. also Stephen S. Conroy, "Sinclair Lewis's Sociological Imagination." Page citations of biographical information in text from Schorer, *Sinclair Lewis: An American Life,* except where noted.

3. Cf. James Lundquist, "The Sauk Centre Sinclair Lewis Didn't Write About," 221–22. Schorer preferred the "externalizing" and "diagnostic" label; see his afterword to *Babbitt,* 326–27. Kazin also said of Lewis (212) that "[n]o other novelist of the time gave so vividly the sense of *not* having been brought up to the constraints, the easy fictions, the veritable rhythm, of modern commercial life" (emphasis mine).

4. Carl Van Doren as cited in Grace Hegger Lewis, *With Love From Gracie,* 74.

5. Lewis's memory in *The Man from Main Street,* 214–15. This collection hereafter abbreviated as *MFMS.*

6. Cf. Clifford Geertz, "Thick Description," 3–30.

7. Cf. my *Labor of Words,* 17–39, 96–101, 116, 196, and the essays in *MFMS,* 193–206.

8. Here Lewis uses "race" both biologically and as a "competition," yet he converts an ethnographic vocabulary ("hyphenation") to half-membership in a "white" collar profession. Contrast W. D. Howells's use of the publishing profession in *The Rise of Silas Lapham;* see the Norton Critical edition (New York: W. W. Norton, 1982), 328, 332–35. On the limits of Howells's own notions of "the commonplace," see esp. Amy Kaplan, *The Social Construction of American Realism,* and Elsa Nettels, *Language, Race, and Social Class in Howells's America,* 108–9.

9. One short-story outline offered to Jack London, called "The New Broom," suggests a self-assessment: the plot tells of a young man "who always makes phenomenally good on a job at first, then, when he is almost beginning to be a master of it, gets tired and either quits or is kicked out." In a folder marked "Plots for Short Stories, apparently sent to Jack London" (SLC). See also Lewis, "Honestly—If Possible," *SEP* 14 Oct. 1916, 36, and Lewis, *The Trail of the Hawk,* 260.

10. Sheet labelled "ROUTINE" in "Miscellaneous Manuscripts and Typed Notes During his Associated Press Period" (SLC). For the assessment of newspaper work and publicity, see the letter to Harcourt, 11 Aug. 1920, in *From Main Street to Stockholm,* 35. This worksheet suggests the collating, wire-service effect in Lewis's novels, where "bulletins" from world-consciousness intrude upon a given scene, as if coming over the Teletype of our own reading. For instance, in *Main Street*'s Chapter 16, during a conversation about creating "a more conscious life," Lewis intervenes with: "At this second, in Buenos Aires, a newspaper editor broke his routine. . . . At this second a clerk standing . . ." and so on. *Main Street,* 198. A similar effect is created in *Babbitt,* 82.

11. Daydream scribble from "Miscellaneous Materials from the Associated Press Years," (SLC). "ROUTINE" also ends with comic, self-satirizing asides—including advice about how not to offend the office "janitress." Lewis's job was "white-handed" work, but it contained threats of subordination. On "personal freedom" in artisan republicanism, see Sean Wilentz, *Chants Democratic,* 92, 101–2. Cf. Grace Lewis, 5–6. Charles Hanson Towne also reports that, while Lewis worked during college on the magazine *Transatlantic Tales,* "[h]e resented four walls and a roof more than anyone I ever have known; yet he had the will to work and accomplished much." Charles Hanson Towne, *Adventures in Editing,* 85.

12. "Scrapbook Containing Book Reviews and Notices" (SLC). While the collection lists these as from Lewis's syndication years, a few derive from a later period. My generalizations in the following must be taken guardedly; Lewis's notes show the stories as having been cut and rewritten by his syndicated papers, and Lewis was taking credit for simply having managed some of the placements. The scrapbook also identifies reviews by "G.S.," doubtless George Soule.

13. The best account of this "wink" is what Neil Harris has called the "operational aesthetic" in *Humbug;* see also Janice Radway, *Reading the Romance,* 193–94.

14. See esp. the series by Algernon Tassin (in which the house of Stokes is quoted

repeatedly), which ran in *The Bookman,* in Feb. to June of 1911: vol. 32: 652–66, and vol. 33: 182–90, 290–302, 405–14. See also the cynically dismissive article by Arthur M. Chase, "The Author and Publicity," *Bookman* 35 (April 1912): 161–63.

15. Alfred A. Harcourt, "Publishing Since 1900," 51–75; this volume also contains Frederick A. Stokes's memoir, 3–47. See also Harcourt's memoir, *Some Experiences.* Here, Harcourt mentions his own interest in contemporary "radical" ideas, which led to a split with Henry Holt, his original employer; see 29–31, 69–70, and 87–89 on "opinion makers." Doran's sense of the "high-water mark" of publicity was Grant Overton's *When Winter Comes to Main Street,* which—even as it covered exclusively Doran authors—was to Doran so "impartial" that it was used as a textbook, the publisher claimed, in university courses. George H. Doran, *Chronicles of Barrabas, 1884–1934,* 347. On the "percolating" strategy, see Harcourt, "Publishing Since 1900," 64, and *Some Experiences,* 87–89; compare Tassin, *Bookman* 33 (April 1911): 187. Frank Luther Mott, however, in *A History of American Magazines,* vol. 4, also points out that Doran, upon finally acquiring *The Bookman,* changed its "Chronicle and Comment" section to the "Gossip Shop." See 422–41.

16. Comfort is promoted in *Have You Come to the Halfway House?: The Story of A Pilgrimage,* Doran pamphlet in (SLC). Later in life, Lewis would hate such testimonials: see anonymous article "Sinclair Lewis Looks at Advertising." Lewis's earlier tastes are suggested by a proposed ad he drafts for Harcourt, which he says should be "short, tactful . . . interesting yet devoid of superlatives," having written that *Main Street* is "*much* bigger than *The Job*—just as true and much better done. It is almost the first book which pictures American small-town life." See the letter to Harcourt, 11 Aug. 1920, in *From Main Street,* 35. I also refer here and subsequently to an exchange in *The Dial:* "'Tainted' Book Reviews," a letter from a "Book Buyer" dated 24 Jan. 1914, *The Dial* 56 (1 Feb. 1914): 97, and the reply by W. E. Woodward, "Syndicate Service and 'Tainted Book Reviews,'" letter to the editor dated 16 Feb. 1914, *Dial* 56 (1 March 1914): 173. See also W. E. Woodward, *The Gift of Life,* 186. See Doran, 339–41, on Lewis during the Doran years.

17. The full dedication mentions five others "[t]hrough Whose Talk at Luncheon" he witnesses life: George Soule, Harrison Smith, Allen Updegraff, F. K. Noyes, and B. W. Huebsch.

18. Christopher Morley, *Parnassus on Wheels,* 44, 46, 72, 74, 126, 129; subsequent page citations in text. The sequel, "Parnassus at Home: An Interview with Roger Mifflin," ran in Doran's *Bookman* 48 (Sept. 1918): 93–102. On the Small Fry club, Christopher Morley, *John Mistletoe,* 158. Morley was directed to Doubleday on the advice of Harry Steger, O. Henry's literary executor; see Helen M. Oakley, *Three Hours for Lunch,* 51.

19. See "Early Publishing Days," *MFMS,* 99–100; see also the letter below to Gordon Ray Young; and the newspaper clipping in his Scrapbook, "An Anti-Toxin For the Tired Business Man" (SLC), which cites a businessman who says, "I never could keep on swinging business deals if I didn't take the stimulant of imagining myself as an adventurer. I'd go stale."

20. Woodward in "Syndicate Service," 173. See also the letter from Lewis to

Gordon Ray Young, 20 Sept. [1915], (SLC), in which Lewis complained: "God but this whole question of reviewing is confused. . . . It seems to me that practically all book-pages in this country are written either by the wife of the managing editor . . . or by a hasty selection of cub reporters, who wear eye glasses and police badges but are only slightly more intelligent."

21. Cf. the clipping on Coningby Dawson to the Lewis letter to Harper & Bros., 15 Oct. 1915 (SLC).

22. "Practical advertising" in memo from Lewis, while at Doran, to Harper & Bros., 15 Oct. 1915. Here Lewis advised his publisher on the promotion of *Trail of the Hawk*. In the 1920s, he would suggest entire paragraphs for Harcourt to "plant" with leading columnists; see the letter to Harcourt, 11 Aug. 1920, in *From Main Street,* 35. Later, he fed Harcourt news copy about *himself* on vacation, working on *Babbitt,* that Harcourt could send out to the papers; see the letter of 12 Feb. 1922, *From Main Street,* 97. On Lewis's fears of intellectual demoralization, see the letter to Jack London cited in Schorer, *Sinclair Lewis: An American Life,* 187.

23. In one, a clerk in a department store, laid off in a depression, learns the power of "will" to heal one's office malaise; he learns to forget the clock, forge ahead, and finally becomes a manager of a branch store in his home town. In another, a perfume demonstrator at a department store performs secret philanthropy by using the tool later praised by Dale Carnegie: her smile. See "The City Shadow," starting in the Oct. 1909 *Nautilus,* and "The Smile Lady," starting in August 1909 (SLC).

24. Morley in *John Mistletoe,* 137. Schorer, *Sinclair Lewis: An American Life,* 216–29; *MFMS,* 100; Sinclair Lewis to Hamlin Garland, 23 Sept. 1915 (SLC); Grace Lewis, 8, 72, 74, 76. See also the "Fifteen Poems to Grace Livingston Hegger, 1912–1913" (SLC), esp. the poem that cites "This antic and disquiet life of mine."

25. See Lewis to Harper & Bros., 15 Oct. 1915 (SLC), and Lewis to Gordon Ray Young, 20 Sept. [1915], (SLC).

26. The Yale collection contains Lewis's Socialist party of New York membership card, fully stamped from his joining on 16 Jan. 1911 to April 1912; his mailing address is Stokes. In folder entitled "Miscellaneous Material."

27. Quotations in this paragraph from Stuart Sherman and D. J. Dooley in Dooley's *The Art of Sinclair Lewis,* 53–54, and Schorer, *Sinclair Lewis: An American Life,* 159, 178, 181, 184; see also 29–31, 46. See also Schorer's lament, in which he declares that it is perhaps "futile" to "approach any Lewis novel as a work of art" (357). Critics in the 1950s and 1960s generally downplayed Lewis's socialist commitments as a form of adolescent rebellion. See, for instance, Sheldon N. Grebstein, "The Education of a Rebel: Sinclair Lewis at Yale." The standard source on Lewis's intellectual debts is Arthur B. Coleman, "The Genesis of Social Ideas in Sinclair Lewis."

28. Lewis's protagonist in *Trail of the Hawk* suggests the special twist the author put on the war experience: "And then a thing like this war comes and our bread and butter and little pink cakes are in danger, and I realize we're not free at all; that we're just like all the rest, prisoners, dependent on how much the job brings and how fast the subway runs." *The Trail of the Hawk,* 369–71. Hereafter cited in text.

29. On potboiling, see Schorer, *Sinclair Lewis: An American Life,* 239, and Doo-

ley, 53. See also Dooley, 17–95; Vernon L. Parrington, *Sinclair Lewis,* 21–23; Walter Lippmann, "Sinclair Lewis," in Mark Schorer, ed. *Sinclair Lewis: A Collection of Critical Essays,* 84–94 (hereafter cited as *Critical Essays*); Sheldon N. Grebstein, *Sinclair Lewis,* 37 ff.; Thomas Reed West, *Flesh and Steel,* 116–131; and John T. Flanagan, "A Long Way to Gopher Prairie." Cf. also Clara Lee Moodie, "The Short Stories and Sinclair Lewis' Literary Development."

30. This article is reprinted in *MFMS,* 327–39; quote from p. 329. On Lorimer and Lewis, see Schorer, *Sinclair Lewis,* 228–229. On Norris's view, see E. H. Cady, *The Realist at War,* 219; "romance" quotation from Norris in W. D. Howells and Frank Norris, *Criticism of Fiction & The Responsibilities of the Novelist,* 200.

31. A Lewis diary entry from 9 April 1908 (SLC) confirms this reading of *The Octopus*. Lewis calls the book "solid, massive big. Might make a 'Red' of one, had it stopped with the meeting in Boomerville. Bumbaum, whom I met on campus, commented on its repetitions unfavorably. Moi, I think they give it a vividity."

32. Cf. Dooley, 27, and Schorer, *Sinclair Lewis,* 217.

33. Reviews cited in following are contained in Patrick Parrinder, *H. G. Wells,* 189–94, 220–22, and 239–45. For a summary of Wells's visits, see Richard L. Rapson, *Britons View America*. Cf. Schorer, *Sinclair Lewis,* 181–82, 210–11; Dooley, 19; and Grebstein, *Sinclair Lewis,* 379. Contrast Coleman, 8 ff. Our best account is that of Martin Light, "H. G. Wells and Sinclair Lewis," but even Light emphasizes a debt to Wells's optimism; cf. Light's treatment in *The Quixotic Vision of Sinclair Lewis,* 23.

34. See Schorer, *Sinclair Lewis,* 51, 59, 77, 113, 178, 179.

35. On socialist views, see esp. Richard W. Fox, "The Paradox of 'Progressive' Socialism." On S.P. battles during these years, see David A. Shannon, *The Socialist Party of America,* 62–80. For the Greenwich Village tale, see Lewis's preface to *The History of Mr. Polly*.

36. Quotations from H. G. Wells, *Anticipations,* 91, 93, 94, 102, 108. Cf. Norman MacKenzie and Jeanne MacKenzie, *The Fabians,* 250, and Stanley Pierson, *British Socialists,* 115, 306.

37. Quotations from H. G. Wells, "The Middle-Class Man and Socialism," 169, 170, 176.

38. Will Levington Comfort, *Midstream,* 108, 183–86, 242–43, 279, and *passim*. See also p. 198 for the "Thought Power" ideas that must have attracted Lewis as well.

39. Lewis's principal contributions were for the journal *The Nautilus,* founded in 1898 by Mrs. Elizabeth Towne in Holyoke, Massachusetts. Mrs. Towne had praised indigenous radicals like Edward Bellamy; the "wildest dreams of socialism," she wrote, "were prophecy." Cf. Donald Meyer, *Positive Thinkers,* 33–37, 44; Quimby disciple quote on 36, and Mrs. Towne on 199; see also Schorer, *Sinclair Lewis,* 150, 159–60.

40. By and large, Wells was interpreted by American reviewers as working within the Dickensian tradition, depicting what Mencken called "the average Englishman," or the lower middle classes. Lewis's comments throughout his career indicated a similar reading; at times he said he unconsciously mistook Wells for Dickens and vice versa. See Wells's reference to "Bumble" in "The Contemporary Novel" in H. G.

Wells, *An Englishman Looks at the World*, 164–65.

41. To Walter Lippmann, Wells's exemplification of this type only made him more popular: he "typified" modern man himself, "his weaknesses and his constant relapses, his tentative hope and his overwhelming tasks." See Parrinder, 221, for Lippmann's review in the *New Republic*, Oct. 1914. On "individualised human beings," see Wells, *An Englishman Looks at the World*, 162. See also Van Wyck Brooks, *The World of H. G. Wells*, esp. 25, 52–53. On Polly, see H. G. Wells, *Mr. Polly*, 199–200, 201, 208, 293.

42. See Peter Weiler's comments on a similar use of the "New World" by William Clarke, in "William Clarke," 82. Quotations from "The Contemporary Novel" in Wells, *An Englishman Looks at the World*, 148–69. "Multiple personality" quoted in Pierson, 309–10, from *New Worlds for Old*. On "collective consciousness," see Wells, *First and Last Things* (1908), as quoted in David C. Smith, *H. G. Wells: Desperately Mortal*, 89.

43. Quotations from *Mr. Polly*, 261, and *MFMS*, 248–49.

44. Lewis to Gordon Ray Young, 20 Sept. [1915] (SLC) (emphasis mine); portion cited in Schorer, *Sinclair Lewis*, 226. Quotation on Una from Lewis, *The Job: An American Novel*, 5. Subsequent citations in text.

45. Lewis, *The Job*, 235; see also the speech of Mr. Fein, 308–9.

46. Lewis, "Honestly—If Possible," pp. 28, 30, 33–34, 37. Subsequent citations in text. The parallels to the marriage of the McPhersons in Anderson's novel are worth noting; Lewis, too, dedicated *The Job* to his wife Grace Hegger, identifying her as the one "WHO HAS MADE 'THE JOB' POSSIBLE AND LIFE ITSELF QUITE BEAUTIFULLY IMPROBABLE."

47. See esp. *New Worlds for Old*, 313–14, for Wells's dismissals of the traditional liberal doctrine of "equality" as a "thing of the past." On "myth" in Lewis, see his depiction of Carol Kennicott's quest for a "more conscious life," or "Utopia *now*," against the "sterile oligarchy" of the "cash register." *Main Street*, 197, 260. H. L. Mencken noticed a "clinical" attitude in Wells's *Mr. Polly;* contrasting Wells with Dickens, Mencken complained that "Mr. Wells loves [Polly] no more than a bacteriologist loves the rabbit whose spine he draws out through the gullet." See Parrinder, 179. For Bourne's view of the "flimsiness" in the "fabric" of Wells's vision, see Parrinder, 240.

48. E. J. Hobsbawm, *Labouring Men*, 266.

49. Contrast the letter from Lewis to Van Doren in *MFMS*, 136–41, and Grace Lewis, 74, with the letter to Gordon Ray Young cited above. Lewis shifted from the novel form to short stories so that he would not have to submit to explicit, discouraging, and arbitrary in-house reviews. Lewis also knew what a *Post* story was, as evidenced by his advice to London regarding plot outlines (SLC). For an early discussion of this dimension of Lewis's exaggeration—if not the "double-take" I am describing—see T. K. Whipple, "Sinclair Lewis," in Schorer, *Critical Essays*, 71–83.

50. "Commutation: $9.17," *SEP*, 30 Oct. 1915, 32–33, 68.

51. "If I Were Boss," *SEP*, 1 Jan. 1916, 5–7, 36. On the revolving door, see Robert L. Blanchard, *Around the World With Van Kannel*, 81, 85.

52. As a sign of Lewis's slipping faith, see "Spiritualist Vaudeville," *Metropolitan* 47 (Feb. 1918): 19–23, 64–65, 66–73, 75; cf. also Meyer, 37. When Lewis left Doran,

Kathleen Norris remembered his shouting that he was "a free man," having "escaped from bondage." Schorer, *Sinclair Lewis,* 229.

53. "Honestly—If Possible," p. 37. Cf. Schorer, *Sinclair Lewis,* 239; see also Stephen S. Conroy, "Sinclair Lewis's Plot Paradigms."

54. "Snappy Display," *Metropolitan* 46 (August 1917): 7–8, 68, 71. Compare Lewis to C. B. Tinker, 31 Dec. [1916] (SLC). "Might and Millions," *Metropolitan* 50 (June 1919): 30–32, 41–42; "Slip It to 'Em," *Metropolitan* 47 (Feb. 1918): 26.

55. "Jazz," *Metropolitan* 48 (Oct. 1918): 23–25, 52, 55–57. On Lewis's own skills at mimicry, see Grace Lewis, 92.

56. "Getting His Bit," *Metropolitan* 48 (Sept. 1918): 12–13, 58–59; "Might and Millions," *Metropolitan* 50 (June 1919): 30–32, 41–42; "Slip It to 'Em," *Metropolitan* 47 (March 1918): 26–28, 34–36, 38–39.

57. Cf. the fine essay by Joel Fischer, "Sinclair Lewis and the Diagnostic Novel"; see also Schorer, *Sinclair Lewis,* 797.

58. See Lewis's interest in developing, out of his early Egyptology, a "more or less scientific study of men (*Homines*); of human nature; of mankind; using people as text books. It would be a sort of 'practical psychology.' Study their mental, moral & physical natures; prevalence & effect of different habits; opinions & knowledge of death, God, the church; politics . . . and other points ad infinitum. My method of study would be by using ears & eyes; asking things delicately by disguising them in innocent sounding questions" (Schorer, 62). In *Main Street,* Carol reads anthropology volumes "with ditches of foot–notes" (16); the field is mentioned again as among the "really stirring ideas that are springing up today" (143); "cynical anthropologist" friends (423) are given the "long view," much to their credit, in the framework of Carol's decision to wait for change across the "hundred generations" (432).

59. Lewis here apparently used domestic manuals and magazine fare—like *The American Magazine* and the *Post*—as well as real estate manuals and what he called "pompous" psychology pamphlets sent to him by Harcourt. See the letter of 27 July 1921, *From Main Street,* 80.

60. *Babbitt,* 11, 14, 23, 37, 66, 316, 319. Further citations in text.

61. Lewis's parodies of modern commodities are often mistaken for antitechnological diatribes; in fact, George is repeatedly faulted for not having the technical knowledge of anything that he promotes. Conversely, Seneca Doane praises technological development. To Lewis, this lack of expertise is the source of the degradation of the commodity itself and consequently its inability to provide "freedom," as in the Todd stories; see *Babbitt,* 84–85.

62. Lewis repeatedly argued that he felt an affiliation with these "little people," as Ferber did. See "Mr. Lorimer and Me."

63. Upton Sinclair would praise *Babbitt*'s "muckraking"; reviewers and readers seemed to follow Lewis's lead, saying he actually wrote from a "love of Main Street" and a belief in its "inherent power" (Schorer, *Sinclair Lewis,* 300). Most revealing, perhaps, was Sherwood Anderson's ambivalence. Upon reading *Main Street,* he wrote Lewis and dubbed the novel with his favorite honorific: "You've sure done a job."

But later, he found Lewis to be joyless and journalistic. See Schorer, *Sinclair Lewis*, 278–81.

64. See Geertz, "Thick Description," 14.

65. In *Babbitt*, Virginia Woolf wrote, "[w]e turn on the taps and the water runs; we press a button and cigars are lit and beds warmed" ("American Fiction," 2–3).

66. On Roosevelt's role, see Christopher Lasch, "The Moral and Intellectual Rehabilitation of the Bourgeoisie."

67. On *Babbitt*'s sales, see Schorer's afterword to the Signet edition of *Babbitt*, note on 357. See also the synopses in *Book Review Digest* for 1922, and Thomas S. Hines, Jr., "Echoes from 'Zenith': Reactions of American Businessmen to *Babbitt*."

Afterword: Within the White Collar Perimeter

1. On this interaction of "horizons," see Lawrence Buell, *New England Literary Culture*, 9.

2. See the attribution of science to Robert Grant by Mary Moss, "Significant Tendencies in Current Fiction," *Atlantic Monthly* 95 (May 1905): 692–93; Jane Tompkins, *Sensational Designs*, xvi; Philip Fisher, *Hard Facts*, 3.

3. On this point, see my "Containing Multitudes," 489.

4. Our best account of this training narrative function is Richard Brodhead, "Sparing the Rod"; see esp. 71–74, 79. Compare Tompkins, 156 ff.

5. "Fine power" from Tompkins, 156, quoting Harvey Sacks.

6. By now it is commonplace for historians to cite Raymond Williams's genealogy of the word "class" in *Keywords* as moving from any "*ad hoc* term of grouping" (53), especially educational (along with "rank"), to a term representing the social divisions of the Industrial era. In fact, the fictions I have examined reflect a modest return of the sense of class as heterogeneous ranking under the arithmetic typologies I have outlined. Williams in fact, did note (57) the ambiguous and uneven character to this term, derived in his view from the "variation between a descriptive grouping and an economic relationship" (58).

7. Cf. Edith Wharton, "The Great American Novel," 646.

8. This is apparent in the recent debate over the "oppositional" character of artisan republicanism, notably under the Knights of Labor; contrast esp. John Patrick Diggins, quoting Samuel Gompers in "The Misuses of Gramsci," 41, and Denning, *Mechanic Accents*, 165. The fuller debate in this same volume—including Leon Fink, T. J. Jackson Lears, and others is also discussed in Palmer, *Descent into Discourse*, 111–118.

9. Lukács makes this observation about bourgeois ideology in relation to the French Revolution: "[A]s the bourgeoisie came to power . . . it could no longer carry through its own ideology: it could not apply the idea of individual freedom to the whole society without the self-negation of the social order . . . it was impossible for the bourgeois class to apply its own idea of freedom to the proletariat. The unsur-

passable dualism of this situation is the following: the bourgeoisie must either deny this ideology or employ it as a veil covering those actions which contradict it." From *Marxism and Human Liberation*, as quoted in Cathy Davidson, *Revolution and the Word*, 218. Cf. Benjamin DeMott, *The Imperial Middle*, 149–69. Cf. the remarks of Stuart Blumin, *Emergence of the Middle Class*, 8–11, 285–90, and Anthony Giddens, *The Class Structure of the Advanced Societies*, 111, 185–86. For a different angle on this problem, see Herbert Gans, *Middle American Individualism*.

10. Robert S. Lynd, *Knowledge for What?* 59; epigraph from 57.

11. Raymond Williams, "Culture is Ordinary," reprinted in *Resources of Hope*.

Bibliography

Ade, George. *Chicago Stories.* Edited by Franklin J. Meine. Chicago: The Henry Regnery Co., 1963.

Adorno, T. W. "Veblen's Attack on Culture." In *Prisms.* Translated by Samuel and Shierry Weber. Cambridge: M.I.T. Press, 1981.

Agnew, Jean-Christophe. "A Touch of Class," *democracy* 4 (1983): 59–72.

American Magazine.

Ammons, Elizabeth. "The Engineer as Cultural Hero and Willa Cather's First Novel, *Alexander's Bridge,*" *American Quarterly* 38 (1986): 746–60.

———. "Going in Circles: The Female Geography of Jewett's *Country of the Pointed Firs,*" *Studies in the Literary Imagination* 16 (1983): 83–92.

Anderson, David D. "Sherwood Anderson's Grotesques and Modern American Fiction," *Midwestern Miscellany* 12 (1984): 53–65.

———. "Sherwood Anderson's Moments of Insight." In *Critical Essays on Sherwood Anderson.* Edited by David D. Anderson. Boston: G. K. Hall, 1981.

Anderson, Sherwood. *Letters to Bab: Sherwood Anderson to Marietta D. Finley, 1916–1933.* Edited by William A. Sutton. Urbana: University of Illinois Press, 1985.

———. *Marching Men.* Edited by Ray Lewis White. Cleveland: Case Western Reserve University Press, 1972.

———. "The New Note: 1913," *Little Review Anthology.* Edited by Margaret Anderson. New York: Horizon Press, 1953.

———. *The Sherwood Anderson Reader.* Edited by Paul Rosenfeld. Boston: Houghton Mifflin Co., 1947.

———. *Windy McPherson's Son.* Chicago: University of Chicago Press, 1965.

———. *Winesburg, Ohio.* New York: Penguin, 1960.

Anderson, Wroe. "Charles Coolidge Parlin," *Journal of Marketing* 21 (1956): 1–2.

The Arena.

Aron, Cindy Sondik. *Ladies and Gentlemen of the Civil Service: Middle-Class Workers in Victorian America.* New York: Oxford University Press, 1987.

The Atlantic Monthly.

Benson, Susan Porter. *Counter Cultures: Saleswomen, Managers, and Customers in American Department Stores, 1890–1940.* Urbana: University of Illinois Press, 1986.

Bergman, Frank. *Robert Grant.* Boston: Twayne, 1982.

Berkhofer, Robert. "Clio and the Culture Concept." In *The Idea of Culture in the Social Sciences.* Edited by Louis Schneider and Charles M. Bonjean. Cambridge: Cambridge University Press, 1973.

Berthoff, Werner. *The Ferment of Realism.* New York: Cambridge University Press, 1965.

Bettleheim, Bruno. *The Uses of Enchantment: The Meaning and Importance of Fairy Tales*. New York: Knopf, 1977.

Bier, Jesse. *The Rise and Fall of American Humor*. New York: Holt, Rinehart, & Winston, 1968.

Bingham, Alfred M. *Insurgent America*. New York: Harper, 1935.

Blanchard, Robert L. *Around the World With Van Kannel*. New York: Van Kannel Revolving Door Co., 1930.

Bledstein, Burton J. *The Culture of Professionalism: The Middle Class and the Development of Higher Education in America*. New York: Norton, 1976.

———. "Discussing Terms: Professions, Professionals, Professionalism," *Prospects* 10 (1985): 1–45.

Blodgett, Geoffrey. *The Gentle Reformers*. Cambridge: Harvard University Press, 1966.

Bloomfield, Maxwell H. "Law: the Development of a Profession." In *The Professions in American History*. Edited by Nathan Hatch. Notre Dame: University of Notre Dame Press, 1988.

Blumin, Stuart. *The Emergence of the Middle Class: Social Experience in the American City, 1760–1900*. New York: Cambridge University Press, 1989.

———. "Explaining the New Metropolis: Perception, Depiction, and Analysis in Mid-Nineteenth Century New York City," *Journal of Urban History* 11 (1984): 9–38.

Bok, Edward. *Successward: A Young Man's Book for Young Men*. New York: Fleming H. Revell Co., 1895.

The Bookman.

Boris, Eileen. *Art and Labor: Ruskin, Morris, and the Craftsman Ideal in America*. Philadelphia: Temple University Press, 1986.

Borus, Daniel. *Writing Realism: Howells, James, and Norris in the Mass Market*. Chapel Hill: University of North Carolina Press, 1989.

Bourne, Randolph. "Sociologic Fiction." In *Randolph Bourne: The Radical Will*. Edited by Olaf Hansen. New York: Urizen Books, 1977.

Bowlby, Rachael. *Just Looking: Consumer Culture in Dreiser, Gissing, and Zola*. New York: Methuen, 1985.

Braverman, Harry. *Labor and Monopoly Capital: The Degradation of Work in the Twentieth Century*. New York: Monthly Review Press, 1974.

Briggs, Asa. "The Language of 'Class' in Early Nineteenth Century England." In *Essays in Labor History*. London: Macmillan, 1960.

Britain, Ian. *Fabianism and Culture: A Study in British Socialism and the Arts*. New York: Cambridge University Press, 1982.

Brodhead, Richard. "Sparing the Rod: Discipline and Fiction in Antebellum America," *Representations* 21 (1988): 67–96.

Brooks, Cleanth, Jr., and Robert Penn Warren. *Understanding Fiction*. New York: F. S. Crofts & Co., 1943.

Brooks, Van Wyck. *The Confident Years, 1885–1915*. New York: E. P. Dutton, 1952.

———. *New England: Indian Summer, 1865–1915*. New York: E. P. Dutton, 1940.

———. *The World of H. G. Wells*. London: T. Fisher Unwin Ltd., 1915.

Brown, Deming. *Soviet Attitudes Toward American Writing*. Princeton: Princeton University Press, 1962.

Brown, JoAnne. "Professional Languages: Words That Succeed," *Radical History Review* 34 (1986): 33–51.

Buell, Lawrence. *New England Literary Culture*. Cambridge: Cambridge University Press, 1986.

Burnett, Whit, ed. *This Is My Best*. New York: Dial Press, 1942.

Butler, Nicholas Murray. *The American As He Is*. 1908. Reprint. New York: Scribners, 1941.

Cady, E. H. *The Realist at War*. Syracuse: Syracuse University Press, 1958.

Calkins, Ernest Elmo. *Modern Advertising*. New York: D. Appelton and Company, 1905.

Calverton, V. F. *The Liberation of American Literature*. 1932. Reprint. New York: Farrar, Strauss & Giroux, 1973.

Cameron, Ardis. "Bread and Roses Revisited: Women's Culture and Working-Class Activism in the Lawrence Strike of 1912." In *Women, Work, and Protest*. Edited by Ruth Milkman. London: Routledge & Kegan Paul, 1985.

Carby, Hazel. *Reconstructing Womanhood: The Emergence of the Afro-American Woman Novelist*. New York: Oxford University Press, 1987.

Carter, Paul A. "Horatio Alger Doesn't Live Here Anymore." In *Another Part of the Twenties*. New York: Columbia University Press, 1977.

Chametzky, Jules. "Elmer Rice, Liberation, and the Great Ethnic Question." In *Our Decentralized Literature: Cultural Mediations in Selected Jewish and Southern Writers*. Amherst: University of Massachusetts Press, 1986.

Chandler, Alfred D. *The Visible Hand: The Managerial Revolution in American Business*. Cambridge: Belknap Press, 1977.

Clifford, James, and George E. Marcus, eds. *Writing Culture: The Poetics and Politics of Ethnography*. Berkeley: University of California Press, 1986.

Cohen, Lizabeth. "Encountering Mass Culture at the Grassroots: The Experience of Chicago Workers in the 1920s," *American Quarterly* 41 (1989): 6–33.

Cohn, Jan. *Creating America: George Horace Lorimer and the Saturday Evening Post*. Pittsburgh: University of Pittsburgh Press, 1989.

Cole, Margaret. *The Story of Fabian Socialism*. Stanford: Stanford University Press, 1961.

Coleman, Arthur B. "The Genesis of Social Ideas in Sinclair Lewis," Ph.D. dissertation, New York University, 1954.

Coles, Robert. *The Middle Americans: Proud and Uncertain,* Photographs by Jon Erikson. Boston: Little, Brown, 1971.

Collection of American Literature, Beinecke Rare Book and Manuscript Library, Yale University, New Haven, Conn.

Comfort, Will Levington. *Midstream: A Chronicle at Halfway*. New York: George H. Doran Company, 1914.

Conroy, Stephen S. "Sinclair Lewis's Plot Paradigms," *Sinclair Lewis Newsletter,* 5–6

(1973–74): 4–6.

———. "Sinclair Lewis's Sociological Imagination," *American Literature* 42 (1970): 348–62.

Corbin, John. *The Return of the Middle Class*. New York: Scribners, 1922.

The Critic.

Croly, Herbert. *The Promise of American Life*. Cambridge: Belknap Press, 1965.

Crowley, John. "The Education of Sherwood Anderson." In *Sherwood Anderson: Centennial Studies*. Edited by Hilbert H. Campbell and Charles E. Modlin. Troy, N.Y.: Whitston Pub. Co., 1976.

———. ed. *Winesburg, Ohio: New Essays*. New York: Cambridge University Press, forthcoming.

Crozier, Michel. *The World of the Office Worker*. Translated by David Landau. Chicago: University of Chicago Press, 1971.

Culler, Jonathan. *Structuralist Poetics: Structuralism, Linguistics, and the Study of Literature*. London: Routledge & Kegan Paul, 1975.

Culver, Stuart H. "What Mannikins Want: *The Wonderful World of Oz* and *The Art of Decorating Dry Goods Windows*," *Representations* 21 (1988): 97–116.

Current Opinion.

Curti, Merle. "The Changing Concept of 'Human Nature' in the Literature of American Advertising," *Business History Review* 41 (1967): 335–57.

Davidson, Cathy. *Revolution and the Word: The Rise of the Novel in America*. New York: Oxford University Press, 1986.

Davies, Margery W. *Woman's Place is at the Typewriter: Office Work and Office Workers, 1870–1930*. Philadelphia: Temple University Press, 1982.

Davis, Robert H., and Arthur Butler Maurice, *The Caliph of Bagdad*. New York: D. Appleton, 1931.

Dell, Floyd. *Intellectual Vagabondage*. New York: George H. Doran, 1926.

DeMott, Benjamin. *The Imperial Middle: Why Americans Can't Think About Class*. New York: William Morrow and Company, 1990.

Denning, Michael. *Mechanic Accents: Dime Novels and Working-Class Culture in America*. New York: Verso, 1987.

DeVault, Ileen A. *Sons and Daughters of Labor*. Ithaca: Cornell University Press, 1990.

The Dial.

Diggins, John Patrick. The Misuses of Gramsci," *Journal of American History* 75 (June 1988): 141–45.

Dimock, Wai-chee. "Slippery Connections," *American Literary History* 2 (Spring 1990): 131–143.

Ditsky, John. "Sherwood Anderson's *Marching Men:* Unnatural Disorder and the Art of Force," *Twentieth Century Literature* 23 (1977): 102–14.

Dolmetsch, Carl R. *The Smart Set: A History and Anthology*. New York: Dial Press, 1966.

Dooley, D. J. *The Art of Sinclair Lewis*. Lincoln: University of Nebraska Press, 1967.

Doran, George H. *Chronicles of Barrabas, 1884–1934*. New York: Harcourt, Brace & Co., 1935.

Douglas, Ann. *The Feminization of American Culture*. New York: Knopf, 1977.

Dreiser, Theodore. *Plays of the Natural and the Supernatural*. 1916. Reprint. London: Constable & Co., 1930.

———. *Sister Carrie*. New York: Signet, 1961.

Dublin, Thomas. *Women at Work: The Transformation of Work and Community in Lowell, Massachusetts, 1826–1860*. New York: Columbia University Press, 1979.

Durham, Frank. *Elmer Rice*. New York: Twayne, 1970.

Eagleton, Terry. *Criticism and Ideology: A Study in Marxist Literary Theory*. London: Verso, 1978.

Edwards, Alba M. *Population: Comparative Occupation Statistics for the United States, 1870 to 1940*. Washington: U.S. Government Printing Office, 1943.

Ehrenreich, Barbara. *Fear of Falling: The Inner Life of the Middle Class*. New York: Pantheon, 1989.

———, and John Ehrenreich. "The Professional-Managerial Class." In *Between Labor and Capital*. Edited by Pat Walker. Boston: South End Press, 1979.

Elwood, William. "An Interview with Elmer Rice on Expressionism," *Educational Theatre Journal* 20 (1968): 1–7.

Ermarth, Elizabeth Deeds. *Realism and Consensus in the English Novel*. Princeton: Princeton University Press, 1983.

Estes, J. Worth. "The Pharmacology of Nineteenth Century Patent Medicines," *Pharmacy in History* 30, No. 1 (1988): 3–18.

Ferber, Edna. *Buttered Side Down*. New York: Stokes, 1912.

———. Collection, The State Historical Society of Wisconsin, Madison, Wis.

———. *Dawn O'Hara*. New York: Stokes, 1911.

———. *Emma McChesney & Co*. New York: Stokes, 1915.

———. *The Girls*. New York: Doubleday & Page, 1921.

———. *A Peculiar Treasure*. New York: The Literary Guild of America, Inc., 1939.

———. *So Big*. New York: Doubleday & Page, 1924.

Fischer, Joel. "Sinclair Lewis and the Diagnostic Novel: *Main Street* and *Babbitt*," *Journal of American Studies* 20 (1986): 421–33.

Fisher, Philip. *Hard Facts: Setting and Form in the American Novel*. New York: Oxford University Press, 1985.

Flanagan, John T. "A Long Way to Gopher Prairie," *Southwest Review* 32 (1947): 403–13.

Forcey, Charles. *The Crossroads of Liberalism: Croly, Weyl, Lippmann and the Progressive Era, 1910–1925*. New York: Oxford University Press, 1961.

Forty, Adrian. *Objects of Desire: Design and Society, 1750–1950*. London: Thames & Hudson, 1986.

The Forum.

Fowler, Nathaniel C., Jr. *Grasping Opportunity*. New York: Sully & Kleinteich, 1917.

Fox, Richard. "The Paradox of 'Progressive' Socialism: The Case of Morris Hillquit,

1901–1914," *American Quarterly* 26 (1971): 127–40.
———, and T. J. Jackson Lears, eds. *The Culture of Consumption: Critical Essays in American History 1880–1980*. New York: Pantheon, 1983.
Fox, Stephen. *The Mirror Makers: A History of American Advertising and Its Creators*. New York: Morrow, 1984.
Frank, Waldo. "Land of the Pioneer." In *Our America*. New York: Boni & Liveright, 1919.
Friedman, Melvin J. "Something Jewish Happened: Some Thoughts about Joseph Heller's *Good as Gold*." In *Critical Essays on Joseph Heller*. Edited by James Nagel. Boston: G. K. Hall, 1984.
Fussell, Edwin. "*Winesburg, Ohio*: Art and Isolation," *Modern Fiction Studies*, 6 (1960): 106–15.
Fussell, Paul. *Class: A Guide Through the American Status System*. New York: Ballantine Books, 1983.
Gans, Herbert. *Middle American Individualism*. New York: Free Press, 1988.
Garland, Hamlin. *A Member of the Third House*. 1892. Reprint. Upper Saddle River, N.J.: Gregg Press, 1968.
Geertz, Clifford. *Local Knowledge: Further Essays in Interpretive Anthropology*. New York: Basic Books, 1983.
———. "Thick Description: Toward an Interpretive Theory of Culture," *The Interpretation of Cultures: Selected Essays*. New York: Basic Books, 1973.
Gerson, Barbara. *All the Livelong Day: The Meaning and Demeaning of Routine Work*. New York: Penguin, 1977.
Giddens, Anthony. *The Class Structure of the Advanced Societies*. London: Hutchinson, 1980.
Gieske, Millard L. *Minnesota Farmer-Laborism: The Third-Party Alternative*. Minneapolis: University of Minnesota Press, 1979.
Gilbert, Julie Goldsmith. *Ferber: A Biography of Edna Ferber and Her Circle*. Garden City, N.Y.: Doubleday, 1978.
Gilkeson, John. *Middle-Class Providence, 1820–1940*. Princeton: Princeton University Press, 1986.
Gillam, Richard. "*White Collar* from Start to Finish: C. Wright Mills in Transition," *Theory and Society* 10 (1981): 1–30.
Good Housekeeping.
Gorn, Eliot. *The Manly Art: Bare-Knuckle Prize Fighting in America*. Ithaca: Cornell University Press, 1986.
Gramsci, Antonio. *Selections from Cultural Writings*, edited by David Forgacs and Geoffrey Nowell-Smith. Translated by William Boelhower. Cambridge: Harvard University Press, 1985.
Grant, Robert. *An Average Man*. Boston: J. R. Osgood, 1884.
———. *Bench and Bar in Massachusetts, 1889–1929*. Boston: Commonwealth of Massachusetts: 1930.
———. Collection, Houghton Library, Harvard University, Cambridge, Mass.
———. *Face to Face*. New York, Scribners, 1886.

———. *Fourscore: An Autobiography*. Boston: Houghton Mifflin Co., 1934.

———. "Harvard in the 1870s," *Scribners* 21 (1897): 564–565.

———. *Jack Hall or The School Days of an American Boy*. New York: Scribners, 1893.

———. "Marriage and Divorce," *Yale Review* 14 (1925): 223–38.

———. "Perils of Will-Making," *Scribner's* 64 (1918): 109–15.

———. *Search-Light Letters*. New York: Scribners, 1899.

———. *Unleavened Bread*. New York: Scribners, 1900.

———. *Yankee Doodle*. Boston: Cupples, Upham & Co., 1883.

Grebstein, Sheldon N. "The Education of a Rebel: Sinclair Lewis at Yale," *New England Quarterly* 28 (1955): 372–82.

———. *Sinclair Lewis*. New York: Twayne, 1962.

Greenblatt, Stephen. "Murdering Peasants: Status, Genre, and the Representation of Rebellion," *Representations* 1 (1983): 1–29.

Gunther, John. *Taken at the Flood: The Story of Albert D. Lasker*. New York: Harper & Bros., 1960.

Hackett, Alice P. *Seventy Years of Best Sellers, 1895–1965*. New York: R. R. Bowker, 1967.

Halttunen, Karen. *Confidence Men and Painted Women: A Study of Middle-Class Culture in America, 1788–1850*. New Haven: Yale University Press, 1982.

Harcourt, Alfred A. "Publishing Since 1900." In *The Bowker Lectures on Book Publishing*. 1st Series. New York: The Typophiles, 1943.

———. *Some Experiences*. Riverside, Conn.: Quinn and Boden, 1951.

Harris, Neil. *Humbug: The Art of P. T. Barnum*. Chicago: University of Chicago Press, 1973.

Harrison, Antony H. "Reception Theory and the New Historicism: The Metaphysical Poets in the Nineteenth Century," *John Donne Journal* 4 (1985): 163–80.

Haskell, Thomas L. *The Emergence of Professional Social Science: The American Social Science Association and the Nineteenth Century Crisis of Authority*. Urbana: University of Illinois Press, 1977.

Hatch, Nathan O., ed. *The Professions in American History*. Notre Dame: University of Notre Dame Press, 1988.

Heilbrun, Carolyn. "Edna Ferber" entry in *Notable American Women*. Vol. 4. Edited by Barbara Sicherman, Carol Hurd Green, *et al*. Cambridge: Belknap Press, 1980, pp. 227–29.

Higham, John, and Paul Conkin, eds. *New Directions in American Intellectual History*. Baltimore: Johns Hopkins University Press, 1979.

Hilfer, Anthony Channell. *The Revolt from the Village, 1915–1930*. Chapel Hill: University of North Carolina Press, 1969.

Hines, Thomas S., Jr. "Echoes from 'Zenith': Reactions of American Businessmen to *Babbitt*," *Business History Review* 41 (1967): 123–40.

Hobsbawm, E. J. "Fabianism Reconsidered." In *Labouring Men: Studies in the History of Labour*. New York: Basic Books, 1964.

Hochschild, Arlie Cameron. *The Managed Heart: Commercialization of Human*

Feeling. Berkeley: University of California Press, 1983.

Hoffman, Frederick J. *The Twenties*. New York: Viking, 1955.

Hogan, Robert. *The Independence of Elmer Rice*. Carbondale: Southern Illinois University Press, 1965.

Hopkins, Claude C. *My Life in Advertising & Scientific Advertising*. 1927 and 1923. Reprint. Chicago: Advertising Publications, 1966.

Horowitz, Daniel. "Frugality or Comfort: Middle-Class Styles of Life in the Early Twentieth Century," *American Quarterly* 37 (1985): 239–59.

Horowitz, Stephen P., and Mirriam J. Landsman. "The Americanization of Edna," *Studies in Jewish American Literature* (1982): 69–80.

Horwitz, Howard. "The Standard Oil Trust as Emersonian Hero," *Raritan* (1987): 97–119.

Howard, June. *Form and History in American Literary Naturalism*. Chapel Hill: University of North Carolina Press, 1985.

Howells, W. D. "The Recent Dramatic Season," *North American Review* 172 (1901): 475–77.

———. *The Rise of Silas Lapham*. New York: W. W. Norton, 1982.

———. *W. D. Howells as Critic*. Edited by Edwin H. Cady. London: Routledge & Kegan Paul, 1973.

———, and Frank Norris. *Criticism of Fiction & The Responsibilities of the Novelist*. New York: Hill & Wang, 1962.

Hubbard, Elbert. *Message to Garcia*. n.p: George H. Daniels, 1900.

———. "A Village Industry," *Wisdom* (1907): 255–66.

The Independent.

Jameson, Fredric. *The Political Unconscious: Narrative as a Socially Symbolic Act*. Ithaca: Cornell University Press, 1981.

Jauss, Hans Robert. "Literary History as a Challenge to Literary Theory." In *Toward an Aesthetics of Reception*. Translated by Timothy Bahti. Minneapolis: University of Minnesota Press, 1982.

Johnson, Paul E. *A Shopkeeper's Millenium: Society and Revivals in Rochester, New York, 1815–1837*. New York: Hill & Wang, 1978.

"Journalization." *New York Times Book Review*, 8 April 1917, p. 128.

Juergens, George P. *Joseph Pulitzer and The New York World*. Princeton: Princeton University Press, 1966.

Kaplan, Amy. "'The Knowledge of the Line': Realism and the City in Howells's *A Hazard of New Fortunes*," *PMLA* 101 (1986): 69–81.

———. *The Social Construction of American Realism*. Chicago: University of Chicago Press, 1988.

Kasson, John. *Amusing the Million: Coney Island at the Turn of the Century*. New York: Hill & Wang, 1978.

———. *Civilizing the Machine: Technology and Republican Values in America, 1776–1900*. New York, Penguin, 1977.

Kazin, Alfred. *On Native Grounds*. New York: Reynal & Hitchcock, 1942.

Kelley, Mary. *Private Woman, Public Stage: Literary Domesticity in Nineteenth-Century America*. New York: Oxford University Press, 1984.
Kennedy, David M. *Over Here: The First World War and American Society*. New York: Oxford University Press, 1980.
Kirschner, Don S. "'Publicity Properly Applied': The Selling of Expertise in America, 1900–1929," *american studies* 19 (1978): 65–78.
Kloppenberg, James T. *Uncertain Victory: Social Democracy and Progressivism in European and American Thought, 1870–1920*. New York: Oxford University Press, 1986.
Knight, Grant C. *The Strenuous Age in American Literature*. Chapel Hill: University of North Carolina Press, 1954.
Kocka, Jürgen. *White Collar Workers in America, 1890–1940*. Translated by Maura Kealey. London: Sage Publications, 1980.
Kramer, Dale. *Ross and The New Yorker*. Garden City, N.Y.: Doubleday, 1951.
Kramer, Lloyd S. "Literature, Criticism, and Historical Imagination: The Literary Challenge of Hayden White and Dominick LaCapra." In *The New Cultural History*. Edited by Lynn Hunt. Berkeley: University of California Press, 1989.
LaCapra, Dominick. *History and Criticism*. Ithaca: Cornell University Press, 1985.
Ladies' Garment Worker.
Ladies' Home Journal.
Langford, Gerald. *Alias O. Henry*. New York: Macmillan, 1957.
Lasch, Christopher. *The Culture of Narcissism: American Life in an Age of Diminishing Expectations*. New York: Knopf, 1978.
———. "The Moral and Intellectual Rehabilitation of the Bourgeoisie." In *The World of Nations*. New York: Knopf, 1973.
———. *The New Radicalism in America*. New York: Vintage, 1965.
Leach, Eugene E. "Mastering the Crowd: Collective Behavior and Mass Society in American Social Thought, 1917–1939," *american studies* 27 (1986): 99–114.
Leacock, Stephen. *Essays and Literary Studies*. New York, John Lane, n.d.
Lears, T. J. Jackson. "The Concept of Cultural Hegemony: Problems and Possibilities," *American Historical Review* 90 (1985): 567–93.
———. "From Salvation to Self-Realization." In *The Culture of Consumption: Critical Essays in American History, 1880–1980*. Edited by Richard Fox and T. J. Jackson Lears. New York: Pantheon, 1983.
———. "Some Versions of Fantasy: Toward a Cultural History of American Advertising, 1880–1930," *Prospects* 9 (1984): 349–405.
———. "Uneasy Courtship: Modern Art and Modern Advertising," *American Quarterly* 39 (1987): 132–43.
Levy, David W. *Herbert Croly of the New Republic*. Princeton: Princeton University Press, 1985.
Lewis, Grace Hegger. *With Love From Gracie*. New York: Harcourt, Brace, 1951.
Lewis, R. W. B. *Edith Wharton: A Biography*. New York: Harper & Row, 1975.
Lewis, Sinclair. *Babbitt*. New York: Signet, 1961.

———. *From Main Street to Stockholm: Letters of Sinclair Lewis, 1919–1930*. Edited by Harrison Smith. New York: Harcourt, Brace, 1952.

———. *The Job: An American Novel*. New York: Grosset & Dunlap, 1917.

———. *Main Street*. New York: Signet, 1980.

———. *The Man from Main Street*. Edited by Harry E. Maule and Melville H. Cane. New York: Random, 1955.

———. "Mr. Lorimer and Me," *The Nation*, 25 July 1928, p. 81.

———. Preface to *The History of Mr. Polly*. New York: The Press of the Readers Club, 1941.

———. *The Trail of the Hawk: A Comedy of the Seriousness of Life*. London: Jonathan Cape, 1923.

Lewisohn, Ludwig. Review of *The Adding Machine*. *The Nation*, 4 April 1923, p. 399.

Libbey, Laura Jean. *A Dangerous Flirtation: The Pathetic Romance of a Poor But Very Beautiful Working Girl*. Cleveland: Arthur Westbrook Co., 1897.

Light, Martin. "H. G. Wells and Sinclair Lewis: Friendship, Literary Influence, and Letters," *English Fiction in Transition* 5 (1967): 1–20.

———. *The Quixotic Vision of Sinclair Lewis*. West Lafayette, Ind.: Purdue University Press, 1975.

Lippmann, Walter. *Public Opinion*. New York: Free Press, 1965.

Literary Digest.

Lorimer, George Horace. *Letters from a Self-Made Merchant to His Son*. New York: Grosset & Dunlap, 1902.

Lundquist, James. "The Sauk Centre Sinclair Lewis Didn't Write About." In *Critical Essays on Sinclair Lewis*. Edited by Martin Bucco. Boston: G. K. Hall, 1986.

Lurie, Jonathan. *Law and the Nation, 1865–1912*. New York: Knopf, 1983.

Lynd, Robert S. *Knowledge for What? The Place of Social Science in American Culture*. 1939. Reprint. New York: Grove Press, 1964.

McBriar, A. M. *Fabian Socialism and English Politics*. Cambridge, Eng.: Cambridge University Press, 1962.

McFarland, Gerald W. *Mugwumps, Morals, and Politics, 1884–1920*. Amherst: University of Massachusetts Press, 1975.

McGerr, Michael. *The Decline of Popular Politics: The American North, 1865–1928*. New York: Oxford University Press, 1986.

MacKenzie, Norman, and Jeanne MacKenzie. *The Fabians*. New York: Simon & Schuster, 1977.

Marchand, Roland. *Advertising the American Dream: Making Way for Modernity, 1920–1940*. Berkeley: University of California Press, 1985.

Martin, Robert L. *H. L. Mencken and the Debunkers*. Athens: University of Georgia Press, 1984.

May, Henry. *The End of American Innocence*. Chicago: University of Chicago Press, 1964.

May, Lary. *Screening Out the Past: The Birth of Mass Culture and the Motion Picture Industry*. New York: Oxford University Press, 1980.

Mayer, Arno J. "The Lower Middle Class as a Historical Problem," *Journal of Modern History* 47 (1975): 409–36.

Meisel, Martin. "Shaw and Revolution: The Politics of the Plays." In *Shaw: Seven Critical Essays*. Edited by Norman Rosenblood. Toronto: University of Toronto Press, 1971.

Metropolitan Magazine.

Meyer, Donald. *The Positive Thinkers: Religion as Pop Psychology from Mary Baker Eddy to Oral Roberts*. New York: Pantheon, 1980.

Michaels, Walter Benn. *The Gold Standard and the Logic of Naturalism: American Literature at the Turn of the Century*. Berkeley: University of California Press, 1987.

Milkman, Ruth, ed. *Women, Work, and Protest: A Century of U.S. Women's Labor History*. Boston: Routledge & Kegan Paul, 1985.

Mill, John Stuart. *On Liberty, Representative Government, and the Subjection of Women*. London: Oxford University Press, 1966.

Miller, Arthur. *Theater Essays of Arthur Miller*. Edited by Robert A. Martin. New York: Viking Press, 1978.

Mills, C. Wright. *White Collar*. New York: Oxford University Press, 1951.

Milne, Gordon. *The Sense of Society: A History of the American Novel of Manners*. Rutherford, N.J.: Fairleigh Dickinson University Press, 1977.

Minneapolis Labor Review.

Minneapolis Sunday Tribune.

Montgomery, David. *Beyond Equality: Labor and the Radical Republicans, 1862–1872*. New York: Vintage, 1972.

———. "White Shirts and Superior Intelligence." In *The Fall of the House of Labor*. New York: Cambridge University Press, 1987.

Moodie, Clara Lee. "The Short Stories and Sinclair Lewis' Literary Development," *Studies in Short Fiction* 12 (1975): 99–107.

Morley, Christopher. *Human Being*. New York: Doubleday, Doran & Co., 1932.

———. *John Mistletoe*. Garden City: Doubleday, Doran & Co., 1931.

———. *Parnassus on Wheels*. Philadelphia: J. B. Lippincott Co, 1917.

Mott, Frank Luther. *A History of American Magazines*. 5 vols. Cambridge: Harvard University Press, 1938–68.

Mouscher, Karen-Elisabeth. "Sherwood Anderson: The Early Advertising Years." Ph.D. dissertation, Northwestern University, 1986.

Moyle, Seth. *My Friend O. Henry*. New York: H. K. Fly Co., 1914.

Nettels, Elsa. *Language, Race, and Social Class in Howells's America*. Lexington: University of Kentucky Press, 1988.

New Republic.

New York World.

Nolte, William H. *Henry L. Mencken: Literary Critic*. Middletown, Conn.: Wesleyan University, 1966.

Nye, David E. *Image Worlds: Corporate Identities at General Electric, 1890–1930*. Cambridge: M.I.T. Press, 1985.

O. Henry. Collection, Greensboro Historical Museum and Library, Greensboro, N.C.
———. Collection, Greensboro Public Library, Greensboro, N.C.
———. *The Complete Works of O. Henry*. 2 vols. Garden City, N.Y.: Doubleday & Co., 1953.
———. *Postscripts*. New York: Harpers, 1923.
———. *Waifs and Strays*. Garden City: Doubleday, Page, 1925.
O. Henry Papers. New York: Doubleday, n.d..
Oakley, Helen M. *Three Hours for Lunch*. New York: Watermill Publishers, 1976.
Oppenheimer, Martin. *White Collar Politics*. New York: Monthly Review Press, 1985.
Ossowski, Stanislaw. *Class Structure in the Social Consciousness*. Translated by Sheila Patterson. New York: Free Press of Glencoe, 1963.
The Outlook.
Overton, Grant. *When Winter Comes to Main Street*. New York: Doran, 1922.
Page, Charles H. *Class and American Sociology: From Ward to Ross*. 1946. Reprint. New York: Schocken Books, 1969.
Palmer, Bryan D. *Descent into Discourse: The Reification of Language and the Writing of Social History*. Philadelphia: Temple University Press, 1990.
Palmieri, Anthony F. R. *Elmer Rice: A Playwright's Vision of America*. Cranbury, N.J.: Fairleigh Dickinson University Press, 1980.
Parrinder, Patrick. *H. G. Wells: The Critical Heritage*. London: Routledge & Kegan Paul, 1972.
Parrington, Vernon. *The Beginnings of Critical Realism in America, 1860–1920*. New York: Macmillan, 1940.
———. *Sinclair Lewis: Our Own Diogenes*. Seattle: University of Washington Book Store, 1929.
Pattee, Fred Lewis. *The Development of the American Short Story: An Historical Survey*. New York: Harper & Bros., 1923.
———. *Side-Lights on American Literature*. New York: Century Co., 1922.
Phillips, William L. "How Sherwood Anderson Wrote *Winesburg, Ohio*," *American Literature* 33 (1957): 7–30.
Pierson, Stanley. *British Socialists: The Journey from Fantasy to Politics*. Cambridge: Harvard University Press, 1979.
Pike, Cathleen. *O. Henry in North Carolina*. Chapel Hill: University of North Carolina Library, 1957.
Pinsker, Sanford. *The Schlemiel as Metaphor: Studies in the Yiddish and American Jewish Novel*. Carbondale: Southern Illinois University Press, 1971.
Pitkin, Hannah Fenichel. *Representation*. New York: Atherton Press, 1969.
Pollay, Richard W. "The Subsiding Sizzle: A Descriptive History of Print Advertising, 1900–1980," *Journal of Marketing* (1985): 24–37.
Pope, Daniel. *The Making of Modern Advertising*. New York: Basic Books, 1983.
Printer's Ink.
Publisher's Weekly

Radway, Janice. *Reading the Romance: Women, Patriarchy, and Popular Literature.* Chapel Hill: University of North Carolina Press, 1984.

Rapson, Richard L. *Britons View America: Travel Commentary, 1860–1935.* Seattle: University of Washington Press, 1971.

Rascoe, Burton. *We Were Interrupted.* Garden City, N.Y.: Doubleday, 1947.

Reizenstein, Elmer L. "Some Lame and Impotent Conclusions," *New York Times,* 11 April 1915, Sec. VII, p. 6.

Retail Clerks' International Protective Association Advocate.

Rice, Elmer. Collection, Harry Ransom Humanities Research Center, University of Texas at Austin, Austin, Texas.

———. Introduction to *Other Plays & Not for Children.* London: Victor Gollancz Ltd., 1935.

———. *Minority Report: An Autobiography.* New York: Simon & Schuster, 1963.

———. "Mr. Rice States His Case," *New York Times,* 12 Feb. 1933, Sec. IX, p. 3.

———. "The Public Censorship," *New York Times,* 29 Jan. 1922. Sec. VI, p. 1.

———. *Seven Plays.* New York: Viking, 1950.

———. "Sex in the Modern Theatre," *Harpers* 164 (1932): 665–73.

———. *The Subway.* New York: Samuel French Ltd., 1929.

———. *3 Plays.* New York: Hill & Wang, 1965.

———. "To the Dramatic Editor," *New York Times,* 1 April 1923, Sec. VII, p. 2.

———. "Towards an Adult Theatre," *Drama Magazine,* 21 Feb. 1931, pp. 5, 18.

———. "Zero et Shrdlu," In *Masques, Cahiers d'Art Dramatique.* Edited by Hanry-Jannett, Paris, n.p., 1927.

Richardson, Dorothy. *The Long Day: The Story of a New York Working Girl—As Told By Herself.* New York: Century Co., 1906.

Rideout, Walter. "Sherwood Anderson." In *Fifteen Modern American Authors: A Survey of Research and Criticism.* Edited by Jackson R. Bryer. Durham: Duke University Press, 1969.

Rodgers, Daniel T. "In Search of Progressivism," *Reviews in American History* 10 (1982): 113–32.

———. "Upstairs, Downstairs." Review of Blumin, *Emergence of the Middle Class, New Republic* 202 (5 Feb. 1990): 40–42.

Rosenberg, Charles E. "Sexuality, Class and Role in 19th Century America," *American Quarterly* 35 (1973): 131–53.

Rothman, David. *The Discovery of the Asylum: Social Order and Disorder in the New Republic.* Boston: Little, Brown, 1971.

Ryan, Mary P. *Cradle of the Middle Class: The Family in Oneida County, New York, 1790–1865.* New York: Cambridge University Press, 1981.

St. Nicholas.

Saroyan, William. "O What a Man Was O. Henry," *Kenyon Review* 29 (1967): 671–75.

Saturday Evening Post.

Saturday Review of Literature.

Schickel, Richard. *Harold Lloyd: The Shape of Laughter.* Boston: New York Graphic

Society, 1974.

Schiller, Dan. *Objectivity and the News: The Public and the Rise of Commercial Journalism*. Philadelphia: University of Pennsylvania Press, 1981.

Schorer, Mark, ed. *Sinclair Lewis: A Collection of Critical Essays*. Garden City, N.Y.: Doubleday, 1962.

———. *Sinclair Lewis: An American Life*. New York: Dell, 1961.

Schorske, Carl. *Fin de Siécle Vienna: Politics and Culture*. New York: Vintage, 1981.

Schudson, Michael. *Discovering the News: A Social History of American Newspapers*. New York: Basic Books, 1978.

Scribner, Charles. Collection, Firestone Library, Princeton University, Princeton, N.J.

Seltzer, Mark. "The Naturalist Machine." In *Sex, Politics and Science in the Nineteenth Century Novel*. Edited by Ruth Bernard Yaezell. Baltimore: Johns Hopkins University Press, 1986.

Sennett, Richard, and Jonathan Cobb, *The Hidden Injuries of Class*. New York: Vintage, 1972.

Shaeffer, Robert K. "A Critique of the 'New Class' Theorists: Towards a Theory of the Working Class in America," *Social Praxis* 4 (1976/77): 75–99.

Shannon, David A. *The Socialist Party of America*. New York: Macmillan Co., 1955.

Shaughnessey, Mary Rose. *Women and Success in American Society in the Works of Edna Ferber*. New York: Gordon Press, 1977.

Shaw, Albert. *The Outlook for the Average Man*. New York: Macmillan Co., 1907.

Shaw, George Bernard. "The Fabian Society." In *Essays in Fabian Socialism*. London: Constable & Company, Ltd., 1932.

———. *Major Critical Essays*. 1932. Reprint. London: Constable & Company. 1955.

Sherman, Stuart P. *Points of View*. New York: Scribner's, 1924.

Silbey, Marilyn McAdams. "Austin's First National and the Errant Teller," *Southwestern History Quarterly* 74 (1971): 478–506.

Sinclair, Upton. *Bill Porter: A Drama of O. Henry in Prison*. Pasadena: Upton Sinclair, 1925.

"Sinclair Lewis Looks at Advertising," *Advertising and Selling*, 15 May 1929, pp. 17–18, 60, 62, 64–66.

The Smart Set.

Smith, C. Alphonso. *O. Henry*. 1916. Reprint. New York: Chelsea House, 1980.

Smith, David C. *H. G. Wells: Desperately Mortal*. New Haven: Yale University Press, 1986.

Smith, J. Percy. *The Unrepentant Pilgrim: A Study of the Development of Bernard Shaw*. Boston: Houghton Mifflin, 1965.

Smith, Judith. "The 'New Woman' Knows How to Type: Some Connections Between Sexual Ideology and Clerical Work, 1900–1930." Paper presented at the Berkshire Conference on Women's History, 1974.

Smith-Rosenberg, Carol. "The Female World of Love and Ritual: Relations Between Women in Nineteenth Century America." In *Disorderly Conduct: Visions of*

Gender in Victorian America. New York: Knopf, 1985.

Society of Arts and Sciences, *O. Henry Memorial Award Prize Stories*. Garden City, N.Y.: Doubleday, 1921.

Sorel, Edward. "The World of Gluyas Williams," *American Heritage* (1984): 50–57.

Stansell, Christine. *City of Women: Sex and Class in New York, 1789–1860*. New York: Knopf, 1986.

Stark, Steven. "A perfectly average American," *Boston Globe*, 28 May 1990, p. 13.

Stearns, Peter. "The Middle Class: Toward a Precise Definition," *Comparative Studies in Society and History* 21 (1979): 377–96.

Stein, Leon. *Out of the Sweatshop: The Struggle for Industrial Democracy*. New York: Quadrangle, 1977.

Stenerson, Douglas. "Short-Story Writing: A Neglected Phase of Mencken's Literary Apprenticeship," *Menckeniana* 30 (1969): 8–13.

Stocking, George W. *Race, Culture, and Evolution: Essays in the History of Anthropology*. New York: Free Press, 1968.

Strom, Sharon. "We're No Kitty Foyles." In *Women, Work, and Protest: A Century of U.S. Women's Labor History*. Edited by Ruth Milkman. Boston: Routledge & Kegan Paul, 1985.

Stuckey, W. J. *The Pulitzer Prize Novels: A Critical Backward Look*. Norman: University of Oklahoma Press, 1966.

Susman, Warren, " 'Personality' and the Making of Twentieth-Century Culture." In *New Directions in American Intellectual History*. Edited by John Higham and Paul Conkin. Baltimore: Johns Hopkins University Press, 1979.

Sutton, William A. *The Road to Winesburg: A Mosaic of the Imaginative Life of Sherwood Anderson*. Metuchen, N.J.: Scarecrow Press, 1972.

Sykes, Robert H. "The Identity of Anderson's Fanatical Farmer," *Studies in Short Fiction* 18 (1981): 79–82.

Taylor, Walter F. *The Economic Novel in America*. Chapel Hill: University of North Carolina Press, 1942.

Tebbel, John. *George Horace Lorimer and the Saturday Evening Post*. Garden City, N.Y.: Doubleday, 1948.

Thompson, E. P. *The Making of the English Working Class*. New York: Pantheon, 1963.

———. *The Poverty of Theory and Other Essays*. London: Merlin, 1978.

Thurber, James. *The Years With Ross*. Boston: Atlantic Monthly Press, 1959.

Tichi, Cecilia. *Shifting Gears: Technology, Literature, Culture in Modernist America*. Chapel Hill: University of North Carolina Press, 1987.

Toman, Marshall. "Nonsense and Sensibility: Negation in the Novels of Joseph Heller." Ph.D. dissertation, Boston College, 1988.

Tompkins, Jane P. *Sensational Designs: The Cultural Work of American Fiction*. New York: Oxford University Press, 1985.

Tomsich, John. *A Genteel Endeavor: American Culture and Politics in the Gilded Age*. Stanford: Stanford University Press, 1971.

Towne, Charles Hanson. *Adventures in Editing*. New York: D. Appleton & Co., 1926.

Trachtenberg, Alan. *The Incorporation of America: Culture and Society in the Gilded Age*. New York: Hill & Wang, 1982.

U.S. Bureau of the Census. *Historical Statistics of the United States, Colonial Times to 1970,* Part I. Washington: U.S. Bureau of the Census, 1975.

Van Doren, Carl. *The American Novel, 1789–1940*. New York: Macmillan, 1940.

———. *Contemporary American Novelists, 1900–1920*. New York: Macmillan, 1922.

———. "O. Henry," *Texas Review,* 2 (1917): 248–59.

———. *Three Worlds*. New York: Harper & Bros., 1936.

Veysey, Laurence. "Higher Education." In *The Professions in American History*. Edited by Nathan O. Hatch. Notre Dame: University of Notre Dame Press, 1988.

Walden, Daniel. "Miller's Roots and His Moral Dilemma: or, Continuity from Brooklyn to *Salesman*." In *Critical Essays on Arthur Miller*. Edited by James J. Martin. Boston: G. K. Hall, 1979.

Walker, Pat, ed. *Between Labor and Capital*. Boston: South End Press, 1979.

Wallas, Graham. *Human Nature in Politics*. 3rd ed. New York: Knopf, 1921.

War Camp Community Service, *A Retrospect: How a Nation Served Its Sons in Army and Navy Through Organized Community Hospitality*. New York: War Camp Community Service, 1920.

Warner, Sam Bass, Jr. *The Province of Reason*. Cambridge: Harvard University Press, 1984.

Weaver, R. A. "*The Adding Machine*: Exemplar of the Ludicrous," *Players* 49 (1974): 130–33.

Webb, Howard W., Jr. "The Development of a Style: The Lardner Idiom," *American Quarterly* 12 (1966): 482–92.

Weiler, Peter. "William Clarke: The Making and Unmaking of a Fabian Socialist," *Journal of British Studies* 14 (1974): 77–108.

Wells, H. G. *Anticipations*. New York: Harper & Bros., 1902.

———. *An Englishman Looks at the World*. London: Cassell & Company, Ltd. 1914.

———. *History of Mr. Polly*. New York: Press of the Readers Club, 1941.

———. "The Middle-Class Man and Socialism." In *New Worlds for Old*. New York: Macmillan, 1913.

Wertheimer, Barbara Mayer. *We Were There: The Story of Working Women in America*. New York: Pantheon, 1977.

West, Thomas Reed. *Flesh of Steel*. Nashville, Tenn.: Vanderbilt University Press, 1967.

Westbrook, Robert. "Politics as Consumption." In *The Culture of Consumption*. Edited by Richard Wightman Fox and T. J. Jackson Lears. New York: Pantheon, 1983.

Wharton, Edith. *A Backward Glance*. New York: Appleton, 1934.

———. "The Great American Novel," *Yale Review* 16 (1927): 646–56.

White, Percival. *Advertising Research*. New York: D. Appleton, 1927.

White, Ray Lewis. "Mencken's Lost Review of *Winesburg, Ohio*," *Notes on Modern American Literature* 2 (1978): Item 11.

Wiebe, Robert H. *The Search for Order, 1877–1920*. New York: Hill & Wang, 1967.

Wiener, Martin J. *Between Two Worlds: The Political Thought of Graham Wallas.* Oxford: Clarendon Press, 1971.

Wilentz, Sean. *Chants Democratic: New York City and the Rise of the American Working Class, 1788–1850*. New York: Oxford University Press, 1984.

Williams, Raymond. *Keywords: A Vocabulary of Culture and Society*. N.p.: Fontana, 1976.

———. *The Long Revolution*. New York: Columbia University Press, 1961.

———. *Marxism and Literature*. New York: Oxford University Press, 1977.

———. *Problems in Materialism and Culture: Selected Essays*. London: Verso, 1980.

———. *Resources of Hope*. Edited by Robin Gale. London: Verso, 1989.

Williams, William Wash. *The Quiet Lodger of Irving Place*. New York: E. P. Dutton, 1936.

Wilson, Christopher P. "American Naturalism and the Problem of Sincerity," *American Literature* 54 (1982): 520–27.

———. "Broadway Nights: John Reed and the City," *Prospects* 13 (1989): 22–39.

———. "Coming to Terms with *The End of American Innocence*," *American Intellectual History Newsletter* 12 (1990): 33–39.

———. "Containing Multitudes: Realism, Historicism, American Studies," *American Quarterly* 41 (1989): 466–95.

———. *The Labor of Words: Literary Professionalism in the Progressive Era*. Athens: University of Georgia Press, 1985.

———. "Markets and Fictions: Howells' Infernal Juggle," *American Literary Realism* 20 (1988): 2–22.

———. "The Rhetoric of Consumption." In *The Culture of Consumption*. Edited by Richard Fox and T. J. Jackson Lears. New York: Pantheon, 1983.

———. "Tempests and Teapots: Harriet Beecher Stowe's *The Minister's Wooing*," *New England Quarterly* 58 (1985): 554–77.

Wolin, Sheldon. "What Revolutionary Action Means Today," *democracy* 2 (1982): 17–28.

Women's Home Companion.

Woodward, W. E. *The Gift of Life*. New York: E. P. Dutton & Co., 1947.

Woolf, Virginia. "American Fiction," *Saturday Review of Literature,* 1 Aug. 1925, p. 1–3.

The World's Work.

Wright, Erik Olin. *Class, Crisis and the State*. London: Lowe & Brydore, 1978.

Yates, Norris W. *The American Humorist*. Ames: Iowa State University Press, 1964.

Young, Stark. Review of *The Adding Machine, New Republic* 34 (4 April 1923): 164–65.

Index

WE DON'T TALK ABOUT LAST NIGHT

J. S. COOPER

Created with Vellum

BLURB

From *New York Times* Bestselling Author J. S. COOPER comes a new hot standalone billionaire romance.

He's the Smuggest, Sexiest, Most Arrogant Man I've Ever Met, and He's Totally Off-Limits

An Alpha Male Who Wants His Way

Jacob Joshua Edwards is my sworn enemy. I've hated him for years, even though I've always been attracted to him. When my father's business goes under, he makes a deal with Jacob's father to save the company. Only the deal is not one that benefits the family in my eyes. My father arranges for my sister to marry Jake so that the deal becomes a merger as opposed to a takeover.

A Rebel with a Cause

As far as I'm concerned, the merger is the worst thing that can happen to the family, and I'm determined to find my own way in life. I plan to escape the night after the big celebration, but I allow myself one confrontation with Jacob to let him know what I really think about him. Only nothing goes according to plan. Soon, I'm caught up with him in a way I never expected.

Secrets, Lies & Even Hotter Nights

Jacob has a proposal for me that is very tempting. One that could enable me to help my family and stop the merger. However, Jacob is playing a high-stakes game that I'm not quite ready for. As bombshell secrets and lies make their way to the surface, I'm left wondering if I'm a contestant in the game or a pawn that's being played.

PROLOGUE

"You can call me Jake, you know," he said, a smirk on his face. His dazzling green eyes seemed to pierce into my soul. As I stared at his too-handsome face, I wondered if he were some sort of fallen angel, sent to earth to annoy the living daylights out of me.

"I'd rather call you by your Christian name, Jacob." I waited to see if he would burst into flames at my use of the word "Christian."

No such luck.

"Well, Tiff..." He paused and laughed, a low, rumbling sound that made my stomach flutter. I hated how my body betrayed me when I was around him.

"My name is Tiffany."

"But I think I prefer Tiff, so I'll go with that." Smugness dripped off his tongue.

"I don't care what you prefer, Jacob Joshua Edwards."

"Ooh, you're saying my full name now. I kind of like it." He took a step closer to me, and my heart started racing as if it were in the rapid-beat Olympics.

"What are you doing?" I said as he leaned down and

touched my lips with his thumb. His thumb felt warm and slightly rough as he caressed my lower lip. I swallowed hard.

"What do you think I'm doing?"

I stepped back, swatting his hand away. "You can't touch me like that."

"Why? Does it make you scared that the big bad wolf might eat you up?"

"I'm not a little girl. I'm not scared of big bad wolves. I am twenty-five years old. And you can't touch me like that because it's not appropriate."

"Okay," he said, stepping back, "If that's what you want."

"That is what I want." I glared at him, wondering how he could be so confident and smug when faced with my death stare. Men richer than him had faltered in the face of my stares. Even teachers had stepped back, but he didn't seem to be bothered at all.

"So, then, I will bid you adieu, Miss Tiffany."

"You're leaving?" I looked at him with surprise. The room was packed, and the party had just begun.

"I'm not leaving. But I shall go and talk to other women that do want to get to know me better."

"Psh, I doubt there's many of them." I rolled my eyes. "And also that's highly inappropriate given that this is your—"

"It's a pity, you know," he interrupted.

"What's a pity?"

"That you're not interested in calling me Jake. I think I could lighten you up quite a bit. You're a spitfire, aren't you?"

"I don't need to lighten up, thank you very much."

"Oh, I think you do." He chuckled.

"What's so funny?" I snapped, wanting to be inside of his head.

"I don't think you want to know." He shook his head and licked his lips.

"Tell me." I knew I should have just let him go. I knew that I shouldn't engage with him. He was an asshole, a jerk, my sworn enemy. But I just couldn't stop myself.

"I think there are three things you need in your life right now," he said, staring at my lips.

I swallowed hard. "Oh yeah, and what are they?"

"I don't think I should tell you. I think I should show you. Don't they say that actions speak louder than words?"

I took a slow sip of my vodka martini. "Fine, show me."

"Really?" His eyes sparkled and widened almost imperceptibly. "You surprise me."

"Why do I surprise you?"

"I thought you were all talk and no action."

"I'm not."

"Then leave with me."

"We can't just leave," I objected. "The party has just begun."

"Yes, the party has just started, but I can do whatever I want." He shrugged. "I am Jake Edwards, after all."

"But the party is for you."

"No," he said, "the party is not for me. The party is for your sister."

"But—"

"Shh." He pressed a finger against my lips and winked. "Come with me, Tiffany, if you dare."

He moved his finger from my lips and walked away. I stood there immobile for a couple of seconds. He didn't even look back to see if I was following as he made his way through the packed room. People tried to talk to him, but he didn't stop. Finally, he reached the entrance of the hallway and walked out.

I'm not sure what came over me, but I started walking quickly to catch up. I knew it was crazy, I knew I was asking for trouble, but how could I not follow him? He had dared me, after all.

I made my way to the entrance and looked to the left and then to the right. He was gone, and I didn't know where he was. I took a deep breath and turned to go back into the room.

"I knew you would come." Suddenly he was next to me, his eyes twinkling with laughter.

"Where did you come from? You weren't here just now." I blinked at him in surprise.

"It's a magic trick," he replied. "I'm Houdini. In and out, just like that."

"In and out just like that, huh? Is that your motto in life?" I smirked at him.

"Wouldn't you like to know?" He winked again, more seductively this time.

"No." I shook my head quickly.

"Liar." He grabbed my hand and squeezed it. "I know exactly what you want, Tiffany."

"Excuse me?"

"And I know exactly what you need as well. Come on."

And like a fool, I followed him. This was what happened when you drank too many vodka martinis on an empty stomach. I could hear my father's voice coming from the room that I'd just left, cheering and celebrating. I started to feel a little bit guilty. What the hell was I doing? I knew I was making a huge mistake, but I couldn't stop myself.

"We shouldn't be doing this, Jacob."

"I said to call me Jake."

"We shouldn't be doing this, Jake," I said, even as I continued following him down the hallway.

"There are many things we shouldn't be doing, Tiffany. But we can't let that stop us, can we?" He rounded the corner, me still at his heels.

Three things he'd said I needed, three things I'd said I wanted. I had no idea what they were. But I had to find out, no matter what the cost was.

wanted me to do was to sit at the dining room table and look pretty.

I had other ideas.

I was going to make it so that Jacob and his father wanted nothing to do with our family. Maybe my family couldn't see beyond the dollar signs, but I could. Aside from his good looks, he was a bastard. The couple of times that he'd been to the house and the main office, he'd looked down on all of us with his superior smile and practically sneered at us. My hand itched to slap him, but I knew if I did, my dad would absolutely kill me. I had other plans, though. I would just have to be very secret about them.

I had grown up confident and self-assured knowing I was Tiffany Newton. Some said that my family was descended from Sir Isaac Newton, though I didn't know if that was true. History stated that he'd never had any children, but I knew that there were always events that happened behind closed doors that most people never knew about in every family. What I did know, though, was that my family was held in high regard in the community. My great-great-grandfather had come over from England with barely a penny to his name, and he'd made something of himself. And he'd passed his business on to his son, who had grown it and passed it on to his son. With each generation, the fortune grew larger and larger...until it came to my father.

My father had squandered everything. The company was close to collapse, and the family was on the verge of bankruptcy. My father cared only about his image and status, not his family—and certainly not his employees.

He had Bentleys and Rolls Royces, a Lamborghini, a Ferrari, several Mercedes, and BMWs. We had so many cars, I had lost count. We had a penthouse in New York, a mansion in LA, a chateau in Paris, a townhome in London, a beach home in Mallorca—he even financed an island in the Caribbean.

And yet none of the properties made any money. He wasn't business savvy at all. I'd offered to help. I was naturally business savvy. I always had been, since I was a little girl, but my father wasn't about to take advice from a twenty-five-year-old woman. As the youngest Newton, my job was to look pretty and smile and flirt with whichever men he wanted me to. Not that I obeyed, of course. I wasn't that sort of woman. And maybe that's why my father didn't like me much. I certainly wasn't the favorite.

"Tiffany, are you not ready yet?" My father's voice interrupted my thoughts as I sat in the library.

"Ready for what, Dad?"

"I told you, Jacob Joshua Edwards and his father are coming to meet your sister." He couldn't hide the anger in his voice. My father had been as bad an actor as he was a businessman.

"Okay, and why do I have to be ready?" I loved being difficult. It gave meaning to my otherwise boring days.

His dark eyebrows drew together. "You will be in the same room as the Edwardses. We have an impression to make. Our whole family will be there to greet them."

"But I don't want to greet them. I don't want to be there while you offload Monique like she's cattle." Monique was my older sister. She was beautiful, but she didn't have much of a brain. All she cared about were designer handbags, shoes, and makeup. If she wasn't my sister, I'd have absolutely hated her. Instead, I quietly despised her. She was a puppet in my father's hands. She did whatever he wanted, whenever he wanted. I thought it was pathetic, and I knew I would never let him manipulate me in that way.

"She's not cattle." He gave me his death stare, the death stare that I'd inherited. Frankly, I thought that my death stare was far superior.

"Okay, not cattle then. A pig or a sheep or a horse. Whatever you sell at auction."

"I am not selling your sister at auction. You should be happy that it wasn't you."

"But he wouldn't want me." I laughed. "You know that, Dad."

"I know." He turned his nose up. "No man would want to have to put up with a—" He paused.

"What were you going to say, Dad?" I smiled at him sweetly. I loved it when he showed me just how much he hated me. Most daughters would cry knowing they were hated by their father, but I actually reveled in it. It was something to be proud of. I didn't respect the man, so it made me feel good that he didn't like me. It meant that I was doing something right.

"I just hope that you can find yourself a suitable husband before it's too late." He looked me up and down. "You are getting on in years Tiffany. You know that, right?"

"Getting on in years? I'm twenty-five!"

"Exactly. And you're not married. You have no kids. What use are you to me?"

"So that's my only worth to you? To get married and to have kids?" I stared at him. "Seriously, Dad? Don't you wish I was a boy?"

He pressed his lips together. It grated on him that he'd had no sons. And he'd tried. Not just with my mother, but with plenty of other women—we all knew about his affairs. But he'd never sired a boy, just my sister and me. There may have been some other bastard children out there, but none of them were men. If they had been, they'd have been welcomed into the family a long time ago.

"Your sister's very lucky that Jacob wants to marry her. I worked very hard for this merger."

"Dad, you sold your soul to the devil, and for what? To keep the family business name? Who even cares? Newton Enterprises has been around for hundreds of years and..."

"And what?"

"We're not even Newton Enterprises anymore. We're part of the Edwards Conglomerate."

"We shall keep our name, though. And perhaps I have some other tricks up my sleeve." He smirked. "But that's nothing for you to worry your sweet little head about."

"You know nothing in my head is sweet, Father. What's your plan?"

He looked at me for a few seconds, calculating. "Let's just say that old man Edwards thinks he's got one on me, but he doesn't. Your sister, she'll marry the Jacob boy, but—" He shrugged. "We shall see what happens next."

"What are you planning on doing, Dad?"

"Nothing," he said innocently. "Why would you think I would plan on doing anything?"

"You're not going to have her poison him or something, are you?"

His eyes narrowed, and I realized that I was either right or very close. I let out a low sigh. My father was stupid. Murder? He'd murder just to keep the family name? I hated Jacob Joshua Edwards, the smarmiest, most arrogant man I'd ever met in my life. But even I didn't want him murdered. He didn't deserve that.

"Dad, I—"

"Go and change," he ordered. He turned on his heel and left the room.

I closed the book in front of me and left it on the table. I'd come back to read it later. The library was my favorite room in the house, filled with thousands of old books. I loved to read. It was my favorite pastime, but now I needed to charm a family that I hated.

I wasn't sure how much longer I could live this farce. I didn't want to be around these people any longer, and I didn't have to be. I was capable of making my way on my own, and I had decided that it was time. I wasn't going to stick around to see the fall of the Newton family. And I sure wasn't going to stick around to see the rise of the Edwards family, either.

TWO

"Hey, Tiffany, what do you think of this dress?" My sister Monique walked into my bedroom wearing a low-cut black dress.

"Um, you're not wearing a bra."

"Well, I don't need to wear a bra. My breasts are pert and perky." She smirked at the mirror and hefted her "perky" breasts in her hands. "And I haven't even had plastic surgery."

"Yes, you did." I rolled my eyes and turned away.

"No, I did not. Take that back, Tiffany."

"Monique, you had plastic surgery on your nose. You also had a boob job. You used to be an A and now you're a C. Remember? I went with you."

"Oh, yeah." She laughed and twirled her peroxide blond hair around her manicured fingers. "I forgot about that. You did come with me, didn't you?" She looked at my chest. "You could do with some implants yourself."

"I don't think so. I'm a 36C naturally. If I went any bigger, I'd have a backache."

"You do need to lose some weight, that's true." She looked at me with contempt.

Gosh, how I hated her. She was my older sister, and it would've been nice if we'd had some sort of special relationship, but we really didn't. I'd always been there for her, but she'd always looked down on me, and frankly, I was over it.

"So what do you think of my dress?" she asked again.

"I think you look kind of slutty," I said honestly, "but if that's the look you're going for..."

"Don't be jealous, Tiffany, just because I'm marrying Jacob Edwards. Of course, you'll be lucky if you ever get married, short of pulling in some hobo off the street."

"Yeah. That's my only option."

"Well, it's not like Jacob would ever want someone like you."

"It's not like I would ever want someone like *him*," I pointed out. "Do you actually need anything? I need to get dressed as well."

"Oh, you're not wearing that?" She took in my jeans and t-shirt.

"No. Dad wanted me to change, so that's what I'm going to do."

"I don't know why Dad cares what you look like. They don't care about you. They've come to meet me."

"Okay, Monique. Is there anything else?" I knew I shouldn't let her rile me up, but her words had annoyed me so much that I decided to wear something extra cute and sexy. I wasn't going to flaunt my tits like she was, of course. I didn't want to look like a stripper. I didn't care what the Edwards family thought of me, but I needed to take Monique down a peg or two.

"Tiffany, you know what I was thinking?" Monique put a hand on the back of my chair.

"What?"

"I was thinking that perhaps I'll bring you with me to my new house."

"Excuse me?" I stared at her, not knowing where she was going with this. Did she really think I'd want to go with her to her new house?

"Yeah. I was thinking that I might need a maid, you know." She giggled. Or maybe cackled would be more accurate.

"I don't need to be a maid, and I certainly wouldn't be a maid for you." I looked her up and down. "You're a mess."

"Yes. And that's why I need a maid because *I* can afford one. *You* can't afford shit. That's why you *have* to get married. I don't have to marry anyone. I want to marry Jacob. This is the answer to all my dreams. Don't you get that, Tiffany? I'm marrying Jacob Joshua Edwards, the most handsome man in the city."

"Okay. Whatever."

Arguing would have been futile. Jacob and his brother Nico were probably the most sought-after bachelors in the city. Every woman who knew them talked about them, but I couldn't stand either one of them, especially Jake. I'd met him many years ago and he'd been such an asshole to me that I'd never forgotten it and I never would. I would never like him or his brother.

"Well, I'm going now." She looked at me. "I'll see you later."

"Bye, Monique."

"Yes. Tiffany, you do that."

"Do what? What are you talking about?"

"Oh, nothing. Nothing." She fluffed her hair. "You wouldn't get it."

"Wouldn't get what? Your sentence didn't even make

sense."

"*You* don't make sense and everyone knows it." And with that, she flounced out of the bedroom.

I quickly closed the door behind her, locked it, then sat down on my bed. Sometimes I felt like a princess locked in a tower, only I wasn't a princess and this wasn't a tower, and there was certainly no Prince Charming coming to save me. How had I been born into this horrible family? My father was horrible. My sister was horrible, and I could barely remember my mother. She'd died a long, long time ago. Sometimes I wondered if she was still alive if things would've been different.

Maybe Monique would've been normal and nice and sweet, the sort of oldest sister that I wanted. Maybe our dad would've been kinder and calmer and more generous with his time and affection.

But there was really no point thinking about what could have been because it would never happen. I grabbed my phone and called my best friend Polly. She was the only one that could make me feel better when I'd had a run-in with Monique.

She answered on the second ring. "Hey, Tiffany, how's it going?" She sounded out of breath.

"Not bad. What are you up to?"

"I was just running on the treadmill," she gasped. "Oh my gosh! That was rough."

"No way. You were running?"

"Well, kind of." She giggled.

"What do you mean kind of?"

"I mean, I was doing a fast walk."

"You were doing a fast walk? Or you were running?"

"Okay, fine. I wasn't running, and I wasn't doing a fast walk. I was walking really slow at two-and-a-half miles per hour, but I have not worked out in ages, and it really took it out of me."

"Oh, Polly." I giggled. "You are too much."

"I know. I need to get in shape," she moaned. "I was going to go on Weight Watchers, but I figured maybe, just maybe, I would wait for Weight Watchers and start working out first. I mean, you can't do both."

"I think you could do both if you really wanted to."

"Well, you know me. If I try and do both of them at the same time, I won't do either."

"That's true," I agreed. "But you really don't need to lose weight at all."

"I do. I tried to put on my jeans the other day and they were so tight the button popped."

"Oh no, Polly!"

"I know," she moaned. "Can you believe it? I really need to lose weight."

"Can't you just buy bigger jeans?"

"I can, but I don't want to go up another size. I want to be slim and beautiful, like you."

"Polly, you're gorgeous!"

"Yeah, but I don't want to be plus-size-friend gorgeous. I want to be model gorgeous."

"Polly, you're gorgeous just as you are, and trust me, I'm no model."

"Yes, you are," she insisted. "You're the most beautiful girl in town."

"Oh my gosh, Polly, really?" I burst out laughing. "Don't make me choke from laughing so hard, and certainly don't let Monique hear you say that, or she'll kill you."

"Oh, Monique," Polly huffed. "I can't stand her. When she looks in the mirror, it does everything it can to not crack."

And that was why Polly was my best friend. She always had my back.

"Can you come over this evening?" I asked her hopefully.

"This evening, why?"

"Because Jacob Joshua Edwards is coming with his father."

"Oh..." Polly knew all about the deal that my father had made. "Is his brother going to be there, too?"

"Nico?" I was surprised that she brought him up. She hated Nico as much as I hated Jake.

"I was just wondering if he was going to be there, but I mean, I don't really care," she said quickly. "I was just curious. And you know, they say curiosity killed the cat, but I'm not a cat, so—"

"Hey, Polly, what is going on?" I interrupted her ramblings. My friend could be ditzy at times, but this had come out of nowhere.

"What do you mean what's going on? Nothing's going on. I was just saying."

"Do you have a crush on Nico Edwards?"

"Nico Edwards? What? Me? A crush? No way. He'd never be interested in someone like me. He probably dates catwalk models. In fact, I'm sure he does."

"Oh my gosh, Polly, you do have a crush on him," I said softly. "You want to come over then and see him?"

"No, there's no way he'd be interested."

"Girl, you can do so much better than Nico Edwards. Trust me."

"I don't think so. He's so gorgeous," she said. "I hate it. That's why I want to lose weight."

"You don't need to lose weight to get someone like Nico

Edwards. Trust me. If you wanted him, you could have him."

"No, I couldn't. Have you seen the girls he goes on dates with?"

"No, and frankly, I don't care."

"He dates girls even hotter than his brother, and everyone wants to be with his brother, Jake."

"Jake is disgusting. He's a pig."

"You still hate him?"

"Of course I still hate him. You know he's a jerk."

"I mean, I remembered that you didn't like him because what happened again?"

"I told you what happened." I started getting angry just thinking about our running in the past.

"I kind of forgot."

"What do you mean you forgot? How could you forget? He's my sworn enemy!"

"You kind of have a lot of sworn enemies, Tiffany," she pointed out. "I mean, I hate to say it, but..."

I started laughing. "Okay. I mean, maybe I have one or two."

"Maybe you have ten or twenty." She giggled. "Sorry, I don't want to get put on the list, but..." She paused.

"You would never get put on the list, Polly. You're my best friend in the world."

"I know," she said. "And you're my best friend in the world, too."

"I know," I said. "But don't you remember what happened?"

"Not really. Remind me."

"Okay, I was at a boutique, and he was there with one of his girlfriends, and I was trying on a dress, and I came out to show Monique. You know what he said to me?"

"No. What did he say again?"

"He said to me, 'Just because a pig can wear a dress doesn't mean that it should.'"

"Ouch." I could practically hear her cringing. "That wasn't very nice, was it?"

"It was horrible. He's such a fucking jackass. I can't stand him. Just because he thinks he's so rich and hot. Well, I'll tell you he is an asshole."

"But at least you're not marrying him."

"Oh, thank God. If my dad would've even thought to hook me up with him—" I shuddered just thinking about it. "No way in hell I'd ever marry him. I'd cut off his balls before I had anything to do with him."

"Really?" She sounded surprised. "I bet he has gorgeous balls."

"I doubt it very much."

"Well, you've heard the rumors, right?"

"What rumors?"

"That he's packing," she said in a loud whisper.

"You don't have to whisper." I laughed.

"I know," she said. "But I don't want to say the words."

"What? You don't want to say that you've heard that he has a large cock? Trust me, I'm sure that's just a rumor. Any man that has a rumor going that he has a large cock most probably started it himself. I bet you he's two inches long, if that."

"You think so?" She giggled.

"I know so. Come on. He's good-looking, rich, drives a nice car—there's no way he has a big cock on top of all that. No way at all."

"I guess we'll never know." Polly paused. "Unless you think Monique will tell us."

"I don't even want to hear anything about Monique. I

can't wait for her to get out of the house. She is such a bitch."

"Do you think she'll love him and they'll be happy together?"

"Polly, I love you, and I know you always see the best in everyone, but come on now. Do you really think those two are going to fall in love? Each one is a bigger user than the other one. That marriage is doomed. I almost feel bad for them."

"Oh, Tiffany." She giggled. "It's not that bad. They might fall in love. Maybe it won't be so bad."

"Yeah, it will be, but hey, come over and keep me company."

"Are you sure your dad won't mind?"

"Who cares if he minds? I just can't deal with all of these people by myself."

"Okay," she relented. "I can be there in an hour."

"Perfect. Wear something nice, okay?"

"What do you mean by nice?"

"I mean a sexy dress."

"Why?"

"Okay. Maybe not sexy, but what's something that you think will get Nico's blood racing?" I giggled.

"Oh my gosh, I'm not going to make a pass at Nico, Tiffany! That's ridiculous."

"You don't have to make a pass at Nico. We just have to show Jake and Nico that just because we're not on their hookup list doesn't mean that we're not equally hot."

"True," she said. "Okay. I'll see you later. Bye."

"Bye." I hung up and walked to my closet. I had no idea why I wanted Jake to find me attractive. Maybe because I knew it would give me a certain satisfaction to have him drooling over me, knowing he could never have me.

THREE

"Oh, Polly, I'm so thankful you're here." I hugged my best friend as she entered the house. Her long blond hair was curled in loose ringlets, and her cheeks were dusted with a shimmering gold bronzer. She looked amazing if slightly overdone for an at-home dinner.

"Hey, are they here yet?" She looked around, and I could see a heavy layer of shimmering blue eyeshadow on her eyes. I bit my tongue to stop from laughing. Polly looked like she was ready for a nightclub. She had understood the assignment, but maybe she had gone a bit over the top.

"You mean Jacob, Nico, and their father?" I shuddered. "Not yet, thank God."

"Oh, okay. Does your dad know I'm coming?"

"No." I grinned.

"Oh, Tiffany, why didn't you tell him?"

"It's fine. He's not going to turn you away."

"He's turned me away plenty of other times."

"It's fine," I said. "Trust me, he's only concentrating on Monique right now. He needs for this to work out."

"But it's already agreed upon, right?"

"Yeah," I shrugged, "I guess so. I don't know why I'm needed at this dinner."

"Yeah," she said, "it's kind of crazy. You read about this stuff happening in the old days, but you never actually think that it's going to happen to someone you know."

"What do you mean?"

"Like an arranged marriage." She looked wistful. "Though sometimes I kind of wish that I was in an arranged marriage."

"What? Why?"

"Just so I'd have someone to marry." Her blue eyes were sad. "I mean, let's be real. I don't exactly have many prospects."

"Polly, are you joking? Guys fawn over you."

"Yeah, but only because my father's rich, not because they actually want me."

I grabbed her by the shoulders. "Polly, I'm not going to accept this talk. Okay? You are absolutely gorgeous. And you've always been gorgeous. I don't know why you don't see that."

"You have to say that. You're my best friend."

"I am your best friend, but you know I'm brutally honest, right?"

"Yeah. That's true." She wrinkled her nose and laughed. "I mean maybe if I lost ten or twenty or thirty pounds, I'd be gorgeous."

She was curvy in all the right places. She was absolutely stunning, in fact. But if she was comparing herself to the stick-thin models that she saw in magazines, of course she'd feel that way.

"Girl, if you really want to lose some weight, which I don't think you need to do, then we should go running together," I suggested. "I could stand to lose ten pounds as well. Let's say we both go on a diet. Yeah," I nodded to myself, "that will help me because if I'm going to run away, then—"

"You what?"

"Shh!" I grinned. "I didn't tell you, did I?"

"What do you mean, run away?" She laughed. "You're twenty-five, Tiffany. Wouldn't it just be moving out?"

"You don't move out in this family, you know that. I've tried several times to leave, and you know my father. He, well, he just won't let me."

"That's just so weird." She shook her head. "I just don't get it."

"Of course you get it. Your dad won't let you move out, either."

"I know, but that's because I'm an heiress." She bit down on her lower lip. "Sorry." She winced. "I didn't mean to rub that in your face."

"Girl, don't worry. The last thing I would want to be is an heiress. I mean, I'm glad for you that you are. One of us has to have some money, but girl, could you imagine if I was an heiress? The men that would be after me! I'd probably have to become some sort of an assassin or something."

"You're funny, Tiffany." She giggled, her blond curls bouncing around her face.

"What? It's true." I heard the sound of a car approaching the house, and I grabbed her hand. "Hurry. We need to get out of here."

"Why?"

"I think they've arrived. And I certainly don't want to be the ones greeting them at the door."

We hurried to the library. I closed the heavy carved wooden door behind us, and we sat down. "I've been reading this really good book recently." I went over to the table and picked up the leatherbound book I'd been reading earlier.

"Um, you know I love books, but now is not the time to talk about them," she said. "I want to talk about Nico and our plan for the night."

"What plan for the night?"

"You said you were going to help me flirt or something?" She looked at me hopefully.

"So you *are* interested in him?"

"I mean, I wouldn't say I'm interested in him so much as I'm interested in seeing if he's interested in me."

"Oh, Polly." I laughed at her. Polly was a true romantic, and she took any and every opportunity she had to try and find romance in her life, even if it was at what I considered a dinner for my enemies. I couldn't stand Nico, I couldn't stand Jacob, and I couldn't stand their father. But if Polly wanted to try and get her flirt on with Nico, who was I to say no? And maybe, just maybe, it would make the evening more interesting. Otherwise, it would just be my dad fawning embarrassingly over the Edwardses.

This whole situation was embarrassing—and infuriating. I felt like we were begging them for help. Worse was knowing that I had ideas that could help but being ignored because I was just a woman.

I sighed. "Fine, we'll get your flirt on with Nico."

"And will you flirt with Jacob?" She grinned.

"Oh, ew! One, that would be totally inappropriate because he's about to marry my sister, and two, I absolutely can't stand him."

"But wouldn't that make it even more enjoyable?"

"What do you mean even more enjoyable?"

"Making him fall for you when you're not even interested in him? Man, that would be like watching the mighty Midas fall or something."

"I didn't think about it like that," I said, "but I just don't know if that's a good idea. Plus, if Monique were to catch me flirting with him, she'd kill me."

"Monique's a bitch." She shrugged. "I hate to say it, she's your sister and all, but I just don't even know how you guys have the same DNA. How did you come out so wonderful and she come out as such an airhead?" She rolled her eyes. "She's so ditzy and fake."

"I know," I agreed. "She's awful. But hey, she'll be Jacob Joshua Edwards's problem soon." I giggled. "Actually, maybe that's all the payback that he needs. Living with Monique will be hell on earth."

Polly shuddered. "Yeah. I'd hate to live with her. Even when we had sleepovers when we were younger, I hated seeing her. She was always so mean. And her friends were even meaner."

"I know. It's like they created the meanest girls in the world club."

The doorbell rang, and Polly's eyes widened. "Oh my gosh. They're officially here."

"Okay." I took a deep breath. "We'll stay in here for ten minutes, and then we'll go out to the dining room. I don't want any of them to think that we rushed out to greet them like they were some sort of royalty."

And by *them*, I meant Jake.

FOUR

The house was ominously quiet as we waited in the library. Each second that passed felt like an eternity.

"Where do you think they went?" Polly asked me, a slightly scared expression on her face.

I didn't know why she was scared. It wasn't like Jake and his father had come to take over her family home.

"I don't know where they've gone." I was a little perplexed.

All of a sudden, I wished we weren't hiding out in the library. I should have been brave enough to venture to the front door and welcome them. I should have gone out to meet the enemy like a soldier heading into battle. I should've let him know that I wasn't the surrendering type.

Instead, I'd retreated like a coward. I chewed on my lower lip, annoyed at myself.

"You okay, Tiffany?" Polly gave my arm a gentle squeeze.

"I'm okay." I nodded. "I just don't think it was the right move to stay in here."

I was about to say more when I heard a knock on the

door. I froze, and I could see that Polly had gone slightly pale.

"Who is it?" I called out.

The door opened, and there stood Jake. He stared at me through dark, foreboding eyes, and I looked back at him, taking in his appearance. It wasn't right that he should be so good-looking. How could someone so cruel be so attractive?

"I came to see where everyone was," he said as he stepped into the library and walked toward myself and Polly.

"I'm Jake." He held his hand out toward me.

I ignored it. "I know."

"Good." He didn't seem fazed by my rudeness. He looked around the library. "Impressive." He looked at the books and then at me. "Do you read a lot?"

"Yes," I snapped.

"Shame," he said in a low voice.

"What do you mean, shame?"

"I mean, it's a shame that you like to read because once I take over this house, this library will be gone." He smirked at me. "Books. Who needs them these days? There are computers and Kindles."

"What?" I gasped in shock. What he was saying was a sacrilege to paperbacks and hardbacks all over the world. "There's nothing like reading a book, a physical book," I insisted, horrified.

"Wouldn't know." He shrugged.

"What?" Polly spoke up. "You've never read a real book?"

"What do you think?" He looked at her and raised an eyebrow, then looked back at me as if to say, *Is your friend as dumb as you?* Or maybe he was saying, *Are you as dumb as your friend?*

"You won't get rid of this library." I shook my head. "I won't let you."

"And who are you to stop me?" He walked past me toward the large window on the other side of the room. "There's a lot of nice, natural light that comes in here."

"It's dark. How would you know?"

"I can just tell. This window is facing north, and there's always a lot of sun on the north side during the day."

"You think you're smart, don't you?"

"I don't have to think about anything." He flashed me a cold smile. "This will be my house, and I can do with it what I want."

"So, that's how you're going to greet me? You're just going to come in here and tell me that you're taking over my family's library. Not even a, 'How are you doing? Nice to meet you. Nice to see you again. Why, don't you look nice tonight?'" I paused as a smile spread over his face. "What's so funny?"

"You've got a mouth on you, don't you, Tiffany?" He walked up to me, stopping just inches from me. "Boy, do you have a mouth on you." He stared at my lips. "Very nice."

I didn't bother responding to him. Instead, I looked over at Polly, who looked like she wished she were anywhere but here. I almost wished the same thing. She wasn't backing me up and telling him off. Instead, she was submissive.

I realized that as much as I loved her, I couldn't afford to be submissive, not in a situation like this.

I stepped up into Jacob's face. "I'm not scared of you, you know. You might be marrying my sister, and you might be saving my family's business, but you don't own me. I can do whatever I want. I can come and go as I please. I can—"

"When you're in this house, you'll do as I say," he said firmly.

"Who do you think you are?"

"Who do I think *I* am? Who do *you* think I am, Tiffany, that you think you can talk to me like that?"

"You think I should be scared of you? Do you think I should bow down to you?" I gave him a little curtsy. "Am I to be your servant, your maid, your piece on the side?"

"My piece on the side?" He raised an eyebrow and grinned. "Are you offering those services?"

"Never." I took a step back. "I'd rather live in the street than be touched by you."

"Really?" His eyes were glinting now.

It was weird how gray they looked when he was thinking. Unfortunately for me, I couldn't tell what he was thinking. Was he impressed by my bravado? Did he think I was a fool? Did he want to get rid of me?

My hands were trembling, and I put them behind my back. The last thing I wanted him to see was how much he affected me, and it wasn't just because I hated him. Part of me enjoyed being in his space. I had a physical reaction to being near him. I hated it, but I couldn't deny it.

"This conversation is getting old. I think we should go to dinner." He walked past me again toward the door. "We can talk later."

"I don't need to talk to you. I'm not part of this transaction."

He paused and looked over his shoulder at me.

"Oh, but that's where you're wrong, Tiffany. You're the reason for this transaction in the first place."

FIVE

Polly looked like she'd just seen a ghost. "Well, what was that all about?" she asked me, looking at me through narrowed eyes.

"I have no idea."

"Why did he say that you're the very reason for the transaction?"

"I don't know. But thanks for that just now," I said, a little bit annoyed.

"What?" She sighed. "Oh, I'm sorry. I didn't mean to freeze up like that. But you know I'm absolutely awful in situations like this."

"Yeah, but I needed you to have my back just now. He basically steamrolled me."

"I know, girl, but I just didn't know what to say. I mean, he's gorgeous."

"Yeah, he's gorgeous. But he's an asshole."

"Yeah, but he's sort of an asshole that you don't mind."

"What does that mean, Polly?"

"I know. I'm crazy." She sighed. "But do you think he's really going to get rid of the library?"

"He said he was going to, and I don't have any reason to disbelieve him."

"Maybe he was just saying that to get a reaction."

"Why would he want a reaction from me?" I shook my head. "I mean, he and I, we have nothing. He's here to marry my sister. If anyone, he should be trying to get a reaction from her."

"True. But she wouldn't care if he got rid of the library."

"No. The only thing she'd care about is if he got rid of the mirrors."

Polly laughed at that. "Tiffany, don't. That's horrible."

I laughed a little, too. "Hey, I never said I was nice." The laughter died away. "But I guess we should get to the dining room before he gets rid of who knows what else."

"Do you think your dad will let him?"

"My dad doesn't care. He just wants the money."

"I really wonder how you're related to them," Polly said as we left the room.

"You're telling me. Sometimes I feel like Cinderella in a story gone wrong."

"Yeah," she said. "He has to be your dad, right? Because your mom was your mom."

"Yeah, my mom was my mom."

"I know you miss your mom, girl." Polly gave me a sad smile.

"Honestly, I barely remember her." I shrugged. "I was so young when she died."

"I know. But imagine if she were here. She wouldn't want this for you or Monique."

"I like to think that if my mom were here, she would have divorced my father a long time ago." My lips twisted in a sneer. "He's a good-for-nothing. I hate to say that about my own dad, but gosh, I would never want to be with someone like him."

"Me either. Monique would not want to be with someone like him, either, right?" Polly said.

"Who knows? Monique is an idiot."

"It's so sad. I just don't know how you guys can be sisters," Polly said.

"Me neither. But let's not talk about that now. Let's go and face the music."

"We don't really have to go," Polly said. "Hopefully. I mean, it's not like you're marrying the man."

"I'm not, but this is my home. It's been in my family for generations. And I'm not going to let him just destroy everything, especially not the library."

"You still think your grandfather hid something here?" Polly asked me, a question in her eyes.

I nodded. "I do. I know it's folklore. But..." I shrugged. "My grandma believed it."

"But your grandma was kind of out of it, right?"

"She had dementia," I admitted. "And yeah, so she said things that didn't always make sense, but I remember there was one thing she used to say all the time."

Polly looked at me as we made our way toward the dining room. "What was that?"

"'Everything that glitters is not gold, but all that's gold is yours.'"

"What do you think she meant by that?"

"No idea," I said. "But there were so many things she said and so many secrets I think she was hiding, and I just want to get to the bottom of it all. And I think the answers lie in the library."

"Why, though?"

"There are so many books, and my grandma told me she

and my granddad met at the library. Remember? They used to exchange notes."

"Yeah, but..."

"I just think it has a meaning okay?" I pressed my lips together as we entered the dining room.

My father was standing at one side drinking a gin. My sister was laughing at something that Jake was saying. Nico was standing next to Jake, his face emotionless. I saw Polly look over at him, her eyes hovering on his face for a moment too long, and I knew that her crush went far deeper than I'd realized.

"There you are, Tiffany." My father smiled politely, but it didn't reach his eyes. He was mad at me. He thought I should have been there to greet our guests. He was standing next to Jake's dad, who was staring at me as well. There was a different look in his eyes.

"Good evening, Polly." Jake's father, Brian, looked me over. He was a tall, handsome man, with jet black hair and steely blue eyes, but there was something austere and creepy about his expression, and I wondered why so many women fell for his charm. He looked like a psychopath to me.

"Good evening." I gave him a pointed look. "This is my best friend, *Polly*."

"Oh, yes, yes, yes," Jake's dad corrected himself. "I meant good evening, Tiffany." He smiled, but the expression in his cold eyes never changed.

"Uh-huh." I looked at Polly. "That was weird. Why would he make a mistake like that?" I could see in Polly's face that she was confused as well. I didn't bother lowering my voice, either. I wasn't embarrassed that he would hear me calling him out.

"Hi." Polly waved timidly. "I am Polly. I'm Tiffany's best friend. I hope you don't mind that I came."

"If we did mind, would you leave?" Nico approached us. His green eyes flickered over me dismissively before turning to Polly. He looked her up and down for a few seconds, smirked, and turned to his father.

I could see Polly blushing; her face was a deep shade of red, and I really hoped she would get it together. "Well, it wouldn't really be up to you, would it?" I said to Nico, speaking up for myself and my best friend. "Seeing as you don't live here, and this is not your house."

"But it will be my family's house soon," he said, smirking at me. "And as such, I think I have a say in who comes and goes, don't you?"

I looked over at Jake, who was staring at me now. Monique had her hand on his shoulder. And for some reason, that made me furious. What was she thinking? Didn't she understand that this family did not have our best interests at heart? Though in my heart of hearts, I knew she didn't care.

"I think it's time for us to eat," my father said. He rang a little bell, and two servants stepped in carrying platters. We all took our places at the dining room table. Polly was on my left-hand side and, surprisingly, Jake was on my right.

"You don't have to sit next to me." I sniffed at him. "I'm not going to run away."

"I didn't think you would," he said. "But I wanted to make sure that you ate all your vegetables."

"Excuse me?"

"I mean, there's no dessert for a girl who doesn't eat her veggies, right?"

I stared at him for a few seconds, wondering what the hell he was talking about. I wanted to retort something back at him, but I felt like that was what he wanted—and I didn't want to give him what he wanted.

Instead, I turned to Polly. "Thanks for coming."

"No worries," she said. She looked across the table at Nico and lowered her voice. "He can't stand me. Can he?"

"Why do you say that?"

"Because he looks at me as if..." She sighed. "It doesn't matter. I wouldn't want to be a part of his family anyway."

"You got that right, girl. Neither would I."

"Well, you will be, kind of," she said. "When Monique marries Jake, you'll be their sister."

"Ugh." I shuddered. "I'll never be their sister, trust me."

"But Tiffany, you—"

"Polly," I said, lowering my voice, "I have a plan. And let's just say the last thing that Jake and his family will get is my house and my inheritance."

Polly swallowed hard and nodded. I could tell she was worried about what I just said, and I knew that she would try and talk me out of my idea, but I wouldn't let her. This was about self-respect. This was about life or death. This was about who I was as a person. I may not have been a princess in a castle. I may not have been a queen waiting for her king. But I was a damsel in distress. The only difference between me and the damsel in fairytales is I wasn't waiting for Prince Charming to come and save me. I was willing to grab the sword and cut off the dragon's head myself. And as I turned to look at Jake, I knew that he was the dragon that I had to slay.

SIX

"So, Jake is handsome, isn't he?" Polly said to me as we left the dining room after dinner.

"He's okay." I frowned at her. "Don't tell me you have a crush on Jake now?"

"Of course not!" She shook her head quickly. "I mean, they're both handsome, but Nico just has that little bit extra, you know."

"As far as I'm concerned, they both suck."

"I mean, they do, and their dad, *eww*," Polly said under her breath.

"Why are you whispering?"

"Because the walls have ears, and I sure don't want them hearing me talking about them."

"It's fine, and no one cares either way. And did you see my sister? She was flirting with Jake *and* Nico *and* their dad."

"I know." Polly sounded wistful. "It must be nice to have self-confidence like that."

"She's a slut." I rolled my eyes and then sighed deeply. "Wanna go to the library, seeing as this is possibly one of the last times we'll get to go in?"

"Oh, don't be so melodramatic. He won't really tear down the library."

"Do you think?"

"Girl, I do."

Tears welled in my eyes. "You know, my mom loved this library. She used to bring me here when I was a kid, and she used to read me stories and tell me about adventures we would go on together when I got older." I bit my lower lip to stop myself from crying.

"I'm sorry." Polly touched me softly on the arm. "I know you miss her."

"I do. I miss her so much." My mother had been dead for twenty years, and while each day had gotten slightly better, the grief had never left me, especially seeing as my dad hadn't even waited six months after she died to get married again. He'd been married five times since she'd passed away, and I was pretty sure he was moving on to his next wife soon, a horrible woman by the name of Angelina.

"Do you want to talk about it?" Polly said gently.

"No." I squared my shoulders. "There's no point in me getting sad and crying and feeling sorry for myself. I feel like I'm Cinderella in a super-twisted version of the story, only my evil stepsister is my real sister, and my father is the wicked stepmother. And Prince Charming," I laughed bitterly, "well, there is no Prince Charming in this story. There's only another evil villain."

"But maybe there will be a Prince Charming," Polly said softly. "Maybe you'll meet someone and he'll whisk you away, and..."

I shook my head. "I don't believe in fairy tales. And honestly, I don't need a prince to whisk me away. I can save myself. I mean, this situation is pathetic. It happened because my family needed saving. And look, what good is it doing to any of us? I mean, maybe Polly..."

"What?"

"I'm sorry. I'm just confused and upset. I meant to say Monique."

"I was wondering," Polly said, with a rueful laugh. "I mean, I'm not doing anything to help, and I certainly have not got any princes coming after me."

"Nico's not a prince, girl. Trust me."

"You were saying earlier that you thought I should go after him."

"For fun, not for anything serious. That family is trouble, mark my words. The craziness is just getting started. I have a bad feeling, Polly."

I sank into the nearest chair and buried my face in my hands, feeling literally ill. My stomach was queasy, and my skin felt clammy. I couldn't believe that my beloved sanctuary, the only place I went to feel comforted and warm, was going to be taken away from me. It was the final straw. I was done. I was absolutely done with my family, and I was done with Jake. I was going to make him pay because I knew he didn't care about the library. This house was huge, and he could have his pick of rooms. He was doing this to spite me. He was doing this to let me know that he controlled me and my life. Well, I'd show him. No one controlled me. No one could hurt me.

In fact, I'd play a little game of my own, and we'd see who would come out on top.

SEVEN

"I'm going to be such a beautiful bride, aren't I?" Monique walked into my bedroom as I was getting ready for the party. She spun around in her long, flowing black dress then paused to admire herself in my mirror. "I am the most beautiful woman I've ever seen," she murmured, toying with the diamond necklace around her throat.

I stared at her in disbelief. How could she be so vain? She looked down at the front of her dress and squeezed her breasts together. They were practically falling out, but I knew that's exactly how she wanted it. "I am a fucking bombshell. I could have any man that I wanted." She turned to me, a look of pity on her face. "I'm sorry." She wrinkled her nose. "I guess can't all be gorgeous, can we?"

"I guess not," I said, rolling my eyes as I grabbed my dress. "Well, I'm going to change now and try and pretty myself up. Even if I do look like a pig."

"No, you don't look like a pig." She paused and tapped her finger carefully against her forehead. "A cow, maybe."

"Excuse me?"

"Moo. Moo." She laughed. Why she was so mean and

nasty? What had I ever done to her? "You and Polly can just play in the corner or something and leave early. This is my engagement party, and I want to ensure that I am the belle of the ball and you two don't distract anyone with your stupid, childish behavior."

"I'm twenty-five years old, Monique." I glared at her. "And I'll do whatever I want whenever I want. This is my house just as much as it is yours."

"No, it's not." She shook her head. "My fiancé will be taking over the family business and this house, so it'll be his house and my house, not yours. You'll be lucky if I even let you stay." She tilted her head up. "Now be a dear and zip me up at the back." She turned around.

"What?"

"I said zip me up at the back, or do you not understand English, Moo Moo?"

I grabbed the zip at the bottom of her back and pulled it up. It wasn't going. She wasn't fat, but the dress was too tight and small for her.

"This is not going to—"

"Zip me up!" she snapped.

"Breathe in."

"I don't need—"

"Breathe in." She breathed in, and I quickly pulled it up about halfway. "This is not going to work. You're too—"

I was going to say *fat*, but I knew how vindictive she could be. Who knew what she would do? I'd be out of this hell hole sooner or later, but I wanted to go of my own accord, not because Monique ran me off. I didn't need her focusing her spite on me.

"I don't think it's going to go up, Monique."

"Do my dress up, or I will burn the books in the library before we change—"

"Fine." I thought quickly. "If you get out of the dress, I can let out the seam slightly. That might give us a bit more room." I looked at my watch. "I don't have much time."

"That's not—"

"If you want to wear that dress, Monique, take it off and let me fix it."

"Fine," she said. "Unzip me."

I unzipped her. The dress fell to the ground, and she stepped out of it. She was wearing a thong, no bra, and tall black heels. She turned around and smirked at me, her peroxide-blond hair shimmering under the ceiling light.

"Yes, this is what perfection looks like." She gave me a dismissive look. "I'm going to my bedroom. Bring me the dress when you're done."

"You're welcome."

She didn't reply. She just walked out of my room and down the hall, practically naked. I stared after her for a few seconds and then pulled my trusty Singer sewing machine out of the closet. I wasn't exactly a seamstress, but I knew how to sew basic things. I'd do my best with the dress. Part of me was tempted to take my scissors and cut the dress up, but I knew that I couldn't have her damaging the library or the books. They were my only connection to my mother. I could remember being a young child and sitting with her on the couch reading. She'd loved me. She'd absolutely adored me, and she'd love reading, and that was the only real memory I had of her.

I quickly got to work on the dress, praying that it would work. I didn't have much time to get ready myself, but it didn't really matter what I looked like. I grabbed my phone and texted Polly to make sure that she was on her way. I sighed when I got her response saying that she was going to be late. That sucked. I'd be all by myself without a friend in the world, but I knew how to handle myself, and if I didn't enjoy the party, I'd disappear. Once I'd made my own entrance, no one could make me stay.

I took my foot off the pedal and hurried to Monique's room with the dress. I didn't bother knocking and walked in. She was sitting at her vanity, her back to me, on the phone.

"I wish she were here already so we could fuck," she was saying. "My pussy is—"

I cleared my throat so she'd know I was there. She turned and glared at me. "Don't you knock, you imbecile?"

"I thought you wanted your dress, but I guess you're on the phone?" I raised an eyebrow. She stared at me, not even embarrassed.

"Leave my dress and go." She turned around dismissively, and I dropped her dress on the bed. "Thanks."

"You're welcome," I muttered under my breath as I walked to the door. I stopped outside the door and listened.

"Yes, I want to fuck you badly, too," she said. "Soon." She giggled. I rolled my eyes and hurried back to my room. So Jake was calling her already, huh? I should have known that he was a dog. All he wanted was sex, and I should have known that Monique would give it up even to a man who obviously didn't love her or even care for her. He just wanted the power. He just wanted to take over our family business, and everyone was giving it to him so easily. My dad didn't care. Monique didn't care. No one cared about the legacy of the family. No one cared about our house or the library. I bit down on my lower lip. I couldn't allow myself to get upset. I had to go through with the party and pretend everything was okay.

I had to think of a way to ruin their plans because I needed to save this house. I put on a dress that I'd found at a department store. It wasn't expensive or even particularly new, but it suited me. It was a midnight blue with sparkling sequins. It was a bit old-fashioned, but I liked it. I slipped on my black heels and stared at my reflection in the mirror. My eyeshadow made my eyes look green tonight even though they were really hazel. I had a gold bronzer dusted on my cheekbones, and I looked quite pretty and adult. I reminded myself of my mother.

I had only three photographs of her that I kept near and dear to me, and I spoke to her every day. Sometimes she even came to me in my dreams, which I thought was odd because I couldn't remember a full conversation I'd ever had with her in real life.

I could hear the music and people talking in the house. I had to go and mingle before my father came to my room and told me off. I headed downstairs, texting Polly as I went: **Hurry. Mayday. Mayday. Hurry!**

I entered the large ballroom on the main floor and was shocked by the number of people that there. I'd known it was going to be a large party, but I still hadn't expected so many. People were drinking champagne and wine and laughing as the servants weaved through the crowd with trays of drinks and canapés. I looked around to see if there was anyone I'd want to talk to. I saw Nico standing in the far corner with his father. Our eyes met for a moment, and then he looked away dismissively. I hoped that Polly would soon get over her crush on him. His father looked cold and austere as usual, staring at his phone. He was an asshole, but his sons were even bigger assholes.

Monique was standing next to my father, a glass of champagne in her hand, laughing about something. She had on diamond earrings that I'd never seen before, and I wondered where she'd gotten them from. I was about to go and get myself a drink when I felt the presence of someone next to me.

"Thinking?" said a deep voice.

I looked up at Jake and rolled my eyes. "No, I was talking."

"In your head?"

"No, I was talking out loud out."

He chuckled slightly, his green eyes gazing over me, flittering up and down my body, making me grow warm. A warm smile spread across his lips. "You clean up nice."

"Likewise," I said, looking him over and trying to sound bored. He was wearing a tuxedo, and he looked absolutely gorgeous. It was unfair that the nastiest men were always so handsome. He was like the devil in an Armani suit.

He grabbed two glasses of champagne from a passing server and handed one to me. "So, what are your plans for the evening?"

"I think my plans for the evening are to not kill myself, to be quite honest," I replied. "Yours?"

"Wouldn't mind fucking," he said, staring me directly in the eyes.

"Okay." I took another sip of champagne, trying not to squirm under the intensity of his gaze. "I'm sure Monique will be happy to help."

"I'm sure she would." He took a step closer to me.

"You're a really nasty man, aren't you?"

"Depends how you're using the word nasty." He lowered his voice. "Why? Do you want to know just how nasty I can be?"

"Are you flirting with me?" I raised an eyebrow at him. "I know you're not flirting with me."

He shook his head. "Flirting would imply a level of

interest that I don't have in you. So no, I'm not flirting. But I did have a question for you, Tiffany."

"What's your question?"

"I think—" He stopped and looked around the room. "I think that we should discuss it somewhere else."

"Discuss what somewhere else?"

"My proposition."

"What proposition? You just said you had a question. How is a question a proposition? How—"

"You need your mouth stuffed. You know that, right?"

"What's that supposed to mean?"

"You need your mouth stuffed so you can't talk so much crap."

"Stuffed?" I took another sip of my champagne. "Stuffed with what?"

"I can think of several things I'd like to stuff your mouth with." He winked. "Maybe a silk scarf or some strawberries or oysters or—" He looked down at his crotch. "Nine inches of...you know."

Involuntarily, I followed his gaze toward his crotch. I could see that he was hard, and I swallowed. He wasn't really nine inches, was he? He couldn't be, I thought as I looked back at his face.

He grinned. "Wouldn't you like to know?" It was like he could read my mind.

"Not really." I scoffed. "Had bigger, had better. Don't need you."

"Liar," he said softly as he ran his fingers down my arm. "I doubt you've had bigger or better, or anything close to what I offer." He blew into my ear. "I could make you cum right here, right now, Tiffany Newton."

My eyes widened, and I took a step back. "Don't touch me and don't blow in my ear."

"Or what? You'll cum?" He chuckled and looked around the room. "Follow me if you know what's good for you."

He turned and walked away from me.

I stood there for a few seconds, unsure what to do. I wasn't one to back down from a challenge, but Jake seemed like bad news. But then he didn't know who he was messing with, either. An idea suddenly popped into my head, an idea that could bring him to his knees.

I downed my champagne quickly and put the empty glass on a nearby table. I swallowed hard and walked back toward the exit of the room. I'd see what he had to say. I'd see what his proposition was, and then I'd make a decision.

I didn't know if I was being brave or just stupid, but I had very little to lose. That thought was all I needed to make my way out of the room. When I got outside, I looked to the left and to the right; I'd lost him. But no, there he was, standing at the end of the corridor beckoning me toward him. I started walking, wondering what I was walking toward.

EIGHT

I'd almost reached Jake when he turned and walked into another room that was full of people.

"What are you playing at, Jacob?" I muttered as I followed him. I'd thought he wanted to talk to me alone. There was nothing I hated more than feeling like I was being played. He handed me a vodka martini, and I stared at him in surprise. How did he know I'd been drinking them while getting ready for the party?

"You can call me Jake, you know," he said, a smirk on his face. His dazzling green eyes seemed to pierce into my soul. As I stared at his too-handsome face, I wondered if he were some sort of fallen angel, sent to earth to annoy the living daylights out of me.

"I'd rather call you by your Christian name, Jacob." I waited to see if he would burst into flames at my use of the word "Christian."

No such luck.

"Well, Tiff..." He paused and laughed, a low rumbling sound that made my stomach flutter. I hated how my body betrayed me when I was around him.

"My name is Tiffany."

"But I think I prefer Tiff, so I'll go with that." Smugness dripped off his tongue.

"I don't care what you prefer, Jacob Joshua Edwards."

"Ooh, you're saying my full name now. I kind of like it." He took a step closer to me, and my heart started racing as if it were in the rapid-beat Olympics.

"What are you doing?" I said as he leaned down and touched my lips with his thumb. His thumb felt warm and slightly rough as he caressed my lower lip. I swallowed hard.

"What do you think I'm doing?"

I stepped back, swatting his hand away. "You can't touch me like that."

"Why? Does it make you scared that the big bad wolf might eat you up?"

"I'm not a little girl. I'm not scared of big bad wolves. I am twenty-five years old. And you can't touch me like that because it's not appropriate."

"Okay," he said, stepping back. "If that's what you want."

"That is what I want." I glared at him, wondering how he could be so confident and smug when faced with my death stare. Men richer than him had faltered in the face of my stares. Even teachers had stepped back, but he didn't seem to be bothered at all.

"So, then, I will bid you adieu, Miss Tiffany."

"You're leaving?" I looked at him with surprise. The room was packed and the party had just begun.

"I'm not leaving. But I shall go and talk to other women that do want to get to know me better."

"Psh, I doubt there's many of them." I rolled my eyes. "And also that's highly inappropriate given that this is your—"

"It's a pity, you know," he interrupted.

"What's a pity?"

"That you're not interested in calling me Jake. I think I could lighten you up quite a bit. You're a spitfire, aren't you?"

"I don't need to lighten up, thank you very much."

"Oh, I think you do." He chuckled.

"What's so funny?" I snapped, wanting to be inside of his head.

"I don't think you want to know." He shook his head and licked his lips.

"Tell me." I knew I should have just let him go. I knew that I shouldn't engage with him. He was an asshole, a jerk, my sworn enemy. But I just couldn't stop myself.

"I think there are three things you need in your life right now," he said, staring at my lips.

I swallowed hard. "Oh yeah, and what are they?"

"I don't think I should tell you. I think I should show you. Don't they say that actions speak louder than words?"

I took a slow sip of my vodka martini. "Fine, show me."

"Really?" His eyes sparkled and widened almost imperceptibly. "You surprise me."

"Why do I surprise you?"

"I thought you were all talk and no action."

"I'm not."

"Then leave with me."

"We can't just leave," I objected. "The party has just begun."

"Yes, the party has just started, but I can do whatever I want." He shrugged. "I am Jake Edwards, after all."

"But the party is for you."

"No," he said, "the party is not for me. The party is for your sister."

"But—"

"Shh." He pressed a finger against my lips and winked. "Come with me, Tiffany, if you dare."

He moved his finger from my lips and walked away. I stood there immobile for a couple of seconds. He didn't even look back to see if I was following as he made his way through the packed room. People tried to talk to him, but he didn't stop. Finally, he reached the entrance of the hallway and walked out.

I wasn't sure what came over me, but I started walking quickly to catch up. I knew it was crazy, I knew I was asking for trouble, but how could I not follow him? He had dared me, after all.

I made my way to the entrance and looked to the left and then to the right. He was gone, and I didn't know where he was. I took a deep breath and turned to go back into the room.

"I knew you would come." Suddenly he was next to me, his eyes twinkling with laughter.

"Where did you come from? You weren't here just now." I blinked at him in surprise.

"It's a magic trick," he replied. "I'm Houdini. In and out, just like that."

"In and out just like that, huh? Is that your motto in life?" I smirked at him.

"Wouldn't you like to know?" He winked again, more seductively this time.

"No." I shook my head quickly.

"Liar." He grabbed my hand and squeezed it. "I know exactly what you want, Tiffany."

"Excuse me?"

"And I know exactly what you need as well. Come on."

And like a fool, I followed him. This was what happened when you drank too many vodka martinis on an empty stomach. I could hear my father's voice coming from the room that I'd just left, cheering and celebrating. I started to feel a little bit guilty. What the hell was I doing? I knew I was making a huge mistake, but I couldn't stop myself.

"We shouldn't be doing this, Jacob."

"I said to call me Jake."

"We shouldn't be doing this, Jake," I said, even as I continued following him down the hallway.

"There are many things we shouldn't be doing, Tiffany. But we can't let that stop us, can we?" He rounded the corner, me still at his heels.

Three things he'd said I needed, three things I'd said I wanted. I had no idea what they were. But I had to find out, no matter what the cost was.

I almost didn't care that it was his engagement party to my sister. I wanted to bring both Jake and Monique to their knees. They both deserved it.

"So are you going to tell me what you wanted to say?" I followed him into an empty room that none of the family ever really went into that held old antiques.

The smirk on his face annoyed me. His green eyes seemed to be piercing right into my soul, and I had a feeling that I'd made a huge mistake following him into this room.

"Close the door," he ordered.

I didn't move.

"I said close the door, Tiffany."

"I don't have to do what you say. You're not the boss of me."

"Oh, I very much think I am the boss of you."

"In your dreams," I sneered.

"Perhaps," he said. He walked past me and slammed the door closed.

"Why did you close the door?"

"Because you didn't."

"Okay. What are you doing here, Jake? Why am I here?"

"There are three things you need, Tiffany Newton."

"You keep saying that, but you haven't said what they are."

"I'm about to tell you. Be patient."

"I am being patient."

"One," he touched his index finger, "you need good sex. Two," he touched his second finger, "you need to run your family business. And three," he touched his ring finger, "you need to walk on the edge." He stared at me as if challenging me, and then he smiled. "And I can help you with all three."

I scoffed. "Number one, I don't need good sex. Number two, why would I care about running my family business? And number three, people who walk on the edge usually fall. And I don't want to fall, thank you very much."

"Don't want to live on the wild side, Tiffany?"

"No. Do you?"

"I already do." He grinned. "That's why I'm in here with you at my own engagement party."

"Why are you marrying my sister?" I asked. "You don't need her. Your family has money. You're a handsome man."

"So you think I'm handsome?"

"Obviously you're handsome. That doesn't mean I want you."

"I think you do want me. But continue."

"I just don't understand why you're in this situation."

"I have my own reasons."

"What, just so you can fuck Monique?"

"I don't need to marry her to fuck her. Did you see how she acts when she's around me? She can't keep her hands off me." He laughed. "Shit, she'd blow me in front of everyone at this party if I wanted her to."

"And you'd like that?"

He shrugged. "It's got nothing to do with 'like' or 'love.' You should know that."

"I know you don't love her. I don't think you could ever love anyone other than yourself."

His expression grew cold. "You might be right about that. But do you care?"

"What do you mean, do I care?"

"Do you care if I love your sister or not? She doesn't seem to treat you very well, or even like you all that much, going by what she's said to me."

"What has she said to you?" I was curious.

"I don't think you want to know."

"I do, actually. I wouldn't be hurt."

"I don't think you'd be hurt. You seem...hard."

"I seem hard?"

"Yeah." He nodded. "I thought when I first saw you years ago that you would be a soft, easily destructible sort of person. But you're not, are you?"

"No, I'm not. I'm not my sister, and I'm not my father, and I don't back down to anyone."

"Good," he said with a smile.

"Why is that good?"

"Because it wouldn't be fun if it was easy."

I stared at him for a few seconds, wondering what that meant. What was going on here? Why was he here with me? "I don't understand why you're propositioning me when you've already got my sister."

"She's easy." He shrugged. "You, though...you're a challenge."

"Okay, I'm a challenge. You think you can just come into my house, threaten to tear down my library, and then I'm going to sleep with you?"

"Did I say that I wanted to sleep with you?"

"You just said that I need good sex."

"Did I say the good sex was going to be with me?" He raised an eyebrow and shook his head. "You assume many things, Tiffany. And that's your first problem."

"My *first* problem. I suppose that means you think I have more?"

"Oh, I know you have more." He undid his bow tie and started unbuttoning his shirt.

"What are you doing?"

"I hate wearing suits." He threw his bow tie onto the table behind him and undid several buttons, revealing a tan, chiseled chest.

"You're going to take off your jacket and your shirt at a party?"

"No." He shook his head. "Did I take anything off? I just unbuttoned my shirt."

He reached down to the button of his dress pants. Was he really going to take his pants down? Was that why we were here? Did he expect me to give him a blow job? Did he think I was that I was desperate?

"Do you think I'm going to blow you?"

"Blow me?" His lips twitched. "Why? Do you want to blow me?"

"No." Although as I said the word, an idea came to my mind. I could blow him and then take a video of it. Imagine if I showed everyone Jake in the study, getting blown by his sister-in-law. Not even Monique would stand for that. She'd be so embarrassed. It would be amazing. I pulled my phone out of my purse and played with it. He promptly grabbed my hand.

"I know what you're thinking," he said, staring deeply into my eyes.

"Oh?" I blinked innocently. "What am I thinking?"

"Do you think you're going to video me? Do you think that I would let you video me?" He laughed. "You're an amateur. You can't play the games that I play, Tiffany."

"I'm not looking to play any games with you."

"I think you are," he said, his lips coming dangerously close to mine. "I think as much as you hate me, you want me as well." His lips pressed against my neck, and I shivered. He brushed his fingers against the skin on my arm. "I think," he whispered as he kissed along my collarbone, "that you like playing this game. I think that you wouldn't mind getting caught."

"I don't need to get caught."

"I know you don't need to get caught, but I think you'd like to get caught." He stepped back and looked me up and down. "I could have this dress off you within five seconds. I could have you flat on your back, your legs in the air over my shoulders, my mouth on your pussy, fucking you with my tongue. I could have you screaming my name, begging me for more." He winked at me. "I can tell that you're thinking about it, wondering if I would do it. I can tell you're wondering if you would push me away, if you would say no. You wouldn't say no." His beautiful lips curled in an arrogant smile. "No one says no to me."

"Then I would be the first." I kept my voice in control, hoping that my face didn't betray my thoughts, but my gaze dropped to his mouth. What would it feel like to be pleasured by him?

He was right: I did hate him. But he was also right that I was attracted to him. And it would be fun to play and toy with him. It would be fun to be played and toyed with. But I would not let him know that. I would not let him have the upper hand. I had to think carefully about how I was going to play this.

"I find you very attractive, Tiffany."

"And...?"

"Think about my proposition."

"I don't really understand what your proposition is. You just told me that there are three things that I need. What's the proposition?"

"I can help you get all three."

"You can help me get all three? If I want good sex, I can easily get it. If I want to run my family business, well...there are ways. And I don't want to walk on the edge. Why would I want to walk on the edge when I could climb a mountain?"

"Shh..." He pressed a finger against my lips. "You have no idea how dangerously close you are to imploding."

"I don't really know what that means."

"I know you don't." He winked. "And that's why I'm here."

"To help me stop from imploding?"

"No." He chuckled. "I'm not here to stop anything."

I didn't understand what he was talking about or why we were here. I needed to get out of there.

I put my hand on his chest to push him away, but the moment my fingers touched his bare skin, I felt his breath hitch. He hadn't expected me to touch him. He'd thought he had the upper hand.

I pushed his shirt to the side and ran my fingers across his nipples. I leaned forward and kissed his chest and then took his nipple in my mouth. I sucked for a moment, then ran my tongue down toward his belly button. I dropped onto my knees and pressed my mouth against his crotch, feeling his cock growing hard through the material. I smiled to myself. Men were so easy.

I stared up at him with wide, innocent eyes. He stared back, his own eyes dark and veiled. He was shaken; I'd gotten to him. I pressed the palm of my hand against his cock and squeezed, and he groaned softly.

I stood up. "There are three things you need as well, Jake."

"Are you going to tell me what those are?"

"Maybe one day." I winked at him, then lifted my dress up. I pulled my panties down, stepped out of them, and slipped them into his pocket as I leaned forward and kissed him on the cheek. "Have a good evening, Jake. Don't think about me too much."

I bit on his earlobe and tugged slightly. He gasped and grabbed my hand, but I pulled away.

"You've got a piece of me to keep you for the night. And trust me, that's all you're ever going to have."

I spun around and left the room, closing the door behind me, and hurried down the corridor before he could catch up with me. I couldn't believe I'd given him my panties, but the look on his face had made it worth it. His expression had told me that I now had the upper hand, and that's just how I liked it. He'd thought he was bringing me to my knees, but I was bringing him to his. He was not going to have the upper hand.

I wondered what he would do with my panties—if he'd sniff them, if he'd use them to pleasure himself, if he'd throw them away.

It didn't matter. I knew he'd been shocked by what I'd

done. Frankly, I was shocked myself. But I felt a freeness, a crazy sense of liberation, as I walked down the corridor and back into the ballroom. Monique was chatting to two women, showing off a diamond ring on her hand that I hadn't seen before. Her lips curled in disdain when she saw me.

I just smiled at her and thought, *You're going down.*

NINE

I looked away from Monique and around the room. There were so many people, yet I felt like I was the only one there. I wished that Polly would hurry up. She would absolutely not believe what I'd just done.

Out of the corner of my eye, I saw Monique walk toward me. What was she thinking? Normally, she'd ignore me at an event like this.

"Why are you wearing that dress?" she hissed, looking me up and down.

"What's wrong with my dress?"

She looked at my neckline. "You're almost showing your breasts."

"And?" I shrugged.

"I thought you didn't like looking like a slut."

"I look like you, though, don't I?" I gave her a lazy smile, and I could tell it pissed her off. I liked making people angry, especially people like Monique and Jake.

"You think you're going to upstage me, don't you?" She crossed her arms over her chest. "In your slutty dress, but you can't upstage me. I'm a blond bombshell. Don't you know that blondes have more fun?"

"You're a peroxide blonde," I sneered. "Give it a couple of hours and your roots will start showing."

"You're a bitch," she said.

"You ain't seen nothing yet, Monique."

I walked away, my heart racing even faster. I couldn't believe that I'd finally said how I felt to her, but it felt amazing. I'd humored her for years, and I was sick of it. I didn't know why she'd hated me all our lives, but I wasn't going to put up with it anymore. I was just about to head to my bedroom when my father rang a bell.

"Attention everyone, attention!" he shouted into the room.

People were still talking, so he rang it louder. When he still didn't get people's attention, he grabbed a megaphone. I paused. He wasn't seriously going to speak through one of those, was he?

"Attention, everyone," he shouted, and the room hushed. "Now that I have your attention, let us make it through to the dining room where we shall feast on lobster and steak."

I rolled my eyes at no one in particular. I wondered if Jake was there and what he was thinking about my father's display, but I didn't see him. Monique stood in the middle of the room, smiling proudly. Brian Edwards, Jake's dad, stood nearby, looking around the room with his steely blue eyes.

Why had he gotten involved with this?

"Hey, I'm here!" Polly rushed up to me and squeezed my hand.

"Hey, Polly, it's so good to see you." I blinked a little at the sight of her long white dress.

Panic spread over her pretty face. "What? Do I not look good?"

"You look beautiful, Polly." I didn't know whether to tell her what I was thinking.

"Tell me, Tiffany. You know you can't keep a straight face."

"You look like you're at your wedding," I admitted, half smiling. "Sorry. I mean, you look amazing."

"Oh, I knew I shouldn't have worn white," she groaned. "I just thought it made me look best. And everyone normally wears black to look thinner, and I didn't want to be that girl that was ashamed of her curves." She looked around the room. Guests were streaming toward the dining room. "What did I miss?"

"You missed a lot, but trust me, you look gorgeous."

Just then, Jake entered the room through the far door. Nico was behind him, whispering something to his brother. Jake caught my eye and nodded. I nodded back.

Polly saw the exchange and gave me a curious look. "What was that about?"

"I'll tell you later," I half-whispered.

Nico then looked toward us. I saw him looking at me, dismissively, and then his gaze went to Polly. He studied her for a moment and then headed toward us. I groaned inwardly. Why did this guy always make a beeline for Polly? It was like he knew she had a crush on him and he wanted to get every little bit of attention that he could from her.

He stopped in front of her. "Why, Polly, that's your name? Right?"

She smiled at him. "Yes. Hello, Nico."

"I didn't realize that you were the bride." He smirked.

She glanced nervously at me. "Sorry, what?"

Nico looked at me. "Was this your idea, Tiffany? Try and get Jake to marry Polly instead of your sister? I don't think it will work."

"You're an asshole, you know that, Nico?"

"I've been called far worse things." He laughed. "But how much for them?" he asked Polly.

"How much for what?"

"I mean, I know Jake got them for free, but I was assuming that you'll probably want something."

"Jake got what for free?" Polly said.

My ears buzzed. Jake hadn't told Nico, had he? My cheeks warmed as Nico looked at me, a superior glint in his eyes, and I knew that he knew.

Fair play, Jacob Joshua Edwards, I thought to myself. I thought I'd been on top when I'd left him. But he'd brought me down by telling his brother. You couldn't feel superior knowing that other people knew what you'd done.

"Your panties, of course." Nico's voice dripped with disdain. "I mean, you and Tiffany are best friends, right? I assume what one of you does, the other one does?"

"What?" Polly looked at me. "What is he talking about, Tiffany?"

"You need to leave, Nico."

"Why? It's only fair, isn't it? That I also get a pair? I am his brother. You know, I have just as much say in what happens in the family business." He smirked. "I can take your library away as well."

Until now, I hadn't realized how much hatred I was capable of feeling. I couldn't believe that Jake had told him everything—but then why would I have thought that he'd feel any sort of loyalty to me?

Nico looked back at Polly. "A hundred dollars for the panties."

"You want to give me a hundred dollars for my *panties*?" Polly stared at him with wide eyes. I stood there silently praying that she wouldn't accept the money or start crying. The last thing I needed was for Polly to let me down again.

"Well, I mean, I can throw in an extra twenty, if you really need it," he said. I wanted to slap him, but I knew I couldn't fight Polly's battles for her.

Polly blinked. "Unfortunately..."

"Yes?" He took a step closer.

"I'm not wearing any panties." She smiled sweetly. "So that would be a waste of a hundred and twenty dollars." She turned to me. "Now, Tiffany let's find a drink, okay? And let's see if there are any gentlemen at this party for me to dance with."

"Sounds good."

I was so proud of my best friend. I didn't know where that had come from, but I couldn't have asked for anything better. I could tell from the stunned expression on Nico's face that he was shocked.

Take that, Nico Edwards, I thought to myself. I grabbed Polly's hand and pulled her to the other side of the room.

"Where did that come from?" I whispered. "That was amazing."

"I don't know where it came from," her face was bright red, "but what the hell? You gave Jake your panties? What is going on?"

"Girl, you don't even want to know. I'll you more later, but..." I gave her a quick hug. "I am so proud of you. You really put him in his place."

"Thanks, Tiffany. He's a jerk. Like, a real jerk. He's hot, but I don't want anything to do with him. I don't care if he likes me or not."

I stared at her in amazement. "Where is my best friend? And what have you done to her?"

She laughed. "Hey, I know I was acting like a fool earlier because I was just completely smitten by Nico. But after how Jake spoke to you and how Nico spoke to me, I went home, and I realized that I need more of a backbone, and I need to be here for you. I'm trying my best. I mean, I nearly peed my pants right there. I'm not going to lie."

"So you do have panties on?"

"Come on now, Tiffany, of course I have panties on. I have granny panties on. You know me."

I burst out laughing. "Oh my God, I love you, Polly." And then I realized that the room was almost empty. "Oh, shit. We have to go through to dinner. I'm sure Dad is going to make some sort of speech."

"Do we have to go?" Polly said. "I don't know if I can face Nico again right now. What if he comes back and asks for my bra or something?"

"He won't." I shook my head. "Trust me. Did you see the look on his face? You took his breath away. You were incredible."

"I'm guessing you took Jake's breath away as well if you gave him your panties."

"Yeah, I think I did." I snickered, remembering the look on Jacob's face. "We're going to take these Edwards men down. You know that, right?"

"We?" She raised an eyebrow.

"Yeah. Jake and Nico think they're the shit. And they're not. They might be able to take over my family business and even my house, but we'll show them that they can't take us over. Come on."

We headed toward the dining room, Polly taking a

couple of deep breaths. I could tell that she was completely out of her element, but then, so was I.

"I need a drink, Tiffany," Polly whispered.

"We'll get one when we sit down," I said. We walked into the dining room, and I looked around the long table that had been set up. There must have been at least forty people sitting down and only two empty seats. I groaned when I realized who they were next to.

One of us would have to sit next to Nico and the other one would have to sit next to Jake.

"Oh shit," I said. "I'm sorry, Polly."

"What?" And then she saw the empty spots. "Oh, no."

"It's okay. We got this. Put a huge smile on your face and walk like a catwalk model."

"I can barely walk in these heels, girl. I'm lucky if I don't trip, let alone look like a catwalk model."

"Fine. We'll walk slowly."

We walked over to the table and stood next to the chairs. I looked at Jacob, and then Polly looked at Nico. They stared at us for a few seconds, then stood up and pulled the chairs back.

"Thank you," I said to Jake, a little surprised that he'd gotten the hint. I'd been looking forward to making a comment about his manners.

"You're welcome." He sat down. "A gentleman does pull the chair for a lady. Not that you're a lady."

"You can stop there," I hissed under my breath.

"Do you want to know what I did with them?"

"Aside from telling your brother about them?" I looked over to the right and saw that Polly was staring straight ahead. Nico was talking to a gentleman on his other side.

"What? I'm not to tell my brother that you gave me your

panties?" He grinned. "Do you think I'm a man or a eunuch?"

I felt his fingers on my leg under the table, and I slapped his hand away.

"What the hell are you doing?"

"I figured you gave me your panties for a reason. I'm smart. I get it." Undeterred by the slap, he moved his hand back, trailing his fingers up my thigh.

"What are you talking about?"

"Easy access," he whispered.

"You're an idiot. You know that, right?"

"Why are you scared, Tiffany Newton?" His fingers grazed even higher. And my body went still. He was so close to my most intimate spot, and I didn't know what he was going to do. It felt dangerous and sexy. And I felt completely out of my element.

"Do you want to know something, Tiffany?"

"What?"

"I wish it was my tongue there right now."

"Excuse me?"

"I wish it was my tongue there instead of my fingers. I sniffed your panties, and let's just say, I'm ready to feast."

"You're absolutely disgusting, aren't you?"

"Is it disgusting to make you come with my tongue? I'd love for you to sit on my face."

"You're at an engagement party, *your* engagement party to my sister. And you're telling me that—"

We were interrupted by the sound of my father, ringing another bell.

Dad stood up. "Good evening, everyone. Thank you for coming. I am so happy and proud to announce my daughter Monique Newton's engagement to Jacob Joshua Edwards, first son of Brian Edwards." He gestured at Jake. Monique was sitting next to Brian, Jake's dad. I was surprised at the seating arrangements.

"Please raise your glasses for the happy couple!" Dad said.

"Cheers," I said, weakly holding up my glass. Then I gasped as I felt Jake's fingers in between my legs, rubbing lightly.

"What the hell do you think— Ohh..."

He started rubbing my clit. I sat back in the chair and closed my eyes for a few seconds. Shit, why did it feel so good?

"Do you have any words, Jake?" My father looked right at Jake.

Jake chuckled and shook his head. "I don't think so. At this time."

I wondered how he was able to talk with a straight face as he played with me under the table.

"Oh, come on, Jake. You must have something to say." My father looked meaningfully at Jake.

Jake appeared to be giving it some thought as he slipped a finger inside me.

"Oh, shit," I mumbled under my breath.

"Sorry, what?" Jake said to me with a smile as he continued to play with me. I glared at him.

"Stop it!" I whispered under my breath.

"I wouldn't do that if I were you," he said through a broken smile. "People will wonder why you're making that face."

"Jake?" My father interrupted our conversation.

"Well, I just like to say thank you for the hospitality. It is always a pleasure being here for the Newton sisters—and my aim in life is to provide as much pleasure as possible."

He continued to play with me as he talked. I finally

pushed his hand away. He turned to me with a smile. "To Tiffany who has made me feel at home in her home, and to Monique," he smiled across the table, "who knows how to make a man feel welcome in any circumstances, thank you. And may we all enjoy the meal."

Monique was staring at Jake with wide eyes and grinning. Was she actually in love with him? Part of me felt bad, but it was hard to feel guilty when she was such a bitch. I knew that she didn't really love anyone other than herself.

"Congratulations, Jake and Monique!" Nico said loudly, and everyone cheered and clapped.

I turned to Jake and glared at him. "Don't you ever do that again!"

"I thought you enjoyed it. I mean, you felt like you enjoyed it. You looked like you enjoyed it. Are you telling me you didn't enjoy it?"

I knew the answer to that question. I *had* enjoyed it. My blood was running through my body like it never had before, pounding in my ears. I knew I didn't want it to stop. I wanted more from Jake.

But I was playing with fire, and it was all too likely that I'd be the one to get burned. I needed to figure it out before I was in over my head. I pulled my chair back and stood up quickly.

"Polly, come with me, please," I said over my shoulder as I left the room. I needed to talk to her. I needed to make a plan. And I had to do it away from the Edwards men. I had to figure out how to play the game without getting too emotionally involved myself.

TEN

"What are you doing, Tiffany?" Polly gasped as we exited the large dining room.

"Come with me." I pulled her toward my bedroom.

"I'm hungry, though," she said, almost tripping in her heels.

"I'll get you some food later. We need to leave."

"What do you mean we need to leave? What's going on? I'm so confused."

"Look, I think we're in over our heads with Jake and Nico."

"You think?" She laughed as we got to my room.

I closed the door behind us. "Yeah. Go and get my suitcase from the closet."

She opened my closet door. "Which one? You want your Tumi or the Louis Vuitton?"

"No. No. Neither of them. The black one in the corner."

"Oh, okay." She grabbed the black suitcase from the corner and dragged it out. "Isn't this the case that your mom gave you when you were young?"

"Yeah, I have some photo albums in there I need to pack," I said, opening my closet drawers and pulling out clothes.

"Are you going somewhere?" she asked me.

"Yeah, and you're going to drive me."

"I am?"

"Yeah. I have an idea. It's not fully fleshed out yet, but obviously, Jake and Nico think they hold all the power in this situation, right?"

"They do, though. They're so gorgeous and rich—"

"Forget about their looks. Jake thinks he can control me and my sister and my father, and Nico probably thinks he can control you."

"He's an asshole," she said. "He's a real asshole. Just because he's cute doesn't mean that—"

"It's okay, Polly. I understand. You still like him."

"I mean, just a little bit." She sighed. "Is it that obvious?"

"Girl, I know you, and you've had a crush on him forever. You're not just going to lose it in two days."

"I know, but what do I do?"

"Listen to me," I said. "They have all the power over my dad and my sister, and that's fine. They can have that power because you know what?"

"No. What?" She shook her head.

"These men, these Edwards men, they need power over all of us. I've realized that. They won't feel right until they have it."

"All of us? Me too?" she squeaked.

"Yeah." I nodded. "I don't know why, but you know how Jake's dad called me Polly? I thought he was just doing it to be rude and pretend like he didn't know who I was because I was in nothing. But it made me think, 'Why did he say *your* name?' He could have said Sarah or Ann or Linda. But he didn't. It was your name on the tip of his tongue, which means that you are important to whatever their plan is."

"But why am I important?" she said. "I'm no one. I'm not a Newton."

"You're not a Newton, but you're not no one. You're my best friend. And your parents are rich."

"Yeah. So?"

"So maybe that matters to them. I don't know. I haven't figured it all out. I don't have the answers, but Jake seems to want to take me down, and Nico definitely seems interested in taking you down."

"You think so? He barely acknowledges me."

"Girl, as soon as he saw you, he walked right up to you."

"Yeah. And he dissed me and said, 'Are you a bride?' Like really? I know you said it looks like a gown, but—" She sighed. "I never should have worn this dress."

"But the thing is he noticed. I'm a woman, and so of course I notice because we always notice stuff, but men don't notice anything."

"So what do you think it means?"

"I don't know, but I feel like we've got power here. We can take these men down."

"We can?"

"Yeah. I just need to figure out how."

"Is that why you gave Jake your panties?"

"I guess so." I sighed. "Girl, he does things to me."

"What do you mean?"

"I mean—oh, I hate to admit this, but I'm attracted to him. There's something about him. I'm drawn to like a moth to a flame, and I know he's going to burn me if I get too close, but I just can't stop myself."

"Oh, boy. Do you like him?"

"No, I don't like him. Attraction doesn't mean like, it just means—I don't know, lust?" I shrugged. "Maybe... maybe I just want to be with him sexually."

"Like, you're going to sleep with him?"

"I don't want to sleep with him. Well, that's a lie. I do want to sleep with him, but I don't want to give him the satisfaction."

"You could fuck him and leave him." She grinned.

"I could, but would that give me the upper hand? Or would that give him the upper hand?"

"I don't know." She shrugged, looking a little helpless. "So what are we going to do?"

"You're going to take the Ford Mustang. The red one, not the black one."

"I am?"

"Yeah. And you're going to drive me to your house."

"But won't they look for you at my house?"

"I'll just be there tonight. Then I'll go somewhere else."

"Okay. Okay...I'm nervous, Tiff."

"It's okay. You're strong. You're much stronger than I thought you were."

"I'm stronger than I thought I was as well." She smiled as she slipped her heels off. "Can I borrow a pair of your shoes? My feet are absolutely killing me."

"Of course. Take a pair of the Nikes in the cupboard. Feel really comfortable."

"Okay." She opened the closet again. "Tiffany?" she said, looking back at me.

"Yeah?"

"We're going to succeed, right?"

"Oh yeah. We're definitely going to succeed. We're two badass bitches."

"Yeah, we are. We're the biggest, baddest bitches in all the world," she agreed.

"Okay," I said, "here's what you're going to do. You're going to go to my father's study, and you're going to grab the keys in the top right-hand drawer."

"Oh, no. Do I have to go by myself?"

"It'll be fine. He's in the dining room showing off to everyone. He's not going to go."

"I know. But..."

"And if he comes in, which he won't, just say you're looking for me."

"He's not going to believe that."

"Trust me. He thinks you're a ditz. He'll believe it."

"Thanks, Tiffany. That makes me feel better." She laughed.

"I'll finish packing, and I'm going get some money from the safe, then I'll meet you out front in fifteen minutes."

"Isn't his safe in the study?" she asked hopefully.

"No." I shook my head. "It's in his bedroom, but I know the combination lock, so I can get in. Go now, okay?"

"Okay."

"I'll meet you outside."

"Okay." She still looked a little dubious. "I'll see you soon. Wish me luck."

"You got this, girl," I said.

I gave her a quick hug and pushed her out the door. Was this really the smartest move? I wasn't sure, but I knew I couldn't be in this house. I couldn't be around Jake and Nico any longer and especially not Monique. She was going to make me do something that I was going to regret.

I finished packing and hurried toward my father's room. I was glad there were so many people in the house because he'd be occupied until late in the night. I went to the back of his walk-in closet, moved the painting to the side, and turned the combination lock: 75, 33, 108. The lock popped open.

"Thank you, God," I whispered.

My father wasn't the sort of person to change anything, and for once, that made me happy. I took out a couple of stacks of hundred-dollar bills and then closed the safe. I couldn't take too much money, or he'd definitely notice. I hurried back to my room and slipped the money into the suitcase. I'd have to go down the back stairs. I couldn't risk anyone seeing me. I hurried down the back stairs and out the back door and made my way to the front.

To my relief, the red Mustang was sitting there, the engine purring. I ran up to it, opened the door, and slid in. The car sped off before I'd fully closed the door.

Too late, I realized that it wasn't Polly in the driver's seat.

"What are you doing?" I screeched.

"I'm driving you where you'd like to go, ma'am." Jake flashed me a wicked grin.

"You're not Polly. Where's Polly?"

"She's on her way home."

"What you mean she's on her way home?"

"Nico's driving her home."

"What? How?"

"You didn't think I would just let you slip out of the room and leave, did you?" The car picked up speed.

"You let me out right now. I want to go home."

"I don't think you want to go home. You've got a suitcase. Looks like you want to leave."

"So what's it got to do with you?"

"You can't just leave."

"I can leave."

"I say you can't."

"Why do you care? You're marrying my sister."

"I care, Tiffany. Trust me. I care."

"What did you tell my father when you left?"

"I didn't tell him anything."

"What are you going to do with me?"

"I'm going to take you where you want to go."

"Take me to Polly's house."

"No, that's not where you want to go."

"Of course it's where I want to go. That is where I was headed."

"We're going to my place," he said softly.

I snorted. "That's the *last* place I want to go."

He turned on the radio and proceeded to ignore me. I sat there huffing and puffing. I couldn't believe it. What had gone wrong? I had been trying to get away from him, and I certainly didn't want to be at his house. The last thing I needed was to be anywhere near him.

ELEVEN

I suppressed a yawn as Jake turned the car onto the highway. I was tired and nervous, and I didn't want to say anything else until Jake said something.

I hoped Polly was okay. I felt bad for her. She was probably freaking out.

"What's wrong?" Jake looked over at me.

"Nothing. Why do you ask?"

"Because you look like you're about to cry."

"Trust me, I'm not about to cry," I snapped. "I was just thinking about Polly and how worried she must be."

"She's fine. I didn't hurt her."

"Really?"

"Do I look like the sort of man that would harm a woman?"

"Yes," I said.

"Not if she didn't want me to."

It took me a moment to understand what he was saying. "That's disgusting."

"I take it you've never enjoyed the pleasure of pain."

"I'm not a masochist."

"Are you a sadomasochist?"

"Same difference." I turned away from him and looked out of the window. This banter was so weird. This whole situation was. "Why are you taking me to your house?"

"I'll tell you when we get there," he said softly. "Why were you leaving?"

"What do you mean, why was I leaving?"

"Simple question. You seem smart enough to be able to answer it."

"I needed to go and think."

"Think about what?"

"None of your business. I can have my own private thoughts."

"Touché," he said.

He was quiet then, and I was glad about it. I turned to face the front of the car again and realized that we had passed the city limits. We were going north of the city to the countryside. I looked at him in surprise.

"You don't live in the city?"

"Nope."

"You're not going to say anything other than that?"

"Nope."

I let out a deep sigh.

"Polly will be okay. She's being driven home by Nico," he said again. "You don't have to worry."

"I'm even more worried now."

"Why? My brother won't hurt her."

"Your brother seems to be even more vindictive and nasty than you. She is not like me. She can't handle someone like Nico."

"What do you think Nico will do to her?"

"I don't know," I said, my voice harsh, "but if he hurts her in any way, I will come for him."

He chuckled. "I guess I'll have to tell Nico that."

"Yeah, you tell him what I said."

"Is that a threat, Tiffany?"

"No, that's a promise."

"You sound like a female Godfather." He laughed out loud. "Oh my, you are very different from what I expected."

"You are not different to what I expected at all."

Which was a lie. I mean, I had expected him to be cruel and vindictive, but I hadn't expected him to have flashes of humor and compassion—not to mention that undeniable chemistry between us.

Obviously, I'd known he was handsome, but I'd never expected to be drawn to him. It annoyed me that I couldn't control my feelings, that I wanted to touch him, that the way he filled out his suit made me swallow hard. I bit my lip nervously as we pulled off the highway and onto a small country road.

"Where are we going?" I asked. There were no lights and the road was bumpy underneath us. "Is this even a real road?"

"I think so. The car is going, isn't it?"

"I mean, it's going, but—" We turned a corner, and I gasped as a huge, brightly lit manor came into view. "You live here?"

"I do." He pulled up next to a Range Rover and turned off the engine. "Home sweet home. Let's get out." He opened his door and got out of the car.

I sat there, unwilling to let him boss me around. He walked over to my side of the car and opened the door.

"I said, 'Let's get out.'"

"What's the magic word?"

He raised an eyebrow. "I kidnapped you, and you expect a please?"

"So you admit you've kidnapped me."

"Well, it's not like I've put a gag over your mouth or handcuffed you or blindfolded you. And you did get into the car willingly."

"In other words, it's about as lame as a kidnapping as you could get. Why did you kidnap me?"

"Are we going to go back and forth all night, Tiffany?"

"I want some answers."

"Get out of the car and you'll get your answers."

"Fine." There wasn't much point in just sitting in the car. "So, what now?"

"Now we go into the house," he said. "Now we talk."

I strode toward the front door, Jake chuckling behind me. I ignored him and turned my attention to the manor. It wasn't the sort of place I'd have expected him to live. I pictured him in some penthouse downtown with a view of the city. This was a country manor. Far out and isolated.

As I approached the front door, it opened. A tall man with a bald head and a large nose stepped forward.

"Good evening, Ms. Newton."

I stared at him in surprise. How had he known my name?

"And good evening, sir," he said to Jake, as Jake stepped up behind me. "The evening went well, I take it."

"Yes. Thank you very much for asking, Hamilton." Jake turned to me. "Tiffany, this is Hamilton, my butler."

"Nice to meet you. How did he know my name?" I asked Jake.

"I told him, of course."

"So you told him you were going to kidnap me?" I wondered if Hamilton would come to my aid if I needed him.

Jake laughed. "I didn't kidnap you. You're walking on

your own two feet, aren't you? In fact, you walked to the door faster than I did." He looked at Hamilton. "You're dismissed for the night."

"Thank you, sir. Is there anything I can get for you before I retire?"

"No, that's fine."

Hamilton gave him a quick bow and then left.

"This is so weird." I frowned at him. "Why do I feel like I'm in the manor in the English countryside?"

"I don't know. Why do you feel that way?"

"Because you have a butler with an English accent and you're American. I'm just all sorts of confused."

"I can tell," he said, his eyes roving over my body. "So, first things first. I don't want to marry Monique."

"What?" I was taken aback by this sudden confession. "What do you mean you don't want to marry Monique? She's your fiancée. Tonight was your engagement party."

"That was the plan that your father came up with." He shrugged. "We just needed to get our foot into the door, but I don't want to marry Monique."

"But you were on the phone with her earlier tonight about how much you wanted to fuck."

He raised an eyebrow. "I was?"

"Yes. I heard her talking to you."

"You heard her talking to someone, but it wasn't me." His lips curled. "But that doesn't surprise me. I'm sure she has many men."

I frowned, trying to remember the conversation. Hadn't she said she'd see him later? But I suppose that meant she'd see him after the party. I wasn't really surprised, either. I sighed. "So you don't want to marry Monique, but what am I doing here?"

"I want to make a deal with you, Tiffany."

"Oh, hell no," I said quickly, "I'm not marrying you." He burst out laughing. "What's so funny?"

"You are. Of course, I don't want to marry you. That's not the deal I want to make with you."

"Then what is?"

He took a step forward and touched my lips gently with one finger. I couldn't suppress a shiver of excitement as he moved his mouth closer to mine.

"I will give you everything you need if you just do one thing for me," he said softly.

I swallowed hard and closed my eyes. His lips, warm and soft, pressed against mine for a lingering moment before he pulled away. I almost melted to the ground. The kiss had lasted only a few seconds, but those few seconds had been electrifying.

"Open your eyes, Tiffany."

"My eyes are open," I said, blinking.

He started laughing again. "If I didn't know better, I'd say you'd never been kissed."

"I've been kissed many times."

"I said, 'If I didn't know better.'"

"How do you know?"

"Ah, there are many things I know about you, Ms. Tiffany Newton."

"Well, that's creepy. So you want to kiss me and then you'll tell me everything?"

He started laughing again. "Do you think one kiss is all I want?"

"So you want to sleep with me?"

"I do want to sleep with you, but you want to sleep with me as well." He ran his fingers across my shoulders. "No, Tiffany. What I want from you is not physical. What I need from you is not physical, but now is not the time or the place."

"So, what does that mean?"

"You'll know what I want when I'm ready to tell you."

"Why do I feel like we're going around in riddles here? You know what? Take me home. This is absolutely ridiculous."

"But you don't want to go home, do you? You were running away."

"I was running away from this entire situation because it's crazy."

"No, you weren't. You were running away because of me," he said softly. His lips pressed against my hair. I stilled, as his tongue circled my ear and he blew gently into it. "You're scared of me," he whispered. "You're scared that I will give you everything you never knew you needed and everything you never knew you wanted."

"I don't even know what that means," I mumbled.

"It means that you want me as badly as I want you."

"I don't want you—"

"Liar." His fingers moved to the back of my dress, and I felt him tug gently on the zipper. "I can pull this down in one fell swoop and your dress will fall to the ground." He smiled at me with dazzling eyes. "All you have to say is say yes or no."

"Yes or no to what?" I knew exactly what he was suggesting, but I was trying to create some time to think.

"You're not a fool, Tiffany." He took a step back. "What's your answer?"

He pulled my panties out of his pocket and brought them up to his face. He sniffed them. "I know what I want," he said. "I want a lot more than your panties in my face. I want to smell and taste all of you."

"I don't know," I said, shaking my head. "This is not what I had planned. I mean, I hate you."

"What we are going to do—well, at least what I hope we're going to do—has nothing to do with liking or loving or hating," he said. "In fact, what we're going to do, we don't even have to talk about again."

"Really?"

"Really," he said with a smile. "Let me pleasure you, Tiffany."

"But I hate you."

"I don't like you, either, but that doesn't mean I don't want to fuck you."

"Is that why you brought me here?" I said, surprised.

"Do you really want to know the answer to that?"

"Of course."

"Okay. You can ask me one question and I'll answer it, but only one."

There were so many questions in my mind, and yet there was one I needed the answer to more than anything. "Okay." I took a step forward and began undoing the buttons of his shirt.

He looked at me with surprise in his eyes. "You always do something I'm not expecting."

"I'm hard to predict," I told him. "Take off your jacket."

He took his jacket off. I reached up and slipped his shirt off his shoulders as well. My gaze was drawn like a magnet to his naked chest, so manly and masculine.

"What's your question, Tiffany?"

"How did your butler know my name?"

"Honestly? That's what you want to know?"

"Yes."

"Because I have pictures of you in my office." From the look on his face, he was telling the truth.

I frowned. "Why do you have pictures of me in your office?"

"I told you. One question."

"But—"

"But nothing." He undid his belt buckle and then unzipped his pants. He slipped his shoes off, and his pants fell to the floor so that he was standing there in a pair of black silk boxers.

"Did I say you should take off your pants?" I asked him.

"No, but you're not the boss of me." He took a step forward and looked at me one more time. I felt his hand move to the back of my dress, and once again it was on my zipper.

"So, Tiffany, is the answer yes or no?"

TWELVE

Every possible answer flew through my mind. A million different ways to say no. A billion different ways to say yes. My hands itched to slap him, or even punch him, but I just stood there. My heart beat alternately fast and slow as if it didn't know whether it should get excited or not.

"I do have all night, but I'd rather get an answer sooner than later," Jake prompted, and for a moment, I saw the man that other women saw, handsome, carefree, charming, and funny. The sparkle of his smile was outmatched only by the devious glint in his eyes. I almost forgot that this was all a game. I almost forgot that this was the man who wanted to steal and destroy my library. The man who thought nothing of hurting me.

I would not let him take my library, and I would not let him take me. At least not every part of me. I'd play his game, but I wouldn't let him steal my soul. My beloved library would always remain mine.

"I suppose I can give you a partial yes."

"There's no such thing as a partial yes, Tiffany. You're all in or you're all out."

"I'm not all in." I shook my head, feeling my hair swaying down my back. I felt stiff and unsure as I stood there, and I only hoped he couldn't read my body language well. Inside me, two forces were battling for control, and I didn't know which side would win. "Anyway, I thought you said you weren't going to try to blow my mind and show me all the ways of the sexual world."

"Things change." His gaze, filled with desire, bore into me, and need rippled through me in response. "What is it you want, Tiffany Newton?"

I answered before I'd fully thought my question through. "I just really want to go on a date."

Jake raised one eyebrow. "A date?"

He looked taken aback, almost as taken aback as I felt. I repressed a sigh. Why had I decided to be open with him?

"Yeah. I want to go on a date. Not with *you*." I laughed, pretending that the idea sounded awful. "I mean with a true gentleman, a man who would woo me. A man I could actually fall for."

"Oh, because a date with me would be so bad?" His words were light, but there was a defensive undertone to his voice. He hadn't liked what I'd said, and that made me happy.

"Well, it wouldn't be great." I shrugged nonchalantly. "You don't seem like the romantic type, like the sort who'd sweep a woman off of her feet."

"Oh, yeah?" He pressed his lips against my temple, and I tried not to melt into him. "You don't think a date with me would be absolutely fantastic?"

"I think it would be absolutely, fantastically horrible." I was lying through my teeth. In truth, I wondered what it would be like to go on a date with Jake, to be the object of his affections, to be someone he wanted to please. I wondered if he even had the ability to be kind and complimentary.

He stroked my cheek. "What are you thinking?"

"I'm thinking that I can't even imagine you dating."

"You can't imagine me dating. Really? Why is that?"

"Because I don't believe a kind word has ever left your mouth."

"Really?" He smirked. "I see."

"That's your answer? 'I see'?"

"What else would you like me to say, Tiffany?"

"Maybe you could give me some examples of compliments that you've given to women."

"Is that your way of telling me you want a compliment? Is that your way of telling me that if I tell you how beautiful you are," he pressed his lips against my neck, "and if I tell you how silky your hair feels," he ran his fingers through my long, dark hair, "and if I," he blew into my ear, "tell you how sweet you smell..."

"What?" I said, flustered by the seductive attention.

"If I tell you all those things," he whispered, "will you say yes?"

I swallowed hard. "You're full of shit, aren't you, Jake?"

"I think I'm full of something." He gave me a lazy smile and kissed me again. I couldn't stop myself from kissing him back. He was so attractive, so devastatingly sexy. He growled against my lips as his fingers made their way to my waist and down to my ass. He squeezed my buttocks and pushed me in toward him so that I could feel his hardness against my stomach.

"I want you, Tiffany." He sank his teeth gently into my lower lip and tugged slightly.

I was breathless, my nipples at attention, and I was

getting wet between my legs. "So you can show me what I've been missing?"

"Oh, I can show you a lot more than that," he said, stroking the side of my arm. "So, Tiffany?"

"Yes," I murmured.

"Yes?" He took a step back. Immediately, I felt bereft at the loss of him near me.

"Yes, Jake."

"Really?" He flashed that cocky smile.

I flushed. "Don't tell me this was all part of some sick—"

"No," he said. "Take your clothes off."

"What?" I hadn't expected him to say that.

"If you want to go through with this, take your clothes off."

"I'm surprised you don't want to take my clothes off. I'm—"

"Take your clothes off." He undid the rest of the buttons on his shirt, and I watched as he took off every single item of clothing. Finally, he shed his boxer shorts, and my gaze was drawn to his gigantic cock. He was hard and thick, and I wanted to touch him. I reached down to stroke him, but he shook his head.

"Take your clothes off, Tiffany," he said.

I decided not to think about it and simply pulled my dress off. I stood there naked, noticing the way his eyes narrowed as his gaze roamed over my body. "You're hot."

"Thank you? Is that what you said to my sister as well?"

"That's kind of sick, isn't it?" he said.

"What do you mean?"

"I mean, that's a perverse question to ask. Is that what I said to your sister? Would you want me to have said that to your sister? Would it make you feel good to know I said your sister was hot, or would you want me to say that I didn't say that to your sister?"

"I'm just guessing you said that to her. I'm sure you say that to all the women."

"No, I don't."

I glared at him. He wasn't answering my question. I didn't care if he'd told my sister she was hot. The real question was, had he seen my sister naked? Had he slept with my sister? It was sick and perverse, and I knew I couldn't go through with it if he had.

I hated her. I hated her more than anything, but I wasn't that sort of woman. I mean, yeah, it was cruel of me to sleep with Jake knowing he was engaged to my sister, but he didn't care about her. And as far as I knew, she didn't really care about him, either. She'd been on the phone with someone else—unless Jake had been lying, which I didn't think he had been. He had no reason to lie, especially not to me. He didn't care about hurting my feelings. He didn't care what I thought.

So Monique was sexting and chatting with someone else, someone else she was possibly fucking. Did it matter if her fiancé cheated as well? Of course it did, and of course it was wrong that it was with me, but I didn't feel bad. Maybe something in me was flawed, maybe something in me had been broken, but I didn't feel so much as a whisper of guilt. I wanted to be with him; I just couldn't be with him knowing he'd been with her as well.

"You're thinking awfully hard," Jake said. "And you're not even naked yet."

"I need to know," I whispered.

"What do you need to know? We both know your sister's attractive. She could have any man that she wanted."

"And that includes you?"

"Are you asking if..." He took a step forward and reached his hand over to my bare shoulder. I felt his fingers grazing along my bra strap and down my back to the clasp of my bra. He nibbled lightly on my earlobe. "Are you asking, Tiffany, if I undid her bra like this?" he said as he unclasped it. The bra fell to the ground. He grinned at me. "Is that what you're asking?"

I was naked now. My panties were in his pocket. My dress and bra were on the floor. His fingers played with my nipples, and I gasped as he sucked hard, tugging on my nipple in a sharp burst of pleasure mixed with pain.

"Ouch!" I pushed him away.

He laughed. "That didn't hurt." He slid his fingers between my legs and rubbed my clit. "Are you asking if I touched her like this?"

"You're sick," I murmured, but I didn't stop him.

"I'm not sick." He shook his head. "You're the sick one if you're enjoying this, thinking that I did this to your sister as well."

I blanched at his comment as his fingers slipped inside of me. I closed my eyes, and I held onto his shoulder as he pleasured me. I cried out softly as he added another finger, moving in and out and in and out.

He pulled his fingers out. "I didn't fuck Monique."

My eyes flew open. "You didn't?"

"No," he said. "I would say I'd never seen her naked, but that would be a lie."

"So you came close to fucking her?" I bit my lower lip. I couldn't lie. I was hurt.

"No." He shook his head. "I haven't come close to fucking her."

"So, how did you see her naked?"

"She sent me photos, of course. Several photos. I guess

she likes to pleasure herself, and she wants me to see what I'm missing."

My eyes widened. "She sent you pictures of her masturbating?"

"That doesn't surprise you, does it? I would think you better than anyone knows what Monique is like."

"Nothing surprises me when it comes to her. Well, I guess I'm surprised that we're sisters."

"Sometimes the things we can't believe are the things that aren't actually believable."

"What does that mean?"

"It doesn't mean anything." He looked me up and down.

"I hate you, you know."

"No, you don't." He raised his gaze to my eyes. "You think you hate me, but you don't hate me."

"Yes, I hate you."

"You wouldn't be here if you hated me."

"You kidnapped me. You made me come."

"I made you take off your panties and give them to me. I made you take off your dress and stand here naked. I made you want to sleep with me."

"I don't— I..." I paused. "My feelings have nothing to do with me wanting to be pleasured. Men aren't the only ones that seek pleasure, you know."

"I know." He grinned. "And that's why we're here." He grabbed my hand and pulled me toward him. He twirled me around as if I were a ballerina doing a pirouette, and I stopped in front of him, just staring at him, wondering who this strange man was. "So, tonight."

"Yes?"

"We can do what we want. We take a pause from everything. And tomorrow..."

"Yes?"

"Tomorrow, we don't talk about it."

"What do you mean, we don't talk about it?"

"We don't talk about it."

I realized he thought he had the upper hand. He thought he was controlling me, and so I did what I knew I had to do to shock him.

I grabbed his hands and pulled him toward the bed. He grinned as I pushed him down on the mattress and grinned even wider when I clambered on top of him. I leaned down to press my lips against his as my breasts brushed back and forth on his chest. The hairs on his chest tickled me, and I giggled as I kissed my way down his stomach to his abdomen. I could feel his harsh intake of breath as my lips met the tip of his cock. I looked up at him with sultry eyes and winked before my head moved further down.

I took him into my mouth, and I sucked all of him inside as deep as I could. I played with his balls as I sucked on his cock, and I could taste the sweat, salty and masculine, on his skin. I loved it. I loved being in control.

He grunted and growled, his fingers tangling in my hair as he moved my head back and forth on his cock. I sucked until I could tell he was close to coming, then I kissed my way back up his chest, and he groaned, looking at me with dark and lustful eyes.

"What are you doing, Tiffany?" His voice was ragged with desire. I pressed my fingers against his lips and moved my pussy back and forth on his cock so the tip of him was stroking my clit. "Tiffany, I'm—"

"Shh." I leaned down and kissed him before shifting back abruptly and filling myself with his cock. He groaned as I rode him. I dug my fingers into his shoulders as I sat up and rode him like a cowgirl on a stallion. He reached up and played with my breasts as I rode him. Within minutes, he was shuddering in my arms as he came and I was screaming my release.

He flipped me over onto the mattress and kissed me, his fingers running to my clit and rubbing quickly until I came as well. He growled as he kissed me passionately.

"That wasn't meant to happen like that," he said.

"Says who?" I grinned at him. I was a formidable opponent, and he had to know that I was not a little girl playing games. I may have only been twenty-five, but I knew what I wanted and I knew how to get it.

"I came inside of you, you know."

"I'm on the pill." I shrugged. "It's fine."

He raised his eyebrows. "You're very unlike anyone I've ever met before, Tiffany Newton."

I smiled sweetly. "Tell me something I don't know."

THIRTEEN

I woke up and realized that I was in the room alone. In fact, the house was deathly quiet. Had Jake left me in his house by myself? I realized if he had, I would have the opportunity to be nosy and snoop. I got out of the bed quickly, looking around for something to put on. I was naked, and though I wasn't shy about my body, I didn't particularly want to walk around in the nude, just in case I happened upon someone. I pulled a shirt out of Jake's closet and put it on.

I stood in the doorway and listened. There was still no sound. I tiptoed down the hallway and was about to enter one of the rooms on the right when a woman in a maid's uniform walked down the hall toward me.

"Good morning, Ms. Newton," she said. Her expression was carefully neutral.

"Oh! Good morning. I didn't know there was anyone here."

"I am always here," she said. "There's a car waiting for you when you're ready to leave."

"I can leave?" I was surprised. "So I wasn't a prisoner?"

"Of course you can leave."

"Is Jake here?"

"He's gone out for the day. Business," she replied. "I can give him a message if you would like."

"No." I shook my head. "I can get him my own message if I really need to send him one."

"Very well. Would you like some breakfast?"

"No."

There was something unnerving about this woman. The way she stared at me, the way her eyes didn't blink, the way she'd known my name. And it wasn't her words or even her tone. More, it was what she hadn't said. It was in the way she didn't smile. She thought I was a floozy. She thought I was just one of those women that... I stopped thinking about what she thought. It didn't matter.

"Tell the driver I'll be ready in ten minutes," I said.

"Yes, Ms. Newton." She turned around.

She walked back down the hallway and away from me. I waited to see if she'd look back to make sure that I didn't enter one of the rooms, but she didn't. I suppose she knew that the mere fact that she was present in the house would stop me. I wasn't brave enough to explore, knowing there was someone else there, especially someone like her.

I hurried back to the bedroom, and I found my clothes on the floor where they'd fallen last night. I pulled them on quickly, then went into Jake's bathroom and splashed my face. I didn't even bother to look through any drawers. I didn't dare.

I went back down the hallway and entered a large foyer. The house was beautiful. I'd noticed that it was nice last night, but I hadn't realized just how immaculately clean it was and beautifully decorated it was. It looked like it could have been in a magazine. I wondered if Jake had designed it himself.

The maid appeared out of nowhere again. "The car is outside for you, ma'am."

I almost wondered if she was a figment of my imagination. I pinched myself and caught my breath at the pain.

"Are you okay, ma'am?" she asked.

"I'm fine."

I stepped out the front door. A Mercedes was waiting with a chauffeur standing next to the back door. Of course. A Mercedes and a chauffeur, only the best for Jake.

I thought about the previous night, how I'd been so reckless, how I'd taken control, how I'd felt like I was in charge of everything. But once again, Jake had gotten the upper hand. I hadn't expected to wake up without him there, a stranger in someone else's home. I'd expected him to try and seduce me and almost wished for it. But I hadn't even noticed when he'd gone. I'd slept straight through the night.

I walked to the car, and the chauffeur opened the door.

"Good morning, Ms. Newton."

Did everyone know my name? I slid into the back seat, and he closed the door behind me. He got into the front and pulled off.

"I assume I'm taking you home," he said.

"Yes." I nodded, wondering if he'd asked me where I lived, but it seemed he didn't need the address.

So Jake had told them all about me. What had he said? Who did they think I was? Did they know he was engaged to my sister? Did they think I was some sort of slut, some sort of homewrecker? Did they even care?

We were at my house within forty-five minutes. The chauffeur got out to open the back door for me.

"Have a nice day," he said.

"You too," I replied. I took a deep breath as I headed to my own front door.

I wondered what Monique and my father would say. Would they be pissed, concerned, or anxious? Or would they even have noticed that I was gone?

I opened the front door gingerly and stepped inside. No one rushed out to greet me. I walked through to the kitchen, wondering if my father and sister were worried or if they might even have called the police.

I entered the kitchen and saw my father on the phone. He barely glanced at me. And as I stood there, I realized he hadn't even known I was gone. They hadn't even checked on me. They didn't even care.

"Good morning, Dad!" I said loudly.

He glared at me and pointed to the phone.

"Wonderful night it was last night, wasn't it?"

"I'm on the phone, Tiffany," he hissed.

I rolled my eyes and headed toward the fridge. "I wonder where Monique is?" I said, keeping my voice raised.

"I'm right here."

I looked around. Monique was sitting at the kitchen table eating a piece of dry wheat toast.

"I didn't see you," I said. "Were you even looking for me?"

She glanced at me as she nibbled her toast. "You're still wearing your dress from last night? Tacky. I need to get ready." She got up. She didn't even care that I had been gone all night. "David is coming over to speak to me."

"David? Jake's father?"

"Yes," she said. "Do you have a problem with that?"

"No, I don't have a problem with that. I'm just curious."

"Curiosity killed the cat. You know that, Tiffany."

She put the toast down on her plate and stood up. "Do me a favor."

"Um, yeah?"

"Do the dishes."

"Why would I do your dishes?"

"Because you should get used to your station in life."

"My *station* in life?" I glared at her. I so badly wanted to tell her I'd fucked her fiancé just the evening before.

"I'm going to get ready." She gave me an infuriating little smile and left the room.

I looked at my father. "Did you hear what she just said to me? Did you?"

"I'm on the phone, Tiffany," he snarled.

Furious, I turned on my heel and headed for my bedroom.

When I got there, I flopped onto my bed and started laughing hysterically. I'd been kidnapped, and no one had noticed or cared. And then I remembered Polly. She would be worried. Maybe even frightened. In fact, I didn't even know if she was okay. I quickly grabbed my phone and called her.

"Polly!" I said as soon as someone answered the phone.

"No," a deep voice said, "it's not Polly."

"Who is this?" The back of my neck prickled. Was Polly okay?

"I think you know who this is, Tiffany," the voice said, and then the phone went dead.

Had that been Jake? But why would Jake have Polly's phone? I called the number again, and it rang several times.

"Hello," Polly said breathlessly.

"Oh my God. Polly, are you okay?"

"I'm okay. Tiffany, is that you?"

"Yes. What happened last night?"

"I don't even know. I..." She lowered her voice, "I can't talk right now."

"Who answered your phone just now, Polly?"

"It was Nico," she said.

"You're with Nico? Are you okay?"

"I'll call you back later. Okay?"

"Polly, I'm worried about you. I—"

"I'll call you in an hour. Stay by your phone."

She hung up. I stared at the phone in shock. Had Polly slept with Nico? Of course, if she had, who was I to judge? I'd slept with Jake.

What were these brothers up to? I didn't understand, but I knew I had to get to the bottom of it. If not for myself, for Polly. She was too innocent and sweet to get involved with the likes of them.

FOURTEEN

I paced back and forth in my room, waiting for Polly to call me back. I had absolutely no idea what was going on, and I was apprehensive and nervous. I thought I could win this, but I'd realized I didn't even know what game I was playing. I needed to tell Polly what had happened last night. I needed her to know everything, and I needed her to know that Nico couldn't be trusted, just like Jake couldn't be trusted.

My phone rang, and I grabbed it immediately. "Hey, Polly?"

"No," a familiar voice drawled. "It's me."

"Jake?"

"That's me."

"What's going on?"

"I just wanted to remind you of something."

"Remind me of what?"

"To remind you we don't talk about last night."

"What do you mean we don't talk about last night?"

"I mean, no one knows about last night."

"Okay...?"

"And that includes your friend, Polly."

"Why can't I tell her? She's my—"

"Listen to me carefully. Polly cannot know about last night."

"Why? And why is Nico there with her?"

"Nico's with her?" He paused. I could tell that he was surprised.

"Yeah. I called her already, and Nico picked up the phone and—"

"Nico picked up Polly's phone?"

"Yeah. Didn't you know they were together?"

He cleared his throat. "Of course I knew."

"You didn't know."

"Of course I knew," he said again.

"Sure. So why is he there?"

"You need to understand one thing, Tiffany."

"What's that?"

"As much as you think as you're in control of this situation, you're not."

"I never thought I was in control—"

"Listen to me carefully, Tiffany. I can help you get your family business."

"What? How?"

"Do you want it?"

"Of course I want it. But why would you help me get it?"

"I have my reasons."

"And those reasons are?"

"For me to know."

"And am I going to find out?"

"No," he said.

I bit back some choice curse words. "So you're going to help me get my family business? What do I need to do?"

"Go to the library."

"Go to the library for what?"

"I've left you something."

"What did you leave me? A pair of edible panties?"

He chuckled. "Why would I leave you a pair of edible panties?"

"I don't know."

"I can get you some vibrating ones if you want."

"No, thank you."

"Actually, I might like that. With a little remote control I keep."

"You wish."

"I do wish. And if you want your family business, then you will wear them whenever I say."

"You don't control me. You can't tell me what to do or what to wear."

"I think you'd like it, though."

"Excuse me?"

"Remember, you need to spice up your life."

"I don't need to spice anything up."

"Yes, you do," he cut me off. "Now go to the library."

"Um, I'll go when I'm ready."

"I know you'll go as soon as we get off the phone."

"You don't know that."

"Trust me, Tiffany Newton, I know you very well."

"Whatever. Anyway, I have to go."

"Just remember," he breathed.

"What?"

"We don't talk about last night—to *anyone*."

He hung up. I stared at my phone, confused. Why did he care if I told Polly that I slept with him? I chewed on my lower lip as I stared at the door. I wanted to go to the library and see what he'd left me, but I didn't want to rush there because I knew that was exactly what he wanted me to do. And I didn't want to play into his hands. Not that he'd know I'd rushed right away.

I was still debating whether to go when the phone rang again. "Hello?"

"Hey, it's me," Polly said softly, and I sighed in relief.

"What the hell is going on, Polly?"

"Girl, I told you to meet me out front, and I went to get the keys and he was waiting for me."

"Who was waiting for you? Nico?"

"Well, Nico and his brother, Jake. And...I'm sorry. Are you okay?"

"I'm fine," I said. "I was just a little shocked when I got into the car and it was Jake and not you."

"I know. Nico drove me home."

"And he stayed the night?"

"No. No, he didn't. He just dropped me home and left. He didn't even try anything."

"So, why did he pick up your phone?"

"He showed up this morning..." She sounded edgy.

"What's wrong?" I asked quietly.

"It was just weird. He showed up, and he said that I wasn't to tell anyone about what happened last night."

"What do you mean?"

"I guess about them taking you?" She sounded uncertain. "I don't know, but he was in my bedroom when I woke up."

"He was in your bedroom?"

"Yeah. And I don't even know how he got into the house. My parents certainly wouldn't have let him in and—" She sighed. "What's going on with you? What happened to you and Jake?"

"He took me to his house," I said.

"Oh. And?"

"Okay. Listen to me carefully, Polly."

"Yeah?"

"There's something I have to tell you."

"Okay."

"And I'm not meant to tell you."

"Okay. You're scaring me."

"I know." I paused as a text message came through. I stared at the screen in shock and my jaw dropped. "Oh my God," I said out loud.

"What? What is it?"

"I just got a text from Jake."

"Okay, and what did he say?"

"It says, 'We don't talk about last night.'" I looked wildly around the room. "He's either tapped my phone or he's tapped my room or— Let me call you back, okay, Polly?"

"Okay. You're really scaring me, Tiffany."

"Not as much as I'm scaring myself. I'll speak to you later."

I hung up and texted Jake back immediately. "Did you tap my phone?"

"No. I don't work for the CIA or the FBI."

"Did you bug my room?"

"Did I bug your room?" he responded. "No."

"How did you know I was on the phone with Polly?"

"Go to the library."

"No."

"You can type no as much as you want. We both know you're going to go."

I didn't text him back. I powered the phone off and sat on the bed. What the hell was going on? This was a lot more complicated than I'd assumed. And I was beginning to think I'd made a mistake. Maybe I shouldn't have slept with Jake last night. Maybe that had been exactly what he wanted. Maybe I had played right into his hands.

I jumped up. I had to see what was in the library. I couldn't wait any longer. I ran down the hallway to the library and opened the door.

As soon as I walked in, I saw it on the table.

FIFTEEN

I took a deep breath, trying to calm my racing. I stared for a long moment at the table, then I reached out and gingerly picked up the photograph that was lying next to a stack of books. Beside it, there was an envelope with my name on it. But it was the photo that took all my attention.

It was of me and my mother when I was just a baby. I couldn't believe how young and beautiful and happy she looked. She was staring at me with adoration in her eyes, and my heart felt like it was going to break.

"Oh, Mama," I whispered to the photo. "I wish you were still here. I wish I could talk to you. I wish things had been different."

Tears welled up in my eyes. I'd never gotten to have a proper relationship with my mother. I'd never gotten to tell her about crushes and boys or my dreams for the company and my dreams for life or to tell her about how I wanted to travel and see the world. She didn't know who I was. She didn't know the person I'd become. Not only had I missed out on so much, but she had as well.

"Oh, Mama," I said again and clutched the photograph

to my heart. I pulled it back and stared at it for a few seconds, my mind going a million miles a minute. How had Jake gotten this photo, and why had he left it on the table? I picked up the envelope and opened it quickly to read the letter inside.

"Tiffany," it read, "I doubt you've ever seen this photograph before, and I wanted you to have it. You may think of me as an enemy, but I am more of a friend than anyone else right now. I am your best bet and the answer to all of your prayers. Work with me, trust me, and you shall see the triumph. Jake."

I reread the letter and frowned. I didn't understand why he thought he could help me or even why he wanted to help. People didn't do something for nothing, and certainly not men like Jake. And if he had really wanted to help me, why would he become engaged to my sister? Why wouldn't he have asked to become engaged to me? He could have offered to marry me, told me that he'd give me the business, and I would've agreed. But no, that's not what he'd done.

I read the letter once more, wondering exactly what was going on. I wanted to call Polly again, but I knew she was confused about her own situation. Why had Nico gone to her house this morning, and why didn't Jake know? Were Jake and Nico really after the same thing? And what did Polly have to do with it? Was she involved just because she was my best friend, or was there something else going on here? I was so confused, and yet I was also captivated. I had to know more.

I also wanted a repeat of the night before.

My legs still tingled when I thought about the way he'd touched me and looked at me. I could still remember how he smelled—all man, not like anyone I'd ever been with before—and the way our bodies had seemed so in tune with each other. It was just physical, of course, but it had felt fantastic. I had wanted the night to never end.

I was standing there when I heard a car coming up the driveway. I looked out of the window and watched as Jake's father got out of his car and adjusted his tie. He was here to see Monique.

What was Monique up to? If Jake's father was making plans with Monique, and Jake was making plans with me, who was the one being fooled, me or Monique? Logic told me I was the one that was being played, and yet I felt like somehow I was still in control.

I looked down at my mother's photo again. I could almost hear her voice warning me to be careful. I could almost feel her lips upon my forehead, telling me how much she loved me.

One of my only memories of my mother was her singing a song to me, a song that had the most beautiful melody. I could still remember the way her eyes had gazed at me, the way she loved me. It was weird to have a memory from that age. I couldn't remember anything else, but I could remember her singing about the morning and how much she loved me.

As I stood there in my beloved library, I could hear her voice whispering to me, "Be careful, my dear. Be very careful who you give your heart to. I can only pray it won't be a man like your father."

I blinked. That was a fresh memory. That was one I hadn't recalled before. So my mother had known my father had been a scoundrel.

I pressed my lips together. My mother had been heartbroken. My father had broken her heart, and that's why he didn't care about me. That's why he was never there for me; he'd never been there for my mother, either. I wasn't even sure that he loved Monique, but Monique probably didn't care because she loved no one other than herself.

I went back to my room, shut the door, and called Polly again.

"Hey. Is everything okay?" she said when she picked up.

"Can you come over?" I asked her.

"Now?"

"Yeah," I said. "We have to talk in person." I hung up and waited.

SIXTEEN

"Hey, Polly. Thank you so much for coming." I was outside when she pulled up. I gave her a quick hug and pulled her to the side of the house.

"What's going on? You're frightening me."

"I'm scaring you?" I raised an eyebrow. "Really?"

"Well, not you, Tiffany, but this whole situation."

"Girl, trust me. I know. It's just really complicated."

"So, what exactly is going on?"

"Look, last night, Jake and I slept together."

"Ooh! Was it good?"

"Yeah, but that's not what we're going to talk about. Jake says he wants to help me get the family business."

Polly's brow furrowed in confusion. "Your family business? The one that your dad runs?"

I nodded. "Let's be real. My dad does not know what he's doing, and neither does Monique."

"But how are you going to get the family business? Isn't the reason Jake is marrying Monique is so that his father can take over?"

"I know, so that's why I don't really understand what

Jake was saying. But also, when I was in the library, I found this." I handed her the photo. She looked at it.

"Is that your mom and you when you were a baby?"

"Yes."

"I've never seen this photo before," she said softly.

"Me either. Don't you get it?"

"What?" she said.

"Something else is going on here, something that I just don't understand, and Jake and his family are at the bottom of it all. I need to figure out what's going on."

"I don't trust him, Tiffany. You know you don't trust him, either."

"I don't trust him. He always seems to be two steps ahead of everything that I'm doing. But..."

"But what?"

"But I need to play along with him. I need to figure out what this is all about."

"But Tiffany, what if it's nothing good?"

"Well, what would it matter? It's not like my life is going all that well now."

"I know, but—I just don't know what to say!" Polly groaned. "This is just all too much. I just feel so confused."

"Are you confused because of what's going on with me? Or because of what's going on with you and Nico?"

"Girl, I just don't even know how to feel about Nico. He's so cold and cruel and mean, but there's a side to him I can't help feel attracted to."

"Trust me, Polly, I understand what you mean. That's the way I feel about Jake. One part of me absolutely hates him and the other part of me is so drawn to him, I can't keep my hands off of him. It's absolutely crazy."

"At least you got to be with Jake. At least he wanted to be with you, too."

"Girl, we're not together. We had sex. And yes, it was the most amazing, mind-blowing sex I've ever had in my life, but it means nothing."

"You sound different, Tiffany." There was a new depth of wisdom in Polly's eyes, and I realized she looked more mature than I normally thought of her.

"What is it, Polly?"

"I don't know. I just feel like this whole situation has aged us both a million years."

"Well, hopefully not in appearance." I grinned, and she laughed.

"Is there a reason we're not going to your room?"

"Come." I led her through the backyard to the gazebo and took a seat. "I think my room might be bugged. Maybe several rooms in the house."

"Why?"

"Because nothing makes sense. Jake knows too much. He seems to be in my head, and he's obviously not in my head. He's not psychic, so..."

"So you think he's hearing what you're doing and saying?" she said. I nodded. "Don't you think he would have bugged here as well?"

"No, not the gazebo. He wouldn't have been able to get to the gazebo unseen."

"I guess." She looked doubtful. "But," she bit her lower lip, "he could be listening through your phone."

"I know," I said. "That's why I don't have it on me." I showed her my empty pockets, and her eyes widened.

"Where is it?"

"It's upstairs in my room, turned off." I shrugged. "I heard sometimes they can still hear even if the battery's dead, but I don't know. It's not like I'm the queen of espionage."

"You could join the CIA or the FBI."

"No, thanks." I snorted. "Way too much danger in those situations, and I'm not one for danger."

"True." She grinned. "You're just one for the passionate sex."

"Really, Polly?"

"What? You slept with him, not me."

"Come on, now. What would you have done if it was Nico?"

"I would've slept with him in a heartbeat."

"Well, don't. I know that you have feelings for him—"

"I don't have feelings for him," she protested.

"Yeah, you do. I'm not saying you're in love with him, but I know you, Polly. If you sleep with him, you're going to develop even deeper feelings."

"But isn't that what you've done with Jake?"

"No, trust me. I don't have any feelings for Jake." Which was a slight lie. I definitely was thinking about him differently, and I hated that about myself. It was a weakness that I felt women had that men didn't.

When women got intimately close with a man, they developed more feelings and made more allowances. When men slept with a woman, it was just sex. It meant nothing. It didn't mean that he would treat her better. And I wasn't going to let Jake get to me like that.

"I'm worried, Tiffany," Polly whispered. "I just don't know what to do."

"I know. Me either." I gave her the photograph again. "I want you to take this with you."

"What?"

"I don't know. In case anything happens, I don't want it to be in the house."

"You want me to take it?"

"Yeah. I know you have a safe in your room."

"You want me to put it in my safe?"

"Yeah. Your parents' house is monitored. No one's going to get in there, except for a smooth criminal. No one's going to steal anything. Nico and Jake have no reason to show up. They don't have an excuse to gain access to your house like do with mine."

"But he gave you the photo. Why would he steal it?"

"He gave me the photo to let me know he has something on me, that he has information. This is his way of getting the power back." I chewed on a fingernail. I had never really taken the power, but in my mind, I was on my way.

"So you want me to put it in my safe?"

"Yeah," I said. "I want you to put it in your safe. You should go now."

"What? I just got here."

"I know. I didn't want to tell you on the phone that this is what I wanted you to come for. I need to go inside."

"Why? What's going on?"

"Jake's dad's there, and I need to find out what he's talking about with my dad. I need to know what deals are taking place."

"Okay. You sure you don't want me to come with you?"

"I'm sure," I said. "This is something I need to do alone, okay? I'll text you when I get done for the evening."

"Oh?" she said. "From your phone?"

"No, I'm going to get a burner."

"What? How?"

"Don't worry about it, okay? I've got resources."

"Hold on." She shook her head and opened her handbag. She pulled out two different phones.

"What are you doing?"

"You know my dad gave me two phones, the phone that

we speak on and the satellite emergency phone, just in case." She handed me the thick black phone. "This is the satellite emergency phone. You press this red button, no matter where you are, and someone will come and save you. You hear me?"

"You can't give this to me. Your dad—"

"He doesn't have to know. I want you to have this, okay?"

"Okay. Thank you."

"It's okay. You can text me on this as well. No one has been in my phone. Trust me."

"I love you, Polly. You're the best friend a girl could ever ask for."

"I love you too, Tiffany. Now be safe, okay?"

"Okay. Now hurry. You leave and go home, and I'm going to go in and see if I can see what's going on inside."

"Okay. Be safe."

"I will." I hugged her. "I need to sort this out. If not for me, then for my mother's memory."

"I understand, Tiffany," she whispered in my ear. "And if anyone can do it, you can."

SEVENTEEN

I crept along the corridor toward my father's study. I could hear him talking to someone, and I quickened my pace. I stopped right before the door and pressed my ear against it.

"I told you, that will not be acceptable!" My father's voice was loud and angry. I frowned. It surprised me he was talking to Jake's dad like that. "No, I don't have that yet. She has not agreed to it." I realized then that he wasn't speaking to someone that was in the room with him. He was speaking on the phone. So where was Jake's dad?

I tiptoed down the hallway to a window at the front of the house. Jake's father's car was still in the driveway. Where was he? He wasn't in the study with my father unless my father was having a conversation on the phone with someone else in front of him.

I went down the stairs and was headed toward the kitchen when I heard Monique laughing. She was in the room at the back.

As I crept toward the door, her laughter got louder. I was about to push open the door and see what was going on when a hand slammed over my mouth and pulled me back. I tried to scream and bit down.

"Ow!" a voice growled into my ear, and I froze. I recognized that voice. He let go of my mouth and turned me around. "Be quiet!" he hissed.

"Jake?" I stared up at him in surprise. "What are you doing here?"

"What do you think?" he said. He tugged on my hand. "Let's go to your room."

"No. I was about—"

"I would advise you not to do that, Tiffany. Let's go to your room."

"I don't—" My eyes widened when I saw he had a ball gag in his hand. "What are you doing with that? Are you—" Before I knew what was happening, he had pushed the ball gag into my mouth and wrapped it around my head. I heard a click. I tried to get the gag off, but I couldn't. I couldn't even say anything. I glared at him in hatred.

He winked at me and laughed as he led me toward the stairs. "Hurry. We don't want anyone to see us," he said. I walked as slowly as possible, but he squeezed my hand, and I increased my pace until we were on the top landing.

When we got to my bedroom, he closed the door behind us, then pushed two bookcases in front of it. I stared at him in surprise. They were heavy bookcases. I couldn't believe he'd been able to do that all by himself. Then he walked over to me and undid the gag.

I spat it out and slapped him. "What the fuck do you think you're doing?" I said. "Why are you here?"

He rubbed his cheek, but he looked more amused than hurt. "I think you know why I'm here, Tiffany."

"Don't you ever put a ball and gag in my mouth again!"

"Or what?" Before I could answer him, he pulled me

into his arms and was kissing me. I melted into his arms, unable to stop myself from kissing him back. I ran my fingers down his chest, loving the rippling feel of his hard muscles. I hated how much I was attracted to him.

He pushed me down onto the bed, pulled down my pants along with my panties, then unzipped himself.

"You're fucking gorgeous, Tiffany," he said. He stepped forward and rubbed the head of his cock against my clit, and I closed my eyes and moaned. Then he was sliding inside of me, and I was gripping the sheets.

There was nothing sweet or romantic about this. It was all about lust and pure sexual want, but I couldn't deny him. I couldn't say no. I loved the feel of him inside of me.

He thrust into me, hard and deep, then leaned forward and kissed me as he continued to fuck me. He straightened himself slightly, and I felt his thumb rubbing my clit as he continued to fuck me hard. I knew I wouldn't last long.

"Wait a sec." He suddenly stopped, laughter in his eyes. He pulled out his phone and made a call as he continued to fuck me.

"What the hell are you doing?" I asked.

He didn't answer, just put the phone on speaker as he continued to bring me to orgasm.

"Hello? What is it?" I recognized my father's voice, and my eyes widened.

"It's Jake." He chuckled into the phone.

"Yes? What do you want, Jake?"

"I was just saying thinking how grateful I am, so I called you to say thank you."

"Thank me for what?"

"Giving me your daughter." His lips twisted in a smile.

I wanted to push him off of me, but I was so close to orgasm. He started flicking my clit with his fingernail, and I moaned out loud. He pressed his finger against my lips and shook his head. I bit my lip, whimpering as he continued to fuck me.

"So, is there anything else that you want, Jake?" My father sounded annoyed.

"No, just wanted to say thank you for welcoming me into your home." My father grunted in response. "I just wanted you to know that I enjoy every second of being inside." He winked at me and then hung up on my father.

"What the fuck was that?" I gasped. "That's sick, you know that? How could you—" And before I could say anything else, he was thrusting into me harder, his thumb rubbing my clit faster and faster until I was exploding and he was exploding inside me as well. I screamed out loud in ecstasy. I couldn't stop myself.

As he pulled his dick out of me, he chuckled. "This isn't a love story, Tiffany. Remember, I'm always four steps ahead, and you're going to love every single moment of this ride." He winked at me, zipped himself up, and then headed back toward my door.

He pushed the bookshelves to the side and opened the door, walking out just as confidently as he'd walked in. I groaned, rubbing my eyes as I sat up and pulled my pants back up. That had been the fucking hottest sex I'd ever had in my life, but I knew I was in way over my head, and I did not know what I was going to do next.

EIGHTEEN

The birds were chirping outside when I woke up the next morning. My inner thighs were sore, and I stretched as I made my way out of the bed. I couldn't quite believe what had happened yesterday, but I was glad that it had.

Maybe I was sick in the head. Maybe having grown up in a family like mine had made me into a weirdo. I didn't know what it was, but I absolutely loved the freeing sexual nature of being with Jake. I couldn't believe that he'd called my father. I didn't know if it had been to show my father he had the upper hand or to show me. What I did know was that he was very much in control of the situation.

I made my way down to the kitchen, yawning and wishing I had gotten more sleep. I smelled pancakes and smiled to myself. I loved blueberry pancakes more than anything. There was no one in the kitchen as I entered, and I frowned, surprised that none of the cooks or maids were there. But there was a plate on the island, and I assumed it was for me.

"Good morning, Tiffany." My father walked into the kitchen as I grabbed a pancake.

"Hi, Dad," I said, not really knowing what else to say.

"Jake and Nico and their father are coming over tonight for dinner to discuss some business."

"Okay. Do I have to be there?"

"No. You don't."

"If I want to be there, can I be there?"

"No, this will be a dinner for your sister and myself."

"But—"

"But nothing. You weren't exactly very hospitable at the last party we gave, were you?" He walked past me to grab some coffee. "You and Polly can do whatever you two do together."

"What's that supposed to mean?"

"I don't know," he poured his coffee without looking at me, "but maybe you should think about finding a husband."

"So, you're going to marry me off as well, then?"

"I'm not trying to marry you off." He shot me a disdainful glance. "I'm just saying—"

"It's fine, Dad." I wasn't sure why my dad hated me so much. I mean, I knew why I hated him, but I didn't know why he hated me. In a weird way, it was a point of pride that he didn't like me. If he had liked me, it would've made me wonder what was wrong with me. He was the sort of evil bastard that only liked other evil bastards, so at least that was some reassurance that I wasn't a completely horrible person.

"Well, I'm going to go back to my room and get ready for the day," I said, taking a bite of the pancake and walking past my father.

"You do that, then," he said.

I made my way to the room, frowning. He hadn't even made a comment about me eating the pancake directly from my hand, which surprised me because he was the sort of person who cared about crumbs and mess. Something was distracting him. I wondered who he'd been talking to the evening before. What had Jake's dad had been doing in the house? Who had Monique had been talking to? So many secrets, and I knew none of them.

I got to my bedroom and turned on my phone, not the one that Polly had given me but my own personal one, and called Jake. Maybe he'd give me some answers. But the phone just rang and rang. I was about to hang up when he suddenly answered.

"Hello?" His voice was terse.

"It's me, Tiffany."

"I know. What do you want?"

"Is that how you greet a woman you fucked twice?"

"If you want me to treat you better, I say we fuck one more time."

"Just one more time?" I couldn't believe I was flirting with him. What had come over me?

"Well, I mean, if you want to fuck two more times, I'm okay with that as well. Or three or four or ten."

"You're a bastard."

"I know," he said. "Remember, I'm not the hero of your story. I'm the villain."

"Okay. And you know what happens to the villain, right?"

"No. You tell me."

"The villain always loses, Jake, in fairy tales."

"You don't still believe in fairy tales, Tiffany, do you?"

"Why are you coming over for dinner tonight?"

"That's what you call to ask me?"

"I know that you and your dad and Nico are coming over to dinner to discuss something with my dad and with Monique. I want to know what."

"You don't think it has to do with the upcoming wedding?"

"So you're still going through with it?"

"I didn't say that."

"I'm really confused here, Jake. I don't really understand what's going on."

"I told you you're on a need-to-know basis, and you don't need to know right now." He lowered his voice. "Don't get involved, Tiffany. Just stay back. I will take care of everything. You just need to do what I tell you to do."

"Where did you get that photo from with me and my mom?"

"Don't ask me any questions."

"So, what, I'm just meant to be like a marionette? You pull my strings and then I act, but otherwise, I just sit there?"

"Yes," he whispered. "That's exactly what happens."

"You're an asshole. I just want—"

"I know what you want, Tiffany."

"Oh, yeah. What's that?"

"You want me to come in your mouth."

"*What?*"

"You want to take my cock into your mouth, and you want me to come, and you want to swallow."

"You're disgusting. No, I don't want that."

"You're thinking about it right now, though, aren't you?"

"No, I am not," I lied.

He chuckled. "You know what I thought about when I went to bed last night?"

"No."

"You sitting on my face, coming, screaming my name as I licked you."

"Enough!" I cut him off.

"What? Don't you like the sound of that? Don't you want me to eat you out?"

"I don't get you, Jake. I don't get what this is about."

"This is about us righting a wrong," he said softly. "This is about you getting what you want and me getting what I want."

"But you don't know what I want."

"I think I do," he said. "Aside from me, of course."

"I don't want you."

"I know you don't want me—aside from in your bed."

"You think I care about having you in my bed?"

"You care about having me inside of you."

"You know what? I'm going." I hung up the phone quickly and powered it off. I was flushed, both furious and turned on. I hurried to the bathroom and took my clothes off so that I could step into the shower. I closed my eyes as the water poured down on my skin, and I screamed. Not loudly because I didn't want my dad to hear, but I screamed to let out the anger and the frustration and the pent-up hostility that I held toward Jake. How could I feel so turned on and so pissed off at the same time?

Part of me wanted to go to Monique and my father and tell them that Jake couldn't be trusted. *He's sleeping with me. He doesn't care about Monique. He doesn't have our best interests at heart.* But I knew it was pointless; they didn't have my best interests at heart, either. I was stuck between the devil and the deep-blue sea, and I felt like I didn't really have a choice. Either way, I was going to lose. Either way, I was going to burn. I just didn't know how high the flames were going to fly.

NINETEEN

There are times when you have to be a spy. And while I definitely wasn't a covert CIA agent, I knew how to slip around the house sight unseen, seeing as I'd been doing it most of my life.

I heard the doorbell ringing and the sounds of Nico, Jake, my father, Monique, and Jake's dad talking. I stayed in my room until I heard them all go to the dining room, then I slipped down the stairs and made my way to the living room, which was next to the dining room. There was a door all the way at the back of the living room that led to the dining room so that if one were in the living room, they could just slip into the dining room. I cracked the door and listened.

"So, it's been such a lovely evening. I wonder if we could go dancing," Monique said. I wasn't sure who she was talking to.

"Not tonight, Monique." I couldn't pin down the voice. It wasn't my dad who'd responded, and it wasn't Jake. Was it Nico? Why would Nico be telling Monique that she couldn't go dancing tonight?

"There's something that we should discuss," Jake said.

I tensed. Was he going to tell them?

"Yes?" My father's voice was terse.

"We need to go over the contracts and the deals that we currently have in place before the wedding."

"About that," my father said. "I'm going to need more money."

The room went silent, and I held my breath. What was my father doing?

"I said I'm going to need more money," my father continued. "About ten million more."

"This is not what we discussed," Jake said, and I was surprised because why was he the one talking? Why wasn't his father talking?

"Well, it might not be something we discussed previously, but..." My father held something up in his hand. I couldn't see what it was. "You see this?"

"Yes."

"It's an SD card," my father said, "and on it is a video, a certain video that I don't think your father would want getting out."

"What's on the video?" Jake said.

"Shall I tell him, or do you want to tell him?" my father said.

"That's enough." Jake's father sounded angry.

"What is it?" Nico said, as oblivious as I was.

"Hold on. Marmaduke!" my father called out. "Marmaduke, come here."

One of the older servants walked into the room. "Yes, sir. How may I help?"

"Get me the laptop that's in the kitchen, please."

"Yes, sir. Right away, sir." Marmaduke hurried out of the dining room and then came back a moment later with a laptop. My father powered it on and inserted the SD card into the laptop. The screen changed, and I could see blurred images of people in a video. I couldn't hear exactly what was being said or see it clearly. I wished I could get closer, but I knew I couldn't get caught.

"What is this?" Jake said.

"What is this? What do you think?" My father turned the volume up, and all I could hear were the sounds of moans and groans. He then stopped it and closed the laptop. "So, your move." He grinned. "I want three million more dollars." He stood up. "Excuse me, I think I have somewhere else to be right now." My father left the room, fortunately in the opposite direction from me.

Jake, Nico, Jake's dad, and Monique were left sitting at the table.

"What's going on here?" Nico said.

"He's playing a game," Jake's dad said.

"Well, I don't think it's funny." Monique jumped up. "I don't think it's funny at all." She ran out of the room after our dad.

I stood there watching the three men. Neither one of them said anything. And then I saw Jake looking up and over directly at the door. I pulled back quickly. Had he seen me?

What had been on the video, and why did neither of them seem concerned? What was my dad up to? Everything was confusing to me, and I knew unless I got some answers, I was in for a world of drama.

TWENTY

I hurried back up the stairs, hoping that Jake wouldn't intercept me in the corridor. I did not know what was going on. I badly wanted to know what my father had shown them. I decided not to go back to my bedroom right away, just in case Jake came to find me there. I made my way to the library instead.

There was a note on the table for me in another envelope. Had Jake come to the library?

I felt uneasy as I walked toward the table. What had he left me this time? I stopped in front of the table and then picked up the envelope. I opened it carefully. And once again, there was a small note and another photograph. This time, the photograph was of just my mother. She wasn't facing me, but I could tell it was her just from the way that she stood and the way her hair hung in one braid down her back. She was standing next to a man who was looking at her with a warm smile. He was no one I recognized, and I wondered who he was.

I pulled out the note and skimmed it. It said, "Trust me,

there's no need to spy." So he had seen me. But if he'd seen me spying on him from the living room, how had he been able to get this note into the library so quickly? There had only been a matter of minutes since the moment I'd closed the door and then made my way up here. So he'd either known that I was going to spy or he'd seen me spying and acted quickly.

I was out of my depth. I heard footsteps and froze. Was he coming to see me now? My breathing was erratic and my heart was racing, but the footsteps continued past the library. Quickly, I ran to my room and called Polly from her satellite phone.

"Hey, is everything okay?" she answered immediately.

"Girl, something strange is going on."

"I know. We've been saying that."

"No, I mean much stranger than we even thought."

"How is that possible?"

"I don't know, but...hold on," I said as I heard what sounded like a little cry coming from outside my window.

I rushed to the window and looked out. "Monique," I said out loud.

"What?" Polly said.

"Monique, she's leaving. She's running in heels. She's dressed up."

"Where's she going?"

"I don't know." I thought for two seconds and then ran out of my room. "Polly?"

"Yes?"

"I'm going to follow Monique. Something weird is going on here."

"What do you mean you're going to follow her?"

"She's sneaking out, and she never sneaks out."

"How do you know she's sneaking out?"

"Because there's a car pulling up to the driveway and she's running toward it. She's not driving. Let me call you back, okay?"

I hung up quickly and then ran to the garage. I got into my car and then sped down the driveway. I was able to see the car that Monique had gotten into pulling out of the driveway, and I decided to follow it. I saw another car leaving after me, and I wondered if it was Jake. Was he going to try and kidnap me? Did he want to have his wicked way with me again?

"Where are we going?" I said under my breath as I followed her. And why was she leaving by herself? Did my father know? Did Nico and Jake know? What was going on?

I followed Monique's car into the center of town, where she got out. The car sped off. So it wasn't someone she'd known; it was an Uber or a taxi or something. It was then that I realized that she was dressed in a silver sequined outfit. That was not what she'd been wearing at the dinner. She walked up to the door, which had nothing on it but the word "Deep."

I chewed on my lower lip for a few seconds, debating what to do. A man stepped out from the door and ushered her in. And then the door closed and they were both gone. I decided to park and got out of the car. I hurried over to the entryway I'd seen her go into.

I called Polly quickly.

She picked up immediately. "What's going on?"

"I need you to do me a huge favor."

"Oh, no. What's the favor, Tiffany?"

"I need you to come into town, okay?"

"Okay. Why?"

"I'll let you know. You need to bring two dresses, the sexier the better, and you need to bring two wigs."

"What?"

"We're going somewhere and we have to look good."

"Where are we going?"

"I don't know."

"What do you mean you don't know?"

"Monique has just gone into a place called Deep. I don't know what it is, but she was all dressed up. If we're going to get in, we have to be dressed up as well."

"Then why do we have to wear wigs?"

"Because I don't want anyone to recognize us."

"But—"

"Please, Polly."

"Fine. Where are you?"

"I'll send you the GPS location when we hang up, okay?"

"Okay."

"And please, be fast."

"I will. Are you going to be okay, Tiffany?"

"Yeah," I said. "I'm going to be fine. You just need to get here as soon as possible."

I hung up and waited outside the door for a few seconds. I pressed my ear against it to see if I could hear anything, but there was no sound. I stared at the building. There were no windows. What was Deep? And what was Monique doing there?

I spied a coffee shop across the street. I'd have to sit somewhere while I waited, and it would give me a good vantage point to make sure that Monique didn't leave. I hurried in, ordered a coffee, then took a seat at the window. I sent the GPS information to Polly, and then I just stared.

All I could do was wait now, but I needed to figure out

what was going on. I needed to figure out what the messages Jake was sending me meant, and I needed to figure out what Monique's part in all of this was because nothing was as it seemed.

And I had a feeling that Monique was the key to everything.

TWENTY-ONE

"Polly, there you are!" I turned as she walked into the coffee shop with a large bag over her shoulder. "I've been waiting for you."

"Well, it took me a while to find two wigs and two dresses that I thought would be good. And then I had to find heels because I assumed if we're wearing dresses, we have to wear heels—"

"I know, you're a godsend." I gave her a big hug. "Now, come on. Let's go to the restroom and change."

"Can I get a coffee at least?"

"No, girl. We don't have time. We have to go and see what's going on inside Deep."

"But I'm thirsty—"

"I promise I'll get you a drink at Deep, okay?"

"But you don't even know what Deep is. What if they don't have drinks?"

"Everywhere has drinks, Polly."

"Fine," she said. "Come on. I brought a few choices of dresses. Black, red, and navy blue."

"You're amazing." We quickly changed and put on our

wigs. She put on a long red wig, and I put on a long blond wig. We applied our makeup, and I stared at her. "You look really hot."

"So do you, too. We don't look anything like ourselves." She giggled.

"That's the point. We don't want anyone to recognize us."

"Okay. And why is Monique there?"

"I told you, I don't know why Monique is there. That's why we're going to find out. Now, come on, Polly. We don't have time. Time is of the essence. In fact, for all I know, she left while we were getting changed."

"Okay. Come on, then," she said.

We headed out of the coffee shop and crossed the street. We stood outside the door to Deep, and I knocked twice.

"Are you sure this is the place?" Polly looked around. "This doesn't even look like anything."

"Trust me. This is the place."

No one came to the door, so I knocked again. I chewed on my lower lip. Was I in the wrong place? Had I remembered it wrong?

A moment later, the door opened and a tall guy that I recognized from earlier in the evening stood there. "Can I help you?"

"Yeah, my friend and I were hoping to get in," I said in a sexy, sultry voice.

"Get in where?"

"Deep," I said. "This is Deep, right?"

"Yeah. I don't recognize you. I've never seen you here before."

"That's because this is my first time. I wanted my friend here to experience it, you know?"

He stared at me for a few seconds, and then he looked over at Polly. "I think you've got the wrong place, ma'am."

"We're here for a good time," Polly said, twirling her hair. She pushed her breasts up, and my jaw almost dropped. I'd never seen Polly acting this flirtatious before in my life.

"Oh, yeah?" the guy said as he looked at her and stared at her breasts. "A good time, huh?"

"Yeah. And you know, maybe even you and I could have a good time tonight. Later, if you're free." Polly pressed her lips together, and my eyes widened. Was this guy really going to fall for that?

"Okay, come on." He opened the door wider and ushered us in. He closed the door behind us, and Polly squeezed my hand. We were in darkness for a few seconds before he switched the light. "Follow me, ladies."

As we walked farther into the building, I could hear the sound of loud music. Where were we? He stopped suddenly and then opened a door. "Have a good night," he said. "And I hope to see you later." He winked at Polly.

We stepped into a huge room with disco lights that was packed with people. "Where are we?" I whispered to Polly as I looked around.

"I think this is some sort of nightclub," she said. "Whoa, this is crazy. I've never seen anything like it before in my life."

"Me either," I said. I looked over to the right, and I could see a group of men and scantily clad women with their noses on the table. "Fuck, I think they're doing cocaine," I said.

"Wow," Polly said.

"No coke for us."

"I know. Trust me, I know."

There was a stage at the front of the room with a group of women on it dancing. I looked away, and then my gaze snapped back to the stage. One of the girls dancing at the front was wearing a silver sequined dress. My jaw dropped.

"Oh my God."

"What? What is it?" Polly followed my gaze. "Oh my gosh. Is that Monique?"

"I think so. Come on," I said as we headed into the room. I didn't want Monique to see me, so I kept my distance.

A beautiful brunette in a bikini walked up to us. "You girls want some drinks?"

"Yes, please. What do you want, Polly?"

"Rum and Coke please."

"Yeah, two rum and Cokes."

We sat down at a little table about fifty yards from the stage. "Shit. That's Monique," I said.

"It sure is," Polly agreed. "What's she doing here?"

"I have absolutely no idea."

The lights dimmed, and Monique was suddenly the only one on the stage. She began swaying her hips back and forth. Her dress slid to the ground so that she was standing there in only a thong and see-through bra.

"Oh my gosh." Polly's eyes were like saucers. "I think your sister's a stripper."

We stared at each other in shock. This was certainly not what I'd expected to find out tonight. Why was Monique stripping? And why did she look like she was enjoying it?

I watched as she unclasped her bra and threw it into the crowd. A tall man with blond hair jumped up and caught it. Monique walked to the front of the stage and blew him a kiss. Then the lights flickered again, and she was gone.

"What the...?" Polly said.

I shook my head, confused. Then I saw Monique, hand in hand with a tall man, disappearing through a door in the back.

"What's going on?" I whispered. "Is my sister a prostitute?" My heart pounded in my ears.

I had absolutely no idea who anyone in my life really was.

TWENTY-TWO

"Oh my gosh, Tiffany. You don't really think that Monique could be a prostitute, do you?" Polly stared at me with wide eyes.

I shrugged. "I mean, we just saw her dancing on a stage, stripping, and now she's gone into a room with some guy. I just don't know what to think. Like, why would she do this?"

"She didn't look like she was hating it." Polly made a face. "I know she's your sister and—"

"Girl, trust me, she may be my sister, but there's no love lost there, unfortunately. And I agree, she looked like she was having a good time. When she took her bra off, it seemed like she was enjoying teasing the men that were sitting at the front."

We both paused as the waitress returned with our drinks. "Thank you," I said. "How much?"

"No charge." She smiled. "Feel free to go on stage if you want."

"About that..." I said casually.

"Yeah?"

"Can anyone just go up on the stage?"

"You sign up on a list," she explained. "Normally, you sign up in advance, but for two hotties like you," she winked, "I'm sure the manager can make an exception."

"Okay, thanks."

"So do you want to sign up?"

"Um, not right now." I shook my head quickly. Polly looked like she was about to faint. "But thank you."

"You're welcome," she said. "And if you want another drink, just stop me or any other waitress, okay?"

"Okay."

The waitress continued on her way, and I looked at Polly. "Do you think I should have asked her more questions? Do you think that she would've given me any answers?"

"I don't know," Polly said. "She seemed very helpful, but I mean, we're not even really meant to be here. So maybe if she thought that we didn't really know what was going on, she wouldn't want us to stay."

"That's true." I nodded. "So—"

Just then, an older lady walked up to me. She was wearing a short white dress and had long blond hair. Her blue eyes looked cold and calculating. "Tiffany?"

"Yeah?" I stared at her in surprise. How did this lady know my name?

"You're surprised, I know. You don't know me. And I really don't know you." She shook her head. "But you look just like your mother."

"I do? You knew my mom?"

"Yeah." She looked around quickly. "It's a pity, you know."

"What's is?"

"That your dad was a bastard and a cheat."

"I know," I said. "I guess everyone knows, huh? I wish she would've been able to be with someone better than him."

"I know," the lady said. "But there's a lot of us women that wish we could have been with someone different."

"You could say that again," Polly said with a laugh. "I guess we really don't choose who we love."

I glanced at Polly, wondering what she was talking about and hoping it wasn't Nico.

"I know where you're coming from," the woman said. "The things we do for love. Still, I'm sorry that he died."

"Sorry. What?" I stared at her in confusion.

"I said I'm sorry that your father died."

"Um, my dad died? No, he's alive. He's—"

She looked panicked all of a sudden. "Hey, well, it was nice seeing you. Um, I've got to go."

"Wait, what? No. Can I ask you a few questions? What are you talking about that my dad died? Are you talking about my mom? But—"

"I have to go, sorry. I didn't realize you didn't know everything. I have to go." And with that, she backed away and left.

I stared at Polly, who was looking at me with the same confused expression on her face. "What's going on here, Tiffany? Do you think she had you confused for someone else?"

"I don't know. She said I look exactly like my mom. She knew my name. She had to know it was me."

"But then why did she say your dad was dead? Your dad's not dead unless he died within the last hour, and we just didn't know."

I grabbed my phone and called my dad's number. It rang and rang, and my heart started beating. Was my dad dead? And then he answered it. "Yes, Tiffany. What do you want?"

"I was just calling to make sure that you were okay," I said softly.

"I'm fine." And then he hung up.

I put the phone away. "So that was my dad. Still alive and still a jerk."

"Girl, I don't want to be here anymore." Polly looked nervous. "I don't know what's going on, but I feel like we're going down a rabbit hole and maybe we don't want to go any further."

"I know. I know you're scared, and I'm scared, too, but let's drink our drinks and then..." An idea came to me. "Let's go to that room. Let's see if we can figure out what's going on with Monique."

"Are you sure you want to do that, Tiffany? Because whatever we see, we can't unsee."

"I know," I said. "But I need to do this. I need to do this or I won't be able to sleep or move on with my life. Something a lot bigger is going on here, Polly. Something bigger than I ever could've imagined. And I think Jake is in on it. I think—I just don't know. I don't want to be one of those conspiracy theorist people, but stuff isn't making sense."

"I know," Polly said. "I know."

"And I want to get to the bottom of it. You understand, don't you?"

"Yes, but I'm scared. And my parents wouldn't like it if they knew I was here."

"You can go, Polly. You don't have to stay. I'll be okay."

"Are you kidding?" She stared at me. "You're my best friend. I would never leave you in this situation. I may be scared, but I'm not going to leave you by yourself. I always have your back. You know that, right, Tiffany?"

"Thanks, Polly." I squeezed her hand. "Come on. Let's drink up and let's go to that room and see what's going on."

"Okay." She took a gulp of her rum and Coke. "But I think I'm going to need another ten drinks tonight because I'm feeling completely out of my element here."

"Don't worry." I laughed. "You can have as many drinks as you want. I think I'm going to need them as well."

We got up and made our way toward the back of the club so that I could have a look and see what Tiffany was up to. I could see the different men and women watching us as we walked by, and I wondered if they were hoping we would get on the stage. We looked hot, but I also knew there was no way in hell either one of us would be going on the stage and stripping.

TWENTY-THREE

We stood outside the door that Monique had gone through and looked at each other. Polly's expression was uneasy, and I knew that she was worried about what we would find out next. It seemed like something new popped up every day, and none of it made sense. I didn't know what was going on with Jake. I didn't know what was going on with Nico. I didn't know what was going on with Monique. I didn't know what was going on with my father.

And now I was starting to wonder if I knew what was going on with Polly.

She'd been my best friend since childhood, and she'd always been an open book, but there was something different about her. She was clearly out of her element here, but she seemed stronger than usual. It was as if something was going on in the background that I didn't know about. I refused to believe that Polly knew more than I did, though. I knew I could count on her to always tell me if there was something I needed to know.

"What are we going to do?" Polly whispered as we stood there.

"I guess we should see what's going on inside the room."

"But what if your sister sees us? Then she'll know we followed her. What if she tells your dad? And what if he gets mad?"

"So what?" I shrugged. "What can they do? They've already turned over my house and my family's business to Jake's father. What more can they do? They've already ruined my life."

"Your life's not ruined, Tiffany."

"Everything's about to change."

"But is that really so bad?" she asked softly.

"What do you mean?"

"I mean, I don't really know when you've ever truly been happy," she said. "And I love you. You're my best friend. And we have fun times, but I feel like you're a princess locked in a castle and your father is the evil king, and your sister is an evil stepsister, and you just don't ever do anything to get out of that situation."

Her words stung me. "What do you mean I don't do anything? My whole life I've been fighting just to be able to be me. Shit, do you know what I went through just to be able to go to college?"

"Look, I know your dad is an asshole, and I know your sister sucks, but nothing is going to change that, right?"

"I don't get what you're saying, Polly."

"I am saying that maybe..." She sighed. "Never mind."

"No, tell me what you were going to say."

"Now's not the time or the place." She shook her head. "If we're going to go in there, then maybe we should do that now."

"Okay." Heart racing, I pushed the door open slightly. It creaked loudly and I froze, but the sound of loud music in the room covered the noise.

"What's that song?" Polly asked.

"I don't know. It sounds like some sort of old rock and roll song." I pushed the door open a little bit more and peeked inside.

The room was very dark. There were two candles on a nightstand, and in the middle of the room was a bed. I could see bodies on the bed and hear groaning and gasping noises.

"Oh my gosh, I don't know if I can look." I glanced back at Polly. "I don't know if I am ready for this. I know I hate her, but still, she's my sister."

"We don't have to." Polly put a gentle hand on my shoulder.

"I need to." I stepped inside the room, holding the door open so that Polly could peek as well.

They were definitely having sex, and it looked like Monique was on top. She was bouncing up and down and moaning, then she leaned forward to kiss the man she was humping. He tugged her hair, and she screamed as he grabbed her hips and moved her up and down. I took a careful step forward, then froze when I realized who she was on top of.

I grabbed Polly and closed the door. My heart was racing, and I felt as if all the blood had drained from my face.

"What is it, Tiffany?" Polly asked me. "What is it? Why do you look like that?"

"I just saw who Monique was with." I felt as if I were a zombie, like I was living in some weird alternate reality.

"Who was it, Tiffany? Don't leave me hanging. Who was it?"

I swallowed hard. "Jake—" I started, but I couldn't force the words out.

"Jake? She's with Jake? Your Jake?"

"He... He's not my Jake," I stuttered.

"Oh my God. Your sister's fucking Jake? What a—"

"No, no," I interrupted her.

"Not Jake. It's Jake's— Oh my God." Polly's face crumpled like she might cry. "It's Jake's brother, isn't it? She's with Nico."

I shook my head. "No," I said, "it's not Nico. It's Jake's dad."

TWENTY-FOUR

"You have got to be kidding me!"

I could tell Polly was as shocked as I was. "Do I look like I'm kidding you?"

What the fuck? I could not believe what I had just seen. Monique was sleeping with Jake's dad. I thought back to all the interactions between the two of them, and suddenly I realized that this wasn't something new. This had been going on for a long time.

I didn't get it. Why would Monique marry Jake if she was sleeping with Jake's father? Had she been sleeping with him before my dad had come up with the idea of marrying her off to Jake? I tried to remember how it had all come up. Had it been my father's idea or had it been Monique's? Nothing was making sense.

"What should we do?" Polly said. I was about to open my mouth when I saw the older woman from before approaching us. She walked quickly and looked behind her shoulder to make sure no one was watching.

"You shouldn't be here," she said under her breath.

"Sorry, what?" I said.

"You shouldn't be here. I shouldn't even be talking to you, but she was my friend, you know? Your mother and I weren't best friends or anything, but she was a good friend of mine."

"Okay. If she was a good friend of yours, will you tell me what you meant when you were saying that my dad died?"

"Look, I know that this must come as a shock to you. I don't understand how you haven't been told the truth, but then I'm not friends with anyone in that circle anymore. I don't even know exactly what went on but..."

"What's your name? Can you—"

"I can't afford to tell you my name." She squeezed my hand. "Please just get out of here. If they see you, if anyone knows—" She pulled me toward the exit.

"I don't really understand what you're talking about, and you're kind of scaring me." I glanced at Polly and then back to the woman. "What's going on here? I saw my sister and—"

"Listen to me very carefully, Tiffany. Before he died, your father—your real father—he cheated on your mom with her best friend."

"What?" I shook my head. "No, that's not possible. No."

"Yes," she said. "They ran away together." She lowered her voice. "They died in a car accident."

"What? No, but that doesn't make sense. My dad's at home. I just talked—"

"He's not your dad, Tiffany. That's all I can say. Please leave."

Just then, we heard the door behind us open. I turned, and I saw Jake's dad leaving the room. His eyes met mine, and I knew he'd seen me. And so did the woman. She stepped back quickly and melted into the crowd.

Jake's father hesitated, and I wondered if he was going to come up to me and say something to me, but instead, he followed the woman and blended into the crowd himself.

"Should we go and speak to Monique?" Polly asked me as we stared at the half-open door.

"And say what?" I said. "No, I need to think. I'm so confused, Polly. I just don't know what to think."

"Call Jake."

"And say what?"

"Just call him."

"Okay." I grabbed my phone and called him. He answered on the second ring.

"Tiffany, how are you?"

"I am okay," I said, but my voice cracked. "What are you doing?"

"Are you calling to have phone sex?"

"No, I'm not. Of course not."

"Okay. You sound agitated."

"I just saw something, and I don't know what to think, but I think you should know."

"What did you see?"

"I saw your dad."

"Okay?"

"And Monique."

"And this should mean something to me?"

"They were having sex, Jake."

He started laughing then. "Do you think I care, Tiffany?"

"What? But—"

"Where are you?"

"What, what do you mean?" I didn't want to tell him where I was.

"Where are you?"

"Nowhere. I have to go." I hung up quickly and looked at Polly. "I don't think he's of any use."

"What did he say when you told him that you saw Monique with his dad?"

"He just laughed. He *laughed*, Polly. She's nothing to him. Just like me. I'm nothing to him. We're nothing to him. And I have a bad feeling that Monique is nothing to them, either, even if she feels like she's in control."

"Should we go and talk to her?"

"No," I said, "I don't want her to know that we've seen. Let's go." I grabbed Polly's hand and hurried down the corridor so that we could get out of there before Monique came out.

"Do you think what that lady was saying was true?" Polly said from behind me.

I turned to her, chewing on my lower lip. "I wish I knew. I wish I knew the truth."

TWENTY-FIVE

Polly called me as I was pulling up the driveway. I answered quickly. "Hey, what's going on?"

"I was just checking on you to make sure that you got home okay."

"Yeah, I did. Just arrived. Are you home?"

"Yeah, I'm in my room. Wiping off my makeup. My mom saw me when I came in, and she nearly went berserk."

"What do you mean?"

"She wanted to know why I was dressed up like a hooker."

"You didn't look like a hooker, Polly." I laughed.

"I know. How are you feeling? Really?"

"I mean, I'm feeling kind of confused, and I just don't know what is going on in the world anymore, but aside from that..."

"I know. It's crazy."

"It does seem completely absurd, doesn't it? I mean, how can my dad not be my dad? He's always been my dad." I sighed. I stopped the car and turned off the ignition. "Though sometimes..."

"Yeah?"

"Sometimes I've wondered why he doesn't love me."

"You know he loves you. He's your dad."

"Polly, he's never shown any real love toward me. He's never shown any positivity toward me. Maybe it's because I'm not his kid."

"But why wouldn't he have told you that? It doesn't make sense."

"I know."

"And Tiffany," Polly's voice was urgent, "we don't know if that lady was telling the truth. I mean, who knows? For all we know, she works for Monique or she's Monique's friend or she knows Jake's dad and they're doing this just to get you all upset and discombobbled."

"Discombobbled." I laughed. "What's that?"

"You know what I mean. Discombobulated."

"I know what you mean. And that thought did cross my mind as I was driving home. But it just doesn't make sense. Like why would Monique pretend that our dad wasn't my dad?" I paused. "Oh my gosh. Something just struck me."

"What?"

"What if he's not Monique's dad, either?"

"Oh, shit! You think?"

"Girl, I don't know anymore. I just don't know." I sighed. "But let me call you back later. Okay? I'm about to go in the house, and I don't want anyone to hear me walking in."

"What do you mean, anyone? Monique was still at the club when we left."

"Yeah, but I don't want my dad to see me looking like this and wondering where I've been." I'd changed back into my regular clothes, but I still had a face full of makeup on.

"Okay, well, I'll call you back later." I hung up, got out

of the car, and opened the front door. I listened for a few seconds before I made my way up the stairs. The house was deathly quiet.

It reminded me of a scene in a horror movie, the heroine creeping through a spooky old house moments before the killer jumped out at her. I laughed silently to myself. It did almost feel like I was living in a horror movie. I walked along the landing and thought about going to the library to see if Jake left me any notes or photographs, but I didn't.

Instead, I continued on to my bedroom. I opened the door and turned the light on. As soon as I switched the light on, I heard a noise to the right of me, but before I could turn, something hit my head and everything went black.

I WOKE up with a splitting headache in an unfamiliar room. I groaned as I pushed myself into a sitting position.

Gradually, it all came back to me. Someone had been in my room; they'd hit me and had brought me here. And where was here? I looked around the room. Everything was a deep gray. On the TV in front of me, there were scenes of a little girl and a woman running around.

I got up and tried the door. It was locked, of course. I banged on it. "Let me out, please!" I shouted. "Let me out!"

But there was no response. Whoever had brought me here wasn't ready to let me know yet.

I screamed, but that didn't change anything. Had Jake kidnapped me? If he'd done it once before, who was to say he wouldn't do it again? But the first time he hadn't tried to hide what he was doing, and he certainly hadn't hit me on the head.

I looked around the room again to see if there were any

clues. This time I noticed a bunch of papers on the table next to the TV. I walked over to the papers and looked at them. There was a yellow Post-it note on the front page with the words "Sign me" scrawled on it.

I blinked in confusion and looked through the papers quickly. It appeared to be some sort of contract signing over my inheritance to a corporation I'd never heard of before in my life.

Were Jake and his father planning to kill my father? Was that why he wanted me to sign the papers? Because I had no inheritance until my father died. I had nothing. That's why I still lived with him.

The flickering images on the television caught my attention.

There was a man running, a handsome man, a man who looked familiar, but I didn't know why. And then I saw the child he was running with. I gasped. The child was me.

I sat on a chair that was directly in front of the TV and watched. A moment later, my mother came on the screen. She played with me as the man watched them lovingly. Was that my father, my real father? He looked like he adored us. He looked like he would never want to leave us.

The throbbing in my head was getting worse. I was torn between the urge to cry and the desire to sleep. Who had brought me here? And why were they showing me this video?

It had to be Jake. He had given me the photos. And now he was showing me the video. He was going to keep me here. He was going to keep me here forever.

"The joke's on you!" I shouted. "I have no inheritance. I have nothing. It's all my father's." And then I paused. Was it my father's?

Was it my father's—or was it my other father's? I didn't

understand, but I didn't care. I knew I just wanted to get out of there. I walked up to the table again, grabbed the pen, and signed and initialed each page.

"I've done it," I yelled. "Please just let me out!" No response. I went to the door and banged some more. "I've signed the contract. Please! Let me out!" Nothing.

I walked back to the chair and started crying. My head was pounding now, and my back was starting to ache. I looked around the room to see if there was anything to eat or drink. I would've killed for a Motrin, but there was nothing, not even a bottle of water.

I wasn't sure if whoever had brought me here wanted me to die or what they wanted from me. All I knew was that I was feeling tired again. And my head was hurting. I closed my eyes and let the blackness overcome me once more.

TWENTY-SIX

"Tiffany! Tiffany!"

I heard my name, and I wasn't sure who was calling me. Was I dreaming? Was it a nightmare?

"Tiffany, where are you? Tiffany!"

My eyes flew open. It wasn't a dream. Someone was calling me.

"Tiffany!"

The voice came closer, and I recognized it.

"Polly?" I got up, still blinking. "Polly, I'm in here!"

The door was ajar. Someone had opened it. They must have opened it while I'd been asleep, but why hadn't they let me know? I stepped outside of the room and saw Polly running down the corridor.

"Oh my God, Tiffany. You're okay!" She hugged me to her. Her face was red, and I could tell she'd been crying.

"What's going on, Polly? How are you here?"

"Someone texted me. I don't know who. They just said, 'Get to this address. Tiffany's there and she needs you.' I was so worried! What are you doing here, Tiffany?"

"I don't know what's going on. When I got home last night—I think it was last night."

"Last night?" Polly looked at me. "Where did you go last night? I was texting you."

"We went to the club. Remember?"

"No." She shook her head. "That was two days ago, Tiffany."

I put a hand to my head. "Oh my God. No way. Well, anyway, that night, when I got home, someone hit me over the head as soon as I got into my room and..." I chewed on my lower lip. "Come." I opened the door wide and pointed at the TV. "Look at that."

"I don't know. I think we should just go. What if they come and they do something to us? What if they lock us in the room?"

"Just look quickly. I'll stand guard outside the room. Just look at the TV," I said.

Polly sighed and walked into the room and stared at the TV.

"Is that you?" she said.

"Yes. It's me. And that's my mom."

"Wow. Where's this video from?"

"I have no idea."

"And look, there's a man in the video." I pointed at the screen.

"Who's that?" Polly said, looking at me with wide eyes.

"I don't know. I think it could be my real dad."

"So you think it's true, then?" She hurried out of the room and pulled me down the corridor with her.

"I don't know."

We ran down the long corridor to the main door and stepped outside into some sort of industrial lot. I didn't recognize it at all. "Where are we?"

"We're near the wharf," Polly replied. "Come quick. My car is over here." She grabbed my hand, and we ran to her car. I jumped in the passenger seat, and she hit the gas, looking more relieved the farther away we got. "Where should we go? Should I take you home?"

"I don't know. I'm frightened. I don't know what to do, Polly. Everything's just going out of control, and I think it might be Jake that kidnapped me. I think he's the one that hit me. He's cruel. I mean, I knew he was horrible, but I didn't know he could be this evil."

"Are you sure?" she said. "You really think it's Jake?"

"Yes. I think it's him. I think that... There's something he wants from me. There's something he wants from my family, and I just don't understand."

"What are you going to do?"

"I want your phone."

"What?"

"Not to keep. I want to call Jake. I need to ask him if it was him that did this to me."

"Are you sure?"

"Yes," I said. "Please, Polly."

"Okay." She handed me her phone. "I'm just going to keep driving, okay? I'm not sure where to go. I don't want to take you home."

"I know. It's okay. Maybe we can get something to eat. I'm really hungry."

"Sorry. I should have thought of that."

"There's nothing for you to be sorry about. You saved my life."

"No, I didn't. Someone wanted to make sure you're okay. Someone texted me. I just wish I knew who."

I let out a deep sigh, and then I put Jake's number into

the phone. How crazy that I'd memorized it already. He answered after three rings.

"Hello? Who is this?"

"Jake?" I said coldly. "It's Tiffany."

"Tiffany." His voice softened. "What's going on?"

"You tell me, Jake. You've got the papers now."

"What papers?" He sounded confused.

"You know what papers. Stop playing. You're not a good actor. You hurt me, Jake. You probably gave me a concussion."

"What are you talking about?"

"You kidnapped me again. You just left me in a room. I was banging on the door and crying and—"

"Tiffany, slow down. What are you talking about? What happened? What room? Who kidnapped you?"

"You mean it wasn't you?" A chill washed over my body. I saw Polly looking at me, her face anxious.

"He says it wasn't him," I said to Polly.

"Who were you talking to?" asked Jake.

"I'm talking to Polly. She found me. We're in her car."

"I need to meet up with you, Tiffany. We need to chat."

"What? No, you got what you wanted—"

"Please."

"Just admit it, Jake. It was you. You trapped me. You just want to take over the business. Wasn't it enough that you're marrying Monique? Isn't it enough that you're taking everything that I love away from me?"

"I don't know what you think I did, Tiffany, but I did not kidnap you last night."

"It was two nights ago," I said. "You hit me over the head."

"It wasn't me. I swear to God. Meet me."

"No, I don't trust you."

"Meet me in a public place. Bring Polly. We need to talk."

"What are we going to talk about? I don't want to talk to you."

"Please, Tiffany."

"Fine. We're going to go and get breakfast. You can meet us at the restaurant."

"Where are you going?"

"Where are we going, Polly?"

"I'm not sure yet."

"She's not sure yet."

Jake groaned impatiently. "Meet me at Annie's Kitchen, okay? It's on Eighth Street."

"Annie's Kitchen?" I looked at Polly. "Do you know it? He says it's on Eighth Street."

"Yeah," she said. "I know it."

"Fine," I said, "we'll meet you there."

"Good. And are you okay, Tiffany?" He sounded concerned, which surprised me.

"I'm fine. At least I hope so. Not that you care."

"I care more than you think. I care more than you know. Meet me there."

And with that, he hung up. I was silent for a moment, then I looked at Polly. "He said it wasn't him."

"Do you believe him?" she asked. "If it wasn't him, who was it?"

"I don't know, Polly. None of this makes sense. None of this makes any sense whatsoever."

TWENTY-SEVEN

"Hey."

I looked up at the sound of Jake's deep voice. He was as handsome as ever, but I couldn't muster so much as a smile.

"Hi," I replied. I can tell that he wasn't pleased with the tone of my voice, but I didn't care.

"Hello, Jake," Polly said, a snark to her voice that I'd never heard before. I looked at her in surprise. I guess Polly thought it was Jake as well.

"Can I have a seat?" he asked.

"If you must," I said, not moving down on my side of the booth. Polly didn't move, either. We both just stared at him.

"Or I could just stand here."

"Fine." I slid down, and he sat next to me.

"I didn't kidnap you, Tiffany." His voice cracked slightly, and I looked at him in surprise. "You need to believe me. I didn't take you."

"Well, then if you didn't take me, who did?"

"I don't know. That's something we need to get to the bottom of. What exactly happened?"

"I came home, and when I went into my room, someone

hit me over the head. I woke up in a locked room. There was a TV on a table in front of me with some sort of video playing. I don't know how, because there was no DVD player or anything, but it was images of my mother and me and some man. And I know you've been giving me photos of my mom."

"I have," he said, nodding.

"So I assumed it was you. I was screaming, and I was shouting. I was banging on the door, and no one came to help me." Tears pricked my eyelids. "I thought I might die there."

Polly reached over and squeezed my hand. "Oh my God, Tiffany. It sounds absolutely horrible. I'm so sorry."

"That wasn't me, Tiffany," Jake insisted. "I would not do that to you."

"How am I supposed to believe that? You're freaking engaged to my sister!" I almost shouted. I could see people from across the restaurant looking at me, and I sighed. "I guess I should lower my voice."

"That would be helpful." Jake offered me a wry grin. "But if you need to scream and shout, you can. You're not embarrassing me."

"Well, thank you."

"You're welcome," he said.

We stared at each other for a couple of seconds, and as I looked into his eyes, I realized that I didn't think it was him. I didn't like him and I didn't trust him, but he wasn't a liar. He was cold and he was calculating, but he wasn't cruel. I really didn't think he would harm me.

"So what's really going on here, Jake? Because I just don't understand. Why have you been giving me pictures of my mother, and why are you marrying my sister? And why did a woman last night—well, two nights ago—tell me that my dad isn't my dad?"

Jake let out a deep sigh. "I swear to you, it wasn't me. I swear to you. Look, my family did want to take over your corporation. I'm not lying about that. That's why I agreed to the deal with your father." He chuckled. "Well, the man who claims to be your father."

I stared at him through narrowed eyes. Did he know more than he was letting on? "Why did you want my family's company so badly? There are so many different companies that you could have. I just don't understand."

"We wanted to take the company and run it into the ground," he said softly. There was a bleakness to his tone, and I felt my heart breaking.

"Why, though?"

"I wanted to destroy you," he said, as calmly as if he just said that the sky was blue or the leaves and the trees were green. "I wanted to destroy you, and so did Nico."

"Why? Why did you guys want to destroy me? And when you say me, did you mean me and my father and my sister, or just me?"

"Your father is not your father." He swallowed. "Your real father, he ran off with my mother."

"What?" My jaw dropped, and I stared at him in shock. "What do you mean?"

"Your father and your mother were friends with my parents. And actually, when you were a baby, I met you." He sighed. "But your dad and my mom, well, they had an affair and they ran off together, and your father killed my mom."

"What? But my... *What?*" I said. "I don't understand."

"I mean, he didn't murder her. They were in a car crash." He clenched his fist, and he looked at me. "And I grew up hating your father. I grew up hating everything about him. So I grew up hating you."

"But he isn't me."

"I know that, but you have to understand. My mother was my life. I loved her, and she wouldn't have left us. I don't care what anyone says. But she died, and it was your father who killed her. And I swore to myself that I would make anyone related to him pay, and you were what was left, you and the house and the business."

"But what do you mean? How is that going to hurt me? It's not my business. It's my father's."

"No, Tiffany. Don't you understand? It was your real father's business, your real biological father's business. When he left, your mother met your stepfather. He was a charmer, a snake oil salesman, and he said he would help her run the business. Your father, when he died, he left everything to you."

"But what about Monique?"

"Monique is not your sister. Your stepfather already had Monique when he met your mother, and you became, I guess, a blended family until your mother died and your stepfather was left to raise you."

"What? So he's never been my father, and Monique isn't my sister?"

"No, and they both know that." Jake sighed. "Your father is a slimy man and your sister is even slimier, but it was you I wanted to hurt."

"But then why marry Monique? Why not try to marry me?"

"You didn't know," he said softly. "And your father, well, he's practically run the company into the ground already. And I know you love your home more than anything else. I've been studying you for years. I know how much you love your books and that library, and I just wanted to make you hurt."

"Well, you've done that. You've hurt me."

"I'm sorry, Tiffany. I didn't know who you were, and I shouldn't have blamed you for the sins of your father. You have to believe me. I would not have harmed you."

I stared at him, not knowing what to say, when suddenly Polly spoke. I'd almost forgotten she was there.

"So if you didn't kidnap and hurt her, who did?" she said. The three of us stared at each other, all of our eyes questioning, all of our eyes thinking, all of our eyes wondering.

We had no idea what was going on, and I didn't know if I would ever be the same ever again.

TWENTY-EIGHT

"So then, is Nico the one that kidnapped Tiffany?" Polly asked.

I could tell from the look on her face that the answer really mattered to her. I stared at Jake to see if his expression would give any tale-tell signs.

"No." Jake shook his head. "Not at all."

"But Nico wanted revenge on me as well, right?" I asked.

"Yes, but I'm the one that spearheaded this." Jake looked at me. "And it wasn't me."

"So, then who was it?" I was getting pissed off now.

"I don't know. I just know it wasn't me or Nico."

"Could it have been your dad?" Polly asked Jake.

"I don't know," Jake admitted. "You have to remember that my dad loved my mom just as much as your mom loved your dad. And when she left him, when she cheated, it broke him."

"It broke him enough to want to destroy my life?" I stared at Jake, tears welling up in my eyes.

"This was my idea," Jake said softly. "I'm the one that

talked my dad and Nico into it." He sighed. "But I didn't have to convince them too hard."

"Why is your dad sleeping with my..." I stopped myself from saying *sister*. "Sleeping with Monique?" I said. "What the fuck?"

"My dad likes young, beautiful women. And if they throw themselves at him, so much the better."

"Monique threw herself at your dad? Monique likes powerful men, but she was going to marry you?"

"She cares about me as much as I care about her. You know this wasn't a love match. You know that the marriage was never going to happen, right?" He took my hand, and I pulled it away from him quickly.

"I just don't know anything anymore. I need to go home. I'm sure my dad and Monique must be worried about me."

"I don't know if that's a good idea," Polly said. "Neither one of them called me and asked me if you were with me, so that means either they didn't notice you were missing or they just didn't care."

"Or it means that your dad was the one who did it." Jake sounded angry. "No, you're not going home."

"Excuse me!" I glared at him. "Who are you to tell me not to go to my own home?"

"I'm not letting you go back to that house. If your dad was the one that had you kidnapped, who knows what he could do!"

"It doesn't matter. I need to go home."

"You're staying with me. We need to speak to an attorney because you said you signed a contract signing over your stake in the business, right?"

"Yeah, so?"

"So, if it's your dad, that means you've given him legal

possession of your company. It means you've given away all your money and your house and everything."

"No," I said quietly. "It doesn't."

"What do you mean?"

"Because I didn't sign my name properly." I smiled at him bitterly.

"What?" He frowned. "What do you mean?"

I laughed. "I'm not stupid. I wouldn't just sign a contract without knowing the implications. I signed the papers Minnie Mouse."

"What?" Polly said. "No way!"

"Yeah. Whoever locked me up was stupid. So then maybe it was my dad. They must not have even read the signature properly, because I didn't sign my name. No way I would have signed my name to something like that."

"That's my girl," Jake said with a smile. "I'm proud of you."

"It wasn't you, was it?" I looked at him. And then I knew one hundred percent in my heart that he was telling me the truth. "It wasn't you."

"No, it wasn't."

"But you wanted to destroy me—"

"I didn't know who you were when I came up with the plan. I didn't know you. I hadn't interacted with you. I hadn't fallen for you."

"And now?"

"And now I don't want to destroy you. Now. I want..." He paused and sighed.

"What?"

He looked at Polly, who was leaning in eagerly.

I crossed my arms over my chest. "Whatever you say to me, you can say in front of Polly."

"This isn't a conversation we should be having now. We

don't even know who's behind what's going on. I can guarantee it's not Nico. But if it's my dad..." Jake sighed. "I just don't know what's next. My dad is very powerful, and..."

"And what?"

"I won't let him hurt you, Tiffany. I won't let anybody hurt you."

"But you would choose him over me. He's your dad."

"It's not going to come to that. I want you to stay with me. I want you to come home with me."

"What about what I want?"

"This isn't the time to be arguing. We need to figure out who tried to harm you. We need to try to figure out who's trying to steal your business."

"Well, you were trying to hurt me, and I didn't even know."

"Come with me, please, Tiffany."

"Okay," I said softly. "I'll come with you. I will stay with you, but not forever."

"I didn't ask you forever." He grinned.

"I know. I know. I didn't mean it like that," I said quickly, hoping that he didn't think that I thought we were going to get engaged, or married, or something like that.

I wasn't crazy. I knew he wasn't offering me his undying love, or even a lifetime. I knew he was just offering to protect me for now, but it felt so much more than that. It felt like the world was spinning around me, and I was out of control. I was losing every single thing that was important to me. My whole identity was gone. If Monique wasn't my sister and my father wasn't my father, then who was I?

"What was my dad's name?" I asked. Jake grimaced. "You don't have to tell me now. I suppose it must be painful for you to think about him."

"I didn't know your father," Jake said. "I mean, I

remember bits and pieces from when I was young, but obviously I was a child myself, and I didn't know him on that level. My father knew your father and..." His jaw tightened. "He doesn't talk about it. He doesn't talk about my mom, either. But I remember her. I remember her taking me and Nico to the park and taking us to the store to get burgers and milkshakes. And I remember every night she would hug me and kiss me on the forehead, and we'd look out the window and watch the stars and the moon. And she'd sing me lullabies and hold my hand. And she'd whisper in my ear, 'My darling Jacob, I love you to the moon and back. I loved you more than a million stars in the sky.'" His voice cracked, and he looked down at the table.

I was taken aback by how vulnerable he was being. I almost wondered if it was an act, but I knew deep inside that it wasn't. He'd loved his mother, and the fact of losing her had caused him to try and destroy me. The memory of his mother was so strong in his mind that it had formed who he was.

I felt sad, sad for Jake and sad for myself. Our lives had been ruined, forever twisted by a horrible betrayal that had led to a terrible car accident.

"I'm sorry," I said. "I know it's not my fault. And I know that it doesn't mean anything, but for what it's worth, I'm sorry."

"No." He shook his head. "It's me who should be sorry. It's me who took this down a bad path. If anything, I should have tried to protect you. I should have been there for you. I can't imagine what it was like losing your father and then losing your mother and being brought up by a man who despised you with a sister who hated you. I'm sorry. I should have protected you instead of trying to destroy you."

"You surprise me," Polly said.

We both looked at her.

"I do?" Jake said.

"You sound remorseful," she said. "I never would've believed it if I hadn't seen it. I should go now, let you guys talk with each other."

"You don't have to go," I said quickly.

"I do," she said. "I think there's a lot more that needs to be said between the two of you. And I think it can't be said with me here."

"But Polly—"

"You'll tell me later."

There was a maturity in her that I'd never seen before. I couldn't help wondering if it was something I'd chosen not to see.

"I love you, Tiffany." She got up. "Take care of my best friend, Jake, okay?"

"I will."

She looked at me. "And call me once you get to Jake's place so I know you're okay."

"I will," I said. "I love you, Polly."

"I love you, too." And with that, she was gone.

"She's a good friend to you," Jake said.

I nodded. "She's the best."

"You do believe me, right? You do trust me?"

"Yeah." I nodded. "I do."

"When you called me, when you told me what had happened, I was so worried." He clenched his fists. "You know that, right?"

"I do," I said sincerely. He leaned forward and gave me a quick kiss on the lips. "What was that for?"

"It's something I've been wanting to do since I got here."

"Really?"

"Yeah. But I didn't want to do it in front of Polly, just in case."

"Just in case what? Are you worried she'd say something?"

"No, I was more worried that I might caress your breast or pull your hair." He winked at me. "And I didn't want her to feel like she was seeing something she shouldn't."

"Jacob!" I blushed and looked at him. "You're so bad!"

"I'm not as bad as I want to be. We should go back to my place."

"What, now?"

"Yeah."

He squeezed my thigh under the table, and I trembled. "What are you doing?"

"I want you. And I know this is crazy, and it's totally inappropriate, but I want you so badly. I just want to touch you and taste you and feel you and be inside of you." His eyes were dark with desire.

"Then what are we waiting for?" I said softly.

"You want me, too?" I nodded. He grabbed my hand and pulled me up out of the booth. "Let's go."

"But we haven't even eaten—"

"Doesn't matter." He pulled out a hundred-dollar bill and left it on the table. "Let's go."

We left the restaurant and walked toward a black Jeep Cherokee. He pushed me against the car and kissed me passionately. I moaned at the sensation of his lips on mine and his arms around my waist. I kissed him back, loving the feel of his hard body against mine. His erection pressed into me, and I gasped as his hand slipped up my blouse and caressed my breast.

"I want you so badly," he groaned against my lips.

It was hot, and it was sexy. And I didn't care who was walking by and witnessing. I wanted him just as badly.

"Let's go back to your place, Jake," I whispered.

He grinned as he pulled away. "Let's do it. I can't wait to have you in my bed again."

TWENTY-NINE

Jake's lips pressed against my skin, warm and luscious. I started to unbutton his shirt. He chuckled as my fingers fumbled.

"It's not funny," I said. "Take off your shirt."

"Why? Do you want to have your wicked way with me?"

"I think you want to have your wicked way with me." I blinked innocently at him. "I feel like little Red Riding Hood and the wolf is about to eat me."

"Oh, I'm going to eat you, all right," he growled and pushed me back on the bed. I giggled as he crawled on top of me and kissed me on the lips. The way he stared into my eyes made me feel alive, as if I were the only woman in the world.

"You are delectable, Tiffany," he murmured as he kissed down my throat. My breath hitched as he began unbuttoning my blouse, then he pulled me up and ripped it off of me. My bra came off just as quickly. I closed my eyes as he pushed me back into the bed, covering my nipple with his lips. He made me feel as if I were on fire. I felt feverish as he sucked and bit and chewed. I tangled my fingers in his hair and pulled.

"You want me, don't you, Tiffany?" he gasped as he kissed back up to my lips, and his eyes pierced into my mine, dark and hot.

"You know I want you, Jake," I moaned as his tongue slipped into my mouth. His fingers glided over my stomach before slipping into my panties where he began to rub me ever so gently. I spread my legs wider and gasped as he slipped a finger inside of me. I just loved the touch of him. I just...

His phone rang, and he pulled back.

"I should get that," he sighed.

"No," I groaned, not wanting him to leave me for one second.

"It's not my regular phone." He got up. "It's a number only Nico has." He picked up a phone from the top of the dresser. "Yeah, what's up?"

He slipped the finger that had just been inside of me into his mouth and sucked. I grinned at him, beckoning him to come back to the bed. He walked back and sat down on the mattress, stroking my breast as he listened to whatever Nico was saying.

"Are you sure?" he said tersely, and I frowned. "There's a note. Read it to me. I am here with Tiffany, Nico. It's okay. She wasn't involved. She was kidnapped. She thought it was me. So then, it definitely wasn't that. Fuck. I'm going to put you on speakerphone, okay?" He pressed a button and then held it down. "Nico's just gone to get the letter. But something's happened."

"What? You're scaring me. Is it Polly? Oh my God, please tell me it's not Polly."

"No." He shook his head. "It's my dad."

"What do you mean?"

"My dad's been kidnapped." He ran his hand through his hair. "So I guess we know, then."

"What?" I said, staring at him confused.

"It was your stepfather. He kidnapped you, and now he's taken my dad."

"But what... Why? I don't understand."

"Greed. Maybe he wanted to get one up on my dad, too." He shrugged. "Nico's gone to get the paper that he found."

"Okay." I could feel myself growing cold, my desire from earlier having left my body. Jake pulled me toward him and kissed me on the forehead.

"It'll be okay. I promise," he said. I wondered at how he could find it in himself to comfort me when it was his father that had been kidnapped.

"Okay, I'm back," Nico said.

"Okay, you're on speaker."

Nico cleared his throat. "So, it's on a plain piece of A4 lined paper."

"Just read the goddamn note, Nico. I don't care what fucking paper it's on," Jake snapped.

"Fine, dude. It says, 'I have your father. He will not be harmed unless you go to the police. I want ten million in cash within twenty-four hours. Call this number once you have the money."

"What the fuck?" Jake said.

"You're telling me, dude," Nico said. "What the fuck is going on?"

"He must have realized," I said suddenly.

"Realized what?" Nico said through the phone.

"He must have realized that I wrote Minnie Mouse on

the contract. He must have realized he's not getting my company. That must be why he's done it."

"You're right." Jake nodded. "Fuck. How dangerous do you think your dad is?"

"He's not my dad, remember?"

"Sorry, your stepdad."

"I don't know." I shook my head. "But then, I feel like I don't really know anything."

"You're not thinking about giving him the money?" Nico asked.

"What choice do we have?" Jake sighed. "It's not like we don't have ten million to spare."

"It's the principle of the thing, Jake." Nico sounded pissed. "Dad would not want us giving that asshole ten million dollars."

"Yeah, but Dad also wouldn't want to die."

"I say we hunt that fucker down and we kill him."

"We don't even know where he is." Jake paused. "Unless he's at the house. No, he wouldn't be dumb enough to stay at the house."

"You never know," I pointed out. "He's not the sharpest tool in the shed. I mean, he took my father's company and he ran it into the ground."

"That's true." Jake nodded. "Okay, Nico, we're going to come over there. We'll be there in thirty minutes. Actually, maybe an hour."

"An hour? Why an hour?"

"Doesn't matter." Jake hung up the phone and stared at me.

"You're not thinking about actually having sex still, are you?" I stared at him with wide eyes.

He grabbed my hand, placed it on his crotch, and squeezed. "I'm just still fucking hard as hell, so..."

"Jake, you just found out your dad's been kidnapped!"

"Yeah, but if I'm horny, I'm not going to be able to concentrate." He shrugged. "So, what you say?"

"Jake, we just found out your dad's been kidnapped. I'm not about to fucking bounce up and down on your cock."

"I love it when you talk dirty to me." He chuckled. "But you're right. We need to get over to Nico's and fucking figure this shit out. Once I get ahold of your dad, that's it, girl."

"He's not my dad, so I really don't care."

"Fair enough," he said.

He pulled me toward him and kissed me hard. I was wet and wanted to have sex just as badly as he did, but I knew I'd never forgive myself if we fucked now and then something happened to his dad. We had to get over to Nico's as soon as possible, so we could figure out what to do next. I grabbed the side of his face and kissed him gently on the lips, then pushed him away.

"I want you just as badly as you want me, Jake, but we have to go now."

"I know." He nodded and stood up and stretched. "But fuck it, I'm going to have blue balls for the rest of the fucking night."

"I know," I said, laughing. "You kind of deserve it."

"Why?" he growled.

"For being an asshole all those times that we met previously."

"Fair enough." He flashed me that cocky grin. "Let's go."

THIRTY

"I thought you guys were going to be here in another half hour," Nico said as he opened the door.

"Nope, we're here now," Jake said as he made his way into the house. I followed behind him, but Nico still stood there.

"Is Polly here as well?" he said, looking outside.

I shook my head. "Why would Polly be here?"

He shrugged. "No reason, I figured she's like your twin or something. You're always together."

"She's my best friend, and she is like a sister to me, but I don't want her to be in danger."

"Not from my father?"

"Your father—or *you*." I stared him down. I wanted him to know that I didn't want him to mess around with Polly. She was in too deep as it was. She already liked him, and I knew she wasn't strong enough to sleep with a man like Nico and then walk away. I didn't trust that he was the sort of man who could commit to anyone, and I was sure he'd break her heart.

"I was just asking," he said as he slammed the door shut. "So, what do we do?"

"You know, I saw your dad at a club the other night with my sister, and he saw me," I said as we made our way into the living room. The house surprised me. It was modern yet homey. It had a womanly touch to it, and I wondered if Nico had chosen the furnishings himself or if he'd had an interior designer.

Jake and I sat on a cream linen couch and Nico sat on a tan leather armchair to our right.

"So my dad saw you. What does that mean?" Nico's voice was gruff. "He's the one that's been kidnapped."

"Well, if your dad saw me, who's to say that my dad doesn't know about Monique and your dad?" I sighed. "I'm never going to stop calling him my dad, am I? I hate myself for it because—"

"It's okay. Don't be so hard on yourself." Jake squeezed my arm. He gave me a loving look, and I smiled back at him gratefully.

"It's just weird knowing that the man I've been calling Dad for pretty much all of my life isn't my real father, and my sister's not my sister. It's just a mind fuck."

"So you know, then?" Nico's gaze darted to me.

"Yeah, I know." I glared at him. "I know that my dad and your mom ran away together. I know that they died in a car crash. I know that my dad and my sister lied to me about who I was, and I know that you and Jake wanted to destroy me and hurt me, even though it wasn't my fault."

Nico shrugged again nonchalantly. "Hey, it's a shit show, right?" He stood up. "I need a drink. Anyone else want anything?"

"I'll have a lime soda," I said.

"Give me a whiskey," Jake said. Nico nodded as he headed toward a bar at the back of his living room.

Jake offered me an apologetic smile. "You have every right to be mad," he said softly. "I'm not upset at you, and Nico isn't upset at you, either."

"I heard that," Nico said. "And who's to say I'm not upset at her for shouting at me in my own home?"

"Nico!" Jake chastised him, and Nico chuckled.

"What? What, are we all best friends now? Shit, didn't you literally just find out that we set you up?"

"What do you mean, you set me up?" I blinked and stared at Jake, and he cursed under his breath. "What's going on? What do you mean you set me up?"

Nico coughed discretely. "Oops, my bad. Guess you didn't know everything."

"What's he talking about, Jake?"

"So, look." Jake swallowed hard. "I know you're not going to like this, but I promise that after the first time, I changed my mind—"

"What are you talking about?"

He sighed. "Okay, so like I said, Monique and I were never going to get married."

"Um, you were engaged?" I reminded him.

"Yeah, we were engaged, but it was never going to happen." He shook his head. "I was never going to marry Monique. I don't care about Monique. It was you I wanted to hurt."

"Okay, and?"

"So I needed to get to closer to you. Becoming engaged to Monique brought me into your life."

"I see."

"I wouldn't have had that access unless it was through

the family. I wouldn't have been invited into your home so many times."

"Okay." I stared at him through narrow eyes. "And so, what, you wanted to hurt me? Is that why you came into the library that day and said you were going to get rid of it?"

"Yeah." He ran his hands through his hair. "Okay, look, there's more to it than that."

"What you mean, there's more to it than that?"

"I wanted to seduce you."

"Okay..." My heart started to race.

"I wanted you to fall for me." He sighed as he stared into my eyes. "And I wanted you to find out about your mother. That's why I was leaving the photos. I have photos of all of us. I was going to gradually give you more and more hints so you'd figure out the truth. But by the time you figured it out, I wanted you to be head over heels in love with me and," he cursed under his breath, "then I was going to break your heart."

Nico walked over to us with the drinks. "There's nothing more painful than a broken heart," he said, an evil smile on his face. He handed me my drink, and then he handed a drink to Jake. "We thought the best way to destroy you would be to hurt you with something inside, something that would break your heart, and what's the thing that breaks your heart the most?"

"Love," I said bitterly. I stared at Jake. "So you slept with me as part of the revenge as well? It was all about revenge, every single part of it?"

"The first time, yes. But after that—you have to believe me."

"Why should I believe you, Jake?" I stood up and paced the room. "I just don't even know what to think anymore. You had sex with me so you could get me to fall for you so you could break my heart? Well, joke's on you, Jake, because I would never fall for a man like you, never."

He jumped up and walked toward me, but I pointed at him. "Stay away from me."

"I promise you, it wasn't just about that. When I went to sleep with you the first time, when I flirted and I took you with me, it was about more than revenge. I felt a connection to you. The more I got to know you, the more I liked you. I loved the fire in your eyes, and I knew from the first time I slept with you that it was no longer about me getting revenge and trying to hurt you. It was about more than that—"

"I don't believe you, Jake. Why should I believe you? Every single time we have a conversation or something happens, something new comes out. What are you going to tell me next?" Tears stung my eyes. I didn't want to be there. I wanted to be at home in my bed, curled up, crying. "I want to go home."

"You can't go home, Tiffany. It's not safe."

"I want to go home. I don't care. Let the man that I call my father do whatever he wants to do to me. He can't hurt me anymore. You've won, Jake. Don't you get it? You've won."

"I haven't won anything, Tiffany. The last thing I want to see is you hurt. The last thing I want to see is you crying, and I can't stand the thought of you getting hurt." He walked over and pulled me into his arms. "Don't you get it, Tiffany? I'm falling for you. I've fallen for you. This is about more than that now."

"It might be for you," I said, "but it's not for me." I pushed him away hard and looked over at Nico. "If Jake won't take me home, you take me home."

"Why would I go against my brother's wishes?"

"Because if you don't, I will tell Polly everything I know about the both of you, and I will poison her mind so much that she won't even look at you, let alone talk to you again."

Nico stiffened visibly and his face went pale, then he shrugged carelessly. "I don't care about Polly. Poison her mind against me, whatever." He took a sip of his drink.

Was I wrong? Had my brain lied to me? Was he not as interested in Polly as I'd thought? And then I saw it; his fingers were gripping his tumbler so hard that his knuckles were white. He did like Polly. He liked her a lot more than he was letting on. Maybe he was even lying to himself, but I could tell. I knew.

I didn't know what had gone on between the two of them because Polly had been secretive, but I knew that her feelings had deepened for him, and it looked like his feelings for her had deepened as well. He was falling in love with my friend. I loved her, and I wanted her to be happy, and I knew happiness didn't lie with Nico.

"Take me home, Jake," I said.

"I can't do that. I can't."

"Then come with me, check the house, and make sure that my father isn't going to do something to me, but I'm not going to stay here with you and Nico. I don't trust either of you. I don't like either of you. I want to go home."

"Tiffany, please." He looked at me beseechingly. "Please listen to me, please."

I shook my head. "If you're telling the truth and everything changed for you, then you'll take me home because I need to be away from you right now. I need my space."

THIRTY-ONE

"Where the hell do you guys think you're going without me?" Nico put his drink down and headed toward the door with us.

"What? You're not coming," I snapped.

"Like hell I'm not coming." He glared at me. "Your father has kidnapped my father. As much as I hate you and you hate me, the simple fact of the matter is he's got my father, and he wants three million."

"Three million?" Jake cleared his throat. "I thought you said ten million?"

"Well, the initial drop can be three million."

"What are you talking about? What initial drop?"

Nico sighed. "I called the number, okay?"

"You called the number?" Jake was pissed.

I stared at the two of them, and I wondered if they were going to get into a fistfight right in front of me. I would have loved to watch Jake beat up Nico. There was something about Nico's cocky arrogance that got to me even more than Jake's ego.

"I was worried, okay? And, look, sometimes kidnappers

don't play fair. So I had a number, I called. I have three million in the safe."

"You keep three million dollars in your safe?" I stared at him, my eyes wide.

"Yeah, that's chump change," he sneered. "They said it would be okay."

"So was it my dad?" I asked.

"I don't know. Whatever they were speaking through was some sort of voice changer. Sounded like a robot. I couldn't even tell if it was a man or a woman."

"Oh my gosh. What have you done?" Jake moaned. "So now they definitely think that they're getting the money."

"We just need Dad back. We can't lose another parent, Jake." Nico sighed. "I'm coming with you. If your stepdad has my father at your house, I'm getting him back."

"My stepdad's not that stupid. I mean, I know I said he was, but... He wouldn't bring your dad to my house if he was kidnapping him. Does that even make sense? He's going to get a voice changer to use on phone, yet he's just going to have your dad in my house? No, he wouldn't do that. He's not there."

"So then you won't mind if we come and just check, will you?" Nico said. "I'll drive."

"No," Jake said, "I'll drive."

"No, you won't. You just had a whiskey."

"You were drinking, too."

Nico rolled his eyes. "Ginger ale, brother, ginger ale."

"Fine. You can drive."

"What?" I stared at Jake. "You're going to let him come with us to the house?" I'd made it clear that I didn't want Nico anywhere near me. I didn't care if they were brothers or not.

"We're both armed," he said. "If something goes down, two guns are going to be better than one. It'll be okay."

"Whatever," I said, shaking my head and crossing my arms. I wanted to call Polly to tell her everything that I'd found out, but now was not the time. "Let's go, then."

We drove in silence toward my house. As I sat in the back seat, I wondered if my father would have run away with their mother if he'd known everything that was going to happen. Would he have regretted what he put me through? Would he have regretted what he put them through? Was it worth it? Was love really worth it?

I thought about what I'd learned about Jake, and my heart broke even more. Obviously, I hadn't slept with him because I thought we were madly in love, but I thought it'd been because our mutual attraction was so intense that neither one of us could deny our feelings for the other. But now, I realized that it had only been me. Jake had just been using me. He had wanted me to fall for him, and I hated to admit it, but a part of me had already fallen. I felt something for him that I couldn't explain. It was like he'd poisoned my blood, and I knew I wouldn't be able to get him out, no matter how many bad things I learned about him.

I wasn't going to cry in the back seat. I wasn't going to break down. I needed to get it out without him there. I needed to scream and shout and punch and let out all my frustration and hurt and anger. My own father's betrayal meant less to me than Jake's. Jake had somehow gotten into my heart, and now he was twisting each ventricle tighter and tighter. I almost felt like I couldn't breathe.

"We're here," Nico said, and I felt the car stop.

I blinked as I looked outside the window and realized that was my house in front of us. I hadn't even realized we'd been driving for so long.

"So, what's the plan?" I said from the back seat. I knew better than to just go marching through the front door like I normally did.

"We go through a side entrance," Jake said softly. "No one will be manning the side entrance."

"We don't know that," Nico said.

"I'm pretty confident," Jake said. "Come on."

We got out of the car. "You know, if my dad's home and he has your dad, he will know we're here already," I pointed out. "You didn't even turn off your lights when you came up the driveway."

"There was a reason for that," Nico said.

What possible reason could he have had for alerting my father to the fact that someone was approaching?

"And are you going to tell me what that reason was?" I prompted.

"No." He shook his head. "You're on a need-to-know basis, and you don't need to know."

"Are you freaking kidding me right now?"

"Listen to me, Tiffany," he said, "for all I know, you are involved in my father's kidnapping. For all I know, you were never really kidnapped in the first place, and this is some sort of long con."

"What!" Instinctively, I looked to Jake for support. "Is he serious? Are you serious, dude? Jake, please tell me you don't think the same thing. Please tell me!"

He took my hands in his and kissed me lightly on the lips before stepping back. "I know you would never do such a thing, Tiffany." There was a bleakness in his voice. "Forgive Nico. He doesn't know you like I do, but I know your heart." He smiled at me softly. "You're full of love, and compassion, and humor, and resilience, and strength, and vitality. You're honest, and you're sweet, and you're strong, and you're beautiful, and you're weak, and you're all the things that make you the woman that I've...become very attached to..." His voice trailed off, and I wondered if he had been planning on saying something else.

I wondered, but I stopped myself from hoping. I wasn't going to hope for something that could never be true.

Nico came and stood next to his brother.

"You'll have to forgive me, Tiffany, if you are innocent, but I haven't fucked you, so I don't have sex on the brain when I look at you. I just have my own common sense. Why would you and my father both be kidnapped? It doesn't make sense. So, either you weren't kidnapped and you are in on this, or something else is going on with our father. And of the two of you, I trust my father."

"Well, let's just say out of the two of you," I looked from Nico to Jake, "I don't trust either of you." I saw Jake's lip twist, but I didn't care. I wanted to hurt him as much as he hurt me. It was going to be a long time before I could forgive and forget everything that had happened. I would probably never be able to forget.

We walked along the periphery of the house until we made it to the side door. I opened it, and we crept inside.

"I can't believe that you guys leave your doors open."

"No one comes here," I said. "We're in the middle of nowhere."

"True, but still. Your father has to have plenty of haters aside from us."

"Perhaps," I said, "but come on, let's go."

We made our way into the house, and I was surprised to hear music playing. "So someone's home. I bet it's Monique," I said. But then I listened to the music. It was Vivaldi, and I knew that Monique never listened to classical music. Only my father listened to classical music.

"I think it's my dad," I said, looking at the two men.

"Get to the back," Jake said, putting me behind him. "We go first."

We crept down the corridor, and we could hear the music coming from upstairs. We made our way up the stairs, and I pointed to the right to indicate where my father's bedroom was. We crept toward his bedroom, and with each step, I felt more and more scared. But if my dad had kidnapped their father, what if he was about to die? I didn't love him. And I knew he didn't love me. And I knew he'd lied to me my entire life, but I didn't want to see him die, not this way.

As we got to my father's bedroom, we could all see that the door was open. My father was standing there, packing shirts into a suitcase.

"Put your hands up!" Jake ran into the room with Nico behind him, their guns drawn.

Dad turned around, shock on his face.

"What the hell is going on here?" He looked at the guns and then he looked back at me. "Tiffany, what is this?"

"I know, Dad. We all know."

"You all know what?"

"Where are you going, sir?" Jake nodded toward the suitcase.

"What do you mean, where am I going? I'm going to Barbados."

"You're going to Barbados? What, with the three million that Nico was going to give you?"

"What the hell are you talking about? Why would Nico be giving me three million?"

"You've got my dad. Where the fuck is my dad?" Nico grabbed him by the collar of his shirt. "Do you want me to beat the answer out of you?"

"Hey, guys, back off!" Dad said angrily. "I have no idea what the hell's going on here, but you need to back the fuck off. Get those guns away from me. I have no idea where your father is. And what three million?"

"Dad, I know the truth. Stop lying."

"What fucking truth are you talking about?"

"I know you're not my real father. I know my mom and my real dad!" My voice broke. I couldn't continue.

"She knows that her real dad ran off with our mom," Jake said somberly. "She knows that her dad died. She knows that the company that you've run into the ground was hers. She knows why you kidnapped her and tried to force her to sign a contract, relinquishing the entire company to you. What you didn't count on was that she would be smart and that she would sign it Minnie Mouse."

"What the hell are you talking about?" Dad looked at me. "So, fine. I'm not your real father. You had no other parents. You were an orphan. I didn't have to bring you up, you know. I was helping you."

"By spending her fortune and trying to steal it?" Jake said angrily.

"Hey, the stock market took some dips and turns. I did my best," he shrugged, "but I sure didn't kidnap you. What the hell are you talking about? And what contract? And who's Minnie Mouse?"

He was genuinely confused. He had no idea what we were talking about. I touched Jake softly on the back.

"I don't think it was him. I don't think that he kidnapped me, and I don't think he has your father."

"No, I don't have your father. Why would I take your father? We had a deal so that you and Monique could get married. Why would I need three million from Nico when I was going to get twenty-five million from your father?"

"But you knew that the marriage was never going to go ahead," Nico said. "You knew that once Jake found out about Monique and my dad—"

"What are you talking about?" Dad looked more and more confused.

Slowly, I shook my head. "Guys, he doesn't have your father. It's someone else."

"But who?" Jake looked at Nico. "Who else could it be, Nico?"

"I don't know." He shook his head. "I'm clueless. Who else stands to gain?"

"Let's think about this," Jake said. "First, Tiffany was kidnapped. And now Dad has been kidnapped. So someone who would want something from both of them."

"Yeah, and he's standing in this room with us!" Nico shouted.

"But we know it's not him," Jake said. "So who else could it be?"

And then suddenly, it hit me. Suddenly, I knew all along who was behind everything, and it made sense. It actually made sense.

"I know who has your father," I whispered. "I know who has him."

They stared at me, and I let out a deep sigh.

"It's Monique. It has to be Monique."

THIRTY-TWO

Jake and I looked at each other for a few seconds, and then he turned toward my stepfather. "Where's Monique?" I could hear the anger in his voice, but I could also hear the acceptance. He knew just as well as I did that she had to be behind this. There was no one else.

"I don't know. I'm not her keeper." My stepfather took a step backward.

"I think you're not telling the truth." Nico approached my stepfather. "You need to tell us where Monique is."

"Look, Monique couldn't kidnap anyone," my stepfather sputtered. "Think about it. She's a pretty little dainty thing." I rolled my eyes at his choice of words. "Do you really think she could kidnap your father, one of the wealthiest men in the city?" It was his turn to sneer. I could hear the disdain in his voice. "Really? Do you really think Monique is capable of that all by herself?"

"Then you obviously had something to do with it as well," Nico said, getting angrier.

"Why? Why would I do that?"

"Because I signed the contract with the wrong name and you aren't going to get my company," I pointed out.

"The company's not worth anything, Tiffany. You're lucky I was even trying to help provide for you."

"Excuse me?"

"The company's not worth anything. What don't you understand? I didn't need to own your company. I was getting twenty-five million dollars."

"But what?" I looked at Jake. "Is it really not salvageable? Is it—"

"Remember? I told you I can help you with your family business. Remember I told you I can help you get it."

"Vaguely," I said, staring at him.

"Nothing is lost, okay?" He squeezed my hand, and I nodded. I realized then that my heart was thawing. I was falling in love with this man. I'd never thought it could happen, especially not with someone like Jake, but it had. I was falling deeply and irrevocably in love with him.

He wasn't as bad as I'd initially thought. He wasn't the evil fox trying to eat me up or the werewolf having his wicked way with me. Maybe in the beginning he'd been that, but he was trying to help me. He had changed. He had feelings for me. I truly believed that.

And maybe he didn't love me yet, but maybe one day he would. And maybe one day he wouldn't, and that would be okay. Everything wasn't always black and white.

"Dad," I said walking up to my stepfather, "please, where's Monique? He's their father, and everything has just gone horribly wrong. It's over. Where are they?"

"I don't know."

"Then call her, Dad. She'll pick up for you." And I knew it was true. Monique and my stepfather had the sort of relationship that other children envied. They were close.

They adored each other. She was the apple of his eye, and I'd always been jealous. I'd always wondered why she was the chosen one, and now I knew. She was his actual blood daughter, and I was no one to him. "Please call her."

He looked me in the eyes, and I could tell that he was thinking hard. "I won't press charges," I said softly, gritting my teeth, "if you do the right thing now." I could see that he wanted to argue, but there was a guilty glint in his eyes that told me that this wasn't the first time he'd broken the law. He knew he had to be careful. I wanted to make him pay, but it was more important to get Jake's father home safe and sound.

"Fine," he said. "I'll try calling her."

"On speaker," Jake said, and my stepfather sighed.

The phone rang twice before she answered. "Hi, Daddy. What's going on?"

"Hi, darling," he said softly. "Where are you?"

"I'm just taking a little break for the weekend."

"I know, but," he paused as he looked at us, "I was wondering if..."

"You were wondering what, Daddy?"

"So, Jake might know about you and his father."

She gasped. "Oh no, Daddy. He's not going to call off the wedding, is he?"

"I don't know, but his father isn't around right now for him to ask questions and..."

"Oh, Daddy." She giggled. "I know. He's with me this weekend."

"He is?"

"Yeah. We're spending the weekend together."

"Voluntarily?"

"What do you mean, Daddy?" She sounded nervous. "Oh, boy. Did they call you?"

"Did who call me, Monique? What have you done?"

"Oh, Daddy. They did call you, didn't they?"

"Monique, you need to tell me what you've done. Did you kidnap their father?"

"Of course not, Daddy. I just used my brains."

"What do you mean?"

"So, Jake's dad wanted to take me away for the weekend, and I said okay, so we're staying at a very exclusive hotel in Chicago."

"Okay."

"And, well, I thought to myself, 'Maybe I'll pretend that I've kidnapped him,' because I knew he wasn't going to tell his sons that he was with me because they wouldn't approve."

"Maybe you'd pretend that you'd kidnapped him? What?"

"I stole his phone." She giggled. "So he can't answer any calls. Yeah. I mean, I'll give it back by the end of the weekend. I just had to make sure that Jake and Nico didn't get in contact with him. I left a letter at his place so that they thought he was kidnapped, and I said that they needed to give me ransom money before the forty-eight hours were up so I'd get the money before he came home. Perfect, right?"

"Oh, Monique." Her father sighed. "You didn't think it through."

"I did what you said, Daddy. I had Tiffany sign the contract, and that little bitch wrote Minnie Mouse." My stepfather looked at all of us with wide eyes. So he *had* been involved in my kidnapping. "So we're not going to get her company."

"Tiffany, don't," Jake hissed as I reached for the phone.

My stepfather looked at me. "Monique, I have to go now."

"Okay, Daddy. Well, if I get the three million or the twenty-five million, I'll let you know, okay?"

"Okay."

"Love you."

"Stay safe, Monique."

"I will." She giggled and hung up. We all stood in the room in silence for a few seconds.

Jake cleared his throat and stepped toward my stepfather. "You need to tell me the truth right now. And you need to tell it to me now, or I won't be responsible for my actions."

"Okay," my stepfather said, "maybe I knew about Tiffany being kidnapped." He looked at me with no remorse in his eyes. "We needed her to sign the damn papers. We're being investigated by the SEC, and they wanted to go back through the paperwork, and I couldn't have that happen. I couldn't have everything come falling down around me."

"Why? What did you do?"

"Let's just say there's a couple of papers that I forged that I didn't want to get out." He shrugged. "So yeah, we had you kidnapped. It was Monique's idea to have you sign the contract. She said you'd sign anything to get out of the room. And then we thought about the videos that we had of you and your mom and your dad, and well, we figured what with everything else going on, maybe that would make you think it was Jake or Nico or something. But I guess you figured it out."

"Who hit me?" I said softly.

"What are you talking about? No one hit you."

"Who hit me over the head that night?"

He sighed. "It was Monique, okay?"

"Why did she hit me?"

"She's jealous of you. She has nothing. You understand that? She has nothing. She has to whore herself out to their father because we have nothing and you have everything."

"What do I have? You've run my business to the ground."

"You always had Jake," he said softly.

I stared at him. "What are you talking about?"

"I knew Jake didn't want Monique. He wanted you. Every time he came over, his eyes were on you. Every time he had a moment to be around you, he was there. He didn't pay that much attention to Monique. He didn't watch her out of the corner of his eye. He didn't try to get to know her. I knew this had nothing to do with him wanting Monique. It had everything to do with him wanting you—and she deserves something, too, you know!"

I swallowed without answering. There was nothing left to say, absolutely nothing at all. "I want to go," I said. I looked at Jake. "I want to go."

"Okay," he said. "Want to go to your room first and get some stuff?"

"Yeah." I nodded. "Please."

"You go," he said. "I need to speak to daddy dearest here."

"What are you going to do?"

"Don't worry, I'm not going to beat him up or kill him. I'm going to do something far worse than that." He looked at my stepfather. "You need to be out of this house within the next forty-eight hours, and so does Monique. When my father comes back from this little trip, I'm going to tell him everything. As I'm sure you're aware, my father has bimbos all around town. Monique is nothing to him. He will leave her, and she will not get a penny from me or my brother or my father. And you will not get a penny from us, either."

"What am I supposed to do? We don't—"

"I don't care." Jake's voice was deathly quiet. "Get out of this town, and we won't press charges against you. However, if I hear about you sniffing around, if I hear your name in any of my circles, I will destroy you like an ant under a magnifying glass in the hot summer sun. Do you understand me?"

"Yeah." My stepdad nodded. "I understand."

I stared at him for a few seconds, almost feeling bad for him but not quite, before leaving the room. I headed to my bedroom where I pulled out one of my mother's old suitcases from the closet and looked around my room. There were so many things that I wanted to take with me, so many things that I loved, but I knew I could only go with one suitcase, so I had to choose my favorites. I heard a noise behind me and looked behind my shoulder. It was Jake.

"Pack what you need for a couple of nights and then we'll come back."

"No." I shook my head. "I don't want to come back here."

"You don't want to live here?" He raised an eyebrow. "But you love it. The library..."

"No, there are too many bad memories here. I need to start over." I sighed. "Maybe I'll find a studio apartment somewhere and get a job and start over. I've got about ten grand in the bank and..."

"No. You're not going to do that, Tiffany."

"What do you mean I'm not going do that?"

"You're not going to find a studio apartment. You're not going to find a job. You're not spending the ten grand you have in the bank, and I'm not letting you leave your home."

"I don't want to be here, Jake."

"Then you don't have to be here. We'll go somewhere else."

"What do you mean we'll go somewhere else?"

"I meant that we will take every book from that library and put them in a new library in a new house."

"What?" I said. "I can't afford a new house—"

"I can."

"What do you mean, you can?"

"Don't you understand, Tiffany? Yes, this started as a game. This started as a lust for revenge, but I love you. I love you more than I ever thought was possible. I love you more than the stars in the sky. I love you more than I can even tell you, and I'm not going to let anyone hurt you. I am going to protect you, and I want to give you everything that your heart desires. I want you to have a library bigger than the New York Public Library system."

Joy bubbled up inside me. "You know that's not possible, right?" I laughed.

"I've got enough money to make it possible."

"Oh, Jake." I wrapped my arms around his neck and kissed him.

He pulled back after a moment. "Are you okay?"

"No." I took a deep breath. "But I will be." I smiled at him softly, and he kissed me again, pulling me into him.

"I love you, Tiffany," he whispered in my ear. "I love you so much."

I looked into his face, and I smiled warmly, letting all the love that was in my heart flow out. "I love you, too, Jacob Joshua Edwards. I love you more than the stars in the sky. I love you more than the moon and the entire universe."

"Do you mean it?" he asked. He looked like the most handsome, wonderful prince I ever could have imagined.

"I mean it more than you'll ever know."

"Thank you." We just stood there for a few seconds before he pulled me back toward him and kissed me deeply. "Now, hurry up and pack this bag because I need to get you back to my place. There's something we have to do."

I giggled. "You're too much. You know that, right?"

"I do," he said, "but I want to show you just how much I can be."

"But I have a question." I gave him an innocent smile.

"What's that?"

"Can we talk about what we do tonight or will it be a secret?"

I laughed as he pulled me back into his arms and caressed my face and hair. The love in his eyes was evident, as was the lust, and I was excited to get back to his place so that we could keep on making new memories.

THIRTY-THREE

One Month Later

"Where are we going?" I frowned as Jake led me down a dark alley. He shushed me and shook his head. "We're not going to a sex shop, are we?" I asked him suspiciously. I watched him as he chuckled, but still he didn't give anything away. I felt a slight buzz of excitement as we passed seedy store after seedy store. I never would have ventured down this alley by myself, but I wasn't scared with Jake. In fact, I'd never been more comfortable with anyone before in my life. Not even Polly. Jake made me feel safe and loved, and I couldn't believe just how much I'd shared with him about my inner thoughts, dreams, and wishes. "Jake, tell me now! Where are we going?"

"You're so impatient, Tiffany." He squeezed my hand.

"Are you taking me to..."

"I think you want me to take you to a sex club." He laughed. "Something you've been fantasizing about?" He raised an eyebrow and licked his lips. "Do you want to seduce me or something?"

"Are you saying you don't want me to seduce you?" I

gave him my most innocent look. "Shall we stop making love until we get married?"

"We're not getting married until next year." He growled and stopped dead in the alley. I saw two men sitting on the ground behind us and stared at Jake with a worried expression.

"Should we stop here?" I leaned forward and whispered. I tried not to look at the two men, even though I could see that they had taken a keen interest in us.

"Why not?" Jake grabbed me around the waist and pulled me in toward him.

"Jake, this is not a good spot."

"I won't let anything happen to you. You're safe with me."

"I know, but..." I paused as Jake leaned forward and kissed me hard. "What are you doing?" I gasped as I felt his hands on my ass. "Jake."

"What?" He grinned. "I want to make sure that you're not planning on making me wait until next year to make love again?"

"Why? Wouldn't you wait?"

He growled as he pulled me against his body, and I felt his erection against my stomach. "I would wait, but it would be hard. Very, very hard." He kissed me on the cheek. "And we'd have to bring the wedding forward." He sucked on my lower lip, and I moaned slightly. "To, like, next week."

"Jake." I giggled. "Really?"

"Really." He nodded solemnly. "We would fly to Vegas and Elvis would marry us."

"Oh, Jake." I laughed. "An Elvis wedding?"

"And we'd honeymoon in a suite with a heart-shaped bed and a huge tub." He smiled. "With a mirrored ceiling.

And we could watch ourselves as we fucked like bunny rabbits."

"I don't want to see my jiggles and wiggles." I shook my head. "No thanks."

"I love to watch you jiggle," he whispered in my ear. "I'm so hard right now."

"Jake." I pulled away from him. "We should leave. I do not want to have sex in this alleyway, no matter how horny you are."

"Boo." Jake laughed and pulled away. "Come on, let's go."

"But where are we going?" I pleaded with him. "Tell me, Jake."

"We're nearly there." He shook his head. "Come on, beautiful."

"Fine." We continued down the alleyway until we finally stopped outside a doorway. "Uhm, where are we?" I looked at the dark windows and swallowed hard. What was going on behind those dark blinds?

"Let's go in and we shall see." Jake winked and rang the doorbell.

"Jake..."

"Do you trust me?"

"Yes." I nodded.

"Good." He smiled in his loving way, and I felt my heart melting. It was still strange to me how wonderful and sweet Jake was. To the outside world, he was a handsome, curt, and foreboding man. But to me, he was absolutely a teddy bear. He was the most romantic man I'd ever met in my life and so protective of me. Every single day, he did something to show me how much he regretted his plan to destroy me and my life. Every single day, he did something to prove to me that he loved me. And every single day, he made me laugh. We were both still heartbroken over what my father and his mother had done, but we knew it had nothing to do with us.

"Hello?" An elderly man with white hair opened the door. He had kind eyes as he surveyed us. "Can I help?"

I stared at Jake and licked my lips nervously. This couldn't possibly be a sex club, could it? Jake grinned at me and winked as he held his hand out.

"Hi, we spoke on the phone. I'm Jacob Joshua Edwards."

"Oh, yes. Mr. Edwards." The man nodded and then looked at me. "You must be Tiffany?"

"Yes." I nodded in surprise.

"Come on," he said and stepped back. Jake walked in first, and then I walked in behind him. "Welcome to my lair."

"Your lair?" I stared at Jake, who was grinning.

"So hold on. I'll be right back." The man nodded and disappeared.

"What's going on, Jake?" I glared at my gorgeous boyfriend.

"You'll see." He pressed his finger to his lips.

"So it was published in 1969 by Roberts Brothers, Boston." The old man walked back into the room, wearing a white pair of gloves. He had two terracotta cloth brown books in his hands. "They are, of course, first editions."

"Of course." Jake nodded.

"What are they?" I asked, my heart racing.

"*Little Women* by Louisa May Alcott." The man grinned. "Jake said he wanted to surprise you."

"Oh?" My heart was racing as I glanced at him. "You bought me the first edition of *Little Women*?"

"You said it was one of your favorite books." He beamed at me. "I wanted you to have it."

"But I'm sure it was expensive." I frowned.

"Ten grand worth of book." The old man grinned and then pressed his lips together. "Oh sorry, I didn't think..." He looked over at Jake, who was frowning.

"Jake, no, that's too much for a book."

"No, it's not." He shook his head. "Do you not love the book?"

"I do love the book, but I do not want you to spend that much on a book. That's just too much money."

"Not if it makes you happy." He stepped forward and shook his head. His eyes were shining as he gazed at me. "Do you know how happy you make me? How being in your presence makes me feel like the luckiest man in the world. I want to spoil you. I want your every dream and desire to come true."

"Jake, I love you as well, but that doesn't mean that—"

"Tiffany, I can more than afford it." He cut me off. "Let me spoil you. Let me treat you to gifts that make you happy. Your whole life you've never had anyone take care of you and love you and spoil you. Let me do that for you."

"But I don't need anything, other than you. I love you, Jake. You mean more to me than anything else."

"I know." He grinned. "And that's what makes me want to spoil you even more."

"I'm the luckiest woman in the world." I beamed at him. "I can't believe how lucky I am."

"I know the feeling because I feel the same." He kissed me softly. "There's nothing more that I want or need. Having you in my life. Loving you. Being with you. Planning the rest of my life with you. That's everything to me."

"You're everything to me," I said, kissing him back. "You

are everything my heart has ever desired." And as we stood there staring at each other, I knew that there was nothing else in the world I could want for. I had found the perfect man for me, and I knew we could battle everything in life together.

Thank you for reading We Don't Talk About Last Night. Please join my mailing list here to never miss any of my new releases. Please leave a review if you enjoyed the book.

CPSIA information can be obtained
at www.ICGtesting.com
Printed in the USA
BVHW061538120522
636888BV00005B/81

9 798201 935382